Enhancing Performance, Efficiency, and Security Through Complex Systems Control

Idriss Chana
ESTM, Moulay Ismail University of Meknès, Morocco

Aziz Bouazi
ESTM, Moulay Ismail University of Meknès, Morocco

Hussain Ben-azza
ENSAM, Moulay Ismail University of Meknes, Morocco

A volume in the Advances in Systems Analysis, Software Engineering, and High Performance Computing (ASASEHPC) Book Series

Published in the United States of America by
    IGI Global
    Engineering Science Reference (an imprint of IGI Global)
    701 E. Chocolate Avenue
    Hershey PA, USA 17033
    Tel: 717-533-8845
    Fax: 717-533-8661
    E-mail: cust@igi-global.com
    Web site: http://www.igi-global.com

                    Library of Congress Cataloging-in-Publication Data

Names: Chana, Idriss, 1978- editor. | Bouazi, Aziz, 1963- editor. |
    Ben-azza, Hussain, 1964- editor.
Title: Enhancing performance, efficiency, and security through complex
    systems control / edited by Idriss Chana, Aziz Bouazi, Hussain Ben-azza.

Description: Hershey PA : Engineering Science Reference, 2024. | Includes
    bibliographical references. | Summary: "This book showcases new ideas,
    methodologies and technologies that can improve the design, modeling and
    control of complex systems, leading to better performance, efficiency
    and safety"-- Provided by publisher.
Identifiers: LCCN 2023034562 (print) | LCCN 2023034563 (ebook) | ISBN
    9798369304976 (hardcover) | ISBN 9798369304983 (paperback) | ISBN
    9798369304990 (ebook)
Subjects: LCSH: Automatic control--Case studies.
Classification: LCC TJ213 .E585 2024 (print) | LCC TJ213 (ebook) | DDC
    629.8/95--dc23/eng/20231226
LC record available at https://lccn.loc.gov/2023034562
LC ebook record available at https://lccn.loc.gov/2023034563

This book is published in the IGI Global book series Advances in Systems Analysis, Software Engineering, and High Performance Computing (ASASEHPC) (ISSN: 2327-3453; eISSN: 2327-3461)

British Cataloguing in Publication Data
A Cataloguing in Publication record for this book is available from the British Library.

All work contributed to this book is new, previously-unpublished material. The views expressed in this book are those of the authors, but not necessarily of the publisher.

For electronic access to this publication, please contact: eresources@igi-global.com.

Advances in Systems Analysis, Software Engineering, and High Performance Computing (ASASEHPC) Book Series

Vijayan Sugumaran
Oakland University, USA

ISSN:2327-3453
EISSN:2327-3461

MISSION

The theory and practice of computing applications and distributed systems has emerged as one of the key areas of research driving innovations in business, engineering, and science. The fields of software engineering, systems analysis, and high performance computing offer a wide range of applications and solutions in solving computational problems for any modern organization.

The **Advances in Systems Analysis, Software Engineering, and High Performance Computing (ASASEHPC) Book Series** brings together research in the areas of distributed computing, systems and software engineering, high performance computing, and service science. This collection of publications is useful for academics, researchers, and practitioners seeking the latest practices and knowledge in this field.

COVERAGE

- Computer System Analysis
- Parallel Architectures
- Distributed Cloud Computing
- Engineering Environments
- Computer Networking
- Storage Systems
- Network Management
- Performance Modelling
- Virtual Data Systems
- Software Engineering

IGI Global is currently accepting manuscripts for publication within this series. To submit a proposal for a volume in this series, please contact our Acquisition Editors at Acquisitions@igi-global.com or visit: http://www.igi-global.com/publish/.

Titles in this Series

For a list of additional titles in this series, please visit: www.igi-global.com/book-series

ODE, BVP, and 1D PDE Solvers for Scientific and Engineering Problems With MATLAB Basics
Leonid Burstein (ORT Braude College of Engineering, Israel (Retred))
Engineering Science Reference • © 2024 • 300pp • H/C (ISBN: 9781668468500) • US $245.00

Digital Technologies in Modeling and Management Insights in Education and Industry
GS Prakasha (Christ University, India) Maria Lapina (North-Caucasus Federal University, Russia) and Deepanraj
Balakrishnan (Prince Mohammad Bin Fahd University, Saudi Aabia)
Information Science Reference • © 2024 • 320pp • H/C (ISBN: 9781668495766) • US $250.00

The Software Principles of Design for Data Modeling
Debabrata Samanta (Rochester Institute of Technology, Kosovo)
Engineering Science Reference • © 2023 • 318pp • H/C (ISBN: 9781668498095) • US $270.00

Investigations in Pattern Recognition and Computer Vision for Industry 4.0
Chiranji Lal Chowdhary (Vellore Institute of Technology, Vellore, India) Basanta Kumar Swain (Government
College of Engineering, Bhawanipatna, India) and Vijay Kumar (Dr B R Ambedkar National Institute of Technology Jalandhar, India)
Engineering Science Reference • © 2023 • 276pp • H/C (ISBN: 9781668486023) • US $270.00

Cyber-Physical System Solutions for Smart Cities
Vanamoorthy Muthumanikandan (Vellore Institute of Technology, Chennai, India) Anbalagan Bhuvaneswari (Vellore Institute of Technology, Chennai, India) Balamurugan Easwaran (University of Africa, Toru-Orua, Nigeria)
and T. Sudarson Rama Perumal (Rohini College of Engineering and Technology, India)
Engineering Science Reference • © 2023 • 182pp • H/C (ISBN: 9781668477564) • US $270.00

Cyber-Physical Systems and Supporting Technologies for Industrial Automation
R. Thanigaivelan (A.K.T. Memorial College of Engineering and Technology, India) S. Kaliappan (Velammal
Institute of Technology, India) and C. Jegadheesan (Kongu Engineering College, India)
Engineering Science Reference • © 2023 • 444pp • H/C (ISBN: 9781668492673) • US $270.00

Perspectives and Considerations on the Evolution of Smart Systems
Maki K. Habib (American University in Cairo, Egypt)
Engineering Science Reference • © 2023 • 419pp • H/C (ISBN: 9781668476840) • US $325.00

IGI Global
PUBLISHER of TIMELY KNOWLEDGE

701 East Chocolate Avenue, Hershey, PA 17033, USA
Tel: 717-533-8845 x100 • Fax: 717-533-8661
E-Mail: cust@igi-global.com • www.igi-global.com

Table of Contents

Detailed Table of Contents

Chapter 1

Chaymaâ Boutahiri, Laboratory of Computer Science, Applied Math and Electrical
    Engineering (IMAGE), EST, Moulay Ismail University, Morocco

Ayoub Nouaiti, Laboratory of Computer Science, Applied Math and Electrical Engineering
    (IMAGE), EST, Moulay Ismail University, Morocco

Aziz Bouazi, Laboratory of Computer Science, Applied Math and Electrical Engineering
    (IMAGE), EST, Moulay Ismail University, Morocco

Abdallah Marhraoui Hsaini, Laboratory of Computer Science, Applied Math and Electrical
    Engineering (IMAGE), EST, Moulay Ismail University, Morocco

Wind energy emerges as a promising solution for electricity generation, circumventing greenhouse gas emissions. However, the complexities of establishing wind energy conversion systems in a laboratory setting have spurred researchers to contemplate the utilization of wind turbine emulators. These latter afford the capability to accurately replicate the behavior of an actual wind turbine. In this chapter, an intricate description of the selected wind turbine emulator is provided, consisting of a DC motor regulated by a DC-DC buck converter. This converter is controlled by the PWM pulses generated by the wind turbine model. Proficient control of the DC motor allows electric sinusoidal voltage and current to be produced by the asynchronous generator in accordance with the adopted wind profile. Subsequently, the emulator undergoes rigorous implementation and thorough analysis within the MATLAB/Simulink environment to validate the efficiency of its system.

Chapter 2

Imane Cheikh, LIMAS-Lab, Faculty of Sciences Dhar El Mahraz, Sidi Mohammed Ben
    Abdellah University, Morocco

Khaoula Oulidi Omali, National School for Computer Science and Systems Analysis,
    University Mohammed V, Morocco

Mohammed Nabil Kabbaj, LIMAS-Lab, Faculty of Sciences Dhar El Mahraz, Sidi
    Mohammed Ben Abdellah University, Morocco

Mohammed Benbrahim, Faculty of Sciences, Sidi Mohammed Ben Abdellah University, Morocco

Digital twin (DT) plays a key role in smart industry by being one of the most useful technologies which has the ability to attach the physical space with the cyber space. On the other side of the coin, manipulator robots have also played an essential role in industrial processes, especially that robots are embedded with sensors and actuators that can lead to a smart control. In this study, generalities about digital twin are mentioned; moreover, the relationship between digital twin and the control of manipulator robots is explained step by step. A simulation study has been employed to the universal robot UR10 applying the sliding mode control. This project shows that the cyber space is beneficial for creating a simulated smart industry by observing real-time state of the process, testing different decisions in simulation before performing the required actions directly in the real system, and acting with different situations.

Chapter 3

Tahiri Omar, Sidi Mohamed Ben Abdellah University, Morocco
Herrou Brahim, Sidi Mohamed Ben Abdellah University, Morocco
Sekkat Souhail, ENSAM, Moulay Ismail University, Morocco
Khadiri Hassan, ENSAM, Moulay Ismail University, Morocco

Design is a predominant phase in the life cycle of any product. Referring to a number of reviews, this chapter cites design support tools, focusing in particular on security system and operational safety. It tried to define these two notions (safety, security) as well as the difference between them. It proposed a design aid model that can be adopted by designers in the design phases of new systems, or during their life cycle, based on the "Teorija Reshenija Izobretateliskih Zadatch" (TRIZ) and Failure Modes Vulnerabilities and Effect Analysis (FMVEA) methods. In the first instance, the authors' model enables newly-designed products to give impetus to production systems, for which they use the resolution matrix for technical contradictions. Secondly, it enables these systems to be improved, for which they suggested adopting the FMVEA method tables.

Chapter 4

Sekkat Souhail, ENSAM, Moulay Ismail University of Meknès, Morocco
Ibtissam El Hassani, ENSAM, Moulay Ismail University of Meknès, Morocco
Anass Cherrafi, Cadi Ayyad University, Morocco

The concept of circular economy (CE) aims to promote sustainable resource utilization, minimize environmental impacts, and create societal, economic, and business value. Simultaneously, the fourth industrial revolution or Industry 4.0 (I4.0) offers companies the opportunity to enhance their operational efficiency. Various process models have been proposed to assist companies in developing a digitalisation strategy roadmap. This chapter presents a thorough analysis of how CE utilizes I4.0 technologies to transition from a conventional linear economy to a circular one. The authors have then first proposed a generic three-stage process to establish a I 4.0 strategy roadmap, then conducted an exhaustive review of the latest literature on CE and I4.0 theory to explore the interrelation between these concepts and ascertain the extent to which I4.0 technologies facilitate progress towards a more sustainable industry.

Chapter 5

Meryeme Bououchma, Laboratoire des Techniques Industrielles-(FST), USMBA-Fez, Morocco
Brahim Herrou, Laboratoire des Techniques Industrielles-(EST), USMBA- Fez, Morocco

The primary goal of any organization or company is to guarantee good performances as far as all sectors are concerned in order to achieve operational excellence at all levels. This can only be achieved through the prior integration of the customer satisfaction function, in which the offer quality is considered as the main determinant. Thus, the launch of new complex and innovative products becomes necessary through developing new products or improving existing ones that meet specific customers' needs, since they have become more conscious and selective in the products they buy, while respecting the triptych cost quality time. In that context, the authors review three quality management tools that are widely used for that purpose—AF, QFD, and FMEA—before defining the advantages and disadvantages of each one, as well as relationships or potential interactions between them.

Chapter 6

Touria Jdid, Faulty of Sciences, Sidi Mohamed Ben Abdellah University, Morocco
Idriss Chana, ESTM, Moulay Ismail University of Meknès, Morocco
Aziz Bouazi, ESTM, Moulay Ismail University of Meknès, Morocco
Mohammed Nabil Kabbaj, LIMAS-Lab, Faculty of Sciences Dhar El Mahraz, Sidi
    Mohammed Ben Abdellah University, Morocco
Mohammed Benbrahim, Faulty of Sciences, Sidi Mohamed Ben Abdellah University, Morocco

Estimating and controlling the COVID-19 pandemic is essential to reduce the spread of the disease and help decision-making efforts in combating public health crises. However, the potential presence of multiple dynamic changes in the reported count data or the occurrence of another wave of the pandemic emerges as a challenge for simulating the evolution of the disease over a long period. In this chapter, to account for the dynamic changes in the COVID-19 curves, the authors propose a rate function based on multiple branches of a logistic function. They assumed in a compartmental model that the recovery and disease transmission rates are time-dependent, and they assign to each the rate function. Then, they apply the model to daily COVID-19 data on infection counts in Morocco between March 2, 2020 and December 31, 2021 using curve fitting through the Nelder-Mead optimization method. The simulation outcomes demonstrate the model's ability to replicate the COVID-19 pandemic in Morocco over two waves, with the goodness of fit depending on the number of logistic branches composing the rate function.

Chapter 7

Houda Bentarki, Moulay Ismail University, Morocco
Abdelkader Makhoute, Moulay Ismail University, Morocco
Tőkési Karoly, Institute for Nuclear Research, Hungarian Academy of Sciences, Hungary

The acousto-optic couplings mechanisms are investigated theoretically in photonic and phononic crystals with simultaneous band gaps. The authors have focused on the acousto-optic couplings inside a phoXonic cavity by taking into account two coupling mechanisms, the photo elastic effect and effect of movement of the interfaces. They discuss the symmetry of modes to distinguish those that don't interfere in an efficient way. They calculate the modulation of the frequency of the photonic mode during a period of acoustic oscillations with a finite element method (FE) (COMSOL®Multiphysics). The two mechanisms presented in the numerical calculations produce additive or subtractive effects in total acousto-optical coupling while depending on whether they are in phase or out of phase.

In the field of channel coding theory, there are two main branches. The first is related to the design and construction of codes capable of facilitating identification of errors at the receiver despite potential alterations during transmission; this is known as the encoding operation. The second branch focuses on developing mechanisms for correcting errors caused by the transmission channel, by devising valid and suitable algorithms; this is known as the decoding operation. The authors have delved into both aspects. In the first part, a novel method for constructing good linear codes is studied. It is based on the Hadamard matrix, which shares the same structure as the kernel of polar codes, and on the generator matrix of several existing linear codes. In the second part, a new decoding algorithm is proposed. This involves adapting the SSCL polar code decoder to decode the codes designed in the first part, as well as some of the most well-known block codes.

All over the world, the increase in the use of transport systems is defined as the cause of traffic problems reflected mainly by the increase in the number of road accidents due to poor traffic management. In order to ensure an intelligent mobility and transport and thus in the trend of building smart cities, the interest has turned to the development of the internet of vehicles (IoV). The IoV communication network involves the evolution of vehicle connectivity enabling the exchange of real-time traffic data between vehicles, with their environment and everything related to it, through different network technologies. Given the complexity of the IoV, it is necessary that its environment is secure, reliable, and protected against attacks, and that it allows the diffusion of information throughout the network. The blockchain technology allows the securing of different data transactions exchanged between IoV nodes, given its provision of several cryptographic techniques and that it provides a distributed, transparent, and highly confidential database. In order to expand the area of the covered network, long-range (LoRa) designed for low power wide area networks (LPWANs) is used to ensure simultaneous and long range transmissions. This chapter presents an IoV-based architecture that integrates blockchain technology to cover the database security aspects and the LoRa network as a service for vehicle tracking that allows to collect information from different vehicles including location in order to be able to prevent the presence of road accidents with the aim of warning, alleviating traffic and minimizing the risk of having others. For its implementation, this system is based mainly on the measurement of the speed of vehicles to detect the deceleration or blockage of traffic in order to identify the presence of accidents.

Okacha Amraouy, Faulty of Sciences, Sidi Mohamed Ben Abdellah University, Morocco
Yassine Boukhali, Faulty of Sciences, Sidi Mohamed Ben Abdellah University, Morocco
Aziz Bouazi, Moulay Ismail University, Morocco
Mohammed Nabil Kabbaj, Faulty of Sciences, Sidi Mohamed Ben Abdellah University, Morocco
Mohammed Benbrahim, Faulty of Sciences, Sidi Mohamed Ben Abdellah University, Morocco

In recent years, IoT has been increasingly applied in agriculture to transform traditional farming practices into smart and precision agriculture (PA) that are more efficient, productive, and sustainable. However, its implementation in agriculture faces several challenges, including network coverage, reliability, lack of flexibility, and scalability. To address these challenges, current research has focused on developing new communication protocols and technologies, along with several IoT architectural design patterns, especially those based on SOA, which play a crucial role in designing service-oriented solutions. This chapter presents comprehensive and impactful solutions for blockchain-based IoT applications in PA. It proposes novel models combining IoT, blockchain, fog and cloud computing for the development of decentralized applications with independent, autonomous, and interoperable functionalities and services based on the SOA approach. Also, technical challenges, research directions, and the recent advances towards an optimized blockchain-based IoT ecosystem for PA are presented.

P. Kanimozhi, IFET College of Engineering, India
A. R. Jayasri, IFET College of Engineering, India
T. Ananth Kumar, IFET College of Engineering, India
S. Arunmozhiselvi, DMI-St. John the Baptist University, Malawi

Water management is critical for long-term development and the preservation of essential natural resources. Traditional water management strategies are becoming increasingly ineffective in dealing with developing water shortages and the need for efficient resource allocation. The incorporation of smart contracts, which are supported by blockchain technology, presents a viable answer for reshaping water management techniques. When combined with internet of things (IoT) devices that give real-time data on water use, quality, and environmental conditions, a powerful alliance is formed that has the potential to alter traditional water management practices. The concept of smart contracts self-executing agreements with established rules that trigger automatic activities upon the fulfillment of specific criteria lies at the heart of this fusion. The use of blockchain technology has emerged as a disruptive option to alleviate water scarcity and ensure equal distribution in the goal of sustainable water management.

Abir Sajji, Faculty of Sciences, Ibn Tofail University of Kenitra, Morocco
Yassine Rhazali, ESTM, Moulay Ismail University of Meknes, Morocco
Youssef Hadi, Faculty of Sciences, Ibn Tofail University of Kenitra, Morocco

The model-driven architecture (MDA) approach revolves around the development of multiple models, including the computation independent model (CIM), the platform independent model (PIM), and the platform specific model (PSM). Web applications have gained popularity for their capabilities. To address the need for robust user interfaces independent of technical details, the interaction flow modeling language (IFML) was introduced. This study focuses on model transformations within MDA, specifically from CIM to PSM via PIM. Metamodels for BPMN and IFML were created using Eclipse, and shift rules were applied with ATL. Webratio, an IFML implementation tool, was used to generate GUIs. A case study on after-sales service with CRUD features demonstrated the practical application of MDA. This research enhances understanding of MDA in web application development, enabling developers to create user-friendly interfaces. It serves as a valuable resource for software engineering professionals, providing insights into MDA's practical implementation and impact on web application development.

Chapter 13

N. Jothy, SRM Valliammai Engineering College, India
Komala James, SRM Valliammai Engineering College, India
N. Subhashini, SRM Valliammai Engineering College, India
A. K. Mariselvam, SRM Valliammai Engineering College, India

In the modern era, the issue of vehicle parking has become a significant concern in substantial investments. The conventional approach of locating available parking spaces by manually searching through multiple lanes has proven to be both time-consuming and labor-intensive. Furthermore, it requires parking safely and securely, eliminating the risk of being towed, and at a reduced cost. To tackle this challenge, a cutting-edge parking control system has been developed. This system incorporates secure devices, parking control gates, time and attendance machines, and car counting systems. These features play a crucial role in ensuring the safety of parked vehicles and effectively managing the fee structure for every vehicle's entry and exit. By leveraging IoT-powered technologies, it simplifies the process of locating available parking spaces by providing real-time information, reducing the manual effort required. With IoT, parking management is revolutionized, offering drivers a seamless and secure parking experience while optimizing operational efficiency for parking operators.

Chapter 14

Aissa Ben Yahya, Faculty of Sciences, Moulay Ismail University of Meknes, Morocco
Hicham El Akhal, Faculty of Sciences, Moulay Ismail University of Meknes, Morocco
Abdelbaki El Belrhiti El Alaoui, Faculty of Sciences, Moulay Ismail University of Meknes, Morocco

The security of embedded systems is deteriorating in comparison to conventional systems due to resource limitations in memory, processing, and power. Daily publications highlight various vulnerabilities associated with these systems. While significant efforts have been made to systematize and analyze these vulnerabilities, most studies focus on specific areas within embedded systems and lack the implementation of artificial intelligence (AI). This research aims to address these gaps by utilizing support vector machine (SVM) to classify vulnerabilities sourced from the national vulnerabilities database (NVD) and specifically targeting embedded system vulnerabilities. Results indicate that seven of the top 10 common weakness enumeration (CWE) vulnerabilities in embedded systems are also present in the 2022 CWE Top 25 Most Dangerous Software Weaknesses. The findings of this study will facilitate security researchers and companies in comprehensively analyzing embedded system vulnerabilities and developing tailored solutions.

Chapter 15

Imen Fourati Kallel, Ecole Nationale d'Electronique et des Télécommunications de Sfax
(ENET'Com), Tunisia
Mohamed Kallel, Ecole Nationale d'Electronique et des Télécommunications de Sfax
(ENET'Com), Tunisia

Artificial intelligence has become widely and increasingly used in various advanced applications, notably classification, optimization, object recognition, and segmentation. Recently, it has been extended into watermarking techniques. It brings some approaches implying innovative security means, which are adjusted to new communications and information technologies. As it generally believed that the use of artificial intelligence in digital watermarking schemes could revolutionize the way digital data is protected. This chapter is about an overview of recent developments in artificial intelligence techniques utilized for watermarking. It begins with the watermarking background. Next, it represents a review of machine and deep learning watermarking techniques followed by a delineation of their advantages and disadvantages. In this light, the main problems are pinpointed with a suggestion of some possible discussed and highlighted solutions. The last point of this chapter is about outlining future research directions.

Chapter 16

Oumayma Rachidi, ENSAM, Moulay Ismail University of Meknes, Morocco
Ed-Dahmani Chafik, ENSAM, Moulay Ismail University of Meknes, Morocco
Badr Bououlid, ENSAM, Moulay Ismail University of Meknes, Morocco

Real-time object detection represents a major part in the development of advanced driver assistance systems (ADAS). Pedestrian detection has become one of the most important tasks in the field of object detection due to the increasing number of road accidents. This study concerns the design and implementation of a Raspberry Pi 4-based embedded stereovision system to detect 80 object classes including persons and estimate 3D distance for traffic safety. Stereo camera calibration and deep learning algorithms are discussed. The study shows the system's design and a custom stereo camera designed and built using 3D printer as well as the implementation of YOLOv5s in the Raspberry Pi 4. The object detector is trained on the context object detection task (COCO) 2020 dataset and was tested using one of the two cameras. The Raspberry Pi displays a live video including bounding boxes and the number of frames per second (FPS).

Chapter 17

Jaouad Boudnaya, Moulay Ismail University, Morocco
Hicham Laacha, Moulay Ismail University, Morocco
Mohamed Qerras, Moulay Ismail University, Morocco
Abdelhak Mkhida, Moulay Ismail University, Morocco

Predictive maintenance is a maintenance strategy based on monitoring the state of components to predict the date of future failure. The objective is to take the appropriate measures to avoid the consequences of this failure. For this reason, the authors determine the remaining useful life (RUL) which is the remaining time before the appearance of the failure on the component. It is an important approach that allows the prediction of aging mechanisms likely to lead components to failure. In this chapter, a new methodology for predicting the remaining useful life of components is proposed using a data-driven prognosis approach with the integration of machine learning. This approach is illustrated in a battery case study to predict the remaining useful life.

Chapter 18
*Marouane Zaizoune, Laboratory of Industrial Technologies, Faculty of Sciences and
Technologies, Sidi Mohamed Ben Abdellah University, Morocco*
*Brahim Herrou, Higher School of Technology, Sidi Mohamed Ben Abdellah University,
Morocco*
Hassan Khadiri, ENSAM, Moulay Ismail University, Morocco
Souhail Sekkat, ENSAM, Moulay Ismail University, Morocco

The purpose of this study is to use the neural networks method in order to build a neural network system that studies and determines the cause of non-conformities. Companies are regularly confronted with quality problems stemming both from assembly mistakes and also during upstream stages in the process, like design, logistics, technical, and industrial support. These problems would sometimes reach the end customer inducing huge losses for the companies in term of costs and reputation. Therefore, an improvement of non-conformities detection systems as well as the identification of their causes is necessary, which is the purpose of this chapter. First, per the authors, this chapter discusses non-conformities in the industrial field and the management of quality problems. Then, the neural networks method is presented, as well as a review in its recent development and its applications. As a result, the steps to building the neural network system to study non-conformity causes are defined and described.

Preface

Enhancing Performance, Efficiency, and Security Through Complex Systems Control emerges as a culmination of collaborative efforts aimed at addressing multifaceted challenges in contemporary engineering. Within these pages lies a compendium of meticulously selected scientific articles, each representing a vital building block in the quest for solutions to pressing issues in system control. This book stands as a testament to the pivotal role of research in unraveling complexities and charting pathways toward enhanced performance, efficiency, and security within our intricate systems.

The significance of research within these domains cannot be overstated. It serves as a compass guiding engineers, academics, and industrialists through the labyrinth of challenges that define our technological landscape. At its core, this compilation seeks to confront the intricacies of complex systems, offering insights and methodologies that promise to unravel their complexities. From the augmentation of electrical engineering paradigms to the precision of modeling and control systems, and from the nuances of information and image processing to the transformative potential of artificial intelligence, each chapter within this volume embodies a step forward in solving intricate problems plaguing our systems.

The urgency of these problems cannot be ignored. Our industries, our technological infrastructures, and our societal frameworks rely heavily on the stability, efficiency, and security of complex systems. Yet, they face incessant challenges—challenges that necessitate innovation, collaboration, and groundbreaking research. The chapters in this book, meticulously evaluated and refined, are not mere scholarly pursuits; they are beacons illuminating the paths toward solutions. They harbor the potential to revolutionize the way we approach system design, modeling, and control, offering tangible methodologies and technologies that can alleviate the burdens faced by engineers and practitioners in their daily endeavors.

This compilation does not exist in isolation; it stands as a catalyst for progress within scientific research. Its potential to seamlessly integrate into ongoing investigations and inspire fresh inquiries is profound. By presenting new perspectives and methodologies, it endeavors to foster collaborations and spark transformative advancements. As readers engage with its contents, we invite them to not only absorb the knowledge within these pages but also to envision and embark upon new research trajectories. It is through this collaborative effort and the relentless pursuit of knowledge that we aspire to forge a future where complex systems are not just controlled but optimized, fortified, and capable of meeting the evolving demands of our world.

ORGANIZATION OF THE BOOK

Chapter 1: Wind Turbine Emulator Based on DC Motor

This chapter delves into the emulation of wind turbines using a DC motor regulated by a buck converter. It details the precise control of the motor to generate sinusoidal voltage and current, mimicking the behavior of an actual wind turbine. The chapter meticulously validates the emulator's efficiency through rigorous implementation and analysis within the MATLAB/Simulink environment, offering insights into its effectiveness in replicating wind turbine behavior.

Chapter 2: The Usefulness of Digital Twin in Manipulator Robot Control

Exploring the intersection of Digital Twin technology and manipulator robots, this chapter elucidates the pivotal role of Digital Twin in smart industries. Focusing on its integration with manipulator robots, the chapter employs a simulation study employing the Sliding Mode Control on the universal robot UR10. The study underscores the benefits of the cyber-physical integration in simulating industry scenarios before practical implementation, contributing significantly to smart control paradigms.

Chapter 3: Design Flowchart for Operational System Safety

Detailing design support tools for safety and operational systems, this chapter presents a design aid model based on TRIZ and Failure Modes Vulnerabilities and Effect Analysis (FMVEA) methods. It emphasizes the model's utility in both initiating and improving systems, utilizing the resolution matrix for technical contradictions and FMVEA method tables for enhancing safety and security in system designs.

Chapter 4: Integrating Circular Economy Concerns Into Industry 4.0 Roadmaps of Companies – A Literature Review

This chapter offers a comprehensive analysis of how Circular Economy (CE) leverages Industry 4.0 (I4.0) technologies. It proposes a generic three-stage process to establish I4.0 strategy roadmaps and reviews the literature exploring the interrelation between CE and I4.0. Highlighting the role of I4.0 technologies in transitioning to a more sustainable industry, this chapter serves as a valuable resource in exploring the symbiosis between these concepts.

Chapter 5: Literature Review on Quality Management Methods in Product Design

Focusing on operational excellence, this chapter reviews three widely used quality management tools— AF, QFD, and FMEA—emphasizing their role in developing or improving products to meet customer needs. It evaluates the advantages, disadvantages, and potential interactions between these tools, providing insights crucial for enhancing product quality and customer satisfaction.

Chapter 6: Tracking of COVID-19 Pandemic for Multi-Waves Using a Compartmental Model With Time-Dependent Parameters – A Sum of Logistic Branches

Addressing the complexities of modeling the COVID-19 pandemic, this chapter proposes a rate function based on multiple logistic branches to simulate dynamic changes in COVID-19 curves. Employing a compartmental model, it demonstrates the model's effectiveness in replicating Morocco's COVID-19 evolution, showcasing its adaptability in capturing multiple epidemic waves.

Chapter 7: Signatures of the Mode Symmetries in Sapphire phoXonic Cavities

This chapter explores acousto-optic couplings mechanisms in phoXonic cavities, investigating mode symmetries and frequency modulation of photonic modes during acoustic oscillations. Through numerical calculations and finite element method simulations, it evaluates the additive or subtractive effects of different coupling mechanisms, shedding light on their efficient interference.

Chapter 8: A New Approach to Construction and Decoding of Linear Block Codes Based on Polar Codes

This chapter navigates through two fundamental aspects of channel coding theory—code construction and decoding. It introduces a novel method for constructing linear codes based on Hadamard matrices and existing linear codes' generator matrices. Additionally, it proposes a new decoding algorithm adapting the SSCL polar code decoder to decode these designed codes, presenting advancements in both code construction and decoding operations.

Chapter 9: IoV-Based Blockchain Over LoRa for Accident Detection

Highlighting the need for smart transportation systems, this chapter introduces an architecture integrating IoT, blockchain, and LoRa technologies for accident detection in the Internet of Vehicles (IoV). Detailing the secure environment achieved by blockchain and the extensive coverage provided by LoRa, it offers a system capable of collecting and managing real-time information from vehicles to enhance road safety.

Chapter 10: Blockchain-Based IoT for Precision Agriculture – Applications, Research Challenges, and Future Directions

Addressing challenges in IoT implementation in agriculture, this chapter proposes novel models integrating IoT, blockchain, Fog, and Cloud computing for Precision Agriculture (PA). It focuses on decentralized applications and services based on Service-Oriented Architecture (SOA) principles, offering insights into creating an optimized blockchain-based IoT ecosystem for sustainable and efficient agriculture.

Chapter 11: Smart Contracts for Enhanced Water Resource Management

This chapter investigates the integration of smart contracts, supported by blockchain technology, into water resource management. Combining IoT devices for real-time data collection with self-executing smart contracts, it illustrates a promising approach to reshape traditional water management practices, ensuring efficient resource allocation and addressing water scarcity.

Chapter 12: IFML-Based Graphical User Interfaces Generated From BPMN up to PSM Level

Focused on enhancing user interfaces through Model Driven Architecture (MDA), this chapter explores the transformation from CIM to PSM via PIM using Interaction Flow Modeling Language (IFML). By detailing model transformations and their practical application, it serves as a valuable guide for developers in creating user-friendly interfaces in web applications.

Chapter 13: Efficient Parking Solutions Powered by IoT and Transportation Integration

Addressing challenges in conventional parking systems, this chapter introduces a cutting-edge parking control system driven by IoT technologies. Detailing the integration of secure devices, control gates, and real-time information, it streamlines the process of locating available parking spaces, optimizing operational efficiency for parking operators while offering drivers a seamless parking experience.

Chapter 14: Machine Learning-Based Collection and Analysis of Embedded Systems Vulnerabilities

Focusing on the security of embedded systems, this chapter utilizes support vector machine (SVM) to classify vulnerabilities sourced from the National Vulnerabilities Database (NVD). It identifies common vulnerabilities in embedded systems, providing insights for security researchers and companies to comprehensively analyze vulnerabilities and devise tailored solutions.

Chapter 15: Intelligent Watermarking for Data Security – An Overview

This chapter explores the intersection of artificial intelligence and digital watermarking techniques. Beginning with a background on watermarking, it reviews machine and deep learning watermarking techniques, discussing their advantages and disadvantages. By pinpointing challenges and proposing potential solutions, the chapter offers an overview of recent developments in utilizing artificial intelligence for data security through watermarking.

Chapter 16: Design of a Real-Time Integrated System Based on Stereovision and YOLOv5 to Detect Objects

Focused on real-time object detection, this chapter details the design and implementation of an embedded stereovision system using a Raspberry Pi 4. Addressing pedestrian detection as a critical task, it covers stereo camera calibration, deep learning algorithms, and the utilization of YOLOv5. The study showcases the system's capability to detect and estimate the 3D distance of 80 object classes, contributing to advancements in traffic safety.

Chapter 17: Prediction of Remaining Useful Life of Batteries Using Machine Learning Models

This chapter introduces a data-driven prognosis approach with machine learning for predicting the Remaining Useful Life (RUL) of batteries. Demonstrated through a case study on batteries, it illustrates the application of machine learning in predicting the lifespan of components, offering a methodology to aid in predictive maintenance and efficient resource management.

Chapter 18: Literature Review on the Study of Non-Conformity Causes Using Neural Networks

Concluding the chapters, this study employs neural networks to comprehensively study and determine the causes of non-conformities in industrial settings. It reviews non-conformities in the industrial field, management of quality problems, and presents neural networks as a method to enhance non-conformity detection systems. The chapter outlines the steps in building a neural network system to study the causes of non-conformities.

IN SUMMARY

In closing, *Enhancing Performance, Efficiency, and Security Through Complex Systems Control* epitomizes a collective endeavor to navigate the complexities inherent in our technological landscape. This compilation, meticulously crafted and curated, stands as a testament to the collaborative spirit of researchers, practitioners, and academics working tirelessly to unravel the intricacies of complex systems.

As editors, we recognize the immense significance of this collective effort. The diverse themes explored within these pages mirror the multidisciplinary nature of the challenges we face in engineering and related disciplines. It is our fervent belief that this compilation, with its wealth of insights and methodologies, will serve as a cornerstone for innovation and problem-solving within our domains.

We extend our deepest gratitude to the contributors whose dedication and expertise have fueled the creation of this comprehensive resource. Their commitment to excellence and their pioneering research have illuminated pathways toward optimized system performance and fortified security. Moreover, we extend our gratitude to the readers—students, researchers, engineers, and practitioners—whose pursuit of knowledge and dedication to advancement drive the continual evolution of our field.

As the pages of this book become a gateway to new perspectives, methodologies, and collaborative opportunities, we encourage our readers to not only absorb its contents but also to embrace the spirit of inquiry and innovation it embodies. Let us venture forward, armed with the insights gleaned from this compilation, and forge a future where the control and optimization of complex systems become not just aspirations, but tangible realities.

Thank you for embarking on this journey of exploration and discovery with us. Together, let us continue pushing the boundaries of knowledge, innovation, and progress within the intricate tapestry of complex systems control.

Warmest regards,

Idriss Chana
ESTM, Moulay Ismail University of Meknès, Morocco

Aziz Bouazi
ESTM, Moulay Ismail University of Meknès, Morocco

Hussain Ben-azza
ENSAM, Moulay Ismail University of Meknès, Morocco

Chapter 1
Wind Turbine Emulator Based on DC Motor

Chaymaâ Boutahiri

Laboratory of Computer Science, Applied Math and Electrical Engineering (IMAGE), EST, Moulay Ismail University, Morocco

Ayoub Nouaiti

Laboratory of Computer Science, Applied Math and Electrical Engineering (IMAGE), EST, Moulay Ismail University, Morocco

Aziz Bouazi

Laboratory of Computer Science, Applied Math and Electrical Engineering (IMAGE), EST, Moulay Ismail University, Morocco

Abdallah Marhraoui Hsaini

Laboratory of Computer Science, Applied Math and Electrical Engineering (IMAGE), EST, Moulay Ismail University, Morocco

ABSTRACT

Wind energy emerges as a promising solution for electricity generation, circumventing greenhouse gas emissions. However, the complexities of establishing wind energy conversion systems in a laboratory setting have spurred researchers to contemplate the utilization of wind turbine emulators. These latter afford the capability to accurately replicate the behavior of an actual wind turbine. In this chapter, an intricate description of the selected wind turbine emulator is provided, consisting of a DC motor regulated by a DC-DC buck converter. This converter is controlled by the PWM pulses generated by the wind turbine model. Proficient control of the DC motor allows electric sinusoidal voltage and current to be produced by the asynchronous generator in accordance with the adopted wind profile. Subsequently, the emulator undergoes rigorous implementation and thorough analysis within the MATLAB/Simulink environment to validate the efficiency of its system.

DOI: 10.4018/979-8-3693-0497-6.ch001

I. INTRODUCTION

In recent times, global energy consumption has witnessed a substantial surge. This has spurred researchers to seek solutions that can offset this increase while also taking into consideration the impacts of climate change (Kirikkaleli, 2021; Pérez-Lombard, 2008; Sadorsky, 2009; Garcia, 2016).

Wind energy stands out as one of the solutions capable of generating power without emitting green-house gases. It serves the purpose of converting kinetic energy into mechanical energy, and subsequently into electrical energy. Nevertheless, the intricacies involved in installing wind energy conversion systems within laboratory settings have prompted researchers to contemplate the utilization of a wind turbine emulator (Wen, 2021; Aljarhizi Y. a., 2023; Garg, 2018; Dekali, 2021).

Several pivotal reasons have contributed to the adoption of this emulator. Firstly, it enables the test-ing of their functionality without being constrained by various wind conditions. Additionally, it ensures maximum energy efficiency and heightened reliability. Furthermore, it plays a role in diminishing costs and development timelines by circumventing costly and time-intensive field testing phases. The emula-tor also proves instrumental in assessing the resilience of wind turbines under extreme weather condi-tions. It establishes a secure framework that fosters the development and fine-tuning of cutting-edge control algorithms. These algorithms empower wind turbines to dynamically adapt to fluctuations in wind patterns, thus optimizing their electricity production output. Moreover, it streamlines the process of simulating interactions between wind turbines and the electrical grid (Taveiros, 2013; Moussa, 2019; Aljarhizi Y. a., 2020).

In summation, the modeling of a wind turbine emulator assumes a pivotal role in propelling the ad-vancement of wind energy. It not only facilitates performance optimization and heightened reliability but also promotes a seamless integration into the global electrical network. These strides make a substantial contribution towards the transition to a more sustainable energy future firmly rooted in renewable sources.

The wind turbine emulator allows for the replication of the wind turbine's behavior, through precise modeling of each of its components, including the blades, the generator, the electrical converter, and the control systems, among others. It can generate various operational scenarios dependent on a simulated weather conditions. Furthermore, it incorporates control strategies identical to those employed in real wind turbines to respond consistently to wind variations. The emulator also enables the calculation of electrical power generated based on the simulated wind speed.

The choice of motor type for the wind turbine emulator presents a range of emulator options. Gen-erally, three categories of motors are commonly used: direct current motors, induction motors, and synchronous motors (Moussa, 2019).

Direct current motors remain the preferred choice for wind turbines due to their control via the armature current, allowing for a direct correlation with the machine's generated torque. This enables precise control of speed and torque, which is crucial in a wind context. Moreover, they can replicate variations in wind speed and optimize energy production. Furthermore, their control is well established, thus facilitating their implementation. DC motors are widely adopted due to their simplicity of control and outstanding performance (Martínez-Márquez, 2019; Benaaouinate, 2019).

On the other hand, induction emulators are known for their robustness and ability to adapt to vari-able loads. They operate on the principle of electromagnetic induction, making them well-suited for the changing conditions encountered in wind applications. While their control may be more complex, they offer excellent control flexibility and high reliability (Mousarezaee, 2020).

As for synchronous machine emulators, they stand out for their ability to accurately replicate the dynamic behavior of a real wind turbine. They operate on the principle of synchronization between the emulator's rotation speed and that of the emulated wind turbine. This synchronization allows for a precise simulation of wind speed variations and the ability to respond to load changes. They are used to operating the turbine at low speed with direct drive. The absence of rotor current results in high efficiency (Mousarezaee, 2020).

The choice between these different types of emulators will depend on the specific requirements of the application. The right emulator choice is crucial to ensure the proper functioning and optimal performance of a wind system. Each of these emulators offers distinct advantages, and the final decision will depend on the project's priorities.

In this chapter, a description of the wind turbine model is presented, along with its mathematical equations. Furthermore, a comprehensive depiction of the employed wind turbine emulator, comprising a combination of a DC motor, a buck converter and a self-excited induction generator, is provided. The emulator is rigorously implemented and subjected to a thorough analysis within the MATLAB/Simulink environment to validate its system effectiveness.

II. THE ADOPTED SYSTEM

The diagram in Figure 1 illustrates the configuration of the Wind Turbine Emulator (WTE) employing a DC motor. To authentically replicate the behavior of a wind turbine utilizing a DC machine and its control system, a specific setup was adopted. This setup incorporates a DC-DC buck converter responsible for regulating the armature voltage of the DC motor. Control signals, generated by the wind emulator model in the form of PWM impulses, are used to control this converter. Consequently, variations in the armature voltage induce corresponding changes in the speed of the DC motor. Which makes it possible to obtain a mechanical torque which depends on the wind speed and varies over time in the same way as the torque of the in the wind turbine. The DC motor subsequently drives an asynchronous generator, which provides electrical energy using a capacitor unit.

Figure 1. The adopted system

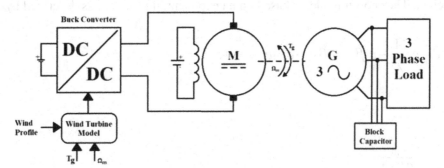

A. Wind Turbine Model

A wind turbine is designed to capture and convert the wind energy into usable electrical energy. At the heart of the turbine are its aerodynamic blades, used to capture the kinetic energy of the wind. They are attached to a central hub that allows them to rotate in response to the wind's movements. At the top of the turbine is the nacelle, which houses the electrical generator. The generator is the crucial component that transforms the mechanical energy from the blades into electricity. In order to increase energy production, the turbine is elevated in height by the tower to capture wind energy at altitudes where wind speed is higher (Wen, 2021; Aljarhizi Y. a., 2023; Garg, 2018; Dekali, 2021).

The power generation process begins when the wind blows and turns the turbine blades. The blades then transmit the mechanical energy to the generator through the hub. The generator converts this mechanical energy into electrical energy.

To be able to study, control, and test the wind energy conversion system on a simulation platform, it is necessary to mathematically model it. This model must accurately describe the real mechanical dynamics of the turbine blades.

The power extracted by the wind turbine is given by the following equation:

$$P_w = \frac{1}{2} A \rho V_w^3 C_p (\lambda, \beta) \tag{1}$$

This power depends on the wind speed, denoted as V_w^3, as well as the power coefficient (C_p), which are influenced by parameters such as air density (ρ), the swept area (A, calculated as πR^2), and the turbine's radius (R).

The power coefficient Cp is determined by both the Tip-Speed-Ratio ($\lambda = \dfrac{\Omega R}{V_w}$) and the blade pitching angle (β), where Ω is the angular velocity. In the scientific literature, various numerical approximations have been devised to derive an expression for the coefficient Cp. Additionally, extensive research efforts have been undertaken to ascertain the most suitable form of Cp. Some studies have developed functions that provide an approximate representation of the actual power coefficient curve. Nonetheless, polynomial, sinusoidal, and exponential function models are typically employed for modeling the power coefficient. The chosen model is based on an exponential function, as described by equations:

$$C_p(\lambda, \beta) = c_1 \left(c_2 \frac{1}{\lambda i} - c_3 \beta - c_4 \beta^{c_5} - c_6 \right) e^{-c_7 \frac{1}{\lambda i}} + c_8 \lambda \tag{2}$$

With,

$$\frac{1}{\lambda i} = \frac{1}{\lambda + c_9 \beta} - \frac{c_{10}}{\beta^3 + 1} \tag{3}$$

The selected coefficient values (c_i) are determined by the specific design of the wind turbine. Their respective values are: c_1=0.5175, c_2=116, c_3=0.4, c_4=0, c_5=0, c_6=5, c_7=21, c_8=0.0068, c_9=0.08 and c_{10}=0.035.

The validated model is assessed using Matlab/Simulink, incorporating the parameters outlined in Table 1.

Table 1. Parameters of the wind turbine model

Parameters	Values
Rated power	10 kW
Cut-in wind speed	3.0 m/s
Rated wind speed	10 m/s
Rotor diameter	7.1 m
Gear	7
Number of blades	3

As depicted in Figure 2, multiple curves have been plotted corresponding to different pitch angles. Nevertheless, this paper will exclusively focus on the curve associated with β=0°. This curve corresponds to a designated optimal value of λ, denoted λ_{opt}=8.1, determined by achieving the highest power coefficient (Cp_{max}=0.48).

Figure 2. Power coefficient

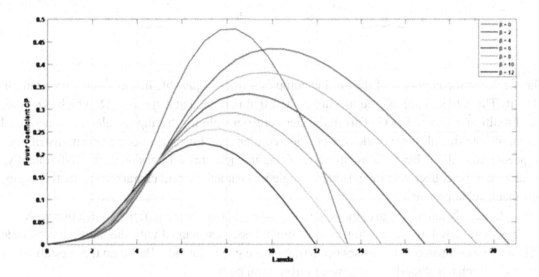

Considering the aerodynamic power equation, the wind turbine's aerodynamic torque T_w is derived by dividing the accessible power by the turbine's rotational speed (Ofualagba, 2008; Ragheb, 2011; Manyonge, 2012).

$$T_w = \frac{1}{2} \frac{\grave{A}\acute{A}R^2 V_w^3 C_p (\text{»},^2)}{©} \tag{4}$$

Figure 3 illustrates the mechanical power and torque characteristics of the wind turbine in relation to both angular velocity and wind speed, with assumed values of $\beta=0°$ and $\lambda=8.1$ (resulting in Cp=0.48). The points of the highest power and torque represent the most optimal operational conditions. This graphic serves as a crucial reference for refining and designing exceptionally efficient wind energy systems.

Figure 3. Mechanical power and torque

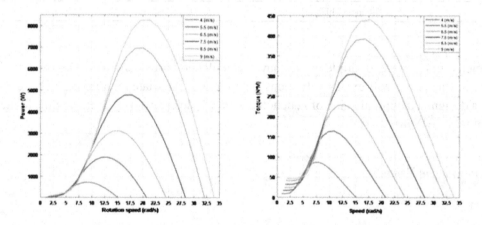

The mechanical component of the turbine comprises three adjustable blades, each with a length denoted as R. These blades are affixed to a drive shaft that is rotated at a speed of Ω, which is connected to a gain multiplier denoted as G. This multiplier is responsible for driving the electric generator. It is important to note that all three blades are considered identical. Furthermore, a uniform distribution of wind speed across all the blades is assumed, resulting in equal thrust forces on each. Consequently, the three blades can be collectively modeled as a single mechanical system characterized by the aggregate of their mechanical properties.

Due to the aerodynamic design of the blades, it is assumed that their coefficient of friction with respect to the air is extremely low. As a result, any frictional losses associated with the blades are considered negligible when compared to the losses occurring on the generator side. Based on these established assumptions, a mechanical model for the wind turbine can be derived.

The mechanical torque experienced by the asynchronous machine differs from the wind torque due to the necessity of accounting for both the inertia specific to the wind turbine and the viscous friction inherent to its structure. Mathematically, this relationship can be expressed as follows, where *J* represents the inertia of the wind turbine, and *f* represents the wind turbine's friction:

$$\frac{T_t}{G} - T_g = J\frac{d\Omega_m}{dt} + f\Omega_m \qquad (5)$$

$$J = \frac{J_t}{G^2} + J_g \qquad (6)$$

In this article, T_t and T_g refer to the torques exerted by the turbine and generator, respectively. Meanwhile, J_t and J_g represent the inertias of the slow-speed (turbine side) and high-speed (generator side) shafts, respectively.

The dynamic model of the wind turbine can be illustrated using the diagram depicted below:

Figure 4. Overall wind turbine model

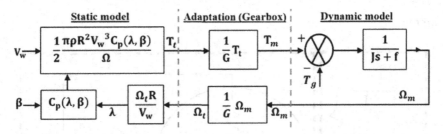

B. DC-DC Buck Converter and DC Motor

The turbine's performance is replicated employing a separately excited DC motor. In order to alter the motor's rotational speed, the supply voltage undergoes modification through a DC-DC buck converter (show Figure 5). This converter transforms a constant DC voltage into an adjustable output voltage dependent on the duty cycle ($\alpha = \dfrac{U_{chopper}}{U_{in}}$)of the chopper. The duty cycle is derived from the wind turbine model and is compared with a triangular signal to derive the pulse width modulation (PWM) signals. These signals are then utilized to control the transistor of the DC-DC buck converter, consequently regulating the armature voltage of the DC motor (Mohammed, 2017).

To accurately reproduce the behavior of a wind turbine using a direct-current motor, it is imperative to carry out an in-depth study of the various characteristics of this machine. This requires modeling its physical behavior using equations. The direct-current machine can be represented by a set of electrical, electromechanical, and mechanical equations. Figure 6 shows the equivalent model of the separately excited direct-current motor.

The parameters U_a and U_e refer to the voltage across the armature and inductor, respectively. Correspondingly, I_a and I_e represent the current flowing through the armature and inductor, respectively. The variables R_a, L_a, R_e and L_e denote the resistances and inductances associated with the armature and inductor components. Additionally, E signifies the electromotive force (EMF) in the system (Taveiros, 2013; Himani, 2015).

Figure 5. DC-DC buck converter and DC motor

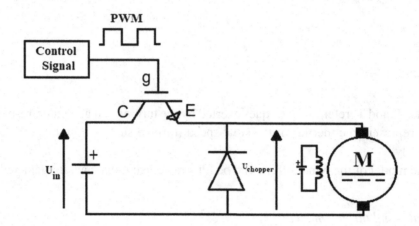

Figure 6. DC motor

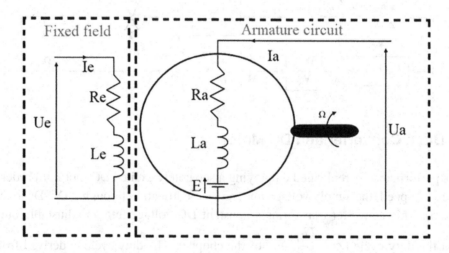

The electrical equations of the motor are:

$$U_a = R_a I_a + L_a \frac{dI_a}{dt} + E \qquad (7)$$

$$U_e = R_e I_e + L_e \frac{dI_e}{dt} \qquad (8)$$

With:

$$E = L_m I_e \Omega = K_e \Omega \qquad (9)$$

The magnetic flux generated by the inductor winding remains constant, characterized by the relationship $K_e = K_c = L_m I_e = \varphi_e$. Here, Ω represents the rotor's angular velocity, while L_m stands for the mutual inductance between the excitation and armature circuits.

The mechanical equation is:

$$T_{em} = T_r + f\Omega + J\frac{d\Omega}{dt} = K_c I_a \tag{10}$$

The symbol J signifies the rotor's moment of inertia, a crucial parameter in rotational dynamics. Additionally, the coefficient of friction is denoted by the variable f.

C. Self-Excited Induction Generator (SEIG)

The self-excited induction generator (SEIG) represents a major advancement in the field of autonomous electrification. It uses a conventional induction motor as the basis, exploiting the principle of electromagnetic induction. When the rotor rotates at a speed greater than that of the rotating magnetic field, an electromotive force is induced in the stator, provided it has a remanent magnetic field. This force is accumulated until reaching the nominal value thanks to a bank of capacitors, thus transforming the motor into a self-excited generator.

Figure 7. Self-excited induction generator

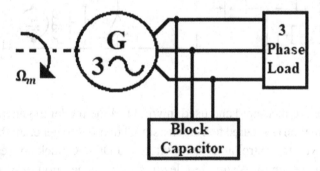

In short, the self-excited induction generator (Figures 7 and 8) offers an innovative solution for autonomous electrification. It opens new perspectives in industrial applications and isolated power systems, providing valuable electrical autonomy where access to an external excitation source is restricted (Aljarhizi Y. a., 2020).

Where X_1 and X_2 are respectively the stator and rotor reactances. And R_s and R_r the stator and rotor resistance. For the magnetizing inductor is represented by X_m, the capacitor by Z_c and the slip velocity by S.

Figure 8. Equivalent circuit with resistive load and excitation capacitance

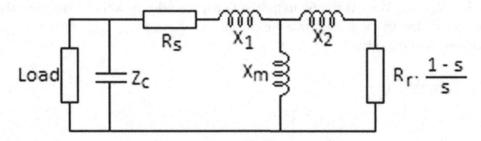

III. THE ADOPTED CONTROL METHOD

This study introduces a wind turbine simulation system tailored for wind power generation applications. The mathematical representation of this wind turbine model is provided to emulate the behavior and performance of an actual wind turbine. Equations 1 to 6 presents the resulting wind turbine model.

Figure 9. The adopted control

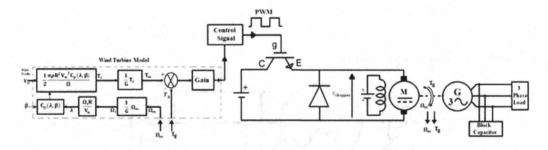

The speed and torque are measured and used in wind turbine model to generate a reference signals. The generated signals are then compared to a carrier signal in order to generate the PWM signals. These PWM signals are employed to control an IGBT switch in a DC-DC buck converter. Consequently, the armature voltage of a DC generator is supplied, leading to the generation of mechanical torque dependent on the wind speed. This torque is then used to drive the self-excited induction generator, Figure 9 illustrate the adopted control method.

IV. SIMULATION RESULTS

This section outlines the system simulation implemented using Matlab/Simulink, as depicted in Figure 10. The setup comprises a 1.5 KW self-induction generator powering a load with a resistive load. This generator is driven by a 1.5 KW DC motor, which is controlled using a DC-DC buck converter. The converter is regulated by a wind turbine model that generates a signal, compared with a carrier signal, to produce SPWM waves to control an IGBT switch in a chopper. The purpose of this simulation was to analyze how the wind turbine model responds when subjected to varying wind speeds. Figures 11 and 12 present the obtained results. The adopted system is illustrated as follow.

Figure 11 depicts the outcomes observed in the selected scenario, varying between [4 m/s–9 m/s]. The speed attains its peak within the range of [60 rad/s–150 rad/s] for each variation. Similarly, the ratio track the reference wind profile, ranging from 0.4 to 0.9.

Figure 10. Simulink model diagram of the proposed system

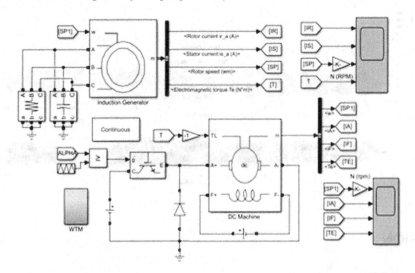

Figure 11. Simulation results: (a) wind profile (m/s), (b) wind turbine speed (rad/s), (c) ratio α

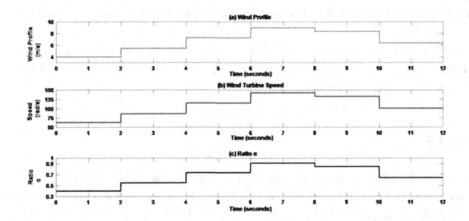

Figure 11 illustrates that the generated speed by the wind turbine model tracks the wind profile. Similarly, in Figure 12, the generator speed varies in accordance with changes in the wind profile, exhibiting different frequencies. As for the voltage and current of the induction generator, these signals present sinusoidal behavior, and their frequency adjusts according to the frequency generated by the wind turbine model. These observed results demonstrate the effectiveness of the adopted system. In comparison to the results obtained in Mhamdi Taoufik (2018), the outcomes of the adopted system are remarkable, providing clear affirmation of the benefits and advantages associated with utilizing the adopted control.

Figure 12. Simulation results: (a) generator speed (Rpm), (b) generator voltage (V), (c) generator current (A)

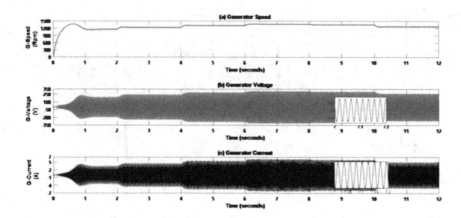

V. CONCLUSION

In this study, a wind turbine emulator has been introduced. It's based on a DC motor drive, a self-excited induction generator to produce electrical energy. The DC motor is controlled via a DC-DC buck converter, supplied with a PWM pulse. This pulse is obtained by comparing a carrier signal with the signals generated by the wind turbine model. The system reproduces the behavior of a wind turbine using a variable wind turbine profile.

The obtained results demonstrate the efficiency of the adopted system, for speed and torque. The delivered voltage and current are variable according to the wind speed. Future work will focus on further enhancing control techniques efficiency.

REFERENCES

Aljarhizi, Y. a. (2020). Static Power Converters for a Wind Turbine Emulator Driving a Self-Excited Induction Generator. In *2020 1st International Conference on Innovative Research in Applied Science, Engineering and Technology (IRASET)* (pp. 1--6). 10.1109/IRASET48871.2020.9092319

Aljarhizi, Y. a. (2023). Optimized Wind Turbine Emulator based on an AC to DC Motor Generator Set. *Engineering, Technology & Applied Scientific Research*, 10559–10564.

Benaaouinate, L. a. (2019). Emulation of Wind Turbine for Standalone Wind Energy Conversion Systems. *Modeling, Identification and Control Methods in Renewable Energy Systems*, 227-244.

Dekali, Z. a. (2021). Experimental implementation of the maximum power point tracking algorithm for a connected wind turbine emulator. *Revue Roumaine Des Sciences Techniques—Serie Electrotechnique Et Eneretique*, 111-117.

Garcia, J. H., Cherry, T. L., Kallbekken, S., & Torvanger, A. (2016). Willingness to accept local wind energy development: Does the compensation mechanism matter? *Energy Policy*, *99*, 165–173. doi:10.1016/j.enpol.2016.09.046

Garg, H. a. (2018). Design and Simulation of Wind Turbine Emulator. In *2018 IEEE 8th Power India International Conference (PIICON)* (pp. 1-6). 10.1109/POWERI.2018.8704424

Himani, G. a. (2015). Modelling and Development of Wind Turbine Emulator for the Condition Monitoring of Wind Turbine. *International Journal of Renewable Energy Research*, 591-597.

Kirikkaleli, D. a. (2021). Do public-private partnerships in energy and renewable energy consumption matter for consumption-based carbon dioxide emissions in India? *Environmental Science and Pollution Research, 28*, 30139-30152.

Manyonge, A. W. (2012). *Mathematical modelling of wind turbine in a wind energy conversion system: Power coefficient analysis*. Academic Press.

Martínez-Márquez, C. I.-B.-M.-G.-S.-C., Twizere-Bakunda, J. D., Lundback-Mompó, D., Orts-Grau, S., Gimeno-Sales, F. J., & Seguí-Chilet, S. (2019). Small Wind Turbine Emulator Based on Lambda-Cp Curves Obtained under Real Operating Conditions. *Energies*, *12*(13), 2456. doi:10.3390/en12132456

Mhamdi Taoufik, B. A. (2018). Stand-alone self-excited induction generator driven by a wind turbine. *Alexandria Engineering Journal*, *57*(2), 781–786. doi:10.1016/j.aej.2017.01.009

Mohammed, H. a. (2017). Simulation and experimental verification of PID controlled DC/DC buck converter in wind energy conversion system. In *2017 4th IEEE International Conference on Engineering Technologies and Applied Sciences (ICETAS)* (pp. 1-6). IEEE.

Mousarezaee, E. a. (2020). Wind turbine emulator based on small-scale PMSG by fuzzy FOC. In *2020 21st international symposium on electrical apparatus & technologies (SIELA)* (pp. 1-4). 10.1109/SIELA49118.2020.9167128

Moussa, I., Bouallegue, A., & Khedher, A. (2019). New wind turbine emulator based on DC machine: Hardware implementation using FPGA board for an open-loop operation. *IET Circuits, Devices & Systems*, *13*(6), 896–902. doi:10.1049/iet-cds.2018.5530

Ofualagba, G. a. (2008). Wind energy conversion system-wind turbine modeling. In 2008 IEEE power and energy society general meeting-conversion and delivery of electrical energy in the 21st century (pp. 1-8). doi:10.1109/PES.2008.4596699

Pérez-Lombard, L., Ortiz, J., & Pout, C. (2008). A review on buildings energy consumption information. *Energy and Building*, *40*(3), 394–398. doi:10.1016/j.enbuild.2007.03.007

Ragheb, M. a. (2011). Wind turbines theory-the betz equation and optimal rotor tip speed ratio. *Fundamental and advanced topics in wind power*, 19-38.

Sadorsky, P. (2009). Renewable energy consumption and income in emerging economies. *Energy Policy*, *37*(10), 4021–4028. doi:10.1016/j.enpol.2009.05.003

Taveiros, F. E. (2013). Wind turbine torque-speed feature emulator using a DC motor. In *2013 Brazilian Power Electronics Conference* (pp. 480--486). 10.1109/COBEP.2013.6785159

Wen, Q. a. (2021). A comprehensive review of miniatured wind energy harvesters. *Nano Materials Science*, 170-185.

Chapter 2
The Usefulness of Digital Twin in Manipulator Robot Control

Imane Cheikh
LIMAS-Lab, Faculty of Sciences Dhar El Mahraz, Sidi Mohammed Ben Abdellah University, Morocco

Khaoula Oulidi Omali
National School for Computer Science and Systems Analysis, University Mohammed V, Morocco

Mohammed Nabil Kabbaj
iD https://orcid.org/0000-0002-6478-1892
LIMAS-Lab, Faculty of Sciences Dhar El Mahraz, Sidi Mohammed Ben Abdellah University, Morocco

Mohammed Benbrahim
Faculty of Sciences, Sidi Mohammed Ben Abdellah University, Morocco

ABSTRACT

Digital twin (DT) plays a key role in smart industry by being one of the most useful technologies which has the ability to attach the physical space with the cyber space. On the other side of the coin, manipulator robots have also played an essential role in industrial processes, especially that robots are embedded with sensors and actuators that can lead to a smart control. In this study, generalities about digital twin are mentioned; moreover, the relationship between digital twin and the control of manipulator robots is explained step by step. A simulation study has been employed to the universal robot UR10 applying the sliding mode control. This project shows that the cyber space is beneficial for creating a simulated smart industry by observing real-time state of the process, testing different decisions in simulation before performing the required actions directly in the real system, and acting with different situations.

1. INTRODUCTION

For the first time, the notion of Digital Twin was suggested by Professor M. Grieves of the University of Michigan in 2003 (Grieves 2016). Then, it started attracting more attention by the end of 2011, when technology knew a rapid growth, specifically by the evolution of simulation technologies, internet of things, big data, sensor innovations, etc. In 2012, NASA considered the usefulness of the implementation

DOI: 10.4018/979-8-3693-0497-6.ch002

of digital twin to improve the performance of air force vehicles (Glaessgen and Stargel 2012). Two years later, Digital Twin was no longer just a theoretical idea, but moved into reality in some manufactories (Grieves 2014). Currently, the reason which has further encouraged the improvement of digital twin is that this concept not only restricted to the aerospace industry, but can be used in many different fields (Tao et al. 2019). In 2025, Gartner predicts that 25 enterprises using Digital Twin will earn 1\$ billion in revenue and in 2027, Gartner also estimates that 40 percent of the companies over the world will be using Digital Twin (Attaran and Celik 2023).

Digital Twin was given different definitions in several articles. Generally, it defines the relation between the physical and virtual objects. Depending on the type of the digital Twin, the cyber simulation space represents and reflects the physical space based on constant transmission data and real-time sensor data and it can trigger or observe the functioning of the physical world containing real devices (Negri et al. 2020). Consequently, this technology leads to improve performance and processes of industries and also allows the quick detection of physical problems which will facilitate finding solutions (Attaran and Celik 2023). Moreover, manipulator robots are commonly used in many industries to accomplish different tasks especially the more complexed ones. Hence, it is undeniable that they play a key role in their process. Therefore, starting to employ the digital twin concept to control the manipulator robots will have a great advantage in the improvement of many industries. Nowadays, many researches employ digital twin in robotic field. As an example, in the article (Matulis & Harvey 2021), the authors used digital twin to train a robot arm with reinforcement learning in the cyber space to complete a desired task and finally apply this training in the physical space. However, there is a limited number of writings using the robot operating system software with digital twin to control robots.

Manipulator robots are typical nonlinear and time varying dynamical systems. Therefore, the conventional linear control strategies are not satisfying the control of these robots. In literature, there are many conventional nonlinear methods to control manipulator robots such as feedback linearization (Deluca 1988), force control (Mason 1981), Sliding Mode Control (Slotine & Li 1991), backstepping (H.-J. Shieh and C.-H.Hsu, 2008), etc. However, some of these methods aren't robust enough to unexpected disturbances or to uncertainties (Kali et al. 2016). Yet, since 1980, the theory of the sliding mode control has been acknowledged by its practical simplicity and its robustness which is opposed to the uncertainties, disturbances and the variations of parameters (Slotine & Li 1991). Despite those advantages, the fundamental disadvantage of this approach relates to the chatter phenomenon due to high-frequency oscillations near to the sliding surface S used in the controller with a switching function Signum. To reduce the problem of chattering with the same precision and performance, there are several functions that can be used such as saturation function that will be applied in this study (Ömür 2021).

The goal of this chapter is to prove that using digital twin in the control of manipulator robot would obviously be of great benefit in the improvement of smart industries. It will lead to develop optimal solutions through simulation in virtual world and optimal manufacturing by increasing product quality, stability and accuracy. It will induce to high durability of the physical components by predictive diagnosis and analytical assessment. For instance, in case of faults in the robot manipulator, Digital Twin can be used to detect those faults by data analysis and monitoring (Omali et al. 2021). Nevertheless, controlling robot manipulators poses different challenges by using Digital Twin. The main challenges to discuss afterwards are about the representation of the robot manipulator in the digital space and how to manage communication, data analysis and simulation of two sliding mode control methods.

The remaining five sections of this chapter are set up to handle the aforementioned challenges. The intended goals of this study are listed in the first section. Then, the second section mentions the digital twin generalities. Afterwards, the third section considers the system description and the methodology used as well as the sliding mode controller design. The fourth section contains the simulation on the universal robot 10 by using the robot operating system framework, GAZEBO simulator and Matlab-Simulink for coding. And the last section is representing the examination of the simulation's outcomes.

2. OBJECTIVES OF THE STUDY

For implementing Digital Twin to control the manipulator robot using the robot operating System framework, Gazebo as a simulator and Matlab Simulink as a coding tool, there are several steps to follow which are described below.

2.1 Steps Diagram

The diagram of the manipulator robot's control by implementing Digital Twin is minutely shown in Figure 1. It is starting by designing the digital robot, then controlling the robot with Matlab and Simulink. After that, the simulation of the robot using Gazebo is done and finally the connection between the hardware, the software and the simulation is completed.

Figure 1. Diagram of the manipulator robot's control based on digital twin

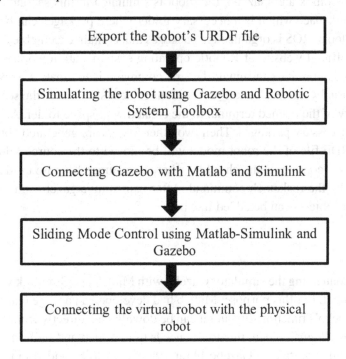

2.2 First Step

The first step is to export the manipulator's robot unified robot description format file (URDF). This file is written with XML format to describe a robot model by giving a detailed kinematic and dynamic description of the robot, collision model and a visual representation of the robot. The joints of the robot connect the link and joint elements with each other so as to connect each joint to its parent link and its child link. On one hand, each link element in the URDF is specified with its mass, its inertia tensor and its center of mass in order to describe the dynamic's corresponding robot component. On the other hand, each joint element in the URDF file is represented with the position *xyz* and the orientation roll, pitch and yaw to indicate the translation and the rotation respectively of the $(k-1)^{th}$ joint to the kth joint.

The URDF with XML format is the standard format that can be used within ROS and can be simulated using ROS simulators like Gazebo, RVIZ and MoveIt.

To extract the URDF file of the corresponding robot using SolidWorks is a good option. It starts by drawing the robot model before using SolidWorks URDF exporter plugin to convert the model parts into a URDF file and the connection between two parts of the robot is detected as a joint automatically (Feder et al. 2022).

Designing its own URDF File might not be simple for the user, it needs mathematics for every robot description. Providentially, Xarco language can be used to simplify the structure of URDF file by specifying constants, doing mathematics and using macros.

2.3 Second Step

Using robotic system toolbox and Gazebo, the robot is simulated in this second stage. The first thing to do is to create a workspace which is a necessary folder where packages can be modified, built and installed using catkin tools. ROS is organized in packages that contain executable files for each purpose.

According to the official website of Robotic operating system, catkin workspace is created by executing three commands in a linux terminal: the first command is to create a workspace folder named "name_workspace", usually named "catkin_ws" with its folder "src". Then, the second command needs to change the directory of the opened terminal to the created workspace folder. And the final command leads to build all the necessary packages. Then two other folders are generated "build" and "devel".

Thereafter, the URDF file of the robot model will be moved to the source folder of the workspace created. This file already contains a launch folder where two launch files are used to simulate the robot in Gazebo and RVIZ by the roslaunch command. After launching a gazebo simulation, the world file can be saved and many objects can be added like box.

2.4 Third Step

This step is based on connecting the simulator Gazebo with Matlab and Simulink which is used to model the controller of the robot. For this purpose, Matlab had developed a package Gazebo plugin which has direct access to all Gazebo's functionality and it can be downloaded directly from Matlab with the command *"packageGazeboPlugin"*. Then, this folder needs to be added and built in the linux platform. In addition, the plugin folder contains a Gazebo library that needs to be added in the world file saved of the gazebo launched file.

Moreover, IP address and the port number are used to connect Gazebo that is located in the Linux virtual machine with Matlab-Simulink which is installed in windows. Using Robotics System Toolbox, Gazebo Pacer is used to ensure successful synchronization of the simulation times between Gazebo and Simulink.

2.5 Fourth Step

In this study, Simulink is employed to simulate real-time trajectory tracking using Gazebo while also modeling the robot's dynamics and controlling the robot using the Sliding Mode Controller to obtain the desired position. It will be divided into four main Simulink blocks:

- Gazebo Pacer.
- End effector desired position xyz and orientation roll, pitch and yaw.
- Control with joint torque as an output.
- Gazebo Robot with joint output from Gazebo and joint torque input from the controller.

2.6 Final Step

Connecting the virtual system that Gazebo had simulated to the physical system is the basis of this step. The real robot and the simulated robot require shadowing which means synchronization so that every movement in the real robot can be visualized directly in the cyber space. Given the progress in the communication technology and in data storage, all the data received from the manipulator robot has been transferred via a suitable communication channel and it may be stored in the cloud to track the evolution of the robot. However, this step will lead to either monitor the physical space or directly take the action on behalf of the robot according to the chosen type of the digital twin (Saracco 2019).

3. DIGITAL TWIN GENERALITIES

This section is reviewing the basic concepts, the mostly used communication protocols, the data representation, and the types of the digital twin.

3.1 Basic Concepts

The simulation technology has been developed for years and the traditional simulations are commonly used to test scenarios for the system so as to have possible conclusions. In another way, digital twin can be used not only for simulation, but also for monitoring the real system and can cooperate directly with the physical space. This dissimilarity between digital twin and the traditional simulations is due to the real-time communication between the physical space and the cyber space by using the system sensors to gather data that will be analyzed by digital twin. In addition, the system's prevision detects the level of the performance, the defects and environment changes in order to provide real-time feedback of the system and to take quick decisions and actions. For this reason, data is gathered from the physical space by employing digital twin and with it, DT can control, optimize and also predict the system's functionality.

The architecture of the Digital Twin is categorized into three parts: physical space, cyber space and the communication between them (Tao et al. 2019). Whilst the physical space represents the real system with different sensors and actuators, the cyber space is a replica of this physical system and it is used for tests and evaluations. Nevertheless, the physical environment can change during the system operation. In this case, the digital twin can detect this change by analyzing the data and then trying to find new control models by performing simulation in the cyber space before guiding the physical space to perform an action.

3.2 Digital Twin Types

The Digital Twin is classified as four types: Digital Twin Instance (DTI), Digital Twin Aggregation (DTA), Digital Twin Prototype (DTP) and Digital Twin Environment (DTE).

A particular digital twin's type that gathers data from the physical system is the DTP. After that, the DTP transfers these data to the digital system only in one-way flow. However, it does not allow data transmission in the other direction, that is, from a digital system to a physical one. Consequently, this particular sort of digital twin is only utilized for system monitoring and does not have the permission to manage or control it (Rasheed et al. 2020).

The DTI is a digital twin's form that enables data transmission from the digital system to the real one, in contrast to the digital twin prototype. Therefore, this type cannot handle the data flow from the cyber space to the digital one. In order to help the real system respond appropriately to changes in the environment, the DTI is used to forecast a result through simulation experiments (Haag & Andrel 2018).

The term DTA has been proposed as a grouping of the existing DTIs including additional mechanisms for data collection from the physical space. Additionally, the digital system's prediction results can be used to manage the physical space (Jones et al. 2020).

The DTE contains multiple cyber and digital spaces; it is commonly used to manage big systems and cooperate in the group of physical systems operations. In addition, a synchronization mechanism is needed between the different digital systems used (Haag & Andrel 2018).

In this project, the main focus is on the DTA, but with only one DTI to control the manipulator robot.

3.3 Digital Twin Data Representation

The format and structure in which data is recorded, saved, and represented inside a digital twin system are referred to as "Digital Twin Data Representation". The type of data being gathered and the unique needs of the digital twin application determine the data representation to be used. Here are four typical methods for digital twin data representation (Qian et al. 2022):

Digital Twin Definition Language consists on the following six properties: (a) Interface: a component's fundamental data such as the element ID, the element type, the display constituent, etc. Aspects from parent interfaces can be inherited by child interfaces, for example, addresses from the parking lot can be inherited by the components of charging stations; (b) Telemetry: data transmitted from any Internet of things based on digital twin component (processed data generated by DT models, raw data produced by IoT devices, etc.); (c) Property: the state of Internet of things based on digital twin component (e.g., whether the system is read-write or read-only). This may potentially include all of the different DT's conditions (such as whether the data between the two DTs is coherent, etc.); (d) Command: actions any DT may comprehend; (e) Relationship: it is the link connecting the DTs (for instance, the connection relating the robot with the environment where it works); (f) Component: the elements that are present in the digital twin, such as detectors, gateways, and cyber systems. Based on the aforementioned six elements, this data representation method may be built from a number of DTs having a common structure and data, allowing for easy data transfer across DTs (Qian et al. 2022).

Another open-source project, FIWARE, supports the transfer of DT data as well as the analysis of contextual data from multiple IoT components. Contextual data collecting, processing, and change notification processes are all covered by the FIWARE NGSI data modeling standard. An object-oriented data protocol called FIWARE NGSI employs context objects to represent real-world and digital items. A data model that NGSI offers permits data interchange across several DTs. Additionally, it employs NGSI-LD to express the connections between various objects and JSON-LD for developing to standardize the data structure (Condo et al. 20222022).

A modeling tool which may extract details from unstructured data is OPC Unified Architecture. It also establishes the paradigm for data transfer and interpretation across different systems. Additionally, it offers a method for going through every data and examining its semantics. To make data management in the DT architecture simpler, OPC UA provides data manipulation. Additionally, it has monitoring features that let the DT system oversee the status of all the controlled sensors (Qian et al. 2022).

A DT structure known as the feature-based DT framework allows the DT system to communicate data depending on the information relating the DT components. Furthermore, data exchange across various DT models as well as across digital and physical systems is made possible by this framework (Qian et al. 2022).

3.4 Digital Twin Communication Protocols

The information is transferred between sensors, actuators, other devices and between systems through communication protocols. There are commonly used protocols such as Modbus TCP/IP Protocol, OASIS standard messaging protocol (MQTT), Constrained Application Protocol (CoAP) and Ultra Reliable Low Latency Communication (URLCC).

TCP/IP, a communication protocol, is usually used in the industry; User Datagram Protocol (UDP) and Transmission Control Protocol (TCP) are used to represent it for connectionless service and connection service, respectively. Both of them are employed to deliver messages between the objects using the IP protocol which delivers packets within the network. The most significant advantages of TCP/IP protocol are its data protection as well as its reliability in transferring data and applying operations (Bohuslava et al. 2017; Qian et al. 2022).

MQTT is a messaging system that is based on the TCP protocol. It consists of MQTT clients (sensors, etc.) and MQTT brokers which manage client-client communication and transmit commands to actuators. The communication between devices is managed via MQTT messages characterized by their optimizing headers. Furthermore, MQTT protocol can also ensure data transmission reliability (Qian et al. 2022).

The communication protocol CoAP works with the Hypertext Transfer Protocol HTTP to transfer data and it is usually used in web applications. It uses the protocol UDP and provides a publish and subscribe mechanism to obtain continuous data from sensors. Therefore, CoAP can be employed to communicate between the system devices (Qian et al. 2022).

URLCC is based on the 5G wireless protocol which makes it a fast information exchanger but it can attain low reliability and latency. With the aim to improve this drawback, URLCC uses three mechanisms:

the first one is for estimating the channel, the second one is for transmission diversity and the third one is for reducing the error rate (Qian et al. 2022).

In this project, the communication protocol used is the TCP/IP protocol to achieve reliable data transfer between Gazebo simulation and Matlab-Simulink.

4. MODELING AND CONTROL

4.1 Robot Modeling

The dynamics of an n-link robot manipulator or arm robot are usually represented by the Euler-Lagrange system with the well-known equation:

$$M(q)\ddot{q} + C(q,\dot{q})\dot{q} + G(q) = \tau + \tau_d \tag{1}$$

where $q, \dot{q}, \ddot{q} \in \Re^n$ are respectively the vectors of the joint position, the joint velocity and the joint acceleration; $M(q) \in \Re^{n \times n}$ is the manipulator inertia matrix which is symmetric and positive definite; $C(q,\dot{q}) \in \Re^n$ gathers the Coriolis and centripetal torques vector; $G(q) \in \Re^n$ is the gravitational torques vector, $\tau \in \Re^n$ is the input torque vector applied to the actuators and τd describes the disturbances.

Denoting that $x_1 = $ q and $x_2 = \dot{q}$, the equation (1) can be rewritten as follows:

$$\begin{cases} \dot{x}_1 = x_2 \\ \dot{x}_2 = f(x,t) + g(x,t)u(t) \end{cases} \tag{2}$$

where the state variable is represented by x = $[x_1, x_2]^T$,

$$f(x,t) = -M(q)^{-1}\left[C(q,\dot{q})\dot{q} + G(q) - \tau_d\right]$$

is the nonlinear dynamics that can be uncertain and the disturbances, the control matrix is $g(x,y) = M(q)^{-1}$ and the control input is $u(t) = \tau$.

4.2 Bounds of the Control Matrix

The robot manipulator's dynamic is only an approximation of the system's applications in real life. Thus, the first step before designing the controller is to determine the bounds of the inertia matrix. In that case, the experimental approach is used to find the inertia matrix bounds using the following formula (Emami et al. 1998):

$$I_{bound} = \frac{\ddot{q}\left[\tau(q,\dot{q},\ddot{q},t) - \tau(q,\dot{q},0,t)\right]}{\ddot{q}^2} \tag{3}$$

The bounds of the inverse matrix g(x,t) are then:

$$g_{min} = \frac{1}{I_{max}}$$

$$g_{max} = \frac{1}{I_{min}} \tag{4}$$

$$g_{min}I < g < g_{max}I$$

Geometrically, the bounds can be defined as:

$$\hat{g} = \sqrt{g_{min}g_{max}} \tag{5}$$

And the control gain margins are as below (Slotine & Li 1991):

$$\beta = \sqrt{\frac{g_{max}}{g_{min}}} \tag{6}$$

The result of combining the equation (5) and (6) is:

$$\beta^{-1}I \le \hat{g}g^{-1} \le \beta I \tag{7}$$

Furthermore, the desired control gain margins βd are defined similary as β.

4.3 Bounds of the Robot's Dynamic Uncertainty

The nonlinear function $f(x,t)$ combines the system uncertainty including joint friction and it is not precisely known. In reality, it can be estimated by $\hat{f}(x,t)$ designed as (Kali et al. 2016):

$$\hat{f}(x,t) \approx f(x,t-L) \tag{8}$$

where L is an estimation time delay which is a positive real number.

Therefore, the imprecision between $f(x,t)$ and its estimate $\hat{f}(x,t)$ should be bounded by F which is known as:

$$\left| \hat{f}(x,t) - f(x,t) \right| \le F \tag{9}$$

F is defined as the maximum of $\Delta F = \left| \hat{f}(x,t) - f(x,t) \right|$.

4.4 Sliding Mode Control

As a robust control method, the sliding mode control approach can be used for dynamic systems with the identical number of inputs and outputs. In this chapter, we consider the manipulator robot with the dynamic equation (1) and (2) to design SMC.

The sliding surface vector of second order nonlinear system is chosen as:

$$S = \dot{e} + \lambda e \tag{10}$$

where $e=x_{1d}-x_1$ is the position error vector and x_d is the desired position; $\lambda=diag(\lambda_1,\ldots,\lambda_n)$ is the sliding coefficient with λ_i are positive constants and $S=[S_1,S_2,\ldots,S_n]^T$ with S_i is the sliding surface for $i\in[1,n]$ (Kali et al., 2016).

4.4.1 Controller Design

The complete design for controlling the robot manipulator is shown in the following block diagram in Figure 2.

Figure 2. Block diagram of the manipulator's control with sliding mode controller and gazebo simulation

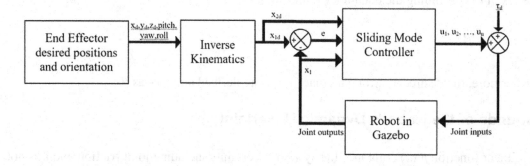

In the sliding mode controller block, the control input "u" has to be designed so that the error vector and its derivative can reach to the sliding surface. To accomplish this aim, the necessary condition to design the control law is:

$$S\dot{S} < 0 \tag{11}$$

The widely used $\dot{S}$ to satisfy the condition (11) is:

$$\dot{S} = -K\, sign(S) \tag{12}$$

where $K=diag(k_1,\ldots,k_n)$ with k_i for $i\in[1,n]$ are positive constants, and sign(S) represents the signum function of the sliding surface S and it is defined as (Kali et al. 2016):

$$Sign(S)=\begin{cases}1, & if\ S>0 \\ 0, & if\ S=0 \\ -1, & if\ S<0\end{cases}\tag{13}$$

According to the equation (10), the time derivative of the sliding surface is (Omali et al., 2022):

$$\dot{S}=\ddot{e}+\lambda\dot{e}$$
$$-K\ sign(S)=\ddot{x}_{1d}-\ddot{x}_1+\lambda\dot{e}\tag{14}$$
$$-K\ sign(S)=\dot{x}_{2d}-\dot{x}_2+\lambda\dot{e}$$

By replacing $\dot{x}_2$ from the equation (2) into (14):

$$-K\ sign(S)=-f(x,t)-g(x,t)u(t)+\dot{x}_{2d}+\lambda\dot{e}\tag{15}$$

In consequence, the controller is determined as:

$$u(t)=g^{-1}\left(-f(x,t)+\dot{x}_{2d}+\lambda\dot{e}\right)+g^{-1}K\ sign(S)\tag{16}$$

On that account, the controller consists of two terms: u_{eq} and u_s where u_{eq} is the sufficient controller to keep the state on the sliding surface S and u_s is the switching controller.

And with the use of the estimations of the inertia matrix and the dynamics uncertainty f, the equivalent control is defined as:

$$u_{eq}=\hat{g}^{-1}\left(-\hat{f}(x,t)+\dot{x}_{2d}+\lambda\dot{e}\right)\tag{17}$$

Then the controller can be defined as:

$$u=u_{eq}+u_s$$
$$u_s=g^{-1}K\ sign(S)\tag{18}$$

4.4.2 Stability Analysis

The principle of Lyapunov is employed in order to prove the stability of the aforementioned system. On that account, the Lyapunov function is proposed as follows:

$$V = \frac{1}{2}S^2 \tag{19}$$

The time derivative of the Lyapunov function candidate (19) including the use of the equation (15) can be written as (Kali et al. 2016):

$$\dot{V} = S\dot{S}$$
$$= S\left(-f - gu + \dot{x}_{2d} + \lambda\dot{e}\right) \tag{20}$$

Therefore, the equation (18) is used to replace the control u(t) by its expression so that the equation (20) can be rewritten as:

$$\dot{V} = S\left(-f - g\hat{g}^{-1}\left(-\hat{f} + \dot{x}_{2d} + \lambda\dot{e}\right) - K\ sign(S) + \dot{x}_{2d} + \lambda\dot{e}\right)$$
$$= S\left(\left[-f + g\hat{g}^{-1}\hat{f}\right] + \left(1 - g\hat{g}^{-1}\right)\left(\dot{x}_{2d} + \lambda\dot{e}\right) - K\ sign(S)\right) \tag{21}$$

Rewrite the dynamics uncertainties as:

$$-f = -f + \hat{f} - \hat{f} \tag{22}$$

Then the equation (21) becomes:

$$\dot{V} = S\left(\left[-f + \hat{f}\right] + \left[1 - g\hat{g}^{-1}\right]\left(-\hat{f} + \dot{x}_{2d} + \lambda\dot{e}\right) - K\ sign(S)\right)$$
$$= S\left(\left[-f + \hat{f}\right] + \left[1 - g\hat{g}^{-1}\right]\hat{g}u_{eq} - K\ sign(S)\right) \tag{23}$$

The condition bellow needs to be held to prove the stability of the system:

$$\dot{V} < 0 \tag{24}$$

To make this condition more stringent, $\dot{V}$ can be less than a negative number which is:

$$\dot{V} < -\mu|S| \tag{25}$$

with μ is a strict positive constant.

According to the equations (23), (9), (7) and the condition (25), the gain K can be designed:

$$K \geq \mu + F + \hat{g}(1 - \hat{g}^{-1}g)\,|u_{eq}| \tag{26}$$

In addition, the equations (7) and (6) yield the gain of the switching controller Us:

$$K = \mu + F + \hat{g}(1 - \beta^{-1})|u_{eq}| \tag{27}$$

4.4.3 Chattering Effect

Despite the Sliding Mode Control's benefits, the chattering effect is a significant obstacle to this approach. It is due to the switching time delays of the control input near to the sliding surface and it can wear out the system actuators by high-frequency oscillations. To mitigate this phenomenon, several methods can be employed such as:

- The hysteresis function technique.
- The boundary layer technique.
- Higher-order sliding mode control method.
- The state observer technique.

In this chapter, the method employed to decrease the chattering phenomena is the time varying boundary layer technique. The idea behind this technique is to use a saturation function (Sat) in place of the sign function in the control input. This function presents a smooth transition around the sliding surface using a time varying boundary layer with a thickness φ. In addition, it leads to reducing the control signal's discontinuity near to the sliding surface S.

Hence, the controller in the equation (16) using the boundary layer technique can be defined as:

$$u(t) = u_{eq} + g^{-1}\left(K\,sat\left(\frac{S}{\varphi(t)}\right)\right) \tag{28}$$

where the saturation function is determined by the following definition:

$$sat\left(\frac{S_i}{\varphi(t)}\right) = \begin{cases} sign(S_i), & if\ |S_i| > \varphi(t) \\ \frac{S_i}{\varphi(t)}, & if\ |S_i| < \varphi(t) \end{cases} \tag{29}$$

The traditional boundary layer technique uses a constant thickness φ. Moreover, it is important to choose carefully the thickness φ, because if the boundary layer is too large, it may give rise to undesirable errors. However, if it is too small, it may not efficaciously eliminate chattering effect (Komurcugil et al 2021). For this reason, Slotine proposed a time-varying thickness φ so as to achieve better elimination of the chattering (Slotine & Li 1991).

To determine the variation of φ, a balance condition is given by (Slotine & Li 1991):

$$\begin{cases} \dfrac{d\varphi}{dt} + \lambda\varphi = \beta_d K\left(q_d\right), & if \ \ K\left(q_d\right) > \dfrac{\lambda\varphi}{\beta_d} \\[4mm] \dfrac{d\varphi}{dt} + \dfrac{\lambda}{\beta_d{}^2}\varphi = \beta_d K\left(q_d\right) & else \end{cases} \tag{30}$$

where $K(q_d)$ is the gain of the switching controller with $q=q_d$.

Overall, sliding mode control is an effective method for controlling the manipulator robots even in the presence of external disturbances and dynamic uncertainties. And with the use of the chattering reduction techniques, the sliding mode control can be applied to achieve robust control for manipulator robots.

5. SIMULATION ON THE UNIVERSAL ROBOT UR10

This section contains two simulations on the universal robot UR10 using Matlab Simulink software for coding the sliding mode controller, Robot operating System framework (ROS) for accessing the UDRF File of the UR10 and Gazebo as a simulation environment and as a digital twin cyber space to mirror the behavior of the real robot UR10.

Figure 3. Digital universal robot UR10

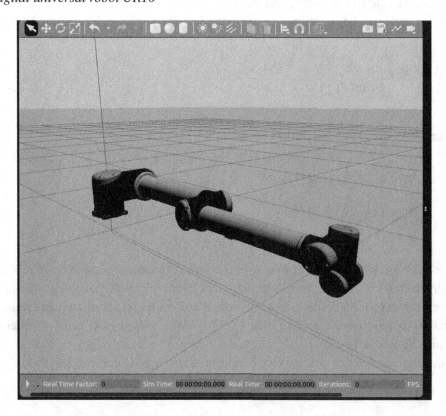

5.1 The Cyber Space Creation

The URDF file can be manually developed, as described in section one, or exported from SolidWorks as the initial step in generating a digital representation of the manipulator robot. Otherwise, the universal robots company offers a range of open-source robot models where the robot UR10's URDF file can be found.

Following the second step of section one, the digital model of the universal robot UR10 can be simulated via Gazebo as a virtual replica of its physical model. The figures 3 and 4 represent both of the digital and physical models of the robot UR10 which have similar parameters, components and characteristics.

Figure 4. Physical universal robot UR10

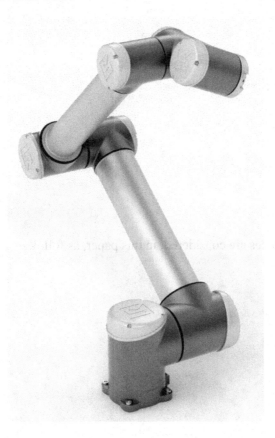

5.2 Dynamic Model

According to the equation (2), the dynamic of the manipulator robot UR10 with 6-DOF is given by:

$$
\begin{cases}
\dot{x}_1 = x_7 \\[4pt]
\dot{x}_2 = x_8 \\[4pt]
\dot{x}_3 = x_9 \\[4pt]
\dot{x}_4 = x_{10} \\[4pt]
\dot{x}_5 = x_{11} \\[4pt]
\dot{x}_6 = x_{12} \\[4pt]
\dot{x}_7 = f_1(x,t) + \displaystyle\sum_{i=1}^{6} g_{1i} u_i \\[10pt]
\dot{x}_8 = f_2(x,t) + \displaystyle\sum_{i=1}^{6} g_{2i} u_i \\[10pt]
\dot{x}_9 = f_3(x,t) + \displaystyle\sum_{i=1}^{6} g_{3i} u_i \\[10pt]
\dot{x}_{10} = f_4(x,t) + \displaystyle\sum_{i=1}^{6} g_{4i} u_i \\[10pt]
\dot{x}_{11} = f_5(x,t) + \displaystyle\sum_{i=1}^{6} g_{5i} u_i \\[10pt]
\dot{x}_{12} = f_6(x,t) + \displaystyle\sum_{i=1}^{6} g_{6i} u_i
\end{cases}
\tag{31}
$$

In addition, the disturbances are considered, in this paper, as follows:

$$
\tau_d(t) =
\begin{cases}
e^{-5t} * \sin(2t) \\[4pt]
\cos(2t) \\[4pt]
\cos(2t) \\[4pt]
0 \\[4pt]
0 \\[4pt]
0
\end{cases}
\tag{32}
$$

The objective is to guarantee that the end effector arrives to the desired position and orientation x_d, y_d, z_d, *roll, pitch,* and *yaw* with a very small error e in a limited convergence time t_c. Using the inverse kinematics solver from Matlab-Simulink software, the desired position and orientation of the end effector are transformed to the six desired joints positions. The initial joint positions are given in Table 1 and the desired positions and orientations x_d, y_d, z_d, *roll, pitch,* and *yaw* of the end effector, considering certain reaching times and velocities constraints, are given in Table 2.

The goal is to track the desired trajectory $p_1 = x_d$, $p_2 = y_d$, $p_3 = z_d$ and the desired velocity $\dot{p}_1 = \dot{x}_d$, $\dot{p}_2 = \dot{y}_d$, $\dot{p}_3 = \dot{z}_d$ starting from an initial position p_{i0} to a desired position p_{if} for $i \in [1,3]$ in a specific reaching time with velocity constraints. To do so, the chosen trajectory is a cubic polynomial trajectory (Craig 2005):

$$p_i(t) = a_{i3}(t-t_0)^3 + a_{i2}(t-t_0)^2 + a_{i1}(t-t_0) + a_{i0} \tag{33}$$

where

$$a_{i0} = p_{i0}$$

$$a_{i1} = \dot{p}_{i0}$$

$$a_{i2} = \frac{3}{t_f^2}\left(p_{if} - p_{i0}\right) - \frac{2}{t_f}\dot{p}_{i0} - \frac{1}{t_f}\dot{p}_{if}$$

$$a_{i3} = -\frac{2}{t_f^3}\left(p_{if} - p_{i0}\right) + \frac{1}{t_f^2}(\dot{p}_{i0} + \dot{p}_{if})$$

Table 1. UR10's joints initial positions

Joint	1	2	3	4	5	6
Initial Position (rad)	$x_1(0)=0$	$x_2(0)=1.22$	$x_3(0)=2.44$	$x_4(0)=0$	$x_5(0)=0$	$x_6(0)=0$

Table 2. Desired positions and orientations of the UR10's end effector at specific reaching times with velocity constraints

End Effector	x_d	y_d	z_d	Roll	Pitch	Yaw
Desired position and orientation (rad)	[0.5, 0.5, 0.8, 0.8]	[0.5, 0.7, 0.5, 0.7]	[0.125, 0.15, 0.175, 0.2]	π	-1.22	1.57
Reaching times t_f (sec)	[0.5, 2, 3.5, 5]					
Velocity constraints (rad/s)	[0, 0.75, 0.5, 0]					

5.3 Calculation of Bounds

For the robot UR10 with 6 DOF, a PD controller was applied using Matlab-Simulink and Gazebo to find the bounds below.

According to the equation (3), the inertia bounds for the purpose of getting the end-effector in the desired position and orientation are:

$$I_{max} = 3.79 \left[kgm^2 \right]$$
$$I_{min} = 0.08 \left[kgm^2 \right]$$

(34)

The bounds of the inverse matrix g(x,t), using the equation (4), are then:

$$g_{min} = 0.26$$
$$g_{max} = 12.5$$
$$g_{min}I < g < g_{max}I$$

(35)

With the equation (5), the geometrical bounds are:

$$\hat{g} = 3.57 \; and \; \hat{g}^{-1} = 0.28$$

(36)

And according to the equation (6), the control gain margins are calculated as below (Slotine & Li 1991):

$$\beta = 6.93 \; and \; \beta^{-1} = 0.14$$

(37)

$$\beta^{-1}I \leq \hat{g}g^{-1} \leq \beta I$$

(38)

Furthermore, the desired control gain margins β_d is:

$$\beta_d = 7.71 \; and \; \beta_{d\text{-}1} = 0.13$$

(39)

5.4 Sliding Mode Controller Simulated on UR10

The sliding mode control law used for controlling the universal robot UR10 is given in the equation (16). For more details, the switching gain matrix $K = diag(k_i)$ is chosen according to the equations (8), (27), (36) and (37) so that $k_i = \mu + F_i + \hat{g} (1 - \beta^{-1}) |u_{eq_i}|$ for $i \in [1,6]$ where:

- F_i is calculated experimentally for each joint by being the bound of the uncertain dynamics $f(x,t)$ and its estimation $\hat{f}(x,t) = f(x,t-L)$ with L=0.03s.
- μ is a strict positive number.
- $\hat{g}$ and β^{-1} are known.
- u_{eq_i} is calculated experimentally for each joint according to the equation (17).

The parameters chosen for this simulation are $\lambda = diag(11, 11, 11, 11, 11, 11)$ as the sliding coefficient and $K = diag(10.43, 42.38, 53.77, 40.53, 7.48, 20.80)$ as the switching gain after its calculation.

Therefore, the desired trajectory vs the real trajectory tracked by the UR10's end effector and the simulation results are depicted in Figure 5, Figure 7, Figure 8 and Figure 9.

5.5 Sliding Mode Controller With Boundary Layer Simulated on UR10

The simulation of the universal robot UR10 using the Sliding Mode Controller with time-varying boundary layer is given in the equation (28). Furthermore, the balance condition mentioned in the equation (30) is used to determine the time varying thickness $\varphi(t)$.

The parameters chosen for this simulation are $\lambda=diag(11, 11, 11, 11, 11, 11)$, $K=diag(10.43, 42.38, 53.77, 40.53, 7.48, 20.80)$ and $K_d=diag(20, 29.28, 49, 26, 10.3, 19)$ which is the desired switching gain. The switching gain K is chosen according to the equation (27) and the desired switching gain is also calculated with this equation by using the desired parameters.

Hence, Figure 6, Figure 10, Figure 11, and Figure 12 show the comparison between the desired trajectory and the real trajectory tracked by the UR10's end effector and the outcomes of this simulation.

Table 3. Comparative study

Control Method	Convergence Time t_c (s)	Error (rad) at t_f	Chattering Effect	Disturbances
Sliding Mode Controller with Sign(S)	2	*At t=5s, the errors of the joints are chattering.* $e_i \cong \alpha 10^{-2}$ *for i∈[1,6] where α is a real number.*	Excessive	Robust
Sliding Mode Controller with time-varying boundary layer	0.6	$e_1(t_f)= -3.2*10^{-3}$ $e_2(t_f)= -9.9*10^{-3}$ $e_3(t_f)= -6.5*10^{-3}$ $e_4(t_f)= -2.8*10^{-3}$ $e_5(t_f)= -2.6*10^{-3}$ $e_6(t_f)= -3.9*10^{-3}$	Reduced	Robust

Figure 5. Desired trajectory vs. real trajectory of the UR10 end effector using SMC without the boundary layer

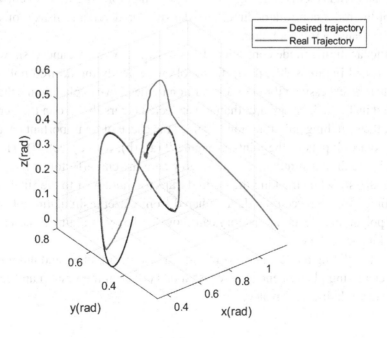

Figure 6. Desired trajectory vs. real trajectory of the UR10 end effector using SMC with time-varying boundary layer

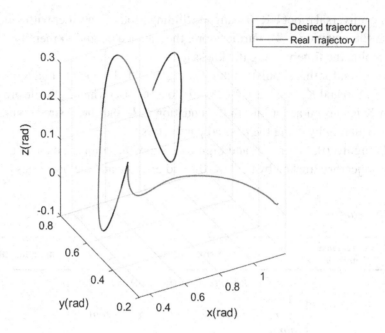

5.6 Analysis of the Simulation's Results

In this chapter, the use of digital Twin has proved its great utility in controlling the UR10 robot with the sliding mode control. On the one hand, the digital space represented by Gazebo shows the mirror of the realistic representation of the robot's behavior and provides real data from the digital sensors and actuators. On the other hand, Matlab-Simulink gathers the data from Gazebo, comes up with the control input for each joint and sends them to the digital actuators. Therefore, digital twin allows the user to test different actions of the robot controllers directly in the simulated version instead of working with the real robot which may cause a robot's failure.

For the conventional sliding mode controller, the states x_1, x_2, x_3, x_4, x_5, and x_6 shown respectively in Figure 7 (b), (d), (f) and Figure 8 (h), (j), (l) didn't follow correctly the desired polynomial trajectory because of the actuators' excessive vibration. In addition to the above explanations, the errors of the six joints, as mentioned in Table 3, are greater than the expected errors that are in the permissive range of 10^{-3}. Furthermore, the switching gain function "sign" is the cause of an important chattering effect that was shown in the control inputs of the joints in Figure 9 (a), (b), (c), (d), (e), (f). This effect was also clearly visualized in the digital simulation by Gazebo where the end effector of the UR10 robot oscillates rapidly and endlessly while tracking the desired trajectory and near to the final desired position.

Moreover, a comparison between the data gathered from Gazebo simulation of the real trajectory and the generated polynomial desired trajectory can show markedly in Figure 5 the vibration of the end effector while tracking trajectory.

In consequence, the sliding mode control is robust against disturbances and unknown dynamics but in real world, the chattering phenomenon can cause a bad effect in the system and real damage to the actuators which reduces their performance.

Figure 7. SMC tracking without the boundary layer of position and error for joints 1, 2, and 3

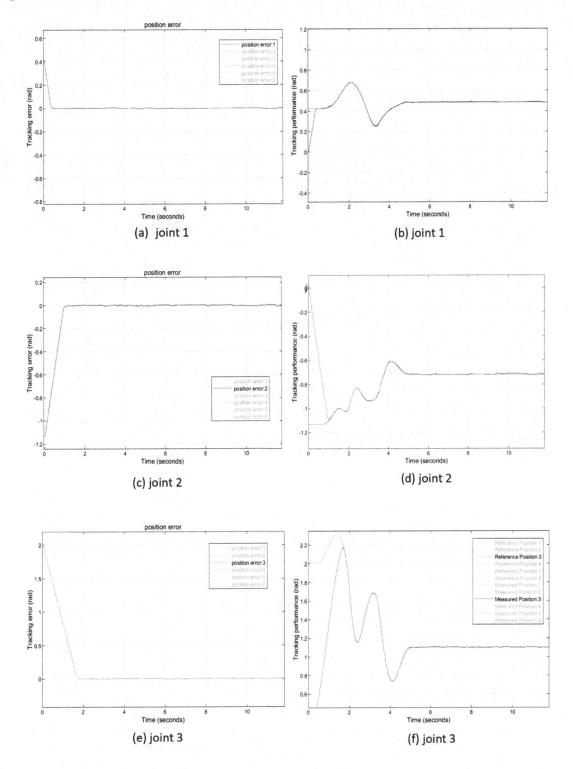

Figure 8. Tracking position and error for joints 4, 5, and 6 using SMC without the boundary layer

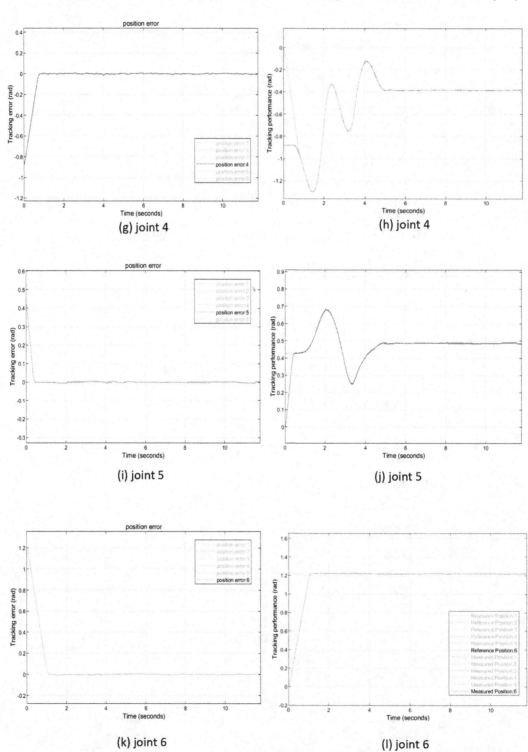

Figure 9. Control input using SMC without the boundary layer

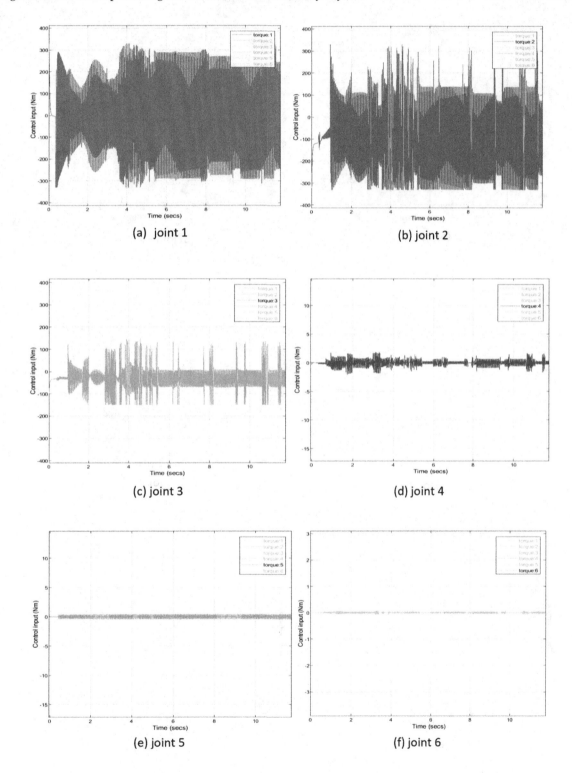

(a) joint 1

(b) joint 2

(c) joint 3

(d) joint 4

(e) joint 5

(f) joint 6

Figure 10. Tracking position and error for joints 1, 2, and 3 using SMC with time-varying boundary layer

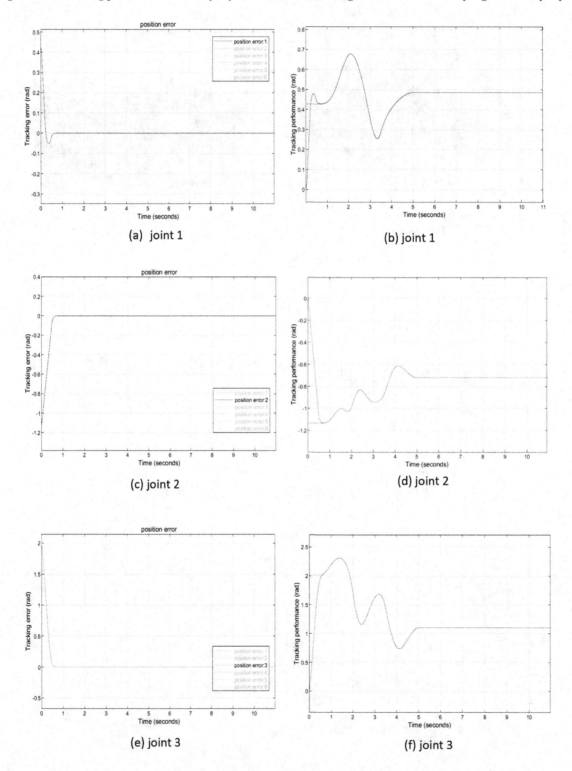

(a) joint 1

(b) joint 1

(c) joint 2

(d) joint 2

(e) joint 3

(f) joint 3

Figure 11. Tracking position and error for joints 4, 5, and 6 using SMC with time-varying boundary layer

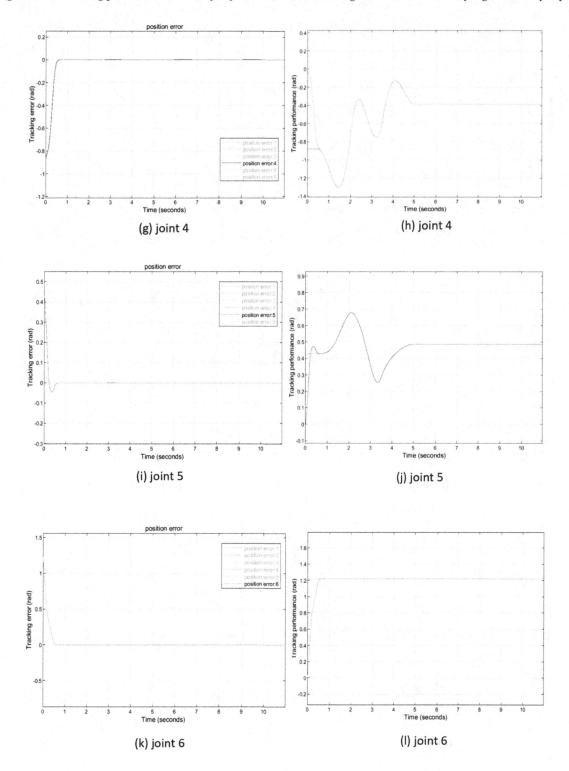

Figure 12. Control input using SMC with time-varying boundary layer

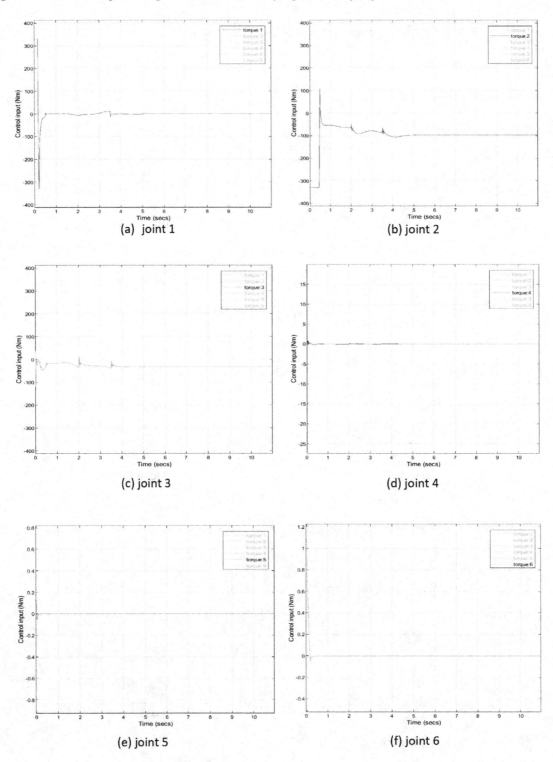

For the conventional sliding mode controller with time-varying boundary layer, the states x_1, x_2, x_3, x_4, x_5, and x_6 depicted respectively in Figure 10 (b), (d), (f) and Figure 11 (h), (j), (l) followed properly the desired references in an acceptable time t_c=0.6sec. According to Table 3, the error of each joint is considered as an acceptable range of error. Furthermore, the tests done on the digital space with the boundary layer method with a constant thickness and with the same method with time varying thickness validates that the second method is much more efficacious in reducing the chattering effect than the first method. In addition, the Figure 12 confirms that the chattering is negligible in the control inputs of the six joints of the robot UR10.

Moreover, a comparison between the data gathered from Gazebo simulation of the real trajectory and the generated polynomial desired trajectory can show in Figure 6 that the chattering effect is clearly reduced while the end effector is tracking the desired trajectory.

Using Digital Twin, a comparative study between controlling the robot with two methods, the Sliding Mode Controller using the switching function Sign(S) and the Sliding Mode Controller using a time-varying boundary layer, is established in Table 3.

From the above analysis, the method SMC with time-varying boundary shows that the error converges to an acceptable range of error in a limited time. Moreover, the chattering effect is negligeable in comparison with the conventional SMC with the sign function where the chattering effect is very excessive. This is the reason why the error is important even after the convergence time and the robot UR10 simulated in Gazebo doesn't stop vibrating. In addition, the two methods tested were both robust to the disturbances.

6. CONCLUSION

This paper illustrates the contribution of the digital twin as an interesting and smart technique to control the manipulator robot. The objective of this method is not only to monitor the real-time manipulator's operation but also to test actions through simulation in the virtual space of the robot. Furthermore, the results of this simulation require analysis in order to improve better solutions before applying them in the physical space. On that account, the performance of the manipulator robot will be enhanced and its components lifetime will be extended due to the predictive diagnosis. In addition, digital twin will lead to optimal manufacturing with high quality, efficiency and accuracy.

To create the digital twin of the manipulator robot, the following steps were followed. The first step was to design exactly the same robot digitally by using SolidWorks and then export the URDF file of the modeled robot or by developing manually a URDF file. In this chapter, the URDF file of the UR10 robot was open source, so it was downloaded. The second step is to create a package of this URDF file in the ROS's workspace. Then, using the Gazebo's launch file, the world where the robot is visualized needed to be safeguarded so as to open it with the GazeboPlugin library. Once the aforementioned steps were completed, Matlab and Simulink were able to communicate with Gazebo via the address IP of the virtual machine. The third step was to develop the chosen controllers for the robot using Matlab and Simulink. Then, the tests of these controllers were done directly on the digital robot already created. The final step will be in the future research; it consists in connecting the robot in Gazebo with the real robot.

For controlling the universal manipulator robot UR10 in the digital space, two controllers were presented and simulated using Gazebo, ROS and Matlab-Simulink. The first method used is the sliding mode controller. In compliance with Lyapunov stability, the switching gain had been designed so that the control input was to be stable. As seen in simulation results, the sliding mode controller gave rise to an excessive chattering effect even if it is a robust method. This effect can lead to the system's instability and can damage the actuators of the robot. In order to reduce the effect of chatter, the second method had been simulated which is the sliding mode controller with time-varying boundary layer. In addition to that, a balance condition had been mentioned to design the time varying boundary layer thickness. As a result, it has been proven that this method reduces the chattering effect and that the error converges to a tolerable value in an acceptable time.

REFERENCES

Attaran, M., & Celik, B. G. (2023). Digital Twin: Benefits, use cases, challenges, and opportunities. *Decision Analytics Journal*, 6, 100165. doi:10.1016/j.dajour.2023.100165

Bohuslava, J., Martin, J., & Igor, H. (2017). TCP/IP protocol utilisation in process of dynamic control of robotic cell according industry 4.0 concept. *2017 IEEE 15th International Symposium on Applied Machine Intelligence and Informatics (SAMI).* 10.1109/SAMI.2017.7880306

Conde, J., Munoz-Arcentales, A., Alonso, A., Lopez-Pernas, S., & Salvachua, J. (2022). Modeling Digital Twin Data and architecture: A building guide with FIWARE as enabling technology. *IEEE Internet Computing*, 26(3), 7–14. doi:10.1109/MIC.2021.3056923

Craig, J. (2005). Trajectory generation. In J. Craig (Ed.), *Introduction to robotics: Mechanics and control* (pp. 201–229). Pearson Education. https://ci.nii.ac.jp/ncid/BA68143739

DeLuca. (1988). Dynamic control properties of robot arms with joint elasticity. *Proceedings of the 1988 IEEE International Conference on Robotics and Automation*, 1574-1580.

Emami, M. R., Goldenberg, A. A., & Türksen, I. B. (1998). A robust model-based fuzzy-logic controller for robot manipulators. *Proceedings of the 1988 IEEE International Conference on Robotics and Automation, 3*, 2500-2505. 10.1109/ROBOT.1998.680717

Feder, M., Giusti, A., & Vidoni, R. (2022). An approach for automatic generation of the URDF file of modular robots from modules designed using SolidWorks. *Procedia Computer Science, 200*, 858–864. doi:10.1016/j.procs.2022.01.283

Glaessgen, E., & Stargel, D. (2012). The Digital Twin Paradigm for future NASA and U.S. Air Force Vehicles. *53rd AIAA/ASME/ASCE/AHS/ASC Structures, Structural Dynamics and Materials Conference; 20th AIAA/ASME/AHS Adaptive Structures Conference.* 10.2514/6.2012-1818

Grieves, M. (2014). *Digital twin: manufacturing excellence through virtual factory replication.* White paper, 1, 2014. pp. 1–7.

GrievesM. (2016). *Origins of the Digital Twin Concept.* Florida Institute of Technology. doi:2016.10.13140/RG.2.2.26367.61609

Haag, S., & Anderl, R. (2018). Digital Twin – Proof of Concept. *Manufacturing Letters*, *15*, 64–66. doi:10.1016/j.mfglet.2018.02.006

Jones, D., Snider, C., Nassehi, A., Yon, J., & Hicks, B. (2020). Characterising the Digital Twin: A Systematic Literature Review. *CIRP Journal of Manufacturing Science and Technology*, *29*, 36–52. doi:10.1016/j.cirpj.2020.02.002

Kali, Y., Saad, M., Benjelloun, K., & Benbrahim, M. (2016). Sliding Mode with Time Delay Control for Robot Manipulators. In Studies in systems, decision and control (pp. 135–156). doi:10.1007/978-981-10-2374-38

Komurcugil, H., Biricik, S., Bayhan, S., & Zhang, Z. (2021). Sliding mode control: Overview of its applications in power converters. *IEEE Industrial Electronics Magazine*, *15*(1), 40–49. doi:10.1109/MIE.2020.2986165

Mason, M. T. (1981). Compliance and force control for computer-controlled manipulators. *IEEE Transactions on Systems, Man, and Cybernetics*, *11*(6), 418–432. doi:10.1109/TSMC.1981.4308708

Matulis, M., & Harvey, C. (2021). A robot arm digital twin utilising reinforcement learning. *Computers & Graphics*, *95*, 106–114. doi:10.1016/j.cag.2021.01.011

Negri, E., Berardi, S., Fumagalli, L., & Macchi, M. (2020). MES-integrated digital twin frameworks. *Journal of Manufacturing Systems*, *56*, 58–71. doi:10.1016/j.jmsy.2020.05.007

Omali, K. O., Kabbaj, M. N., & Benbrahim, M. (2021). Fault detection and isolation using sliding mode observers with sensor fault in robot manipulator. *International Journal of Digital Signals and Smart Systems*, *5*(2), 182. doi:10.1504/IJDSSS.2021.114560

Omali, K. O., Kabbaj, M. N., & Benbrahim, M. (2022). Fault-tolerant control with high-order sliding mode for Manipulator Robot. *International Journal of Power Electronics and Drive Systems*, *13*(3), 1854. doi:10.11591/ijpeds.v13.i3.pp1854-1869

Ömür Bucak, İ. (2021). An in-depth analysis of sliding mode control and its application to robotics. IntechOpen eBooks. doi:10.5772/intechopen.93027

Qian, C., Liu, X., Ripley, C., Qian, M., Liang, F., & Yu, W. (2022). Digital Twin—cyber replica of Physical Things: Architecture, applications and future research directions. *Future Internet*, *14*(2), 64. doi:10.3390/fi14020064

Rasheed, A., San, O., & Kvamsdal, T. (2020). Digital Twin: Values, challenges and enablers from a modeling perspective. *IEEE Access : Practical Innovations, Open Solutions*, *8*, 21980–22012. doi:10.1109/ACCESS.2020.2970143

Saracco, R. (2019). Digital Twins: Bridging physical space and cyberspace. *Computer*, *52*(12), 58–64. doi:10.1109/MC.2019.2942803

Shieh, H., & Hsu, C. (2008). An adaptive Approximator-Based backstepping control approach for Piezoactuator-Driven stages. *IEEE Transactions on Industrial Electronics*, *55*(4), 1729–1738. doi:10.1109/TIE.2008.917115

Slotine, J. E., & Li, W. (1991). Sliding Control. In *Applied Nonlinear Control* (pp. 276–307). Prentice-Hall International. http://ci.nii.ac.jp/ncid/BA11352433

Tao, F., Zhang, H., Liu, A., & Nee, A. Y. (2019). Digital Twin in industry: State-of-the-art. *IEEE Transactions on Industrial Informatics*, *15*(4), 2405–2415. doi:10.1109/TII.2018.2873186

Chapter 3
Design Flowchart for Operational System Safety

Tahiri Omar
Sidi Mohamed Ben Abdellah University, Morocco

Sekkat Souhail
ENSAM, Moulay Ismail University, Morocco

Herrou Brahim
Sidi Mohamed Ben Abdellah University, Morocco

Khadiri Hassan
ENSAM, Moulay Ismail University, Morocco

ABSTRACT

Design is a predominant phase in the life cycle of any product. Referring to a number of reviews, this chapter cites design support tools, focusing in particular on security system and operational safety. It tried to define these two notions (safety, security) as well as the difference between them. It proposed a design aid model that can be adopted by designers in the design phases of new systems, or during their life cycle, based on the "Teorija Reshenija Izobretateliskih Zadatch" (TRIZ) and Failure Modes Vulnerabilities and Effect Analysis (FMVEA) methods. In the first instance, the authors' model enables newly-designed products to give impetus to production systems, for which they use the resolution matrix for technical contradictions. Secondly, it enables these systems to be improved, for which they suggested adopting the FMVEA method tables.

INTRODUCTION

In the life cycle of any process, a design phase is essential. That said, as in the case of production systems, the design study, or feasibility study of the latter, has taken on greater importance in intelligent industry. There are two aspects to it: the first is the material part of the company that produces goods, it's all about products and materials; the second is the system as a whole; the hardware system, human resources and organizational structure.

With the multitude of design methods to be found in the literature (Hampson, 2015; Choulier, n.d.; Herrou & Elghorba, 2005; Beauvallet & Houy, 2009), the choice of one among them is more difficult than it appears. The aim of this section is to propose a design aid method which will give priority to operational safety in the production process, and in particular to the security of goods and people in the production system to be designed.

DOI: 10.4018/979-8-3693-0497-6.ch003

The aim of this study is to find a model that we would like to develop further, by introducing algorithms with iterations that will enable us to continuously improve the system under study.

In the first part of this chapter, we attempt to define design according to the literature, focusing on maintenance and innovation. This is followed by a non-exhaustive presentation of design support methods, with a comparative table of the methods presented.

The second part is devoted to defining safety and security by reference. We then refer to the model proposed by Robin (Cressent et al., 2009) called MéDISIS; a method for integrating safety analysis into systems engineering; (in French: Méthode D'Intégration des analyses de Sdf à l'Ingénierie Système) based on the SysML method. Then we presented the tools used for the design model presented by Nabdi and Herrou (2017). The result of this analysis was to propose a model integrating the two previous approaches, in an attempt to improve the design of production systems. Finally, we have outlined the problems that our model may encounter, and the prospects for this work.

1) Design of Production Systems

a) Design, Definition

Design Review

Deneux (2002) considered that design is a process made up of three essential phases:

- Understanding and identifying the problem to be solved;
- The search for a solution;
- Choice, in order to satisfy the design intent, which translates into a finalized design project.

According to Sénéchal et al. (2003), the product design process consists in transforming the flow of information (in the form of the Functional Specification FS) in a way that accurately represents the evolution of the product. The author has summarized the design activity in the actigram shown in Figure 1.

The same author identified the following non-exhaustive elements: corporate strategy, market constraints, design and production resources, as elements that influence the design process. And here, we can cite the impact of the COVID-19 pandemic, which affected customers' purchasing power, as well as the price of raw materials, which exceeded all limits.

Figure 1. Design activity
Source: Sénéchal et al. (2003)

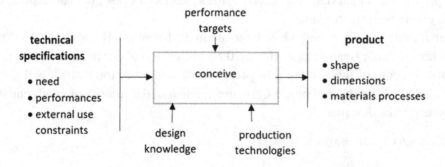

Toussaint (2010) presented the time-saving benefits of adopting integrated engineering instead of sequential engineering. Despite this dazzling gain, the organization of design sequences still needs to be defined to optimize the design phase.

Bounouar (2020) has classified these robotic systems into three sub-families: autonomous systems, enabling tasks to be performed without human intervention; cobotic systems, where human presence is required; and collaborative manipulator robots, performing the same tasks as humans and occupying the same spaces.

Despite the need for robotized systems in production processes, the human factor remains a decisive link, especially when it comes to decision-making, which must take into account the hazards of the process, which will undoubtedly cause considerable financial loss to the company.

Schumacher (2020) in his article cited eleven principles for a successful development framework; applicability, Duration, Result, Direction, Trends, Simplification, Consistency, Levels, Self-similarity, Selectivity, Weighting. This classified the futuristic industrial framework into three levels: human, technological and organizational. Figure 2 shows a development of the first level of this classification.

Lameche (2018) proposed a general approach to the design of a manufacturing system, starting with the design of the product to be manufactured, followed by the design of the process, and ending with the design of the production system. Figure 3 shows, in addition to these three design phases, the control phase which must be planned during and after the three phases mentioned above.

For Debongnie (2007), the design must meet the requirements of functionality, reliability or viability and cost, as developed in his document.

Maintenance in the Design Process

In the design of production systems, maintenance takes up a very important space, given the malfunctions that the system may undergo, which may be foreseen (by performing a diagnostic analysis of the system), or unforeseen (accidental). In his article, Mattioli (2018) treated system maintenance, mentioning both predictive and corrective maintenance, the latter of which can be costly for the company. Even late predictive maintenance will have the same consequences. Hence the importance of early predictive maintenance (need for Prognosis), which accompanies corrective maintenance (need for Diagnosis).

Optimizing the manner and scheduling of these two types of maintenance can lead to cost-relevant results for the process under analysis. Figure 4 shows an overall view of how well the system functions when these two types of maintenance are adopted.

According to Mattioli et al. (2018), prognostic or diagnostic methods require knowledge of the system to be analyzed. These methods have been based on one of three approaches: adopting a physical model, being data-driven or relying on experience.

It can be said that, taking maintainability into account from the earliest phases of system design will enable the development of decision-support resources in the case of a diagnosed or prognosticated malfunction of the designed system (Mattioli et al., 2018).

Figure 2. Futuristic industrial work environment
Source: Schumacher et al. (2020)

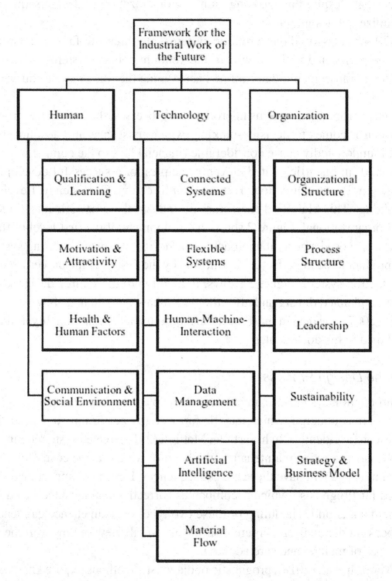

Innovation

Another issue that needs to be addressed in the design phase is innovation, which can be decisive in the adoption of one design model and not another. Given the meteoric rise of computer tools that help design new systems or products, innovation is the means that can be decisive for a company's viability. In this context, design can be classified into two types (Sénéchal et al., 2003): *Routine design*, where we seek to design or implement a new product or a new implementation, in which case it's up to the process to structure the organization or cooperation between the players, and the passage of information between the different phases is framed by established rules. *The Innovative Design*, it's the organization that encourages action, and the production and flow of information that takes place in real time throughout the process.

Figure 3. General design approach for a manufacturing system
Source: Lameche (2018)

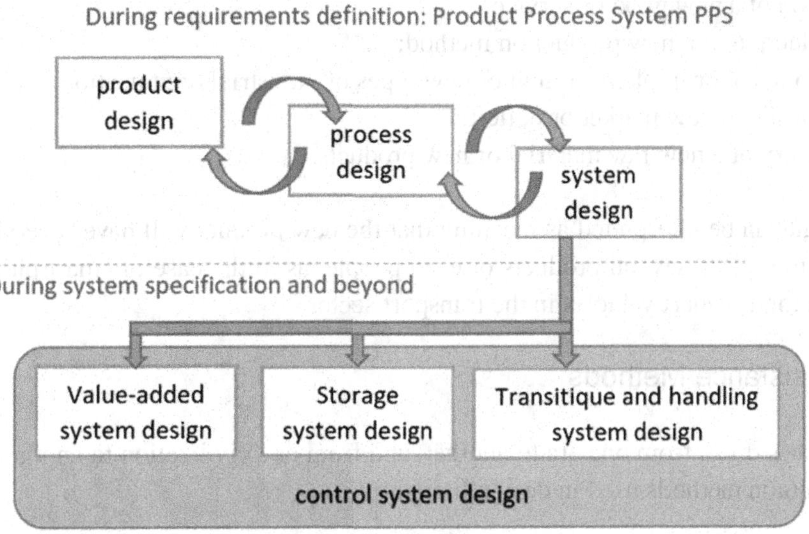

During requirements definition: Product Process System PPS

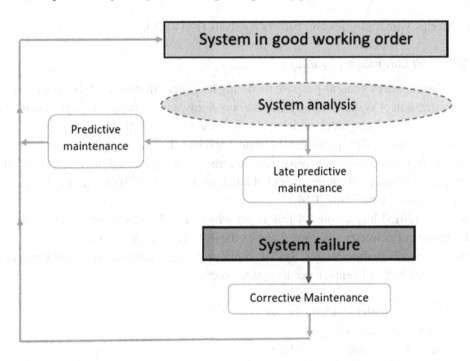

Figure 4. Correct operation of the system through adoption of predictive and corrective maintenance

Schumpeter (1935) proposed five categories of innovation in the first quarter of the 20th century:

- The creation of a new good or service;
- The introduction of a new production method;
- The development or implementation of new types of industrial organization;
- The conquest of a new market or outlet;
- The discovery of a new raw material or new products.

The last point can be interpreted as meaning that the new product will have several functionalities, or will be able to replace several products or even people, as in the case of smart phones in the communications sector, or smart vehicles in the transport sector.

b) Design Assistance Methods

Design approaches differ from one era to another, and from one civilization to another. Here are a few of the most common methods used in design literature:

- Systems Modeling Language (SysML)
- TRIZ;
- LEAN.
- Failure Modes Vulnerabilities and Effects Analysis (FMVEA).

Systems Modeling Language (SysML)

SysML is one of a number of general-purpose modeling languages that support the specification, design, analysis and verification of systems, taking into account hardware, software, data, personnel, procedures and equipment. SysML is a graphical modeling language with a semantic basis for representing requirements, behavior, structure and properties of the system and its components. What's more, it is specifically designed for industrial systems such as aerospace, automotive and production systems. SysML was thus born as an extension of the UML object-oriented language to cover all stages in the design of complex, heterogeneous systems" (Chalfoun, 2014).

Kyle Hampson (2015) has defined 4 pillars on which SysML modeling is based: Requirements, Structure, Behavior et Parametrics. Figure 5 shows these 4 pillars in more detail

For modeling an information model, SysML remains a better solution than (Guillerm et al., 2012) summarized its contribution in eleven points that we recite:

- Common language understandable by all;
- Modeling of a wide range of systems;
- Rigorous traceability (analysis possible);
- Careful expression of requirements;
- Visible allocation of requirements on the model;
- Functional and structural allocation, ...;
- Good interface definition;
- Integration and association of test cases directly with modeling;

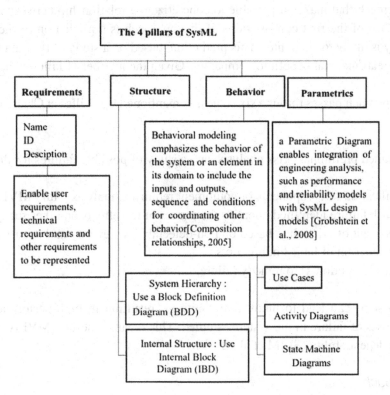

- Addition of information relating to risks and expected safety properties;
- A complete database enabling modifications, improvements or re-engineering;
- A single modeling language will facilitate data management.

The SysML language can be a good platform for the development of design tools or design aids, given the various advantages it provides. Changyong Chu et al (2022)present a system model in Figure 6, which highlights the advantages of this modeling tool, which is simple

Teorija Reshenija Izobretateliskih Zadatch Method (TRIZ)

The TRIZ method has been developed in the former Union of Soviet Socialist Republics (USSR) since 1946 by its inventor Genrich Altshuller. The method is a problem-solving approach which began with the analysis of invention patents (over 2 million patents "analyzed"), leading to design problem-solving tools. The method underwent two periods of development: from 1946 to 1985, the period of development under its founder G. Altshuller. Since 1946, development in the context of perestroika, and subsequently "westernization" with the help of computer tools (Choulier, n.d.).

According to its founder, the TRIZ method is based on two essential notions: Ideality and Contradictions. Figure 7 presents these two notions (Choulier, n.d.) and can be used in all fields.

Failure Modes Vulnerabilities and Effects Analysis (FMVEA)

FMVEA is an approach that makes it possible to concretize the relationship between cause and effect in various fields. One of the first contributions of this approach is a prediction of the events that the system under study is likely to encounter. This prediction, based on a study of the data from the system in question, is of great financial benefit to companies. Given the number of failures they can overcome or even avoid.

The FMVEA approach passes through six stages, as mentioned by Grilles et Claudia (Lasnier, 2011; Wagner, 2009):

- Step 1: A detailed preliminary risk analysis, and a study of possible failures for the system and its interfaces.
- Step 2: Identification of components or equipment requiring analysis with FMVEA.
- Step 3: For each failure identified, identify the causes of the effects on other subsystems.
- Step 4: Assessment of criticality, based on non-detectability, severity and occurrence.
- Step 5: Determination of fault-finding tools.
- Step 6: Proposal of action(s) to remedy failure.

These last two steps can lead to innovative solutions, resulting in high-performance systems by minimizing the causes of failure in the systems studied. This means that the FMVEA approach plays a key role in system dependability (SLIM et al., 2019).

The LEAN Approach

Thanks to the Toyota Production System (TPS), the three major international press agencies (Reuters, Associated Press and Agence France Presse) awarded the Japanese brand Toyota the top spot in 2007, after General Motors (GM) had dominated the market since 1931. This miracle strategy, which researchers have dubbed "lean management", has prompted them to clarify concepts, practices and foundations. The two concepts on which this strategy is based are (Ohno & Setsuo, 1988): Just-in-time (JIT), which means that the company delivers the product on time, at the right moment, with a quality that meets the specifications. Autonomy, whereby the company's employees will be encouraged to improve the quality of the products/services sold, rather than eliminating them (scrap), by instilling precise procedures to this effect. Shingo (1989)identified the objective associated with the two concepts of this strategy as non-waste. Which Godefroy and Thomas (2009) have classified into seven types: Overproduction, waiting times, unnecessary transport or handling, unnecessary machining, stocks, unnecessary movements and defective production. Hence the term "no superflows", or "waste reduction", which is the obvious meaning of the term Lean in literature.

Lyonnet (2010) has summarized the Lean approach in six associated concepts, which we have grouped together in Figure 8, based on what exists in the literature; for further details, please consult his thesis.

Figure 6. Collaborative optimization model in the SysML model
Source: Chu et al. (2022)

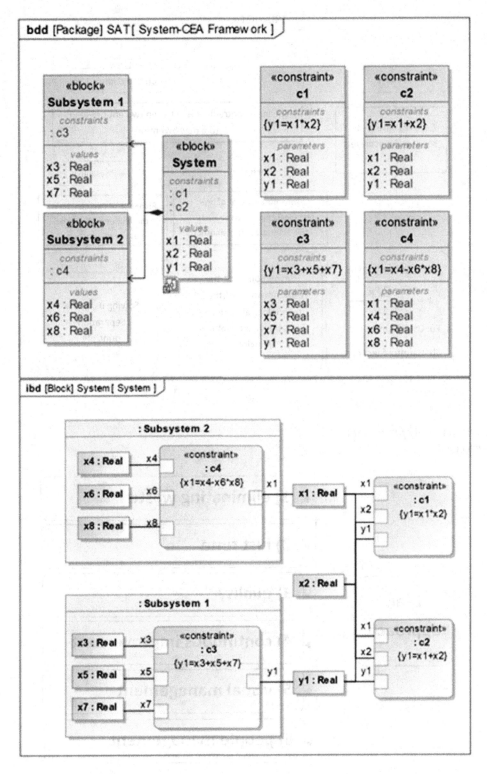

Figure 7. TRIZ method concept

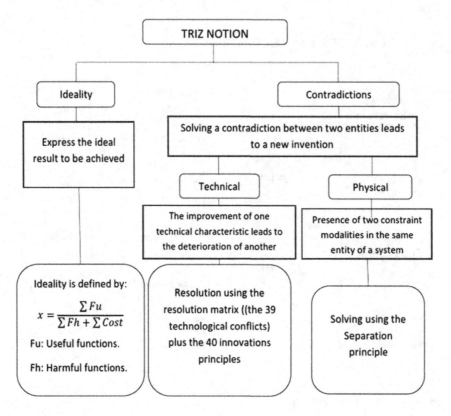

Figure 8. The six concepts of lean
Source: Lyonnet (2010)

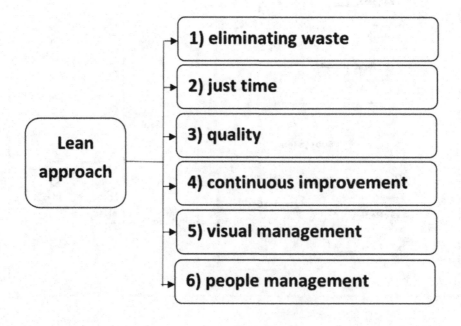

To use this approach, Lyonnet (2010) raised the question of how to implement the concepts of this approach, since it was not possible to standardize the implementation of these most dazzling concepts; sequential or simultaneous. Dombrowski et Mielkea (2013) discussed a methodical approach called Lean Leadership, in which workers are at the heart of improving the production system, rather than focusing solely on the methods and tools used. According to the literature, the five basic principles of this approach are (Dombrowskia & Mielkea, 2013):

- Improvement culture;
- Self development;
- Qualification;
- Gemba (workshop management, decisions based on first-hand knowledge);
- Hoshinkanri (customer orientation, objectives aligned at all levels).

c)   Comparison of design aid methods

Table 1 compares the above methods, giving their principles, advantages and disadvantages.

Table 1. Summary table of design assistance methods (not exhaustive)

Method	Author(s)	Principle	Benefits	Disadvantages
SysML	(Rland Renier & Raphael Chenouard, 2011) (Romaric Guillerm and al. 2012) (Changyong Chu et al. 2022) (Kyle Hampson, 2015) (Imad Chalfoun 2014) (Grobshtein et al., 2008) (Composition relationships, 2005)	"graphical modeling with a semantic basis for representing the requirements, behavior, structure and properties of the system and its components..." (Imad Chalfoun 2014)	+Comprehensible to all; +Modeling of a wide range of systems;	-Probability of difficulty in modelling complex systems;
TRIZ	(Denis Choulier) (Souad Nabdi & Brahim Herrou, 2017) (Nabdi S. & Herrou B. 2018)	Based on two essential notions: Ideality and Contradictions	+Reduced series changeover times ;+Algorithme bien précis de résolution ;	-The need for continuous improvement of the technological conflict resolution matrix, given the constant emergence of new problems and new technologies.
FMVEA	(Galina Samigulina & Zarina Samigulina, 2020); (Brahim Herrou& Mohamed Elghorba, 2005)	Collect information from the system under study;	+ensure safety of system operation;	-apply the approach to a concrete system;
The LEAN Approach	(U. Dombrowskia & T. Mielkea, 2013); (Godefroy Beauvallet & Thomas Houy, 2009)	Based on Just-in-Time (JIT) and Autonomy (improving quality instead of eliminating).	+Continuous improvement; + Non-waste;	-Limit the concepts to be considered;

Conclusion

A means of modeling the manufacturing process which takes into account all the players (material, human ...) will enable us to design an optimized global process, understandable by all those involved, is welcome for the design of the production system. But a combination of modeling and design aids will certainly produce more satisfactory results. With this in mind, a study of a real production system will be desirable.

2) Taking Safety Into Account in the Design of Production Systems

a) Definitions, Safety, Security

The dictionary definition of industrial safety is (Wiktionnaire 2023a): "All the technical provisions, human resources and organizational measures inside and outside industrial installations, designed to prevent malicious acts from inside or outside, and to mitigate the consequences of accidents."

However, one definition of industrial security (Ecology, Industry) is Wiktionnaire (2023b): "All technical provisions, human resources and organizational measures internal to industrial facilities and activities, designed to prevent accidents or mitigate their consequences."

Despite the many definitions we come across, the terms safety and security are confused most of the time. As a result, we can still say that a system operating safely means that it must be safe and reliable during the use phase of its life cycle, without being affected by external elements that can damage it or make it unsafe. However, when we talk about security, we must ensure that external hazards will not affect the system in question during operation, or that their effects are not too harmful. A consideration illustrated by Figure 9, presents safety as the consequences of an accident originating from the system on its environment, whereas security refers to what is caused by malevolence without consideration of the System – Environment (S-E) dimension.

Figure 9. Safety and security terms
Source: Pietre-Cambacedes (2010)

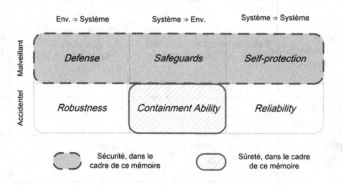

However, in 2002, AFNOR (n.d.-a). defined dependability as "all the properties that describe availability and the factors that condition it: reliability, maintainability and maintenance logistics".

Another definition of safety is dependability (AFNOR, n.d.-b), which classifies safety as one of the parameters characterizing the dependability of a system. The other parameters according to this definition are: reliability, maintainability and availability. This is the definition we will adopt for the remainder of our development.

b) Production System Issues-Safety and Security

Technological development is reflected in our day-to-day lives, whether in the visible form of goods (gadgets, means of transport, etc.), or in the invisible form of the means used to create or manufacture these products. The latter are the fruit of well-developed production systems based on new technologies, and such development adds to the causes affecting the safety and security of these same systems.

Consideration of operational safety requires an analysis of the system's behavior, by observing its behavior and noting all the functional and dysfunctional details. This leads to two possibilities mentioned in the literature: formal validation and the search for failure scenarios (Cressent et al., 2009). In the same review, to carry out an operational safety analysis, two phases are required: the qualitative phase "requires the creation and incorporation of new knowledge going beyond the functional view of the system", and the quantitative phase, in which the knowledge gathered in the previous phase is exploited. Robin Cressent et al. (2009) proposed a method he dubbed MéDISIS (Méthode d'Intégration des analyses de Sûreté de fonctionnement à l'Ingénierie Système), for analyzing malfunction phenomena in system design. Figure 10 presents this method, which can be summarized in 3 phases: firstly, the dysfunctional component and its influences (impacted requirements) are identified; secondly, formal models are described with assistance; finally, a tool-based analysis of these models is carried out in order to validate the requirements. The design continues after exchanging data during these three phases with a Dysfunctional Behavior Database (DBD) of the system.

Figure 10. The MéDISIS method
Source: Cressent et al. (2009)

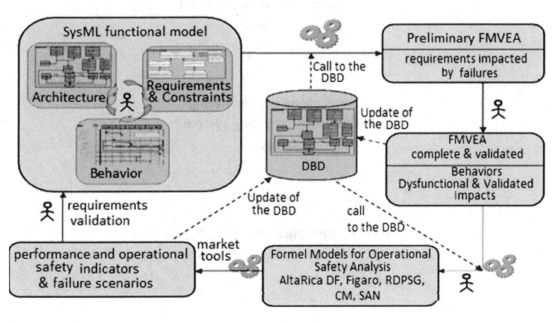

In their work, Nabdi and Herrou (2017) have proposed a model for integrating maintainability and availability in the design phase, using the TRIZ tool to analyze contradictions in this preliminary phase of the product/system life cycle.

3) Design Model Proposal

An analysis of certain models, such as the one cited previously by Robin Cressent et al. (2009) and Rland Renier & Raphael Chenouard (2011) has enabled us to propose a System failure mode analysis approach (Figure 11) in which an analysis of a system's failure modes based on problems encountered, using the FMVEA method in the first instance, then from there we will conduct a complete analysis in order to draw performance and reliability indicators, analyzing failure scenarios.

Figure 11. System failure mode analysis approach

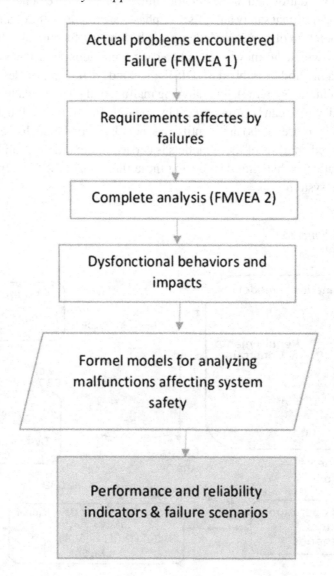

Nabdi and Herrou (2017) in their work, presented a design model that presents the three phases of design, namely, conceptual, architectural and detailed design using the TRIZ method, based on the contradiction resolution matrix. The proposed model in Figure 12 presents a flowchart that starts from the manifestation of the user's need to the prototyping of the final product, passing through a phase of oscillation between design and requirements acquisition.

Figure 12. Product design flowchart

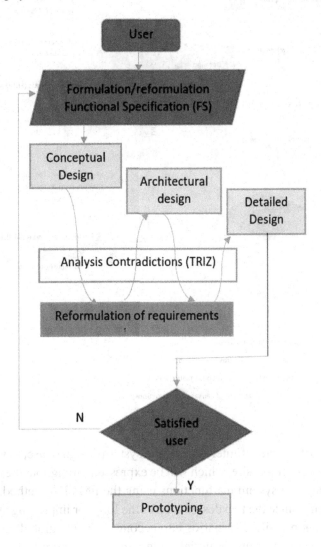

By combining these two models, we have proposed the model shown in Figure 13, which represents the design process. On the one hand, to design a new product, based on a need expressed by a manufacturer. And on the other hand, to improve it by trying to overcome the failures that the production system in question may encounter. The two loops, design and improvement, exchange information with an up-to-date database, enabling production systems to be designed and operated in complete safety.

Figure 13. Flowchart for operational system safety

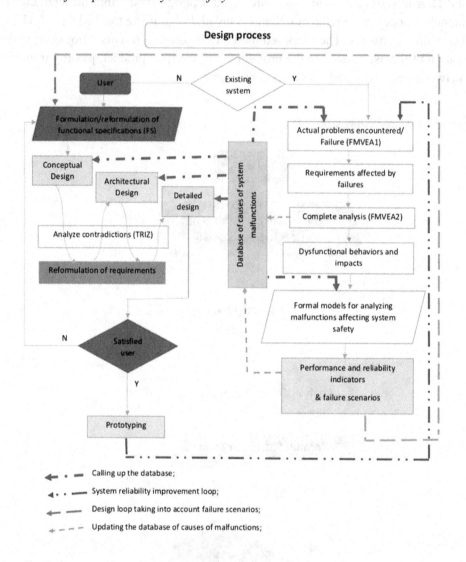

The proposed model will iterate infinitely during the system design phase, as well as during its operation. First, by analyzing the user's desire, which will be expressed throughout the design phase, using the TRIZ tool. Then, by analyzing system malfunctions using the FMVEA method. This approach can be called "Integrated Design", since the two design loops - the loop for improving system operating safety, and the design loop for taking failure scenarios into account - are integrated into each other. This will enable continuous improvement, from the initial design phase of the production system, right through to the end of its life.

FMVEA analysis will enable us to present the system's vulnerabilities, so that the group of research engineers can find a suitable remedy for each case. This will ensure safe operation, and hence the safety of people and property.

CONCLUSION AND OUTLOOK

In this chapter, we have tried to review the design aids available in the literature (non-exhaustive), in order to create our own design aid model, based on existing tools. This has enabled us to propose a model based on the two methods TRIZ and FMVEA, in order to improve the operational safety of the system to be designed.

Data analysis algorithms can be adopted for the development of our model. We are now trying to improve this model, while integrating algorithms for risk identification and analysis.

REFERENCES

Wiktionnaire. (2023). https://fr.wiktionary.org/wiki/s%C3%BBret%C3%A9_industrielle

Hampson, K. (2015). Technical evaluation of the Systems Modeling Language (SysML), Conference on Systems Engineering Research. *Procedia Computer Science, 44*, 403 – 412.

AFNOR. (n.d.-a). *NF EN 13306 et NF X 60–500, fiabilité maintenabilité disponibilité, recueil des normes françaises*. Author.

AFNOR. (n.d.-b). *Afnor ; fiabilité maintenabilité disponibilité, recueil des normes françaises, afnor-ute*. Author.

Beauvallet, G., & Houy, T. (2009). L'adoption des pratiques de gestion lean Cas des entreprises industrielles françaises. Revue française de gestion, 7(197), 83-106.

Bounouar, Béarée, Siadat, & Benchekroun. (2020). *Vers un cadre méthodologique de conception des systèmes humains-robots*. 13ème Conférence Internationale de Modélisation, Optimisation et Simulation (MOSIM2020), Agadir, Maroc.

Brahim, H., & Mohamed, E. (2005). L'AMDEC un outil puissant d'optimisation de la maintenance, application à un motocompresseur d'une PME marocaine. CPI'2005, Casablanca, Morocco.

Choulier & Drãghici. (n.d.). *TRIZ: une approche de résolution des problèmes d'innovation dans la conception de produits*. Academic Press.

Chu, C., Yin, C., Shi, S., Su, S., & Chen, C. (2022, June). Multidisciplinary Modeling and Optimization Method of Remote Sensing Satellite Parameters Based on SysML-CEA. *Computer Modeling in Engineering & Sciences*, 20.

Composition relationships. (2005). *Composition relationships. Introduction to Rational Systems Developer*. IBM Rational Systems Developer Info Center. http://publib.boulder.ibm.com/infocenter/rsdvhelp/v6r0m1/index.jsp?topic=%2Fcom.ibm.xtools.modeler.doc%2Ftopics%2Fccompasn .html

Cressent, David, Idasiak, & Kratz. (2009). *Apport de SysML à la modélisation des systèmes complexes à fortes contraintes de sûreté de fonctionnement*. ITT 09 (Technological Innovation and Transport Systems 2009), Oct 2009, Toulouse, France.

Debongnie, J. F. (2007). Université de Liège, Faculté des sciences Appliquées, Institut Mécanique (Liège.). *Chemin des Chevreuils*, *1*, B-4000.

Deneux, D. (2002). Méthodes et modèles pour la conception concourante. Université de Valenciennes, habilitation à diriger des recherches, Valenciennes, France.

Dombrowskia, U., & Mielkea, T. (2013). Lean Leadership fundamental principles and their application. Forty Sixth CIRP Conference on Manufacturing Systems 2013. *Procedia CIRP*, *7*, 569–574.

Grobshtein, Y., & Dori, D. (2008). *Evaluating Aspects of System Modeling Languages by Example: SysML and OPM*. Israel Institute of Technology.

Imad. (2014). *These: Conception et déploiement des Systèmes de Production Reconfigurables et Agiles (SPRA)*. Academic Press.

Juliette, Pierre-Olivier, & Reydellet. (2018). *L'intelligence artificielle au service de maintenance prévisionnelle*. 4ième conférence sur les Applications Pratiques de l'Intelligence Artificielle APIA, Nancy, France.

Lameche. (2018). *Proposition d'une méthodologie pour la conception des systèmes de production reconfigurables et d'un outil associé d'aide à la décision par simulation de flux* [Thesis]. Université de Nantes, Soutenue.

Lasnier, G. (2011). *Sûreté de fonctionnement des équipements et calculs de fiabilité*. Lavoisier.

Luis, T. (2010). *Modèles et méthodes pour une conception hautement productive orientée vers la fabrication: application à l'ingénierie routinière de pièces plastiques* [Thesis]. Université de Technologie de Belfort-Montbéliard-UTBM.

Lyonnet, B. (2010). *Amélioration de la performance industrielle: vers un système de production Lean adapté aux entreprises du pôle de compétitivité* [Thesis]. Arve Industries Haute-Savoie Mont-Blanc.

Nabdi, S., & Herrou, B. (2018). Contribution to Integrating Maintainability into Preliminary Design. *Triz, Engineering Journal*, *22*(5).

Ohno, T., & Setsuo, M. (1988). *Just-In-Time: For Today and Tomorrow*. Diamond, Inc.

Pietre-Cambacedes. (2010). *Des relations entre sûreté et sécurité* [Thesis].

Renier, R., & Chenouard, R. (2011). *De SysML à MODELICA aide à la formalisation de modèles de simulation en conception préliminaire*. 12ème Colloque National AIP PRIMECA, France.

Romaric, Hamid, & Nabil. (2012). *Base De Connaissances Sysml Pour La Conception De Systemes Complexes Surs De Fonctionnement*. Academic Press.

Samigulina, G. (2020). Development of Industrial Equipment Diagnostics System Based on Modified Algorithms of Artificial Immune Systems and AMDEC Approach Using Schneider Electric Equipment. *2020 International Conference on Industrial Engineering, Applications and Manufacturing*.

Schumacher, Pokornib, Himmelstoßa, & Bauernhansla. (2020). *Conceptualization of a Framework for the Design of Production Systems and Industrial Workplaces*. Academic Press.

Sénéchal, O. (2003). *Le cycle de vie du système de production. Evaluation des performances des systèmes de production.* Lavoisier.

Shingo, S. (1989). *A Study of the Toyota Production System from an Industrial Engineering Viewpoint.* Productivity Press.

Slim, Houssin, & Coulibaly. (2019). Une approche d'intégration de la méthode SMED dans la conception des systèmes de production. *16e Colloque National S-mart, Les Karellis,* (73).

Souad, N., & Brahim, H. (2017). *Integration de la maintenabilité en phase préliminaire de conception en se basant sur la théorie TRIZ. 3ième Congrès International du Génie Industriel et du Management des Systèmes (CIGIMS'2017), May 2017.* Meknès.

Schumpeter, J. (1935). Théorie de l'évolution économique. Traduction française Dalloz, Paris.

Wagner, C. (2009). *Specification risk analysis: Avoiding product performance deviations through an fmea-based method* [Thesis]. L'université téchniques, München, Allemagne.

LIST OF ABBREVIATIONS

BDD: Block Definition Diagram
DBD: Dysfunctional Behavior Database
FMVEA: Failure Modes Vulnerabilities and Effects Analysis
GM: General Motors
IBD: Internal Block Diagram
JIT: Just-in-Time
Sdf: Operability Safty (Sûreté de Fonctionnement)
SysML: Systems Modeling Language
TPS: Toyota Production System
TRIZ: Teorija Reshenija Izobretateliskih Zadatch Method
USSR: Union of Soviet Socialist Republics

Chapter 4
Integrating Circular Economy Concerns Into the Industry 4.0 Roadmaps of Companies:
A Literature Review

Sekkat Souhail

iD https://orcid.org/0000-0003-0514-0179

ENSAM, Moulay Ismail University of Meknès, Morocco

Ibtissam El Hassani

ENSAM, Moulay Ismail University of Meknès, Morocco

Anass Cherrafi

Cadi Ayyad University, Morocco

ABSTRACT

The concept of circular economy (CE) aims to promote sustainable resource utilization, minimize environmental impacts, and create societal, economic, and business value. Simultaneously, the fourth industrial revolution or Industry 4.0 (I4.0) offers companies the opportunity to enhance their operational efficiency. Various process models have been proposed to assist companies in developing a digitalisation strategy roadmap. This chapter presents a thorough analysis of how CE utilizes I4.0 technologies to transition from a conventional linear economy to a circular one. The authors have then first proposed a generic three-stage process to establish a I 4.0 strategy roadmap, then conducted an exhaustive review of the latest literature on CE and I4.0 theory to explore the interrelation between these concepts and ascertain the extent to which I4.0 technologies facilitate progress towards a more sustainable industry.

DOI: 10.4018/979-8-3693-0497-6.ch004

INTRODUCTION

Industry 4.0 (I4.0) and Circular Economy (CE) have emerged as prominent and extensively discussed subjects in recent decades. The Circular Economy (CE) entails a production and consumption model focused on the reuse, repair, and recycling of materials and products to minimize environmental impacts. Embracing a circular economy involves waste elimination, prolonging product lifespans, and fostering the regeneration of natural systems. On the other hand, Industry 4.0 (I4.0), often referred to as the fourth industrial revolution, signifies a manufacturing revolution propelled by technological advancements, such as big data and connectivity, analytics, human-machine interaction, and robotics. The integration of technologies like IoT, Big Data, and augmented reality can empower manufacturing companies to enhance process performance. To effectively implement Industry 4.0, companies need to establish a strategic vision, develop a roadmap, and translate this vision into practical projects.

This chapter undertakes a Literature review to explore the correlation between the concepts of Circular Economy and Industry 4.0. The question we want to address is whether there is a relationship between the concept of CE and I4.0 technologies. We therefore want to know how I4.0 technologies are being used to influence the CE approach on the one hand, and on the other, how CE-related domains can be covered by I4.0 technologies. We will therefore begin by proposing a generic three-stage process to establish a I 4.0 strategy roadmap, then we will review the most recent literature on CE and I4.0 theory to determine the extent to which I4.0 technologies are facilitating progress towards a more sustainable industry and to develop an innovative framework that enable companies to create an I4.0 Roadmap that adequately incorporates ecological concerns.

The chapter is structured as follows: Section 2 provides a brief theoretical background on the Circular Economy Concept. Section 3 introduces the fourth industrial revolution technologies. Section 4 presents a generic process model for developing an Industry 4.0 strategy roadmap. Section 5 conducts a literature review of the Circular Economy and Industry 4.0 concepts, aiming to identify the interrelation between them and assess the extent to which I4.0 technologies contribute to building a more sustainable industry. Finally, the last section presents conclusions drawn from the study and outlines potential goals for future research.

THE TWO LIFE CYCLES OF CIRCULAR ECONOMY

The Circular Economy (CE) presents a production and consumption model centered on reusing, repairing, and recycling existing materials and products to minimize environmental impact, making it a pivotal strategy for achieving sustainable development. Sustainable development, a United Nations principle, seeks to balance economic growth, environmental protection, and social well-being. Transitioning to a circular economy entails waste elimination, prolonging product lifespans, and regenerating natural systems. This shift expands the conventional linear economy into a closed-loop system, aligning the product life cycle with the natural life cycle (Zbicinski, Stavenuite, Kozlowska, & van de Coevering, 2006). This section provides a concise theoretical background of the CE concept.

The concept of sustainable development today emphasizes economic and social progress, as well as safeguarding the environment for future generations. The Brundtland Report in 1987 (Brundtland, et al., 1987) defined sustainable development as development that meets present needs without compromising future generations' ability to meet their own needs. The CE model is instrumental in achieving sustainable development. It is based on lifecycle perspective to reach sustainability. The product life cycle encompasses the stages from extraction or creation of raw materials to product disposal, while the natural life cycle involves the continuous loop of growth and decay of organic materials. In the product life cycle, raw materials are extracted and processed from natural resources, followed by production, distribution, and use of the product. When the product reaches the end of its useful life, options like remanufacturing, reusing components, recycling materials, or proper disposal in a landfill are available. Conversely, the natural life cycle involves the decomposition of organic materials, which can serve as nutrients for new growth in the ecosystem, creating a sustainable loop.

However, certain materials, such as minerals, are non-renewable resources and form over extended time frames. When used in industrial materials, they cannot be readily recreated within short periods through natural processes. Consequently, disposing of mineral-based industrial materials in landfills can lead to the accumulation of harmful wastes. Figure 1 illustrates the intersection of the two life cycles, where natural materials are utilized in industrial products and organic materials are reintegrated into the natural cycle, contributing to a holistic circular economy approach.

Figure 1. Relation between product life cycle and natural cycles

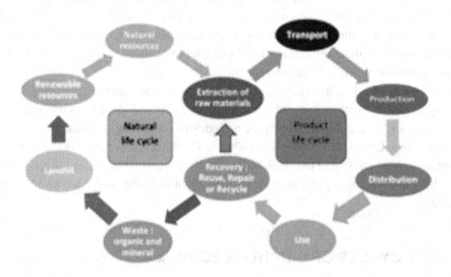

Current model used by most industries is linear economy system which boils down to: Take, Make and Dispose. Extract resources, process them into products, dispose of after use as waste. The waste after use ultimately goes back to the earth and is, generally, toxic, unusable or takes long to biodegrade. Our economy runs on this linear chain of events. Linear economy system is not sustainable at all. From the life cycle perspective (Figure 1), by implementing closed-loop systems, we can minimize the extraction of new resources and reduce waste generation by maximizing the recovery and reuse of materials. Organizations committed to Circular economy use several concepts and tools such as Eco-design and Cradle-to-Cradle. In Cradle-to-Cradle approach (MBDC, 2021) a product is designed so that its materials and components can be repurposed or recycled indefinitely. This makes products "circular" and reduces their environmental impacts. Eco-design tools also called Design For Environment (DFE) (Ulrich & Eppinger, 2008) helps organizations to create better products by choosing materials carefully and by enabling proper recovery options so that the materials used in products can be reintegrated either into the product life cycle or into the natural life cycle. Among Eco-design challenges there is, elimination of the use of non-renewable natural resources (materials and energy) especially synthetic and inorganic materials that do not decay quickly and toxic wastes that are not part of natural life cycles. Now we have presented a theoretical background of CE Concept, we will move on to present I4.0 Technologies and describe a generic process model for establishing a I 4.0 strategy Roadmap.

THE FOURTH INDUSTRIAL REVOLUTION

The fourth industrial revolution, also known as Industry 4.0 or I4.0, has given rise to novel manufacturing methods. This transformation involves intelligent products and machines operating as autonomous entities, leveraging real-time data, embedded software, and internet connectivity within a value creation network. To successfully navigate this digital shift, companies must formulate a roadmap for Digitalization. This section provides a concise theoretical overview of Industry 4.0 and presents a generic process model for devising an effective I4.0 strategy roadmap.

Nowadays, we are witnessing a new industrial revolution (Lu, 2017). Indeed, the first revolution was characterized by the introduction of steam power as a primary source of energy. The second revolution was marked by the widespread adoption of electricity and saw the development of assembly line production. The third revolution was characterized by the emergence of information technology (IT), electronics, and automation. Currently, a new industrial revolution called Industry 4.0 or the fourth industrial revolution, will once again change the profile of industry.

Figure 2. Enabling technologies of Industry 4.0

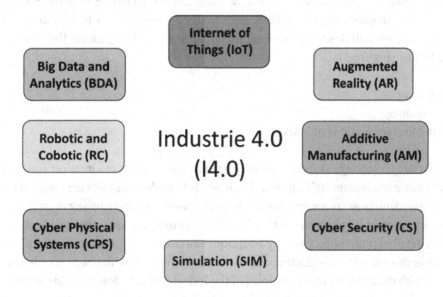

The core concepts of Industry 4.0 originated as part of a strategic initiative by the German government aimed at fostering the digital transformation of factories. Many other nations have since developed their own policies and measures to financially and structurally support digitalization within companies. These initiatives involve all stakeholders along the value chain, including universities and training programs. Similar strategies have been proposed in other industrialized countries, such as "Factories of the Future" in Europe, "Industrial Internet" in the USA, and "Internet +" in China. Industry 4.0 is underpinned by a group of enabling technologies, including Cyber Physical Systems (CPS), Internet of Things (IoT), Additive Manufacturing, and Robotics (Lu, 2017; Alcácer, Rodrigues, Carvalho, & Cruz-Machado, 2022). These technologies have the potential to address various challenges in the manufacturing process and can significantly improve process efficiency and product quality (Sekkat & El-hassani, 2021). However, implementing Industry 4.0 is a complex, long-term undertaking that requires substantial commitment and investment.

One significant hurdle is that many companies struggle to fully comprehend the overall concept of Industry 4.0 and its relevance to their business strategy. They face challenges in identifying specific areas of action (Erol, Schumacher, & Sihn, 2016). Success in implementing Industry 4.0 is not solely reliant on the quantity of technology adopted but rather on how selectively and effectively it is integrated into the company's operations.

ROADMAPING TOWARDS DIGTALISATION

To embark on the digitalization journey, careful planning and execution are crucial. Companies must first define a strategic vision, develop a roadmap, and then translate this vision into actionable projects. Several guidelines have been proposed to help companies establish their path towards digitalization (Schumacher, Nemeth, & Sihn, 2019; Erol, Schumacher, & Sihn, 2016; Cotrino, Sebastián, & González-Gaya, 2020). We will in this chapter propose, at first, generic three-stage process to establish a I 4.0 strategy roadmap. This paragraph will describe this road mapping process. The generic three-stage process we propose are as follow (Figure 3):

1. Defining a strategy,
2. Making a roadmap,
3. Formalizing technological standards.

Within the defining a strategy stage a company must assess its current situation and define strategic targets. Indeed, before implementing Industrie 4.0, it needs to understand its current level of digitization and automation and identify areas for improvement. In a second steps a company must define clear goals and objectives for implementing Industrie 4.0 and develop a comprehensive strategy to achieve them. This should include a detailed plan for technology adoption, workforce training, and organizational changes. We advise starting this phase by conducting an awareness campaign, which will enable the company to familiarize itself with the fundamental principles of the Industrie 4.0 vision. This initiative will facilitate the development of the company's comprehension and alignment of general Industry 4.0 concepts with its specific objectives and customer requirements. A company can invite external experts and ask them to explain the conceptual pillars of Industry 4.0 and present relevant best practices. This activity serves as a way for benchmarking and raise awareness for the need for immediate action. Stakeholders are subsequently advised to develop their company specific Industry 4.0 vision in a collaborative way. At this stage we can use a maturity model. It is a tool allowing a company to increase its capabilities over time by comparing its current maturity level to a desired maturity level (Sekkat, El-hassani, & Cherrafi, 2023). The digitalization strategy should therefore be stated in an unambiguous way, but generic enough not to presume the means for reaching the desired outcome.

During the roadmap development phase, a company needs to convert its strategies into tangible projects. This involves establishing project goals, assembling teams, and identifying key milestones. These projects are then assessed and prioritized based on their impact, available resources and potential risks. Implementing Industry 4.0 technologies is not an end, these technologies, rather, aim to improve business processes and avoid waste of non-value adding activities. Therefore, to implement a relevant Industry 4.0 strategy, the company must use new technologies as IT levers. This is why at this stage we are inspired by Business Process Reengineering approach which advises following five major steps to implement an Industry 4.0 technology (Davenport & Short, 1990): develop the business vision and process objectives, identify the processes to be redesigned, understand and measure the existing process, identify IT levers, and design and build a prototype of the new process. To establish the roadmap to I4.0, we advise considering the three strategic perspectives proposed by Erol et al (Erol, Schumacher, & Sihn, 2016): the market, the product and process, and the value network.

Figure 3. Generic three-stage road mapping process towards I 4.0

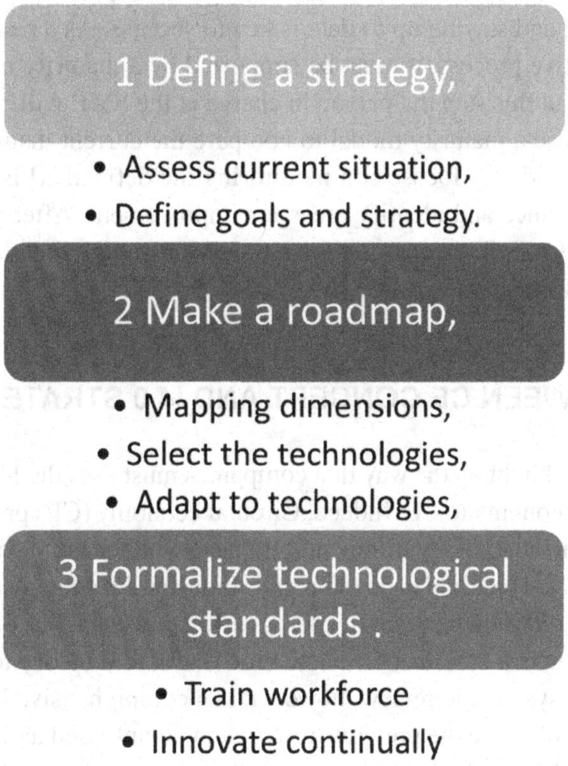

1 Define a strategy,

- Assess current situation,
- Define goals and strategy.

2 Make a roadmap,

- Mapping dimensions,
- Select the technologies,
- Adapt to technologies,

3 Formalize technological standards .

- Train workforce
- Innovate continually

These perspectives are mapped in a top-down fashion, starting with the market perspective to identify potential customer segments, then deriving product characteristics and the processes required to produce them. Finally, by identifying the network of partners needed to produce the product and the players influencing the process. Roadmap projects use technology as an IT lever to improve processes and create value. The company must select the technologies that will help it achieve its objectives, whether hardware (Sensors, Robots, 3D printers) or software (Data analytics, Machine Learning, Automation). This technology selection is essential to successfully implement the transformation to I4.0. To deploy the roadmap, the company must adapt rather than adopt the new industry 4.0 technologies. When we adopt technology, the primary focus is adding that technology to the system, but when you adapt to it, the primary focus is changing the system, whether that requires additional technology or not (Soto, 2018). To adapt to technology, we advise beginning with a prototype and creating a pilot project. Starting small will allow the company to test the technology and processes before scaling up. Once, the prototype shows promising results and the Industrie 4.0 have been successfully implemented in a pilot project, company scale up to other areas.

During Formalizing technological standards stage, a company must define technological standards and implement digital information processes to enhance its competitiveness and adapt to the evolving technological landscape. To Formalize technological standards a company must train her workforce to work with new technologies and processes. This might include training in data analytics, robotics, and automation. She must also collaborate with partners and suppliers to integrate their systems with hers. This will help her create a more connected and efficient supply chain. Finally, she must continue to innovate and explore new technologies and processes that can help her achieve goals. Industrie 4.0 is a constantly evolving field, and staying up to date is key to success. As a result, Industrie 4.0 roadmap implementation is an iterative process, it must be supported by a maturity model (Sekkat, El-hassani, & Cherrafi, 2023). Indeed, at this step the person in charge at the SME will control sustainment during a defined period. He may use a maturity model to compare the current maturity level of the company to a desired maturity level and also focuses on monitoring the defined KPIs to evaluate the impact of Industrie 4.0, track performance and identify areas for improvement. After presenting a CE Concept; and I 4.0 strategy and Roadmap, il the next section we will look at the literature review of the relationship between CE and I4.0 Concepts.

RELATIONSHIP BETWEEN CE CONCEPT AND I4.0 STRATEGY

In this paper we want to shed light on the way that companies must uses the I4.0 technologies to transfer from the traditional linear economy to CE. Indeed, Circular economy (CE) promotes the sustainable use of resources and the minimization of environmental impacts while creating value for society, economy, and businesses. Companies are required to develop their Industry 4.0 strategy and established a roadmap to deploy this strategy. The question we want to address is to know what place they gave to the CE in this strategy. This section conducts a systematic review on CE and I4.0 theory to identify the relationship between these concepts. A systematic review, however, is a comprehensive literature review aiming to find, code, appraise, and synthesize the previous research in an unbiased and well-documented manner (Kraus, Breier, & Dasí-Rodrígue, 2020). This study follows the guidelines for Performing Systematic Literature Reviews in Software Engineering, provided by Barbara Kitchenham from The Department of

Computer Science at Keele University (Kitchenham & Charters, 2007). It is carried out in three main stages as follows:

1. Planning the review, where we have defined the research questions,
2. Conducting the review, where we have searched for, extracted, analyzed, and combined relevant data sources,
3. Reporting the review, where we communicate and discus the results.

In the first stage we have defined the research questions as follow:

- Is there any relationship between CE concept and I4.0 technologies?
- How I4.0 technologies are used to influence CE approach and to move towards a more sustainable industry?
- How CE related areas can be covered by I4.0 technologies?
- How companies use the I4.0 technologies to transfer from the traditional Linear Economy to CE?

In the second stage we conducted the literature review in three steps: first we searched for relevant data sources, then we extracted this information and finally we analyzed and combined the extracted information.

At first step, the search was done by title, keyword, and abstract, and type of publication were journal papers, conferences, book chapters, PHD Dissertation and book reviews. A search was performed within the scientific databases Science Direct, Scopus, Web of Science (WOS), HAL open archive and Google Scholar (GS). Since the methodology aims to consider two separate research topics, the twofold set of keywords obtained from a combination of generic terms such as "Industry 4.0" and "Digitalization", with the corresponding keywords such as "Circular Economy", "Green Operations" and "Sustainable Development" were utilized.

In a second step we extracted relevant data and assess its eligibility. We therefore eliminate irrelevant documents and identify the papers that aim to answer the research questions. Indeed, after reading the abstract and considering general information for all these references, articles that were not directly related to the focus of this research were discarded.

In a third step we analyzed the selected papers. After an in depth reading of these papers, we classified them according to two criteria: type and application field. For the first criterion we found three classes:

- A first class were reviews for works published in recent years (Piscitelli, et al., 2020; Rosa, Sassanelli, Urbinati, Chiaroni, & Terzi, 2020; Arsova, Genovese, & Ketikidis, 2022; Javaid, Haleem, Singh, Suman, & Gonzalez, 2022; Patil, Dwivedi, Abdul Moktadir, & Lakshay, 2023)
- A second class were presenting frameworks, and few of them focused on mathematical models (Wang & Wang, 2019; Hallioui, Herrou, Santos, Katina, & Egbue, 2022)
- A third class were study cases applied to frameworks proposed or frameworks that proposed study cases (Martín-Gómez, Aguayo-González, & Bárcena, 2018).

Since case studies and proposed Frameworks associated with the deployment of CE and Industry 4.0 may concern a company, a supply chain, or a whole country we have categorized selected papers based on application field. This classification approach enables a comprehensive analysis of the literature and provides a basis for identifying trends, knowledge gaps, and potential areas for further research. So, based on this second criterion we categorized the papers on four levels:

- Company level: In this category papers explore how businesses can integrate circular principles into their operations and leverage advanced technologies to optimize production, resource utilization, and waste management (Vacchi, Siligardi, Cedillo-González, Ferrari, & Settembre-Blundo, 2021), (Javaid, Haleem, Singh, Suman, & Gonzalez, 2022).
- Industrial zone level: Papers in this category assess how collaborative efforts among multiple companies in a particular geographical area can lead to shared infrastructure, resources, and increased efficiency through the adoption of digital technologies (Martín-Gómez, Aguayo-González, & Bárcena, 2018). Other papers extend their study to regional scales, where governments and local authorities play a significant role. They discuss policy frameworks, collaborative initiatives, and the development of smart cities or regions that promote circularity and digital transformation (Arsova, Genovese, & Ketikidis, 2022).
- Supply chain level: Papers in this category investigate how circular practices and digitalization can enhance transparency, traceability, and collaboration across the various stages of a supply chain, including sourcing, production, distribution, and end-of-life management (Wang & Wang, 2019). Certain Papers focus on specific industrial sectors. For example, the automotive industry may explore the adoption of circular business models and smart manufacturing technologies to enable remanufacturing and closed-loop material flows (Yadav, Luthra, Jakhar, Mangla, & Rai, 2020) (Grati, Loukil, Boukadi, & Abed, 2023).
- National or global level: These papers analyze policy frameworks, systemic changes, and international collaborations to facilitate the transition towards a circular and digitally enabled economy (Dantas, et al., 2021), (Khan & Kabir, 2020), (Šebestová & Sroka, 2020).

In the third stage we will present and discus the paper selected. Dantas et al (Dantas, et al., 2021) conducted a systematic literature review to explore the potential of the combination of circular economy (CE) practices and Industry 4.0 (I4.0) technologies in achieving the Sustainable Development Goals (SDGs). The SDGs were established by the United Nations General Assembly in 2015 as part of the Post-2015 Development Agenda, aiming to create a global development framework beyond the Millennium Development Goals. Private businesses play a crucial role in accelerating the implementation of sustainable practices outlined in the United Nations Agenda 2030. Their contribution often involves innovation, skilled personnel, and adaptability. Research suggests that private sector engagement creates mutually beneficial outcomes for businesses, society, and the environment. Consequently, industries have shifted from traditional production methods to innovative technologies to pursue the 17 SDGs. The review encompassed 50 peer-reviewed papers that examined the link between CE and I4.0, in relation to sustainability. The findings highlight the significance of the CE-I4.0 nexus in advancing the SDGs, as it integrates cutting-edge technologies with novel circular production and business models, thereby offering opportunities to address the SDG targets highlighted in this study.

Yadav et al (Yadav, Luthra, Jakhar, Mangla, & Rai, 2020) proposed a novel framework to address challenges in Sustainable Supply Chain Management (SSCM) by integrating Industry 4.0 and circular economy-based solutions. Their research involved identifying 28 distinct SSCM challenges and 22 corresponding solution measures. To gauge the intensity of these challenges, they employed a multi-criteria decision-making approach, establishing links between challenges and solutions. The applicability of the framework was then tested using a case study of an automotive organization based in the Republic of India. The findings highlighted managerial and organizational challenges, along with economic challenges, as critical factors influencing SSCM adoption.

Rosa et al (Rosa, Sassanelli, Urbinati, Chiaroni, & Terzi, 2020) conducted a systematic literature review to explore the relationship between Industry 4.0 (I4.0) and Circular Economy (CE). The papers were classified based on CE-related areas (DISAS Disassembly, RECYC Recycling, REMAN Remanufacturing, RESOU Resource Efficiency, REUSE Reuse, etc.) and I4.0-related technologies (AM Additive Manufacturing, BDA Big Data and Analytics, CPS Cyber-Physical Systems, IOT Internet of Things, SIM Simulation, etc.). The study developed an innovative framework that elucidated the connections between I4.0 and CE, as well as identified potential research avenues. The analysis indicated that certain I4.0 technologies, such as AM, BDA, and IOT, were more prevalent in specific CE domains, though the influence of I4.0 technologies on CE was evident across the board.

Martín-Gómez et al (Martín-Gómez, Aguayo-González, & Bárcena, 2018) created a framework for Circular Economy (CE) that focuses on the sharing of resources within Eco-Industrial Parks at the Meso-level. Their approach involves developing an ontological framework based on industrial metabolism. The ontology is constructed using the Ontology Web Language and is integrated into an architecture that utilizes bio-inspired Multi-Agent Systems (MAS). To apply this integrated model, the researchers conducted a case study on the product life cycle, specifically a workbench. They aimed to establish the metabolic pathway of the workbench within an eco-industrial park. By incorporating MAS into their framework, they successfully established a Smart Eco-Industrial Park (SEIP).

Wang and Wang (Wang & Wang, 2019) introduced Digital Twin for the Waste Electrical and Electronic Equipment (WEEE) recovery to support the manufacturing/remanufacturing operations throughout the product's life cycle, from design to recovery. The Waste Electrical and Electronic Equipment (WEEE) recovery can be categorized into two types: recycling at the material level and remanufacturing at the component level. Indeed, the WEEE recovery face the challenges of diversified individuals, lack of product knowledge, and distributed location. They used the latest ICT and developed the international standard-compliant data models to support WEEE recovery services with high data interoperability. The feasibility of the proposed system and methodologies were validated and evaluated during implementations in the cloud and cyber-physical system.

Tavera Romero et al (Tavera-Romero, Castro, Ortiz, Khalaf, & Vargas, 2021) conducted an in-depth review on circular economy and Industry 4.0 to establish the relationship between these concepts. Among the identified topics, the three pillars of sustainable development were included. The researchers found a lack of studies addressing the impact of CE on the societal pillar of sustainable development, as well as a dearth of information on the mechanisms used to measure the effects of CE implementation on people. Consequently, the authors concluded that there is currently insufficient research on how individuals are being prepared to transition from the linear economy to a circular economy, which is becoming increasingly important for societies worldwide.

Vacchi et al (Vacchi, Siligardi, Cedillo-González, Ferrari, & Settembre-Blundo, 2021) developed a circular eco-design model for the Italian ceramic tile manufacturing industry, integrating Industry 4.0 technologies, smart data, Life Cycle Assessment (LCA) methodology, and material microstructural analysis techniques. They implemented an integrated MES, ERP, and PLC system to enhance production efficiency. By utilizing LCA-based Dynamic Eco-design, they evaluated the environmental impacts of different resource inputs and identified the formula with the least significant impact on the ceramic body composition. Throughout the ceramic production process, sensors connected via cabling or Wi-Fi collected process data and transmitted them to the Manufacturing Execution System (MES). The circular eco-design model utilized the abundant process-related data (Big Data) collected by line sensors connected to the MES, which integrated with the Enterprise Resource Planning (ERP) system. A Business Intelligence (BI) application selected critical data (Smart Data) from the ERP for real-time Life Cycle Inventory (BI-LCI), forming the basis for conducting environmental impact assessments using Dynamic Life Cycle Assessment (LCA). Initially, the model was simulated to define five alternative scenarios for raw material supply compared to the current production method. These scenarios were then validated in laboratory-scale and pilot environments, demonstrating that selecting appropriate raw material transport systems significantly improves the environmental performance of ceramic products.

In conclusion, after thoroughly examining the relevant academic papers, it becomes evident that there is a consensus among the authors regarding the interconnected nature of Circular Economy (CE) and Industry 4.0 (I4.0) due to their mutual dependence. The impact of I4.0 technologies on CE has been consistently confirmed. However, the literature review reveals existing gaps concerning the challenges and implications that both society and individuals must confront to successfully transition from a linear to a Circular Economy model, ensuring sustainability at the organizational, supply chain, industrial sector, or national level (Tavera-Romero, Castro, Ortiz, Khalaf, & Vargas, 2021). Moreover, it is worth noting that the current Maturity Models fail to incorporate Circular Economy and the three pillars of Sustainable Development Goals, particularly those related to social development goals. As a result, there is a need for further research and comprehensive assessment models to address these critical aspects and facilitate a smoother transition towards Circular Economy principles.

CONCLUSION AND PROSPECTS FOR THE FUTURE

This chapter presents a literature review of the concepts of Circular Economy (CE) and Industry 4.0 (I4.0). The review involved a comprehensive analysis and synthesis of various academic sources, including case studies, literature reviews, and proposed frameworks and methodologies. Through this process, the relationship between CE and I4.0 was identified, revealing correlated behavior, and indicating that I4.0 technologies significantly influence the CE concept. It is evident from the review that companies need to strengthen the integration of environmental dimensions into their industrial strategies. Simultaneously, it is crucial for public authorities, governments, and the international community to play an active role in encouraging and supporting companies to adopt this approach. Drawing from the findings of this literature review, our future work will focus on developing an innovative framework that seamlessly integrates the principles of I4.0 and CE. This framework aims to enable companies to create an I4.0 Roadmap that adequately incorporates ecological concerns.

REFERENCES

Alcácer, V., Rodrigues, J., Carvalho, H., & Cruz-Machado, V. (2022). Industry 4.0 Maturity Follow Up Inside an Internal Value Chain: A Case Study. *International Journal of Advanced Manufacturing Technology*, *119*(7-8), 5035–5046. doi:10.1007/s00170-021-08476-3

Arsova, S., Genovese, A., & Ketikidis, P. H. (2022). Implementing circular economy in a regional context: A systematic literature review and a research agenda. *Journal of Cleaner Production, 368*, 133117. doi:10.1016/j.jclepro.2022.133117

Brundtland, G. H., Khalid, M., Agnelli, S., Al-Athel, S. A., Chidzero, B., Fadika, L. M., . . . Botero, M. M. (1987). *Our common future*. World Commission on Environment and Development.

Cotrino, A., Sebastián, M. A., & González-Gaya, C. (2020). Industry 4.0 Roadmap: Implementation for Small and Medium-Sized Enterprises. *MDPI. Applied Sciences (Basel, Switzerland), 10*(23), 8566. doi:10.3390/app10238566

Dantas, T. E., de-Souza, E. D., Destro, I. R., Hammes, G., Rodriguez, C. M., & Soares, S. R. (2021). How the combination of Circular Economy and Industry 4.0 can contribute towards achieving the Sustainable Development Goals. *Sustainable Production and Consumption, 26*, 213–227. doi:10.1016/j. spc.2020.10.005

Davenport, T., & Short, J. (1990). The New Industrial Engineering: Information Technology and Business Process Redesign. *Sloan Management Review*, 11–27.

Erol, S., Schumacher, A., & Sihn, W. (2016). Strategic guidance towards Industry 4.0 – a three-stage process model. *International Conference on Competitive Manufacturing 2016 (COMA16)*.

Grati, R., Loukil, F., Boukadi, K., & Abed, M. (2023). A blockchain-based framework for circular end-of-life vehicle processing. *Cluster Computing*, 1–14. doi:10.1007/s10586-023-03981-4

Hallioui, A., Herrou, B., Santos, R. S., Katina, P. F., & Egbue, O. (2022). Systems-based approach to contemporary business management: An enabler of business sustainability in a context of industry 4.0, circular economy, competitiveness and diverse stakeholders. *Journal of Cleaner Production, 373*, 133819. doi:10.1016/j.jclepro.2022.133819

Javaid, M., Haleem, A., Singh, R. P., Suman, R., & Gonzalez, E. S. (2022). Understanding the adoption of Industry 4.0 technologies in improving environmental sustainability. *Sustainable Operations and Computers, 3*, 203–217. doi:10.1016/j.susoc.2022.01.008

Khan, I., & Kabir, Z. (2020). Waste-to-energy generation technologies and the developing economies: A multi-criteria analysis for sustainability assessment. *Renewable Energy, 150*, 320–333. doi:10.1016/j. renene.2019.12.132

Kitchenham, B., & Charters, S. (2007). *Guidelines for Performing Systematic Literature Reviews in Software Engineering*. Technical Report EBSE 2007-001 Keele University and Durham University Joint Report. Récupéré sur https://www.elsevier.com/__data/promis_misc/525444systematic reviewsguide.pdf

Kraus, S., Breier, M., & Dasí-Rodrígue, S. (2020). The art of crafting a systematic literature review in entrepreneurship research. *The International Entrepreneurship and Management Journal, 16*(3), 1023–1042. doi:10.1007/s11365-020-00635-4

Lu, Y. (2017). Industry 4.0: A survey on technologies, applications and open research issues. *Journal of Industrial Information Integration, 6*, 1–10. doi:10.1016/j.jii.2017.04.005

Martín-Gómez, A. M., Aguayo-González, F., & Bárcena, M. M. (2018). Smart Eco-Industrial Parks: A Circular Economy Implementation Based on Industrial Metabolism. *Resources, Conservation and Recycling*, *135*, 58–69. doi:10.1016/j.resconrec.2017.08.007

McDonough Braungart Design Chemistry, M. B. D. C. (2021). *Built Environment Herman Miller*. (MBDC) Récupéré sur https://mbdc.com/case-studies/herman-miller/

Patil, A., Dwivedi, A., Abdul Moktadir, M., & Lakshay. (2023). Big data-Industry 4.0 readiness factors for sustainable supply chain management: Towards circularity. *Computers & Industrial Engineering*, *178*, 109109. doi:10.1016/j.cie.2023.109109

Piscitelli, G., Ferazzoli, A., Petrillo, A., Cioffi, R., Parmentola, A., & Travaglioni, M. (2020). Circular Economy models in the Industry 4.0 era: A review of the last decade. *Procedia Manufacturing*, *42*, 227–234. doi:10.1016/j.promfg.2020.02.074

Rosa, P., Sassanelli, C., Urbinati, A., Chiaroni, D., & Terzi, S. (2020). Assessing relations between Circular Economy and Industry 4.0: A systematic literature review. *International Journal of Production Research*, *58*(6), 1662–1687. doi:10.1080/00207543.2019.1680896

Schumacher, A., Nemeth, T., & Sihn, W. (2019). Roadmapping towards industrial digitalization based on an Industry 4.0 maturity model for manufacturing enterprises. *Procedia CIRP*, *79*, 409–414. doi:10.1016/j.procir.2019.02.110

Šebestová, J., & Sroka, W. (2020). Sustainable development goals and sme decisions: The czech republic vs. Poland. *Journal of Eastern European and Central Asian Research*, *7*, 39–50.

Sekkat, S., & El-hassani, I. (2021). What approach using to digitize quality management? *International Conference on Artificial Intelligence and Emerging Technologies (AIET) 24-25 November 2021.*

Sekkat, S., El-hassani, I., & Cherrafi, A. (2023). *Maturity Models as a support for Industry 4.0 implementation: Literature review. Artificial Intelligence & Industrial Applications A2IA'2023 February 17th and 18th, 2023.*

Soto, F. (2018). *Operational Excellence: The fundamentals for succeeding where others have failed.* Endeavor Management.

Tavera-Romero, C. A., Castro, D. F., Ortiz, J. H., Khalaf, O. I., & Vargas, M. A. (2021). Synergy between Circular Economy and Industry 4.0: A Literature Review. *MDPI. Sustainability (Basel)*, *13*(8), 4331. doi:10.3390/su13084331

Ulrich, K. T., & Eppinger, S. D. (2008). *Product Design and Development* (5th ed.). McGraw-Hill.

Vacchi, M., Siligardi, C., Cedillo-González, E. I., Ferrari, A. M., & Settembre-Blundo, D. (2021). Industry 4.0 and Smart Data as Enablers of the Circular Economy in Manufacturing: Product Re-Engineering with Circular Eco-Design. *MDPI. Sustainability (Basel)*, *13*(18), 10366. doi:10.3390/su131810366

Wang, X. V., & Wang, L. (2019). Digital Twin-Based WEEE Recycling, Recovery and Remanufacturing in the Background of Industry 4.0. *International Journal of Production Research*, *57*(12), 3892–3902.

Yadav, G., Luthra, S., Jakhar, S. K., Mangla, S. K., & Rai, D. P. (2020). A framework to overcome sustainable supply chain challenges through solution measures of industry 4.0 and circular economy: An automotive case. *Journal of Cleaner Production, 254*, 120112. doi:10.1016/j.jclepro.2020.120112

Zbicinski, I., Stavenuite, J., Kozlowska, B., & van de Coevering, H. P. (2006). *Product Design and Life Cycle Assessment.* The Baltic University Press.

Chapter 5
Quality Management, Tools, and Interactions

Meryeme Bououchma
Laboratoire des Techniques Industrielles-(FST), USMBA-Fez, Morocco

Brahim Herrou
Laboratoire des Techniques Industrielles-(EST), USMBA- Fez, Morocco

ABSTRACT

The primary goal of any organization or company is to guarantee good performances as far as all sectors are concerned in order to achieve operational excellence at all levels. This can only be achieved through the prior integration of the customer satisfaction function, in which the offer quality is considered as the main determinant. Thus, the launch of new complex and innovative products becomes necessary through developing new products or improving existing ones that meet specific customers' needs, since they have become more conscious and selective in the products they buy, while respecting the triptych cost quality time. In that context, the authors review three quality management tools that are widely used for that purpose—AF, QFD, and FMEA—before defining the advantages and disadvantages of each one, as well as relationships or potential interactions between them.

INTRODUCTION

Nowadays, it is crystal clear that the primary goal of any organization or company is to guarantee good performances as far as all sectors are concerned, in order to achieve operational excellence at all levels. which generally begins with a culture shift, where all leaders and employees are dedicated for creating not only a quality product but also providing great customer experiences, via the prior integration of the satisfaction function, in which the offer quality is considered as the main determinant. In fact, one of pillars or necessary key points that support the operational excellence are process excellence as well as commitment to quality, which has been considered nowadays a major and permanent concern. On the other hand, within such an actual industrial world, where competition is a key factor in the economic environment of companies, organizations strive to compete in the highly competitive global economy,

DOI: 10.4018/979-8-3693-0497-6.ch005

as the level of competition is increasing day after day. Thus, the launch of new complex and innovative products becomes necessary, through developing new or improving existing products that meet specific customers' needs, since they have become more conscious and selective in the products they buy, while respecting the triptych Cost Quality Time. In other words, companies must match or surpass their competitors' products in terms of quality, price, time, and service in order to survive. Some organizations have achieved impressive results as far as their ability to convert raw materials into goods and services is concerned, through investing in advanced technologies, focusing on efficiency and productivity and establishing a new management policy. However, the organization's ability to develop new products to meet the customer's changing wants and needs has not kept pace, taking in considerations interactions of several functions necessity. Hence, the importance of using quality management tools and methods in product design has been realized. Among the most widely used methods, we will focus on three ones: AF (Functional Analysis), QFD (Quality Function Deployment), FMEA (Failure Mode & Effects Analysis). Thus, the design process is presented as a macro-process based on three complementary points of view: functional features, technical aspects and reliability conditions. Indeed, "AF" is an approach that involves all sectors of the company, whether functional or operational, and it proposes to explain needs and requirements to be met, in terms of technical functions and solutions, which makes it possible to achieve product optimization while meeting the use constraints. Nevertheless, this method remains sometimes difficult to implement. The second tool "QFD" method aims at translating the customer's voice into engineers' jargon to ensure continuous improvement. For this reason, the QFD is fully in line with a global approach for reducing costs and deadlines specific to a Total Quality Action, by revealing the optimal solution to be implemented by the company. It allows to target the necessary parameters to satisfy the customer, build the perceived quality and discover early in the project cycle the sensitive points for which preventive measures should be taken. However, this analysis may have adverse consequences for the company if the conducted study is of poor quality. Furthermore, methodical thinking can make adapting to market needs more complex, as customer's requirements can change quickly. The third method "FMEA" takes into account more precisely the product-process-system triptych. Many authors have pointed out that this method is an extremely powerful tool used for created systems or those in operation. Also, it assists engineers during new systems design stage, in order to verify certain behavioral aspects, and make it possible to anticipate possible uncertainties. This reflection will naturally lead to many technical or organizational solutions to be put in place. However, it does not sometimes make it possible to take into account the combination of several failures whose criticality can be high. As a conclusion, we can note that no approach is really complete to cover all design different steps, since these three methods can be called complementary.

FUNCTIONAL ANALYSIS

Functional analysis is a method that integrates the need that will mark the product characteristics, technical solutions to satisfy its requirements, as well as the topological analysis that lays the groundwork for the future product development. It enables to characterize the functions offered by a product in order to satisfy the user's needs.

Functional analysis of the need: According to AFNOR, a function is defined as the set of actions of a product or one of its constituents expressed exclusively in terms of purpose; while a need is a need or desire experienced by a user. According to AFNOR, functional specifications (CdCF) is a document by which the applicant expresses his need (or the one he is responsible for translating in terms of service functions and constraints), for each of which are defined criteria for the assessment and Each of its levels must have flexibility (Brisco & Wolfgang, 2018).

The functional analysis of the need for a product, system or service basis resides in its potentiality to be valuable by satisfying the expecting benefits for future users. Indeed, it describes the user's point of view, as if the product is a «black box» that must meet expressed needs during its life cycle. For that, the graphical tool, called "horned beast" is used to answer the following questions: At who, or what does the system serve? On who, or what is he operating on? For what purpose?

Figure 1. Horned beast diagram

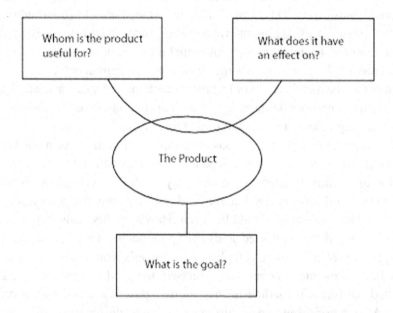

Functions identification: This step is very important during a design process. Indeed, functions reflect the description of the need to be satisfied by the system and they provide guidance for the choice of the different technical solutions to be later analyzed.

Functions of the system are represented via the tool called "octopus diagram", which introduces the system surrounded by external elements in contact with it. In other words, the role of octopus diagram is to define the relationships that might be between elements of the system environment. Thus, service functions, separated into main FP functions, and FC constraint functions are defined. The figure below shows an example of the octopus diagram:

Technical-functional analysis: it aims at analyzing the system from the technical point of view. In fact, it ensures the transition from service functions to technical functions before proposing constructive solutions that will be implemented. For this purpose, the FAST diagram makes it possible to well understand a complex product, and then introduce different scenarios of technical solutions, up to constituent equipment of the product, through answering the questions: Why? When? How? starting from a given function.

Figure 2. Octopus diagram

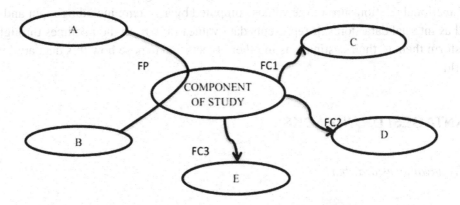

Figure 3. FAST diagram principle

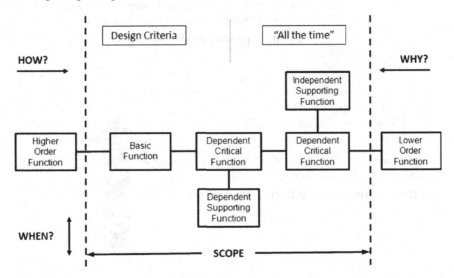

Figure 4. SADT diagram

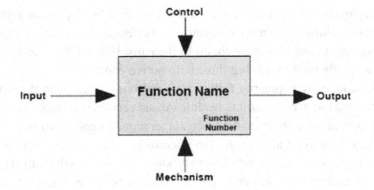

Also, the second tool that might be used is the the SADT diagram, which is an analytical tool that shows the functional relationships of the values computed by a system, including input and output values, as well as internal data stores. It represents data values flow from their sources through processes which transform them to their destinations in other objects and expose how this data are related to the outside world.

FA ADVANTAGES/ DRAWBACKS

Figure 5. FA advantages/drawbacks

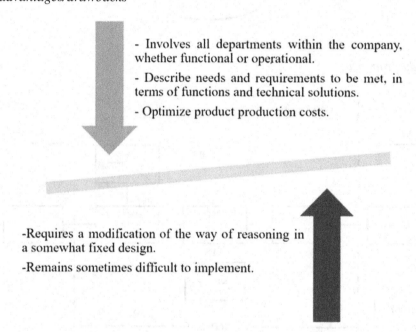

- Involves all departments within the company, whether functional or operational.

- Describe needs and requirements to be met, in terms of functions and technical solutions.

- Optimize product production costs.

-Requires a modification of the way of reasoning in a somewhat fixed design.

-Remains sometimes difficult to implement.

Quality Function Deployment (QFD)

Quality Function Deployment (QFD) was first developed in Japan by Yoji Akao in the late 1960s while working for Mitsubishi's shipyard, as a form of cause and effect analysis. It was later adopted by other companies including Toyota and its supply chain. In the early 1980s, QFD was brought to the United States, where it was mainly used by the big three automotive companies and a few electronics manufacturers. QFD gained its early popularity following numerous successes in the automotive industry. Currently, it has been used in manufacturing, healthcare and service organizations.

Indeed, QFD is a structured approach to define customer requirements and translate them into specific plans. It is about a process and set of tools used to effectively define customer needs and convert them into detailed engineering specifications and plans to produce the products that fulfill those requirements. QFD is used to define customer voice, that might describes these stated and unstated customer needs, since it is captured through a variety of ways: direct discussions, surveys, focus groups, interviews, customer complaints, observations, before convert it into measurable design targets and drive it from the assembly level down through the sub-assembly, production and component process levels.

HOUSE OF QUALITY

The expectations of the user regarding the product are subjective, qualitative and non-technical. Their deployment in product requirements, which are essentially objective, quantitative and technical, is performed through a matrix diagram called House of Quality (Naveiroa & de Oliveira, 2018). QFD is often referred to 'The House of Quality' in the product planning stage because of the shape of the resulting matrix diagram. In fact, lines refer to customers' requirements, while columns contain expected technical characteristics of the new product. Not only does the House of Quality reduce product development time, but it also increases the customer's satisfaction once the product is used.

House of Quality diagrams bring to mind the shape of a house with a rooftop. It should be created using direct customer input if applicable. It is considered the primary tool in QFD, since it serves as a roadmap for describing the journey from initial idea to final product.

The Figure 1 shows an example of a House of Quality of a drone:

Figure 6. An example of a house of quality diagram matrix

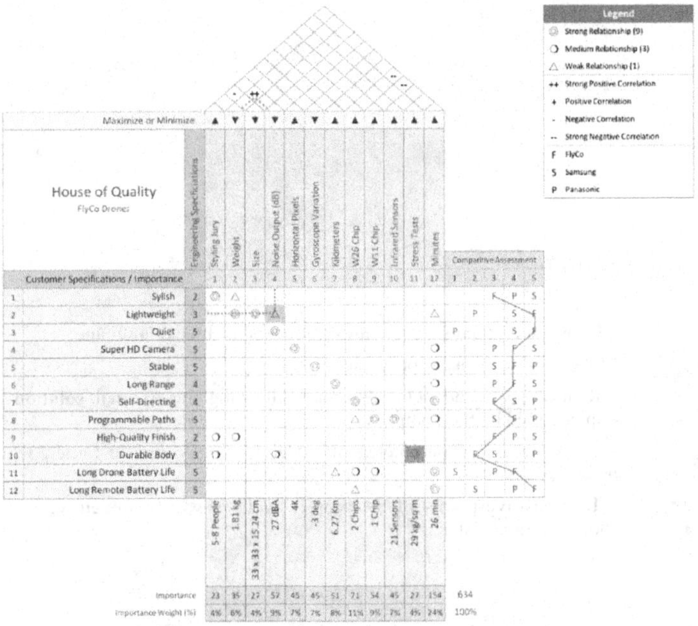

In the left of the matrix, Customer Specifications are listed. They refer to specific priority features on which the customer has set focus. Numbers just to the right represent their importance to the customer on a scale of one to five. Concerning the section Engineering Specifications, it represents engineering methods and technical characteristics needed to satisfy customer requirements.

The center grid containing symbols shows how strong a relationship each customer need has to each technical characteristic. Referring to the Legend, a ◎ indicates a strong relationship with a weight of 9, a ○ is a medium relationship with a weight of 3, whereas a △ is a weak relationship with a weight of only 1.

The top portion, also called the roof of the house, introduce potential conflicts between engineering specifications. Referring to the legend, a ++ indicates a strong positive correlation, a + presents a strong correlation. Oppositely, a – indicates a negative correlation, while a – refers to a strong negative correlation.

Concerning the Importance numbers, as well as Importance Weights, they represent the overall importance after evaluating both engineering relationships and customer importance. Indeed, the product of each customer importance weight and the value of the relationship symbol for each specification and engineering specification is calculated, to obtain these numbers. As shown, the total of all importance weights is 634. The importance weight (%) of each engineering specification is calculated by dividing the total of the concerned engineering specification importance by the total of all importance weights.

Lastly, the right of the matrix shows the Comparative Assessment section. It is a sort of benchmark analysis in which a trending line indicates the position of the product compared to other brand models with similar specifications. For each customer specification, each brand is rated on a scale of 1 up to 5. (1 means poor, 5 represents excellent effectiveness of the brand).

Figure 7. QFD advantages/drawbacks

- Translate customer's voice into engineers' technical language.

- Ensure continuous improvement.

- Reduce costs and delays, through choosing the optimal solution to be implemented by the company.

- Track necessary parameters in order to satisfy the customer, work on perceived quality.

- Tag sensitive points of the project cycle in which preventive measures should be taken later.

- May generate negative consequences for the company if the study carried out is of a poor quality.

- Difficulty to respond swiftly to market changes, as customer requirements can change quickly.

ADVANTAGES/ DRAWBACKS OF QFD METHOD

Failure Mode and Effects Analysis (FMEA)

Very often, faults and defects in products or services are generally detected through extensive testing and predictive modeling that need expensive costs and may add significant delays to schedules. The challenge consists of ensuring that defects never arise since the first time. Thus, failure mode and effects analysis tool is used, in order to identify potential problems and their impact. Its origin goes back to the early 1950's when the technique was utilized in the design and development of flight control systems.

In fact, FMEA is a widely used tool that aims to evaluate design at the initial stage from the reliability aspect. Indeed, "Failure modes" means the way, or mode, in which something might break down, such as potential errors, especially those which may affect the customer. "Effects analysis" refers to analyzing and studying the consequences of those breakdowns. FMEA is a progressive method whose objective is to collect knowledge about possible points of failure related to a product or a service, identify, analyze all possible probabilities a process or a product could fail and define a strategy to prioritize, reduce or eliminate the biggest risks, through ensuring that all failures can be detected, via determining how periodically a failure might happen, and by identifying which potential failures should be prioritized.

When to Perform FMEA

Used within many industries, FMEA is considered as one of the best ways to early analyze potential reliability problems during the development cycle, which make it possible for manufacturers to anticipate issues, take quick actions, reduce recurrent failures and ensure the customer's safety and satisfaction. Therefore, there are several cases when FMEA analysis should be applied, like:

- Analyzing new product, service or process design,
- Planning to perform an existing product or service, in a different way,
- Planning quality improvement for a specific process or improvement goals for an existing product, service or process,
- Analyze, understand and reduce a specific process failures,
- Before introducing control plans for a new or modified process,
- Before using a design or a process in a new environment or application,
- Periodically throughout the life of the process, product, or service, as quality as well as reliability should be regularly examined and improved, in order to optimize results.

Why Perform FMEA

Absolutely, the sooner as possible a failure is detected, the less it will cost. If a failure is discovered late, the impact will exponentially be more disastrous. Thus, FMEA is used to discover a failure at an earliest point in a product or a process design. In other words, it provides many benefits, such as:

- Afford multiple choices to reduce or eliminate potential risks and probable failures at an early step,
- Reduce the frequency of a problem occurrence,
- Avoid poor performance of a product or a service,

- Guarantee high capability and reliability of a product or a service,
- Ensure costs reduction,
- Promotes collaboration among complementary teams, such as design, manufacturing, quality, testing and sales...

Types of FMEA Analyses

There are three main types of failure mode & effects analysis.

- **Design FMEA (DFMEA):** it focuses on how to reduce or perhaps prevent possible system, product or process failures. DFMEA allows engineers to detect early potential failures, define how bad consequences could be, and what measures will be put in place in order to mitigate and prevent failures, so that they can be corrected at optimal cost.
- **Process FMEA (PFMEA):** it identifies failures that may impact product quality, safety and environmental hazards, reduce reliability of the process, or lead to customer's disapproval. In fact, it pinpoints potential risks related to the process, in order to help managers and teams understand probable risks for each process stage as soon as possible.
- **Functional FMEA (FFMEA):** it aims at avoiding potential failures before corrective actions must be employed. It identifies and prioritizes possible functional failure modes.

FMEA Procedure

Process Failure Mode and Effects Analysis is implemented through interrelated steps. As a general process, here is an overview of the FMEA tool steps:

Step 1: Review the process
  ◦ Refer to process flowchart, in order to identify each process component, before listing them in the FMEA table,
  ◦ Create a team of employees with diverse knowledge about the process, product or service, functions and customer's requirements, manufacturing, quality, testing, maintenance, reliability purchasing, sales, customer service, marketing...
Step 2: Brainstorm potential failure modes
  ◦ Review existing documentations about potential failures of each component,
  ◦ Use brainstorming tool to identify other potential failures, via experiences, cumulative knowledge...
  ◦ Generate a list of failures per component.
Step 3: Potential effects of each failure
  ◦ Evaluate the impact of the failure on the final product, service or on one or more steps of the process,
  ◦ It might be more than one effect for each failure.
Step 4: Assign Severity, Occurrence and Detection rankings
  ◦ Severity (S) rating refers to how serious the consequences of the failure. It is usually rated on a scale from 1 to 10, where 1 is insignificant and 10 is catastrophic.

- Occurrence (O) rating estimates the probability of a failure happening. It is usually rated on a scale from 1 to 10, where 1 is quite unlikely and 10 is certain.
- Detection (D) rating defines how well the failure would be detected through controls, or via other detection tools before the customer would be affected. Detection is usually rated on a scale from 1 to 10, where 1 means the control is totally certain to detect the problem and 10 means that no control exists or the control is certain not to detect the problem.

Step 5: Calculate the RPN

- The Risk Priority Number (RPN) is calculated this way: RPN= Severity x Occurrence x Detection

STEP 6: Develop the action plan

- Based on RPN results, prioritize failures and elaborate an action plan (who will do what, and by when) for priority failures that will be worked on.
- Implement the identified improvements.

Figure 8. FMEA advantages/drawbacks

- Powerful tool for complex systems design.

- Pinpoint the critical points of the process.

- Anticipate eventual defects or hazards.

-Implement optimal solutions whether technical and/ or organizational ones.

- Reduce additional costs.

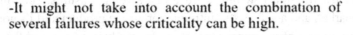

-It might not take into account the combination of several failures whose criticality can be high.

Step 7: Re-evaluate RPN

- Re-evaluate again each of the potential failures after implementing improvements, in order to measure their impact on the final product and the process.

FMEA ADVANTAGES/ DRAWBACKS

Results Interpretation of the Reviewed Tools: Functional Analysis

Nowadays, the competition between companies is becoming more and more intense, which obliges companies to think of creating new products, with more attractiveness, new design based on necessary functions, as well as additional sophisticated characteristics, to ensure their good position in the targeted market, and absolutely satisfy the user's needs. For that reason, functional analysis is used as a decision-making tool, by the project team who builds the solution step by step. In fact, this method promotes dialogue between the different project stakeholders, at all stages of the product cycle. For example, the marketing and sales services are aware of needed functions that are expected by customers, so that they will get satisfaction once they use the future product. Technical department proposes suitable solutions to be implemented and evaluated. Therefore, once all functions are identified, characterized, ordered, prioritized and valued, decision-makers choose the most appropriate solution in terms of profitability, and efficiency. Although the method complexity, it is widely used within organizations as a primary method for new product design. The major tools that support functional analysis are graphical representations whose development and reading are easier. Thus, making the task quite simple and more pleasant.

QFD Tool

OFD has been considered nowadays as one of the important quality management tools, which ensures high quality. Currently, it has been used within several organizations, as a useful improvement tool which helps companies to efficiently improve their product design plans. Many articles in literature deals with QFD benefits after its implementation within the organization. Indeed, not only is it a one of the continuous product improvement methods, but also, it must be a part of the organization quality culture, since QFD benefits surpasses the fact of solving design issues while providing users perfect products (Govers, 2000). In fact, it might be considered as a proactive product development, that promotes teamwork values within the organization, and then it generates so many significant gains. Indeed, getting market informations on a continuous basis through listening to customer's voice, ensures a continuous communication with the targeted market, and a successful introduction of the product and its good position in the market place, via the integration of customer's needs in the product design and the production process, since it is a "customer-driven planning process", as it was described by Eureka and Ryan (1994). In other words, OFD is an efficient process that reflects customers' desires, through involving them in the final product design, and by presenting them the exact product that they need, as if it is designed by themselves rather than the company design, which guarantee their loyalty. Besides, QFD enables the firm to plan and control the product process development. It may optimize design process cycle time, since the product is introduced faster to the market. Moreover, the product quality is improved, as the lower number of required technical changes would absolutely reduce run-up costs and financial waste. It is a way of management (Bluvband & Grabov, n.d.), rather than a simple tool, since it has become a part of the quality management process, as well as the whole organization management vision.

Functional Analysis

It is crystal clear that product quality and reliability are critical key points as far as final products performances are concerned. For that reason, one of the important tools that has been developed so far, and has become widely used is in manufacturing industries during different steps of the product life cycle, and within variety of industries including semiconductor processing, food service, plastics, power plant, software, and healthcare is FMEA method (Sharma & Srivastava, 2018). It has been considered, nowadays, as a proactive tool used to define, evaluate and prevent product and/or process failures. It refers to disciplined engineering which effectiveness remains in the fact that it can be used significantly and on a continuous basis, to get benefits from past experiences with similar products or processes, according to available resources, in order to identify potential failures, before defining risks with greatest concern which must be reduce, or radically prevented, through deploying actions within the organization. Such a method enables the firm to reduce cost waste and time of product development, and then meet final product defined requirements and fulfil customers' needs.

DISCUSSIONS ABOUT THE THREE REVIEWED METHODS

Bringing a new product to life, from an innovant idea with the best chance of succeeding, is very challenging for organizations, especially if it has never been done before. Indeed, new product development refers to the process that goes into bringing a new product to market, or developing an existing one, from brainstorming an idea to understanding if it fits into the market. Even though it seems to be a lengthy process that sometimes requires iteration, it may ensure that the product is the best it can be, that it satisfies customers' needs before it reaches them. Indeed, every new product development commences with research. There are numerous methods to be used, which should include also market research. We will present interactions between three Quality Management Tools that has become widely used in companies, and which their use remains necessary for product development process.

RELATIONSHIPS BETWEEN QUALITY MANAGEMENT METHODS

FA-QFD Relationship

The functional analysis generates the list of customer's requirements which is considered as the first step of QFD tool deployment. In this phase, the QFD shows the relationship between the expected needs and the different technical solutions that the company is likely to put in place to satisfy those needs. Thus, the idea consists of establishing the WHAT (representation of customer's needs) via functional needs analysis results, before taking advantage of the technical functional analysis, for the choice of elementary technical solutions, which make part of the HOW matrix.

On the other hand, it is not very logical to proceed with a QFD without having already carried out a functional analysis to define customer's needs, especially when it comes to a new product design. Nevertheless, such a relationship can make sense, in the case of studying the redesign of an existing product. In other words, a benchmark study might be carried out, in order to identify some functionalities of competitive products which may not be satisfied by the current one, and later study the possibility of adding them through using the functional analysis tool.

FA-FMEA Relationship

FMEA is generally used in the design phase, to verify a new or a modified system, whose the behavior is poorly known. The analysis aims to identify the system potential failures, in order to improve the design and/ or validate a technical solution in relation to customer's needs.

In practice, FMEA is carried out in the phases of the system use or operation. So, it is necessary to well understand the system functions, before analyzing the potential risks of defects and failures. Therefore, the functional analysis constitutes an essential prerequisite for the FMEA.

Besides, customer's needs are described in the product functional specifications (Product CdCF), that contains the service functions, and which must be translated into parameters that can be used by the designer. Indeed, this transformation of the input data is carried out using the functional analysis, which ensures the adequacy between the product functional specifications and the customer's expectations. Moreover, the verification of the adequacy of the technical solutions, that were established by the designer, to the Product CdCF is carried out using FMEA. In other words, FMEA requires a technical functional analysis of the product or the service beforehand.

QFD-FMEA Relationship

QFD offers customer's requirements that have to be met, to ensure their satisfactions, via introducing technical solutions, which must be verified through the FMEA tool, in order to decide whether implement them or not. Otherwise, the relationship between FMEA and QFD goes through the existing relationship between each of these methods and the functional analysis, as shown previously.

CONCLUSION

In this chapter, we introduced literature reviews of three quality management tools (AF, QFD and FMEA) that are widely used by designers, in order to innovate new products or improve existing ones according to customer's requirements changes. Afterwards, we presented some advantages and drawbacks of each method, before defining significant interactions between them. In fact, different features of each tool do not provide a direct comparison, since their expected targets are very different. Furthermore, intrinsic characteristics of each one define their scope of application with a high degree of precision. Thus, the design process is presented as a macro-process based on three complementary points of view, functional features using FA, technical aspects via QFD tool and House of Quality Matrix, and finally reliability conditions through FMEA. In other words, no approach is really complete to cover the different design phases. AF unlocks the system utility, QFD provides technical technologies, FMEA pinpoints probable defects as well as potential risks. To summarize, we can conclude that these three design methods can be called complementary. Hence, their usefulness remains in their integration into a global approach of quality analysis design.

REFERENCES

Bluvband, Z., & Grabov, P. (n.d.). *Failure Analysis of FMEA*. Academic Press.

Brisco & Wolfgang. (2018). Design of a Semi-Automatic Artificial Incubator. *European Journal of Applied Engineering and Scientific Research, 6*(3), 4-14.

Eureka, W.ERyan, N.E. (1994). *The Customer-Driven Company Managerial Perspective on Quality Function Deployment* (2nd ed.). ASI Press/Irwin.

Govers, C. P. (2000). QFD not just a tool but a way of quality management. *J. Production Economics*.

Naveiroa & de Oliveira. (2018). *QFD and TRIZ integration in product development: A Model for Systematic Optimization of Engineering Requirements*. Academic Press.

Sharma, K. D., & Srivastava, S. (2018). *Failure Mode and Effect Analysis (FMEA) Implementation: A Literature Review*. Academic Press.

Chapter 6

Tracking of COVID-19 Pandemic for Multi-Waves Using a Compartmental Model With Time-Dependent Parameters:
A Sum of Logistic Branches

Touria Jdid

https://orcid.org/0000-0002-3919-5402

Faulty of Sciences, Sidi Mohamed Ben Abdellah University, Morocco

Idriss Chana

https://orcid.org/0000-0001-6989-4709

ESTM, Moulay Ismail University of Meknès, Morocco

Aziz Bouazi

ESTM, Moulay Ismail University of Meknès, Morocco

Mohammed Nabil Kabbaj

https://orcid.org/0000-0002-6478-1892

LIMAS-Lab, Faculty of Sciences Dhar El Mahraz, Sidi Mohammed Ben Abdellah University, Morocco

Mohammed Benbrahim

Faulty of Sciences, Sidi Mohamed Ben Abdellah University, Morocco

ABSTRACT

Estimating and controlling the COVID-19 pandemic is essential to reduce the spread of the disease and help decision-making efforts in combating public health crises. However, the potential presence of multiple dynamic changes in the reported count data or the occurrence of another wave of the pandemic emerges as a challenge for simulating the evolution of the disease over a long period. In this chapter, to account for the dynamic changes in the COVID-19 curves, the authors propose a rate function based on multiple branches of a logistic function. They assumed in a compartmental model that the recovery

DOI: 10.4018/979-8-3693-0497-6.ch006

and disease transmission rates are time-dependent, and they assign to each the rate function. Then, they apply the model to daily COVID-19 data on infection counts in Morocco between March 2, 2020 and December 31, 2021 using curve fitting through the Nelder-Mead optimization method. The simulation outcomes demonstrate the model's ability to replicate the COVID-19 pandemic in Morocco over two waves, with the goodness of fit depending on the number of logistic branches composing the rate function.

1. INTRODUCTION

Coronavirus disease 2019 (COVID-19), an illness caused by the novel SARS-CoV-2 virus, was first reported in Wuhan, China, on December 31, 2019. As of July 5, 2023, the worldwide count of confirmed infections exceeded 767 million, with more than 6 million deaths recorded (WHO Coronavirus Dashboard, 2023). Faced with the growing risk of a pandemic, governments have started implementing targeted policies aimed at slowing the transmission of infection, easing the strain on public healthcare systems, and lowering the mortality rate. Combating COVID-19 has encountered increased challenges due to the re-emergence of consecutive waves, following periods of partial containment, in new infection cases, hospitalizations, or fatalities.

In the COVID-19 pandemic, the re-emergence of a new wave of infection in a population is not primarily due to seasonal variations. On the contrary, the way the virus spreads and the subsequent impact on waves is influenced by human behavior, such as adherence to preventive measures, compliance with public health guidelines, mobility patterns, and social interactions. Further, the effectiveness or lack of interventions implemented by local health authorities can contribute to the occurrence and severity of successive waves. When relaxing restrictions, the transmission of the virus tends to increase, whereas reintroducing or strengthening control measures can lead to a decrease in the transmission rate of the virus. A COVID-19 wave typically starts with a gradual rise in cases, reaches a peak where infection rates are at their highest, and then experiences a gradual decline in cases. Similarly, when examining the impact on healthcare systems, such as hospitalizations, intensive care unit (ICU) admissions, or healthcare resource utilization, a significant increase in hospitalizations or overload of healthcare capacity during a specific period indicates the presence of a COVID-19 wave.

Identifying multiple dynamic changes or waves in epidemic count data provides valuable insights into the trajectory of the outbreak, helps evaluate interventions, guides resource allocation, informs public health strategies, and aids in monitoring and forecasting. It is a crucial phase in understanding and effectively responding to an ongoing epidemic and guiding decision-making for future waves or similar outbreaks. This requires a dependable mathematical model and numerical technique to depict the intricate patterns of epidemic curves that exhibit multiple waves. In response to the subsequent waves of the COVID-19 disease observed in many countries, researchers have examined various models in the literature to represent the dynamic changes in COVID-19 curves. These include growth models or diffusion models (Brum et al., 2023; Vasconcelos et al., 2021; Eryarsoy et al., 2021) and compartmental models (Alshammari, 2023; Cacciapaglia et al., 2020) with time-dependent parameters. Our interest goes to compartmental or mechanistic models that consider the key biological features of infectious diseases. The epidemiological parameters of these models can be viewed as constant (time-invariant) or time-dependent.

In this chapter, we used a non-vaccination version of a dynamical model proposed by (Jdid et al., 2023) to estimate and track the COVID-19 pandemic with multiple waves. To achieve this, we first considered all model parameters as time-invariant and fitted the model through a Bayesian approach based on the Hamiltonian Monte Carlo algorithm. This allows us to identify the unknown quantities accurately and run simulations of the model within the first epidemic wave. Second, we considered recovery and disease transmission rates time-dependent, with each rate assigned a rate function consisting of multiple branches of a logistic function. In this case, we calibrate the model to daily infections of COVID-19 data in Morocco between March 2, 2020, and December 31, 2021, using a curve-fitting approach based on the Nelder-Mead method.

The subsequent sections of this chapter are structured as such. A brief review of relevant studies is presented in the next section. Following this, we provide a short description of an epidemic mathematical model introduced by Jdid et al. (2023), which serves as the foundation for this study. Then, we propose our methodology to estimate and track the COVID-19 pandemic with multiple waves. In the final section, we conclude our study.

2. RELATED WORK

The transmission of infectious diseases is commonly described through compartmental models, with the SEIR (Susceptible-Exposed-Infected-Removed) epidemiological model (Bootsma et al., 2007) being the most recognized and extensively utilized framework to analyze various epidemics, including the ongoing COVID-19 pandemic. Studies focused on modeling the COVID-19 disease can be divided into two categories. First, by examining the compartmental model structure, most researchers adopt the classical SEIR model or extend it by incorporating supplementary classes. Second, in terms of model parameters (transition rates), many studies assumed these parameters time-invariant, while others accounted for their time-dependent nature. A summary of the discussed research is provided in Table 1.

The focus of authors utilizing the extended or modified SEIR model with time-independent parameters is to evaluate the effectiveness of implementing vaccination programs and non-pharmaceutical interventions over one epidemic peak. Adewole et al. (2022) added two compartments (asymptomatic and hospitalized) to the SEIR model. They assumed that the infection rate of asymptomatic carriers is reduced by a variability factor compared to the symptomatic individuals, and hospitalized subpopulation can not transmit the disease to the susceptible class. The model was applied to COVID-19 data in Nigeria from March 27 to September 22, 2020, to investigate the incidence behavior of COVID-19 during and after the lockdown. Acuña-Zegarra et al. (2021) expanded the SEIR model by considering two classes of infectious individuals, one for asymptomatic cases and another for individuals displaying symptoms, and incorporating categories to represent vaccination and COVID-19-related fatalities. The model assumed temporal immunity following vaccination and recovery from natural infection and was calibrated on daily and cumulative death counts in Mexico between February 19 and October 31, 2020. Through various scenarios, this study performed simulations to explore the impact of vaccine efficacy, coverage, immunity induced by the vaccine, and natural immunity on vaccination schedules. The aim was to identify policies that effectively reduce the burden imposed by COVID-19. Shen et al. (2021) introduced a mechanistic model derived from the SEIR model, in which they divided the infectious category into five distinct compartments. These compartments included asymptomatic cases, undiagnosed infected with mild clinical signs, undiagnosed infected displaying severe clinical signs, diagnosed individuals with mild COVID-19 symptoms, and diagnosed individuals with severe COVID-19 signs. They also added a compartment for vaccinated individuals and one for deaths related to COVID-19. The model employed data on daily and cumulative COVID-19 cases and deaths recorded from January 26 to September 15, 2020. Its purpose was to assess the vaccine efficacy and the extent of vaccination coverage needed to alleviate the COVID-19 pandemic. This assessment accounted for scenarios where social interactions reverted to levels seen before the pandemic, accompanied by a decrease in the use of face masks.

Compartmental models with time-independent parameters are suitable for modeling one wave with a single peak in the propagation of infectious diseases, so several methods are available to incorporate temporal variations in model parameters. Zelenkov and Reshettsov (2023) used a SEIRV dynamic model to simulate the spread of COVID-19 across four countries from February 16, 2020, to January 9, 2022. They considered four parameters of the model, the force of infection, vaccination rate, the death rate of infectious individuals, and registration probability of infected individuals as time-dependent. The coefficients of these parameters were determined using a genetic algorithm. Papageorgiou and Tsaklidis (2023) constructed a SEIHCRDV compartmental model to capture the temporal changes in COVID-19 dynamics across an extended duration. In their approach, they accounted for the time-varying nature of two parameters: the transition rate from hospital to the Intensive Care Units (ICU) and the hospitalization rate, by considering the stochastic discrete-time form of the model and applying a Kalmen filter to eliminate the noise in the observed data. The model simulated daily COVID-19 cases in France over 400 days. Otunuga (2021) implemented a stochastic SEIRS epidemiological model to depict the evolution of COVID-19 spread, integrating temporal variations into its parameters by considering the temporary immunity rate, symptomatic recovery rate, and transmission rate as time-dependent functions. Utilizing daily infection and recovery COVID-19 data between January 22, 2020, and February 25, 2021, in the United States, a generalized method of moments estimation was applied to determine the unknown quantities and related functions in the model. Sun et al. (2023) presented a modified SEIR model that distinguished between symptomatic and asymptomatic infections. They supposed that the infection rate of asymptomatic individuals is proportional to the one of symptomatic individuals by a factor. The model used COVID-19 data on hospitalization, recovery, and death in four regions to inform about the effective reproduction number and the unobserved, symptomatic, and asymptomatic populations. Employing a data assimilation method based on Ensemble Transform Kalman Filter (ETKF), the authors iteratively updated the model's state variables and the infection rate for symptomatic individuals to capture evolving dynamics over time.

Table 1. Compartmental models reviewed in this study

Reference	Model	Parameters
Adewole et al. (2022)	Extended SEIR	Constant
Acuña-Zegarra et al. (2021)	Extended SEIR	Constant
Shen et al. (2021)	Extended SEIR	Constant
Zelenkov and Reshettsov (2023)	Extended SEIR	Time-dependent
Papageorgiou and Tsaklidis (2023)	Extended SEIR	Time-dependent
Otunuga (2021)	Extended SEIR	Time-dependent
Sun et al. (2023)	Extended SEIR	Time-dependent

In the literature, additional techniques can be found to address the variability of parameters in mechanistic models. However, we cover a limited number of studies among hundreds of publications. This review offers a broad overview of how researchers tracked the pandemic of COVID-19 through compartmental models.

3. MATHEMATICAL MODEL

Following (Jdid et al., 2023), a compartmental model designed to capture COVID-19 characteristics and control measures was adopted in this work. The model structure encompasses nine compartments, Susceptible (S), Exposed (E), Symptomatic Infectious (I_S), Asymptomatic Infectious (I_A), Hospitalized (H), Quarantined (Q), Recovered (R), Dead (D), and Vaccinated (V). Besides, the model analyzed in this paper excludes the vaccination class. The schematic diagram in Figure 1 illustrates the compartmental model without a vaccination strategy.

Figure 1. Diagram illustrating the dynamics of COVID-19 transmission

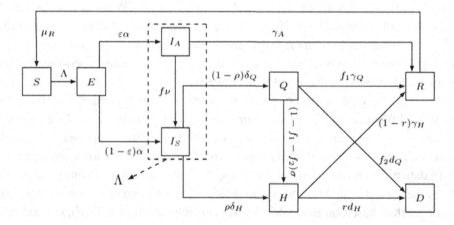

A susceptible person catches the virus when contact with symptomatic or asymptomatic infectious individuals at the infection rates βS and βA, respectively, and becomes exposed. After an incubation time of $(1/\alpha)$, a proportion of exposed people $(1-\varepsilon)$ develop clinical signs and join the symptomatic class, whereas the other proportion (ε) moves to the asymptomatic class. Recovery from COVID-19 in asymptomatic carriers is expected to occur naturally at a rate of γ_A. Symptomatic cases can be admitted to the hospital or self-quarantined at home. There are three potential outflows for those placed in quarantine: admission to the hospital, recovery at a rate of γ_Q, or mortality due to COVID-19. People under hospital care have two possible outflows: either they recover with a rate of γ_H, or they experience COVID-19-related mortality with a rate of dH. Healed individuals, after natural infection, lose their immunity throughout $(1/\mu g)$ and return to the susceptible state. The model exclusively accounts for fatalities caused by COVID-19 in the D class. In Table 2, we summarize all the parameters involved in this model. The dynamics of COVID-19 are defined by the system of Ordinary Differential Equations (ODEs) outlined in Equation (1):

$$\begin{cases} \dot{S} = \mu_R R - \Lambda S, \\ \dot{E} = \Lambda S - \alpha E, \\ \dot{I}_S = (1-\varepsilon)\alpha E + f\nu I_A - (\rho\delta_H + (1-\rho)\delta_Q)I_S, \\ \dot{I}_A = \varepsilon\alpha E - (f\nu + (1-f)\gamma_A)I_A, \\ \dot{H} = \rho\delta_H I_S + (1-f_1-f_2)\sigma Q - (rd_H + (1-r)\gamma_H)H \\ \dot{Q} = (1-\rho)\delta_Q I_S - (f_1\gamma_Q + f_2 d_Q + (1-f_1-f_2)\sigma)Q \\ \dot{R} = (1-f)\gamma_A I_A + f_1\gamma_Q Q + (1-r)\gamma_H H - \mu_R R \\ \dot{D} = rd_H H + f_2 d_Q Q \end{cases} \qquad (1)$$

where, Λ symbolizes the force of infection targeting susceptible individuals, and it is defined as:

$$\Lambda = \frac{\beta_S I_S + \beta_A I_A}{N}, \qquad (2)$$

and N refers to the total population size, such that

$$N = S + E + IS + IA + H + Q + R \qquad (3)$$

4. MODEL FITTING

We present our methodology for fitting the above compartmental model to a second wave of COVID-19 in Morocco in two stages. We consider all parameters time-invariant and adjust the model to the first wave data. Then assume some of its parameters as time-dependent and calibrate it to the data with two waves.

4.1 Data With One Wave

This part introduces a Bayesian inversion method to analyze COVID-19 data during a single wave, aiming to determine the essential unknown quantities in the epidemiological model. This method relies on Bayes' Theorem (Smith, 2013), in which probabilities serve as a fundamental concept to capture the uncertainty in model parameters, enabling the solution of the inverse problem associated with COVID-19. So, the unknown parameters in the model are regarded as random variables with prior probability distributions reflecting our initial knowledge or assumptions about their values before any measurements are observed. The observed data is then used to update the priors and obtain the posterior probability distribution, representing our updated knowledge about the parameters.

Table 2. Description of model parameters

Parameter	Interpretation
βA	Transmission rate from symptomatic to susceptible individuals
βS	Transmission rate from asymptomatic to susceptible individuals.
α	Incubation rate
ε	Fraction of asymptomatic population
f	Proportion of asymptomatic people moving into the symptomatic class
v	Rate at which asymptomatic persons become symptomatic
ρ	Proportion of individuals with COVID-19 symptoms who require hospitalization
δQ	Rate at which symptomatic persons enter quarantine
δH	Transition rate from symptomatic status to hospitalization
σ	Rate of transition from quarantine to hospitalization
f_1	Fraction of individuals in quarantine who recover from the disease
f_2	Fraction of individuals in quarantine who die due to COVID-19
γA	Rate of recovery for individuals in the asymptomatic group
γQ	Rate of recovery for individuals in the quarantined group
γH	Rate of recovery for individuals in the hospitalized group
d_Q	Mortality rate attributed to the disease within the quarantined class
d_H	Mortality rate attributed to the disease within the hospitalized class
r	Fraction of hospitalized patients who pass away due to COVID-19
μR	Rate of waning natural immunity in healed persons

Assuming a given vector $\theta = (\theta_1, \theta_2, \ldots, \theta_q)$ of q unknown parameters and a vector $y = (y_1, y_2, \ldots, y_n)$ of n independent and identically distributed measurements, Bayes' theorem can be expressed as follows

$$\pi(,|\text{y}) = \frac{L(y|,)\pi_0(,)}{\pi(y)}, \tag{4}$$

with

$$\pi(y) = \int L(y|,)\pi_0(,)d,, \tag{5}$$

where $L(y|\theta)$ stands for the likelihood function, $\pi_0(\theta)$ is the prior probability distribution, $\pi(y)$ is the evidence, and $\pi(\theta|y)$ is the posterior distribution.

Given that the evidence $\pi(y)$ acts as a normalizing factor that integrates with one, equation (4) can be rewritten in an alternative form,

$$\pi(\theta|y) \propto L(y|\theta)\pi_0(\theta). \tag{6}$$

Markov Chain Monte Carlo (MCMC) is a computational method used to generate samples from complex probability distributions, especially when direct sampling presents challenges or limitations. MCMC operates by constructing a Markov chain, a sequence of states, eventually converging to a stationary distribution corresponding to the posterior distribution of the quantities to be estimated. One of the robust algorithms used in MCMC simulation is the Hamiltonian Monte Carlo (HMC) algorithm (Betancourt, 2017) which utilizes the concept of Hamiltonian dynamics to explore the parameter space. HMC has several advantages over traditional MCMC algorithms. It efficiently searches the parameter space, resulting in faster convergence and better mixing of the Markov chains. The benefit of this algorithm appears when addressing high-dimensional distributions with complex and correlated structures. However, performing the HMC entails tuning some of its parameters. In this context, the No-UTurn Sampler (NUTS) algorithm has been developed in (Hoffman and Gelman, 2014) to adjust the HMC's parameters automatically. The NUTS algorithm was implemented as the default algorithm in the platform Stan (Stan Development Team, 2017) for statistical modeling.

When modeling count data like the number of infected individuals with a contagious disease, we commonly use the Poisson distribution or the Negative Binomial distribution. As a difference, the Poisson distribution assumes equality between the mean and variance, whereas the Negative Binomial model allows overdispersion. As daily COVID-19 confirmed cases in Morocco present overdispersion, we link the observed data to the model output, the number of symptomatically infected individuals, by a Negative Binomial distribution:

$$y_i \sim NB\left(y_I^E(\theta), \phi\right), \tag{7}$$

where y_i is the data at time $t=i$, $i=1,\dots,n$, $y_I^E(\theta)$ is the value of reported symptomatic infected individuals in the model at time $t=i$, ϕ is the dispersion parameter, $\theta = (\beta_S, \beta_A, f, f_1, f_2, \rho, r, \delta_Q, \phi)$ are the unknown parameters.

In this work, we adjust the dynamical system (1) to daily infection cases of COVID-19 in Morocco, from March 2 to June 10, 2020 (first wave), publically accessible (Mathieu et al., 2020). This adaptation is performed through a Bayesian inversion framework, employing the NUTS algorithm with the R user interface to find the probability distributions and confidence intervals of model parameters. In doing so, we used a Negative Binomial distribution as a likelihood function, assumed a normal distribution for the transmission rates (β_S and β_A), non-informative priors for f, f_1, f_2, ρ, r, and δ_Q parameters, and an exponential distribution for the parameter ϕ. Running the NUTS algorithm, we engage four parallel chains in a process involving 2000 iterations for each chain, where the first 1000 iterations serve as the warm-up phase. The initial conditions for state variables are specified in Table 3, while some parameters are inferred from previous studies, and the remaining parameters are assumed (Table 4).

By calibrating the model, we obtain the mean posterior estimate, standard deviation, and quantiles 5% and 95% of the parameters Θ, as outlined in Table 5. The fitting results are visualized in Figure 2, which includes the model estimation (posterior median) and 95% credible interval at each time point. The model's accuracy is also verified.

Table 3. Initial values of the system variables

Variable	Interpretation	Value	Source
$S(0)$	Number of people initially susceptible	3.78×10^7	(Worldometer, 2023)
$E(0)$	Number of people initially exposed	4	Fixed
$I_s(0)$	Initial count of symptomatically infected	1	Fixed
$I_A(0)$	Initial count of asymptomatically infected	1	Fixed
$H(0)$	Number of people initially hospitalized	1	Fixed
$Q(0)$	Number of people initially quarantined	0	Fixed
$R(0)$	Number of people initially recovered	0	Fixed
$D(0)$	Number of people initially deceased	0	Fixed

Table 4. Values of derived and fixed model parameters

Parameter	Mean Value	95% Confidence Interval (CI)	Source
α	1/5.2	[0.1429, 0.2439]	Li et al. (2020)
ε	0.1790	[0.1550, 0.2020]	Mizumoto et al. (2020)
γA	0.1398	[0.0701, 0.2094]	Tang et al. (2020)
γQ	0.1162	[0.0388, 0.1937]	Tang et al. (2020)
γH	0.0714	[0.0476, 0.0909]	Tang et al. (2020)
μ_R	1/180	–	Fixed
ν	0.5000	–	Fixed
σ	0.1429	–	Fixed
δ_H	0.0314	–	Fixed
d_Q	0.0001	–	Fixed
d_H	0.0010	–	Fixed

Table 5. Mean parameter estimates with standard deviation and quantiles

Parameter	Posterior Mean	Standard Deviation	Quantile 5%	Quantile 95%
β_S	0.2322	0.0346	0.1743	0.2900
β_A	0.5125	0.1936	0.1973	0.8360
f	0.0552	0.0604	0.0027	0.1821
f_1	0.6980	0.1730	0.4283	0.9682
f_2	0.0503	0.0291	0.0055	0.0952
ρ	0.4349	0.0993	0.3122	0.6288
r	0.0497	0.0298	0.0045	0.0958
δ_Q	0.0471	0.0028	0.0417	0.0506
ϕ	5.0307	0.9560	3.6041	6.7314

Figure 2. Fitting model to daily confirmed cases of COVID-19 data for Morocco from March 2 to June 9, 2020 (first wave)

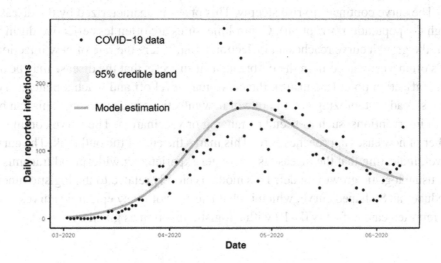

4.2 Data With Multiple Waves

A common approach to investigate multiple wave diffusion (Figure 3) in an isolated region is to adopt an epidemiological mathematical model and enable some parameters to vary over time to account for subsequent infection waves.

Figure 3. Second waves in Morocco. This figure illustrates the presence of multiple waves in daily new cases for Morocco from March 2, 2020, to March 9, 2023.

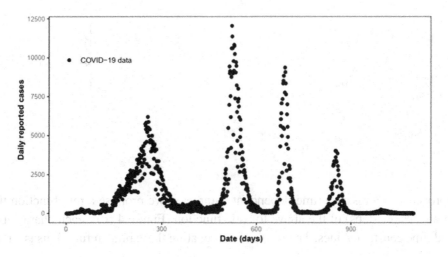

A typical pattern of an outbreak is that the number of reported cases starts slowly, with a small number of initial cases (gestation). As more individuals become infected, the number of new cases each day increases. The curve continues to rise steeply. This phase is characterized by the disease spreading quickly through the population (irruption). Control measures are often less effective during this phase. At some point, the growth curve reaches an inflection point, where the rate of new infections begins to slow down. It's often a critical point in the outbreak, as it suggests that the disease may be achieving its peak. After the inflection point (maturing), the curve may level off and reach a plateau. This assumes that the disease spread is stabilizing and the rate of new infections is decreasing. This can be attributed to public health interventions, such as social distancing or vaccination. The curve continues to decline until the number of new cases approaches zero. This marks the end of the outbreak. The curve reaches a stable, low level, indicating that the disease is no longer experiencing widespread transmission. Figure 4 (a) depicts a usual logistic growth model. This model is closely related to the logistic function (Figure 4 (b)) that produces an S-shaped curve, which is characteristic of many epidemic curves. Therefore, we can represent reported cases of COVID-19 with a logistic function as given by

$$l(t) = \frac{1}{1 + e^{-a(t-t_1)}},$$ (8)

where a is the growth rate or steepness of the curve, which could be positive or negative, and t_1 represents the time of maximum growth. The logistic function achieves its maximum value, 1, when $e^{-a(t-t_1)}$ approaches zero.

Figure 4. (a) A usual S-shape curve of the growth model. (b) Standard logistic function.

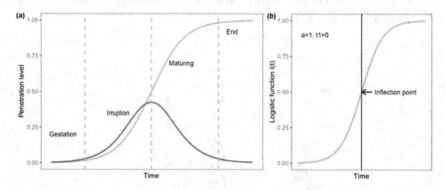

In our approach, to represent a time-dependent parameter, we propose a rate function that consists of multiple branches (or steps) of the above logistic function (Figure 4 (b)), each characterized by different gain and time constant values. The result of aggregating these branch functions is a rate function:

$$RFunct(t) = \sum_{i=1}^{m} \frac{L_i}{1 + e^{-a(t-t_i)}}$$ (9)

In the Equation (9), L_i is the gain of the branch (i), m is the number of logistic branches, a is a constant parameter to be estimated from the data, and the time parameters t_i are expressed as a vector $T = (t_1, t_2, \ldots, t_m)$ of length m, whose elements can be predefined manually. When a noticeable change is detected in the reported data at a given time t_i, the logistic function adjusts its magnitude to explore new parameter values.

Here, to simulate the spread of the second wave in Morocco, we consider disease transmission rates (β_S, β_A) and recovery rates $(\gamma_A, \gamma_Q,$ and $\gamma_H)$ of our model as time-dependent, and we attribute to each of them the rate function given in Equation (9). Other parameter values of the model and initial conditions stemming from the first wave fits (Tables 3, 4, and 5). In the fitting process, we adopted a least-squares error (LSE) based method, where the objective is to minimize the sum of squared errors (SSE) that represents the squares of the vertical distances of the observed measurements from the best-fit curve. Given the data y and the model $\hat{y}$, we express SSE for the set of unknown parameters θ by

$$SSE(.) = \sum_{i=1}^{n} \left(y_i - \hat{y}_T(\theta) \right)^2, \tag{10}$$

Using the Nelder-Mead optimization algorithm (Nelder and Mead, 1965), we aim to minimize the sum $SSE(\theta)$ and determine the optimal parameter values corresponding to the lowest Root Mean Squared Error (RMSE). We coded and performed all our analyses and simulations in R language.

Figures 5, 6, and 7 depict the result of calibrating the system (1) to the daily incidence in Morocco. We considered a rate function with twenty, thirty, and fifty logistic branches in Figures 5, 6, and 7, respectively. Based on the simulations, it is evident that the goodness of fit depends on the number of logistic steps that constitute the rate function. As we augment the number of logistic steps, the simulated curve exhibits improved agreement with the observed data.

Figure 5. Fitting model to daily infections of COVID-19 data in Morocco between March 2, 2020, and December 31, 2021, using 20 logistic branches

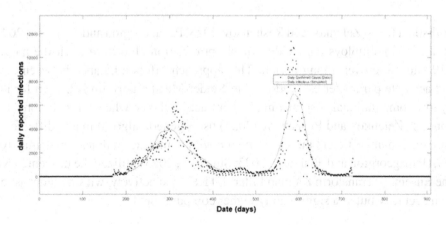

Figure 6. Fitting model to daily infections of COVID-19 data in Morocco between March 2, 2020, and December 31, 2021, using 30 logistic branches

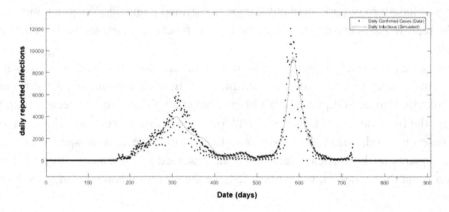

Figure 7. Fitting model to daily infections of COVID-19 data in Morocco between March 2, 2020, and December 31, 2021, using 50 logistic branches

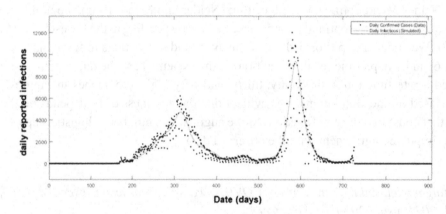

Our study, distinct from (Zelenkov and Reshettsov, 2023; Papageorgiou and Tsaklidis, 2023; Otunuga, 2021; Sun et al., 2023), employs the Nelder-Mead optimization algorithm to fit the model and track the COVID-19 pandemic over a long period. This approach offers a balance between computational efficiency and accurate parameter estimation. The Nelder-Mead algorithm is known for its simplicity and relatively low computational cost, making it an attractive choice when computational resources are limited. In contrast, Zelenkov and Reshettsov (2023) use a genetic algorithm and difference equations, which are computationally efficient but may struggle with complex, nonlinear epidemic dynamics. On the other hand, (Papageorgiou and Tsaklidis, 2023; Sun et al., 2023) utilized the unscented Kalman filter (UKF) and the Ensemble Transform Kalman Filter (ETKF), respectively, within a stochastic framework to achieve high accuracy but at a significantly higher computational cost.

5. CONCLUSION

In this study, our primary objective was to capture and address the dynamic changes observed in CO-VID-19 transmission patterns. To achieve this, we introduce variability into the recovery and disease infection rates and assign a specific rate function to each. This function comprises multiple branches of a logistic function, allowing us to capture the intricate dynamics of COVID-19 transmission by modeling how different factors contribute to the disease's spread over time. By implementing the proposed rate function, we calibrate our dynamic model to the real-world scenario of COVID-19 cases. Our dataset spanned a significant period, from March 2, 2020, to December 31, 2021, thus encompassing several waves and fluctuations in the pandemic's progression. This extended time frame allowed us to capture the full spectrum of changes in COVID-19 incidence throughout the pandemic. The results of our simulations were both revealing and promising. Notably, we observed a substantial improvement in the goodness of fit when we increased the number of logistic branches within our rate function. This key finding highlights the adaptability and effectiveness of our model in capturing the intricate nuances of COVID-19 transmission. It demonstrates the model's capacity to provide valuable insights into the ever-evolving nature of the pandemic, showcasing the potential of employing multiple branch rate functions as a powerful tool in epidemiological research.

ACKNOWLEDGMENT

The National Center for Scientific and Technical Research (CNRST) of Morocco and Sidi Mohamed Ben Abdellah University (USMBA) generously supported this research under grant number Cov/2020/54.

REFERENCES

Acuña-Zegarra, M. A., Díaz-Infante, S., Baca-Carrasco, D., & Olmos-Liceaga, D. (2021). COVID-19 optimal vaccination policies: A modeling study on efficacy, natural and vaccine-induced immunity responses. *Mathematical Biosciences*, *337*, 108614. doi:10.1016/j.mbs.2021.108614 PMID:33961878

Adewole, M. O., Okekunle, A. P., Adeoye, I. A., & Akpa, O. M. (2022). Investigating the transmission dynamics of SARS-CoV-2 in Nigeria: A SEIR modelling approach. *Scientific African*, *15*, e01116. doi:10.1016/j.sciaf.2022.e01116 PMID:35155878

Alshammari, F. S. (2023). Analysis of SIRVI model with time dependent coefficients and the effect of vaccination on the transmission rate and COVID-19 epidemic waves. *Infectious Disease Modelling*, *8*(1), 172–182. doi:10.1016/j.idm.2023.01.002 PMID:36643866

Betancourt, M. (2017). *A conceptual introduction to Hamiltonian Monte Carlo*. arXiv preprint arXiv:1701.02434.

Bootsma, M. C., & Ferguson, N. M. (2007). The effect of public health measures on the 1918 influenza pandemic in US cities. *Proceedings of the National Academy of Sciences of the United States of America*, *104*(18), 7588–7593. doi:10.1073/pnas.0611071104 PMID:17416677

Brum, A. A., Vasconcelos, G. L., Duarte-Filho, G. C., Ospina, R., Almeida, F. A., & Macêdo, A. M. (2023). ModInterv COVID-19: An online platform to monitor the evolution of epidemic curves. *Applied Soft Computing*, *137*, 110159. doi:10.1016/j.asoc.2023.110159 PMID:36874079

Cacciapaglia, G., Cot, C., & Sannino, F. (2020). Second wave COVID-19 pandemics in Europe: A temporal playbook. *Scientific Reports*, *10*(1), 15514. doi:10.1038/s41598-020-72611-5 PMID:32968181

Coronavirus, W. H. O. (COVID-19) Dashboard. (n.d.). https://covid19.who.int

Eryarsoy, E., Delen, D., Davazdahemami, B., & Topuz, K. (2021). A novel diffusion-based model for estimating cases, and fatalities in epidemics: The case of COVID-19. *Journal of Business Research*, *124*, 163–178. doi:10.1016/j.jbusres.2020.11.054 PMID:33281248

Hoffman, M. D., & Gelman, A. (2014). The No-U-Turn sampler: Adaptively setting path lengths in Hamiltonian Monte Carlo. *Journal of Machine Learning Research*, *15*(1), 1593–1623.

Jdid, T., Benbrahim, M., Kabbaj, M. N., Naji, M., & Benboubker, M. B. (2023, January). A New Compartmental Model for Analyzing COVID-19 Spread Within Homogeneous Populations. In *International Conference on Digital Technologies and Applications* (pp. 976-985). Cham: Springer Nature Switzerland. 10.1007/978-3-031-29857-8_97

Li, Q., Guan, X., Wu, P., Wang, X., Zhou, L., Tong, Y., Ren, R., Leung, K. S. M., Lau, E. H. Y., Wong, J. Y., Xing, X., Xiang, N., Wu, Y., Li, C., Chen, Q., Li, D., Liu, T., Zhao, J., Liu, M., ... Feng, Z. (2020). Early transmission dynamics in Wuhan, China, of novel coronavirus–infected pneumonia. *The New England Journal of Medicine*, *382*(13), 1199–1207. doi:10.1056/NEJMoa2001316 PMID:31995857

Mathieu, E., Ritchie, H., Rodés-Guirao, L., Appel, C., Giattino, C., Hasell, J., Macdonald, B., Dattani, S., Beltekian, D., Ortiz-Ospina, E., & Roser, M. (2020). *Coronavirus Pandemic (COVID-19)*. Retrieved from: https://ourworldindata.org/coronavirus

Mizumoto, K., Kagaya, K., Zarebski, A., & Chowell, G. (2020). Estimating the asymptomatic proportion of coronavirus disease 2019 (COVID-19) cases on board the Diamond Princess cruise ship, Yokohama, Japan, 2020. *Eurosurveillance*, *25*(10), 2000180. doi:10.2807/1560-7917.ES.2020.25.10.2000180 PMID:32183930

Nelder, J. A., & Mead, R. (1965). A simplex method for function minimization. *The Computer Journal*, *7*(4), 308–313. doi:10.1093/comjnl/7.4.308

Otunuga, O. M. (2021). Estimation of epidemiological parameters for COVID-19 cases using a stochastic SEIRS epidemic model with vital dynamics. *Results in Physics*, *28*, 104664. doi:10.1016/j.rinp.2021.104664 PMID:34395184

Papageorgiou, V. E., & Tsaklidis, G. (2023). An improved epidemiological-unscented Kalman filter (hybrid SEIHCRDV-UKF) model for the prediction of COVID-19. Application on real-time data. *Chaos, Solitons, and Fractals*, *166*, 112914. doi:10.1016/j.chaos.2022.112914 PMID:36440087

Population by Country. (2023). *Worldometer*. https://www.worldometers.info/world-population/population-by-country/

Shen, M., Zu, J., Fairley, C. K., Pagán, J. A., An, L., Du, Z., Guo, Y., Rong, L., Xiao, Y., Zhuang, G., Li, Y., & Zhang, L. (2021). Projected COVID-19 epidemic in the United States in the context of the effectiveness of a potential vaccine and implications for social distancing and face mask use. *Vaccine*, *39*(16), 2295–2302. doi:10.1016/j.vaccine.2021.02.056 PMID:33771391

Smith, R. C. (2013). *Uncertainty quantification: theory, implementation, and applications* (Vol. 12). Siam. doi:10.1137/1.9781611973228

Stan Development Team. (2017). Stan Modeling Language User's Guide and Reference Manual, Version 2.32.0. Author.

Sun, Q., Miyoshi, T., & Richard, S. (2023). Analysis of COVID-19 in Japan with extended SEIR model and ensemble Kalman filter. *Journal of Computational and Applied Mathematics*, *419*, 114772. doi:10.1016/j.cam.2022.114772 PMID:36061090

Tang, B., Wang, X., Li, Q., Bragazzi, N. L., Tang, S., Xiao, Y., & Wu, J. (2020). Estimation of the transmission risk of the 2019-nCoV and its implication for public health interventions. *Journal of Clinical Medicine*, *9*(2), 462. doi:10.3390/jcm9020462 PMID:32046137

Vasconcelos, G. L., Brum, A. A., Almeida, F. A., Macêdo, A. M., Duarte-Filho, G. C., & Ospina, R. (2021). Standard and anomalous waves of COVID-19: A multiple-wave growth model for epidemics. *Brazilian Journal of Physics*, *51*(6), 1867–1883. doi:10.1007/s13538-021-00996-3

Zelenkov, Y., & Reshettsov, I. (2023). Analysis of the COVID-19 pandemic using a compartmental model with time-varying parameters fitted by a genetic algorithm. *Expert Systems with Applications*, *224*, 120034. doi:10.1016/j.eswa.2023.120034 PMID:37033691

Chapter 7
Signatures of the Mode Symmetries in Sapphire PhoXonic Cavities

Houda Bentarki
Moulay Ismail University, Morocco

Abdelkader Makhoute
Moulay Ismail University, Morocco

Tőkési Karoly
Institute for Nuclear Research, Hungarian Academy of Sciences, Hungary

ABSTRACT

The acousto-optic couplings mechanisms are investigated theoretically in photonic and phononic crystals with simultaneous band gaps. The authors have focused on the acousto-optic couplings inside a phoXonic cavity by taking into account two coupling mechanisms, the photo elastic effect and effect of movement of the interfaces. They discuss the symmetry of modes to distinguish those that don't interfere in an efficient way. They calculate the modulation of the frequency of the photonic mode during a period of acoustic oscillations with a finite element method (FE) (COMSOL® Multiphysics). The two mechanisms presented in the numerical calculations produce additive or subtractive effects in total acousto-optical coupling while depending on whether they are in phase or out of phase.

1. INTRODUCTION

The study of wave propagation in general, and in periodic media in particular, has aroused great interest in the scientific community for several decades. In order for an extension of the notion of band gaps to electromagnetic waves to emerge, it was not until 1987 that photonic crystals were born.

DOI: 10.4018/979-8-3693-0497-6.ch007

Photonic band gap materials or photonic crystals (Joannopoulos et al., 2008; Yablonovitch, 1993) are periodic dielectric structures which have the ability to inhibit the propagation of light in certain directions, for a given frequency range.

In the image of photonic crystals, a composite material whose density and elastic constants are periodic functions of the position, may present, under certain conditions, bands prohibited for acoustic or elastic waves. These are materials with phononic band gaps called phononic crystals (Kushwaha et al., 1993; Pennec, Vasseur, Djafari-Rouhani et al, 2010).

To meet the growing needs to increase the performance of existing components or to propose new components, a new type of periodic structure combining the principle of photonic and phononic crystals which has been named phoXonic crystal (Eichenfield et al., 2009; Maldovan & Thomas, 2006a; Maldovan & Thomas, 2006b; Pennec, Djafari Rouhani, El Boudouti et al, 2010; Pennec et al., 2011; Rolland et al., 2012) was born. It was then expected an improved efficiency with regard to the strong confinement potentially achievable in these structures which present simultaneous photonic and phononic band gaps.

Several applications of these crystals have emerged thanks to these properties, in particular for the production of interesting components in integrated optics such as high quality factor micro cavities, low loss micro guides, laser micro sources, isolation of resonant structures, such as filters and oscillators (El-Kady, 2009), the resolution limited to under-diffraction and acoustic shielding (Lu et al., 2009). The simultaneous existence of photonic and phononic structures has opened a new path in the field of acousto-optic devices (Eichenfield et al., 2009a; Eichenfield et al., 2009b; Gorishny et al., 2005), while seeking to consolidate the principle of photonic and phononic crystal in a single structure called phoXonic crystal. The interest of studying these artificial crystals is to improve the performance of optical devices by controlling the propagation of electromagnetic waves in the presence of elastic waves. During the recent years, the availability of powerful numerical calculation machines has stimulated consider-able interest in the study of acousto-optic couplings mechanisms in phoXonic crystal. In particular, two-dimensional phoXonic crystals have attracted a great deal of attention after publication the pioneering theoretical study of Maldovan and Thomas (Sadat-Saleh, Benchabane, & Baida, 2009; Sadat-Saleh, Benchabane, Baida et al, 2009), which studied theoretically the phononic and photonic band gaps in 2D crystals for a square or hexagonal network of air holes in a silicon matrix. The opening of simultaneous photonic and phononic band gaps in a square periodic array of air holes in a sapphire substrate is studied in this work. The matrix component is chosen to take advantage of the anisotropy of the dielectric tensor in the microwave sapphire regime; the use of anisotropy has the advantage of widening the bandwidth of a cavity, and the reverse is achieved in the case of a cavity intended for a filter design, however, the microwave filters are widely used in radars, satellites, and mobile communication systems. These are typically devices, band pass, or selective bandwidth, with stringent features for insertion losses. The goal is to study the acousto-optic coupling, based on both photo-elastic and opto-mechanical mechanisms, in periodic structures with simultaneous photonic and phononic band gaps. The acousto-optic interaction generates a phonon thanks to the excitation of the cavity by the confinement of the optical wave. The aim in this field being to seek a maximum coupling of this interaction, and this also due to a strong confinement of the waves in the micro cavities. The obtaining of allowed bands in band gaps are also studied in this work, by introducing defects in the periodicity of a super cell, which has led to the propagation of waves appropriate. The frequencies of the localized modes in the first band gap are computed with a finite element method (FE) (*COMSOL®Multiphysics*). However, the Finite Difference Time Domain (FDTD) method was also used in 2010 for the same structure (Bria et al., 2011); the difference with our work is that we have chosen a different network parameter to have localized modes when introducing defects into the perfect structure. The paper is structured as follows. In part 2, the geometry of the crystal is described. Part 3 presents the theoretical investigation of simultaneous photonic and phononic band gaps. In Section 4, we show that very limited optical and acoustic waves exist in a photonic cavity created by a defect in a perfect structure. The fifth paragraph focuses on the study of the acousto-optical interaction and coupling mechanisms in band gap structures. The conclusions are summarized in paragraph 6.

2. THE STRUCTURE OF THE PHOXONIC CRYSTAL

Optical and Acoustic Properties of Simulated Material

To study the variations of the photonic and phononic bandwidths of two-dimensional photonic and phononic crystals, we are going to model a sapphire structure, the elastic and optical properties of which are presented in Table 1.

Table 1. Elastic and optical cubic constants of Sapphire (Al_2O_3) used in numerical simulations. The refractive index (n), the density (ρ), the radius of holes (r), and transverse (c_t) velocity of sound (Renosi & Sapriel, 1994; Yariv & Yeh, 1984).

	n	$\rho(K\,g/m^2)$	s	$C_{11}(N/m^2)$	$C_{12}(N/m^2)$	$C_{44}(N/m^2)$	c_t (m/s)
Sapphire	1.75	3950	11.5	$16.57 * 10^{10}$	$6.39 * 10^{10}$	$7.962 * 10^{10}$	6040

Simulated Structure

In order to account for the main results related to the creation of the photonic band gap, we will study a photonic crystal consisting of a sapphire plate with a mesh parameter $a = 120nm$ on which air cylinders of radius r are periodically deposited $r = 0.465\,a$, and arranged in a square arrangement. The unit cell is reduced in the perfect crystal to a square mesh on side "a" and which includes a single air cylinder in the center (Fig. 1a). The existence of band gaps as wide as possible contributes to the confinement of electromagnetic and elastic waves inside the cavity. In order to fulfill the last condition, we took a filling factor equal to 0.68 (band gap as large as possible), which corresponds to a radius equal to $r = 0.465\,a$, with "a" is the mesh parameter.

The finite element method (FEM) is dedicated for the simulation of phoXonic structures studied in this work. The basis of the Finite Element Method (FEM) is a polynomial approximation of the solution within the finite element tiling space. It is very useful in structural mechanics. A variation method is used in the simulation to obtain the eigen value problem.

Figure 1 shows the unit cell of the perfect crystal, which is reduced to a square mesh of side "a" and comprising a single cylinder of air in the center. The dispersion curves are presented in the reduced Brillouin zone associated to the crystal square lattice, the studied cavity is periodically repeated in the (X, Y) plane with a super-period of

$L = 7* a$, giving rise to a super-cell 7* 7.

3. PHOXONIC BAND GAPS

The band structures of the electromagnetic and elastic waves are shown in Figure 2. It should be noted that for electromagnetic waves, two polarizations are distinguished; Transverse electric (TE) and transverse magnetic (TM), which present respectively an electric field and a magnetic field parallel to the axis of cylinders. The phononic modes propagate in the plane (X, Y) and are composed of a mixture of transverse and longitudinal vibrations.

Figure 1. (a) 2D periodic photonic crystal composed of air cylinders on a sapphire plate. (b) Elementary cell.

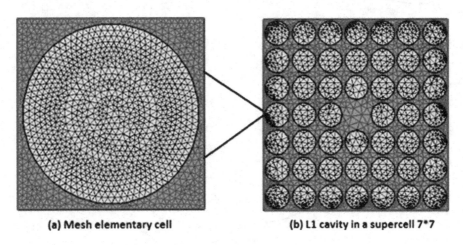

(a) Mesh elementary cell   (b) L1 cavity in a supercell 7*7

The frequencies of the dispersion curves are presented with the reduced unit $\Omega = \omega a/2*c$, with"c" is the speed of light in vacuum for the electro- magnetic waves, whereas it presents the transverse velocity of the sound in Sapphire for elastic waves.

With the filling factor considered, the optical dispersion curves obtained show non- absolute forbidden bands dependent on the polarization of the electromagnetic field, since the TE and TM modes can be excited separately, the TE modes have the electric field polarized in the plane of the waveguide, and TM modes have the polarized magnetic field in the plane of the waveguide. While the phononic dispersion curves have a wide band gap that prohibit the propagation of elastic waves whatever the direction of the incident wave, the existence of the simultaneous photonic and phononic forbidden bands leads to the confinement of the two types of waves within one and the same cavity.

4 PHOXONIC CAVITY IN A TWO-DIMENSIONAL LATTICE CRYSTAL

The band diagram of photonic and phononic structures without defects has been presented in the previous paragraph. It allowed us to find the band gap of a phoXonic crystal. This diagram is obtained by varying the wave vector "k" along the contour defined by the points of high symmetries of the first Brillouin zone of the reciprocal lattice. The purpose of this section is to look for defect modes when breaking the periodicity of the material. The concept of super cell is then used. A super cell consists of several primitive cells.

Figure 2. (Color online) Two-dimensional band structure of a square arrangement of air holes drilled into a sapphire plate

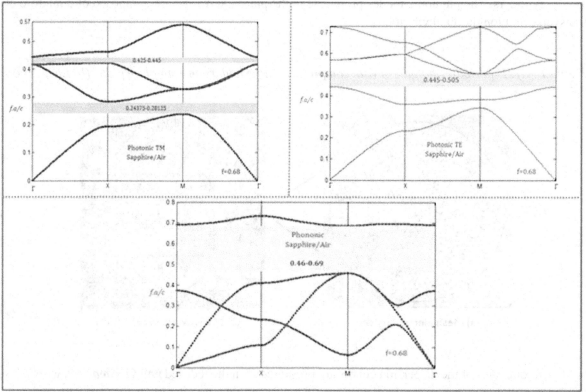

In this case, we have a super cell composed of 7*7 primitive cells in which we created a cavity by filling a hole; the perfect phoXonic crystal is modified then by changing a middle air hole with Silicon in the structure, so a cavity is created.

We present in Figure 3, the mapping of the elastic and electromagnetic field components associated with the photonic and phononic modes located in the forbidden bands, namely 7 optical modes TM, 2 optical modes TE and 5 phononic modes (Fig. 3). The calculated modes present good confinement inside the cavity.

The types of symmetry of the photonic and phononic modes are symmetrical (even (e)) or antisymmetric (odd (o)). The field distributions of the Fig.3 revealed the symmetry of the modes and hence their analysis. Optical modes (b) and (c) are of symmetry (oo), (a) is of symmetry (oo), (a') and (b') are of symmetry (oe) and (eo) respectively. The phononic mode (A) is of symmetry (ee), (B) and (C) are of symmetry (oo). The other two modes (D) and (E) are degenerate; (oe) and (eo) are their respective symmetries of (D). The animations of modes in *COMSOL®Multiphysics* allow us to describe each acoustic mode during a period of vibration.

For mode (A), one of the 2 sides of the cavity is stretched, while the other contracts. Mode (B) is a mode of torsion perpendicular to the axis of the cavity with a counterclockwise rotation in the outer part of the cavity. The animation of mode (C) shows a breathing movement with homothetic deformation of the shape of the cavity. The field distributions of the degenerate modes (D) and (E) are orthogonal.

Figure 3. (Color online) Field maps for the photonic and phononic modes in the (x, y) plane. For each mode of the phononic cavity.

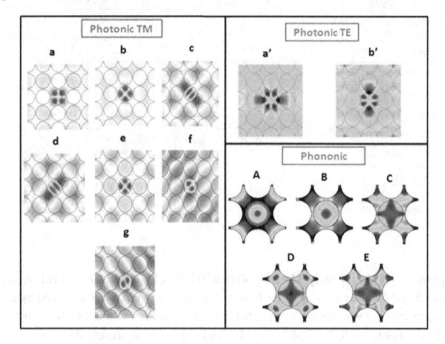

5. ACOUSTO-OPTICAL COUPLING IN A PHOXONIC CAVITY

The photo elastic effect (PE) (Yariv & Yeh, 1984) and the effect of the movement of the interfaces (MI) (Johnson et al., 2002) are two mechanisms that contribute to the acousto-optical interaction, the first corresponds to the changes in the refractive index as a function of the acoustic deformations applied to the material, while the second is due to the variation of the dielectric permittivity in the vicinity of the surface because of the movements of the boundaries during the vibrations of the cavity.

The acousto-optical coupling will be addressed in this section, estimating its amplitude by the modulation of the frequency of the photonic mode during a period of acoustic oscillations. The effect of the acoustic modes (B) and (C) on the photonic cavity modes TE and TM will be studied, namely the modes *a*, *c* and *d* of the magnetic transverse, as well as the mode (*a'*) of the electrical transverse. Horizontal inputs of Figures 4 and

Figure 4. (Color online) Modulation of the TM modes b, c, and d during a period T = 2π/Ω of acoustic oscillations for the phononic modes B and C in the Sapphire matrix. The colors blue, red and green show respectively the effects of movement of the interfaces (MI), photo elastic (PE) and both at once (MI + PE). The blue arrows describe each mode of the phononic cavity during a period of vibration.

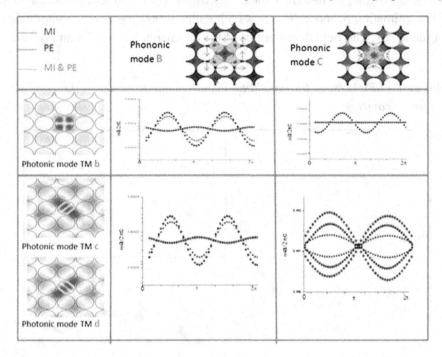

Show the photonic modes, namely TM (Fig. 4) and TE (Fig. 5), while the vertical inputs present the phononic modes *B* and *C*. The coupling of each pair of photon- phonon mode is traced by a curve whose ordinate axis represents the wavelength of the photonic mode $\omega a/2\pi c$ while the abscissa axis represents the period of the phononic mode $T = 2\pi/\Omega$. The blue and red curves represent the contributions of the *M I* and *PE* mechanisms respectively, while the green curves show the whole coupling taking into account both effects. Generally speaking, during an acoustic period, each optical mode oscillates sinusoid ally around its initial frequency before the deformation.

TM Photon-Phonon Coupling

The mode (B) is presented with a counter-clockwise rotation in the outer part of the cavity; it is a mode of torsion perpendicular to the axis of the cavity (Fig. 3). The coupling of the mode (B) with all the photonic modes TM gives curves with simple sinusoidal oscillations, which implies the intervener of a single phonon in the coupling. Figure 4 reveals that the two effects *PE* and *M I* are in opposition of phase which gives a subtractive effect *PE + M I* (Fig. 4 Column on the left). The amplitudes of the oscillations for the two mechanisms PE and MI are dependent on the rates of initial deformation imposed by the phononic mode. In our structure, the maximum deformation in the cavity is taken equal to 1% (0.01). This value has been chosen in order to overcome the increase in time which is caused by an increase in the mesh size. Figure 4 on the right represents the modulations of the frequencies of the TM photonic modes by the acoustic excitation of the mode (C). For the non-degenerate mode (b), the amplitude of the oscillations of the mechanism $M\ I$ is very weak for reasons of symmetry.

With respect to the degenerate modes (c) and (d), the amplitudes are very strong compared to the mode (b).

Figure 5. (Color online) Modulation of the TE modes a' and b' during a period $T = 2\pi/\Omega$ of acoustic oscillations for the phononic modes B and C in the Sapphire matrix. The colors blue, red and green show respectively the effects of movement of the interfaces (MI), photo elastic (PE) and both at once (MI + PE). The blue arrows describe each mode of the phononic cavity during a period of vibration.

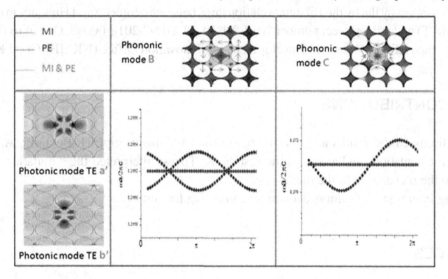

TE Photon-Phonon Coupling

Recall that mode C is essentially a breathing mode that periodically changes the volume of the cavity by a succession of contractions and dilations (see Figure 3). It is non degenerate, with a homothetic deformation, and its breathing movement centered on the center of the cavity considerably varies the volume of the cavity. The coupling of the mode C with the modes a' and b' of polarization TE gives sinusoidal curves where the two effects PE and MI are always in phase which gives an additive total effect (Fig. 5 right column). The same conclusion was obtained in the mode coupling (B) with the degenerate TE photonic modes. All the results obtained for the coupling of the phononic modes with the photonic modes TE give amplitudes of very weak oscillations of the mechanism MI. The reason comes from the fact that the first-order perturbation is zero for reasons of symmetry.

6. CONCLUSION

We have presented theoretical studies of the acousto-optic interaction in 2D Sapphire phoXonic crystal drilled with holes. Our recent works were focused on the acousto-optic couplings inside a phoXonic cavity by taking into account two coupling mechanisms, the photo elastic effect and effect of movement of the interfaces. We have shown that the confinement of both elastic and electromagnetic energies is possible inside a phoXonic cavity. Optomechanical coupling between photonic and phononic modes localized in phoXonic cavities was calculated taking into account two main effects, namely the mobile interface (MI) and photo elastic effects (PE). We deduced that they can be in phase or out of phase and produce additive or subtractive effects in the total optomechanical coupling.

ACKNOWLEDGMENT

The work was support by the by the Bilateral relationships between Morocco and Hungary in science and technology (S&T) under the project number 2018-2.1.10- TÉT-MC-2018-00008. One of us (KT) thanks the support by the National Research, Development and Innovation Office (NKFIH) Grant KH126886.

AUTHOR CONTRIBUTIONS

All authors discussed the results and contributed to the final manuscript. H. Bentarki, A. Makhoute performed the calculations and analyzed the results. K. Tökési interpreted the simulation results and contributes to the preparation of the manuscript.

Competing Interests: The authors declare no competing interests.

REFERENCES

Bria, D., Assouar, M. B., Oudich, M., Pennec, Y., Vasseur, J., & Djafari-Rouhani, B. (2011). Opening of simultaneous photonic and phononic band gap in two-dimensional square lattice periodic structure. *Journal of Applied Physics*, *109*(1), 014507. doi:10.1063/1.3530682

Eichenfield, M., Chan, J., Camacho, R. M., Vahala, K. J., & Painter, O. (2009a). Optome-chanical crystals. *Nature*, *462*(7269), 78–82. doi:10.1038/nature08524 PMID:19838165

Eichenfield, M., Chan, J., Camacho, R. M., Vahala, K. J., & Painter, O. (2009b). A picogram-and nanometre-scale photonic-crystal optomechanical cavity. *Nature*, *459*(7246), 550–555. doi:10.1038/nature08061 PMID:19489118

Eichenfield, M., Chan, J., Safavi-Naeini, A. H., Vahala, K. J., & Painter, O. (2009). Modeling dispersive coupling and losses of localized optical and mechanical modes in optomechanical crystals. *Optics Express*, *17*(22), 20078. doi:10.1364/OE.17.020078 PMID:19997232

El-Kady. (2009). Microfabricated phononic crystal devices and applications. *Measurement Science & Technology*.

Gorishny, Maldovan, Ullal, & Thomas. (2005). Sound ideas. *Physics World*, *18*, 24.

Joannopoulos, J. D., Johnson, S. G., Winn, J. N., & Meade, R. D. (2008). *Photonic Crystals: Molding the Flow of Light*. Princeton University Press.

Johnson, S. G., Ibanescu, M., Skorobagatiy, M. A., & Weisberg, O. (2002). Perturbation theory for Maxwell's equations with shifting material boundaries. *Physical Review E: Statistical, Nonlinear, and Soft Matter Physics*, *65*(6), 066611. doi:10.1103/PhysRevE.65.066611 PMID:12188855

Kushwaha, M. S., Halevi, P., Dobrzynski, L., & Djafari-Rouhani, B. (1993). Acoustic band structure of periodic elastic composites. *Physical Review Letters*, *71*(13), 2022–2025. doi:10.1103/PhysRevLett.71.2022 PMID:10054563

Lu, M. H., Feng, L., & Chen, Y.-F. (2009, December). Phononic crystals and acoustic metamaterials. *Materials Today*, *12*(12), 34–42. doi:10.1016/S1369-7021(09)70315-3

Maldovan & Thomas. (2006a). Simultaneous complete elastic and electromagnetic band gaps in periodic structures. *Appl. Phys. B, 83*, 595-600.

Maldovan, M., & Thomas, E. L. (2006b). Simultaneous localization of photons and phonons in twodimensional periodic structures. *Applied Physics Letters*, *88*, 251907. doi:10.1063/1.2216885

Pennec, Djafari Rouhani, El Boudouti, Li, El Hassouani, Vasseur, Papanikolaou, Benchabane, Laude, & Martinez. (2010). Simultaneous existence of phononic and photonic band gaps in periodic crystal slabs. *Opt. Express, 18*(13), 14301-14310.

Pennec, Y., Djafari Rouhani, B., El Boudouti, E. H., Li, C., El Hassouani, Y., Vasseur, J. O., Papanikolaou, N., Benchabane, S., Laude, V., & Martnez, A. (2011, February). Band gaps and waveguiding in phoxonic silicon crystal slabs. *Zhongguo Wuli Xuekan*, *49*, 100.

Pennec, Y., Vasseur, J., Djafari-Rouhani, B., Dobrzynski, L., & Deymier, P. A. (2010). Two-dimensional phononic crystals: Examples and applications. *Surface Science Reports*, *65*(8), 229–291. doi:10.1016/j.surfrep.2010.08.002

Renosi, P., & Sapriel, J. (1994, May 23). Near-resonance acousto-optical interactions in GaAs and InP. *Applied Physics Letters*, *64*(21), 2794–1994. doi:10.1063/1.111427

Rolland, Q., Oudich, M., El-Jallal, S., Dupont, S., Pennec, Y., Gazalet, J., Kastelik, J. C., Leveque, G., & Djafari-Rouhani, B. (2012). Acousto-optic couplings in two-dimensional phoxonic crystal cavities. *Applied Physics Letters*, *101*(6), 061109. doi:10.1063/1.4744539

Sadat-Saleh, S., Benchabane, S., & Baida, F. I. (2009). *Simultaneous photonic and phononic band gaps in a two-dimensional lithium niobate crystal*. IEEE International.

Sadat-Saleh, S., Benchabane, S., Baida, F. I., Bernal, M.-P., & Laude, V. (2009). Tailoring simultaneous photonic and phononic band gaps. *Journal of Applied Physics*, *106*(7), 074912. doi:10.1063/1.3243276

Yablonovitch, E. (1993). Photonic band-gap structures. *Journal of the Optical Society of America. B, Optical Physics*, *10*(2), 283. doi:10.1364/JOSAB.10.000283

Yariv & Yeh. (1984). *Optical Waves in Crystals*. Academic Press.

Chapter 8
A New Approach to Construction and Decoding of Linear Block Codes Based on Polar Codes

Driss Khebbou

Polydisciplinary Faculty of Safi, Cadi Ayyad University of Marrakech, Morocco

Idriss Chana

ESTM, Moulay Ismail University of Meknes, Morocco

Hussain Ben-Azza

ENSAM, Moulay Ismail University of Meknes, Morocco

ABSTRACT

In the field of channel coding theory, there are two main branches. The first is related to the design and construction of codes capable of facilitating identification of errors at the receiver despite potential alterations during transmission; this is known as the encoding operation. The second branch focuses on developing mechanisms for correcting errors caused by the transmission channel, by devising valid and suitable algorithms; this is known as the decoding operation. The authors have delved into both aspects. In the first part, a novel method for constructing good linear codes is studied. It is based on the Hadamard matrix, which shares the same structure as the kernel of polar codes, and on the generator matrix of several existing linear codes. In the second part, a new decoding algorithm is proposed. This involves adapting the SSCL polar code decoder to decode the codes designed in the first part, as well as some of the most well-known block codes.

DOI: 10.4018/979-8-3693-0497-6.ch008

1. INTRODUCTION

In the field of channel coding theory, two main branches can be identified. The first is related to the design and construction of codes that represent the information to be transmitted, and are capable of facilitating its identification at the receiver despite the alterations it may undergo during transmission; this is known as the coding operation. The second branch focuses on conceiving mechanisms for error correction caused by the transmission channel, by developing valid and appropriate algorithms; this is referred to as the decoding operation. Both operations are grouped under an aspect known as error-correcting codes.

In general, error-correcting codes can be divided into two categories: convolutional codes and block codes. In this paper, we limit our discussion to block codes, which involve breaking down the message to be transmitted into blocks, to which redundancy bits are added and utilized by the decoder to correct transmission errors. A highly significant class of block codes is linear block codes, which leverage algebraic principles to provide a structure that is both algebraically straightforward and less complex. However, the design of linear codes, known for their appealing algebraic structure and substantial error-correction capabilities, remains an open challenge in coding theory. Consequently, working with existing codes may be an intriguing street for constructing linear codes with excellent performance (*Error-Correction Coding and Decoding*, n.d.). In the literature, several works have relied on this principle to construct error-correcting codes with attractive properties, such as the construction X presented by N. Sloane in (Grassl, 2006; Sloane et al., 1972), which essentially involves adding a codeword from an auxiliary code to the existing code.

On the other hand, despite their many appealing properties, most algebraic codes, particularly linear block codes, suffer from a major drawback: the lack of low-complexity, soft decoding algorithms. A well-known soft decoding algorithm for binary linear block codes is the "Ordered Statistics Decoder (OSD)," presented in (Fossorier & Lin, 1995), inspired by the Dorsh algorithm (Dorsch, 1974), which has claimed performances close to those of Maximum Likelihood Decoding (MLD) for many linear block codes. However, these exceptional performances can only be achieved by using Ordered Statistics Decoder with high orders, which implies relatively significant complexity and a substantial memory.

In this work, we aim to summarize our research efforts, which revolve around two main aspects. The first involves proposing a approach for constructing good binary linear codes based on existing codes (Khebbou, Benkhouya, et al., 2021, 2022). The term "good" refers to the optimality of the rate between the bloc message and the redundant part on one hand, and error-correction capability on the other. This method is based on a well-known matrix, the Hadamard matrix (Hadamard, 1893).

The second aspect, introduces a new decoding method by adapting the Simplified Successive Cancellation List (SSCL) of Polar codes (Arikan, 2009), used in the 5G standard, to decode the linear bloc codes designed in the first part and some well-known block codes (Khebbou, Chana, et al., 2021; Khebbou et al., n.d.-b, n.d.-a, 2023; Khebbou, Idriss, et al., 2022). In addition to simplifying and reducing the complexity of the decoding process, the performance evaluation of the proposed decoders demonstrates their advantages over other decoders in the literature, notably OSD, which is considered most suitable for all linear block codes, despite its limitations in terms of complexity and order saturation.

The rest of this paper is organized as follows. In the next section, we will introduce important aspects for describing the proposed construction and decoding methods, such as linear block codes, Polar codes, and their decoding techniques. In the third section, we will describe the method for constructing good binary linear block codes, along with some obtained results and interpretations. In the fourth section, we will explain how to leverage Polar code decoding approach for linear codes, including simulations and result interpretations. In the final section, we will conclude with avenues for future research.

2. BACKGROUND

In the field of digital transmission, we can employ error-correcting codes, denoted in the form (n,k,d_{min}), to effectively reduce the occurrence of errors. The coding process involves transforming a *k-bit* vector called message into an *n-bit* vector called codeword, where n is greater than k. This transformation results in the creation of a code C composed of 2^k codewords of n bits, selected from a set of 2^n possible codewords. These codes are characterized by three key parameters: the codeword length (n), the dimension of the encoded message (k), and the minimum Hamming distance between codewords (d_{min}). This distance plays a crucial role in ensuring that a codeword remains distinguishable from others, even in the presence of noise, enabling efficient error correction.

2.1 Linear Bloc Codes

A binary linear code C of length n and dimension k is a subspace vector over $\mathbb{F}_2^n$. The subspace C is defined as the set of vectors (codewords), which are obtained through linear combinations of the basis vectors. Each basis vector represents a specific bit sequence, referred to as a codeword. The minimum distance of a linear code corresponds to the minimum Hamming weight (number of non-zero bits in codeword) among all non-zero codewords.

The basis vectors form a $k \times n$ matrix, known as the generator matrix, where the rows represent codewords, and each codeword in the linear code C is obtained through linear combinations of these vectors. The structure of this matrix, if the code is systematic, is defined as follows:

$$G_{sys} = [I_k | P] \tag{1}$$

The orthogonal complement of the vector subspace defined by the set of codewords in code C, is a subspace vector of dimension $n-k$, which provides an implicit definition of code C. Its basis forms the parity-check matrix H and is used to check the validity of a received codeword. Starting from equation (1), it is possible to define the matrix H as follows:

$$H = \left[I_{n-k} \mid P^{\mathrm{T}} \right] \tag{2}$$

The matrix H represents the generator matrix of a linear code C^{T}, known as the dual code of C, with dimension $n-k$ and length n. MacWilliams defined a relationship between the two codes called the MacWilliams identity (MacWilliams & Sloane, 1977). To establish this relationship, it is necessary to provide the following definitions:

Definition 1: let $C(n,k)$ be a linear block code, and c a codeword of C. The weight $w(c)$ of the word c is the number of non-zero components of c. And the minimum weight $w(C)$ of the code C is the minimum of the weights of all non-zero vectors in C.

An important combinatorial property of a code is its weight distribution; it is the count of words of each weight.

Definition 2: The weight distributions of a code C represent the number of codewords with weight i in C, denoted as $A_i(C)= \#\{c \in C|\ w(c)=i\}$ for all $1 \leq i \leq n$.

From the weight distribution, it is straightforward to define a polynomial called the weight enumerator polynomial as follows:

Definition 3: The (enumerator) polynomial of the weights of a code C is the polynomial defined as:

$$W_c(x) = \sum_{i=0}^{n} A_i(C).x^i \tag{3}$$

The relation between the weight distribution of a linear code and its dual code can be made by the MacWilliams identity as described in theorem 1.

Theorem 1: (MacWilliams identity). Let C be a code over $\mathbb{F}_q$, and its dual code C^T. Then:

$$W_{C^\mathsf{T}}(x) = q^{-k}.\left(1+(q-1).x\right)^n.W_c\left(\frac{1-x}{1+(q-1).x}\right) \tag{4}$$

With $q=2$ in the binary case.

2.2 Polar Codes

Polar codes ($n=2^m,k$) belong to a category of error-correcting codes constructed by leveraging the symmetrical capacity of polarized channels [5]. In this process, $(n-k)$ binary channels with the lowest reliable, known as frozen bits, are systematically set to zero. Meanwhile, the remaining highly reliable binary channels are utilized as k-bit positions for transmitting information. One distinctive characteristic of Polar codes is their recursive generation, where a code of length n is derived from a code of length $n/2$. The encoding of Polar codes is carried out like any other linear block code, using its generator matrix constructed through Kronecker products of order $log_2(n)$ of the Arikan kernel $G_p = \begin{bmatrix} 1 & 0 \\ 1 & 1 \end{bmatrix}$.

2.2.1 Successive-Cancellation Method

One of the appealing features of Polar codes is their ability to achieve low-complexity decoding. The successive cancellation (SC) decoding method, as described in (Arikan, 2009), enables the attainment of channel capacity with minimal decoding complexity. To facilitate the explanation of this decoding approach, a representation of the Polar code (8, 4) as a binary tree is depicted in Figure 1.

Figure 1. Binary tree representation of (8,4) Polar code: (a) repésentation tree and (b) decoding steps on each node

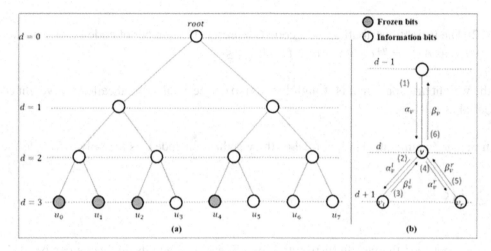

The representative tree of a Polar code consists of $log_2(n)+1$ depth levels d, with each level containing 2^d nodes, as shown in Figure 1.a. The decoding procedure entails traversal of the tree, commencing at the root and proceeding over the tree to reach a leaf node. At each non-leaf node v with a length of n_v, the likelihood ratio (LLR) values propagate from parent to child nodes in the steps illustrated in figure 1.b. In other words, for a node v receiving the LLRs αv The equations (5), (6), (7) and (8) are applied in the order indicated in the figure 1.b.

$$\alpha_{v_i}^l = sign(\alpha_{v_i}).sign\left(\alpha_{v_i+\frac{n_v}{2}}\right).min\left(\left|\alpha_{v_i}\right|,\left|\alpha_{v_i+\frac{n_v}{2}}\right|\right) \tag{5}$$

$$\alpha_{v_i}^r = \left(1-2\beta_{v_i}^l\right).\alpha_{v_i} + \alpha_{v_i+\frac{n_v}{2}} \tag{6}$$

$$\beta_{v_i} = \begin{cases} \beta_{v_i}^l \cdot \beta_{v_i}^r, & i < \dfrac{n_v}{2} \\ \beta_{v_{\left(i-\frac{n_v}{2}\right)}}^r, & i \geq \dfrac{n_v}{2} \end{cases} \tag{7}$$

If v is leaf and frozen βv is 0, else the binary quantized function is used to make a hard decision as follows:

$$\beta_v = \begin{cases} 1, & \alpha_v < 0 \\ 0, & \alpha_v \geq 0 \end{cases} \tag{8}$$

2.2.1 Simplified Successive-Cancellation Method

While the SC decoding is computationally straightforward, the decoder's speed is constrained by the inherently serial nature of the algorithm. Among the significant advancements is simplified successive cancellation decoding (SSC), introduced in (Alamdar-Yazdi & Kschischang, 2011; Hashemi et al., 2016a), achieved by identifying a set of special nodes capable of estimating all dependent bits. The various special nodes are described as follows:

- The root of a subtree in which all leaf nodes are frozen bit nodes is the Rate-0 node. It is obvious that the leaf nodes can be reached without having to go through the tree; the necessary bits can simply be changed to 0.
- The root of a subtree in which all leaf nodes are information bit nodes is called the Rate-1 node. Notably, estimating βv at the current node (Rate-1 node) and taking a Polar transform of βv using the binary qualification equation (8) are similar to going down to the leaf node and estimating the information bits.
- The SPC-node (Single Parity Check node) is equivalent to the root of a subtree, with the exception of the first node, which is a frozen bit node, all leaf nodes being information bit nodes. By calculating βv at the current node and flipping the smallest reliable node, which corresponds to the LLR with the smallest absolute value, such nodes can be decoded. To obtain the estimation at the leaf nodes, a Polar transformation is then applied to βv.
- The REP-node (Repetition node) is equivalent to the root of a subtree, where all leaf nodes except the final one stand in for frozen bits. By adding the LLRs at the current node and guessing the bit corresponding to the repeat node, such nodes can be decoded. To obtain the estimation at the leaf nodes, a Polar transformation is then applied to βv.

The different estimation equations for each type of node are described in (Hashemi et al., 2016a). Additionally, like any List Decoder, SSC can be used in a list form to enhance its performance, particularly in moderate-sized regimes. The updates of path metrics are provided in (Hashemi et al., 2016b, 2017).

2.3 Used Codes

Simulations are a crucial tool for evaluating the performance of such a method. To test our construction and decoding methods, we propose in this paper simulations based on the BCH, ReedMuller, Golay and LDPC codes.

- Bose-Chaudhuri-Hocquenghem (BCH) codes stand as a distinguished subset of cyclic codes, renowned for their robust error correction capabilities. BCH codes are cyclic codes, meaning they possess a specific cyclic shift property. They are constructed using finite fields, and the codeword generation process is based on polynomial arithmetic over these fields.
- Low-Density Parity-Check (LDPC) codes, a product of intensive research in coding theory, represent a pinnacle in error-correcting code design. The defining feature of LDPC codes is their sparse parity-check matrix. This matrix represents the relationships between data bits and check bits. In LDPC codes, each data bit is connected to a small subset of the check bits, resulting in a low-density connectivity structure.

- Reed-Muller codes are defined over binary alphabets and exhibit a rich algebraic structure. They represent a message as coefficients of a polynomial, which is then evaluated at specific points to generate codewords. The order of the Reed-Muller code, denoted by "r", dictates the degree of the polynomial and the error correction capability.

3. NEW METHODS FOR CONSTRUCTING GOOD LINEAR BLOCK CODES

Designing linear block codes with a high Hamming distance for given parameters of dimension k and size n is an ongoing challenge in coding theory. Several studies have leveraged existing codes with a favorable minimum Hamming distance as a foundation for constructing new linear codes. A code is considered "good" if it reaches the limits of Markus Grassl's database, "record" if it surpasses these limits, and "optimal" if it reaches the theoretical upper limit (upper bound). In our research, we propose a method for constructing good binary linear codes, drawing inspiration from the construction of Polar codes and utilizing the Hadamard matrix with the same form of the Arikan Kernel.

3.1 Hadamard Matrix

The Hadamard's matrix is a $n \times n$ matrix with entries of $+1$ or 1, and it is mutually orthogonal for rows and columns (LaClair, 2016), According to the mathematician M.J. Hadamard (Hadamard, 1893), a Hadamard's matrix is a $(+1, 1)$ matrix of dimension n:

$$\mathcal{H}_m . \mathcal{H}_m^{\mathsf{T}} = \mathcal{H}_m^{\mathsf{T}} . \mathcal{H}_m = n.I \tag{9}$$

We can swap out "+1" and "1" for the binary elements "0" and "1" to get the Hadamard matrix. As a result, any combination of columns or rows turns the matrix into another Hadamard matrix. The process used to create the Hadamard matrix of order m is as follows:

$$\mathcal{H}_1 = \begin{bmatrix} 1 \end{bmatrix} = \begin{bmatrix} 0 \end{bmatrix} \tag{10}$$

$$\mathcal{H}_2 = \begin{bmatrix} 1 & 1 \\ 1 & 0 \end{bmatrix} = \begin{bmatrix} 0 & 0 \\ 0 & 1 \end{bmatrix} \tag{11}$$

$$\mathcal{H}_m = \mathcal{H}_2 \otimes \mathcal{H}_{m/2} \tag{12}$$

Where, $\otimes$ denotes the Tensor product, also known as the Kronecker product.

3.2 New Construction Method

The proposed method for constructing good binary linear codes is inspired by the construction of Polar codes. The idea is based on extracting linear codes from the result matrix of the Kronecker product between the redundant part P, defined in equation (1), of the generator matrix of a linear code $C(n,k,d_{min})$ with good properties on one hand, and the Hadamard matrix similar to the Arikan kernel used for Polar code construction on the other hand. The redundant part P described in equation (1), of the chosen code's generator matrix is a $[k \times (n–k)]$ matrix, and the Hadamard matrix of order m has dimensions $m \times m$. Therefore, the result of the Kronecker product between these two matrices will have dimensions $[(m.k) \times (m.(n–k))]$.

Let's A be the result of the Kronecker product. Since the minimum distance of a linear code corresponds to the smallest weight among its codewords, so from A, promising rows in terms of weight (The rows whose weight exceeds the existing d_{min} value in the literature for the suspected code parameters) will be combined to form generator matrices of linear codes that have the potential to be good.

To describe the proposed construction method, let's consider the following notations:

- G: The systematic $n \times k$ generator matrix of a chosen binary linear block code (n, k);
- $\mathcal{H}_m$: The Hadamard matrix with a choosing order m;
- k': The desired dimension of potential good linear block code;
- LB: The lower bound relative to the parameters $\left(m.(n-k), k' \right)$ existing in (Grassl, Markus, n.d.).
- LB_d: The lower bound relative to the parameters $\left(m.(n-k), m.(n-k)-k' \right)$ existing in (Grassl, Markus, n.d.).

The flowchart illustrated in Figure (2) represents the proposed construction process. The construction steps are described as follows:

1) Take from G the redundant part P of dimensions $k \times (n–k)$;
2) Calculate the Kronecker product using the Stage 1 result with $\mathcal{H}_m$;
3) Parse the Kronecker product result so that each resultant row's weight is more than or equal to LB;
4) Create matrices using combinations of k' rows from the Stage 3 output;
5) For each matrix from Stage 4, a multi-threaded process is launched to perform two distinct tasks:
   - The first one directly utilizes the space generated by the candidate linear code C. It involves calculating the minimum distance of C and comparing it with LB. If it is greater than or equal to LB, the code will be considered a good linear code;
   - The second one utilises the orthogonal space of C to obtain information about the minimum distance of its dual code C^{T} .

3.2 Results and Interpretations

The proposed method has been tested on a variety of popular existing codes. Some examples of codes constructed using the method on well-known codes such as BCH codes, Reed-Muller codes, and the Golay code are represented in Tables (1), (2), and (3), respectively.

One of the most important factors in a data transmission system is channel capacity. It shows the fastest possible rate of data transmission between two sites in a system with a low theoretical error probability. Shannon theorized that information can be transferred with a very low error probability at a coding rate $R=k/n$ that is less than the channel capacity. Additionally, he demonstrated that transmission errors are

Figure 2. The process of the new approach for designing good binary linear block codes from an existing code

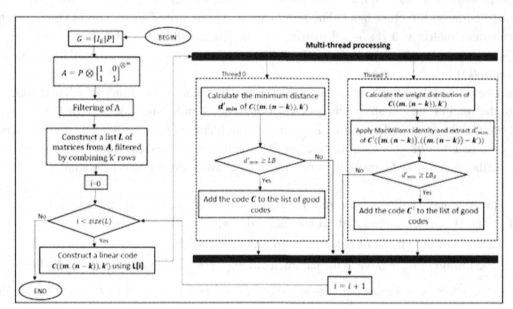

unavoidable when the coding rate **R** is larger than or equal to the channel capacity. In actuality, codes with rates higher than 0.5 have frequently attracted attention. In addition, the majority of the time, the minimum distance of the codes acquired is equal to **LB**, permitting us to recognize them as effective binary linear codes. The selected code is the one with the fewest codewords with the lowest weight in distribution described in equation (3), when many codes are discovered in certain results for the provided **n'** and **k'** and the required minimum distance (**LB**) as found in (Grassl, Markus, n.d.). Though research has some alternative codes with (**LB - 1**), it is important to note that only a small number of codes with the LB have been published in the literature for codes that have not reached **LB**.

4. NEW METHODS FOR DECODING LINEAR BLOCK CODES

Among the criteria for choosing Polar codes for error control in the 5G standard is the appealing complexity of their SC decoding technique and its derivatives. It is a decoding technique with linear complexity. However, this technique suffers from its serial nature, which involves decoding not just one bit at a time. This has been addressed in the previous research by the proposal of the SSC technique, which offers parallel estimation of certain bits. Therefore, our proposal is to adapt this technique for use with linear block codes.

The starting point of our decoding method is the proposition (1), which allows defining an equivalent Polar code for a linear code for using decoding algorithms of Polar code.

Proposition 1: For a binary linear block code $C(n,k)$ and a permutation matrix $\mathcal{P}$, a Polar code C_p with frozen dynamic bits exist, such that the injective mapping between codewords c in C and codewords c_p in C_p is given by:

Table 1. Good binary linear block codes obtained using BCH codes

$R = k'/n'$	n'	k'	d_{min}	LB	BCH Codes	$\mathcal{H}_m$
0,33	12	4	6	6	(7, 4)	m=4
0,5	16	8	5	5	(15, 7)	m=2
0,71	32	23	4	4		m=4
0,72	36	26	4	4	(16, 7)	m=4
0,6	40	24	7	7	(31, 11)	m=2
0,625	40	25	6	6		
0,78	60	47	6	6	(31, 16)	m=4
0,81	60	49	4	4		
0,84	78	66	4	4	(63, 24)	m=2

$$c = c_p . \mathcal{P} \tag{13}$$

4.1 Polar Codes With Dynamic Frozen Bits

In addition to the serial nature of SC decoders, the poor performance of Polar codes in short block lengths is also attributed to their low minimum distances. To address this issue, serial concatenation with an external CRC code was proposed in (Niu & Chen, 2012). Numerical results demonstrate that this approach significantly enhances performance, even without improving the minimum distance of the elementary

Table 2. Good binary linear block codes obtained using Reed-Muller codes

$R = k'/n'$	n'	k'	d'_{min}	LB	R.M Codes	$\mathcal{H}_m$
0,5	16	8	5	5	(8, 4)	m=2
0,56	16	9	3	4		
0,63	22	14	4	4	(16, 5)	
0,59	22	13	4	5		

Table 3. Good binary linear block codes obtained using Golay code

$R = k'/n'$	n'	k'	d'_{min}	LB	Golay code	$\mathcal{H}_m$
0,86	22	14	4	4	(23, 12, 8)	m=2
0,68	22	15	3	4		
0,9	22	17	3	3		
0,93	22	18	2	2		

code. The observation of data precoding with the CRC introduces dependencies among information symbols, which led the authors in (Trifonov & Miloslavskaya, 2013, 2016) to generalize the concept by constructing these dependencies in such a way that the resulting code becomes a subcode of another code with a sufficiently high minimum distance. The generated Polar code is characterized by frozen bits, whose values are no longer fixed at 0 but become a linear function of the preceding information bits. That is, for a linear code with a specific generator matrix G_{aux} of size $k{\times}n$, and G_p is the matrix of the Polar code of size n, the codewords c_p of a Polar code can be generated as follows:

$$c_p = u.G_p = m.G_{aux}.G_p \tag{14}$$

The proof is provided in (Trifonov & Miloslavskaya, 2013).

Based on equation (14), the dynamic frozen bits can be determined by the preceding bits. An example of dynamically frozen bits determined based on an extended BCH code is provided in (Trifonov & Miloslavskaya, 2016), which has been found to have a high minimum distance and excellent performance.

4.2 Transformation of a Linear Block Code Into a Polar Code With Dynamic Frozen Bits

The transformation of a linear block code into a Polar code with dynamically frozen bits allows us to harness the soft decoding performance of the latter. Figure (2) in (Lin et al., 2020) demonstrate how the mapping between code words of the two classes is achieved. On the decoder side, the proposed system offers an alternative path where a suitable soft decoding algorithm is employed based on Polar decoding algorithms. The generator matrix of linear code can be used to define the Polar code with dynamic frozen bits corresponding to a linear block code.

According to (Lin et al., 2020), it is possible to transform the space of a linear code C into the space of a suitable Polar code C_p, using a permutation matrix $\mathcal{P}$. Let G be the generator matrix of the linear code and G_p be the Arikan kernel of length n similar to that of the chosen linear code. The transformation of $G.\mathcal{P}^{-1}.G_p^{-1}$ into reduced row echelon form allows us to define the appropriate Polar code.

So, the Polar code with dynamic frozen bits is obtained by considering the indices of zero columns as the positions of static frozen bits, the columns with a single 1 as the positions of information bits, and the columns with multiple 1s as the positions of dynamic frozen bits whose value is defined based on the 1s in the columns related to the information bits. The mapping between codewords, before encoding and after decoding, is done using the matrix $\mathcal{P}$. An example is illustrated in (Khebbou, Chana, et al., 2021) for BCH code (16,7).

4.3 Adaptation of the SSCL Decoding Technique to Polar Codes With Dynamic Frozen Bits

To leverage the low complexity of Polar code decoding techniques for binary linear block codes, and considering that equivalent Polar codes have dynamic frozen bits, we have proposed an adaptation of the SSCL technique to Polar codes with dynamic frozen bits.

Figure 3. The single parity check tanner graph representation: (a) single parity check with static frozen bit and (b) single parity check with dynamic frozen bit

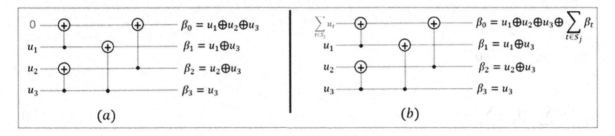

$$(a) \qquad\qquad\qquad\qquad (b)$$

The first step is to transform the linear code into a Polar code with dynamic frozen bits as described earlier. To do this, let's consider the transformation of $G.\mathcal{P}^{-1}.G_p^{-1}$ into reduced row echelon form as follows:

$$A_{RF} = E.G.\mathcal{P}^{-1}.G_p^{-1} \tag{15}$$

where E is the elimination matrix that transforms $G.\mathcal{P}^{-1}.G_p^{-1}$ into reduced row echelon form, it can be obtained from the Gauss-Jordan elimination.

The corresponding Polar code is defined in such a way that the indices of the columns in the A_{RF} matrix, where all elements are zeros, correspond to the positions of the static frozen bits (i.e., their values are fixed at zero). The columns with a single 1 correspond to the information bits, and the rest are considered positions of the dynamic frozen bits. After transforming the codeword from the linear block code to that of the equivalent Polar code using equation (13), the second step is to decode the codeword using the adapted SSCL method. The modifications made to the regular SSCL method pertain to the estimation and updates of the PM (Path Metrics) for an SPC (Single Parity Check) with dynamic frozen bits on one hand, and for dynamic frozen leaf nodes on the other hand. The remaining estimations for other special nodes and standard nodes remain unchanged.

- **SPC with dynamic frozen bit**

If we consider $\mathcal{F}$ as the set of positions of information bits, a dynamic frozen bit in position j has its value determined based on a set of information bits denoted as S_j. In other words, the value of the dynamic frozen bit u_j is defined as follows:

$$\forall j \in \bar{\mathcal{F}} : \exists S_j \subset \mathcal{F} | u_j = \sum_{t \in S_j} u_t \tag{16}$$

If $S_j = \phi$, the bit is statically frozen, meaning $u_j = 0$.

The frozen position of an SPC node is $j=0$. When it is dynamically frozen, its value is defined based on S_0 as shown in Figure 3.b, rather than 0 as shown in Figure 3.a. Its estimation thus depends on the function that specifies the dynamically frozen bit $\sum_{t \in S_0} \beta_t$ as well as on the estimation of the information bits that make up the SPC node. Thus, in the scenario where the parity bit is dynamically frozen, the equations relating to the estimation of β_v returned to the parent node of an SPC node are as follows:

$$\beta_{v_{(i \neq j)}} = \begin{cases} 1, & \alpha_{v_i} < 0 \\ 0, & \alpha_{v_i} \geq 0 \end{cases} \tag{17}$$

$$\beta_{v_{(i=j)}} = \sum_{i=1}^{n_v} \beta_{v_i} + \sum_{t \in S_j} \beta_t \tag{18}$$

The equation for updating PMs also applies to information bits, but it should depend on the linear function that describes the dynamically frozen bit for parity bits. The following is a definition of it:

$$PM_l = \begin{cases} PM_l, & \beta_j = \sum_{t \in S_j} \beta_t \\ PM_l + |\alpha_{v_j}|, & else \end{cases} \tag{19}$$

In Figure (3.a), the estimation of the generated parity check bit statically frozen (fixed at 0) for polar code with length $n=4$ is shown. When the parity check bit is a dynamically frozen bit in an SPC sub-code, its estimation can be achieved as shown in Figure (3.b).

- **Leaf dynamic frozen node**

Unlike a statically frozen bit, whose estimation always remains at 0, if the current node at a position j is a leaf and represents a dynamically frozen bit, the estimation is determined in the following manner:

$$\beta_j = \sum_{t \in S_j} \beta_t = \sum_{i=0}^{k-1} \beta_i . A_{RF_{i,j}} \tag{20}$$

4.4 Results and Interpretations

In order to evaluate the decoding performance of certain linear block codes using the adapted SSCL technique we proposed, we typically consider different list sizes L. We present the frame error rate (FER) as functions of various signal-to-noise ratio (Eb/N0) values in dB, where Eb represents the energy per bit and N0 is the spectral noise density. The simulations were conducted on an additive white Gaussian noise (AWGN) channel using binary phase-shift keying (BPSK) modulation scheme. The performance evaluation of the method we presented has been conducted and compared to the Optimal Soft Ordered Statistics Decoder (OSD) algorithm for binary linear codes, which is the best-known soft decoder for linear block codes. Experiments in the literature confirm that OSD can achieve Maximum Likelihood Decoding (MLD) performance [x], but with high memory requirements and significant computational complexity of $\mathcal{O}\left(nk^2 + 2^r nk\right)$ where r is the order of the OSD decoder.

Being an important class of linear block codes, BCH codes play a crucial role in the field of error-correcting codes. Therefore, we tested our decoding method on this class of linear block codes, namely E-BCH(16,7), E-BCH(32,11), E-BCH(64,16), and E-BCH(64,24). In this paper, we illustrate in Figure 4 FER simulation over a range of SNR for two BCH codes, where part (4.a) is for the E-BCH(32,11) code and part (4.b) is for the E-BCH(64,16) code.

For the E-BCH(32, 11) code, the Polar code with dynamic frozen bits is defined such that $\{u_8, u_{12}, u_{14}, u_{15}, u_{16}, u_{20}, u_{24}, u_{28}, u_{30}, u_{31}, u_{32}\}$ are information bits, $\{u_{22}, u_{23}, u_{26}, u_{27}, u_{29}\}$ are dynamic frozen bits, which are obtained in such a way that:

$$\begin{cases} u_{22} = u_8 + u_{14} + u_{15} \\ u_{23} = u_{12} + u_{15} \\ u_{26} = u_8 + u_{12} \\ u_{27} = u_{12} + u_{14} + u_{20} \\ u_{29} = u_8 + u_{14} + u_{15} + u_{20} \end{cases} \qquad (21)$$

the rest are static frozen bits.

Figure (4.a) illustrates the simulation of the performance of the E-BCH(32, 11) code using the proposed method compared to the OSD. In terms of FER, we observe from figure (4.a) that with a list size of $L=8$, the method we propose partially outperforms the performance of OSD with order $r=1$ starting from $Eb/N0=3$. For a list size of $L=16$, the performance matches that of the saturated OSD with order $r=2$, which represents the saturation order of the OSD in this case. The figure 5 represent the SSCL decoding tree with identified special nodes for Polar code equivalent to E-BCH(32,11). At depth 2, a Rep node is identified, allowing to estimate 8 bits in parallel way. At depth 3, some Rep nodes, SPC node and SPC node with dynamic frozen bits are identified offring a parallel estimation.

For the E-BCH(64, 16) code, we can observe from figure (4.b), which represents the FER performance, that starting from a list size of $L=16$, the adapted SSCL decoding algorithm offers a significant gain compared to OSD with order $r=1$, with a gain estimated at almost 1.5dB. With the same list size, adapted SSCL approaches the performance of OSD with order $r=2$ with a slight overshoot starting from $Eb/N0=3.5$, and it offers a gain exceeding 2dB compared to OSD with order $r=1$. For $L=64$, it allows reaching OSD with order $r=3$ with a slight overshoot starting from $Eb/N0=3$. Note that $r=3$ is the saturation order of OSD for the E-BCH(64, 16) code. In the literature (Lin et al., 2020), OSD with order $r=3$ applied to the E-BCH(64, 16) code achieves the performance of the MLD decoder, which is the case for the proposed method.

To test our method on a variety of other classes of linear block codes, we applied the method to the LDPC code (16,7) and the (16,9) code constructed using the construction method proposed in this paper.

By applying the transformation described above, the equivalent Polar code with dynamic frozen bits for the LDPC(16, 7) code is described as follows: positions *{6, 8, 10, 12, 13, 14, 16}* are dedicated to information bits, positions *{9, 11, 15}* are for dynamic frozen bits, and the rest are positions for static frozen bits. The dynamic frozen bits are obtained in such a way that:

$$\begin{cases} u_9 = u_8 \\ u_{11} = u_6 + u_8 \\ u_{15} = u_{10} \end{cases} \tag{22}$$

By observing Figure (6.a), which represents FER over a range of *Eb/N0*, it can be seen that the OSD with order $r=1$ for the LDPC code (16, 7) achieves the performance of the MLD decoder (Lin et al., 2020), and it slightly outperforms the belief propagation (BP) decoder with 100 iterations. Figure (6.a) confirms that the performance curves of the SSCL decoder proposed in this work coincide with those of the OSD with order $r=2$ and $L=4$. This implies that the proposed approach with $L=4$ reaches MLD decoder performance. Note that $r=1$ is the saturation order for the OSD for the LDPC(16, 7) code.

Figure 4. FER simulation of our method compared to OSD: (a) for E-BCH(32,11) and (b) for E-BCH(64,16)

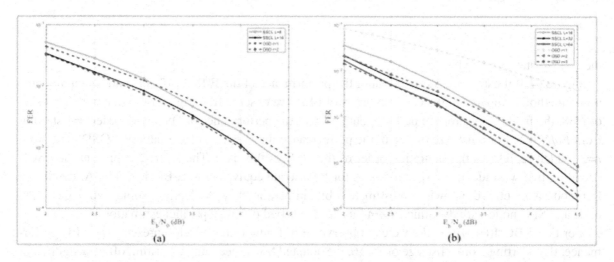

(a)   (b)

Figure 5. The SSCL decoding tree with identified special nodes for polar code equivalent to E-BCH(32,11)

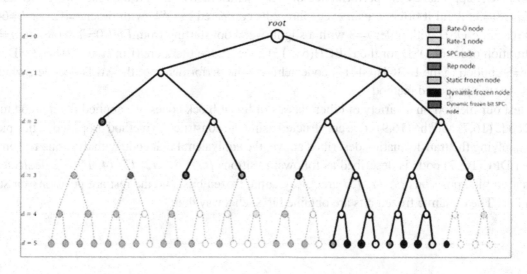

Figure 6. FER simulation of our method compared to OSD: (a) for LDPC(16,7) and (b) for the code (64,16) constructed with the proposed construction method

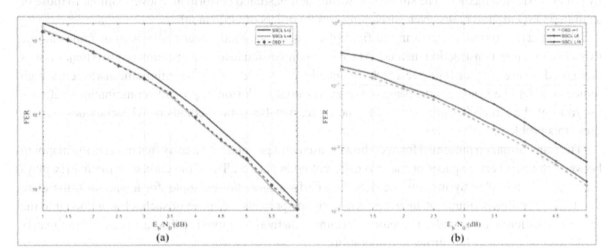

Similarly, the transformation of the (16, 9) code into a Polar code with dynamic frozen bits is obtained in such a way that positions {4, 6, 7, 8, 9, 10, 11, 12, 15} are dedicated to information bits, positions {5, 13, 14, 16} are for dynamic frozen bits, and the rest are positions for static frozen bits. From Figure (6.b), it can be observed that with a list size of $L=16$, the proposed method achieves performance comparable to OSD with order $r=1$ in terms of FER.

The complexity of the OSD scheme is critical $\mathcal{O}\left(nk^2 + 2^r nk \right)$ because complexity affects how much energy a communication system costs. It is clear that the complexity of the Polar code with the SC decoding method is lower than OSD, given that the complexity of the SC decoder simply depends on the block length $\mathcal{O}\left(nlog_2\left(n \right) \right)$. We can take use of the SC technique's low-complexity for a number of popular classes of linear codes due to the application of a derivative which we provide in our works.

6. CONCLUSION

In a segment of our research work, we introduced a novel method for constructing high-capacity binary error-correcting codes. This approach draws inspiration from Polar codes, widely utilized in the 5G standard for error control. It falls within the framework of construction methods based on existing codes. The proposed method employs a Hadamard matrix, similar to the Arikan kernel of Polar codes, in conjunction with the generator matrix of an existing linear code. The exploration leverages the space generated by the candidate code and its dual space through multi-threaded execution, enabling the exploration of larger dimensions in search of good linear bloc codes.

We also addressed the decoding issue by proposing a new method for linear codes. This method adapts a less complex yet highly efficient technique from Polar codes, specifically the SSCL in comparison to OSD. While OSD stands among the most efficient and versatile decoders for linear codes, it is known for its complexity and memory requirements. The method we proposed establishes a connection between the space of a linear code and that of a Polar code to leverage promising decoding techniques. Simulations were conducted on various popular linear codes such as BCH codes, LDPC codes, and those constructed by our construction method. The simulation results demonstrated performance levels similar to those of saturated OSD in most cases, even surpassing certain orders of OSD in others.

The objective of our research in the field of constructing good linear codes is to demonstrate the existence of a new construction method. At a certain dimension level, we encountered two major issues that could be avenues for future research: the challenge of calculating the minimum distance for high dimensions on one hand, and the issue of the exponential explosion of possible combinations between the rows of the Kronecker product result. Therefore, metaheuristic methods or AI techniques can address this problem.

The transformation presented for decoding is based on a permutation matrix that ensures the mapping between the two vector spaces of the two different code classes. Thus, the choice of the matrix plays a crucial role and directly impacts the decoding performance. For example, for a size n=8, there are 8!=40320 possible permutation matrices, and each one projects the space of such a linear code into the space of a different polar code. Therefore, defining a method for targeting the best permutation matrix could also be a subject for further consideration.

REFERENCES

1 Linear codes. (1977). InMacWilliams, F. J., & Sloane, N. J. A. (Eds.), *North-Holland Mathematical Library* (Vol. 16, pp. 1–37). Elsevier. doi:10.1016/S0924-6509(08)70526-9

Alamdar-Yazdi, A., & Kschischang, F. R. (2011). A Simplified Successive-Cancellation Decoder for Polar Codes. *IEEE Communications Letters*, *15*(12), 1378–1380. doi:10.1109/LCOMM.2011.101811.111480

Arikan, E. (2009). Channel Polarization: A Method for Constructing Capacity-Achieving Codes for Symmetric Binary-Input Memoryless Channels. *IEEE Transactions on Information Theory*, *55*(7), 3051–3073. doi:10.1109/TIT.2009.2021379

Dorsch, B. (1974). A decoding algorithm for binary block codes andJ-ary output channels (Corresp.). *IEEE Transactions on Information Theory*, *20*(3), 391–394. doi:10.1109/TIT.1974.1055217

Error-Correction Coding and Decoding. (n.d.). Retrieved October 19, 2022, from https://link.springer.com/book/10.1007/978-3-319-51103-0

Fossorier, M. P. C., & Lin, S. (1995). Soft-decision decoding of linear block codes based on ordered statistics. *IEEE Transactions on Information Theory*, *41*(5), 1379–1396. doi:10.1109/18.412683

Grassl, M. (2006). Searching for linear codes with large minimum distance. In W. Bosma & J. Cannon (Eds.), *Discovering Mathematics with Magma: Reducing the Abstract to the Concrete* (pp. 287–313). Springer., doi:10.1007/978-3-540-37634-7_13

Grassl, M. (n.d.). *Bounds on the minimum distance of linear codes and quantum codes*. http://www.codetables.de

Hadamard, J. (1893). *Resolution d'une question relative aux determinants - in Bulletin des Sciences Mathematiques, Septembre 1893* (1st ed.). See Description.

Hashemi, S. A., Condo, C., & Gross, W. J. (2016). Simplified Successive-Cancellation List decoding of polar codes. *2016 IEEE International Symposium on Information Theory (ISIT)*, 815–819. 10.1109/ISIT.2016.7541412

Hashemi, S. A., Condo, C., & Gross, W. J. (2017). Fast and Flexible Successive-Cancellation List Decoders for Polar Codes. *IEEE Transactions on Signal Processing*, *65*(21), 5756–5769. doi:10.1109/TSP.2017.2740204

Khebbou, D., Benkhouya, R., & Chana, I. (2022). Construction of Some Good Binary Linear Codes Using Hadamard Matrix and BCH Codes. In X.-S. Yang, S. Sherratt, N. Dey, & A. Joshi (Eds.), *Proceedings of Sixth International Congress on Information and Communication Technology* (pp. 523–532). Springer. 10.1007/978-981-16-2377-6_49

Khebbou, D., Benkhouya, R., Chana, I., & Ben-azza, H. (2021). Finding Good Binary Linear Block Codes based on Hadamard Matrix and Existing Popular Codes. *International Journal of Advanced Computer Science and Applications*, *12*(11). Advance online publication. doi:10.14569/IJACSA.2021.0121150

Khebbou, D., Chana, I., & Ben-azza, H. (2021). Simplified successive-cancellation list polar decoding for binary linear block codes. *Journal of Southwest Jiaotong University*, *56*(6), 6. Advance online publication. doi:10.35741/issn.0258-2724.56.6.54

Khebbou, D., Chana, I., & Ben-azza, H. (n.d.-a). *Decoding of the Extended Golay Code by the Simplified Successive-Cancellation List Decoder adapted to Multi-Kernel Polar Code*. Academic Press.

Khebbou, D., Chana, I., & Ben-azza, H. (n.d.-b). *Single Parity Check Node Adapted to Polar Codes with Dynamic Frozen Bit Equivalent to Binary Linear Block Codes*. Academic Press.

KhebbouD.IdrissC.Ben-azzaH. (2022). *Décodage des codes en blocs linéaires par les techniques des codes polaires*. doi:10.13140/RG.2.2.15406.08002

Khebbou, D., Idriss, C., & Ben-azza, H. (2023, May 27). *Adaptation of deep learning-based polar code decoding technique for linear block code decoding*. Academic Press.

LaClair, A. (2016). *A Survey on Hadamard Matrices*. Chancellor's Honors Program Projects. https://trace.tennessee.edu/utk_chanhonoproj/1971

Lin, C.-Y., Huang, Y.-C., Shieh, S.-L., & Chen, P.-N. (2020). Transformation of Binary Linear Block Codes to Polar Codes With Dynamic Frozen. *IEEE Open Journal of the Communications Society*, *1*, 333–341. doi:10.1109/OJCOMS.2020.2979529

Niu, K., & Chen, K. (2012). CRC-Aided Decoding of Polar Codes. *IEEE Communications Letters*, *16*(10), 1668–1671. doi:10.1109/LCOMM.2012.090312.121501

Sloane, N., Reddy, S., & Chen, C.-L. (1972). New binary codes. *IEEE Transactions on Information Theory*, *18*(4), 503–510. doi:10.1109/TIT.1972.1054833

Trifonov, P., & Miloslavskaya, V. (2013). Polar codes with dynamic frozen symbols and their decoding by directed search. *2013 IEEE Information Theory Workshop (ITW)*, 1–5. 10.1109/ITW.2013.6691213

Trifonov, P., & Miloslavskaya, V. (2016). Polar Subcodes. *IEEE Journal on Selected Areas in Communications*, *34*(2), 254–266. doi:10.1109/JSAC.2015.2504269

Chapter 9
IoV–Based Blockchain Over LoRa for Accident Detection

Fatima Zohra Fassi Fihri
Faulty of Sciences, Sidi Mohamed Ben Abdellah University, Morocco

Mohammed Benbrahim
Faulty of Sciences, Sidi Mohamed Ben Abdellah University, Morocco

Mohamed Nabil Kabbaj
iD https://orcid.org/0000-0002-6478-1892
Faulty of Sciences, Sidi Mohamed Ben Abdellah University, Morocco

ABSTRACT

All over the world, the increase in the use of transport systems is defined as the cause of traffic problems reflected mainly by the increase in the number of road accidents due to poor traffic management. In order to ensure an intelligent mobility and transport and thus in the trend of building smart cities, the interest has turned to the development of the internet of vehicles (IoV). The IoV communication network involves the evolution of vehicle connectivity enabling the exchange of real-time traffic data between vehicles, with their environment and everything related to it, through different network technologies. Given the complexity of the IoV, it is necessary that its environment is secure, reliable, and protected against attacks, and that it allows the diffusion of information throughout the network. The blockchain technology allows the securing of different data transactions exchanged between IoV nodes, given its provision of several cryptographic techniques and that it provides a distributed, transparent, and highly confidential database. In order to expand the area of the covered network, long-range (LoRa) designed for low power wide area networks (LPWANs) is used to ensure simultaneous and long range transmissions. This chapter presents an IoV-based architecture that integrates blockchain technology to cover the database security aspects and the LoRa network as a service for vehicle tracking that allows to collect information from different vehicles including location in order to be able to prevent the presence of road accidents with the aim of warning, alleviating traffic and minimizing the risk of having others. For its implementation, this system is based mainly on the measurement of the speed of vehicles to detect the deceleration or blockage of traffic in order to identify the presence of accidents.

DOI: 10.4018/979-8-3693-0497-6.ch009

INTRODUCTION

The amount of people who depend on the vehicles has increased exponentially in today's world. Due to the limited availability of emergency services and the increase in vehicular network, traffic hazards and road accidents have multiplied, resulting in a high death toll and significant material damage.

Intelligent Transport Systems (ITS) have developed rapidly and form the core of intelligent mobility, which ensures traffic management. ITS cover information gathering, detection, device control, data processing and transmission to ground devices via user-specific platforms. ITS has been further enhanced by the Internet of Things (IoT) to enable connectivity between different objects.

The Internet of Vehicles (IoV) is a central IoT theme that has developed from the Vehicular Ad Hoc Network (VANET) based on the connectivity and exchange of information and data between vehicles and their surroundings. The connectivity between vehicles is ensured by intercommunication between vehicles intelligent devices, sensors, and intelligent systems in the environment, as part of ITS. IoV's dynamic architecture and scalability allows all vehicles to interact with each other via the Internet, and enables for those moving to communicate independently of a fixed network infrastructure.

There are five types of IoV communication: vehicle-to-vehicle (V2V), vehicle-to-infrastructure (V2I), vehicle-to-pedestrian (V2P), vehicle-to-cloud (V2C), vehicle-to-sensor (V2S), vehicle-to-road node (V2R) and vehicle-to-network (V2N). In other words, it's vehicle-to-everything (V2X) communication (Figure 1).

Figure 1. Communication V2X. Different communication types for IoV.

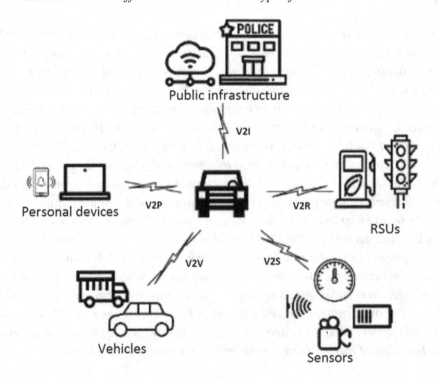

Low-power wide-area network (LPWAN) technologies have recently come into use for IoT-based developments due to their wide range, low energy consumption and high efficiency. LoRa supports wireless networks (WAN) via a LoRaWAN server and has been chosen for mobility services above all for its adequate data throughput and low latency among LPWAN technologies. It would be required for various IoV applications, and its properties make it suitable for all types of V2X communication.

However, in addition to the inability to manage traffic, especially due to the increasing number of nodes accessing the same centralized network, IoV suffers from security and privacy issues related to the storage and management of exchanged information, which are vulnerable to external attacks or malicious users. Blockchain, which provides a distributed, transparent and highly confidential database by recording immutable transactions, is a promising technology in IoV to overcome these constraints.

BLOCKCHAIN VALUE IN IOV

Recently, several researches have been conducted on blockchain technology and its rapid development that has revolutionized intelligent transportation systems. It is considered a decentralized, reliable, secure, transparent and immutable solution that opens up new possibilities for data sharing and management.

The blockchain is a continuous chain of blocks containing the records of its users in a distributed manner. All the information collected is shared between these blocks, which are linked to one another. The block is the basic data unit of the blockchain, generated using cryptographic techniques, and is responsible for recording the valid transaction information confirmed by each peer in the network. All pairs in the network have the same copy of the data, which cannot be modified (Figure 2).

Figure 2. Blockchain. Generic blockchain and blocks generation.

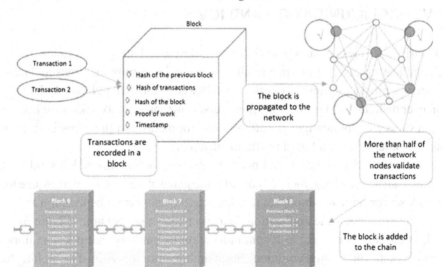

A general approach to integrating blockchain with IoT/ ITS was explained in (Najah et al., 2020) to ensure road safety. In (Singh & Kim, 2018) we used the trust bit shared between all the nodes to strengthen the trust for vehicular networks with the integration of the blockchain for the processing and management of this information. The research (Leo Brousmiche et al., 2018) evoked a hybrid protocol to ensure the security of vehicular data, based on a blockchain consensus that ensures the confidentiality of the data by limiting access to only a restricted number of authorized members. Blockchain is known for its traceability, transparency and confidentiality, which helps in the management of information, meaning its exchange and sharing in real time for ITS as presented in (Sharma et al., 2020). In (Ma et al., 2020) an architecture with ITS and Blockchain that ensures security thanks to its decentralization function was presented. The authors in (Zhao et al., 2022) presented an approach to ensure trust management which is Blockchain based Trust management that relies on the use of a trust factor that will be generated by each vehicle to judge the validity of the messages communicated between them, a new block containing this information is stored and managed by Blockchain.

There are several papers discussing security issues of IoVs, and some papers introduce blockchains and their use in IoVs and propose some architectural setups (Wang et al., 2019; Eltahlawy & Azer, 2021)

Studies (Mendiboure et al., 2020; Queiroz et al., 2020) have focused on the interest of decentralized blockchain technology while explaining its ability to improve the performance of IoVs to ensure security, privacy, and trust management.

In (Tripathi & Ahad, 2019 ; Kapassa et al., 2021) the issues and challenges for the application of blockchain in the IoV domain have been presented. This is important considering that IoVs require multiple communications and applications to provide all required roadside services, leading to an exchange of a vast amount of data between vehicle network entities. This data can be the target of several attacks that lead to potential problems, hence the interest of the blockchain for security.

LORA FOR V2X COMMUNICATION AND IOV

In recent years, various wireless technologies have been developed and standardized for use in Internet of Things (IoT) applications, and more specifically for vehicular communications and hence IoV.

LoRa represents a promising new network (Low Power Wide Area Network, LPWAN) enabling communication over distances of up to a few kilometers. LoRa-based networks have been implemented and deployed in a variety of applications in different environments, but the focus is more on IoV-based applications such as smart cities and road traffic management.

LoRa consists of four main parts: the end nodes (sensors or actuators) which send messages to the gateways and receive an acknowledgement from them, the gateway forwards the message to the network server, the network server removes duplicate messages and performs authentication tasks, and the application server which processes the application data and makes the decision. (Figure 3)

Related work has focused on LoRa as a communication technology that plays an important role in the development of a safe and trusted communication architecture for V2X. The architecture proposed in (Haque et al., 2020) is modular and compact, making it ideal for existing systems without the need for additional hardware. The work presented a reliable and robust architecture for V2X communication with LoRa, which includes design, implementation and real-life testing with prototypes, and the results showed that the LoRa architecture is suitable for V2X communications where vehicle mobility poses particular challenges. In (Asiain & Antolín, 2021), a LoRa-based system for wireless detection of road traffic flow has been developed, focusing on special cases where a slow or stopped flow increases the risk of road accidents. The LoRa system presented provides the speed of vehicles passing through the surveillance zone, enabling the development of traffic signs that adapt their behavior to the speed of vehicles on the road. The authors of (Jurado et al., 2020) presented a prototype for a transit vehicle tracking service based on ITS architecture, built using LoRa between the critical modules, and employed six experiments realized to evaluate the performance of the LoRa network. The results of the work (Bidollahkhani et al., 2023) demonstrate that LoRaWAN can operate successfully in the IoV environment with the two proposed mechanisms. The primary mechanism allows nodes to receive data from a given communication link and the second one is conceived to pull the data from the nodes, and the second one was conceived to retrieve essential information such as connection establishment and closure, successful data transmission or errors.

Figure 3. Long-range wide area networks. Architecture of LoRaWAN.

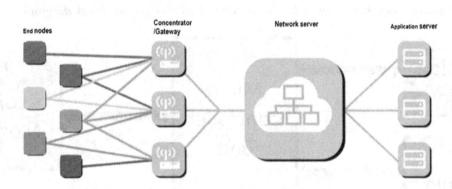

SYSTEM OF ACCIDENT DETECTION

Speed is a very important parameter in driving, and is responsible for most accidents, increasing the associated risk and influencing its severity. Faced with an obstacle or in critical driving conditions, individuals need a certain reaction time to be able to make a decision, react or not, and then carry out the activity. The gap between starting to brake and coming to a complete stop is longer at higher speeds, and is equal to the square of the speed. This means that the probability of avoiding an accident decreases with increasing speed. When an accident occurs, the engine's power is transformed into harmful forces that cause damage to the vehicle and its occupants.

This chapter presents a device for the prevention and detection of road accidents. This proposal is a method which can notice coincidences in a considerably reduced time and which sends basic information to the center, including the geographical coordinates, time and angle in which a vehicle accident has occurred. This information can be communicated in a short space of time to different vehicles in a well-covered area, helping to prevent and therefore reduce risk and save lives. When an accident occurs, the targeted message is automatically sent to the various network components.

The aim of the proposed system is to implement a complete working model using a microcontroller and its interfacing various components used to complete the accident detection system. The system has been modeled on the basis of current technologies, which are predominantly easy to use, but which also give good results.

This system can be described using the following block diagram, including the central core which is the microcontroller with the sensors and the Lora module. (Figure 4)

The Arduino is the microcontroller used to control all the modules we've used in the circuit, and the GPS module represents an important component and integral part of a vehicle's system that gives speed on vehicle positioning and speed. The Arduino is the microcontroller used to control all the modules we've used in the circuit, and the GPS module represents an important component and integral part of a vehicle's system that gives speed and vehicle positioning. The vibration sensor serves primarily as an accident discovery module, sending information to the microcontroller. All the information collected is sent to the Arduino uno, which calculates the data and determines the intensity of the accident. Finally, the LoRa module establishes communications with the remote control unit inside the city.

Figure 4. IoV-based blockchain over LoRa for accident detection system. Block diagram.

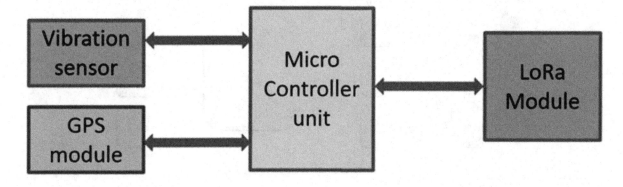

Arduino as Controller Unit

Arduino Uno is a widely used open-source microcontroller board. The one used provides ports for direct connection of electronic components, such as sensors, through 14 (input or output) digital input/output types. The Arduino is the relevant control unit for accident detection in that it collects data from the vibration sensor and GPS, and the output is transmitted by message or in a presentation system. The Arduino gathers information from all modules and, via the LoRA module, sends packets to the collector.

LoRa Module

LoRa is a physical layer technology for long-range wireless communication systems, defined among other LPWA technologies such as SigFox and WiSUN, and distinguished by its robustness to interference, low latency which is very important especially for critical applications requiring real-time response, and long-range coverage (over 10 km). LoRa can cover more than 15 km on the ground and almost 30 km on water, using the 868 MHz ISM band with a transmission power of 14 dBm and the maximum spreading factor (SF) according to real-life experiments carried out (Petajajarvi et al., 2015).

LoRa technology is operated using the LoRaWAN protocol, designed for battery-powered end devices. These are connected to the core network server via a gateway (also known as a base station or concentrator) in a star-of-stars topology. The end devices connect to one or more gateways using LoRa communication, while the gateways and network servers are connected using standard Internet Protocol (IP) connections.

GPS Module

The low-cost Global Positioning System (GPS) has become popular and used in many applications due to its improved accuracy and more affordable cost. It provides excellent navigation performance, even in the harshest environments, thanks to a design that eliminates sources of interference and mitigates the effects of multipath. The GPS module determines the vehicle's position, and the recovered information is sent to the microcontroller.

Vibration Sensor

Vibration measurement is a frequent measurement requirement in a number of areas. The vibration sensor is used to monitor vibration acceleration and speed and employ different mechanical or optical concepts to detect the vibrations of an observed system. Although no direct vibration sensors exist, vibrations will be measured by deducting the values of conventional mechanical or optical quantities indirectly.

Below is a diagram explaining in detail the system's function and describing the interaction between its components in order to avoid road accidents (Figure 5).

SYSTEM LIMITATIONS

The implementation of robust devices and the use of reliable materials will enable a complete system to be deployed in autonomous vehicles, which could be defined as the vehicle's main functionality being an accident warning and prevention system, as well as a system that will be used to locate accident vehicles so that other vehicles in the same area covered by the LoRa network have the information and can possibly take other decisions such as changing the route they are taking, This will help to avoid traffic jams and keep traffic flowing smoothly.

In addition, the high number of conditions and rules implemented by the consensus algorithms used in the application of blockchain to IoV to validate transactions and determine their compliance makes their application complex.

Improvements are still needed, especially regarding the system's non-functional requirements: response time, performance, portability. Research on the application of blockchain for IoV is still ongoing, especially in terms of managing multiple nodes simultaneously, integrating the same network, given the huge increase in the number of vehicle users, which has become indispensable for every human being, as well as integrating the LoRa network to extend the coverage area of the network.

Figure 5. IoV-based blockchain over LoRa for accident detection system. Diagram.

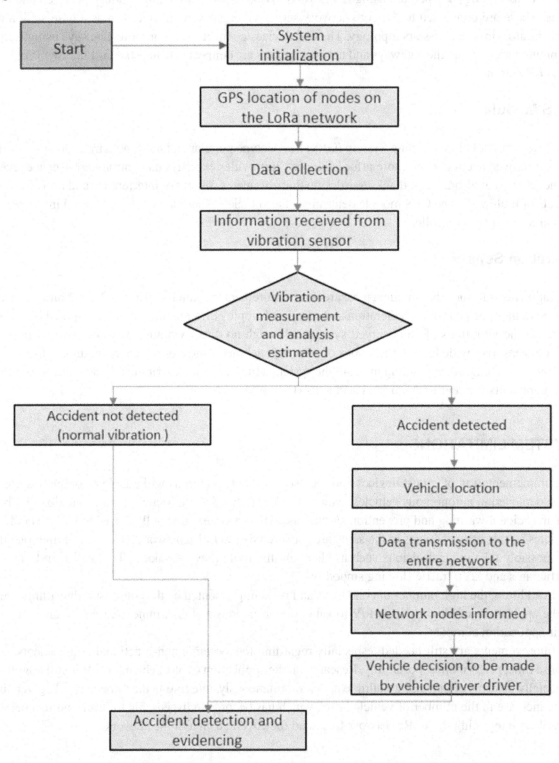

CONCLUSION

In this chapter, as a potential solution to the security limitations of IoVs and to protect the information exchanged between vehicles from attacks and malicious behavior, an accident detection system for IoVs using blockchain technology is presented. LoRa, a low power wide area network (LPWAN) technology chosen for mobility services because of its long range, low operating cost, sufficient data throughput, low latency, and coverage of more than 15 km, was used to apply this system to a well-defined area of the road network. Vehicles connected to a well-defined area covered by the LoRa network will receive information about the existence and location of the accident with this system. This could be enhanced by the implementation of a mobile application that could manage these alerts or even suggest decisions to be taken in the face of a nearby traffic accident.

REFERENCES

Ali, N.A., Taha, A.-E.M., & Barka, E. (2020) Integrating Blockchain and IoT/ITS for Safer Roads. *IEEE Network, 34*(1), 32-37.

Asiain, D., & Antolín, D. (2021). LoRa-Based Traffic Flow Detection for Smart-Road. *Sensors (Basel), 21*(2), 338. doi:10.3390/s21020338 PMID:33419026

Bidollahkhani, M., Dakkak, O., Mohammad Alajeeli, A. S., & Kim, B.-S. (2023). LoRaline: A Critical Message Passing Line of Communication for Anomaly Mapping in IoV Systems. *IEEE Access : Practical Innovations, Open Solutions, 11*, 18107–18120. doi:10.1109/ACCESS.2023.3246471

Eltahlawy, A.M., & Azer, M.A. (2021) Using Blockchain Technology for the Internet of Vehicles. *2021 International Mobile, Intelligent, and Ubiquitous Computing Conference, MIUCC 2021*, 54-61.

Haque, K. F., Abdelgawad, A., Yanambaka, V. P., & Yelamarthi, K. (2020). LoRa Architecture for V2X Communication: An Experimental Evaluation with Vehicles on the Move. *Sensors (Basel), 20*(23), 6876. doi:10.3390/s20236876 PMID:33271857

Jurado Murillo, F., Quintero Yoshioka, J. S., Varela López, A. D., Salazar-Cabrera, R., Pachón de la Cruz, Á., & Madrid Molina, J. M. (2020). Experimental Evaluation of LoRa in Transit Vehicle Tracking Service Based on Intelligent Transportation Systems and IoT. *Electronics (Basel), 9*(11), 1950. doi:10.3390/electronics9111950

Kapassa, E., Themistocleous, M., Christodoulou, K., & Iosif, E. (2021). Blockchain application in internet of vehicles: Challenges, contributions and current limitations. *Future Internet, 13*(12), 313. doi:10.3390/fi13120313

Leo Brousmiche, K., Durand, A., Heno, T., Poulain, C., Dalmieres, A., & Ben Hamida, E. (2018). Hybrid Cryptographic Protocol for Secure Vehicle Data Sharing over a Consortium Blockchain. *Proceedings - IEEE 2018 International Congress on Cybermatics: 2018 IEEE Conferences on Internet of Things, Green Computing and Communications, Cyber, Physical and Social Computing, Smart Data, Blockchain, Computer and Information Technology, iThings/GreenCom/CPSCom/SmartData/Blockchain/CIT 2018*, 1281-1286. 10.1109/Cybermatics_2018.2018.00223

Ma, Z., Richard Yu, F., Jiang, X., & Boukerche, A. (2020) Trustworthy Traffic Information Sharing Secured via Blockchain in VANET. *DIVANet 2020 – Proceedings of the 10th ACM Symposium on Design and Analysis of Intelligent Vehicular Networks and Applications*, 33-40.

Mendiboure, L., Chalouf, M. A., & Krief, F. (2020). Survey on blockchain-based applications in internet of vehicles. *Computers & Electrical Engineering*, *84*, 106646. doi:10.1016/j.compeleceng.2020.106646

Petajajarvi, J., Mikhaylov, K., Roivainen, A., Hanninen, T., & Pettissalo, M. (2015). On the coverage of LPWANs: Range evaluation and channel attenuation model for LoRa technology. *Proc. 14th Int. Conf. ITS Telecommun. (ITST)*, 55-59. 10.1109/ITST.2015.7377400

Queiroz, A., Oliveira, E., Barbosa, M., & Dias, K. (2020) A Survey on Blockchain and Edge Computing applied to the Internet of Vehicles. *International Symposium on Advanced Networks and Telecommunication Systems, ANTS*.

Sharma, A., Awasthi, Y., & Kumar, S. (2020). The Role of Blockchain, AI and IoT for Smart Road Traffic Management System. *Proceedings - 2020 IEEE India Council International Subsections Conference, INDISCON 2020*, 289-296.

Singh, M., & Kim, S. (2018). Trust Bit: Reward-based intelligent vehicle commination using blockchain. *IEEE World Forum on Internet of Things, WF-IoT 2018 - Proceedings*.

Tripathi, G., Ahad, M. A., & Sathiyanarayanan, M. (2019). The Role of Blockchain in Internet of Vehicles (IoV): Issues, Challenges and Opportunities. *Proceedings of the 4th International Conference on Contemporary Computing and Informatics, IC3I 2019*, 26-31.

Wang, X., Zeng, P., Patterson, N., Jiang, F., & Doss, R. (2019). An improved authentication scheme for internet of vehicles based on blockchain technology. *IEEE Access, 7*, 45061-45072.

Zhao, Y., Wang, Y., Wang, P., & Yu, H. (2022). PBTM: A Privacy-Preserving Announcement Protocol With Blockchain-Based Trust Management for IoV (2022). *IEEE Systems Journal*, *16*(2), 3422–3432. doi:10.1109/JSYST.2021.3078797

Chapter 10
Blockchain–Based IoT for Precision Agriculture:
Applications, Research Challenges, and Future Directions

Okacha Amraouy

ⓘD https://orcid.org/0000-0001-7913-5132

Faulty of Sciences, Sidi Mohamed Ben Abdellah University, Morocco

Yassine Boukhali

ⓘD https://orcid.org/0000-0002-9173-7424

Faulty of Sciences, Sidi Mohamed Ben Abdellah University, Morocco

Aziz Bouazi

Moulay Ismail University, Morocco

Mohammed Nabil Kabbaj

ⓘD https://orcid.org/0000-0002-6478-1892

Faulty of Sciences, Sidi Mohamed Ben Abdellah University, Morocco

Mohammed Benbrahim

Faulty of Sciences, Sidi Mohamed Ben Abdellah University, Morocco

ABSTRACT

In recent years, IoT has been increasingly applied in agriculture to transform traditional farming practices into smart and precision agriculture (PA) that are more efficient, productive, and sustainable. However, its implementation in agriculture faces several challenges, including network coverage, reliability, lack of flexibility, and scalability. To address these challenges, current research has focused on developing new communication protocols and technologies, along with several IoT architectural design patterns, especially those based on SOA, which play a crucial role in designing service-oriented solutions. This chapter presents comprehensive and impactful solutions for blockchain-based IoT applications in PA. It proposes novel models combining IoT, blockchain, fog and cloud computing for the development of decentralized applications with independent, autonomous, and interoperable functionalities and services based on the SOA approach. Also, technical challenges, research directions, and the recent advances towards an optimized blockchain-based IoT ecosystem for PA are presented.

DOI: 10.4018/979-8-3693-0497-6.ch010

INTRODUCTION

There is a large number of research in the literature that recognizes the importance of using emerging advanced technologies and data-driven solutions in Precision Agriculture (PA) (Torky & Hassanein, 2020; W. Lin et al., 2020; R. Tanwar et al., 2023). PA refers to a range of tools, systems, and techniques used in modern farming practices, based on the use of Information and Communications Technology (ICT), global positioning system technology, robotics and automation technologies, variable rate technology, satellite technology, geographical information system and remote sensing. These technologies aim to enhance performance, efficiency, productivity, and security across all agricultural functions and services by implementing flexible, intelligent, and precision-controlled systems (Khanal, Fulton, & Shearer, 2017). Today, PA started to rely upon IoT (V. K. Quy et al., 2022), wireless sensor and actuator networks (M. Sultan et al., 2023; Singh & Sharma, 2022; Jihani, Kabbaj, & Benbrahim, 2023), weather monitoring systems, wireless networks (Feng, Yan, & Liu, 2019), smart irrigation and fertilization systems (E. A. Abioye et al., 2020; R. L. Ray et al., 2022; N. Lin et al., 2020), drones (V. Puri et al., 2017; Mogili & Deepak, 2018), Fog/Edge computing (E. Guardo et al., 2018), cloud computing (Ahmed, De, & Hussain, 2018), SOA (Khanna & Kaur, 2019), virtualization and containerization (C. Núñez-Gómez et al., 2021), Artificial Intelligence (AI) (K. Jha et al., 2019), big data analytics (Akhter & Sofi, 2022), and BlockChain (BC) (Y.-P. Lin et al., 2017). Based on these technologies, it becomes possible to create a next-generation internet of smart farming as the backbone of modern agricultural systems and processes. Also, forecasting methods/models and predictive analytic software systems leverage agricultural data, employing data analysis techniques and advanced algorithms to make predictions concerning future outcomes or trends. These predictions are derived from a combination of historical and Real-Time (RT) data, allowing for more accurate and informed decision-making in PA. Thus, advancements in optimization, prediction, and control algorithms have a significant impact on PA (F. Jamil et al., 2022). Prediction algorithms are used to analyze sensing data collected from various sources such as weather stations, satellite imagery, drones, soil sensors, and crop monitoring systems. By applying Machine Learning (ML) and statistical techniques, prediction algorithms can identify hidden patterns, correlations, and trends in the data (K. Jha et al., 2019). They enable farmers to make informed decisions about irrigation scheduling, fertilizer application, disease detection, yield estimation, and pest control. By predicting future outcomes, farmers can optimize their resource allocation, minimize risks, and maximize productivity. Similarly, optimization algorithms process sensing data and other relevant parameters to determine optimal strategies for various agricultural practices. These algorithms utilize mathematical models and optimization techniques to maximize profits or minimize losses. For example, they can optimize crop planting patterns, determine the ideal timing and quantity of irrigation and fertilization, and optimize resource allocation across different fields or crops. Likewise, control algorithms build upon the outputs of prediction and optimization algorithms to implement automated control mechanisms in PA. These algorithms utilize optimal parameters and strategies determined by the optimization algorithms to effectively control actuating devices. Besides these advancements, Decision Support Systems (DSS), data mining, and data analysis, along with the use of web-based DSS, have become significant techniques in managing services in PA. (Z. Zhai et al., 2020). Furthermore, various irrigation decision models have been developed to support farmers in making optimal irrigation decisions (Car, 2018; H. M. Abd El Baki et al., 2018; E. Bwambale et al., 2023; E. A. Abioye et al., 2022). These models take into account factors such as soil moisture levels, weather conditions, crop water requirements, and irrigation system efficiency. By incorporating these models into DDS, farmers can determine the most appropriate irrigation actions and optimize irrigation depth. Also, automation in irrigation canal operations and the use of different irrigation systems can contribute to reducing water losses and improving water supply efficiency in farms. By automating irrigation canal operations, farmers can ensure precise water delivery to crops while minimizing water losses due to leakage or inefficient distribution (S. M. Hashemy Shah-dany et al., 2019). Agricultural robotics has made also significant advancements in PA, enabling various applications and functions. The primary objective of agricultural robotics is not limited to using robots for specific tasks but rather developing multi-functional automatic agricultural vehicles that leverage AI to perform a wide range of operations (M. Wakchaure et al., 2023). Moreover, the development of smart-versatile drone systems has emerged as one of the most important advancements in PA (H. M. Jalajamony et al., 2023; Guven & Parlak, 2022). Remote agricultural monitoring system uses automa-tion and sensing technologies to supervise and manage an IoT-based agriculture sector. However, it's highly vulnerable to various cyber-attacks. Unauthorized parties can attempt to exploit vulnerabilities in the systems infrastructure, software, or communication channels, which can lead to the compromise of integrity, confidentiality, and data availability.

The advent of BC technology and smart contracts enables the creation of distributed ledgers that contains connected blocks of immutable transactions on a decentralized network where honest or dishon-est nodes can communicate with each other directly without the need for intermediaries or centralized authorities. BC technology has emerged as a promising solution to address significant challenges in PA. Its integration with IoT offers several opportunities to mitigate these challenges effectively (T. H. Pranto et al., 2021; T. M. Fernández-Caramés et al., 2018). The combination of BC and IoT will lead to create decentralized and collaborative networks that allow different IoT devices and platforms to communicate and interact with each other securely and seamlessly (M. Shyamala Devi et al., 2019). The result of this combination will move us from only smart farms to the internet of smart farms, providing enhanced control at the network layer. It has the potential to create new opportunities with several benefits and outcomes, such as enhanced security and privacy, improved data integrity and traceability, consensus mechanisms and smart contract-enabled transactions, transparent and tamper-resistant transactions, ef-ficient data sharing and collaborations (A. E. Uddin et al., 2021). In PA, this combination will let us get more autonomy and intelligence in managing agricultural processes in highly efficient and optimized ways. However, building flexible-automated platforms able to accommodate individualized services and meet all the expressed needs in PA remains an important challenge. This challenge necessitates the integration of IoT, BC, AI, cloud and fog/edge computing.

Fog/Edge computing extends the capabilities of cloud computing by bringing distributed comput-ing resources at the edge of the network closer to the data sources or consumers (F. M. Ribeiro et al., 2021), which allows farmers to get a convenient and comfortable approach with low latency, location awareness, very large number of nodes, wide-spread geographical distribution, wireless access, mobil-ity, strong presence of streaming and RT applications (A. Hazraet et al., 2023; U. Sakthi et al., 2023). Also, by harnessing the power of clusters, virtualization, and containerization in the Fog/Edge layer, PA can unlock numerous benefits by achieving flexible ubiquitous computing. However, without uti-lizing BC technologies, the elastic composition between end-devices and cloud computing, based on Fog/Edge computing paradigm, lacks several advantages and faces many challenges. These challenges include maintaining data integrity and traceability, transparency, consensus mechanisms and smart contract-enabled transactions, task offloading, allocate and schedule resources of the Fog/Edge nodes (e.g., power, memory, CPU, storage disks, software capabilities, networking and I/O). Additionally, it struggles in vain to establish a common state with no centralized controller having special privileges, especially in the hybrid collaborative IoT design patterns for PA, which contains a fog computing layer as the backbone of these models, to ensure data flow resilience between fog and cloud during either network availability or unavailability situation, by allowing data persistence in the fog layer and employing various compression techniques to reduce the overall data volume. However, the use of BC, smart contracts and SOA can be leveraged to provide trust, security, orchestration and more benefits as missed links in the Fog/Edge computing paradigm.

A. Research Background

Several research articles on BC-based IoT for PA have been published in recent years (Torky & Hassanein, 2020). BC technology is a decentralized and distributed ledger that allows multiple parties to maintain a shared database without the need for intermediaries or central authorities (A. Reyna et al., 2018). It eliminates the risk of a single point of failure by utilizing distributed P2P networks and smart contracts (A. Dorri et al., 2017), which is essential to create DApps, P2P systems and collaborative approaches in IoT for PA (P. Kochovski et al., 2019). The analysis, research challenges and opportunities, and the necessity of integrating BC in IoT for PA, along with relevant use cases in more details have been provided by (Torky & Hassanein, 2020). However, the authors cannot use smart contracts in their proposed models, and cannot clarify how to avoid the limitations of using smart contracts and BC in IoT for PA as described by (Manoj, Krishnamoorthi, & Narendra, 2023) because smart contracts cannot interact securely with off-chain data sources. Besides, all proposed models by (Torky & Hassanein, 2020) lack a structured approach for systematically providing services to end-users. This can lead to disorganized or inefficient delivery of services, which leads to potential problems or dissatisfaction among users. The same thing for (Y.-P. Lin et al., 2017) because they proposed a model of an e-agriculture system based on BC infrastructure associated with ICT, intended for implementation at the local and regional scale, without explaining how to avoid the aforementioned limitations. Furthermore, a comprehensive review in the field of PA has been conducted by (Khanna & Kaur, 2019) to identify the most prominent IoT-based applications, the authors highlighted the major benefits of using AI with IoT and focused on expanding the capabilities of IoT from IPv4 to IPv6 and other relevant standards capable of supporting the future of IoT and resolving its current issues related to fragmentation. The authors recommend developing a highly scalable IPv6-based SOA that can effectively address challenges such as interoperability, mobility, intelligent distribution among diverse smart components, cloud computing integration, applications, and their services. However, they have not mentioned the benefits of using Fog/Edge computing paradigm, BC technology and smart contracts in their review. The same thing for (K. Jha et al., 2019) because they discussed different automation practices in agriculture, focusing just on IoT, ML, Deep Learning (DL), wireless communications and AI. In the past few years, a prevalent practice involved sending RT sensory data to centralized cloud servers through a reliable communication channel for analysis. However, this approach has encountered several issues, including network congestion, latency, data loss, and increased energy consumption. These problems mainly stem from the large distance between end-users and cloud servers. To overcome these challenges, fog computing has emerged as a solution in a distributed environment. (A. Hazraet et al., 2023) conducted a comprehensive survey encompassing various aspects of fog computing through recent advancements. The authors discussed the layered architecture of the standard fog framework and explored various state-of-the-art techniques for efficiently utilizing the computing resources available in fog networks. Furthermore, an IoT use case scenario was presented to illustrate the process of fog data offloading and resource provisioning in heterogeneous fog networks. Also, the DECENTER fog computing platform has been designed by (P. Kochovski et al., 2019) specifically to support the emerging big data pipelines from the IoT (M. San Emeterio de la Parte et al., 2023). By implementing AI algorithms across the edge/fog and cloud computing continuum, the platform offers several advantages to applications, including enhanced Quality of Service (QoS), and reduced operational costs. Whereas (P. Kochovski et al., 2019) proposed a trust management architecture for ethereum BC-based fog computing platform specifically designed with trustless smart oracles. By establishing trust relationships among stakeholders, entities and services within the platform, the authors highlight the advantages of their approach and showcase the benefits it brings to various aspects of the system. However, the distributed nature of fog/edge computing presents a challenge when it comes to resource orchestration. (C. Núñez-Gómez et al., 2023) presented a Heterogeneous, Interoperable and DistRibuted Architecture (HIDRA), a novel architecture designed for resource orchestration of applications running in fog computing environments, utilizing ethereum BC and smart contracts. The results obtained by the authors demonstrate the minimal overhead introduced to the system and its capability to execute coordinated actions among heterogeneous fog nodes without the need for any central authority's intervention. Furthermore, (T. H. Pranto et al., 2021) proposed a system that utilizes BC technology and smart contracts as the backbone for IoT enabled smart agriculture, integrating IoT devices in both pre-harvesting and post-harvesting stages of agriculture. The authors emphasize the robust mechanism that arises from the collaboration of BC, smart contracts, and IoT. Also, (Q. Zheng et al., 2023) have proved the necessity of using BC, IoT and smart contracts in PA. The authors proposed a BC-based IoT service platform to enhance the efficiency of agricultural service operations. They utilized drone plant protection services as a specific example and devised a novel execution procedure for smart contract-based agricultural services. Also, (M. Pincheira et al., 2021) explores unprecedented use of constrained IoT-based sensing devices as reliable data sources for public ethereum BC platform. The findings were obtained through the real implementation of an irrigation water management use case, revealing that the proposed architecture can be implemented with only a 6% increase in the energy budget compared to normal IoT device operations. The authors achieve this by representing each IoT device as a unique smart contract deployed on the BC. Each smart contract can be seen as a "smart-twin," which refers to a digital replica of a physical object or process, thus representing a "digital twin." This contract comprises both private and public methods. The private methods are responsible for updating the state of the twin on the BC, and can only be invoked by the device that owns the BC identity. On the other hand, public methods offer a standardized interface for other smart contracts to interact with smart-twins, thereby building DApps that directly interact with the twin contracts.

B. Study Objectives

Considering the existing challenges in BC-based IoT for PA as motivation, this chapter conducts a comprehensive study of the proposed architecture for SOA-based IoT, with a particular focus on PA. It is an architectural design making it possible to benefit from BC, IoT, microservices and SOA, fog/edge and cloud computing. Also, it can benefit from software or hardware evolutions at the level of each part of the IoT systems. The chapter aims to explore the challenges and potential solutions, requirements, and benefits of implementing BC and SOA in the context of IoT for PA, along with the major benefits comes from virtualization and containerization technologies, especially when it's implemented in the Network-Attached Storage (NAS) servers. The key research findings of this chapter are "How can optimize the integration between SOA, BC and IoT for total management in PA". An illustrative description of the main contributions made by the two proposed models are presented in Section 4. Additionally, an existing IoT systems for precision irrigation are briefly explained, which is considered as one of the major applications in PA. Moreover, an illustrative description of the Intelligent Irrigation as a Service (2IaaS) system has been performed. This system aims to provide farmers with a comprehensive solution for optimizing their irrigation practices. It is a flexible product-service system presenting individualized solutions for the optimal management of precision irrigation. Its flexibility comes from its adaptation to any type of agricultural operation and any expressed need. It is a system ranging from a simple application to an integrated system with the use of intelligent algorithms, connected instruments, drones, satellite data and BC. Finally, we have briefly explained future trends of BC-based IoT and its potential impact in PA.

C. Manuscript Structure

The rest of the chapter is structured as follows. Section 1 presents a brief overview of IoT and proposed architecture with a focus on the SOA-based model and its intermediate layers. Challenges of building BC-based IoT networks and potential solutions is discussed in Section 2. Section 3 explores how the latest advancements in virtualization and containerization technologies are set to revolutionize the fields of computing and software development. In Section 4, we have proposed two novel models by integrating BC, SOA and IoT in order to allow farmers to present individualized solutions or any expressed need in PA sector. Section 5 discusses several application systems for precision irrigation in PA, along with brief discussion about our 2IaaS system. In Section 6 we have briefly explained research challenges and future directions regarding the integration of BC and IoT technologies, leading to a revolutionary impact on agriculture in the long term. Finally, Section 7 contains the conclusive remarks of the chapter.

1. IOT OVERVIEW AND PROPOSED ARCHITECTURE

The IoT is rapidly transforming various industries, with PA being a key beneficiary. In this context, the integration of IoT into PA has the potential to revolutionize farming practices. IoT plays a pivotal role in the digital transformation of PA, offering optimal solutions for managing its critical applications like precision irrigation and fertilization, although the seamless integration of the required technologies has not yet been fully achieved. IoT represents an evolution that emphasizes greater dependence on remote sensing devices, large volumes of data, and more patterns of interconnected devices within various network topologies. For example, the emergence of IoT solutions in precision irrigation takes the form of a wireless sensor and actuator network connected to the Internet for data collection and triggering actions in remote areas, which enables informed decision-making and provides farmers with the flexibility to select between automated and manual options for taking necessary actions or interventions. This technology seamlessly combines real-time data-driven insights, low-power wireless technologies, remote monitoring and control, large-scale automation, cost reduction in operations, promotes sustainable farming practices, the capability to integrate energy-efficient sensing devices into water distribution systems, and the ability to process the collected data and store it in the cloud (Hafian, Benbrahim, & Kabbaj, 2021, 2023). However, IoT-based systems often operate on centralized architectures and are typically managed by third-party service providers (e.g., The Things Industries, FIWARE, Cisco IoT Cloud Connect, AWS IoT, Microsoft Azure IoT, Kaa IoT, ThingSpeak and much more), leading to significant restrictions on the stakeholders participating in PA management processes. These restrictions can include limited control, dependency on service providers, and restricted data access and ownership, among other potential limitations. As a result, IoT is undergoing a transition from a focus on devices and data technology to actionable intelligence technology. This transition involves increased integration with other technologies, such as fog/edge and cloud computing, BC, cybersecurity, AI and IoT edge analytics, in conjunction with cloud-based analytics. The main goal of these integrations is to empower digital transformation, making IoT communications so powerful, characterized by network capacity and low-power improvement, connectivity loss prevention, no single points of failure, orchestration, coordination, agility and much more. This is achieved by focusing on optimization and mitigating or eliminating the constraints mentioned earlier.

Nowadays, there are ever-increasing efforts to optimize the way of connecting various objects, applications and technologies into a cohesive, simplified, and unified IoT architecture reference model, which means that a flexible layered architecture is very much needed. The main objective is to enable diverse and disparate objects to seamlessly interconnect and communicate via the Internet in more optimized ways. However, the growing number of proposed IoT architectural models has not yet converged to the common-unified reference model. Furthermore, there is no research paper presenting an open and comprehensive IoT-based platform with a unified architecture specifically designed for PA systems, featuring flexible, modular and reusable services, while achieving distributed and decentralized collaboration, processes and management. The goal is to create a powerful and hybrid IoT ecosystem, which takes advantage of both private and public IoT networks to optimize the performance, security and flexibility of an IoT solution in the field of PA. This can be achieved by using a hybrid BC that combines both public and private/consortium BC features. This allows users and stakeholders to access highly customizable solutions with unmatched security, privacy, transparency, autonomy and data integrity, combining the strengths of both public and private/consortium BC configurations. Modular architecture, also known as modular system or modular design, is a design approach or system organization in which a complex system is broken down into smaller, self-contained, loosely coupled and interchangeable components or modules. These modules can be developed, tested and maintained separately, and then combined or integrated to create a complete and functional system. This approach promotes maintainability, flexibility and the efficient development of complex systems by breaking them down into more cohesive and manageable parts.

The preceding points set the stage for understanding the SOA-based IoT proposed architecture, as depicted in Figure 1, which serves as the central focus of this chapter. This architecture introduces two innovative design patterns, as illustrated in Figure 3 and Figure 4, making a significant impact on PA by providing adaptable solutions for various agricultural operations and addressing specific needs. The proposed architecture comprises several layers that work together to harness the power of IoT in PA. It offers a comprehensive and tailored solution designed to meet the specific requirements of PA, aligning with the goals of collaboration, product-services and process management. Furthermore, by implementing this architecture with a primary focus on the utilization of a hybrid BC, it becomes possible to establish a powerful and hybrid IoT ecosystem, which delivers several benefits in the PA sector. This ecosystem has the potential to significantly enhance performance and security while improving the efficiency, productivity and sustainability of agricultural operations. In the following, we will provide a brief discussion of the SOA-based model layers.

Figure 1. SOA-based IoT architecture

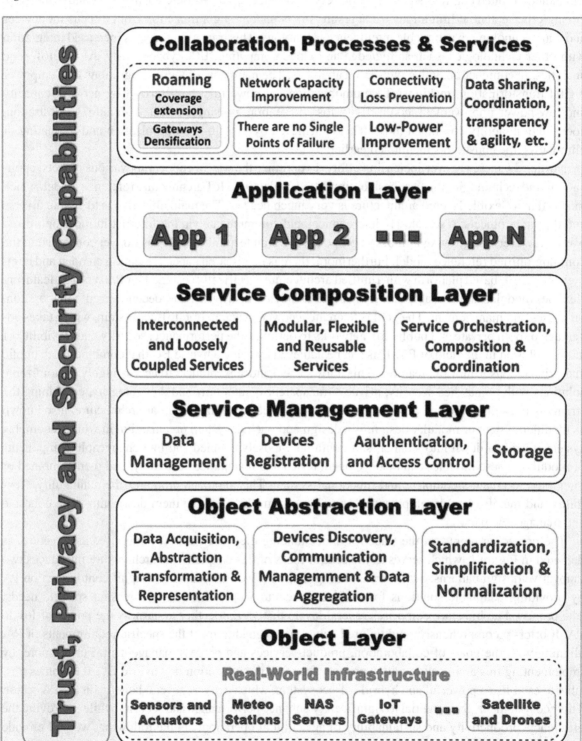

1.1. Object Layer

This layer is responsible for connecting various sensor nodes, including weather stations, drones, satellites, soil moisture sensors, nutrient sensors, water and air quality sensors, crop growth and health sensors, light sensors, and potentially more types of sensors that support PA. It's distributed throughout the farms to gather data and provide RT information's about various environmental factors for further analysis and processing in the service management layer. Also, actuator nodes perform some major-specific tasks in this layer, with the ability to control and manipulate different aspects of agricultural operations based on the received information from the higher layers or local control through mechanisms like farmers. These nodes can include irrigation control nodes (e.g., solar inverters, pumps, irrigation valves, etc.), fertilizer dispensing nodes, crop harvesting nodes, pesticide and herbicide spraying nodes, autonomous robotic nodes, livestock management nodes, and more. It's clear that actuator and sensor nodes play crucial and deterministic roles in monitoring and control strategies, as well as optimizing agricultural operations. The object layer is responsible for data collection, device communication, and basic data processing. It forms the foundation of the IoT ecosystem, enabling physical objects to connect to the digital world, facilitating digitization, and transferring data to the object abstraction layer. Moreover, the big data generated in PA through the IoT applications, as recently demonstrated by (M. San Emeterio de la Parte et al., 2023), is initiated at this layer.

1.2. Object Abstraction Layer

This layer is responsible for transferring the data produced by the object layer to the service management layer through advanced communication protocols (e.g., LoRaWAN, IPv6, MQTT, TCP/IP, etc.) and secure channels or connections. Data can be transferred through various technologies such as LoRa, NB-IoT, LTE, 5G, WiFi, etc. Choosing the right technology depends on several factors and requirements that should be carefully considered for each scenario in PA. Moreover, in order to handle the complexities of heterogeneous objects/devices inherent in IoT systems, the concept of abstraction is used. Abstraction involves hiding unnecessary details and focusing on a general form or common interface and data representation. This is crucial for simplifying data interactions, as well as ensuring security, privacy, and the management of a wide range of IoT components or objects, by storing their encryption and authentication keys in the BC via smart contracts and then managing authorization in a decentralized manner. By abstracting the underlying complexities, developers can work with a simplified and unified view of the IoT ecosystem and harmonize access to different devices by providing a common language and procedure for communication.

1.3. Service Management Layer

This layer is primarily responsible for handling the operational aspects and system-level management of the IoT infrastructure. It includes components that ensure the smooth functioning, coordination and control of the IoT system. In PA, this layer can include tasks such as registration and management of IoT devices, gateways, servers and networks, and data management processes, as well as system monitoring and control mechanisms for managing system-level parameters, security and privacy, access control, service discovery and other relevant aspects. Moreover, the service management layer is responsible for forwarding the processed data, making decisions and delivering the required services over the network layer, while maintaining the accessibility, security, scalability and reliability of IoT components and data.

1.4. Service Composition Layer

This layer sits above the management layer. Its primary function is to facilitate the integration and composition of various services and functionalities offered by the management layer. By leveraging microservices and SOA principles at this layer, it becomes inevitably possible to achieve enhanced modularity, flexibility and interoperability within the IoT architecture for PA. Furthermore, other functions like fog/edge and cloud computing and service management processes are handled at this layer. This layer is responsible for implementing service orchestration and service composition, along with managing services, including those provided by cloud resources, fog/edge devices, and other components of the architecture. It involves composing services, managing their interactions, and ensuring efficient data processing and communication between IoT devices, fog/edge nodes and cloud services. Additionally, this layer enables the modification or replacement of individual services without affecting the entire system, making it loosely coupled and more adaptable to changing requirements.

1.5. Application Layer

This layer focuses on specific applications and services designed for PA. It is the layer where data collected from various sensors and devices are processed, analyzed, and utilized to provide valuable insights and control actions. It typically involves monitoring, data processing and analytics which can be used to inform scheduling decisions, and provide high-quality, effective and efficient product-services to the farmers. Intelligent scheduling and planning in PA involve using the data collected from various sources, such as RT data, weather forecasts and historical data, to determine the optimal timing for different agricultural activities. This can include tasks such as irrigation, fertilization, pest control, harvesting, equipment maintenance, etc.

1.6. Collaboration, Processes, and Services

This layer promotes collaboration among different stakeholders and streamlines various agricultural processes and services. Its main objective is to facilitate cooperation, roaming, data sharing, orchestration and automation of IoT processes, as well as coordination among the various stakeholders participating in PA. Additionally, it manages peer-to-peer processes, workflows, and interactions among different entities within the common agricultural ecosystem. Its plays a critical role in managing interactions between stakeholders and services in a decentralized manner. This layer operates above the application layer and exhibits unique attributes that differentiate it from other layers, because it should take extra care and caution at this sensitive layer. BC and smart contracts play a key role in this layer. Moreover, the use of a hybrid BC, which combines private/consortium and public BC features, can create a hybrid IoT combining cloud-based and fog/edge computing, along with use of SOA-based modular architecture. This enables users and stakeholders to access highly customizable solutions with unmatched privacy, transparency, integrity and security, leveraging the strengths of both public and private/consortium BC configurations. It aims to harness the advantages of both private/consortium and public BC solutions, providing controlled access and freedom simultaneously. In simple terms, some processes remain private, while others are made public.

1.7. Trust, Privacy, and Security Capabilities

It's important to note that trust, privacy and security is a multi-layered and ongoing process. It should be integrated and considered across all layers of the IoT architecture for PA to establish a robust and secure system. Trust, privacy and security in IoT for PA is a critical aspect due to the potential impact of compromised systems or data breaches. the multi-layered assigned to the security can include all the security considerations and capabilities relevant to IoT for PA, such as IoT devices security, networks and data security, authentication and authorization, over-the-air updates, and cybersecurity, along with physical security which aims to protect physical access to critical components such as gateways, servers, and control systems to prevent unauthorized physical tampering or theft.

2. CHALLENGES OF BLOCKCHAIN-BASED IOT NETWORKS AND POTENTIAL SOLUTIONS

Building robust systems of BC-based IoT networks in PA faces several challenges that must be addressed for widespread adoption without any threats or dilemmas. Indeed, optimal automatic data management is one of the major challenges in BC-based IoT for PA, such as effectively managing and processing the vast amount of data generated by IoT devices can be complex. Furthermore, this section outlines additional main challenges, including heterogeneity, scalability and storage limitations, cost, and energy consumption constraints, along with a brief proposal of potential solutions.

2.1. Heterogeneity

The number of IoT end-devices, smart sensors, and embedded devices is increasing daily, with limited resources in terms of computing power, storage capacity, and energy consumption, which make the integration of BC technology in these devices impractical and inefficient. Integrating BC technology in the fog layer, which is closer to these devices, can be a more practical approach compared to integrating it directly into the IoT end-devices themselves. However, heterogeneity is an important issue that arises when deploying and advancing both BC and fog computing. The heterogeneity challenges in fog computing include variations in hardware and software development, operating systems, networking, and the use of various programming languages. Also, data generated from IoT end-devices have different formats, structures, and characteristics, along with the ever-increasing number of wireless communication technologies and IoT communication protocols, which require implementing middleware layers or gateway devices that can handle the translation and adaptation between end-devices and fog computing. BC technology is mostly focuses on addressing challenges related to trust, transparency, and decentralization rather than directly targeting heterogeneity-related issues. SOA provides a standardized and interoperable approach to encapsulating data, IoT services, and process execution, enabling communication that is immune to the heterogeneity of networked things in IoT services. By adopting SOA approach, the heterogeneity challenges can be mitigated. SOA promotes loose coupling between services, allowing them to be developed independently and communicate through standardized interfaces and protocols. This decouples the specific implementation details of each service from the overall IoT system, facilitating interoperability.

2.2. Data Offloading

Data offloading refers to the process of transferring data from one device or system to another, typically with the goal of reducing the workload or improving efficiency. In the context of integrating BC and IoT, data offloading refers to the practice of moving large amount of IoT-generated data from the local devices or sensors to a BC network, because processing and storing these data locally on the devices can be resource-intensive and inefficient. However, it's important to note that offloading all IoT data to the BC may not be feasible or efficient in every scenario due to factors such as scalability, latency and cost. In some cases, a hybrid approach where critical data or metadata is selectively offloaded to the BC, while less important data is processed locally in the fog/edge devices or in the private cloud might be more practical and more efficient, to meet any expressed or expected need for any PA scenarios.

2.3. Storage and Scalability Limitations

Scalability refers to the capability of BC-based IoT solutions to accommodate a growing number of IoT devices, users, and data traffic without a significant degradation in performance. IoT devices and objects in PA generates massive amounts of RT data that needs to be recorded and verified on the BC. However, the current BC infrastructure, besides its inherent characteristics, faces limitations in terms of transaction processing speed and capacity. These limitations make the scalability issues very difficult to address, and could potentially create bottlenecks mainly caused by BC consensus protocols, which may not be suitable for some agricultural scenarios. Also, maintaining multiple copies of the BC across nodes increases redundancy and the overall storage requirement, ensures data integrity and prevents a single point of failure. Storing large amounts of data directly on the BC itself can be inefficient, due to the block size limitations and the need to replicate data across all the nodes. Moreover, scaling BC to serve large amounts of data and transactions is a big technical challenge. Nowadays, addressing scalability challenges is an active and ongoing area of research and development, and several approaches are being explored to enhance scalability and make BC-based IoT more feasible at scale, such as hybrid architectures, use of distributed trust-based architectures, sharding and layer-2 solutions (e.g., Ethereum's Optimism, Arbitrum, Sidechains, etc), off-chain computations, consensus algorithm optimizations, along with the efficient and optimized data structures, such as Merkle trees, can be employed to reduce the size of transaction data stored on the BC, thus improving storage and bandwidth requirements. Besides, implementing data compression techniques or aggregating data before storing it on the BC can help reduce the overall storage requirements. Also, advancements in hardware, such as increased storage capabilities and faster processors especially those based on quantum computing, can potentially contribute to improved BC scalability. In particular, quantum computing has the potential to significantly impact BC technology. Quantum computers leverage quantum bits (qubits) to perform computations, which have the ability to process and manipulate vast amounts of information simultaneously. This computational power can potentially enable more efficient and faster execution of complex cryptographic algorithms, which are fundamental to BC security and consensus mechanisms. Improved processing power offered by quantum computing could enhance the efficiency of consensus algorithms. This could lead to faster block validation and transaction processing, thereby increasing the overall throughput and scalability of BC networks. However, the practical implementation and widespread adoption of quantum computing in the context of BC-based IoT technology still require further research, development, and careful consideration of security aspects.

2.4. Cost and Complexity Constraints

Implementing BC technology in IoT systems requires additional infrastructure with associated costs, such as network nodes, storage capacity, computational power, security measures, scalability solutions and interoperability frameworks or protocols, which leads to cost and complexity challenges. Virtualization and containerization technologies, along with the SOA approach, can help mitigate both cost and complexity challenges. Also, careful evaluation of the specific use case, requirements, and available resources is essential. It may involve selecting the appropriate BC platform, optimizing data storage and transmission, considering alternative consensus algorithms, and leveraging off-chain solutions where applicable. Balancing the benefits of BC technology with the associated costs and complexities is crucial for achieving successful and sustainable BC-based IoT implementations. Operating a BC network involves maintaining and managing the infrastructure required to support it. The associated costs of hardware, software, and ongoing maintenance can be significant, and specialized knowledge and expertise is required. BC networks often require transaction fees to incentivize network participants and prioritize transactions. For example, wheen using ethereum BC platform, which is highly recommended for various IoT applications including smart contracts and DApps, gas fees are incurred for executing transactions and smart contracts on the BC. In the context of IoT, where a large volume of transactions may occur, gas fees can accumulate quickly, and become a considerable cost factor. It's important to carefully consider the cost implications of executing transactions and optimize the usage of gas to minimize expenses. Also, the development of complex smart contracts, can provide powerful functionalities in SOA-enabled IoT systems. However, complex smart contracts may require more computational resources to execute, leading to higher gas fees. Balancing the functionality of smart contracts with their computational complexity is essential to manage costs effectively. Moreover, integrating ethereum BC with IoT and SOA architectures introduces additional complexity. Developing the necessary interfaces, protocols, and standards to enable communication between IoT devices, services, and the ethereum network requires careful consideration. It may involve implementing middleware layers, smart contract APIs, and utilizing existing frameworks and libraries like Web3.js or Ethers.js to interact with the Ethereum BC. The integration process should be well-planned to minimize complexity and ensure smooth interoperability.

2.5. Energy Consumption

The integration of BC and IoT also leads to energy consumption challenges, because BC networks require significant computational power and resources to validate transactions and maintain the network. To optimize the energy consumption of BC-based IoT systems, it should address potential solutions to the previous challenges, especially those focused on addressing complexity, storage and scalability limitations, along with performing computations at the edge of the network (e.g., NAS servers), which is closer to IoT devices, reduces the burden on resource-constrained devices and minimizes energy consumption. Also, developing lightweight consensus mechanisms tailored for IoT devices can minimize energy consumption while ensuring the required level of security and decentralization. Besides integrating renewable energy sources.

3. RECENT ADVANCEMENTS IN VIRTUALIZATION AND CONTAINERIZATION TECHNOLOGIES TO REVOLUTIONIZE COMPUTING AND SOFTWARE DEVELOPMENT

Virtualization technology aims to create and run multiple virtual instances or environments on a single physical machine or server. It enables the utilization of hardware resources more efficiently and allows for the isolation and management of software applications and operating systems. On the other hand, containers are a lightweight form of virtualization that provides isolated environments for running applications. Unlike traditional VMs, containers share the host operating system kernel, allowing them to be more resource-efficient and faster to start and stop. Each container encapsulates the application and its dependencies, creating a portable and consistent runtime environment. Containers have gained immense popularity due to their ability to streamline application deployment and management. Docker is a leading platform and toolset for building, packaging, and deploying DApps as containers. Today's, researchers call for using both docker and kubernetes together, because they serve different purposes and complement each other in managing containerized applications at scale. Docker allows developers to package their applications along with all the necessary dependencies into a single container image. These images can easily share and deploy on any machine that has docker installed. It provides a standardized way to create, distribute, and run containers across different operating systems and environments, ensuring that applications work consistently regardless of the underlying infrastructure. Kubernetes provides the tools for orchestrating and managing containers at scale, because there are some limitations and inconveniences when using docker alone:

- *Orchestration complexity:* Docker does not provide native built-in orchestration capabilities. For example, if you need to manage a cluster of docker hosts, handle scaling, load balancing, and high availability, you would need to rely on external tools like docker swarm or kubernetes;
- *Scalability and load balancing:* Docker swarm, the native orchestration tool for docker, offers basic scaling and load balancing features. However, it may not provide the same level of advanced scaling and load balancing options as kubernetes;
- *Service discovery and load balancing:* While docker swarm provides built-in load balancing, it may not offer the same level of flexibility and advanced features as kubernetes for service discovery and load balancing across multiple clusters or hybrid environments;
- *Limited advanced deployment features:* Docker lacks some advanced deployment features provided by kubernetes, such as canary deployments, blue-green deployments, and advanced rollout strategies. These features are essential for managing complex deployment scenarios and implementing advanced release strategies;

In summary, while docker is excellent for containerization and getting started with container-based applications, it may lack some advanced orchestration and deployment features provided by kubernetes. Kubernetes offers powerful container orchestration capabilities with a more comprehensive solution for managing containerized applications at scale. Indeed, virtualization and containerization technologies offer several benefits for deploying the IoT that will aim to have a real impact on the real world. Quality Network Appliance Provider (QNAP) has redesigned its NAS for IoT. Complete QNAP IoT (QIoT) virtualization are now available for the QNAP virtualization station platform. Virtualization station is a powerful hypervisor integrated into QNAP appliances, enables the creation of a cost-efficient virtualization environment. It supports many operating systems such as Linux, Windows, and QuTScloud. Depending on available system resources, it allows the configuration and operation of multiple virtual machines. It also supports acceleration functions and many resource management, providing an affordable virtualization platform with superb performance. Also, complete QIoT containers are now available for the QNAP container station platform. QNAP container station exclusively integrates Linux Containers (LXC) and Docker lightweight virtualization technologies. Container station provides an ideal platform with countless ready-to-use containerized applications that enable developers to apply, develop and deploy IoT applications quickly. Figure 2 depicts the NAS QNAP based hybrid approach of docker containers and VMs, which is the most suitable for IoT applications.

Figure 2. NAS QNAP-based hybrid approach of docker containers and VMs

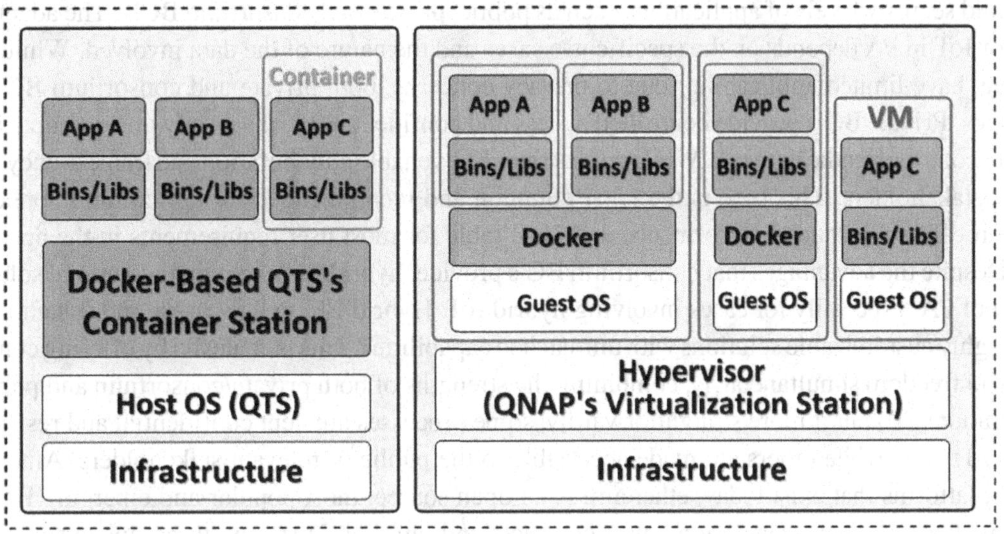

The rapid advances in the IoT and network softwarization have caused the physical network infrastructure to become very complicated to achieve dynamic and flexible solutions for management, distributing software, configuration, and flow scheduling. It shows the necessity to migrate some or all of their network services to a virtualized network infrastructure to enable the next-generation networks with more flexibility, more scalability, reduced resource usage and network operational capital and costs. Virtualized network infrastructure refers to the concept of decoupling network services from the underlying physical infrastructure and implementing them in a virtualized environment. This enables the creation of Peer-to-Peer or hybrid Software-Defined Networking (SDN) and Network Function Virtualization (NFV). In virtualized network infrastructures, Network Functions (NFs) such as firewalls, content filters, traffic load balancers, deep packet detector and intrusion detection systems can be either instantiated on VMs or lightweight containers. Today, it is highly recommended to chain these NFs together to create SFC, which is considered one of the important use cases of NFV and SDN architectures (H. U. Adoga et al., 2022). The major goal of SFC is the flexibility that comes from its adaptation to any type of traffic to traverse diverse network functions along the service chain.

Overall, recent advancements in virtualization and containerization have transformed the way software is developed, deployed, and managed. These technologies offer tremendous benefits, including improved resource utilization, enhanced scalability, portability, faster application deployment, and simplified infrastructure management. As organizations continue to embrace virtualization and containerization, we can expect further innovations and refinements that will shape the future of software development and Information Technology (IT) operations.

4. SOA-BASED HYBRID DESIGN PATTERN: PROPOSED MODEL

BC systems have gained significant attention and popularity in distributed database solutions for the IoT (C. Núñez-Gómez et al., 2021). Three types of BC systems are commonly classified based on the accessibility and security levels of applications such as public, private and consortium BC's. The adaptability of BC for IoT in PA depends on the specific use cases and the nature of the data involved. While public BC's may have limited applicability due to privacy concerns, both private and consortium BC's offer advantages. Private BC's provide controlled access and confidentiality where only one organization has complete control over the network. While consortium BC's enable collaboration and transparency among multiple stakeholders. This type is the most common and recommended for agricultural applications because it offers a balanced performance and is suitable for most user requirements in the agriculture sector. Despite the advantages that consortium BC's provide, hybrid BC's remain the optimal solution in the field of PA, especially for cases involving hybrid IoT. Hybrid BC's allow users and stakeholders to access highly customizable solutions with unmatched capabilities. This is achieved by offering controlled access and freedom simultaneously, combining the strengths of both private/consortium and public BC configurations. To put it more straightforwardly, some processes are kept confidential and restricted to authorized users, while others are made accessible to the public or relevant stakeholders. Among several BC platforms that exist today, ethereum is an open source, most popular and emerging BC based platforms, featuring next-generation smart contracts and building DApps with complete security and availability. Ethereum provides a robust infrastructure for building IoT applications and implementing smart contracts in PA. Its software is built on top of the Ethereum virtual machine (EVM). The EVM serves as a runtime environment for executing smart contracts, which is widely recommended to be written using Solidity programming language (Dannen, 2017). Each smart contract should be compiled into EVM bytecode, a low-level representation of the contract's instructions that can be executed by the EVM. The EVM is responsible for interpreting and executing this bytecode on each ethereum node. The EVM ensures that the execution of smart contracts is deterministic, meaning that it will produce the same results for the same inputs, regardless of the node executing the contract. This consistency is crucial for maintaining the integrity of the BC and enabling trustless interactions. Moreover, BC plays a major role in performing direct or indirect connections between IoT devices. Integrating BC into IoT communications requires identifying the design pattern in which the communication occurs. We have generally proposed one fundamental design pattern as illustrated in Figure 3, to overcome all the expressed needs in BC-based IoT for PA.

Fog computing is a promising approach in IoT. It complements the traditional cloud-based approach, providing a distributed architecture that can handle the increasing demands of interconnected IoT devices. Moreover, implementing BC with Fog computing infrastructure can create a secure and efficient system with reduced latency and real-time processing at the network edge. The data will remain available and resistant to network failures, attacks, unavailable situations and disconnections. It makes it possible to process and analyze data closer to the source, where the endpoints of IoT devices are talking to each other with more reliable interdependence, and processing more data locally in the farms. Fog devices can continue to function and process data even when the network connection to the cloud is disrupted. This offline capability is more valuable in agricultural scenarios where a continuous connection to the cloud cannot be guaranteed, such as remote farms locations or areas with intermittent connectivity. Also, Fog devices can collaborate and share the computational burden, making it easier to scale IoT systems. Furthermore, the integration of Fog and Cloud computing with AI and hybrid BC, results in the development of the SOA-based hybrid design pattern, which can enhance the scalability and efficiency of IoT systems in PA.

BC technology is not designed to store large files efficiently due to inherent limitations in terms of cost-effectiveness, performance and scalability. These limitations make it impractical for many real-world applications. Instead, BC technology serves as a secure and immutable ledger for various purposes, including data transactions, identity and authentication, data integrity, supply chain management, access control, and network and communication management through the use of smart contracts. These contracts can automatically manage network traffic and trigger actions based on predefined conditions. Once they are compiled and deployed on the BC network, they cannot be altered or deleted without the consent of the network participants, making them a reliable source of truth. However, these contracts cannot interact securely with real-world data or external data sources (e.g., web APIs, databases, websites, etc.). This limitation arises from the fact that BC platforms, on which smart contracts are executed, prioritize security, determinism, and immutability. They operate in a closed environment where they can only access data and perform computations on the BC itself. This limitation can be a significant roadblock for applications that require a connection between BC and the external world.

To overcome this limitation, a holistic approach that combines the strengths of hybrid BC with off-chain solutions and other technologies is crucial. In this approach, the Fog nodes act as intermediaries between the BC network and the real-world data sources, enabling secure data ingestion and interaction. Moreover, the entire dataset should be stored off-chain in a network of distributed nodes, whether in the Fog or Cloud. The data should be stored in an encrypted and redundant manner, and the choice of storage location depends on the availability of the Internet and the chosen strategy. Only critical metadata and references are stored on the BC to maintain data integrity and tamper-proof records. This metadata can include information about the data, such as timestamps, data sources, owner and access permissions, as well as supply chain information, land ownership, equipment usage, smart contract logic code, and other critical data, ensuring transparency and trust. The entire dataset can include high-resolution images, drone footage, satellite imagery, and other large data files generated in PA, as well as real-time sensor data, weather information, market prices, and other external data that can be retrieved via APIs and stored off-chain. Smart contracts can interact with external APIs to access this data when needed, and they are employed to manage and enforce access controls, permissions, track data usage, data sharing agreements, and data interactions. Instead of storing the entire dataset on the BC, this technology is employed for data anchoring. This involves storing references to the off-chain dataset, such as keys and cryptographic hashes, on the BC. These hashes act as proofs of data integrity and can be used to verify the authenticity of the data stored off-chain, while avoiding the bloat of the BC itself. This strategy allows users to verify the authenticity and integrity of the data without overwhelming the BC's storage capacity. Additionally, it is essential to encrypt sensitive data before storing it off-chain and provide decryption keys or access permissions through the BC's smart contracts. This way, only authorized users can access the decrypted data.

Overall, this design ensures that all IoT communications are traceable and immutable as defined in BC, creating an auditable and tamper-resistant history of events related to the entire dataset. This transparency and immutability can be valuable in scenarios where data integrity and accountability are critical. It enhances the independence of IoT nodes by allowing each device to interact directly with BC. This design pattern is effective when transactions occur between a variety of IoT devices in different farms to achieve a common management of agricultural systems or scenarios. As a result, a robust data management strategy is needed to ensure that only necessary and unchangeable data is stored in the BC. BC network can be composed of various types of nodes, including physical nodes, virtual nodes and container nodes, which work together to maintain the network's integrity, validate transactions and reach consensus. The combination of these nodes offers flexibility, scalability and resilience to the BC network infrastructure. Moreover, with the help of using node.js technology, a web server can be implemented to enable users to define their individualized requirements and allow managers to efficiently manage the operation and configuration of the entire system. Ethers.js is a popular JavaScript library aims to be a complete, compact and powerful library for interacting with the ethereum smart contracts, BC and its ecosystem, which enables developers to build DApps.

On the other hand, SOA is an architectural style that promotes the creation of modular and reusable services. It emphasizes the separation of concerns and the encapsulation of functionality into distinct services that can be invoked by other components or clients. To implement BC-based SOA encapsulation, it must design smart contract functions as individual services, encapsulating their logic and exposing them as API endpoints. It's possible to create a server-side application that uses ethers.js to interact with the smart contracts and exposes these services to clients. Then, implement a service repository to store and manage information about available services. This will enable clients to discover and interact with these services effectively. Cloud services is used in this design pattern to host APIs, repository services and other required components. The optimal approach for designing the final application through this design pattern is to use both microservices and SOA approaches, as it is highly advised by (Raj & Sadam, 2021). Despite the higher complexity of microservices, their response time for processing the requests is very fast compared to the SOA services. Hence, flexible product services presenting individualized solutions in PA can be provided. In this design pattern, the data needs to be processed and manipulated on the Fog devices and eliminating the necessity of transmitting it back to the cloud. The inclusion of AI will become a key player in this proposed model. It will help IoT devices to perform tasks locally in the farm. BC can be leveraged in this design to provide trust, security and reliability as missed links in the hybrid IoT network where Fog computing approach plays a major role. In contrast, Fog computing can remedy the limitations of BC and IoT regarding computing power, energy consumption, bandwidth and latency. Figure 3 explains the proposed model, which integrates BC, IoT, Fog and Cloud computing into a coherent design pattern. This figure illustrates how BC can function as a data repository and transactions monitor and verifier for different heterogeneous fog networks that are managed remotely by a Cloud. The strength of the hybrid design pattern here is that BC is not only intended for data anchoring and verifying data from different IoT devices, but also extends the functionality to include data anchoring and verification from different complex and heterogeneous fog and cloud networks. This approach provides a strong foundation for designing and implementing secure, efficient, scalable and hybrid IoT solutions in PA. It highlights the synergy between BC, Fog computing, Cloud computing, and AI, offering a holistic solution for the complex requirements of this field.

Figure 3. SOA-based hybrid design pattern: Proposed model

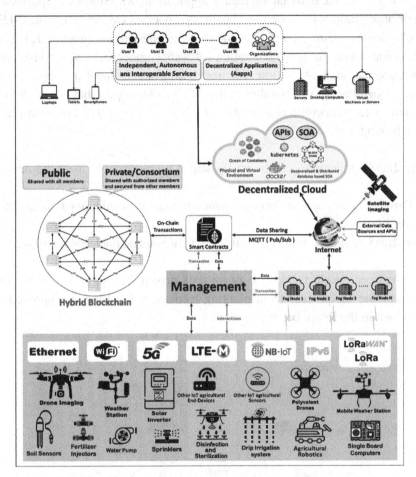

5. IOT SYSTEMS AND APPLICATIONS FOR PRECISION IRRIGATION IN AGRICULTURE

The development of IoT-based application platforms should possess the flexibility to adapt to diverse crops, climates and countries. And some examples of projects and frameworks such as the SWAMP project (C. Kamienski et al., 2018; C. Kamienski et al., 2019), IoT methods are being devised to facilitate smart water management in precision irrigation, with pilot deployments in Italy, Spain, and Brazil. An essential element in enabling the Agriculture Internet of Things is the Wireless Sensor Network (WSN), the Agri-IoT project (S. K. Sah Tyagi et al., 2021) establishes a robust framework by connecting numerous sensor nodes or devices to ensure efficient and seamless communication with improved throughput for intelligent networking. Accomplishing this enhancement requires a smart ML-based resource allocation approach. As the number of deployed devices surges in smart applications such as intelligent irrigation, and smart crop monitoring. The FIGARO (Flexible and Precision Irrigation Platform to Improve Farm Scale Water Productivity) project's (L. Doron et al., 2017) enhance water productivity and improve irrigation practices through a precision irrigation management platform.

IT faces a growing challenge in replacing legacy applications with innovative public cloud solutions that can help their organizations improve their business processes (M. Seifert et al., 2023). Combining IoT and cloud technologies can improve integration between physical resources and cloud services. Software as a service is appropriate for third-generation software engineering and is considered a package of development, execution automation, runtime resource sharing management, and security (Vidhyalakshmi & Kumar, 2014). Recognizes the vast number of irrigation technologies that can be delivered as remote access services, our system 2IaaS offers a number of advantages over traditional on-premises software solutions, these advantages include:

- *Scalability:* 2IaaS applications can be easily scaled up or down to meet the needs of a growing business.
- *Cost-effectiveness:* 2IaaS applications are typically more cost-effective than traditional on-premises software solutions.
- *Ease of use:* 2IaaS applications are typically easy to use and do not require any specialized training.

2IaaS system services enable farmers to make data-driven decisions, optimize their agricultural practices, and streamline the process from planting to market, resulting in improved efficiency and profitability, as shown in the figure below:

Figure 4. 2IaaS services circular flow

- *Data Collection:* Collect data from various sources like sensors, drones, satellites, and weather stations to monitor crop growth and health, dynamic crop water uptake, soil conditions, weather patterns and spatial variability ;
- *Data Analytics*: Analyze the collected data to gain valuable insights and trends that inform decision-making ;
- *Precision Agriculture:* Utilize data insights to provide personalized recommendations for optimized resource allocation, irrigation, and crop management ;
- *Management Software*: Integrate precision agriculture recommendations into a farm management platform to plan and schedule daily tasks efficiently ;
- *Market Access:* Share crop data and quality information to connect farmers with buyers, enabling transparent transactions and better market access.
- *Supply Chain:* Organize logistics and distribution based on sales data, ensuring timely delivery and reduced wastage.

6. FUTURE RESEARCH DIRECTIONS

Over the past few years, limited progress has been made in addressing some challenges systematically. However, the majority of the research issues remain open and necessitate the implementation of efficient problem-solving strategies. In the following sections, we will explore future opportunities in BC-based IoT, as well as the shortcomings that require attention in future research, and how these impact the PA sector in the long term.

6.1. Dynamic and Agile Pricing Models

The design of a dynamic and agile pricing models based on BC and IoT technologies can address evolving expectations in PA, by finding a balanced agreement between the client's expectations of service cost, service quality, operational performance, and service provider's cost. However, developing dynamic and adaptable pricing models presents a major challenge in BC-based IoT systems, as a single pricing model may not be suitable to accommodate the diverse interactions and requirements of farmers and clients. The pricing model variation arises due to the increasing number of proposed IoT architectural models that have not yet converged to the common-unified reference model specific to PA, along with the lack of proper domain expertise, which invoke various migrations in the IoT ecosystem. The field of PA encompasses a wide range of applications and use cases, and there is ongoing research and development in proposing different IoT architectural models to address these specific needs. As a result, there is a lack of convergence towards a standardized reference model that can serve as a foundation for developing a single pricing model. It is important to note that without optimized, standard and unified BC-based IoT architecture reference model in PA, there are only a few-limited number of standard dynamic pricing model techniques exist to tackle the challenges depending on dynamic and agile pricing models, which is often impractical or inefficient. This, in turn, affects the long-term cost-effectiveness and sustainability of precision agriculture.

6.2. Distributed Machine Learning and Distributed Deep Learning

AI has developed rapidly in recent years, enabling more intelligent, sophisticated and more automated systems and applications in PA. It has achieved significant success in effectively managing complex tasks by utilizing protocols, inferences, and decision-making processes that surpass human comprehension. This success is due to large advancements in ML algorithms and hardware optimizations. ML is a subset of AI, involves the creation of techniques and algorithms that can think, act and execute tasks based on the learned knowledge and patterns extracted from historical and RT data, without being explicitly programmed. To achieve accurate predictions, solve more complex problems and take precise actions in PA, algorithms should be trained with vast amounts of data, which require a great deal of computation and could be time consuming to process. This solution could be achieved by Distributed Machine Learning (DML), also known as the distribution of data and algorithms across multiple machines or computing resources to train a ML model or process large-scale data. The distributed nature allows for parallel processing and can potentially speed up the learning process or handle larger datasets. Today, considerable efforts have been devoted to the development DML algorithms, resulting in the proposal of various methods so far. A wide range of ML algorithms can be employed to analyze data and construct data-driven systems, including clustering and classification, DL and deep reinforcement learning, and more. Classification and clustering algorithms are traditional ML methods, and some studies have been made to develop distributed versions of these algorithms, such as distribution of boosting, consensus-based algorithms, K-means algorithms, and many others. However, DL is a subfield of ML that focuses on training artificial neural networks with multiple layers to learn and extract features from data. Furthermore, distributed DL techniques and algorithms are gaining more attention in recent studies for PA, specifically in tasks involving decision-making, resource optimization, and autonomous farming systems. Distributed DL models offer promising opportunities for BC-based IoT systems in PA, allowing farmers to make optimal data-driven decisions. They have been applied to tasks such as autonomous robotic farming, crop management, and irrigation scheduling. On the other hand, traditional DML approaches have received less focus in recent studies, despite their advantageous characteristics and promising results in PA. Deep neural networks exhibit excellent performance, particularly in the IoT distributed systems. Nevertheless, they can pose significant challenges. The interpretability of a model can play a crucial role in providing insights into the relationship between input data and the trained model, which is particularly useful in some PA scenarios. However, achieving interpretability in distributed algorithms remains an open and ongoing challenge. Furthermore, novel challenges emerge when attempting to implement distributed algorithms, encompassing aspects such as the partitioning of data and models, scalability, delay of the slowest nodes, optimality, communication overhead, and aggregation of results. This is already an ongoing line of research that will need to be addressed in the future. Thereby enabling more automation in smart systems and applications, and enhancing decision-making capabilities with more intelligence, specifically in PA.

6.3. Dynamic QoS Requirements

Dynamic QoS requirements in a BC-based IoT system for PA refers to the specific QoS needs that can vary and adapt based on the ability of a system to adapt its QoS parameters in RT to dynamically allocate and manage resources and services based on changing requirements and conditions. It involves optimizing the performance, reliability, and efficiency of the IoT network and applications to meet the specific needs of PA. PA environments are very dynamic, with varying requirements for different tasks and scenarios. Adapting the QoS parameters can be used to tackle complex and dynamic problems in IoT systems. However, dynamic QoS requirements is challenging for heuristic or approximate methods to forecast the QoS needs dynamically for any IoT application. Although the majority of distributed platforms employ static QoS limitations for next-generation IoT applications, the dynamic nature and instability of developing computing devices, like cloud servers and fog nodes, render the traditional static QoS requirement approach unsuitable. To address these challenges, more sophisticated approaches, such as ML models, data-driven analytics, adaptive routing algorithms, dynamic resource allocation, QoS-aware smart contracts, and fog/edge computing can be employed. These methods can leverage historical data, RT monitoring and predictive analytics to better capture the dynamic nature of QoS requirements in IoT applications. By continuously learning and adapting, these approaches can provide more accurate forecasts and improve QoS provisioning in dynamic IoT environments. Moreover, by combining the SOA approach with dynamic QoS requirements, organizations can build flexible and responsive software systems that can adapt to changing conditions and ensure that the desired quality of service levels are maintained. These solutions aim to improve the long-term performance, reliability, and efficiency of IoT systems in precision agriculture, allowing them to adapt and ensure desired quality of service levels as conditions change.

6.4. Integrating Quantum Computing, Blockchain, and IoT

It's important to note that integrating quantum computing into BC-based IoT systems is still an ongoing area of research and development. As quantum computers are expected to become more powerful in the coming years, which poses a threat to the security of existing cryptographic systems. Quantum computing has the potential to revolutionize various fields in BC and IoT technologies, including cryptography and computational efficiency. By integrating quantum computing capabilities, BC-based IoT systems can prepare themselves for the era of quantum computing. This future-proofs the systems and ensures that they remain secure even as quantum computing technologies advance. Quantum computing can potentially break traditional cryptographic algorithms that are currently used in BC and IoT systems. By integrating quantum computing, we can develop and implement quantum-resistant cryptographic algorithms to ensure long-term security against attacks from quantum computers. This integration strengthens the overall security of the IoT ecosystem and protects sensitive data exchanged within BC networks. Also, quantum computing has the potential to optimize the computational aspects of BC networks, improving scalability and efficiency. Quantum algorithms can address complex computations required for consensus mechanisms, transaction verification, and data analysis within the BC. By leveraging quantum computing power, BC-based IoT systems can handle larger volumes of data, process transactions more quickly, and enhance overall system efficiency. In the long term, the integration of quantum computing into BC-based IoT systems will ensures the PA sector's data security, scalability, and system efficiency, which are vital for sustainable precision agriculture.

CONCLUSION

This chapter aims to explore the importance of integrating blockchain and IoT technologies using the SOA approach, and examines the major benefits derived from virtualization and containerization technologies when developing applications and smart systems in precision agriculture. The integration of blockchain technology has shown that it can introduce innovative solutions to tackle long-standing security and performance issues in precision agricultural systems based on the IoT.

In this chapter, we have performed a confident study of blockchain-based IoT with a specific emphasis on the SOA-based IoT architecture, which conforms the actual IoT environment for precision agriculture. This architectural design makes it possible to benefit from blockchain, IoT, microservices and SOA, AI, fog and cloud computing, while remaining adaptable to software or hardware evolutions at the level of each part of the IoT systems. The study aims to explore the challenges and potential solutions, requirements and benefits of implementing blockchain and SOA in IoT for precision agriculture. It presents significant originality in the field of precision agriculture and emerging technologies, while the authors have made an original contribution to research. The proposed architectural models represent valuable contributions that meet the current needs of the agricultural sector. Moreover, the study references several previous works in the field of precision agriculture, IoT and blockchain. Also, existing IoT systems for precision irrigation are briefly explained, along with an illustrative description of the Intelligent Irrigation as a Service system.

Future works will address practical implementations and intelligent optimization issues related to digital solutions for precision agriculture management, specifically focusing on optimal automatic management for precision irrigation in mechanized farms. Hence, future works can contribute to sustainable farming practices, reduce environmental impacts and the waste of resources, the viability of agricultural systems and promote long-term ecological resilience.

REFERENCES

Abd El Baki, H. M., Fujimaki, H., Tokumoto, I., & Saito, T. (2018). A new scheme to optimize irrigation depth using a numerical model of crop response to irrigation and quantitative weather forecasts. *Computers and Electronics in Agriculture*, *150*, 387–393. doi:10.1016/j.compag.2018.05.016

Abioye, E. A., Abidin, M. S. Z., Mahmud, M. S. A., Buyamin, S., Ishak, M. H. I., Rahman, M. K. I. A., Otuoze, A. O., Onotu, P., & Ramli, M. S. A. (2020). A review on monitoring and advanced control strategies for precision irrigation. *Computers and Electronics in Agriculture*, *173*, 105441. doi:10.1016/j.compag.2020.105441

Abioye, E. A., Hensel, O., Esau, T. J., Elijah, O., Abidin, M. S. Z., Ayobami, A. S., Yerima, O., & Nasirahmadi, A. (2022). Precision Irrigation Management Using Machine Learning and Digital Farming Solutions. *AgriEngineering*, *4*(1), 70–103. doi:10.3390/agriengineering4010006

Adoga, H. U., & Pezaros, D. P. (2022). Network Function Virtualization and Service Function Chaining Frameworks: A Comprehensive Review of Requirements, Objectives, Implementations, and Open Research Challenges. *Future Internet*, *14*(2), 59. doi:10.3390/fi14020059

Ahmed, N., De, D., & Hussain, I. (2018). Internet of Things (IoT) for Smart Precision Agriculture and Farming in Rural Areas. *IEEE Internet of Things Journal*, *5*(6), 4890–4899. doi:10.1109/JIOT.2018.2879579

Akhter, R., & Sofi, S. (2022). Precision agriculture using IoT data analytics and machine learning. *Journal of King Saud University. Computer and Information Sciences*, *34*(8), 5602–5618. doi:10.1016/j.jksuci.2021.05.013

Bwambale, E., Abagale, F. K., & Anornu, G. K. (2023). Data-driven model predictive control for precision irrigation management. *Smart Agricultural Technology*, *3*, 100074. doi:10.1016/j.atech.2022.100074

Car, N. J. (2018). USING decision models to enable better irrigation Decision Support Systems. *Computers and Electronics in Agriculture*, *152*, 290–301. doi:10.1016/j.compag.2018.07.024

Dannen, C. (2017). Introducing ethereum and solidity: Foundations of cryptocurrency and blockchain programming for beginners. *Apress Media*. Advance online publication. doi:10.1007/978-1-4842-2535-6/COVER

Doron, L. (2017). Flexible and Precise Irrigation Platform to Improve Farm Scale Water Productivity. *Impact*, *2017*(1), 77–79. doi:10.21820/23987073.2017.1.77

Dorri, A. (2017). Towards an optimized blockchain for IoT. *Proceedings - 2017 IEEE/ACM 2nd International Conference on Internet-of-Things Design and Implementation*, *6*, 173–178. 10.1145/3054977.3055003

Feng, X., Yan, F., & Liu, X. (2019). Study of Wireless Communication Technologies on Internet of Things for Precision Agriculture. *Wireless Personal Communications*, *108*(3), 1785–1802. doi:10.1007/s11277-019-06496-7

Fernández-Caramés, T. M., & Fraga-Lamas, P. (2018). A review on the use of blockchain for the Internet of Things. *IEEE Access : Practical Innovations, Open Solutions*, *6*, 32979–33001. doi:10.1109/ACCESS.2018.2842685

Guardo, E. (2018). A Fog Computing-based IoT Framework for Precision Agriculture. *Journal of Internet Technology*, *19*(5), 1401–1411. doi:10.3966/160792642018091905012

Guven, I., & Parlak, M. (2022). Blockchain, AI and IoT Empowered Swarm Drones for Precision Agriculture Applications. *IEEE 1st Global Emerging Technology Blockchain Forum: Blockchain & Beyond (iGETblockchain)*, 1-6. 10.1109/iGETblockchain56591.2022.10087152

Hafian, A., Benbrahim, M., & Kabbaj, M. N. (2021). Design and Implementation of Smart Irrigation System Based on the IoT Architecture. *Lecture Notes in Networks and Systems*, *211*, 345–354. doi:10.1007/978-3-030-73882-2_32

Hafian, A., Benbrahim, M., & Kabbaj, M. N. (2023). IoT-based smart irrigation management system using real-time data. *Iranian Journal of Electrical and Computer Engineering*, *13*(6), 7078–7088. doi:10.11591/ijece.v13i6.pp7078-7088

Hashemy Shahdany, S. M., Taghvaeian, S., Maestre, J. M., & Firoozfar, A. R. (2019). Developing a centralized automatic control system to increase flexibility of water delivery within predictable and unpredictable irrigation water demands. *Computers and Electronics in Agriculture*, *163*, 104862. doi:10.1016/j.compag.2019.104862

Hazraet, A. (2023). Fog computing for next-generation Internet of Things: Fundamental, state-of-the-art and research challenges. *Computer Science Review*, *48*, 100549. doi:10.1016/j.cosrev.2023.100549

Jalajamony, H. M., Nair, M., Jones-Whitehead, M., Abbas, M. I., Harris, N., & Fernandez, R. E. (2023). Aerial to Terrestrial Edge Communication Using LoRa in Drone-Aided Precision Agriculture. *Southeast-Con*, *722–723*, 722–723. Advance online publication. doi:10.1109/SoutheastCon51012.2023.10115215

Jamil, F., Ibrahim, M., Ullah, I., Kim, S., Kahng, H. K., & Kim, D.-H. (2022). Optimal smart contract for autonomous greenhouse environment based on IoT blockchain network in agriculture. *Computers and Electronics in Agriculture*, *192*, 106573. doi:10.1016/j.compag.2021.106573

Jha, K., Doshi, A., Patel, P., & Shah, M. (2019). A comprehensive review on automation in agriculture using artificial intelligence. *Artificial Intelligence in Agriculture*, *2*, 1–12. doi:10.1016/j.aiia.2019.05.004

Jihani, N., Kabbaj, M. N., & Benbrahim, M. (2023). Sensor fault detection and isolation for smart irrigation wireless sensor network based on parity space. *Iranian Journal of Electrical and Computer Engineering*, *13*(2), 1463–1471. doi:10.11591/ijece.v13i2.pp1463-1471

Kamienski. (2018). SWAMP: An IoT-based smart water management platform for precision irrigation in agriculture. *Global IoT Summit (GIoTS)*. doi:10.1109/GIOTS.2018.8534541

Kamienski, C., Soininen, J.-P., Taumberger, M., Dantas, R., Toscano, A., Salmon Cinotti, T., Filev Maia, R., & Torre Neto, A. (2019). Smart Water Management Platform: IoT-Based Precision Irrigation for Agriculture. *Sensors (Basel)*, *19*(2), 276. doi:10.3390/s19020276 PMID:30641960

Khanal, S., Fulton, J., & Shearer, S. (2017). An overview of current and potential applications of thermal remote sensing in precision agriculture. *Computers and Electronics in Agriculture*, *139*, 22–32. doi:10.1016/j.compag.2017.05.001

Khanna, A., & Kaur, S. (2019). Evolution of Internet of Things (IoT) and its significant impact in the field of Precision Agriculture. *Computers and Electronics in Agriculture*, *157*, 218–231. doi:10.1016/j.compag.2018.12.039

Kochovski, P., Gec, S., Stankovski, V., Bajec, M., & Drobintsev, P. D. (2019). Trust management in a blockchain based fog computing platform with trustless smart oracles. *Future Generation Computer Systems*, *101*, 747–759. doi:10.1016/j.future.2019.07.030

Lin, N., Wang, X., Zhang, Y., Hu, X., & Ruan, J. (2020). Fertigation management for sustainable precision agriculture based on Internet of Things. *Journal of Cleaner Production*, *277*, 124119. doi:10.1016/j.jclepro.2020.124119

Lin, W., Huang, X., Fang, H., Wang, V., Hua, Y., Wang, J., Yin, H., Yi, D., & Yau, L. (2020). Blockchain Technology in Current Agricultural Systems: From Techniques to Applications. *IEEE Access : Practical Innovations, Open Solutions*, *8*, 143920–143937. doi:10.1109/ACCESS.2020.3014522

Lin, Y.-P., Petway, J., Anthony, J., Mukhtar, H., Liao, S.-W., Chou, C.-F., & Ho, Y.-F. (2017). Blockchain: The evolutionary next step for ICT e-agriculture. *Environments (Basel, Switzerland)*, *4*(3), 2076–3298. doi:10.3390/environments4030050

Manoj, T., Krishnamoorthi, M., & Narendra, V. (2023). A trusted IoT data sharing and secure oracle based access for agricultural production risk management. *Computers and Electronics in Agriculture*, *204*, 107544. doi:10.1016/j.compag.2022.107544

Mogili, U., & Deepak, V. (2018). Review on Application of Drone Systems in Precision Agriculture. *Procedia Computer Science, 133*, 502–509. doi:10.1016/j.procs.2018.07.063

Núñez-Gómez, C., Caminero, B., & Carrion, C. (2021). HIDRA: A Distributed Blockchain-Based Architecture for Fog/Edge Computing Environments. *IEEE Access: Practical Innovations, Open Solutions, 9*, 75231–75251. doi:10.1109/ACCESS.2021.3082197

Núñez-Gómez, C., Carrión, C., Caminero, B., & Delicado, F. M. (2023). S-HIDRA: A blockchain and SDN domain-based architecture to orchestrate fog computing environments. *Computer Networks, 221*, 109512. doi:10.1016/j.comnet.2022.109512

Pincheira, M., Vecchio, M., Giaffreda, R., & Kanhere, S. S. (2021). Cost-effective IoT devices as trustworthy data sources for a blockchain-based water management system in precision agriculture. *Computers and Electronics in Agriculture, 180*, 105889. doi:10.1016/j.compag.2020.105889

Pranto, T. H., Noman, A. A., Mahmud, A., & Haque, A. K. M. B. (2021). Blockchain and smart contract for IoT enabled smart agriculture. *PeerJ. Computer Science, 7*, 1–29. doi:10.7717/peerj-cs.407 PMID:33834098

Puri, V., Nayyar, A., & Raja, L. (2017). Agriculture drones: A modern breakthrough in precision agriculture. *Journal of Statistics and Management Systems, 20*(4), 507–518. doi:10.1080/09720510.2017.1395171

Quy, V. K., Hau, N. V., Anh, D. V., Quy, N. M., Ban, N. T., Lanza, S., Randazzo, G., & Muzirafuti, A. (2022). IoT-Enabled Smart Agriculture: Architecture, Applications, and Challenges. *Applied Sciences (Basel, Switzerland), 7*(7), 3396. doi:10.3390/app12073396

Raj, V., & Sadam, R. (2021). Performance and complexity comparison of service oriented architecture and microservices architecture. *International Journal of Communication Networks and Distributed Systems, 27*(1), 100–117. doi:10.1504/IJCNDS.2021.116463

Ray, R. L., & ... . (2022). The Role of Remote Sensing Data and Methods in a Modern Approach to Fertilization in Precision Agriculture. *Remote Sensing (Basel), 14*(3), 778. doi:10.3390/rs14030778

Reyna, A., Martín, C., Chen, J., Soler, E., & Díaz, M. (2018). On blockchain and its integration with IoT. Challenges and opportunities. *Future Generation Computer Systems, 88*, 173–190. doi:10.1016/j.future.2018.05.046

Ribeiro, F. M. (2021). Data resilience system for fog computing. *Computer Networks, 195*, 108218. doi:10.1016/j.comnet.2021.108218

Sah Tyagi, S. K., Mukherjee, A., Pokhrel, S. R., & Hiran, K. K. (2021). An Intelligent and Optimal Resource Allocation Approach in Sensor Networks for Smart Agri-IoT. *IEEE Sensors Journal, 21*(16), 17439–17446. doi:10.1109/JSEN.2020.3020889

Sakthi. (2023). Blockchain-Enabled Precision Agricultural System Using IoT and Edge Computing. *Smart Trends in Computing and Communications*, 397–405. doi:10.1007/978-981-99-0769-4_35

San Emeterio de la Parte, M., Martínez-Ortega, J.-F., Hernández Díaz, V., & Martínez, N. L. (2023). Big Data and precision agriculture: A novel spatio-temporal semantic IoT data management framework for improved interoperability. *Journal of Big Data*, *10*(1), 1–32. doi:10.1186/s40537-023-00729-0 PMID:36618886

Seifert, M., Kuehnel, S., & Sackmann, S. (2023). Hybrid Clouds Arising from Software as a Service Adoption: Challenges, Solutions, and Future Research Directions. *ACM Computing Surveys*, *55*(11), 1–35. doi:10.1145/3570156

Shyamala Devi, M., Suguna, R., Joshi, A. S., & Bagate, R. A. (2019). Design of IoT Blockchain Based Smart Agriculture for Enlightening Safety and Security. *Communications in Computer and Information Science*, *985*, 7–19. doi:10.1007/978-981-13-8300-7_2

Singh, P., & Sharma, A. (2022). An intelligent WSN-UAV-based IoT framework for precision agriculture application. *Computers & Electrical Engineering*, *100*, 107912. doi:10.1016/j.compeleceng.2022.107912

Sultan, M. (2023). UAV-Based Wireless Data Collection from Underground Sensor Nodes for Precision Agriculture. *AgriEngineering*, *5*(1), 338–354. doi:10.3390/agriengineering5010022

Tanwar, R., Chhabra, Y., Rattan, P., & Rani, S. (2023). Blockchain in IoT Networks for Precision Agriculture. *Lecture Notes in Networks and Systems*, *471*, 137–147. doi:10.1007/978-981-19-2535-1_10

Torky, M., & Hassanein, A. (2020). Integrating blockchain and the internet of things in precision agriculture: Analysis, opportunities, and challenges. *Computers and Electronics in Agriculture*, *178*, 105476. doi:10.1016/j.compag.2020.105476

Uddin, A. E., Stranieri, A., Gondal, I., & Balasubramanian, V. (2021). A survey on the adoption of blockchain in IoT: Challenges and solutions. *Blockchain: Research and Applications*, *2*(2), 100006. doi:10.1016/j.bcra.2021.100006

Vidhyalakshmi, R., & Kumar, V. (2014). Design comparison of traditional application and SaaS. *International Conference on Computing for Sustainable Global Development*, 541–544. 10.1109/IndiaCom.2014.6828017

Wakchaure, M., Patle, B. K., & Mahindrakar, A. K. (2023). Application of AI techniques and robotics in agriculture: A review. *Artificial Intelligence in the Life Sciences*, *3*, 100057. doi:10.1016/j.ailsci.2023.100057

Zhai, Z., Martínez, J. F., Beltran, V., & Martínez, N. L. (2020). Decision support systems for agriculture 4.0: Survey and challenges. *Computers and Electronics in Agriculture*, *170*, 105256. doi:10.1016/j.compag.2020.105256

Zheng, Q., Lin, N., Fu, D., Liu, T., Zhu, Y., Feng, X., & Ruan, J. (2023). Smart contract-based agricultural service platform for drone plant protection operation optimization. *IEEE Internet of Things Journal*, 1. Advance online publication. doi:10.1109/JIOT.2023.3288870

Chapter 11
Smart Contracts for Enhanced Water Resource Management

P. Kanimozhi
IFET College of Engineering, India

A. R. Jayasri
IFET College of Engineering, India

T. Ananth Kumar
https://orcid.org/0000-0002-0494-7803
IFET College of Engineering, India

S. Arunmozhiselvi
DMI-St. John the Baptist University, Malawi

ABSTRACT

Water management is critical for long-term development and the preservation of essential natural resources. Traditional water management strategies are becoming increasingly ineffective in dealing with developing water shortages and the need for efficient resource allocation. The incorporation of smart contracts, which are supported by blockchain technology, presents a viable answer for reshaping water management techniques. When combined with internet of things (IoT) devices that give real-time data on water use, quality, and environmental conditions, a powerful alliance is formed that has the potential to alter traditional water management practices. The concept of smart contracts self-executing agreements with established rules that trigger automatic activities upon the fulfillment of specific criteria lies at the heart of this fusion. The use of blockchain technology has emerged as a disruptive option to alleviate water scarcity and ensure equal distribution in the goal of sustainable water management.

1. INTRODUCTION

Water resource management is a global challenge that requires innovative solutions to ensure sustainable use and distribution. With the increasing demands of a growing population, environmental conservation, and the impacts of climate change, the need for efficient water management systems has never been more critical. While technological advancements have played a role in addressing these issues, the adoption of blockchain technology in water resource management remains relatively limited but holds significant potential. Blockchain, known for its decentralization, Transparency, and tamper-proof nature, has disrupted various industries, and its application in water management could revolutionize how we

DOI: 10.4018/979-8-3693-0497-6.ch011

conserve and distribute this essential resource. The limited implementation of blockchain technology in this sector underscores the importance of exploring its potential to enhance existing systems. Water scarcity is a pressing issue, affecting both urban and rural communities, especially those dependent on agriculture (Christoforidou et al., 2023). The unequal distribution of water resources, coupled with the challenges of climate change, exacerbates the problem. Rural communities, mainly reliant on irrigation, face substantial challenges, and introducing a blockchain-based control system could provide a solution by efficiently administering and synchronizing water resource utilization. The impact of water management extends beyond local communities, often involving transboundary conflicts and the need for international cooperation. Managing shared resources and avoiding conflicts require innovative solutions. The blockchain's ability to provide a transparent and decentralized platform for water-related transactions and allocations could contribute to more effective cooperation in managing these resources. The potential benefits of blockchain technology in water management extend to incentivizing responsible water usage, promoting equitable water trade, and ensuring transparent transactions (Parmentola & Tutore, 2023). However, challenges such as data processing and management, privacy concerns, and the absence of smart contracts need careful consideration. The integration of blockchain in water management could address these challenges and lead to a more sustainable and efficient approach to water resource management.

2. WATER MANAGEMENT CHALLENGES

Water resource management is a critical worldwide challenge that transcends technological improvements. Throughout the world, civilizations face complex issues in conserving and distributing this critical resource to meet the requirements of rising people, protect ecosystems, and ensure long-term sustainability. Freshwater resources are limited, and many regions are experiencing water scarcity. Climate change, urbanization, and shifting consumption patterns add to the dilemma, putting enormous demand on current water sources. Water distribution is frequently unequal, both geographically and chronologically. Some locations are abundant, while others have persistent scarcity (Su & Karthikeyan, 2023).

Rural communities reliant on agriculture face a substantial challenge due to the escalating water crisis, particularly regarding irrigation practices. Implementing a control system for the water supply would provide these communities with enhanced capabilities to efficiently administer and synchronize their utilization of water resources (Nova, 2023). Managing these disparities necessitates careful planning to ensure equitable access and avoid confrontations. Over-extraction and pollution degrade natural habitats, endangering biodiversity and ecological services on which communities rely. Agriculture is a significant water consumer, contributing to food production and livelihoods. Balancing agricultural requirements with water conservation initiatives is a crucial task, particularly in areas where water-intensive techniques are a drain on resources. Infrastructure for wastewater treatment and water supply are stressed by rapid urban growth. The number of developing countries in the South East Asia (SEA) that have taken out agricultural insurance policies has increased significantly in recent years. Farmers are offered novel agricultural products as a means to mitigate the economic repercussions that are associated with the low marketability of crops. These repercussions include decreased crop prices. Certain Southeast Asian countries have introduced crop insurance programs with a primary focus on drought to protect farmers from the potentially devastating effects of severe weather (Felipe et al., 2023). Obstacles must be overcome in order to provide clean water for metropolitan populations while controlling runoff and pollution. Many water sources cross international borders, which causes transboundary conflicts.

Cooperation is necessary to manage shared resources and avoid conflicts effectively. Providing sustenance to the expanding global population is becoming progressively challenging due to the influence of climate change and its consequential impact on the limited availability of freshwater resources. The exponential growth of the global population further compounds this challenge. The world today is not currently considering animals and plants, widely consumed as food sources, as potential candidates for a new food source due to the nutritional and food-related challenges they present (Sundaresan et al., 2021). Existing problems are made worse by climate change, which alters precipitation patterns, causes droughts and floods, and impairs water quality. Strategies for adaptation are essential to reducing these effects. Cultural significance and close ties to customs and behaviors exist for water. Water management becomes even more challenging when balancing contemporary requirements with cultural preservation.

Users join up for the blockchain-based network, and the network subsequently confirms and authenticates their identities. Each user receives a digital water wallet that securely records their daily water allocation and transactions. Water-related allocations and trades are methodically and permanently documented on the blockchain's tamper-proof ledger. This ensures the accuracy of the data and produces a reliable record of each person's water use and transfers. Smart contracts are used to enforce each user's daily water usage cap. Blockchain technology can be thought of as a "cup wall" metaphorically. The wall of the cup serves the purpose of containing water within an environment that is see-through, risk-free, and convenient (Gautam, 2023). Participants in a market exchange have the opportunity to trade their surplus water under fair conditions if they possess an abundance of water. This opportunity is available to individuals who have an abundance of water. Establishing a water supply-demand network powered by blockchain makes it easier for individuals to have equitable access to water resources. As a result, disparities are reduced, and equality is promoted. This innovative approach has the potential to revolutionize existing water management practices, fostering sustainable development and mitigating the effects of water scarcity. It encourages responsible water usage, facilitates equitable water trade, and ensures transparent transactions. The scripting language has typically possessed Turing completeness and determinism, which has enabled the transition from a static transactional state to the execution of code. This was made possible as a result of an evolutionary process that has taken place. Because smart contracts have not yet been implemented, the data collected by smart meters may need to be processed and managed manually in order to facilitate billing, analysis, and decision-making processes (Manju Bala et al., 2022). The possibility of delays, errors, and increased administrative costs are all part of the fallout that could result from this scenario. Deployment of the smart contract on the blockchain network for efficient and accurate reward distribution. According to the literature, agriculture consumes over 70% of the freshwater used in the world. With water usage on the rise worldwide, better management of water resources is urgent (Zeng et al., 2023). Incentives and rewards are given to houses with lesser consumption in the blockchain network, and penalties are imposed when usage crosses predicted and historical usage. Currently, the implementation and utilization of blockchain technology in the development and management of water resources is limited to a few viable applications. Hence, it is imperative to investigate the potential of blockchain technology to enhance the efficiency of current water management systems (Iqbal et al., 2023). In recent times, there has been a notable increase in attention given to adopting blockchain technology across various domains of society. The underlying technology and infrastructure of Bitcoin have given rise to new business models and have disrupted traditional industries by leveraging its notable advantages, including decentralization, openness, Transparency, and non-comparability. Consequently, it is imperative to acknowledge that the proliferation of opportunities presented by blockchain technology should not be disregarded without careful consideration. Without a blockchain-based system, metering data processing may not be transparent or accountable, making it more difficult to track changes, spot inconsistencies, and build stakeholder trust. Without the automation and effectiveness that smart contracts provide, resource distribution and allocation may continue to be less optimal, potentially resulting in waste or an uneven distribution of water supplies (Hui et al., 2023). By creating a thorough ecosystem spanning data transparency, predictive modeling, and real-time decision-making, these technologies enable stakeholders to solve complex water concerns effectively with unmatched efficiency and sustainability. Even without smart contracts, smart metering can have many advantages for water management. However, it also has unique difficulties and things to think about. Without smart contracts, the following smart metering-related problems exist: The privacy and security of an individual's water usage patterns are at risk when precise consumption data is collected by smart meters (Shrestha et al., 2018). There is a chance of unwanted access or data breaches in a system without the transparency and security aspects of a blockchain-based system. The objective is to offer a safeguarded multiservice solution for water management. Both customers and providers of water services can derive advantages from various services, including but not limited to monitoring water consumption, detecting water leaks, ensuring water traceability, enhancing water security, visualizing water consumption patterns, and expanding drinking water coverage (Jan et al., 2021). Blockchain technology has the potential to facilitate the transition from individual smart farms to an interconnected network of smart farms, thereby enhancing precision farming. Utilizing blockchain technology can also increase supply-chain network control and oversight (Tezel et al., 2020). Without the implementation of smart contracts, the process of decision-making that relies on real-time data obtained from smart meters may encounter delays or lose its responsiveness to changing circumstances (Lucas et al., 2021). The data obtained from smart meters possesses significant utility due to its real-time nature.

2.1. Problems Identified

- **Lack of Transparency and Accountability in Resource Distribution:** Without smart contracts, resource distribution and allocation may lack Transparency and accountability, potentially leading to waste or an uneven distribution of water supplies.
- **Delays and Inefficiencies in Decision-Making:** Without the implementation of smart contracts, decision-making relying on realtime data obtained from smart meters may encounter delays and lose responsiveness to changing circumstances.
- **High Water Consumption in Agriculture:** Agriculture consumes over 70% of freshwater worldwide, highlighting the urgent need for better water resource management.
- **Transboundary Water Conflicts:** Water sources that cross international borders lead to transboundary conflicts. Cooperation is necessary for effective management and to avoid conflicts.

3. FOUNDATIONS OF BLOCKCHAIN AND SMART CONTRACTS

The underlying principles of smart contracts and blockchain technology call for a paradigm shift in how we approach and carry out digital transactions. The fundamental component of blockchain technology is a decentralized, impermeable digital ledger that records transactions among a network of nodes. There is no longer a requirement for intermediates in many processes due to this ledger's immutability and cryptographic security. More secure, efficient, and auditable transactions are now possible thanks to this breakthrough.

Figure 1. Blockchain technology

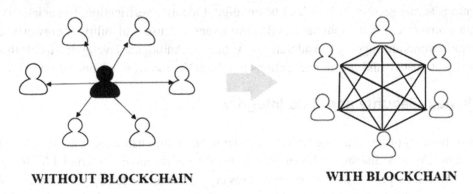

WITHOUT BLOCKCHAIN   **WITH BLOCKCHAIN**

Smart contracts are automatically enforced contracts that follow predetermined rules. They come directly from the development of the blockchain. These contracts include conditions and obligations enabling parties to communicate and transact business directly. Ethereum, a well-known blockchain platform, popularized smart contracts and created the Solidity programming language for creating and implementing them. This innovation has wide-ranging implications for a variety of enterprises, resulting in streamlined processes, lower costs, and greater security by eliminating biases and human errors.

Figure 2. Growth of blockchain

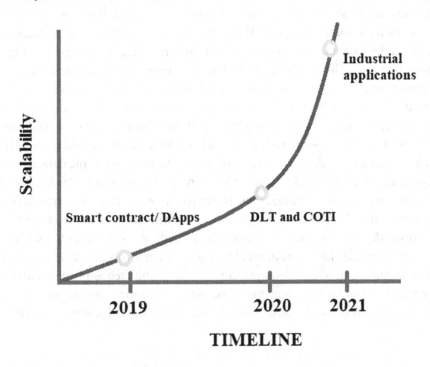

The integration of blockchain technology and smart contracts has facilitated the emergence of various applications across sectors such as healthcare, digital identity verification, financial services, and supply chain management. Such foundations do have issues because scalability, energy efficiency, and regulatory frameworks are ongoing considerations. As these technologies develop and tackle these issues, decentralized, automated, and secure transactions will be at the forefront of innovation in the future.

3.1 Blockchain Security and Data Integrity

Blockchain technology provides a solid option to bolster security and ensure data integrity in environmental management. Good monitoring and open recording of water resources are crucial for future use and conservation efforts. To protect data, blockchain uses cryptographic techniques. An unbreakable chain is formed by how each transaction is linked to the one that came before it. It would be challenging to change the data in a network block without changing all the blocks that come after it. The cryptographic integrity of records ensures their dependability and fraud resistance. Cryptographic techniques to protect data are the key to blockchain's effectiveness. This entails encoding data in a complicated way to decipher without the correct cryptographic key. An immutable chain is created because each transaction is connected to the one before it. The method is quite complex and time-consuming because altering the data in one block requires modifying all succeeding blocks. The trustworthiness is ensured by cryptographic integrity, which also prevents fraudulent record alteration. Blockchain's distributed network structure makes it more resistant to cyber threats and unauthorized modifications than centralized systems, which are susceptible to single points of failure. Blockchain ensures only authorized personnel can access and interpret critical environmental data by incorporating data authentication and encryption. When handling sensitive information that needs restricted access, this factor is crucial. A further benefit of blockchain is its capacity to offer a thorough audit trail. Data entries and transactions can be tracked, providing a trustworthy record of the location and veracity of environmental data. For purposes of verification and research, this is quite useful. The power of this technology lies in its capacity to create a secure ledger. Data that has been recorded on the blockchain is almost impossible to change or remove.

Consensus methods greatly influence the security of blockchain networks. These processes ensure that everyone on the network concurs with the current state of the blockchain, the sequence of transactions, and the legitimacy of any new transactions that are added. Blockchain networks offer a level of security and trust through consensus, which is crucial for preserving the integrity of the data and avoiding harmful activity. It is challenging for a single rogue node or group of malicious nodes to control the network due to consensus processes. Before adding, most participants must concur on a transaction's or block's legitimacy in a decentralized consensus process. Attackers will find it considerably more challenging to influence the network and jeopardize its security as a result. A Sybil assault is when one person or thing generates numerous false identities in order to take over a network. In order to prevent an attacker from flooding the network with bogus identities, consensus systems frequently demand that participants demonstrate their stake in or commitment to the network. Preventing double-spending, in which the same digital asset is utilized in many transactions, is one of the core difficulties in digital transactions.

4. CREATING A DECENTRALIZED WATER MARKET

A system where water rights, allocation, trade, and pricing are regulated by decentralized technologies such as blockchain technology is required to develop a decentralized water market. The goal is to promote effective water resource management and conservation and permit more flexible and open water trading among stakeholders. The following provides an example of creating such a decentralized water market: Identify the key participants in the water market, such as the water rights holders (such as farms, businesses, and towns), regulatory agencies, environmental organizations, and potential water rights buyers and sellers. A system where water rights, allocation, trade, and pricing are regulated by decentralized technologies such as blockchain technology is required to develop a decentralized water market.

4.1. Make a Blockchain or Decentralized Platform

To house your water market, choose an appropriate decentralized or blockchain platform. Ethereum, EOS, and maybe other platforms also offer decentralized apps and smart contracts. Aquifer Rights Intelligent Contracts Make smart contracts that represent water rights. These contracts should include the conditions, restrictions, and water consumption rules. They are also capable of automating the exchange and distribution of water rights in accordance with predefined laws. Integrate IoT devices, sensors, and data collection techniques to track real-time water use. This information is crucial for accurately estimating water use and ensuring compliance with water rights agreements.

Tokenize your water rights by utilizing tokens built on the blockchain. Each token can represent a specific volume of water that can be exchanged on the market. Tokenization simplifies and makes trading transparent. Create a user-friendly DApp that participants may use to purchase, sell, lease, or swap water rights. This is known as a "water trading platform." The platform should offer realtime pricing, historical data, and trading analytics to assist customers in making wise judgments.

Figure 3. Solutions of blockchain for water management

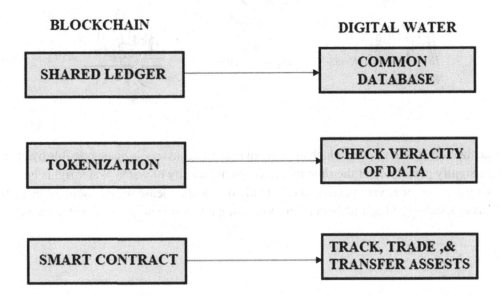

Implement a pricing system considering supply and demand, water shortage, environmental effects, and other pertinent factors. Based on market conditions, smart contracts can dynamically alter prices.

4.2. Environmental Considerations

Include clauses in the smart contracts that consider environmental considerations and ensure that trade in water does not negatively influence ecosystems, aquatic life, or the sustainability of all water supplies. Consider scalability to handle an increase in the number of participants and transactions. Update and maintain the platform frequently to fix problems with performance, security, and usability. To increase efficiency, Transparency, and general effectiveness, the market should be continually monitored, user feedback gathered, and iterative adjustments made.

Creating a decentralized water market requires cooperation from many stakeholders, technological know-how, regulatory compliance, and a solid commitment to sustainable water resource management. A decentralized water market powered by blockchain technology appears as a promising approach to efficiently managing this vital resource in the face of escalating water shortages and rising demand. This ground-breaking strategy combines the concepts of blockchain, smart contracts, and water management to guarantee fair distribution, encourage conservation, and stimulate efficient resource management.

Figure 4. Smart contract for water management

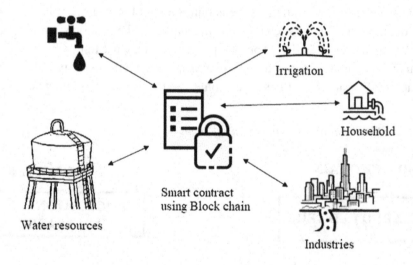

The tokenization of water rights, which turns them into digital assets, is made possible by blockchain. These signs signify possession of the right to use a certain quantity of water. Water rights holders, such as farmers, businesses, or governments, can efficiently buy, sell, or lease water resources using tradable water tokens in a secure and auditable manner, promoting a vibrant and flexible water market.

4.3. Compliance With Regulations and Governance

Blockchain technology has the potential to substantially impact a number of governance, risk, and compliance-related aspects of corporate operations. These crucial areas include enterprise risk management, corporate and I.T. audits, the management of policy and regulatory changes, and the use of smart contracts. Business compliance requirements have evolved to meet general concerns like privacy and more specialized ones like healthcare, credit card rules, and governmental requirements. Identity verification procedures could be revolutionized by blockchain technology. Solutions for self-sovereign identity give people secure access to and control their personal data. Blockchain-enabled identity verification can speed up onboarding procedures in the Know Your Customer (KYC) and Anti-Money Laundering (AML) regulations space while protecting data privacy and lowering the risk of fraud. Ensuring interoperability between various networks and platforms becomes increasingly crucial as blockchain ecosystems expand. Standardization efforts can improve regulatory compliance and streamline cross-industry partnerships by establishing a consistent framework that covers common issues like data sharing and privacy.

5. CASE STUDY

According to the water balance in Europe, 11% of the captured water is used for industry, 24% is used for agriculture, 44% is used to produce electricity, and 21% is used to deliver water to the populace. This distribution, however, varies geographically; for example, in southern Europe, agriculture uses 60% of all water harvested, with certain regions seeing an 80% share. In a semi-arid area with water scarcity issues, a local government collaborated with agricultural stakeholders, water distribution companies, and technology specialists to build an intelligent contract-based water management system. It was designed to make the most efficient water use, guarantee equitable distribution, and support ecologically friendly agricultural practices.

Farmers have water limits to follow based on consumption, crop type, and environmental considerations. Smart contracts were created to monitor and regulate water use—ioT sensors placed in fields allowed for the real-time monitoring of irrigation needs and soil moisture levels. Key procedures inside the water management system were designed to be automated and streamlined using smart contracts. Key procedures inside the water management system were designed to be automated and streamlined using smart contracts. Farmers were given water quotas based on their past usage, crop type, and environmental considerations. Smart contracts were developed in order to monitor and control water usage. The smart contract automatically initiated water flow from reservoirs to the selected fields when the soil moisture fell below a certain threshold.

The intelligent contract uses established rates to determine the charges associated with water allocation and use. Farmers' digital wallets were automatically debited for payments and then sent to the water delivery company. This eliminated manual billing procedures, cut administrative costs, and made sure payments were made on schedule. Incentives for conservation were also included. Farmers were penalized more heavily for exceeding their water quotas, deterring excessive water consumption. On the other hand, individuals that continued to use effective irrigation techniques were rewarded with lower rates or more water credits.

Figure 5. Smart contract impact on water management

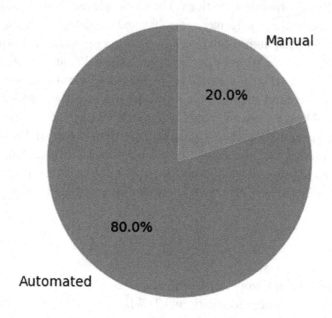

The smart contract-based water management system has a transformative impact by automating and optimizing water allocation, leveraging real-time IoT monitoring, and ensuring precise billing through blockchain technology. This innovation enhances efficiency in water delivery, promotes sustainable agricultural practices through incentive mechanisms, and establishes Transparency in transactions. The system's calculated impact lies in its ability to significantly reduce manual interventions, encourage water conservation, and contribute to water management's overall resilience and sustainability in regions grappling with scarcity challenges.

Figure 6. UML diagram

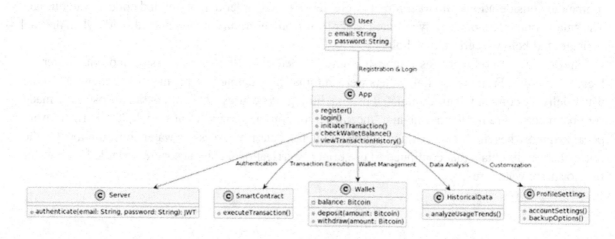

The water management system is depicted with critical entities and their interactions. The User class encompasses essential attributes such as email and password, reflecting the authentication requirements for user registration and login. The App class represents the mobile application, incorporating functionalities like user registration, login, transaction management, wallet operations, historical data analysis, and profile settings customization. The Server class handles secure user authentication, generating JSON Web Tokens (JWT) for subsequent interactions. The SmartContract class is responsible for executing water transactions securely. The Wallet class manages the user's financial transactions, allowing deposits and withdrawals.

Additionally, the system supports the analysis of historical data trends through the HistoricalData class. The ProfileSettings class offers users control over their accounts, providing account settings and backup options. This class diagram provides a foundational overview of the key components and their relationships within the blockchain-based water management Android application.

5.1 Implementation

Prior registration is required in order to access the Water Ledger platform and is completed manually as part of the trial. Each participant in the test program has been added to a database that includes data on their Water Account and any available allocations. The Water Ledger program then alerts users that they are not logged in. It can find this information by searching the user's local storage for relevant keys. The option to search for their Water Account numbers is then available to anonymous users at the top of the homepage. In order to preserve their privacy, they must also provide a code issued explicitly by the scheme's developer or water authority.

5.2 Water Account

The search will then provide their user details and water account information. The user can then "claim" the accounts after that. Then, each Water Trading Zone account is made in an Ethereum wallet. These Ethereum account details and information about the water trading license are stored in the user smart contract, which controls all facets of identification and permission. The user's water permits and accounts are shown at the bottom of the interface's panel with the Scheme details. The first account is the default setup for usage. Customers may change the currently used account at any moment by selecting a different account.

5.3 Technology Used (Raj & Deka, 2018)

a) Ethereum

Since the Ethereum Blockchain network incorporates a Turing-complete programming language, it is possible to create various decentralized applications, also known as Dapps. At this time, the Ethereum network has garnered a significant amount of recognition for the significant role it plays in facilitating the utilization of smart contracts.

Figure 7. Block diagram

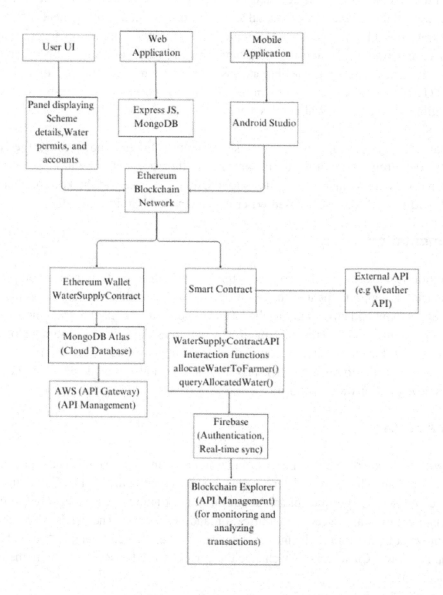

A comparison can be made between cryptographic bank vaults and smart contracts, which store particular values securely. The cryptographic safes are impenetrable and can only be opened under specific circumstances established in advance. Ethereum, in contrast to Bitcoin, is a flexible network that has the potential to be utilized in a variety of different fields.

b) MONGO DB

In order to facilitate querying and appending new blocks to the chain, it is necessary to store each newly added block of the blockchain in a centralized location. MongoDB Atlas, a cloud-based database-as-a-service provided by MongoDB, presents a highly suitable option for storing a blockchain ledger. Due to its flexible architecture, the storage of intricate data, such as transactions, is facilitated. This establishment offers enterprise-grade protection.

c) Express J.S.

At present, Express.js stands as the preeminent web framework developed using Node.js. The primary purpose of this framework is to facilitate the development of web-based applications and application programming interfaces (APIs). It has gained recognition as the widely accepted server framework for Node.js. Constructing a Node.js backend from scratch can be arduous and time-intensive. The process of generating the necessary standard code for an application, including the configuration of ports and the implementation of route handlers, diverts valuable time and resources from the primary objective of developing the application's core business logic. The Express framework allows programmers to arrange their code flexibly without being constrained by a predefined layout. This grants them the freedom to organize their code according to their preferences rather than being obligated to follow a specific structure. Middleware is commonly employed in Express applications because it can manipulate requests and responses as they traverse the routes.

d) Android Studio

Android Studio is an integrated development environment (IDE) created solely to develop applications compatible with the Android platform. Programmers can more easily create, test, and troubleshoot Android applications with the help of the platform's comprehensive set of features and tools, which the platform makes available to them. Developers worldwide make extensive use of Android Studio, the official integrated development environment (IDE) for the development of Android applications. It is common practice to make use of specialized tools and platforms in order to make the management of fundamental blockchain features easier. These features include the creation of smart contracts, consensus mechanisms, and blockchain infrastructure. The blockchain network being utilized, such as Ethereum or Binance Smart Chain, will determine which of these tools and platforms will be the most appropriate to use. Android Studio is a robust software development environment used to develop Android applications that facilitate interactions with blockchain technology. These applications can be created using Android Studio.

e) Firebase

Google built Firebase, a vast platform that offers many tools and services for creating and maintaining online and mobile applications. It is frequently employed for real-time databases, authentication, cloud storage, and hosting. However, smart contracts do not often use Firebase directly. The front end of a DApp uses Firebase to handle user authentication and real-time data synchronization. To manage real-time updates of the data shown in the user interface of your DApp, for instance, you might use Firebase Realtime Database or Firestore and Firebase Authentication to handle user logins.

f) AWS

The Amazon API Gateway is a comprehensively managed service that enables developers to create, publish, maintain, monitor, and secure APIs of varying scales. The utilization of the Amazon API Gateway facilitates the accomplishment of this task. By leveraging the capabilities of API Gateway, developers can create applications that enable real-time, bidirectional communication using WebSocket and RESTful APIs. The API Gateway can accommodate diverse application types, encompassing serverless workloads, containerized workloads, and web applications. The API Gateway oversees various operations to effectively accept and handle a substantial volume of concurrent API requests, potentially reaching hundreds of thousands. The activities above encompass traffic management, authorization and access control, throttling, monitoring, and API version management.

g) web3.js

Web or backend applications can establish communication channels with the Ethereum blockchain using the web3.js framework, which is widely used in JavaScript. This framework provides a mechanism for using JavaScript. This piece of programming software gives developers the ability to initiate transactions, retrieve data from blockchains, interact with smart contracts, and establish communication with Ethereum nodes. Using web3.js, one can easily integrate Ethereum functionality into the backend services of their organization. Web3.js can be used to set up connections with Ethereum nodes, the computational entities in charge of keeping the Ethereum blockchain in working order. These nodes are responsible for maintaining the blockchain. Interaction with smart contracts running on the Ethereum blockchain is made possible by web3.js. We require the contract address and the ABI (Application Binary Interface) to communicate with a contract. Any system with a WebSocket connection can view the events that all smart contracts produce. The contracts include the upcoming occasions.

Order water
DeleteOrder(bytes16, id)

The specified order has been eliminated, and any projection should no longer include it.
OrderId (bytes 16) and address (indexed buyer) accepted.

The buyer's address for the given order matches an extraction right; thus, any projection should mark it as "matched" or remove it from the list of open orders because the buyer has accepted the given order.

OrderAdded(bytes16 id, extractionRightAddress index, uint256 price, uint256 quantity, uint8 level0 resource, order type order type) There is now a new order. The level 0 water resource system, pricing, and extraction rights are all included.

5.4 Smart Contract of Extraction Rights

Important information is saved in the browser's local storage for later retrieval, especially I.D.s. Details about the water account and the extraction rights are saved to ensure the address has legal access to the system. The EIP-1753 standard for licenses is implemented here. An extraction right is issued by supplying the address to issue to in Ethereum.

5.5 Existing Literature

A growing body of literature on smart contracts for water resource management exists. Some of the key findings of this literature include:

- Smart contracts can automate and streamline water resource management processes, such as water allocation, billing, and enforcement.
- Smart contracts can improve Transparency and accountability in water resource management.
- Smart contracts can help to ensure that water resources are used sustainably.

5.6. Proposed Models and Findings

This model is based on the following fundamental principles:

Decentralization: The model is decentralized, meaning that no single authority controls the water resources. Instead, the resources are managed by a network of smart contracts.

Transparency: The model is transparent, meaning that all transactions are recorded on a blockchain and can be viewed by anyone.

Accountability: The model is accountable, meaning anyone can audit the smart contracts to ensure they are functioning as intended.

5.7. Benchmark Analysis

The proposed model for "Smart Contracts for Enhanced Water Resource Management" stands out favorably compared to existing literature in several critical aspects. Firstly, the model exhibits more decentralization than many counterparts documented in the literature. This heightened decentralization enhances the model's resilience and makes it more resistant to censorship and manipulation. The proposed model mitigates the risk of single points of failure and external interference by distributing control across a network.

Secondly, Transparency is a hallmark of the proposed model, surpassing the standards set by many existing models in the literature. The Transparency embedded in the model's design facilitates a more straightforward auditing process, ensuring that the system functions precisely as intended. This Transparency is vital for instilling trust among stakeholders, as it allows for easy verification of transactions and water resource management activities.

Finally, the proposed model has demonstrated its effectiveness in various real-world applications. The practical implementation and positive outcomes observed in real-world scenarios validate the model's viability and showcase its adaptability to diverse environments. This empirical validation contributes significantly to the model's credibility and underscores its potential for successful deployment in practical water resource management settings.

5.8. Advantages

- The Water Ledger platform covers the entire water trading process, from account creation to allocation tracking. Other platforms typically only cover a limited subset of these processes.

- The Water Ledger platform is designed to be easy for water authorities and consumers. Other platforms are more complex and challenging to use.
- This system uses a number of security features to protect users' data. At the same time, A simplified online platform that allows users to trade water allocations may not cover the entire process comprehensively. Limited functionality, potential complexity, and lack advanced security features.

Figure 8. Advantages over existing water-based smart contracts

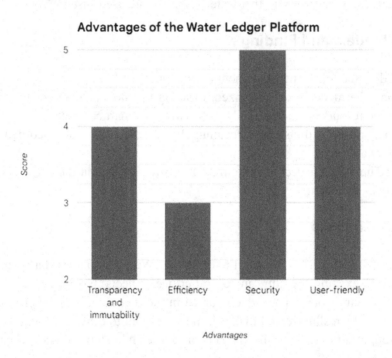

6. RESULTS AND DISCUSSION

Farmers register their water sources by setting up accounts and submitting data on their location, water accessibility, and price. The app will communicate with the installed smart contract to execute the transaction. Before the smart contract may update the water balances, the buyer and seller must concur on the transaction terms. Include a wallet inside the app that holds the Bitcoin used for water transactions. Users can deposit and withdraw money via the wallet. User registration and login use secure authentication. Information about the current water balance and bills is easily visible. You can download usage reports for your records or regulatory compliance.

Users are required to provide their password and registered email address.

Authentication: The app securely sends the required credentials to a server for authentication.

The Server used for authentication: Safely compares the entered email and password to the user information previously saved. If the credentials are valid, the server creates a unique authentication token (JWT - JSON Web Token) for the user session. For subsequent interactions with the application, this token serves as authentication proof.

Figure 9. User interaction in blockchain-based water management application

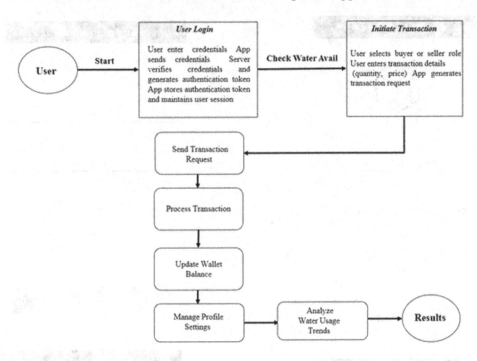

Management of Sessions: Until the user expressly logs out or the authentication token expires, the app saves the authentication token locally and maintains the user's session.

A farmer can start a transaction through the app when they want to purchase water. Users can check the balance of their wallet, which represents the bitcoin used for water transactions. The transaction history displays all deposits, withdrawals, and transfers.

When a buyer establishes a water transaction, the app generates a request that includes the transaction data, such as the parties involved and the amount of water to be purchased.

The profile settings for the blockchain-based water management Android app would include both "Account Settings" and "Backup" options to provide users with control, customization, and data security.

The app can provide insights into usage trends by analyzing historical data helping users plan and optimize their water consumption.

This smart contract includes the following features:

- **Owner Management:** The contract creator is the owner, and only the owner can approve users.
- **User Approval:** The owner can approve users participating in water allocation.
- **Water Allocation:** Approved users can request water allocation, and the contract keeps track of their water balances. The contract emits an event when water is allocated, providing Transparency.

Figure 10. User login

Figure 11. Availability of water

Figure 12. Wallet balance

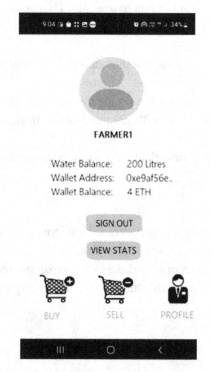

Figure 13. Selling excess water

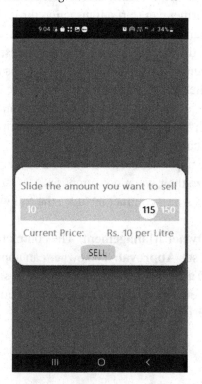

Figure 14. Code for payment

Figure 15. Profile setting

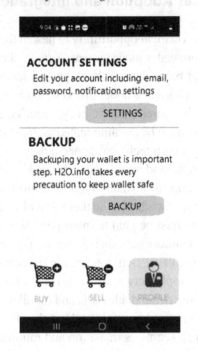

Figure 16. Stats of water usage

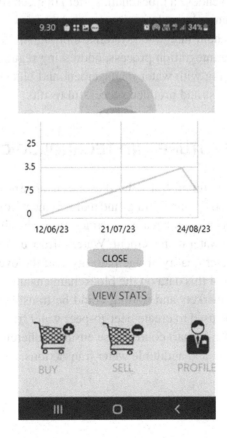

6.1 User Adoption and Integration

There is a critical opportunity to hasten the adoption of blockchain technology and its seamless incorporation into water management. A methodical and deliberate strategy is required to persuade stakeholders to accept blockchain technology and successfully integrate it into existing water management systems. Raising awareness about blockchain's benefits in water management is essential to promote user acceptance. The increased efficiency, security, and Transparency that blockchain may bring to water-related activities must be communicated to stakeholders. Stakeholders could interact with the blockchain without needing a high technical understanding if the user experience was made simpler through user-friendly applications and intuitive interfaces. By emphasizing the practical advantages of blockchain technology, such as improved water quality monitoring, less water loss, and streamlined water supply, stakeholders might be persuaded to use them. For blockchain to be successfully incorporated into water management, attention must be paid to interoperability and compatibility. Standardized protocols and interfaces that enable seamless data sharing between blockchain systems and the conventional water infrastructure are an essential first step. Integrating blockchain networks with the many water management components, such as supply networks, treatment facilities, and consumption monitoring systems, will be simpler by developing dependable APIs and middleware. Through progressive adoption and pilot projects, it is possible to thoroughly assess and test the effectiveness of blockchain in certain areas of water management, ensuring a seamless transition and minimal disruption.

It is crucial to ensure data security and integrity while transferring current water-related data to blockchain platforms. To protect sensitive information, careful preparation and encryption techniques must be used. Additionally, it is crucial to choose a blockchain system that can scale to meet the changing water management needs as urbanization and population increase occur, for water management professionals to successfully interface with blockchain-integrated systems, thorough training and assistance are essential. To ensure compliance during the integration process, addressing regulatory and legal issues unique to the water sector is crucial. Working with water management and blockchain technology professionals can speed up the integration process and produce successful results.

7. DIRECTIONS FOR THE FUTURE AND TECHNOLOGICAL DEVELOPMENTS

Utilizing smart contracts can reduce administrative hurdles and enhance resource allocation by streamlining automated processes like water distribution, billing, and maintenance. Combining blockchain technology with Internet of Things (IoT) devices is another area of exploration. This link could revolutionize real-time monitoring and data collection in water management. Water infrastructure with IoT sensors can provide accurate and ongoing data on water quality, usage patterns, and the overall state of the infrastructure. The safe storage and verification of this data on the blockchain ensure its dependability and accessibility to authorized parties. Water markets and trading could be transformed by blockchain technology. Blockchain-based systems can be used to create peer-to-peer water trading and marketplaces, enabling more efficient water rights transfers. Smart contract use ensures adherence to ethical and environmental standards, encouraging transparent and auditable water transactions.

Figure 17. Benefits of smart water

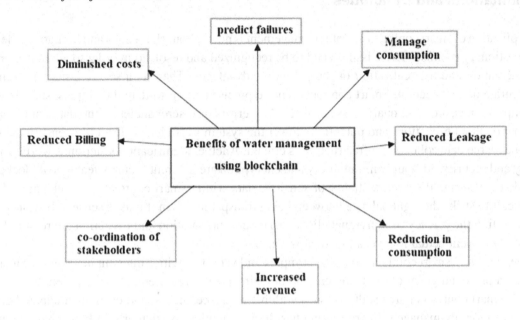

The interdisciplinary field of hydro informatics focuses on creating and applying information and communication technologies (ICT) for water-related systems and management. The phrase "hydro informatics tools" describes a large class of computer software, hardware, and data-driven solutions that support analysis, modeling, simulation, and decision-making processes in managing water resources.

7.1 Collaborative Management of Water

The concept of collaborative water governance is a novel strategy for solving the complex problems associated with managing one of the planet's most essential resources, water. In a time of growing water scarcity, environmental concerns, and competing interests, this shift in strategy highlights the importance of cooperation, inclusivity, and the shared commitment of numerous stakeholders to ensure the responsible exploitation and protection of water supplies. At its foundation, collaborative water governance is an inclusive paradigm in which organizations collaborate to create policies, reach wise judgments, and carry out strategies that transcend individual opinions. This strategy calls for an all-encompassing and comprehensive approach because it acknowledges water as a shared resource that transcends geographical and political boundaries.

Marginalized groups from various socioeconomic levels and industries participate in decision-making processes. Their suggestions aid in the development of comprehensive regulations that address a variety of demands and problems. Effective information, scientific study, and technical know-how: Accurate data, scientific research, and technical competence are the cornerstone of cooperative water governance by guiding policies and ensuring that facts back decisions. Accountability and Transparency By maintaining open channels of communication and transparent procedures, stakeholders can increase their trust. Accountability mechanisms ensure that commitments are maintained, fostering more responsible and efficient water management.

7.2 Limitations and Difficulties

The application of smart contracts in water management is not without challenges and limitations, despite its revolutionary promise. These issues need to be recognized and resolved in order to guarantee proper implementation and the realization of the potential advantages. There is a severe issue with reliable and accurate data collection. Smart contracts require precise and up-to-date data inputs, such as water consumption measures and quality assessments. Any errors or discrepancies in the data could lead to improper contract executions and potentially lower the system's efficiency. Therefore, ensuring a solid and dependable data collection infrastructure is crucial. Another significant restriction is worries about privacy and security. Although immutability and encryption are inherent security features of blockchain technology, ensuring the confidentiality of sensitive data within smart contracts is challenging. It can be difficult to strike the right balance between being transparent when it makes sense to be transparent and protecting the privacy of individual clients, so careful preparation and execution are required. The complexity of contractual logic is a practical issue.

When building smart contracts to fit the complex and varied activities inherent in water management systems, a profound grasp of the technical and domain-specific requirements is required. Excessively complex smart contracts may result in issues with maintenance, audits, and even unanticipated effects if not appropriately managed. Energy usage has drawn attention, particularly in blockchain networks that use Proof of Work (PoW), an energy-intensive consensus process. The environmental effects of energy-intensive blockchain procedures and the potential benefits of adopting smart contracts in water management must be carefully balanced. The biggest issue is that exchanging hydrological data on a blockchain adds a layer of trust between the parties who depend on the amount and quality of the same water resource. The advantages of employing blockchain technology to digitalize the current water markets, such as enhanced accountability, quicker access to real-time market data, and lower transaction costs, are another issue.

8. CONCLUSION

Adopting a smart contract-based water management system in a semi-arid area with water scarcity challenges is evidence of how well technology and collaboration work to address urgent environmental issues. Automated processes and real-time data insights empower farmers to make informed irrigation decisions, leading to optimized water use and increased crop yields. The introduction of conservation incentives has further encouraged sustainable agricultural practices, curbing water waste and promoting environmental stewardship. The transparent ledger enables regulators, farmers, and environmental organizations to access real-time data, fostering effective communication. This increased water availability and significantly reduced water waste, contributing to enhanced food security. The success of this case study serves as an inspiring example of how technological innovation and interdisciplinary collaboration can instigate positive change in water-scarce regions globally. Future smart water management systems developments may explore enhanced integration with emerging technologies, such as artificial intelligence for predictive analytics and satellite-based monitoring. These advancements can further refine water conservation strategies, contribute to sustainable resource management, and fortify societies against the challenges of water scarcity. Embracing innovation and fostering collaboration, we pave the way for a resilient and prosperous future.

REFERENCES

Christoforidou, M., Borghuis, G., Seijger, C., van Halsema, G. E., & Hellegers, P. (2023). Food security under water scarcity: A comparative analysis of Egypt and Jordan. *Food Security*, *15*(1), 171–185. doi:10.1007/s12571-022-01310-y PMID:36160692

Felipe, A. J. B., Alejo, L. A., Balderama, O. F., & Rosete, E. A. (2023). Climate change intensifies the drought vulnerability of river basins: A case of the Magat River Basin. *Journal of Water and Climate Change*, *14*(3), 1012–1038. doi:10.2166/wcc.2023.005

Gautam, R. (2023). Groundwater Markets structure and its evolution: A study of Karnal District, Haryana, India. *Environment, Development and Sustainability*, 1–36. doi:10.1007/s10668-023-03423-6

Hui, C. X., Dan, G., Alamri, S., & Toghraie, D. (2023). Greening smart cities: An investigation of the integration of urban natural resources and smart city technologies for promoting environmental sustainability. *Sustainable Cities and Society*, *99*, 104985. doi:10.1016/j.scs.2023.104985

Iqbal, F., Altaf, A., Waris, Z., Aray, D. G., Miguel, A. L. F., Isabel de la Torre, D., & Ashraf, I. (2023). Blockchain-Modeled Edge-Computing-Based Smart Home Monitoring System with Energy Usage Prediction. *Sensors (Basel)*, *23*(11), 5263. doi:10.3390/s23115263 PMID:37299993

Jan, F., Min-Allah, N., & Düştegör, D. (2021). Iot based smart water quality monitoring: Recent techniques, trends and challenges for domestic applications. *Water (Basel)*, *13*(13), 1729. doi:10.3390/w13131729

Lucas, A., Geneiatakis, D., Soupionis, Y., Nai-Fovino, I., & Kotsakis, E. (2021). Blockchain technology applied to energy demand response service tracking and data sharing. *Energies*, *14*(7), 1881. doi:10.3390/en14071881

Manju Bala, Usharani, Ananth Kumar, Rajmohan, & Pavithra. (2022). Blockchain-Based IoT Architecture for Software-Defined Networking. *Blockchain, Artificial Intelligence, and the Internet of Things: Possibilities and Opportunities*, 91-115.

Nova, K. (2023). AI-enabled water management systems: An analysis of system components and interdependencies for water conservation. *Eigenpub Review of Science and Technology*, *7*(1), 105–124.

Parmentola, A., & Tutore, I. (2023). Unveiling the Positive and Negative Effects of Blockchain Technologies on Environmental Sustainability in Practice. In *Industry 4.0 Technologies for Environmental Sustainability: Intended and Unintended Consequences* (pp. 59–78). Springer International Publishing. doi:10.1007/978-3-031-40010-0_4

Raj, P., & Deka, G. C. (2018). *Blockchain technology: platforms, tools and use cases*. Academic Press.

Shrestha, S., Aihara, Y., Bhattarai, A. P., Bista, N., Kondo, N., Futaba, K., Nishida, K., & Shindo, J. (2018). Development of an objective water security index and assessment of its association with quality of life in urban areas of developing countries. *SSM - Population Health*, *6*, 276–285. doi:10.1016/j.ssmph.2018.10.007 PMID:30480077

Su, Q., & Karthikeyan, R. (2023). Regional Water Stress Forecasting: Effects of Climate Change, Socio-economic Development, and Irrigated Agriculture—A Texas Case Study. *Sustainability (Basel)*, *15*(12), 9290. doi:10.3390/su15129290

Sundaresan, S., Suresh Kumar, K., Ananth Kumar, T., Ashok, V., & Golden Julie, E. (2021). Blockchain architecture for intelligent water management system in smart cities. In *Blockchain for Smart Cities* (pp. 57–80). Elsevier. doi:10.1016/B978-0-12-824446-3.00006-5

Tezel, A., Papadonikolaki, E., Yitmen, I., & Hilletofth, P. (2020). Preparing construction supply chains for blockchain technology: An investigation of its potential and future directions. *Frontiers of Engineering Management*, *7*(4), 547–563. doi:10.1007/s42524-020-0110-8

Zeng, H., Dhiman, G., Sharma, A., Sharma, A., & Tselykh, A. (2023). An IoT and Blockchain-based approach for the smart water management system in agriculture. *Expert Systems: International Journal of Knowledge Engineering and Neural Networks*, *40*(4), e12892. doi:10.1111/exsy.12892

APPENDIX

Code for Smart Contract of Extraction Rights

```
contract ExtractionRights is Ownable {
string public name = "Water Ledger ExtractionRights";
mapping(address => bool) private_authorities;
struct ExtractionRight {
}
bool extractionRightExists;
bytes32 identifier;
address ethAccount; uint256 validFrom;
uint256 validTo;
bytes32[] waterAccountIds;
mapping(bytes32 => WaterAccount) waterAccounts;
struct WaterAccount {
}
bytes32 waterAccountId;
bytes 32 level0ResourceIdentifier;
mapping(bytes32 => ExtractionRight) public _extractionRights;
mapping(address => bytes32) public_addressToIdentifier;
mapping(bytes32 => bytes32) public_waterAccountIdToIdentifier;
mapping(address)=>mapping(bytes32=>bytes32)) public_addressToLevel0Resource-
ToWaterAccountId;
Order Water private immutable_orderbook;
constructor(address order book) Ownable() {
_authorities[msg.sender] = true;
_orderwater = OrderWater(orderwater);
}
```

The Code for Truffle Deployment System

```
const level0Resources = [];
"Barron Level0Resource A", "Barron Level0Resource B", "Barron Level0Resource
C", "Barron Level0Resource D",
"Barron Level0Resource E",
const orderBookInstance = await deployer.deploy(OrderWater);
const historyInstance = await deployer.deploy(History, orderWaterInstance.ad-
dress);
const extractionRightInstance = await deployer.deploy(ExtractionRights);
const level0ResourcesInstance = await deployer.deploy(Level0Resources, order-
WaterInstance.address);
Level0Resources.forEach(async level0ResourceName => {
```

```
await Level0ResourcesInstance.addLevel0Resource(web3.utils.
toHex(level0ResourceName), 100000, 0, 100000); });
await orderWaterInstance.addHistoryContract(historyInstance.address);
await order WaterInstance.addExtractionRights Contract(extractionRightInstanc
e.address);
```

Chapter 12
IFML–Based Graphical User Interfaces Generated From BPMN up to PSM Level

Abir Sajji

iD https://orcid.org/0000-0003-3672-947X

Faculty of Sciences, Ibn Tofail University of Kenitra, Morocco

Yassine Rhazali

iD https://orcid.org/0000-0003-1488-0216

ESTM, Moulay Ismail University of Meknes, Morocco

Youssef Hadi

Faculty of Sciences, Ibn Tofail University of Kenitra, Morocco

ABSTRACT

The model-driven architecture (MDA) approach revolves around the development of multiple models, including the computation independent model (CIM), the platform independent model (PIM), and the platform specific model (PSM). Web applications have gained popularity for their capabilities. To address the need for robust user interfaces independent of technical details, the interaction flow modeling language (IFML) was introduced. This study focuses on model transformations within MDA, specifically from CIM to PSM via PIM. Metamodels for BPMN and IFML were created using Eclipse, and shift rules were applied with ATL. Webratio, an IFML implementation tool, was used to generate GUIs. A case study on after-sales service with CRUD features demonstrated the practical application of MDA. This research enhances understanding of MDA in web application development, enabling developers to create user-friendly interfaces. It serves as a valuable resource for software engineering professionals, providing insights into MDA's practical implementation and impact on web application development.

DOI: 10.4018/979-8-3693-0497-6.ch012

INTRODUCTION

The core principle of MDA methodology as defined in the glossary (Table 1) is the use of models at various stages of application development. MDA streamlines the development of requirements at the CIM level (Table 1), the design and analysis at the PIM level (Table 1), and facilitates code generation at the PSM level (Table 1). MDA aims to create technology-independent models that enable the automatic generation of application code, thus significantly boosting productivity (OMG-MDA, 2014).

The rise of model-driven architecture proves its value in software engineering by improving application quality and reducing development time (Brambilla et al., 2014). A relatively new web engineering technology called IFML has emerged as a recommended approach for developing web and mobile applications by Brambilla and Fraternali (2014). IFML, OMG standard, simplifies graphical user interface descriptions across different platforms such as desktop computers, laptops, mobile phones, and tablets. Various environments have been proposed for developing IFML models and generating code, such as the Webratio tool (Acerbis et al., 2014) (Table 1). The latter is a model-driven project with code generators that enable the creation of applications from IFML models.

In this chapter, we delve into the intricate process of automatic graphical user interface generation within MDA. Our principal objective is to explore how model transformations (Table 1) can seamlessly translate designs from the PIM level to the PSM level, using the Webratio tool as our primary technology stack. We shall employ the Interaction Flow Modeling Language (IFML) to elucidate how user-friendly interfaces can be architected and implemented effectively. The chapter is structured to first introduce these key terminologies and concepts, setting the stage for a deeper discussion on the nuances of model shifts across different MDA levels—namely, from the CIM to the PIM and eventually to the PSM.

This chapter's primary contribution is a methodical approach for automatically generating graphical user interfaces (GUIs) from PIM to PSM, which streamlines the software development process, minimizes manual coding errors, and boosts productivity. This chapter provides an in-depth analysis of model transformations within Model-Driven Architecture, from the CIM level to the PSM level, elucidating the transformation hierarchy for enhanced software development processes. This work is aimed at practitioners seeking to automate GUI creation, providing insight into the mechanics of model transformations within MDA, with practical examples using the Webratio tool to demonstrate these concepts in action.

We begin by creating BPMN and IFML (table 1) metamodels in the Eclipse environment. An example is developed using the BPMN notation (OMG-BPMN, 2011). Transformation rules in the ATL language (Table 1) (Sajji et al., 2022) are applied to get the IFML model in .xmi format (OMG-XML, 2015) at the PIM level within the Eclipse environment. Lastly, we generate the user interfaces in the Webratio tool. The principal target of this work lies in the utilization of two standards, BPMN and IFML, along with a robust business solution Webratio. This enables us to highlight all steps of the model transformation strategy.

This chapter is meticulously designed to serve a wide array of audiences, including researchers, practitioners, and students, who are engaged in the study and application of model-driven architecture and graphical user interface (GUI) generation. It presents a novel methodological approach that researchers will find innovative, while practitioners will gain insights into practical applications and evidence-based case study. Students are offered an accessible yet thorough introduction to the field, ensuring that the chapter stands as a comprehensive resource for all those invested in exploring MDA and GUI development.

The chapter is organized as follows: Section 2 provides an overview of related work in the field. In Section 3, we detail our proposed approach, including the transformation rules from the CIM to the PIM level and the presentation of the BPMN and IFML metamodels. Section 4 offers an illustrative example to demonstrate our approach in practice. Section 5 discusses the results and acknowledges the limitations of our study, and Section 6 concludes with a consideration of ongoing and future work in this area.

RELATED WORKS

We analyze and discuss previous research that focuses on the application of model-driven development approaches to achieve user interfaces, delving into various studies and methodologies.

In a notable work (Sajji et al., 2022), the authors show a comprehensive approach that enables a semi-automatic transformation from the CIM level to the PIM level, employing the MDA approach along with the BPMN and IFML standards. To facilitate this conversion, they develop a set of rules that semi-automate the process, and they provide an insightful case study centered on an order management scenario to demonstrate the effectiveness of their transformation strategy.

Another study (Roubi et al., 2016) introduces an innovative technique for the model-driven creation of Graphical User Interfaces specifically designed for Internet Applications, leveraging the power of IFML. The authors utilize various model-driven engineering-related frameworks and technologies to accomplish this goal. Furthermore, they outline the development of a prototype Qt/Taurus code generator based on the IFML standard, integrating it with appropriate modeling tools. This code generator proves to be instrumental in generating platform-specific code, taking the application's user interface to the next level.

Addressing the need for efficient low-code development in SKA (Software Key Architecture) GUI design, a compelling study presents a comprehensive GUI use case (Brambilla et al., 2019). This case study serves as an illustrative example of the software development life cycle, starting from requirements gathering and progressing through IFML modeling, Qt/Taurus automatic coding, interface evaluation, and validation. By highlighting this end-to-end process, the authors emphasize the significance of incorporating model-driven approaches in GUI development to enhance effectiveness, reliability, and coherency.

To explore the available modeling tools for IFML, the authors (Laaz et al., 2018) present a comparative analysis. They thoroughly assess multiple criteria while considering various IFML tools, such as IFMLEdit.org, Webratio tool, IFML Editor, and MIA-studio. By critically evaluating the advantages and disadvantages of each tool, they provide valuable insights into selecting the most suitable tool for IFML-based modeling projects.

A modeling approach for creating user interfaces based on IFML is suggested in a noteworthy paper by Rong and Liu (2020). The authors outline the benefits of the model-shifting process, highlighting the Webratio tool and the extension of IFML to web applications. Additionally, they present a detailed method for mapping IFML to the design environment, focusing on the creation of IFML-based web applications that fully meet user expectations. This approach simplifies and expedites the process of designing the front-end interface of a project.

Introducing the AutoCRUD plugin for the Webratio tool by (Rodriguez-Echeverria et al., 2018) provides a valuable contribution to automating the development of CRUD operations. By generating IFML specifications, this plugin significantly enhances the efficiency of web developers, streamlining the process of creating and managing basic Create, Read, Update, and Delete functionalities in web applications.

In an ambitious work by Lachgar and Abdali (2014), the authors propose an innovative method for creating user interfaces specifically tailored for mobile applications, with a focus on implementing them using the Android operating system. They introduce a Technology Neutral DSL (Domain-Specific Language) that allows for the creation of graphical user interfaces. This DSL can be cross-compiled to generate native code compatible with various platforms, offering flexibility and scalability in mobile application development.

Another study (Planas et al., 2021) highlights the benefits of model-driven approaches by exploring the development of software applications featuring multi-experience User Interfaces. By raising the abstraction level at which interfaces are defined, developers can achieve faster development cycles, improved deployment, and seamless integration with the rest of the software system and other interfaces. The authors introduce a new Domain-Specific Language (DSL) specifically designed for describing different types of CUIs (Conversational User Interfaces) and showcase how this DSL can be integrated into a comprehensive modeling environment that accurately represents the relationships between the modeled CUIs and other system models.

Huang et al. (2018) researched generating GUI models using static reverse engineering from Android source code. Their objective was to statically generate GUI models for Android applications. The benefit of this static analysis approach, when compared to dynamic methods, is its ability to efficiently derive models that closely mirror the application code's implementation. This can be valuable for areas like model-based testing and code generation.

Waheed et al. (2020) propose a method for stress testing web applications through automated script generation. Their approach incorporates a meta-model designed for automation and employs model-based construction of a system/tool capable of generating test scripts for stress-testing web applications using IFML. This method not only saves time by removing the manual effort required in script production but also aids developers throughout the development process.

Hamdani et al. (2019) introduce an innovative method to automatically generate IFML models from text-based specifications by leveraging natural language processing (NLP) features. They set up a series of NLP rules designed to extract key IFML elements, including view components and events, directly from textual requirements. The effectiveness of their proposed framework is evaluated using case studies of a movie manager and an online bookstore.

These diverse studies shed light on the immense potential and benefits of model-driven approaches in graphical user interface development, offering valuable insights into the methodologies, tools, and techniques employed in this domain. By harnessing the power of models and automation, developers can streamline the UI development process, enhance productivity, and deliver high-quality interfaces that meet the evolving needs of businesses and end-users alike.

PROPOSED METHODOLOGY

The CIM model serves as a comprehensive representation of the application, encompassing both the fundamental business process requirements and clients' specific needs. It remains independent of the technical details associated with implementation. The widely recognized BPMN standard is a powerful tool to define and depict business processes. IFML takes center stage. It offers a comprehensive suite of tools and methodologies that facilitate the graphical representation of user interactions and program behaviors. This standardized approach ensures consistency and clarity throughout the development process.

In our work, we utilized the Eclipse platform, known for its comprehensive features to facilitate the transformation from the CIM level, represented by the BPMN model, to the PIM level, expressed through the IFML model. This process is in line with the principles and guidelines of the MDA approach. Utilizing Eclipse's robust capabilities, we created the BPMN and IFML metamodels, which formed the foundation for our subsequent model transformations.

To begin, we meticulously created the two metamodels BPMN and IFML within the Eclipse environment. These metamodels provided the foundation for the subsequent modeling activities. Next, we established the BPMN model by capturing and formalizing the business processes using BPMN notation. This model was saved in ".xmi" format, using the BPMN metamodel as a reference.

The true essence of our methodology lies in the transformation step, where the CIM level illustrated by the BPMN model is converted into the PIM level represented by the IFML model. This pivotal process is accomplished by following the transformation rules outlined in Figure 1, expressed in the Atlas Transformation Language (ATL). These transformation rules encapsulate the logic and operations necessary to translate the BPMN representations into their corresponding IFML equivalents. Through the application of these rules within the Eclipse environment, we obtain the IFML model, also saved as a ".xmi" file.

Finally, the IFML model, serving as a comprehensive specification of the application's user interfaces, is seamlessly integrated into the Webratio tool. Webratio is a commercial software tool specifically designed to leverage the power of IFML for the automatic generation of user interfaces.

In summary, our methodology encompasses the entire spectrum of model-driven development by employing the BPMN and IFML standards, coupled with the Eclipse and Webratio tools, we streamline the transformation process, ensuring the automatic generation of high-quality user interfaces. This comprehensive approach boosts productivity and enhances overall efficiency and effectiveness.

The Conversion Rules From the CIM Level to the PIM Level

depicts the transformation rules governing the conversion process from BPMN to IFML models. Each rule, crucial for ensuring accurate transformation, is meticulously defined using the Atlas Transformation Language (ATL) and expressed in both human language and a well-structured schema.

To establish a solid foundation for the transformation rules, defining the metamodels at both the PIM and CIM levels is imperative. These metamodels serve as the schema for describing the transformation rules within the ATL language.

At the PIM level, the metamodel captures the essential elements and relationships specific to the IFML model. It provides a comprehensive representation of the concepts, components, and behaviors comprising the application's platform-independent view. This metamodel acts as a reference point for the transformation rules, enabling the conversion of BPMN models to their IFML equivalents. Similarly, the CIM metamodel serves as a fundamental input for defining the transformation rules, ensuring the alignment and consistency of the transformed IFML models with the original BPMN representations.

By establishing clear and well-defined metamodels at both the PIM and CIM levels, we established the transformation rules within the ATL language. These rules serve as the bridge between the two metamodels, dictating the conversion process from BPMN models to IFML models. Through careful analysis, design, and implementation, each transformation rule ensures that the transformed IFML models faithfully capture the essence and intent of the original BPMN models.

In essence, the transformation rules, defined within the ATL language, enable the seamless and accurate conversion of BPMN models to IFML models. By establishing a solid foundation through these metamodels and employing the power of transformation rules, we empower developers to translate high-level business processes and requirements into concrete and actionable IFML models, bridging the gap between conceptual design and practical implementation.

Figure 1a. BPMN to IFML transformation rules

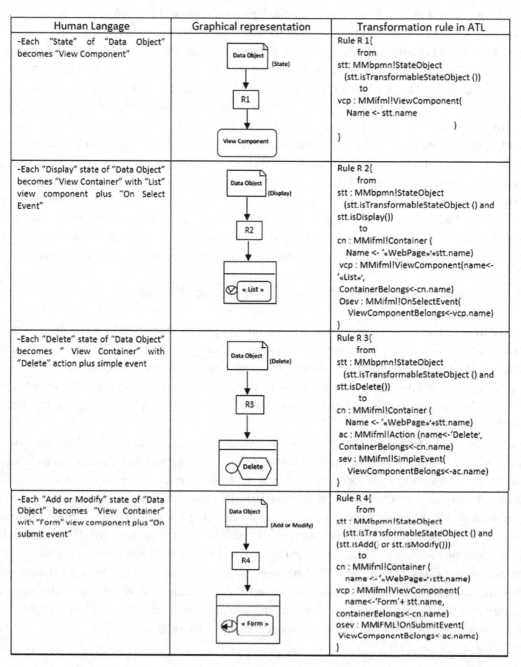

Human Langage	Graphical representation	Transformation rule in ATL

-Each "State" of "Data Object" becomes "View Component"	Data Object (State) → R1 → View Component	Rule R 1{
		    from
		stt: MMbpmn!StateObject
		(stt.isTransformableStateObject ())
		    to
		vcp : MMifml!ViewComponent(
		    Name <- stt.name
		                    )
		}

-Each "Display" state of "Data Object" becomes "View Container" with "List" view component plus "On Select Event"	Data Object (Display) → R2 → « List »	Rule R 2{
		    from
		stt: MMbpmn!StateObject
		(stt.isTransformableStateObject () and stt.isDisplay())
		    to
		cn : MMifml!Container (
		    Name <- '«WebPage»'+stt.name)
		vcp : MMifml!ViewComponent(name<-'«List»',
		    ContainerBelongs<-cn.name)
		Osev : MMifml!OnSelectEvent(
		    ViewComponentBelongs<-vcp.name)
		}

-Each "Delete" state of "Data Object" becomes " View Container" with "Delete" action plus simple event	Data Object (Delete) → R3 → Delete	Rule R 3{
		    from
		stt: MMbpmn!StateObject
		(stt.isTransformableStateObject () and stt.isDelete())
		    to
		cn : MMifml!Container (
		    Name <- '«WebPage»'+stt.name)
		ac : MMifml!Action (name<-'Delete',
		ContainerBelongs<-cn.name)
		sev : MMifml!SimpleEvent(
		    ViewComponentBelongs<-ac.name)
		}

-Each "Add or Modify" state of "Data Object" becomes "View Container" with "Form" view component plus "On submit event"	Data Object (Add or Modify) → R4 → « Form »	Rule R 4{
		    from
		stt : MMbpmn!StateObject
		(stt.isTransformableStateObject () and (stt.isAdd() or stt.isModify()))
		    to
		cn : MMifml!Container (
		    name <- '«WebPage»'+stt.name)
		vcp : MMifml!ViewComponent(
		    name<-'Form'+ stt.name,
		containerBelongs<-cn.name)
		osev : MMIFML!OnSubmitEvent(
		    ViewComponentBelongs<-ac.name)
		}

Figure 1b. BPMN to IFML transformation rules

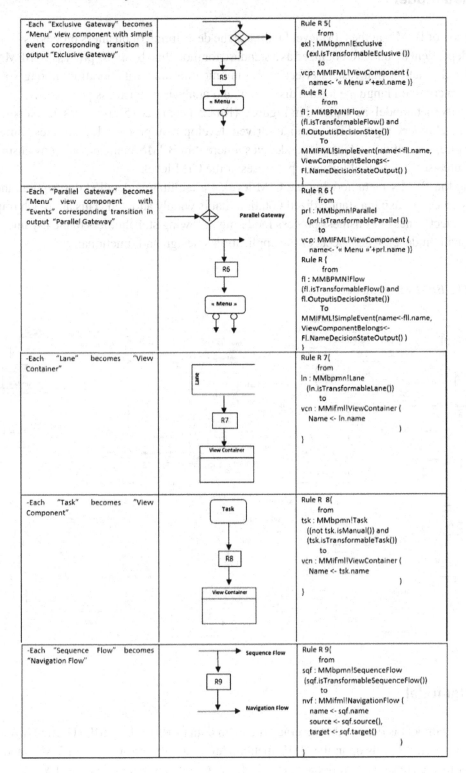

-Each "Exclusive Gateway" becomes "Menu" view component with simple event corresponding transition in output "Exclusive Gateway"		Rule R 5{
		from
		exl : MMbpmn!Exclusive
		(exl.isTransformableEclusive ())
		to
		vcp: MMIFML!ViewComponent {
		name<- '« Menu »'+exl.name)}
		Rule R {
		from
		fl : MMBPMN!Flow
		(fl.isTransformableFlow() and
		fl.OutputisDecisionState())
		To
		MMIFML!SimpleEvent(name<-fll.name,
		ViewComponentBelongs<-
		Fl.NameDecisionStateOutput())
		}

-Each "Parallel Gateway" becomes "Menu" view component with "Events" corresponding transition in output "Parallel Gateway"		Rule R 6 {
		from
		prl : MMbpmn!Parallel
		(prl.isTransformableParallel ())
		to
		vcp: MMIFML!ViewComponent {
		name<- '« Menu »'+prl.name)}
		Rule R {
		from
		fl : MMBPMN!Flow
		(fl.isTransformableFlow() and
		fl.OutputisDecisionState())
		To
		MMIFML!SimpleEvent(name<-fll.name,
		ViewComponentBelongs<-
		Fl.NameDecisionStateOutput())
		}

-Each "Lane" becomes "View Container"		Rule R 7{
		from
		ln : MMbpmn!Lane
		(ln.isTransformableLane())
		to
		vcn : MMifml!ViewContainer {
		Name <- ln.name
		)
		}

-Each "Task" becomes "View Component"		Rule R 8{
		from
		tsk : MMbpmn!Task
		((not tsk.isManual()) and
		(tsk.isTransformableTask())
		to
		vcn : MMifml!ViewContainer {
		Name <- tsk.name
		)
		}

-Each "Sequence Flow" becomes "Navigation Flow"		Rule R 9{
		from
		sqf : MMbpmn!SequenceFlow
		(sqf.isTransformableSequenceFlow())
		to
		nvf : MMifml!NavigationFlow {
		name <- sqf.name
		source <- sqf.source(),
		target <- sqf.target()
		)
		}

BPMN Metamodel

The utilization of BPMN at the CIM level facilitates the description of business processes in a computationally independent manner. Recognized as a standard for modeling business processes, BPMN provides a standardized notation that fosters effective communication and collaboration among stakeholders, establishing a common language for the discussion and analysis of business processes.

The BPMN metamodel, as depicted in Figure 2 (Rhazali et al., 2015), provides developers, analysts, and other stakeholders engaged in the model-driven development process. It facilitates comprehension of the structure, semantics, and interdependencies inherent in BPMN elements, thereby ensuring a consistent and precise depiction of business processes at the CIM level.

Utilizing the BPMN metamodel at the CIM level, we facilitate a detailed description and analysis of business processes using a standardized notation that is widely adopted. This approach improves the clarity and effectiveness of business process modeling, allowing stakeholders to clearly understand the computationally independent aspects of the application's design and functionality.

Figure 2. The BPMN metamodel

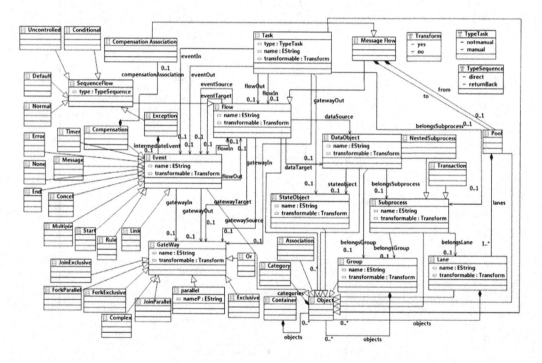

IFML Metamodel

The IFML metamodel is designed to leverage the main data types of the UML (Unified Modeling Language) metamodel. It builds upon the UML metamodel by incorporating a set of UML metaclasses as the basis for its metaclasses. Additionally, the IFML metamodel assumes that the IFML ContentModel is defined using UML.

Figures 3 and 4 provide visual representations of the IFML metamodel's structure and components, illustrating the relationships between metaclasses to aid in comprehensive understanding.

Figures 3 and 4 show the IFML metamodel (Brambilla et al., 2017), (OMG-IFML, 2015), capitalizing on the UML metamodel's data types. This ensures consistency and compatibility with UML-based modeling tools and practices. By aligning with UML, IFML provides a standardized approach for describing and modeling interaction flows and user interfaces. The IFML metamodel, built upon the foundation of UML metaclasses, provides a robust and comprehensive set of constructs for modeling user interfaces and interaction flows. Overall, the IFML metamodel, as illustrated in Figures 3 and 4, provides a structured and standardized framework for modeling interaction flows and user interfaces. By aligning with UML and utilizing its main data types, IFML ensures compatibility, consistency, and interoperability within the broader modeling ecosystem.

Figure 3. IFML metamodel 1

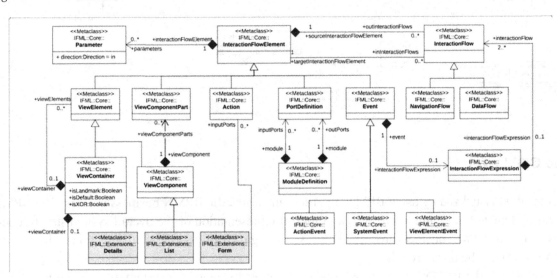

ILLUSTRATIVE EXAMPLE

The after-sales service case study revolves around facilitating CRUD (Create, Read, Update, and Delete) operations for customers who encounter issues with their orders and need to address complaints. The process initiates with user authentication, requiring the input of a username and password. Existing users with registered accounts gain access to a menu offering four key features; adding, modifying, deleting, and consulting a complaint. On the other hand, if a user is not yet registered, they must complete the registration process to avail themselves of the remaining features.

Overall, the after-sales service focuses on addressing customer complaints about their orders. It emphasizes user authentication, menu-driven interactions, and the implementation of CRUD operations to enhance the customer experience, streamline complaint management, and foster effective communication between customers and the service provider.

Figure 4. IFML metamodel 2

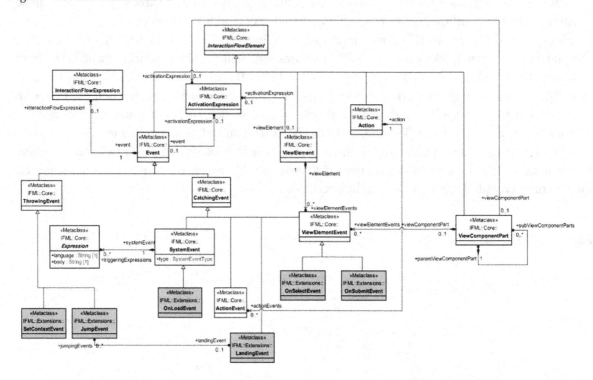

The CIM Level

This level; is visualized by using BPMN diagrams and a specific BPMN business process. The BPMN diagram, depicted in Figure 5, provides a graphical representation of the overall system structure and flow, while the BPMN business process, showcased in Figure 6, offers a detailed depiction of the specific business process being analyzed.

In Figure 5, the BPMN diagram captures the high-level view of the system, illustrating its components, interactions, and dependencies. This diagram serves as a visual guide to understanding the overall architecture and organization of the system, providing a clear overview of how different elements are connected and how information flows within the system.

Moving on to Figure 6, the BPMN business process diagram delves deeper into a specific business process within the system. This diagram presents a systematic representation of the activities, tasks, events, and decision points involved in the defined business process. It allows stakeholders to visualize the sequence of actions and the corresponding flow of information, providing a comprehensive understanding of the process and its various stages.

Together, these BPMN representations at the CIM level provide a powerful means of capturing and communicating the essential aspects of the system. The BPMN diagram offers a holistic view, while the BPMN business process diagram offers a more detailed perspective on a specific process. These visual representations aid in analysis, design, and communication, enabling stakeholders to better comprehend the system's structure, behavior, and operational flow at the CIM level.

Figure 5. BPMN diagram of the case study

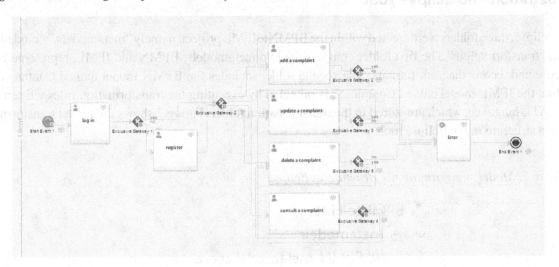

Figure 6. BPMN business process diagram of the case study

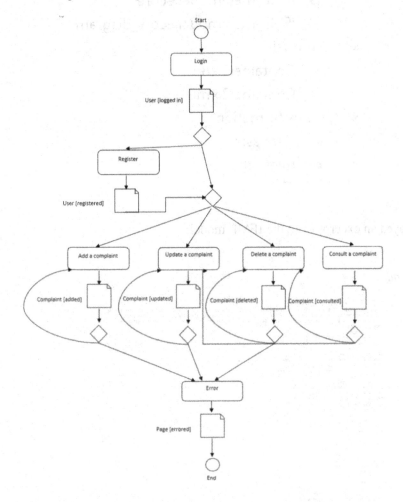

Illustration into Eclipse Tool

In Eclipse, three folders were created within the BPMNtoIFML project, namely "metamodels," "models," and "transformation." The first folder contains the two metamodels, BPMN and IFML, represented in .ecore and .ecore_diagram formats. The second folder includes the BPMN model named Container1, while the IFML model named Container2 is obtained by executing the transformation rules written in the ATL language, which are stored in the transformation folder. Figure 7 shows the model transformation's structure in the Eclipse tool.

Figure 7. Model transformation's structure in Eclipse

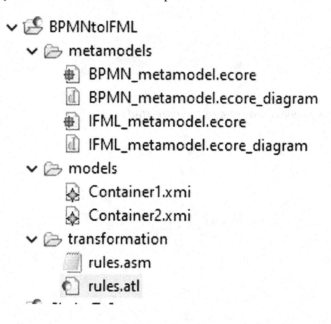

Figure 8 displayed an excerpt from the IFML model:

Figure 8. IFML model

```xml
<?xml version="1.0" encoding="ISO-8859-1"?>
<xmi:XMI xmi:version="2.0" xmlns:xmi="http://www.omg.org/XMI" xmlns:IFML="platform:/resource/BPMNtoIFML/metamodels/IFML_metamodel.ecore">
<ecore:EPackage xmi:version="2.0" xmlns:xmi="http://www.omg.org/XMI" xmlns:xsi="http://www.w3.org/2001/XMLSchema-instance"
    xmlns:ecore="http://www.eclipse.org/emf/2002/Ecore" name="IFML" nsURI="platform:/resource/BPMNtoIFML/metamodels/IFML_metamodel.ecore"
    nsPrefix="IFML">
</ecore:EPackage>
  <IFML:ViewComponent name="user [logged in]"/>
  <IFML:ViewComponent name="user [registred]"/>
  <IFML:ViewComponent name="complaint [added]"/>
  <IFML:ViewComponent name="page [errored]"/>
  <IFML:ViewComponent name="complaint [updated]"/>
  <IFML:ViewComponent name="page [errored]"/>
  <IFML:ViewComponent name="complaint [deleted]"/>
  <IFML:ViewComponent name="page [errored]"/>
  <IFML:ViewComponent name="complaint [consulted]"/>
  <IFML:ViewComponent name="&quot;Menu&quot;1"/>
  <IFML:ViewComponent name="&quot;Menu&quot;3"/>
  <IFML:ViewComponent name="&quot;Menu&quot;4"/>
  <IFML:ViewComponent name="&quot;Menu&quot;5"/>
  <IFML:ViewComponent name="&quot;Menu&quot;6"/>
  <IFML:Event name="no 4"/>
  <IFML:Event name="yes 7"/>
  <IFML:Event name="8"/>
  <IFML:Event name="yes 11"/>
  <IFML:Event name="no 12"/>
  <IFML:Event name="15"/>
  <IFML:Event name="yes 18"/>
  <IFML:Event name="no 19"/>
  <IFML:Event name="22"/>
  <IFML:Event name="yes 25"/>
  <IFML:Event name="no 26"/>
  <IFML:Event name="29"/>
  <IFML:Event name="32"/>
  <IFML:ViewContainer name="login"/>
  <IFML:ViewContainer name="register"/>
  <IFML:ViewContainer name="add a complaint"/>
  <IFML:ViewContainer name="error"/>
  <IFML:ViewContainer name="update a complaint"/>
  <IFML:ViewContainer name="error"/>
```

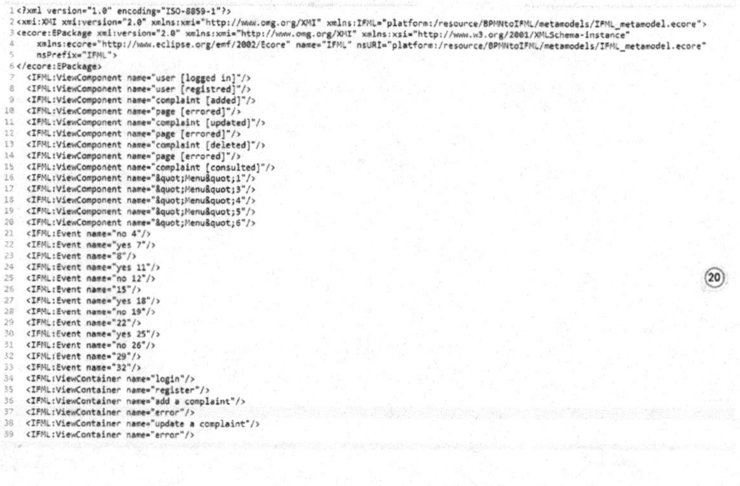

The PIM Level

Among the available options, Webratio stands out as the most powerful commercial tool (Laaz et al., 2018). We choose Webratio for several reasons, including its graphical modeling capabilities, which enable the expansion of IFML components and the design of IFML diagrams specifically for web applications. Additionally, Webratio is built on the Eclipse platform, ensuring seamless integration and providing efficient response times. Furthermore, Webratio is well-suited for academic researchers, making it an ideal choice for our work.

Using Webratio, we successfully obtained the front-end interfaces for the after-sales service, using the IFML language. This was achieved by utilizing the transformation rules from the CIM to the PIM level (Sajji et al., 2022). The development process in IFML follows a systematic approach, starting with modeling the application's domain and then creating an IFML model using the IFML language. Finally, the model obtained is converted into a fully functional web application.

By leveraging the capabilities of Webratio and adhering to the IFML development process, we were able to seamlessly transition from conceptual modeling to the implementation of user interfaces, resulting in a well-designed and functional software system.

Domain Model

It serves as a comprehensive illustration of the information relevant to the application's domain. Instead of introducing a new modeling language for domain modeling, we leverage the widely adopted UML-based standard called IFML. Specifically, we use UML class diagrams to construct the domain model.

In our example, the domain model is depicted in Figure 9 it includes various tables, such as "complaint," "User," "Group," and "Module." It is worth noting that the Webratio tool provides these tables by default, allowing for efficient and streamlined modeling within the application. By utilizing UML, class diagrams, and the Webratio tool's default tables, we can construct a clear and visually accessible representation of the domain model.

Figure 9. Domain model of the after-sales service

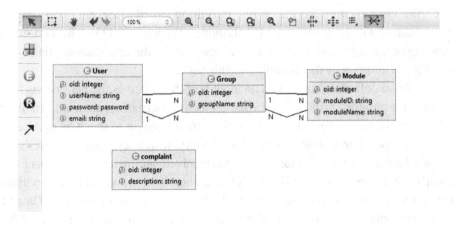

IFML Model

In our example, we focus on two essential elements: the login/registration function and the client's space. These elements play a crucial role in the application's functionality and user experience.

The public page serves as the main entry point for the application. It provides users with options to authenticate themselves by accessing the login page and registering if it is their initial attempt to utilize the application. The public page acts as a gateway for users to access the application's features and services.

If an error occurs during the authentication process, an error message is displayed. Figure 10 displays the visual representation of the "Public" site view, providing the login/registration functionality and the overall layout of the page.

Figure 10. Site view "Public"

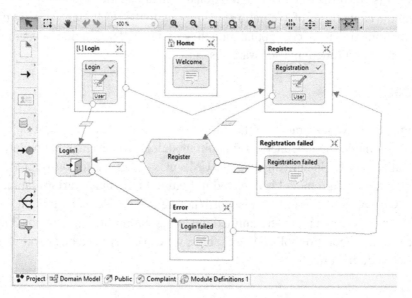

The "Public" site view encompasses an action definition called "Register" that defines a specific business logic associated with an event in the IFML model (Webratio, 2023). This action is responsible for handling the registration process and creating a new user in the application's database. Figure 11 provides a visual representation of the modeling of this action.

The "Register" action definition starts with an input port that receives the parameters from the user's registration form. These parameters include information such as username, password, email, and any other required details. Once the parameters are received, they are passed on to the "Create User" operation.

The "Create User" operation is based on the "User" entity, which represents the user's data structure in the application's database. This operation utilizes the received parameters to create a new user entry in the database, storing the provided information for future authentication and interaction within the system.

To establish a seamless flow of data within the "Register" action, we employed a Data Flow mechanism. This Data Flow enables the transfer of information from the Input Port to the Output Port, ensuring the smooth progression of data between different components of the action.

In this case, the Data Flow connects the input port, which receives the user registration parameters, to the "Create User" operation. This ensures that the necessary information is passed on to the operation for processing and creating the user entry in the database.

Similarly, another Data Flow is established between the "Create User" operation and the output port. This ensures that the processed data or any relevant output from the operation is directed to the output port for further usage or display. The success or failure of the operation execution is handled through designated ports. If all the operations are completed successfully, the action definition proceeds via the "Success" OK Port. On the other hand, if any operation encounters an error or fails to execute correctly, the "KO Port" handles the failed execution and appropriate measures can be taken to handle the error condition.

Figure 11. Action definition "Register"

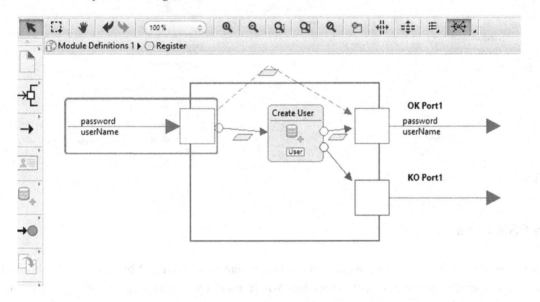

The "Complaint" space serves as a dedicated space for users to perform various operations related to their complaints. These operations align with the CRUD functionalities. Figure 12 illustrates the interface modeling for this section. Within the "Complaint" site view, we have utilized four distinct areas to represent the CRUD operations. Each area consists of pages and action definitions, along with view components such as lists and forms. These components facilitate the interaction between the user and the system.

For the example of adding a complaint. We have a page named "complaint" that contains a form. When the user clicks the "save" button on the form, it triggers the action definition "Add a complaint". This is achieved through a flow that connects the form to the action definition, with the relevant parameters being bound. Upon successful addition of the complaint, the flow directs the user back to the "Add a complaint" page. However, if any errors occur during the process, the user is redirected to an error page to handle the error condition appropriately.

By utilizing flows and parameter binding between the source and target elements, the interface modeling ensures a seamless and intuitive user experience when performing CRUD operations within the "Complaint" section.

Figure 12. Site view "Complaint"

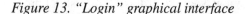

The PSM Level

We will display a selection of graphical user interfaces that were obtained by using the Webratio tool. Figure 13 illustrates the page for authentication, where users can authenticate themselves by entering their username and password. This page serves as the entry point for users to access the application's features securely.

Figure 13. "Login" graphical interface

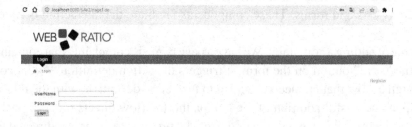

If a user is not yet registered, he is directed to the registration page depicted in Figure 14 This page prompts the user to provide their personal information for creating an account within the system.

Figure 14. "Register" graphical interface

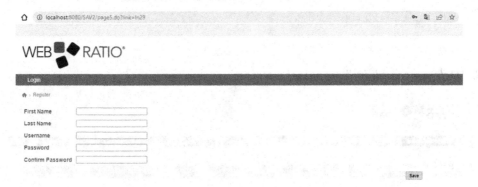

Figure 15 displays an additional interface that allows users to add a complaint. This interface provides a space where users can input the necessary details and submit their complaints. The form is designed to capture the required information accurately for the user.

Figure 15. "Add a complaint" graphical interface

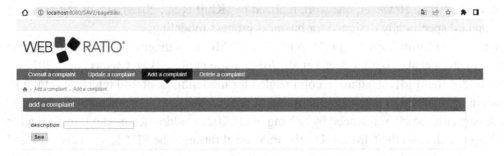

Figure 16. "Consult a complaint" graphical interface

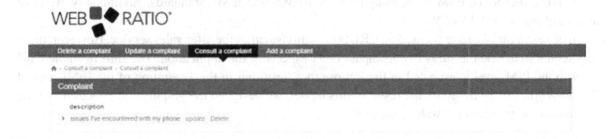

Figure 17. "Update a complaint" graphical interface

Figure 18. "Delete a complaint" graphical interface

DISCUSSION AND LIMITATION

We can observe that the studied works can be categorized into two main groups: those focused on the CIM to PIM shift and those focused on the PIM to PSM shift. Practically all of the works utilize UML diagrams to illustrate the levels of the MDA approach (Rhazali et al., 2018), (Kharmoum et al., 2019), (Arrhioui et al., 2018). However, one work realized by (Khlif et al., 2018), stands out as it employs the BPMN standard specifically designed for business process modeling.

In terms of transformations from PIM to PSM, the UML class diagram is commonly used in most of the works (Erraissi et al., 2020), (Deeba et al., 2018), (Srai et al., 2017), (Betari et al., 2017).

Interestingly, the IFML standard, recommended for modeling front-end interfaces at the PIM level, is not commonly adopted in the works examined, except for the work referenced by Koren and Klamma (2018). A particular work, referenced by (Zhang et al., 2022), addresses model transformations within the MDA approach from the CIM level to the PSM level through the PIM level. This work utilizes two models: one for requirements and another represented by a graph.

Overall, the analyzed papers demonstrate diverse approaches to model conversions within the MDA architecture, with varying emphasis on different levels and standards. Our work covers all model transformation processes. We have successfully implemented transformations from the CIM level to the PIM level and further to the PSM level, using both the BPMN and IFML standards. Additionally, we have leveraged the powerful tool Webratio.

In our example, we have focused on CRUD operations within the after-sales service. However, there is potential to extend the study to encompass other aspects of the application. The shift from the CIM level to the PIM level is executed in the Eclipse tool, resulting in the generation of the IFML model (OMG-XML, 2015). Based on the result of this model, we designed the graphical interfaces using the Webratio tool, to obtain the web application.

While our methodology demonstrates promising results, it is essential to acknowledge its limitations. One of the notable advantages of using IFML modeling is the ability to create front-end interfaces for software programs. The application generation process is highly streamlined. However, it is important to acknowledge that IFML is relatively a new technology, and it may be more suitable for working with smaller applications.

Also, a dependency on specific tools like Webratio, which may not be accessible or suitable for all development environments. Additionally, our approach may encounter difficulties when dealing with highly complex systems where traditional coding might offer finer control. It is also worth mentioning that while we have focused on certain modeling languages like IFML, some other languages and methods were not explored in this work. These limitations represent challenges for future research and should be considered when interpreting the results presented.

CONCLUSION AND FUTURE WORK

The MDA approach significantly reduces development time and effort. In the case of web applications, Webratio's robust architecture is widely used, providing a reliable platform for creating models. With this in mind, our work focuses on highlighting the different model transformations within the MDA approach.

Our methodology follows the principles of MDA and emphasizes the characteristics of each MDA level, particularly the shift from the CIM level to the PIM level using BPMN and IFML standards. The ultimate goal is to generate user interfaces using the Webratio tool. To accomplish this, we create the BPMN and IFML metamodels in the Eclipse tool. We then develop the BPMN model for our illustrative example and apply the transformation rules using ATL language to get the IFML model. Lastly, we generate the graphical user interfaces using the Webratio tool.

The primary aim of our future work is to create a tool that automates the entire transformation process, starting from the CIM level to the generation of graphical interfaces. We intend also to integrate machine learning algorithms to improve the adaptability and personalization of generated GUIs. In addition, comparative studies involving different tools and languages could offer valuable insights into the relative strengths and weaknesses of various methodologies in this rapidly evolving field

REFERENCES

Acerbis, R., Bongio, A., Brambilla, M., & Butti, S. (2015). Model-Driven Development Based on OMG's IFML with WebRatio Web and Mobile Platform. *Lecture Notes in Computer Science*, 605–608. Advance online publication. doi:10.1007/978-3-319-19890-3_39

Acerbis, R., Bongio, A., Butti, S., Ceri, S., Ciapessoni, F., Conserva, C., Fraternali, P., & Carughi, G. T. (2004). WebRatio is an Innovative Technology for Web Application Development. *Lecture Notes in Computer Science*, 613–614. Advance online publication. doi:10.1007/978-3-540-27834-4_90

Arrhioui, K., Mbarki, S., & Erramdani, M. (2018, August 30). Applying CIM-to-PIM Model Transformation for Development of Emotional Intelligence Tests Platform. *International Journal of Online Engineering*, 14(08), 160. doi:10.3991/ijoe.v14i08.8747

Bernaschina, C., Brambilla, M., Mauri, A., & Umuhoza, E. (2017). A Big Data Analysis Framework for Model-Based Web User Behavior Analytics. In J. Cabot, R. De Virgilio, & R. Torlone (Eds.), Lecture Notes in Computer Science: Vol. 10360. *Web Engineering. ICWE 2017*. Springer. doi:10.1007/978-3-319-60131-1_6

Betari, O., Erramdani, M., Roubi, S., Arrhioui, K., & Mbarki, S. (2016, September 23). Model Transformations in the MOF Meta-Modeling Architecture: From UML to CodeIgniter PHP Framework. *Advances in Intelligent Systems and Computing*, 227–234. doi:10.1007/978-3-319-46568-5_23

Brambilla, M., Cirami, R., Gasparini, M., Marassi, A., & Pavanetto, S. (2019, Oct). Code Generation based on IFML for the User Interfaces of the Square Kilometre Array (SKA). *Proc. ICALEPCS'19*, 1307-1311. 10.18429/JACoW-ICALEPCS2019-WEPHA093

Brambilla, M., & Fraternali, P. (2014). *Interaction Flow Modeling Language: Model-Driven UI Engineering of Web and Mobile Apps with IFML* (1st ed.). Morgan Kaufmann Publishers Inc.

Brambilla, M., Mauri, A., & Umuhoza, E. (2014). Extending the Interaction Flow Modeling Language (IFML) for Model Driven Development of Mobile Applications Front End. *Mobile Web Information Systems*, 176–191. doi:10.1007/978-3-319-10359-4_15

Brambilla, M., Umuhoza, E., & Acerbis, R. (2017, September 26). Model-driven development of user interfaces for IoT systems via domain-specific components and patterns. *Journal of Internet Services and Applications*, 8(1), 14. Advance online publication. doi:10.1186/s13174-017-0064-1

Deeba, F., Kun, S., Shaikh, M., Dharejo, F. A., Hayat, S., & Suwansrikham, P. (2018, April). Data transformation of UML diagram by using model-driven architecture. *2018 IEEE 3rd International Conference on Cloud Computing and Big Data Analysis (ICCCBDA)*. 10.1109/ICCCBDA.2018.8386531

Erraissi, A., Banane, M., Belangour, A., & Azzouazi, M. (2020, October 26). Big Data Storage using Model Driven Engineering: From Big Data Meta-model to Cloudera PSM meta-model. *2020 International Conference on Data Analytics for Business and Industry: Way Towards a Sustainable Economy (ICDABI)*. 10.1109/ICDABI51230.2020.9325674

Hamdani, M., Butt, W. H., Anwar, M. W., Ahsan, I., Azam, F., & Ahmed, M. A. (2019). A Novel Framework to Automatically Generate IFML Models From Plain Text Requirements. *IEEE Access : Practical Innovations, Open Solutions*, 7, 183489–183513. doi:10.1109/ACCESS.2019.2959813

Huang, A., Pan, M., Tian, Z., & Li, X. (2018). *Static extraction of IFML models for Android apps*. doi:10.1145/3270112.3278185

Kharmoum, N., Ziti, S., Rhazali, Y., & Omary, F. (2019, June 1). An Automatic Transformation Method from the E3value Model to IFML Model: An MDA Approach. *Journal of Computational Science*, 15(6), 800–813. doi:10.3844/jcssp.2019.800.813

Khlif, W., Elleuch Ben Ayed, N., & Ben-Abdallah, H. (2018). From a BPMN Model to an Aligned UML Analysis Model. *Proceedings of the 13th International Conference on Software Technologies*. 10.5220/0006866606570665

Koren, I., & Klamma, R. (2018). The Exploitation of OpenAPI Documentation for the Generation of Web Frontends. *Companion of the Web Conference 2018 on the Web Conference 2018 - WWW '18.* doi:10.1145/3184558.3188740

Laaz, N., Wakil, K., Mbarki, S., & Jawawi, D. N. (2018, September 1). Comparative Analysis of Interaction Flow Modeling Language Tools. *Journal of Computational Science, 14*(9), 1267–1278. doi:10.3844/jcssp.2018.1267.1278

Lachgar, M., & Abdali, A. (2014, October). Generating Android graphical user interfaces using an MDA approach. *2014 Third IEEE International Colloquium in Information Science and Technology (CIST).* 10.1109/CIST.2014.7016598

Model Driven Architecture (MDA). (2014). Object Management Group. https://www.omg.org/mda/

OMG-BPMN. (2011). *Business Process Model and Notation (BPMN)-Version 2.0.* OMG. Available at: https://www.omg.org/spec/BPMN/2.0/PDF

OMG-IFML. (2015). *Interaction Flow Modeling Language (IFML)- OMG.* Available at: https://www.omg.org/spec/IFML/1.0/Beta1/PDF

OMG-XML. (2015). *XML Metadata Interchange (XMI) Specification.* Available at: https://www.omg.org/spec/XMI/2.5.1/PDF

Planas, E., Daniel, G., Brambilla, M., & Cabot, J. (2021, August). Towards a model-driven approach for multiexperience AI-based user interfaces. *Software & Systems Modeling, 20*(4), 997–1009. doi:10.1007/s10270-021-00904-y

Rhazali, Y., Hadi, Y., Chana, I., Lahmer, M., & Rhattoy, Ab. (2018). A model transformation in model-driven architecture from business model to web model. *IAENG International Journal of Computer Science, 45*, 104–117.

Rhazali, Y., Hadi, Y., & Mouloudi, A. (2015, December 31). A Methodology of Model Transformation in MDA: From CIM to PIM. *International Review on Computers and Software, 10*(12), 1186. doi:10.15866/irecos.v10i12.8088

Rodriguez-Echeverria, R., Preciado, J. C., Sierra, J., Conejero, J. M., & Sanchez-Figueroa, F. (2018, December). AutoCRUD: Automatic generation of CRUD specifications in interaction flow modeling language. *Science of Computer Programming, 168*, 165–168. doi:10.1016/j.scico.2018.09.004

Rong, C., & Liu, X. (2020). IFML-Based Web Application Modeling. *Procedia Computer Science, 166*, 129–133. doi:10.1016/j.procs.2020.02.034

Roubi, S., Erramdani, M., & Mbarki, S. (2016, April 19). A Model-Driven Approach for generating Graphical User Interface for MVC Rich Internet Application. *Computer and Information Science, 9*(2), 91. doi:10.5539/cis.v9n2p91

Sajji, A., Rhazali, Y., & Hadi, Y. (2022, October 1). A methodology for transforming BPMN to IFML into MDA. *Bulletin of Electrical Engineering and Informatics, 11*(5), 2773–2782. doi:10.11591/eei.v11i5.3973

Srai, A., Guerouate, F., Berbiche, N., & HilalDrissi, H. (2017, November 2). Generated PSM Web Model for E-learning Platform Respecting n-tiers Architecture. *International Journal of Emerging Technologies in Learning*, *12*(10), 212. doi:10.3991/ijet.v12i10.7179

Waheed, F., & Azam, F. (2020). Model Driven Approach for Automatic Script Generation in Stress Testing of Web Applications. doi:10.1145/3397125.3397137

WebRatio Learn Center. (2023, February 16). WebRatio. https://my.webratio.com/learn/content?nav=65&link=oln208a.redirect&so=pcu1a

Zhang, L., Pingaud, H., Lamine, E., Fontanili, F., Bortolaso, C., & Derras, M. (2022). A Model-Driven Approach to Transform Business Vision-Oriented Decision-Making Requirement into Solution-Oriented Optimization Model. *Advances and Trends in Artificial Intelligence. Theory and Practices in Artificial Intelligence*, 211–225. . doi:10.1007/978-3-031-08530-7_18

KEY TERMS AND DEFINITIONS

ATL (Atlas Transformation Language): It offers methods to generate target models from a collection of source models.

BPMN (Business Process Model and Notation): Is a visual depiction used to define business processes within a business process model.

CIM (Computation Independent Model): It's a model identified within the Model-Driven Architecture, serving as a cornerstone model. It encapsulates system and software insights from a business-oriented viewpoint.

IFML (Interaction Flow Modeling Language): IFML is a recognized modeling language within software engineering. It offers a collection of graphical notations for visually representing user interactions and the front-end dynamics of software applications.

MDA (Model Driven Architecture): A methodological approach to software design, offering guidelines for organizing specifications that are articulated in the form of models.

Model Transformations: Model transformation provides an automated method to generate platform-specific models from platform-independent ones. The primary objective of leveraging model transformation is to enhance efficiency and minimize errors by automating the creation and alteration of models whenever feasible.

PIM (Platform Independent Model): It's a representation of a software or business system that isn't tied to any particular technological platform for its implementation.

PSM (Platform Specific Model): It's a representation of a software or business system that is tailored to a particular technological platform.

Webratio: It's a low-code application development platform designed for crafting web, and mobile applications 7 times quicker than conventional coding methods.

Chapter 13
Efficient Parking Solutions Powered by IoT and Transportation Integration

N. Jothy

iD https://orcid.org/0000-0003-4786-7034

SRM Valliammai Engineering College, India

Komala James

SRM Valliammai Engineering College, India

N. Subhashini

iD https://orcid.org/0000-0002-3318-3144

SRM Valliammai Engineering College, India

A. K. Mariselvam

SRM Valliammai Engineering College, India

ABSTRACT

In the modern era, the issue of vehicle parking has become a significant concern in substantial investments. The conventional approach of locating available parking spaces by manually searching through multiple lanes has proven to be both time-consuming and labor-intensive. Furthermore, it requires parking safely and securely, eliminating the risk of being towed, and at a reduced cost. To tackle this challenge, a cutting-edge parking control system has been developed. This system incorporates secure devices, parking control gates, time and attendance machines, and car counting systems. These features play a crucial role in ensuring the safety of parked vehicles and effectively managing the fee structure for every vehicle's entry and exit. By leveraging IoT-powered technologies, it simplifies the process of locating available parking spaces by providing real-time information, reducing the manual effort required. With IoT, parking management is revolutionized, offering drivers a seamless and secure parking experience while optimizing operational efficiency for parking operators.

DOI: 10.4018/979-8-3693-0497-6.ch013

INTRODUCTION

The incorporation of Internet of Things (IoT) technology and transportation systems has paved the way for innovative parking solutions that address the challenges faced by cities and urban areas. Assim et al. (2020), proposed IoT-driven parking solutions harness the power of connectivity, data analysis, and real-time information to maximize parking space usage, optimize traffic flow, and elevate the overall parking experience for drivers. By integrating with transportation networks and services, these solutions offer a comprehensive approach to urban mobility.

The IoT-based parking solutions collect and monitor data on the availability of parking spaces, their occupancy status, and the duration of parking sessions in real-time was discussed by Nova et al. (2022). This data is then processed and made accessible to drivers through mobile applications, parking guidance systems, and digital signage. The integration with transportation systems allows for seamless parking-to-transit connections, enabling drivers to find parking spaces near public transportation hubs or ride-sharing pick-up points.

These intelligent parking solutions bring several benefits to cities, drivers, and transportation authorities. Primarily, these solutions enhance parking space utilization by offering precise information about available parking spots, thus reducing the time spent searching for parking and alleviating traffic congestion. This leads to improved traffic flow and reduced emissions, contributing to a more sustainable and eco-friendlier urban environment.

Secondly, Immanuel et al. (2023) proposed IoT-powered parking solutions enhance the parking experience for drivers by offering convenient features such as mobile payment options, parking reservations, and navigation guidance to available parking spaces. Drivers can easily locate, reserve, and pay for parking using their smartphones, eliminating the need for physical payment and reducing the hassle associated with finding parking.

Thirdly, the integration of parking solutions with transportation networks enables seamless connectivity between parking facilities and public transportation services. This integration allows drivers to plan their journeys more efficiently, combining parking with other modes of transportation such as buses, trains, or bicycles. It promotes the use of sustainable and multimodal transportation options, reducing reliance on private vehicles and congestion in city centers.

Furthermore, Rajbhandari et al. (2018) suggested that IoT-driven parking solutions furnish transportation authorities with invaluable data insights, empowering them to make well-informed decisions regarding parking management, infrastructure planning, and traffic policies. Through thorough analysis of parking data, authorities can discern parking patterns, fine-tune parking operations, and introduce demand-based pricing strategies to promote off-peak parking and incentivize the adoption of alternative transportation modes.

In conclusion, the integration of IoT technology and transportation systems in parking solutions offers a transformative approach to urban mobility. Farooqi et al. (2019) elucidated smart parking solutions enhance the efficiency of parking operations, improve traffic flow, and contribute to sustainable transportation. By providing real-time information, seamless connectivity, and data-driven insights, IoT-powered parking solutions are revolutionizing the way cities and drivers approach parking, making urban environments more accessible, convenient, and environmentally friendly.

Causes of Parking Problems

Parking challenges in cities and urban areas arise from a notable discrepancy between the demand for parking spaces (the quantity of cars seeking parking) and the limited availability of parking supply. This disparity can be attributed to several factors, including:

Historical City Planning: Many old and historical cities, especially capitals, were originally designed with narrow streets meant for horse-drawn carts rather than cars. Furthermore, population densities in these cities were much lower than they are today. Due to the inability of these narrow streets to be easily widened or altered, they struggle to accommodate the high density of vehicles for both moving and parking, far exceeding their original capacity.

Activity Concentration: Certain areas, such as central business districts (CBDs) or district centres, frequently see the convergence of various activities and facilities that necessitate a large number of cars. Commercial facilities, office buildings, and governmental institutions are examples of clustering. This concentration increases the demand for parking in these areas.

Miscalculation in New City Planning: In newly planned urban areas, parking demand is frequently underestimated due to an unexpected increase in car ownership, particularly among the upper and middle income classes. This happens when the available mass transit systems fail to attract these population segments for their daily commuting needs, leading to a greater reliance on private vehicles.

Inadequate Parking Infrastructure: In the planning of new cities and urban areas, curb-side parking and on-street parking areas are frequently used, with little provision for multi-level parking structures. The scarcity of dedicated land for multi-story parking facilities becomes a problem, especially in areas with densely packed facilities such as office buildings and commercial centres.

Land Use Changes: In existing cities, the phenomenon of land use invasion and succession causes areas to be converted from low car-dependent uses, such as residential, to high car-dependent uses, such as commercial or business zones. This transition worsens the parking issue because the parking supply does not adequately match the increased demand.

Violation of Building Codes and Zoning Regulations: In many cases, building codes and zoning regulations provide specific uses for areas, as well as parking requirements, such as basement garages. These regulations are frequently violated, resulting in a deviation from the planned calculations for providing sufficient parking spaces in these areas.

Ramasamy et al. (2018) addressed the parking problem in cities and urban areas necessitates a comprehensive approach that takes into account historical constraints, promotes alternative modes of transportation, improves urban planning practises, and effectively enforces building codes and zoning regulations.

Conventional Parking Methodologies

Conventional parking methodologies refer to traditional approaches and solutions used to address parking challenges in cities and urban areas. Here are some common conventional parking methodologies:

1. *On-Street Parking:* This is the most common and widely available form of parking. It involves designating specific areas along the sides of streets for vehicles to park. On-street parking is typi-

cally regulated through parking meters, time restrictions, or permits to manage the parking duration and ensure turnover.

2. ***Off-Street Parking Lots:*** These are designated areas, often privately owned, where vehicles can park. Off-street parking lots can be standalone facilities or integrated into larger developments such as shopping centers, office complexes, or residential buildings. They may charge a fee for parking, and regulations can be enforced to control parking duration and usage.

3. ***Parking Garages:*** Parking garages, also known as multi-story or multi-level parking structures, provide multiple levels of parking spaces within a confined building. These structures efficiently utilize vertical space to accommodate a larger number of vehicles compared to surface parking lots. Parking garages often have ramps or elevators for access between different levels.

4. ***Parking Decks:*** Similar to parking garages, parking decks are multi-level structures that provide parking spaces. However, parking decks typically have open sides, allowing for better natural ventilation and lighting compared to fully enclosed parking garages.

5. ***Parking Structures:*** These are large-scale parking facilities that can include a combination of parking garages, parking decks, and surface parking areas. They are often strategically located in areas with high parking demand, such as downtowns or near major attractions or transit hubs.

6. ***Park-and-Ride Facilities:*** Park-and-ride facilities are designed to encourage commuters to park their vehicles and use public transportation for the remainder of their journey. These facilities are usually located near transit stations, allowing people to easily transfer from their cars to buses, trains, or other modes of public transport.

7. ***Parking Permit Programs:*** Many cities implement parking permit programs to regulate and allocate parking spaces. Permits are issued to residents, businesses, or specific groups, allowing them exclusive parking privileges in designated areas.

8. ***Parking Management Technology:*** *Various parking management technologies are used to* optimize parking space utilization and enhance efficiency. These include automated payment systems, parking guidance systems, occupancy sensors, and mobile applications for locating available parking spaces.

While conventional parking methodologies have been widely used, they often face limitations in meeting the growing parking demand in urban areas. As cities continue to evolve, there is an increasing need for innovative and sustainable parking solutions, such as smart parking systems, shared mobility options, and transportation demand management strategies, to alleviate parking challenges and promote efficient land use.

Automated Parking System

Peyal et al. (20121) explained the automated parking systems utilize technology and mechanical systems to optimize parking space utilization and streamline the parking process. Here are some methodologies commonly employed in automated parking systems:

1. ***Automated Parking Garages:*** Automated parking garages, also known as robotic parking garages or robotic parking systems, use mechanical lifts, conveyors, and platforms to transport vehicles to and from parking spaces. Drivers leave their vehicles at the entry point, and the system automatically

moves and parks the vehicles in designated spaces. When a driver wants to retrieve their vehicle, the system retrieves it and brings it back to the pick-up point.

2. *Puzzle Parking Systems:* Puzzle parking systems, also called puzzle garages, consist of multiple levels of vertically stacked parking spaces. Vehicles are parked on pallets or platforms that can be independently moved horizontally and vertically by automated mechanisms. This system allows for compact parking arrangements and efficient space utilization.

3. *Automated Parking Towers:* Automated parking towers are vertical structures that house multiple levels of parking spaces. They use automated platforms and lifts to transport vehicles vertically within the tower. The system retrieves and delivers vehicles to the designated parking levels and spaces, optimizing space efficiency.

4. *Automated Parking Shuttles*: Automated parking shuttles, also known as shuttle parking systems, are designed for high-density parking. Vehicles are driven onto a platform, and an automated shuttle system transports the vehicle to a vacant parking space within a storage area. The shuttle system efficiently arranges and retrieves the vehicles as needed.

5. *Automated Parking Platforms:* Automated parking platforms are flat or inclined platforms that can move horizontally and vertically to park and retrieve vehicles. These platforms are controlled by automated systems and can be integrated into existing parking structures or built as standalone facilities.

6. *Automated Parking Guidance Systems:* Automated parking guidance systems use sensors and signage to guide drivers to available parking spaces within a parking facility. These systems provide real-time information on parking availability, directing drivers to vacant spaces and reducing the time spent searching for parking.

7. *Smart Parking* Applications: Smart parking applications and platforms utilize digital technology and connectivity to streamline the parking experience. These applications provide real-time parking availability information, allow drivers to reserve parking spaces in advance, and enable cashless payments for parking fees.

Automated parking systems offer benefits such as increased parking capacity, reduced parking footprint, improved parking efficiency, and enhanced user experience. Chu et al.(2023), particularly mentioned the usefulness in urban areas with limited space and high parking demand. By optimizing space utilization and automating the parking process, these systems contribute to efficient and sustainable urban mobility.

ARCHITECTURE OF SMART PARKING SYSTEM

A description of flowchart for the whole process of smart parking IoT is shown in Fig. 1.A smart parking system is an advanced technological solution that aims to optimize the parking experience by efficiently managing and monitoring parking spaces. The architecture of a smart parking system typically involves several key components working together to provide a seamless and automated parking process. Here's an explanation of each component:

1. **Sensors:** Smart parking systems rely on various types of sensors to detect the occupancy status of parking spaces. These sensors can be placed in individual parking spots or in different areas of a parking lot. Commonly used sensors include infrared sensors, ultrasonic sensors, or magnetic

sensors. The deployed sensors detect the real-time presence or absence of vehicles and promptly transmit this information to the central system. Smart parking systems use various sensors to monitor and manage parking spaces efficiently. The choice of sensors depends on factors such as cost, accuracy, and the specific requirements of the parking facility. Some common types of sensors used in smart parking systems are listed below:

(i) *Ultrasonic Sensors:* These sensors use sound waves to detect the presence of a vehicle in a parking space. Ultrasonic sensors are often mounted on the ceiling or on poles and can detect the distance between the sensor and the vehicle. Ultrasonic sensors operate as beam-based sensors, emitting and receiving sound waves with frequencies beyond the human audible range (typically between 20 and 40-50 kHz). These sound waves, often generated by piezo-actuators through a membrane, propagate through the air surrounding the vehicle and bounce back when encountering obstacles. The sensors capture the reflected echo signals, which are then analyzed by a central control unit. By measuring the crossing time, representing the duration for the echo signal to travel from the transmitter to the obstacle and back, the system calculates the distance to the obstacle'

(ii) *Infrared Sensors:* Infrared sensors detect the presence of a vehicle by emitting and receiving infrared radiation. When a vehicle enters a parking space, it interrupts the infrared beams, signaling that the space is occupied.

(iii) *Magnetic Sensors:* Magnetic sensors detect changes in the Earth's magnetic field caused by the presence of a vehicle. These sensors are usually embedded in the pavement and are sensitive to the metal in vehicles. Magnetic sensors contribute to enhancing vehicle safety, efficiency, and convenience by providing valuable data for various systems and applications. Their reliability and versatility make them integral components in modern automotive technology.

(iv) *Radar Sensors:* Radar sensors serve the purpose of identifying the presence of vehicles within parking spaces by emitting radio waves. These waves, upon encountering an object like a vehicle, reflect back to the sensor. By analyzing the reflected signals, the sensor determines whether a vehicle is present. In smart parking systems, these radar sensors are often integrated with IoT capabilities, facilitating communication with a central control system. This connectivity allows for remote monitoring, control, and data analysis, contributing to efficient parking management. By providing precise and real-time information about parking space occupancy, radar sensors play a pivotal role in optimizing parking operations and elevating the overall parking experience.

(v) *Lidar Sensors:* Lidar sensors utilize laser light to precisely measure distances, offering accurate 3D mapping of the surroundings. This capability aids in identifying the presence and dimensions of vehicles within parking spaces. The advanced features of Lidar sensors, including detection, ranging, and mapping, play a pivotal role in enhancing the efficiency, precision, and overall effectiveness of smart parking systems. Integration of Lidar technology elevates the management of parking spaces, delivering advantages to both drivers and operators of parking facilities.

2. **Communication Network:** A reliable communication network is essential for the functioning of a smart parking system. This network enables the transfer of data between different components of the system, including sensors, gateways, servers, and user interfaces. It can be a wired or wireless network, such as Wi-Fi, Bluetooth, or cellular networks.

Figure 1. Process of smart parking IoT

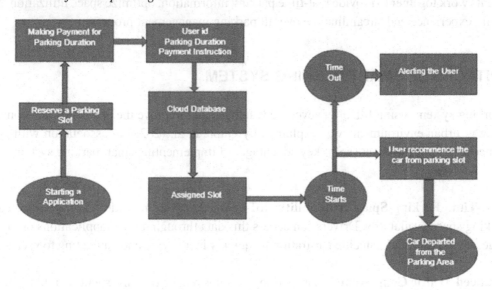

3. **Gateways:** Gateways serve as intermediaries between the sensors and the central server, functioning as data hubs. They receive data from the sensors and facilitate its transmission to the server for processing and analysis. Gateways may also perform data aggregation and pre-processing tasks to optimize the communication between sensors and the server.

4. **Central Server**: The central server is the core component of a smart parking system. It receives real-time data from the sensors via the gateways and processes it to determine the availability or occupancy status of parking spaces. The server may use algorithms and analytics to analyze the data and make intelligent decisions. It also stores and manages the parking-related information and provides APIs or interfaces for other system components and user applications to interact with.

5. **User Applications:** Drivers, parking lot operators, and administrators have interfaces to communicate with the smart parking system owing to user applications. These applications can be mobile apps, web portals, or even in-car navigation systems. Drivers can use these applications to search for available parking spaces, make reservations, and receive navigation instructions. Operators and administrators can monitor the parking status, generate reports, and manage the overall system.

6. **Display and Signage:** Smart parking systems often include digital displays or signage at key locations within a parking facility. These displays can show real-time information about the availability of parking spaces, guiding drivers to vacant spots. They can also provide directions, payment information, and other relevant details.

7. **Payment and Access Control:** To enable seamless payment and access control, smart parking systems may integrate with payment gateways and access control systems. This integration allows drivers to make cashless payments through mobile apps or other means and provides automated access to parking spaces using technologies like RFID (Radio-Frequency Identification) or license plate recognition.

Overall, the architecture of a smart parking system involves a combination of sensors, communication networks, gateways, servers, user applications, displays, and payment/access control systems. These components work together to provide real-time parking information, optimize space utilization, enhance the parking experience and streamline the overall parking management process.

ADVANTAGES OF SMART PARKING SYSTEM

Smart parking systems using IoT offer several advantages that improve the efficiency and convenience of parking in urban environments was explained by Gupta et al. (2022) in association with Artificial Intelligence technology. Here are some key advantages of implementing smart parking systems powered by IoT:

1. **Real-Time Parking Space Availability:** IoT-enabled sensors provide real-time information on parking space availability. Drivers can access this data through mobile applications or digital signage, saving time and reducing frustration by quickly identifying and navigating to vacant parking spots.
2. **Reduced Traffic Congestion:** Smart parking systems reduce the time spent searching for parking by efficiently directing drivers to available spaces. This reduces traffic congestion, as fewer vehicles circulate in search of parking, leading to smoother traffic flow and reduced emissions.
3. **Improved User Experience**: Smart parking systems enhance the overall parking experience for drivers. Lin et al. (2017), revealed the features such as navigation guidance, mobile payments, and parking reservations streamline the process and eliminate the need for physical payment transactions, reducing hassle and increasing convenience.
4. **Efficient Space Utilization**: IoT-powered parking systems optimize parking space utilization by providing accurate occupancy data. This information allows parking operators to effectively manage parking resources, maximize occupancy rates, and identify underutilized areas that can be repurposed for other needs.
5. **Cost Savings:** Smart parking systems help drivers save on parking costs. By providing information on parking rates, discounts, and promotions, drivers can make informed decisions and choose more affordable parking options. Additionally, features like dynamic pricing based on demand can incentivize off-peak parking, offering cost savings to drivers.
6. **Sustainability***:* IoT-powered parking systems contribute to environmental sustainability. They aid in lowering fuel consumption and greenhouse gas emissions by decreasing the amount of time spent looking for parking and reducing traffic congestion was discussed by Lin et al. (2019). The integration with public transit options further promotes sustainable transportation by encouraging the use of alternative modes.
7. **Data-Driven Decision Making:** Smart parking systems generate valuable data on parking patterns, occupancy rates, and user behavior. This data can be analyzed to gain insights into parking demand, peak usage hours, and infrastructure planning. Parking operators and city authorities can make data-driven decisions regarding parking management, pricing strategies, and infrastructure development.
8. **Integration With Transportation Services:** Smart parking systems can be integrated with transportation networks, providing seamless connectivity between parking facilities and public transit services. Mackey et al. (2020), framed the integration that allows the drivers to easily combine

parking with other modes of transportation, promoting multimodal mobility and reducing reliance on private vehicles.

Overall, smart parking systems using IoT technology offer numerous advantages, including real-time information, reduced traffic congestion, enhanced user experience, efficient space utilization, cost savings, sustainability, and data-driven decision making. These advantages contribute to improving urban mobility, reducing environmental impact, and enhancing the overall quality of life in cities.

DISADVANTAGES OF SMART PARKING SYSTEM

Smart parking management systems have a few drawbacks in addition to their many advantages. Here are some potential drawbacks of smart parking management systems:

1. **Implementation Costs:** Setting up a smart parking management system can be expensive. It requires the installation of sensors, cameras, and other infrastructure, which can be costly for parking facility owners or municipalities. The initial investment may pose a financial challenge for some organizations.
2. **Maintenance and Upkeep:** Smart parking systems involve a complex network of sensors, software, and hardware components. Regular maintenance and upkeep are essential to ensure smooth operation. If any part of the system malfunctions, it may require skilled technicians to diagnose and repair the issue promptly, resulting in additional costs.
3. **Technical Challenges:** Various technologies, including sensors, data analytics, and communication networks, are used in smart parking systems. These technologies can encounter technical challenges such as connectivity issues, data synchronization problems, or sensor failures. These issues may disrupt the system's functionality and lead to inaccurate information, causing frustration for users.
4. **Privacy and Security Concerns:** Smart parking systems collect and store data about vehicle movements, parking habits, and user information. Xiang et al. (2022), raises concerns about privacy and security. If the system's data is not adequately protected, it could be vulnerable to hacking attempts or unauthorized access. Maintaining robust cybersecurity measures is crucial to mitigate these risks.
5. **Learning Curve for Users:** Transitioning from traditional parking methods to a smart parking management system may involve a learning curve for users. People who are not familiar with the technology may find it challenging to navigate the system, use mobile apps, or interpret real-time data. This could lead to confusion or delays, especially during the initial stages of implementation.
6. **Reliance on Infrastructure**: Smart parking systems heavily depend on robust infrastructure, including a stable internet connection and power supply. In areas with poor network coverage or frequent power outages, the system's effectiveness may be compromised. Lack of infrastructure support can limit the system's reliability and availability.
7. **Exclusion of Non-Smartphone Users:** Smart parking management systems often rely on mobile apps for user interaction, such as finding available parking spaces or making payments. This can create challenges for individuals without smartphones or those who are not tech-savvy, potentially excluding them from accessing the benefits of the system.

While these drawbacks are present, it is important to keep in mind that many of them can be reduced or eliminated with proper preparation, implementation, and ongoing management of the smart parking system.

INNOVATIONS IN SMART PARKING SYSTEM

1. **AI-Based Predictive Analytics**: AI-based predictive analytics is a powerful technology that has the potential to revolutionize the efficiency and effectiveness of smart parking systems. Krishnan et al. (2022), leveraged artificial intelligence and machine learning algorithms, predictive analytics can analyze historical data, real-time information and various influencing factors to make accurate predictions about parking demand and availability. AI-based predictive analytics can enhance smart parking systems will be addressed in the following:

    a) *Parking Demand Forecasting*: AI algorithms can analyze historical data, such as parking patterns during different times of the day, weekdays, and special events. This analysis helps predict future parking demand, allowing parking operators to proactively manage parking spaces and optimize resource allocation.

    b) *Real-Time Parking Availability Prediction*: AI can process data from various sensors and cameras deployed in parking lots and streets to monitor parking space occupancy in real-time. By analyzing this data, the system can predict which parking spaces are likely to become available soon, helping drivers find open spots quickly.

    c) *Dynamic Pricing*: With predictive analytics, smart parking systems can implement dynamic pricing models based on anticipated demand. During peak times or events, the system can adjust parking fees to incentivize drivers to use alternative transportation or park at off-peak hours, thus reducing congestion.

    d) *Optimized Parking Space Allocation:* Errousso et al. (2020), briefed the AI algorithms that can optimize the allocation of parking spaces based on historical and real-time data. For example, certain areas might experience higher demand during specific times, and the system can adjust the allocation of spaces accordingly.

    e) *Traffic Management and Congestion Reduction:* By predicting parking demand and availability, smart parking systems can help reduce traffic congestion as drivers are directed to available spaces efficiently, avoiding aimless searching for parking spots.

    f) *Personalized Parking Recommendations:* Said et al. (2021), suggested that AI can learn from user behavior and preferences to provide personalized parking recommendations to individual drivers. This could be based on their usual parking habits, preferred payment methods, or other relevant factors.

    g) *Predictive Maintenance:* AI-based predictive analytics can also be applied to parking infrastructure and equipment. By analyzing sensor data and historical maintenance records, the system can predict potential equipment failures and schedule maintenance proactively, ensuring smooth operations and minimizing downtime.

    h) *Integration With Navigation Systems:* AI-driven parking predictions can be integrated into navigation systems or mobile apps, allowing drivers to receive real-time parking availability information and suggested parking locations along their route.

i) *Enhanced User Experience:* By accurately predicting parking availability and streamlining the parking process, AI-based predictive analytics can significantly improve the overall user experience for drivers, making it more convenient and less stressful.

However, it's worth noting that AI-based systems rely heavily on data quality and accuracy. Regular updates and maintenance of sensor networks and data sources are essential to ensure the reliability and effectiveness of the predictive analytics in smart parking systems.

2. **Blockchain Integration:** Smart parking systems might have started exploring the use of blockchain technology to enhance security, transparency, and data integrity for transactions, especially when handling payments and user information. Here's how blockchain integration can impact smart parking systems:

    a) *Secure and Transparent Transaction:* Blockchain's decentralized nature ensures that all parking transactions, such as payments and reservations, are securely recorded on the distributed ledger. This eliminates the need for a centralized authority, reducing the risk of data manipulation or unauthorized access.

    b) *Fraud Prevention:* With blockchain, each transaction is cryptographically linked to the previous one, forming a chain of blocks. This creates an immutable record of parking transactions, making it nearly impossible for fraudulent activities like double-spending or altering records.

    c) *Decentralized Payment System:* Blockchain allows for peer-to-peer transactions without the need for intermediaries. This enables direct payments between drivers and parking providers, reducing transaction fees and processing delays.

    d) *Smart Contracts for Automation:* Smart contracts are self-executing contracts with predefined rules was discussed by Kuran et al. (2015), in the article. They can be utilized in smart parking systems to automate payment processing, reservation validation, and other aspects of parking management. This automation streamlines the parking process and reduces administrative overhead.

    e) *Data Privacy and Ownership:* Blockchain technology allows individuals to have control over their data by providing them with private keys. Users can grant permission to access their data, enhancing data privacy and ownership rights.

    f) *Integration with Digital Wallets:* Leone et al.(2017), framed that by integrating with blockchain technology, smart parking systems can seamlessly connect with digital wallets and cryptocurrencies, enabling cashless and borderless payments for parking services.

    g) *Reduced Administrative Costs:* Blockchain's decentralized nature reduces the need for intermediaries and administrative entities, leading to cost savings for both parking operators and users.

    h) *Auditability and Accountability:* Every parking transaction recorded on the blockchain is timestamped and linked to the previous block, creating a transparent and auditable trail of events. This promotes accountability and can be valuable for resolving disputes or issues related to parking payments or reservations.

    i) *Interoperability and Standardization:* Blockchain can facilitate interoperability between different smart parking systems and applications, creating a standardized platform that enables seamless data sharing and collaboration among various stakeholders in the parking ecosystem.

It's important to note that blockchain integration requires careful consideration of network scalability, energy consumption (especially for proof-of-work blockchains), and user adoption. Additionally, as with any emerging technology, it's crucial to stay updated on the latest developments and security best practices in blockchain implementation to ensure its successful integration into smart parking systems.

3. **Edge Computing for Faster Response:** Implementing edge computing in smart parking systems could reduce latency and enable faster data processing and decision-making, enhancing the overall system's responsiveness. This approach offers several advantages that can significantly enhance the efficiency and responsiveness of smart parking systems:

   a) *Low Latency and Real-Time Processing:* Edge computing reduces data processing delays since the data is analyzed locally, near the parking lot or sensors. This real-time processing allows for immediate responses to changes in parking occupancy, enabling faster updates on parking availability for drivers.

   b) *Bandwidth Optimization:* By processing data at the edge, only relevant and summarized information is sent to the central server or cloud. This reduces the amount of data transmitted over the network, optimizing bandwidth usage and lowering communication costs.

   c) *Improved Reliability:* Decentralizing data processing increases system reliability. If the central cloud server experiences downtime or network connectivity issues, the local edge devices can continue functioning independently, ensuring uninterrupted parking operations.

   d) *Enhanced Privacy and Security*: Edge computing can enhance data privacy and security as sensitive data remains local and is not transferred to a centralized cloud. This reduces the risk of data breaches and unauthorized access to sensitive information.

   e) *Offline Capabilities:* Edge computing allows smart parking systems to operate even when there is limited or no internet connectivity. Local processing ensures that critical parking functionalities remain available, providing a seamless experience for drivers.

   f) *Scalability and Cost Efficiency:* Edge computing can distribute the computational load across various edge devices, making it easier to scale the system as the number of parking spaces and connected devices increases. It also reduces the need for expensive cloud infrastructure, contributing to cost savings.

   g) *Edge-Based AI and Machine Learning*: Edge computing can facilitate AI and machine learning capabilities at the edge, allowing the smart parking system to make intelligent decisions locally without relying solely on cloud-based algorithms.

   h) *Traffic Pattern Analysis:* Edge computing enables real-time analysis of traffic patterns near parking lots, helping to optimize traffic flow and reduce congestion around parking facilities.

   i) *Redundancy and Backup:* By having processing capabilities at the edge, data redundancy and backup mechanisms can be implemented locally, providing an extra layer of protection for critical data.

   j) *Complementing Cloud Computing:* Edge computing doesn't replace cloud computing; instead, it complements it by offloading processing tasks to the edge and utilizing cloud resources for more complex analysis, long-term data storage, and system-wide optimizations.

Overall, edge computing in smart parking systems offers numerous benefits that can lead to more efficient, reliable, and responsive parking management, contributing to a better experience for both parking operators and drivers.

4. **Augmented Reality (AR) Navigation:** Augmented Reality (AR) navigation in smart parking systems is a cutting-edge technology that enhances the parking experience for drivers by providing real-time visual guidance and information. AR overlays digital information onto the physical world, allowing users to see virtual elements superimposed on their surroundings through a device's camera or smart glasses. Here's how AR navigation can be applied in smart parking systems:

    a) *Parking Space Visualization:* AR can display virtual markers or icons directly on the physical environment, indicating the location of available parking spaces. Drivers can see which spots are open and navigate directly to them, reducing the time spent searching for parking.

    b) *Directions and Pathfinding*: AR navigation can guide drivers step-by-step, offering visual cues on the route to follow to reach a chosen parking space. It can also provide turn-by-turn directions to parking entrances and exits within a parking facility.

    c) *Real-Time Parking Availability:* AR can dynamically update the virtual markers based on real-time data from parking sensors, providing accurate information on parking space availability as drivers move through the parking area.

    d) *Parking Reservation and Payment:* AR interfaces can enable drivers to reserve parking spaces or make payments directly from their AR-enabled devices. This seamless integration streamlines the parking process and eliminates the need for physical payment machines.

    e) *Augmented Information about Parking Facilities*: AR can provide additional information about the parking facility, such as operating hours, available amenities, and contact details, creating a more informed and convenient parking experience.

The AR navigation in smart parking systems not only simplifies the parking process but also contributes to reducing traffic congestion, optimizing parking space utilization, and enhancing overall driver satisfaction. As AR technology continues to evolve, its integration with smart parking systems is likely to become more sophisticated, offering an even more seamless and immersive parking experience.

5. **5G Connectivity:** The adoption of 5G technology might have allowed smart parking systems to transmit data faster and support a more extensive network of connected devices and sensors, improving overall system performance. Here are some key benefits and impacts of 5G in smart parking:

    a) *High Data Transfer Speeds:* 5G offers significantly faster data transfer speeds compared to previous generations of cellular networks. This enables real-time communication between parking sensors, cameras, and other connected devices, allowing for more accurate and up-to-date information about parking space availability.

    b) *Low Latency:* 5G networks have lower latency, reducing the delay in transmitting data between devices and the central system. This low latency is crucial for real-time applications, such as real-time parking availability updates and instant response to driver requests.

    c) *Increased Capacity:* 5G networks can handle a much higher number of connected devices simultaneously. In smart parking systems, this means that a larger number of parking sensors and devices can be deployed without overloading the network, leading to more comprehensive parking coverage and better data accuracy.

    d) *Enhanced Connectivity for IoT Devices:* The Internet of Things (IoT) plays a significant role in smart parking systems. With 5G, the connectivity and responsiveness of IoT devices, such as parking sensors and cameras, improve, leading to more efficient and reliable data collection.

e) *Edge Computing Support:* 5G networks' low latency and high bandwidth make them well-suited for edge computing applications. This enables data processing and analysis to occur closer to the source, reducing the need to send all data to centralized cloud servers. Edge computing can enhance real-time parking availability updates and support faster decision-making.

f) *Improved User Experience:* With 5G, drivers can quickly access real-time parking information through mobile apps or in-car navigation systems. The speed and responsiveness of 5G enable seamless reservation, payment, and navigation features, making the parking process more convenient and efficient.

g) *Smart City Integration:* 5G connectivity enhances the integration of smart parking systems into broader smart city initiatives. It enables data sharing and collaboration between different components of a smart city, such as traffic management systems and public transportation, leading to more coordinated urban mobility solutions.

As the rollout of 5G continues to expand globally, we can expect to see further advancements and innovations in smart parking systems, leveraging the full potential of this high-speed, low-latency connectivity to provide more efficient and user-friendly parking solutions.

6. **Environmental Sensors:** Smart parking systems could incorporate environmental sensors to monitor air quality and pollution levels in parking areas, contributing to sustainable urban planning and eco-friendly initiatives. Here's how environmental sensors can enhance smart parking systems:

a) *Air Quality Monitoring:* Environmental sensors can measure air pollutants like nitrogen dioxide (NO_2), carbon monoxide (CO), particulate matter (PM), and ozone (O_3) levels. By collecting this data, the smart parking system can assess the air quality in and around parking areas, alerting users of potential health risks and promoting sustainable urban planning.

b) *Noise Level Monitoring:* Environmental sensors can track noise levels near parking facilities. This information can help identify areas with excessive noise pollution, enabling better city planning and potentially influencing drivers' parking preferences.

c) *Climate Control and Efficiency*: By monitoring temperature and humidity levels, the smart parking system can optimize climate control in indoor parking facilities. This improves user comfort and reduces energy consumption by adjusting heating, ventilation, and air conditioning (HVAC) systems based on real-time data.

d) *Urban Planning and Traffic Management:* Environmental data collected from sensors can contribute to urban planning initiatives. By understanding how parking facilities affect local air quality and noise levels, city planners can implement measures to mitigate negative impacts and optimize traffic flow.

e) *Public Health Awareness:* Smart parking systems can use environmental data to raise public awareness about air quality and noise pollution. Providing this information to drivers through mobile apps or digital displays can encourage eco-friendly transportation choices and reduce emissions.

f) *Parking Guidance and Reservation Optimization:* Environmental sensors can be used to assess parking demand and identify patterns related to specific weather conditions or events.

This data can optimize parking guidance systems and parking space reservation strategies, improving parking efficiency and reducing congestion during peak times.

g) ***Eco-Friendly Incentives:*** Based on real-time environmental data, the smart parking system can offer incentives for eco-friendly vehicles, such as electric cars or low-emission vehicles, by providing them with preferential parking or discounted rates.

h) ***Public Data Sharing***: Environmental data collected from smart parking systems can be shared with local authorities, researchers, and environmental agencies. This information can be used to make informed policy decisions, promote sustainable urban development, and assess the effectiveness of environmental initiatives.

i) ***Real-Time Alerts and Notifications:*** Environmental sensors can trigger real-time alerts and notifications to drivers, parking operators, and local authorities when certain environmental thresholds are exceeded. This can help address immediate concerns and ensure a healthier environment for the community.

Integrating environmental sensors into smart parking systems creates a more comprehensive and sustainable urban infrastructure, aligning with the goals of smart cities and promoting a healthier and more environmentally friendly parking environment.

The efficient car parking is achieved by using a camera which can record the images or provide information as a video stream to monitor the parking area and allocate the free space to the user accordingly. Ahmed et al. (2022), presented the convolutional neural network tool referred as Alexnet comprising of eight layers which includes five convolutional layers and three fully connected layers. In this work, a system display is used to display the availability of the free parking lot. The entrance gate open if and only the space is available for parking else it remains closed. In addition to the space notification, it also displays the total number of the cars parked and the free slot available for parking. The billing is levied based on the parking duration of the vehicle in the slot and the same will be intimated to the driver.

In the article, Huanmei et al. (2023), discussed about the importance given to the traveler's psychology and the factors related to the parking lot allocation. The overall utilization of the parking lot based on the psychological threshold for the reservation of the parking lot provides the satisfaction of the travellers. A well-balanced satisfaction and the utilization of the parking resources is achieved by deciding the psychological threshold appropriately.

APPLICATIONS OF SMART PARKING SYSTEMS USING IOT

Smart parking systems using IoT have numerous applications and offer various benefits in urban environments.

Here are some key applications of smart parking systems powered by IoT:

1. **Real-Time Parking Space Availability:** IoT-enabled sensors installed in parking spaces can detect and communicate the availability of parking spots in real-time. This information is then relayed to drivers through mobile applications or digital signage, allowing them to find and reserve vacant parking spaces quickly and efficiently.

2. **Parking Guidance and Navigation**: IoT-based parking systems can provide drivers with turn-by-turn navigation guidance to available parking spaces. By integrating with mapping and naviga-

tion applications, drivers can be directed to the nearest parking facility with real-time availability updates, minimizing the time spent searching for parking.

3. **Mobile Payments and e-Ticketing**: IoT-powered parking systems enable seamless mobile payments for parking fees. Drivers can use mobile applications to make cashless payments, eliminating the need for physical payment at parking meters. Additionally, e-ticketing capabilities can be integrated into parking solutions, allowing drivers to receive electronic tickets for entry and exit, streamlining the parking process.

4. **Parking Reservation and Pre-Booking:** Smart parking systems can allow drivers to reserve parking spaces in advance, ensuring a guaranteed spot upon arrival. This feature is particularly useful for events, airports, or busy areas where parking demand is high. Drivers can use mobile applications or online platforms to reserve and pay for parking in advance, enhancing convenience and reducing stress.

5. **Parking Analytics and Management**: IoT-based parking systems collect valuable data on parking occupancy, duration, and patterns. This data can be analyzed to gain insights into parking demand, usage patterns, and peak hours. Parking operators and city authorities can use this information to optimize parking management strategies, allocate resources efficiently, and make data-driven decisions regarding pricing, infrastructure development, and enforcement.

6. **Integration with Transportation Systems:** Smart parking systems can integrate with transportation networks and services to provide seamless connectivity between parking facilities and public transit. This integration enables drivers to easily combine parking with other modes of transportation, such as buses, trains, or bike-sharing services. By promoting multimodal transportation, smart parking systems contribute to reducing congestion and improving overall urban mobility.

7. **Sustainability and Environmental Impact:** IoT-powered parking solutions support sustainability efforts by reducing traffic congestion and emissions. By guiding drivers to available parking spaces more efficiently, these systems minimize the time spent circling for parking, which in turn reduces fuel consumption and greenhouse gas emissions. Additionally, the integration with public transit encourages the use of alternative transportation modes, further reducing reliance on private vehicles.

The applications of smart parking systems using IoT technology have the potential to revolutionize urban parking, making it more convenient, efficient, and sustainable. These systems not only benefit drivers by reducing parking-related stress but also provide valuable insights for parking operators and city authorities to optimize parking operations and enhance overall urban mobility.

CONCLUSION

In conclusion, the implementation of a smart parking management system using the Internet of Things (IoT) offers significant benefits and improvements to traditional parking systems. By leveraging IoT technologies, such as sensors, connectivity, and data analytics, smart parking management systems optimize parking space utilization, enhance user convenience, and improve overall efficiency.

Firstly, IoT-based sensors installed in parking lots can detect and transmit real-time data on parking space availability, allowing drivers to quickly locate vacant spots through mobile applications or digital signage. This reduces the time spent searching for parking, minimizes congestion, and enhances the overall user experience.

Secondly, the integration of IoT enables effective parking space management. Real-time data on parking occupancy and patterns can be collected and analyzed, providing valuable insights for parking operators to optimize resource allocation, improve traffic flow, and implement dynamic pricing strategies. This results in better space utilization, increased revenue generation, and reduced environmental impact by minimizing unnecessary driving.

Furthermore, IoT-based smart parking systems offer additional features such as automated payment processing, reservation systems, and personalized notifications, further streamlining the parking experience for users. These systems can also provide data analytics and reporting tools, enabling parking operators to monitor trends, identify bottlenecks, and make data-driven decisions for future planning and infrastructure development.

However, it is important to address certain challenges associated with implementing IoT-based parking systems, such as ensuring data privacy and security, integrating with existing infrastructure, and addressing connectivity issues. Robust security measures must be in place to protect sensitive user data and prevent unauthorized access to the system.

In summary, smart parking management systems using IoT offer numerous advantages, including optimized space utilization, improved user experience, increased revenue, and enhanced operational efficiency. By leveraging IoT technologies, parking management can be transformed, leading to more sustainable, convenient, and intelligent urban environments.

REFERENCES

Alsheikhy, A. A., Shawly, T., Said, Y. F., & Lahza, H. (2022). An Intelligent Smart Parking System Using Convolutional Neural Network. *Journal of Sensors*, *2022*, 1–11. Advance online publication. doi:10.1155/2022/7571716

Assim, M., & Al-Omary, A. (2020). A survey of IoT-based smart parking systems in smart cities. In *3rd Smart Cities Symposium (SCS 2020), Online Conference* (pp. 35–38). 10.1049/icp.2021.0911

Chu, Y., & Li, S. (2023). Application of IoT and artificial intelligence technology in smart parking management. In *IEEE International Conference on Integrated Circuits and Communication Systems (ICICACS), Raichur, India, 2023* (pp. 1–6). 10.1109/ICICACS57338.2023.10099976

Errousso, H., Malhene, N., Benhadou, S., & Medromi, H. (2020). Predicting car park availability for a better delivery bay management. *Procedia Computer Science*, *170*, 203–210. doi:10.1016/j.procs.2020.03.026

Farooqi, N., Alshehri, S., Nollily, S., Najmi, L., Alqurashi, G., & Alrashedi, A. (2019). UParking: Developing a smart parking management system using the Internet of things. Sixth HCT information technology trends (ITT), 214–218. doi:10.1109/ITT48889.2019.9075113

Gupta, A., Singh, G. P., Gupta, B., & Ghosh, S. (2022). LSTM based real-time smart parking system. In *IEEE 7th International conference for Convergence in Technology (I2CT), Mumbai, India, 2022* (pp. 1–7). 10.1109/I2CT54291.2022.9824249

Immanuel, J., Bersha, B., Boomadevi, M., Soundiraraj, N., Narayanan, K. L., & Krishnan, R. S. (2023). An Efficient IoT based Smart Vehicle Parking Management System. In *7th International Conference on Computing Methodologies and Communication (ICCMC), Erode, India, 2023* (pp. 1224–1228). 10.1109/ICCMC56507.2023.10083977

Krishnan, R. S., Narayanan, K. L., Bharathi, S. T., Deepa, N., Murali, S. M., Kumar, M. A., & Prakash, C. R. T. S. (2022). Machine learning based efficient and secured car parking system. In *Recent advances in internet of things and machine learning* (pp. 129–145). Springer. doi:10.1007/978-3-030-90119-6_11

Kuran, M. S., Carneiro Viana, A., Iannone, L., Kofman, D., Mermoud, G., & Vasseur, J. P. (2015). A Smart Parking lot management system for scheduling the recharging of electric vehicles. *IEEE Transactions on Smart Grid*, 6(6), 2942–2953. doi:10.1109/TSG.2015.2403287

Leone, G. R., Moroni, D., Pieri, G., Petracca, M., Salvetti, O., Azzarà, A., & Marino, F. (2017). An intelligent cooperative visual sensor network for urban mobility. *Sensors (Basel)*, 17(11), 2588. doi:10.3390/s17112588 PMID:29125535

Lin, J., Chen, S. Y., Chang, C. Y., & Chen, G. (2019). SPA: Smart parking algorithm based on driver behavior and parking traffic predictions. *IEEE Access: Practical Innovations, Open Solutions*, 7, 34275–34288. doi:10.1109/ACCESS.2019.2904972

Lin, T., Rivano, H., & Le Mouël, F. (2017). A survey of smart parking solutions. *IEEE Transactions on Intelligent Transportation Systems*, 18(12), 3229–3253. doi:10.1109/TITS.2017.2685143

Mackey, A., Spachos, P., & Plataniotis, K. N. (2020). Smart parking system based on Bluetooth low energy beacons with particle filtering. *IEEE Systems Journal*, 14(3), 3371–3382. doi:10.1109/JSYST.2020.2968883

Nova, S. H., Quader, S. M., Talukdar, S. D., Sadab, M. R., Sayeed, M. S., Al Islam, A. B. M. A., & Noor, J. (2022). IoT based parking system: Prospects, challenges, and beyond. In *International Conference on Innovation and Intelligence for Informatics, Computing, and Technologies (3ICT), Sakheer, Bahrain, 2022* (pp. 393–400). 10.1109/3ICT56508.2022.9990838

Peyal, M. M. K., Barman, A., Tahiat, T., Ul Haque, Q. M. A., Bal, A., & Ahmed, S. (2021). IoT based cost effective car parking management for urban area. In *4th International Symposium on Agents, Multi-Agent Systems and Robotics (ISAMSR), Batu Pahat, Malaysia, 2021* (pp. 70–75). 10.1109/ISAMSR53229.2021.9567826

Qin, H., Xu, N., Zhang, Y., Pang, Q., & Lu, Z. (2023). Research on Parking Recommendation Methods Considering Travelers' Decision Behaviors and Psychological Characteristics. *Sustainability (Basel)*, 15(8), 6808. doi:10.3390/su15086808

Rajbhandari, S., Thareja, B., Deep, V., & Mehrotra, D. (2018). IoT based smart parking system. In *International Conference on Innovation and Intelligence for Informatics, Computing, and Technologies (3ICT), Sakhier, Bahrain, 2018* (pp. 1–5). 10.1109/3ICT.2018.8855787

Ramasamy, M., Solanki, S. G., Natarajan, E., & Keat, T. M. (2018). IoT based smart parking system for large parking lot. In *IEEE 4th International Symposium in Robotics and Manufacturing Automation (ROMA), Perambalur, India, 2018* (pp. 1–4). 10.1109/ROMA46407.2018.8986731

Said, A. M., Kamal, A. E., & Afifi, H. (2021). An intelligent parking sharing system for green and smart cities based IoT. *Computer Communications*, *172*, 10–18. doi:10.1016/j.comcom.2021.02.017

Xiang, Z., & Pan, J. (2022). Design of intelligent parking management system based on ARM and wireless sensor network. *Mobile Information Systems*, *2022*, 2965638. Advance online publication. doi:10.1155/2022/2965638

Chapter 14
Machine Learning-Based Collection and Analysis of Embedded Systems Vulnerabilities

Aissa Ben Yahya

(iD) https://orcid.org/0000-0002-5437-2745

Faculty of Sciences, Moulay Ismail University of Meknes, Morocco

Hicham El Akhal

Faculty of Sciences, Moulay Ismail University of Meknes, Morocco

Abdelbaki El Belrhiti El Alaoui

(iD) https://orcid.org/0000-0001-9462-2932

Faculty of Sciences, Moulay Ismail University of Meknes, Morocco

ABSTRACT

The security of embedded systems is deteriorating in comparison to conventional systems due to resource limitations in memory, processing, and power. Daily publications highlight various vulnerabilities associated with these systems. While significant efforts have been made to systematize and analyze these vulnerabilities, most studies focus on specific areas within embedded systems and lack the implementation of artificial intelligence (AI). This research aims to address these gaps by utilizing support vector machine (SVM) to classify vulnerabilities sourced from the national vulnerabilities database (NVD) and specifically targeting embedded system vulnerabilities. Results indicate that seven of the top 10 common weakness enumeration (CWE) vulnerabilities in embedded systems are also present in the 2022 CWE Top 25 Most Dangerous Software Weaknesses. The findings of this study will facilitate security researchers and companies in comprehensively analyzing embedded system vulnerabilities and developing tailored solutions.

DOI: 10.4018/979-8-3693-0497-6.ch014

1. INTRODUCTION

The last few years have seen remarkable progress in a variety of fields, such as astronomy, healthcare, agriculture, connected cars, and smart devices, to name a few. Smart homes equipped with voice-activated digital assistants (Wellsandt et al., 2020) remote patient monitoring systems, and connected cars designed to prevent accidents and collisions are just a few examples of technologies that have made users' lives easier and helped people with disabilities (Gulati et al., 2020) Embedded systems are the basic building blocks and key technologies that make these applications possible. Embedded systems serve as the fundamental building blocks and vital technologies that facilitate the development of various applications. The progress observed in these applications is largely dependent on the advancements in embedded systems, as noted by (Prasad et al., 2021). These systems are designed to operate with limited resources, such as memory, processing power, and energy consumption, as well as operating in harsh environments and using customized components and software, also the absence of standardization makes them vulnerable to cyber-attacks. The vulnerabilities in these systems can be exploited to cause serious harm to human life and privacy. For example, in 2017, the US Food and Drug Administration (FDA) (Hern, 2017) recalled 500,000 pacemakers due to cybersecurity vulnerabilities that could allow hackers to access the device and reprogram it. The vulnerability could lead to the battery running flat or the administration of inappropriate pacing, which could result in the death of the patient. In 2020 a critical vulnerability in a traffic light controller deployed on roads across Europe could cause "sustained traffic chaos" (*Critical Traffic Light System Vulnerability Could Cause 'Chaos' on the Roads*, 2020). While in 2021, Trend Micro (*Connected Cars Technology Vulnerable to Cyber Attacks*, n.d.) reported that connected cars are vulnerable to cyber-attacks that could threaten the safety of drivers and passengers. The report revealed that distributed denial-of-service (DDoS) attacks on Intelligent Transportation Systems (ITS) could overwhelm connected car communications and represent a high risk. Exposed and vulnerable connected car systems are easily discovered, making them at higher risk of abuse. Buffer overflow flaws in the privacy-preserving TPM 2.0 protocol were discovered in March 2023 (Nuspire, 2023), potentially putting billions of IoT devices at risk. In comparison to general-purpose systems, the security of embedded systems is declining, mainly due to their limited resources. As a result, the security measures that are commonly applied in general-purpose systems cannot be utilized in embedded systems. As vulnerabilities in embedded systems (ESs) continue to rise, it has become evident that the security solutions applied to general-purpose systems cannot be used in ESs. Therefore, it is crucial to study and analyze vulnerabilities in ESs to address current issues and prevent future zero-day attacks. Although vulnerability databases hold most of the reported vulnerabilities, they do not provide information on the classification of vulnerabilities into specific categories, such as embedded systems, general-purpose PCs, web browsers, operating systems, or protocols.

The significant advancement achieved in the fields of machine learning (ML) and deep learning (DL) have unveiled opportunities for the automation of classification processes. An exemplary demonstration of this can be seen in the research conducted by (Huang et al., 2019), the authors introduced TFI-DNN model, a novel approach that merges Term Frequency-Inverse Document Frequency (TF-IDF) and information gain (IG) techniques with a Deep Neural Network (DNN) to effectively categorize vulnerabilities into their respective types. (Chen et al., 2020) in the other hand propose a novel framework for classifying vulnerability severity in software development using the term frequency-inverse gravity moment (TF-IGM) instead of the traditional TF-IDF model. TF-IGM shows promise, and feature selection enhances classification performance on various datasets. (Sharma et al., 2021) introduced a vulnerability prioritization system that utilized word embedding and convolutional neural network (CNN) approaches. This system was created with the purpose of categorizing vulnerabilities into three different severity levels: high, medium, and low. It achieved this by analyzing the textual descriptions of vulnerabilities and historical data from diverse vendors. In a separate study conducted by (Wang et al., 2023), they introduced an improved automatic vulnerability classification algorithm. This algorithm incorporates weighted word vectors and a fusion neural network to address the common issue of sparsity in traditional vector representations. The use of ML and DL for vulnerability classification proven to reduce the time between the vulnerabilities report and their analyse by professionals. However, the exist solutions in the literature have only classified vulnerabilities either into their corresponding types defined in Common Weakness Enumeration (CWE) or based on their severity. Therefore, the gap of extracting only embedded system related vulnerabilities is still lacking in previous researches.

To address the aforementioned challenge, our paper aims to classify these vulnerabilities specifically to extract embedded systems related vulnerabilities for further analysis to make it easy for the researchers to forge dedicated solution for these systems. Therefore, this paper presents a machine learning-based automatic system for collecting embedded system vulnerabilities from the National Vulnerabilities Database (NVD) (*NVD - Home*, n.d.) database and analysing them. This system is designed to assist experts in developing tailored solutions within a reasonable time frame for addressing these vulnerabilities. For the training dataset, we utilized the National Vulnerability Database (NVD) as the primary source. The NVD is a vast database that encompasses publicly disclosed vulnerabilities and security exposures. It is fully synchronized with the MITRE CVE list and provides a JSON downloadable version of the database (*NVD - Data Feeds*, n.d.), which is convenient to work with. To extract the training dataset, a Python script was utilized, which employed a white and black list to isolate embedded systems (ES) and general-purpose systems (GPS) related vulnerabilities in the NVD database. Moreover, to facilitate feeding data into the model, the embedded system set was labeled as "es" to denote embedded system vulnerabilities, whereas the general-purpose set was labeled as "classic" to denote vulnerabilities in traditional systems.

The structure of our paper is as follows: In Section II, we present an overview of the existing literature related to our study. The methodology employed to develop our automatic embedded system vulnerability collection system is described in detail in Section III. We present the results of our proposed mechanism and engage in a comprehensive discussion in Section IV. Finally, Section VI provides a summary and concluding remarks for our paper.

2. RELATED WORK

The rise in vulnerabilities affecting ESs, along with the ineffectiveness of solutions developed for general-purpose systems when applied to these systems, makes it imperative to investigate and analyze vulnerabilities specific to ESs in order to develop targeted solutions. However, obtaining sufficient data for a thorough study poses significant challenges, particularly due to the inadequacy of existing vulnerability databases like the National Vulnerability Database (NVD) in providing the necessary information to identify the desired category of vulnerabilities. In order to achieve this objective, researchers have conducted numerous studies (Papp et al., 2015), (Wen et al., 2015), (Välja et al., 2017), (N. Neshenko et al., 2019), (Huang et al., 2019), (Chen et al., 2020), (Blinowski & Piotrowski, 2020), (Nazzal et al., 2022) aimed at categorizing and classifying software vulnerabilities. However, a significant portion of these studies primarily focuses on the general classification of vulnerabilities, with only a limited number specifically targeting the extraction of vulnerabilities in embedded systems. The techniques employed in these studies can be categorized into two groups: traditional techniques and intelligent techniques, where intelligent techniques involve the use of machine learning or deep learning methods. Traditional techniques encompass manual and script-based approaches.

2.1 Traditional Techniques

The manual collection and classification of vulnerabilities in embedded systems (N. Neshenko et al., 2019), (Nazzal et al., 2022), (Välja et al., 2017) yield more accurate and superior results compared to automatic analysis. However, this approach suffers from a significant drawback in terms of time and scope. Manual parsing and collection of vulnerabilities are time-consuming processes, leading to slower analysis. Moreover, due to the long time required, researchers employing this technique often focus on specific types of systems to narrow down the search scope. On the other hand, the automation of vulnerability collection using scripts (Papp et al., 2015) is faster than manual collection. Scripts utilize predefined white and black lists of keywords to gather targeted vulnerabilities. Although this technique is faster, it is limited to collecting vulnerabilities that contain the specified keywords. With the growing number of vulnerabilities published daily, it becomes nearly impossible to determine all the necessary keywords within a reasonable timeframe. Consequently, a mechanism is required to address the increasing vulnerabilities and the diverse range of embedded systems products and vendors.

2.2 Intelligent Techniques

Multiple research studies (Wen et al., 2015), (Huang et al., 2019), (Chen et al., 2020), (Blinowski & Piotrowski, 2020) have been conducted to support and assist security teams in analyzing vulnerabilities and evaluating their impact. The objective is to minimize the time gap between vulnerability reporting and analysis by automating the classification process.

The paper (Wen et al., 2015) introduced a novel framework called Automatic Security Vulnerability Categorization (ASVC) to automate the process of categorizing vulnerabilities into their respective categories. The framework utilizes text mining techniques to match the description of each vulnerability with its corresponding Common Weakness Enumeration (CWE). Also in (Huang et al., 2019) the researchers proposed a new automatic vulnerability classification model (TFI-DNN). The model is based on, Term frequency-Inverse Document Frequency (TF-IDF), information gain (IG), and Deep Neural Network (DNN). The authors used NVD database as the source of their training dataset to learn the model to classify the vulnerabilities into their predicted type. The study conducted by (Chen et al., 2020) introduced a novel weighting mechanism called Term frequency-inverse gravity moment to categorize software vulnerabilities based on their severity. The paper (Blinowski & Piotrowski, 2020) focuses on classifying Internet of Things (IoT) systems based on Common Vulnerabilities and Exposures (CVE). The study aims to identify and categorize vulnerable IoT devices using CVE entries. The author's approach involves manually parsing CVE vulnerabilities with the Common Platform Enumeration (CPE) attribute set to "h," which indicates hardware records. Blinowski and colleagues utilized Support Vector Machine (SVM) for classifying the CVEs. (Sharma et al., 2021) unveiled a vulnerability prioritization system. This system harnessed word embedding and convolutional neural network (CNN) methods to categorize vulnerabilities into three distinct severity levels: high, medium, and low. This classification was achieved by analyzing vulnerability descriptions and historical data from a range of vendors. Expanding upon this line (Wang et al., 2022) proposed SVC-CG, an algorithm for software vulnerability classification. It combines CNN and GRU models to extract local and global features from vulnerability text, improving semantic and grammatical representation. Using Skip-gram Word2Vec, CNN, and GRU, the algorithm outperforms in Macro recall rate, Macro precision rate, and Macro F1-score when evaluated on NVD data, enhancing vulnerability classification efficiency. In another recent study (Wang et al., 2023) introduced an algorithm for software vulnerability classification that tackles high-dimensional sparsity issues. It combines TextCNN and Bidirectional GRU for feature extraction, uses Dropout and Early Stopping for regularization, and employs a Softmax classifier. Experiments on NVD dataset data validate its effectiveness using multiple metrics.

Compared to the studies in the literature, which primarily concentrate on classifying vulnerabilities into their corresponding types as outlined in the Common Weakness Enumeration (CWE) or their severity, our paper presents a distinctive contribution. We distinguish vulnerabilities in embedded systems from those in general-purpose systems, enabling security researchers to focus specifically on the analysis of vulnerabilities within embedded systems and develop tailored solutions for them. Furthermore, we perform a detailed analysis of the results to identify the most prevalent vulnerabilities, assess their severity, and elucidate the prerequisites for their exploitation. This distinction represents a significant gap in the current body of literature.

3. METHODOLOGY

This section presents our methodology for developing a machine learning system specifically tailored to classify vulnerability reports. Our primary objective is to distinguish vulnerabilities in embedded systems from those in general-purpose systems. To train our machine learning model, our primary data source is the National Vulnerability Database (NVD), which serves as a centralized repository with comprehensive information about known software vulnerabilities and their characteristics. It's among the most widely used resources for vulnerability data. However, the NVD database includes Common Vulnerabilities and Exposures (CVEs) that are not suitable for model training. Therefore, we need to filter out these entries from the database during dataset collection. Given the substantial volume of CVEs in the NVD, manual parsing would be impractical and time-consuming. To address this, we employed a script to automate the dataset collection process. Our methodology unfolds in three distinct phases. The first phase focuses on database cleaning, where we remove irrelevant CVEs. In the second phase, we engage in dataset collection. Finally, the third phase revolves around model training.

3.1 Database Cleaning

Our objective was to gather a dataset for training our machine learning SVM algorithm using TF-IDF as the embedding method. SVM is an ideal choice for text classification due to its capacity to handle high-dimensional data efficiently, its non-linearity handling for capturing complex relationships, and its robustness against overfitting, which is crucial when dealing with limited samples in text classification tasks compared to deep learning models which requires large amount of high quality data (Kowsari et al., 2019). TF-IDF, on the other hand, is a widely recognized technique for quantifying the importance of terms within documents, aiding in the identification of relevant and unique terms while reducing dimensionality by filtering out common, uninformative words. Therefore, we focused on the NVD database, which is one of the prominent vulnerability databases. At the time of our research, it contained 202,747 CVE entries, and its size continues to increase regularly. The NVD database can be obtained in a JSON format, as specified in the reference (*NVD - Data Feeds*, n.d.) enabling us to automate the process of cleaning and collecting the data.

The initial database, contains certain CVEs that are unsuitable for training purposes. Hence, these CVEs are excluded before dataset collection. The excluded CVEs fall into three categories: reserved, rejected, and disputed. Reserved CVEs are those that have been reserved by a CVE Numbering Authority (CNA) or a security researcher. As a result, they lack the necessary vulnerability description required for our dataset and are therefore excluded. Rejected CVEs, as explained in the Frequently Asked Questions (FAQ), are not accepted as CVE entries due to various reasons, typically indicated in their descriptions. Consequently, they are also excluded from our dataset. Lastly, disputed CVEs refer to CVEs that have not yet been determined as genuine vulnerabilities. Hence, we also remove these CVEs from consideration. CVEs that are reserved, rejected, or disputed are identified by a specific format keyword present in their description. To eliminate such entries, a script is developed to identify and remove any CVE entry that includes this keyword in its text description. For instance, reserved CVEs will invariably include the keyword "** RESERVED **" in their text description. After applying the cleaning process to the National Vulnerability Database (NVD), we excluded a total of 13,094 CVEs out of the initial 202,747 CVEs. This refinement resulted in a more focused database, which consists of the remaining CVEs that are confirmed as genuine vulnerabilities and are suitable for training our machine learning SVM algorithm. The cleaning process was crucial in creating a dataset consisting solely of valid CVEs, thereby ensuring that the model training will yield more accurate results.

3.2 Data-Set Collection

The dataset used to learn machine learning and deep learning algorithms is of a form of three categories, Embedded systems vulnerabilities (ESV), None embedded systems vulnerabilities (NESV), and unknown (i.e., samples that the models are not trained to classify). Despite the considerable efforts made by the National Institute of Standards and Technology (NIST) to provide comprehensive information on vulnerabilities in the NVD database, there remain significant challenges in accurately classifying them into specific categories. Currently, the database lacks explicit indications regarding the types of vulnerabilities associated with specific domains such as Internet of Things (IoT) devices, supervisory control and data acquisition (SCADA) systems, Industrial IoT (IIoT), connected cars, and more. This absence of information hampers the ability to identify vulnerabilities specifically relevant to embedded systems without prior knowledge of the products and vendors involved.

Within the database, only three CPE indicators are available, namely hardware, operating system, and application. These broad categories encompass vulnerabilities and weaknesses from diverse systems. Consequently, they are insufficient for extracting vulnerabilities that pertain exclusively to embedded systems. Therefore, to extract Embedded System Vulnerabilities (ESV), we employed a similar approach as described in a previous study (Papp et al., 2015) This method involves the utilization of a Python script. In this Python script, we implement a methodology inspired by (Papp et al., 2015) to classify Common Vulnerabilities and Exposures (CVEs) based on a white list and a black list of keywords. The objective is to categorize vulnerabilities into two classes: "embedded system" (labeled as "es") and "genera-purpose system" (labeled as "classic"). The white list is carefully curated with keywords that are specifically associated with embedded systems, including examples such as "DIR-645 Wired," "Amazon

Echo," "MQTT," "Tesla Model S," and "NX-OS." These keywords serve as a reference for identifying vulnerabilities related to embedded systems. Conversely, the black list contains keywords associated with general-purpose systems, which are not of interest for our analysis. These keywords encompass terms like "Windows Desktop," "Dell XPS 13," "Image Magick," and "Xen.". The script proceeds as follows:

1. Download CVEs in JSON format from NVD feeds.
2. Check the CVEs description against the keywords in the white list and black list.
3. If the description contains any keywords from the white list, the CVE is labeled as "es," signifying that it pertains to embedded systems.
4. If the description contains any keywords from the black list, the CVE is labeled as "classic," indicating it's associated with general-purpose systems.
5. Generate a CSV file with two columns: "text" and "label." The "text" column contains the CVE descriptions, while the "label" column specifies whether the CVE is "es" or "classic.".

This script provides a straightforward yet effective approach to automatically collect dataset for model training.

3.3 Models Training

In this paper, SVM algorithm is trained to classify vulnerability reports into either embedded system vulnerability or general-purpose vulnerability, it uses Term Frequency Inverse Document Frequency (TF-IDF) as its word embedding.

3.3.1 Term Frequency-Inverse Document Frequency (TF-IDF)

In natural language processing (NLP), TF-IDF is a widely used numerical statistic that represents the importance of a term within a corpus of documents. It is a feature representation technique that aims to capture the significance of terms in a collection of text data.

TF-IDF combines two key components: term frequency (TF) and inverse document frequency (IDF).

1. Term Frequency (TF):
   ◦ Term frequency measures how frequently a term occurs within a specific document.
   ◦ It quantifies the occurrence of a term by calculating the ratio of the number of times the term appears in a document to the total number of terms in that document.
   ◦ TF provides information about the local importance of a term in a particular document.
2. Inverse Document Frequency (IDF):
   ◦ Inverse document frequency calculates the rarity of a term across the entire corpus.
   ◦ It assigns a weight to a term by computing the logarithm of the ratio of the total number of documents in the corpus to the number of documents containing the term.
   ◦ IDF diminishes the importance of terms that occur frequently across all documents and assigns higher weights to terms that appear rarely.

3.3.2 Data Labeling

Prior to the training phase, the dataset undergoes a labeling process. CVE descriptions that contain one or more keywords related to embedded systems are assigned the label "es", indicating the presence of an embedded system vulnerability. On the other hand, CVEs that lack embedded systems keywords but contain one or more keywords associated with general-purpose system vulnerabilities (GPSV) are labeled as "classic". The labeling process is illustrated in Figure 1.

Figure 1. An example of CVEs labeling as either "es" or "classic" based on the keywords in their description

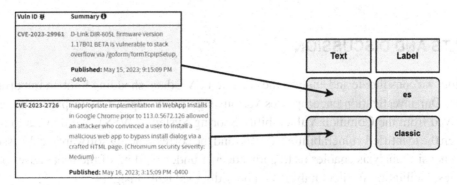

3.3.3 Data Pre-Processing

The textual descriptions of CVE entries in the NVD database encompass various types of information that are not useful as features for extracting embedded systems vulnerabilities from vulnerability databases. To address this, a series of consecutive operations are performed to preprocess the text. These operations include tokenizing, removing stop words, stemming, lemmatization, and converting verbs to their base form. These steps are executed prior to converting the text into vectors.

Tokenizing involves dividing a sentence into its constituent meaningful words. This process helps eliminate unnecessary and irrelevant words, such as stopwords and symbols. Tokenizing serves two purposes: removing unwanted elements and converting the CVE descriptions into vectorized representations.

In natural language processing, certain words may have similar meanings but are expressed in different word forms, such as "organize," "organizes," and "organizing." These variations in word forms can pose challenges during the learning phase. To address this, stemming is employed to unify these different forms into a single feature space. The outcome of stemming can be illustrated as follows:

security researchers are analysing the collected vulnerabilities => security research are analyse the collect vulnerability

To handle word suffixes, we employed the technique of lemmatization. This method removes the suffix from a word and returns its base or dictionary form. By applying lemmatization, we can ensure that words are represented in their standardized format.

3.3.4 Word Embedding

Machine learning algorithms are not capable of directly processing natural language as input; instead, they operate on numerical data. Hence, it is necessary to transform vulnerability descriptions into a vector format. This transformation process, known as Text Embedding or word embedding, involves representing text in a numerical vector representation that can be understood by machine learning algorithms. In our model, we convert the corpus of CVE descriptions into a vector representation to effectively train the models. To accomplish this, we employ the TF-IDF (Term Frequency-Inverse Document Frequency) technique. TF-IDF assigns weights to words based on their frequency in each CVE description and inversely proportional to their occurrence across the entire corpus. By utilizing TF-IDF, we can capture the importance of words within the context of CVE descriptions, enhancing the learning process of our model.

4. RESULTS AND DISCUSSION

In this section, we consolidate and analyze the collected CVE data, shedding light on important findings and insights. Our investigation encompasses various significant aspects, with particular emphasis on metrics derived from the Common Vulnerability Scoring System (CVSS). We delve into the relationships between the identified vulnerabilities (CVEs) and the corresponding software weaknesses (CWEs). This comprehensive analysis enables us to gain a deeper understanding of the root causes behind these vulnerabilities, facilitating further analysis and providing valuable insights.

Furthermore, it is essential to acknowledge that the number of vulnerabilities affecting embedded systems continues to rise each year Figure 2. This escalating trend emphasizes the critical importance of conducting thorough vulnerability assessments and implementing effective security measures to safeguard these systems from potential threats. By collecting and analysing embedded systems vulnerabilities, we can identify patterns, trends, and areas of concern that will aid in devising targeted solutions and enhancing the overall security posture of embedded systems.

Figure 2. Number of CVEs per year

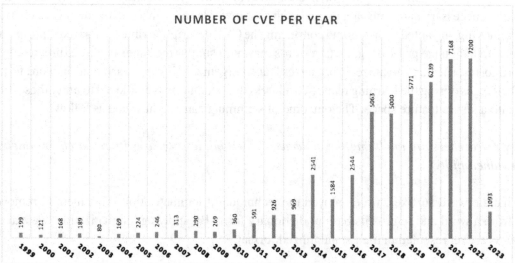

4.1 Evaluation Metrics

We employed standard evaluation metrics commonly used for assessing the effectiveness of our embedded system vulnerability collection system. The details metrics are as follows:

- **Accuracy**: a key metric, represents the overall correctness of the detected vulnerable codes in our system.
  Accuracy = (TP+TN) / (TP+TN+FP+FN)
- **Precision:** measures proportion of correctly predicted positive instances out of all the instances that the model classified as positive.
  Precision = TP / (TP+FP)
- **Recall:** the proportion of correctly predicted positive instances out of all the actual positive instances in the dataset.
  Recall = TP / (TP+FN)
- **F1-score:** F1 score is a metric that combines both precision and recall to provide a balanced evaluation of a model's performance.
  F1score = 2* (precision*recall) / (precision+recall)

4.2 Experimental Setup

We run the experiments in a computer with Xion CPU 2.40GHz and 32G of RAM along with NVIDIA M2000 GPU. The computer uses Ubuntu 21.04 LTS as its operating system. Both Tensorflow version 2.8.0 and Keras version 2.8.0 have been used during our experiments.

4.3 Model Performance

The performance of our SVM model with TF-IDF word embedding is quite impressive. It achieved an overall accuracy of 98.35%, which indicates that it is able to correctly classify the majority of the embedded system vulnerabilities in our dataset.

Precision, which measures the proportion of true positive predictions out of the total predicted positives, is 97%. This means that when our model predicts an embedded system vulnerability, it is correct 97% of the time. This high precision value indicates that our model has a low rate of false positive predictions.

Recall, also known as sensitivity or true positive rate, measures the proportion of actual positives that are correctly identified by the model. In our case, the recall is 98%, indicating that our model is able to capture 98% of the embedded system vulnerabilities present in the dataset. This high recall value suggests that our model has a low rate of false negatives.

F1-score is a measure that combines precision and recall into a single metric, providing a balanced evaluation of the model's performance. Our model achieved an impressive F1-score of 98%, indicating a good balance between precision and recall.

Overall, our SVM model with TF-IDF word embedding demonstrates strong performance in classifying embedded system vulnerabilities.

4.4 Data Analysis

4.4.1 Attack Vector

The attack vector in the context of the Common Vulnerability Scoring System (CVSS) refers to the path or method used by an attacker to exploit a vulnerability in a system. It describes the means through which the attacker gains access to the target system or network to carry out malicious activities.

In the case of embedded systems, the attack vector specifies how the vulnerabilities in these systems are exploited. It indicates whether the attack is launched over a network, locally by physical access, through adjacent systems, or in other ways.

Based on our analysis, as shown in Figure 3, we found that approximately 67.2% of attacks on embedded systems have a network-based attack vector. This means that the majority of the attacks targeting embedded systems are carried out remotely, leveraging network connections to exploit vulnerabilities.

Figure 3. Attack vector

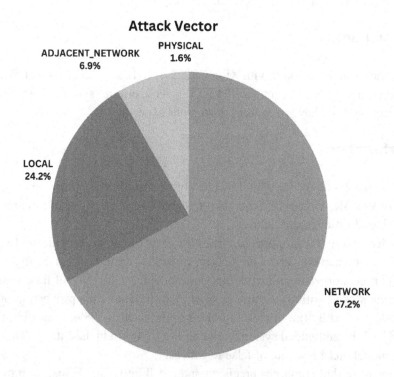

4.4.2 Attack Complexity

Attack complexity, as defined in the Common Vulnerability Scoring System (CVSS), refers to the level of difficulty or effort required for an attacker to successfully exploit a vulnerability. It considers various factors such as the availability of tools or techniques, the knowledge required, and the level of access or privileges needed to exploit the vulnerability. In the case of attacks on embedded systems, we have observed that approximately 87% of the attacks have a low attack complexity, Figure 4. This implies that the majority of the attacks targeting embedded systems are relatively straightforward to execute, requiring minimal technical expertise or specialized tools. Low attack complexity suggests that attackers can easily exploit vulnerabilities in embedded systems.

Figure 4. Attack complexity

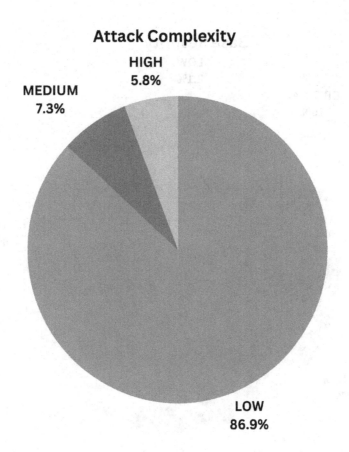

4.4.3 Base Severity

Base severity, in the context of the Common Vulnerability Scoring System (CVSS), represents the overall severity level assigned to a vulnerability based on its intrinsic characteristics. It takes into account various factors, including the impact of the vulnerability, the ease of exploitation, and the potential consequences of a successful attack. Analyzing the attacks on embedded systems, we have determined that approximately 45% of these attacks are classified as having a high base severity as illustrated in Figure 5. This indicates that a significant portion of the vulnerabilities in embedded systems pose a substantial risk and have the potential to cause severe damage or compromise the system's security. Furthermore, around 38% of the attacks on embedded systems are classified as having a medium base severity. This suggests that a considerable number of vulnerabilities in embedded systems have the potential to cause moderate-level impacts and may result in significant disruptions or unauthorized access if exploited.

These findings underscore the critical need for robust security measures, prompt vulnerability patching, and proactive defense strategies to mitigate the risks associated with high and medium severity vulnerabilities in embedded systems. By addressing these vulnerabilities promptly, organizations can enhance the security posture of their embedded systems and reduce the likelihood and impact of successful attacks.

Figure 5. Base severity

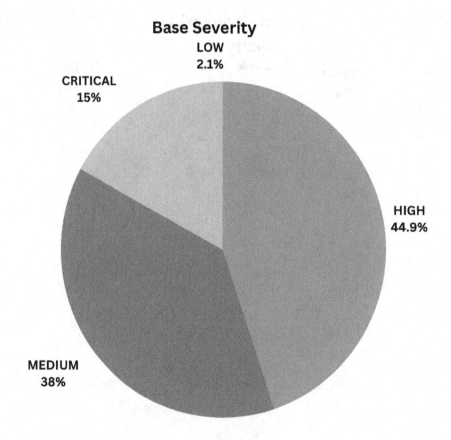

4.4.4 Confidentiality Impact

Confidentiality impact, in the context of the Common Vulnerability Scoring System (CVSS), refers to the potential impact that a successful exploit of a vulnerability can has on the confidentiality of information. It assesses the degree to which unauthorized individuals or entities can gain access to sensitive or confidential data as a result of the vulnerability being exploited. Based on our analysis of attacks on embedded systems, we have found that approximately 55% of these attacks have a high confidentiality impact, see Figure 6. This indicates that a significant portion of the vulnerabilities in embedded systems, when successfully exploited, can lead to the unauthorized disclosure of sensitive information. Such information may include personal data, trade secrets, intellectual property, or other confidential data stored or transmitted by the embedded system. The high confidentiality impact underscores the critical need for robust security measures and data protection mechanisms in embedded systems. Safeguarding sensitive information is crucial to maintaining the trust of users and stakeholders, as well as ensuring compliance with privacy regulations. Organizations should prioritize implementing strong access controls, encryption techniques, and secure communication protocols to mitigate the risks associated with high confidentiality impact vulnerabilities in embedded systems.

Figure 6. Confidentiality impact

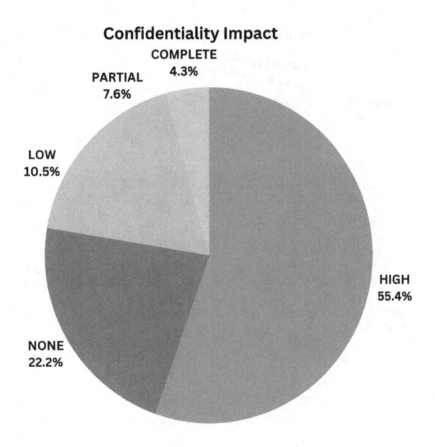

4.4.5 Availability Impact

Availability impact, in the context of the Common Vulnerability Scoring System (CVSS), refers to the potential impact that a successful exploit of a vulnerability can have on the availability of a system or resource. It assesses the extent to which the vulnerability can disrupt or impair the normal functioning or accessibility of the system. Upon analyzing attacks on embedded systems, we have found that approximately 53% of these attacks have a high availability impact, see Figure 7. This indicates that a significant portion of the vulnerabilities in embedded systems, when exploited, can result in a severe disruption of the system's availability. This disruption may render the embedded system inaccessible, unresponsive, or inoperable, leading to significant downtime or loss of service. The high availability impact highlights the critical importance of ensuring the resilience and continuous operation of embedded systems. Organizations need to implement robust measures to mitigate the risks associated with high availability impact vulnerabilities. This includes implementing redundancy, failover mechanisms, backup and recovery strategies, and effective monitoring and incident response procedures. By prioritizing the availability of embedded systems, organizations can minimize the impact of attacks and maintain the desired level of service and functionality.

Figure 7. Availability impact

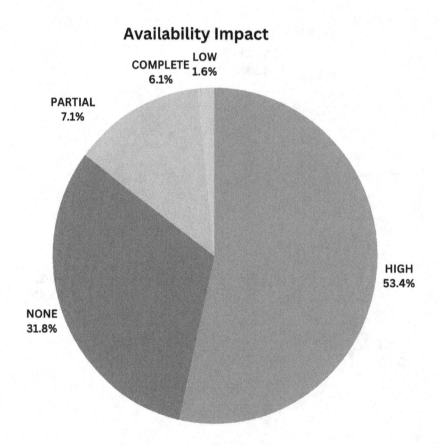

4.4.6 Integrity Impact

Integrity impact, in the context of the Common Vulnerability Scoring System (CVSS), refers to the potential impact that a successful exploit of a vulnerability can have on the integrity of a system or data. It assesses the extent to which the vulnerability can result in unauthorized modification, alteration, or destruction of information or system components. Upon analyzing attacks on embedded systems, we have found that approximately 46% of these attacks have a high integrity impact, see Figure 8. This indicates that a significant portion of the vulnerabilities in embedded systems, when exploited, can lead to severe integrity violations. Such violations may involve unauthorized modification of critical data, tampering with system functionality, or compromising the overall integrity and trustworthiness of the system. The high integrity impact emphasizes the critical need for robust security measures to protect the integrity of embedded systems. Organizations should focus on implementing measures such as access controls, encryption, secure coding practices, and system integrity checks to mitigate the risks associated with high integrity impact vulnerabilities. By safeguarding the integrity of embedded systems, organizations can ensure the accuracy, reliability, and trustworthiness of their operations and data.

Figure 8. Integrity impact

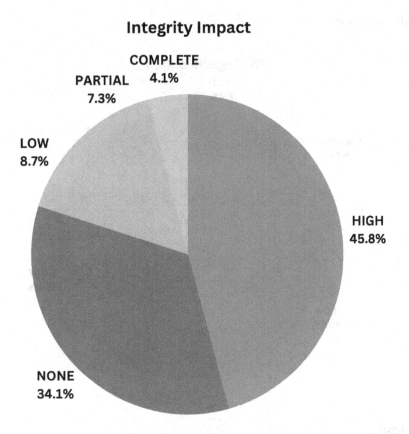

4.4.7 Privileges Required

Privileges required, in the context of the Common Vulnerability Scoring System (CVSS), refers to the level of access or privileges that an attacker must possess in order to exploit a vulnerability successfully. It evaluates whether the vulnerability can be exploited without any special privileges (None), with some user-level privileges (Low), or with elevated administrative or system-level privileges (High). Based on our analysis of attacks on embedded systems, we have observed that approximately 57% of these attacks have None as the required privileges, see Figure 9. This indicates that the majority of the vulnerabilities in embedded systems can be exploited without the need for any specific access rights or privileges. Attackers can potentially exploit these vulnerabilities without having any prior elevated permissions. The high percentage of attacks with None as the required privileges highlights the importance of implementing strong security measures even for low-privileged accounts. It implies that all users, including those with limited privileges, should follow security best practices, and organizations should enforce principle of least privilege to restrict unnecessary access rights. By adopting security practices such as privilege separation, access controls, and regular security updates, organizations can reduce the risk of exploitation for vulnerabilities that require no privileges. This proactive approach helps in mitigating the potential impact of attacks on embedded systems and protecting sensitive data and critical functionalities.

Figure 9. Privileges required

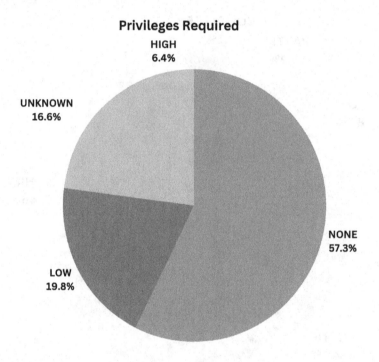

4.4.8 CWE Analysis

During our analysis of embedded system vulnerabilities, we discovered a noteworthy correlation with the 2022 CWE Top 25 Most Dangerous Software Weaknesses. Out of the top 10 CWEs identified in the embedded system vulnerabilities, 7 of them were consistent with the CWEs listed in the 2022 CWE Top 25, as can be seen in Figure 10. This alignment highlights the significance and relevance of the identified weaknesses in the context of embedded systems. The CWE Top 25 is a widely recognized and authoritative list that outlines the most critical software weaknesses posing potential risks to various systems. The fact that a significant proportion of the CWEs found in our analysis of embedded system vulnerabilities align with this list indicates the importance of addressing these weaknesses to enhance the overall security of embedded systems. By focusing on the identified CWEs, we can prioritize mitigation efforts and allocate resources effectively. This targeted approach allows for a more proactive and efficient response to potential threats and vulnerabilities. Furthermore, this correlation underscores the need for industry-wide attention and collaboration to address these common weaknesses, driving advancements in embedded system security and reducing the overall risk landscape. By addressing these top CWEs, organizations can significantly improve the security posture of their embedded systems, mitigating the risk of exploitation and potential impact on critical operations. Implementing best practices, secure coding guidelines, and rigorous vulnerability assessments can go a long way in reducing the prevalence and impact of these software weaknesses in embedded systems.

Figure 10. Top 10 CWEs

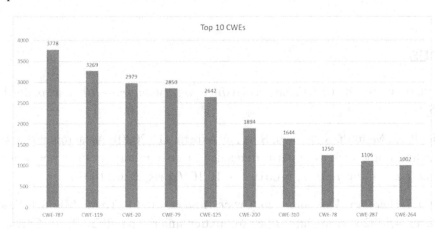

5. CONCLUSION

This paper proposes an automated system based on machine learning for extracting vulnerabilities related to embedded systems. The system aims to facilitate the collection of such vulnerabilities from databases, enabling further analysis and faster development of tailored solutions. The proposed method involves constructing a dataset from a vulnerability database such as NVD, which is then used to train the machine learning model for automatic extraction of embedded system vulnerabilities.

The training dataset is sourced from the NVD database, and the TF-IDF word embedding technique is applied to extract meaningful features from the vulnerability text descriptions. SVM, a machine learning algorithm, is utilized to extract Embedded System Vulnerabilities (ESV) from the NVD database. The combination of SVM and TF-IDF achieves an impressive accuracy of 98.35%. Despite the promising outcomes of this study, it's not limitations free. Some of the limitations of our work is absence of large dataset, incapability of capturing long context dependent vulnerability descriptions, also the current TF-IDF embedding technique must be enhanced to catch semantic meanings. Therefore, there are opportunities for further improvement in various areas, including optimizing hyperparameters and refining scripts to collect large amount of data, and enhancing TF-IDF embedding method. The future work can be outlined as follows:

- **Enhancing hyperparameters:** While we are confident in the selection of hyperparameters in this paper, we recognize the importance of further research to explore alternative hyperparameter configurations that could potentially enhance the performance of the models.
- **Refining script:** Due to the continuous growth and evolution of embedded systems vendors and industries, new devices and applications are constantly being introduced. Consequently, it be-

comes necessary to periodically update the keywords in our script to ensure its effectiveness in identifying relevant vulnerabilities. By keeping the script up to date with the latest industry developments.

- **Enhance TF-IDF embedding technique:** The current TF-IDF technique struggles with lengthy, context-dependent text and lacks semantic understanding which is necessary for vulnerability classification

REFERENCES

BlinowskiG. J.PiotrowskiP. (2020). *CVE based classification of vulnerable IoT systems*. doi:10.1007/978-3-030-48256-5_9

Chen, J., Kudjo, P. K., Mensah, S., Brown, S. A., & Akorfu, G. (2020). An automatic software vulnerability classification framework using term frequency-inverse gravity moment and feature selection. *Journal of Systems and Software*, *167*, 110616. doi:10.1016/j.jss.2020.110616

Connected Cars Technology Vulnerable to Cyber Attacks. (n.d.). Trend Micro | Newsroom. Retrieved November 4, 2023, from https://newsroom.trendmicro.com/2021-02-16-Connected-Cars-Technology-Vulnerable-to-Cyber-Attacks

Critical traffic light system vulnerability could cause 'chaos' on the roads. (2020, June 9). The Daily Swig | Cybersecurity News and Views. https://portswigger.net/daily-swig/critical-traffic-light-system-vulnerability-could-cause-chaos-on-the-roads

Gulati, U., Ishaan, & Dass, R. (2020). Intelligent Car with Voice Assistance and Obstacle Detector to Aid the Disabled. *Procedia Computer Science*, *167*, 1732–1738. doi:10.1016/j.procs.2020.03.383

Hern, A. (2017, August 31). Hacking risk leads to recall of 500,000 pacemakers due to patient death fears. *The Guardian*. https://www.theguardian.com/technology/2017/aug/31/hacking-risk-recall-pacemakers-patient-death-fears-fda-firmware-update

Huang, G., Li, Y., Wang, Q., Ren, J., Cheng, Y., & Zhao, X. (2019). Automatic Classification Method for Software Vulnerability Based on Deep Neural Network. *IEEE Access : Practical Innovations, Open Solutions*, *7*, 28291–28298. doi:10.1109/ACCESS.2019.2900462

Kowsari, K., Meimandi, K. J., Heidarysafa, M., Mendu, S., Barnes, L. E., & Brown, D. E. (2019). Text Classification Algorithms: A Survey. *Information (Basel)*, *10*(4), 150. doi:10.3390/info10040150

Nazzal, B., Zaid, A. A., Alalfi, M. H., & Valani, A. (2022). Vulnerability classification of consumer-based IoT software. *Proceedings of the 4th International Workshop on Software Engineering Research and Practice for the IoT*, 17–24.

Neshenko, N., Bou-Harb, E., Crichigno, J., Kaddoum, G., & Ghani, N. (2019). Demystifying IoT Security: An Exhaustive Survey on IoT Vulnerabilities and a First Empirical Look on Internet-Scale IoT Exploitations. *IEEE Communications Surveys and Tutorials*, *21*(3), 2702–2733. doi:10.1109/COMST.2019.2910750

Nuspire, T. (2023, March 30). The Ongoing Rise in IoT Attacks: What We're Seeing in 2023. *Security Boulevard*. https://securityboulevard.com/2023/03/the-ongoing-rise-in-iot-attacks-what-were-seeing-in-2023/

NVD - Data Feeds. (n.d.). Retrieved May 18, 2023, from https://nvd.nist.gov/vuln/data-feeds

NVD - Home. (n.d.). Retrieved May 18, 2023, from https://nvd.nist.gov/

Papp, D., Ma, Z., & Buttyan, L. (2015). Embedded systems security: Threats, vulnerabilities, and attack taxonomy. *2015 13th Annual Conference on Privacy, Security and Trust (PST)*, 145–152.

Prasad, D., Rahul Reddy, P., Sreelatha, B., Jeevan Reddy, K., Jayabalan, S., & Kumar Panigrahy, A. (2021). Recent developments in code compression techniques for embedded systems. *Materials Today: Proceedings*, *46*, 4128–4132. doi:10.1016/j.matpr.2021.02.643

Sharma, R., Sibal, R., & Sabharwal, S. (2021). Software vulnerability prioritization using vulnerability description. *International Journal of System Assurance Engineering and Management*, *12*(1), 58–64. doi:10.1007/s13198-020-01021-7

Välja, M., Korman, M., & Lagerström, R. (2017). A study on software vulnerabilities and weaknesses of embedded systems in power networks. *Scopus*, 47–52. Advance online publication. doi:10.1145/3055386.3055397

Wang, Q., Gao, Y., Ren, J., & Zhang, B. (2023). An automatic classification algorithm for software vulnerability based on weighted word vector and fusion neural network. *Computers & Security*, *126*, 103070. doi:10.1016/j.cose.2022.103070

Wang, Q., Li, Y., Wang, Y., & Ren, J. (2022). An automatic algorithm for software vulnerability classification based on CNN and GRU. *Multimedia Tools and Applications*, *81*(5), 7103–7124. doi:10.1007/s11042-022-12049-1

Wellsandt, S., Foosherian, M., & Thoben, K.-D. (2020). Interacting with a Digital Twin using Amazon Alexa. *Procedia Manufacturing*, *52*, 4–8. doi:10.1016/j.promfg.2020.11.002

Wen, T., Zhang, Y., Wu, Q., & Yang, G. (2015). ASVC: An Automatic Security Vulnerability Categorization Framework Based on Novel Features of Vulnerability Data. *Journal of Communication*, *10*(2), 107–116. doi:10.12720/jcm.10.2.107-116

Chapter 15
Intelligent Watermarking for Data Security:
An Overview

Imen Fourati Kallel

Ecole Nationale d'Electronique et des Télécommunications de Sfax (ENET'Com), Tunisia

Mohamed Kallel

Ecole Nationale d'Electronique et des Télécommunications de Sfax (ENET'Com), Tunisia

ABSTRACT

Artificial intelligence has become widely and increasingly used in various advanced applications, notably classification, optimization, object recognition, and segmentation. Recently, it has been extended into watermarking techniques. It brings some approaches implying innovative security means, which are adjusted to new communications and information technologies. As it generally believed that the use of artificial intelligence in digital watermarking schemes could revolutionize the way digital data is protected. This chapter is about an overview of recent developments in artificial intelligence techniques utilized for watermarking. It begins with the watermarking background. Next, it represents a review of machine and deep learning watermarking techniques followed by a delineation of their advantages and disadvantages. In this light, the main problems are pinpointed with a suggestion of some possible discussed and highlighted solutions. The last point of this chapter is about outlining future research directions.

INTRODUCTION

Artificial intelligence (AI) is the process of developing and implementing a number of techniques designed to enable computers to imitate human intelligence. Artificial intelligence (AI) offers many benefits and can have a significant impact on various sectors for improving efficiency and productivity, and for making faster and more accurate decisions. In this context machine learning and deep learning has become a promising solution for solving various intelligence related problems. It can be actively used for watermarking (Cox,2002) which is defined as a technique that involves inserting a message, logo or

DOI: 10.4018/979-8-3693-0497-6.ch015

signature into digital data. The objective is to make it possible to verify the assertion of ownership, the content authentication or the copy Control. Watermarking techniques based on artificial intelligence algorithms are called Intelligent Watermarking (IW) techniques.

Classic watermarking techniques have been the subject of a great deal of research and overview. (Cox, 2002), (Podilchuk, 2001), (Mahto,2021),(Kumaraswamy,2020). However, a limited number of studies have been concerned with intelligent watermarking. In his book (Pan, 2004), Pan gives a general introduction of digital watermarking by focusing on its areas of use, categories and other various characteristics. He ends with listing a number of classic watermarking methods. Solely, the last part of his book is kept for intelligent watermarking methods in which he covers soft computing and machine learning. Nonetheless, the AI methods were merely recognized within a classic framework. In (Singh, 2022), Singh reviews watermarking properties, applications and attacks. Generally, he reviews various watermarking techniques in the space and frequency domains by pinpointing the transition from the classical techniques into the new ones featuring with soft computing. He investigates grey scale and colour images in addition to a video. Wu (Wu, 2014) examines watermarking techniques by shedding light on the optimization algorithms, also known as soft computing, and by processing the three methods of the genetic algorithms (GA) (Katoch, 2021), the particle swarm optimization (PSO)(Clerc, 2010),and the differential evolution (DE)(Opara, 2019). They are detailed and compared, essentially by showing their advantages and disadvantages, each apart.

The aim of this book chapter is to provide an overview of intelligent watermarking for digital data. This chapter presents a detailed study of watermarking using current and popular technologies, such as artificial intelligence, soft computing, machine learning and deep learning. It also presents a general introduction to watermarking, the type of watermark, the insertion domain, the extraction schema and the most used watermarking applications. The major role and contributions of advanced technologies in watermarking are also underlined. A range of existing WI techniques is presented and the contributions of the studied approaches are discussed and compared. Finally, the book's chapter highlights the advantages and disadvantages of these WI techniques, opening the way to new research directions in this new area.

This chapter is organized by an introductory entry. Section 2 is retrospective by referring to watermarking background as a field standing on its legs. Section 3 is about surveying intelligent watermarking techniques, ranging from machine to deep learning usages. A detailed discussion is presented in Section 4 while some concluding remarks are listed in the last section.

THE BACKGROUND OF WATERMARKING DOMAIN

With the widespread of technology, the transfer of digital documents into networks has become increasingly of a great importance. It is practically essential not only to ensure security during data transfer but also to establish a reliable exchange of information. In this context, its use in watermarking is very demanding, particularly in hiding subliminal information in a digital document, which guarantees a secure service for copyright, integrity, traceability, non-repudiation, and even for informative reasons.

The classic watermarking scheme consists of two distinct stages: watermark insertion and extraction. The first stage happens when a message or mark is inserted imperceptibly into the cover medium before transmitting it via a public channel. However, during the extraction stage, watermarking algorithms are used to find and extract the previously inserted mark.

The mainly considered technical constraints when developing a high-performance watermarking techniques are robustness, insertion capacity and imperceptibility.

- The insertion capacity of a watermarking technique is the ratio between the size of the watermark to be dissimulated and the size of the used cover medium. In the spatial domain, insertion capacity is expressed as the number of watermark bits inserted per pixel (bpp). In the transformed domain, it is expressed as the number of watermark bits, which are inserted per coefficient (bpc).
- The robustness is the power to recover the embedded mark even if the watermarked image has been manipulated by attacks. Attacks can be manifested in different contexts. It may be intentional by attempting to destroy and remove the watermark in the watermarked image. It can occur unintentionally by applying the watermarked image before or during the transmission interval without aiming either to alter the watermarked image, as in the case of image processing operations used to optimize the quality of the watermarked image.

To assess robustness, different attacks are applied to the watermarked image. The next step is embodied in extracting the watermark and comparing it with the original watermark. It is possible to use qualitative evaluation, which consists of assuring the comparison with the naked eye. In addition to the qualitative assessment, several metrics have been stated in the literature such as Bit Error Rate (BER) and Normalized Cross Correlation (NCC).

- The imperceptibility refers to the visual quality of the watermarked image. In fact, it is necessary to avoid distorting the quality of the cover image.

The imperceptibility of the watermark plays a significant role in affirming whether an image has been visually degraded by the insertion of the mark or not. The value of this role varies widely from one application to another. To assess imperceptibility, it is possible to use qualitative evaluation, which consists of comparing the quality of the watermarked image and its similarity to the original image with either the naked eye or the use of different metrics (Sara, 2019), measuring the fidelity between the watermarked image and the original image. The measurement tools indicate the degradation of the image after its integration, such as maximum Peak Signal to Noise Ratio (PSNR) and Structural Similarity Index(SSIM) used to find similarities between the cover and the watermarked image.

Developing a watermarking algorithm involves finding the best compromise between these three main characteristics, according to the application in question. In addition to these characteristics, other features can be taken into consideration like computational speed, time complexity, security and reversibility.

The complexity of a watermarking technique stems from its intricate algorithm, which is used to insert and/or detect the mark. The application of a watermarking technique in real-time requires low complexity. Security rests on the ease with which data is detected, removed, and manipulated by a hacker. Reversibility is a specific requirement for certain fields such as medical image watermarking (Kallel, 2009). In addition to the three important watermarking requirements mentioned before, reversibility is basically taken into account because any distortion occuring in this type of data can lead to an erroneous diagnosis.

As shown in Figure 1 digital watermarking systems can be classified into several taxonomies, with reference to their applications and requirements. Digital watermarking is applicable to several types of data, such as text (Kamaruddin, 2018), audio (Furon, 2000), 3D (Kallel, 2023),video (Yu, 2018), and image (Kallel, 2022). Nevertheless, this work sheds light specifically on image watermarking.

Based on perceptibility, watermark can include a visible logo or text. It may also be imperceptible to the human eye. Visible watermarking is printed on cover images as the case of company logos orlogo for channels. In this scenario, the watermark is easily removed by simple cropping; it significantly degrades the visual quality of the cover image whereas an invisible watermark is used for security reasons.

The watermark can be inserted either into spatial or transform domains. Concerning the spatial domain, the watermarking insertion process is simply manipulated and got directly into the pixel of the image. The transform is applied to the cover image before inserting the watermark. Several transformations can be used in particular the Singular Value Decomposition (SVD), the Discrete-Cosine Transform (DCT) and the Discrete-Wavelet Transform (DWT). The watermark is embedded into the transform coefficient. Briefly, the use of watermarking techniques in the transform domain is more robust than in the spatial one. It is possible to get a hybrid watermark insofar as both insertion domains are used to take the advantage of their benefits.

Regarding robustness, the watermarking methods are classified into three degrees: fragile, semi-fragile and robust. Actually, the robust watermark resists several processing operations and attacks. In fragile watermarking, the signature is extremely sensitive to any modification of the watermarked data. Fragile watermarking is generally used to verify the integrity of data (Kallel, 2006). Semi-fragile watermarking combines the properties of fragile and robust watermarking. It is an intermediary situation in which the watermark is robust to a specific set of attacks, but fragile to others (Kallel, 2008). With respect to, the extraction watermarking schemes, there are three different types of watermarking methods. They are non-blind, semi-blind, and blind. The blind techniques do not require the cover image while extracting the embedded watermark; they are the most practical. The semi-blind watermarking techniques do not require the cover image. Rather, they require the watermark itself, or the secondary information, notably the secret key to obtain the watermark. For the non-blind extraction techniques, the original image is required. Although the blind methods ensure enhanced robustness, their applications are limited.

Watermarking techniques can be used to achieve several security objectives. Each objective requires some appropriate properties. Some of them are mentioned earlier.

In copyright protection, the owners or the rightful claimants of an image are able to give legal proof of their properties, even if the image has been attacked. Confidentiality ensures that the information included in the system is uniquely accessible to the authorized users. Authenticity guarantees that the received information from the subject is identical to the supplied one while integrity prevents the corruption or destruction of data processed by the system.

Classical digital watermarking techniques rely on manual processes and human intervention, particularly for the selection of the insertion zones, which can be time-consuming and sources of error. However, the integration of AI into the digital watermarking schemes could revolutionize the way of how digital data is protected.

Inspired by the success of artificial intelligence in computer vision applications, several watermarking techniques have been developed. These techniques have been extensively investigated in recent years, with outstanding results compared to classical watermarking ones. Indeed, intelligent algorithms can be used in watermark insertion, extraction, and in both them. They optimise the insertion process, the extracted watermark quality, or the trade-off between image quality and robustness. In this work, the authors distinguish between two families of learning-based image watermarking methods, namely machine learning and deep learning.

Figure 1. Digital watermarking classification

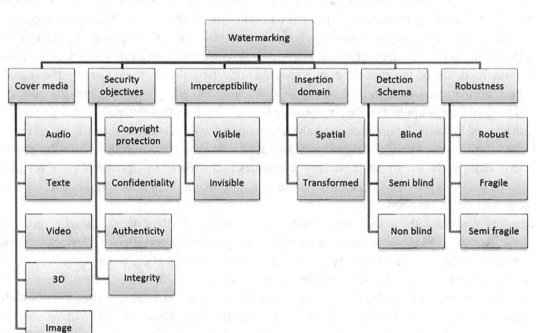

Figure2. Machine learning and deep learning

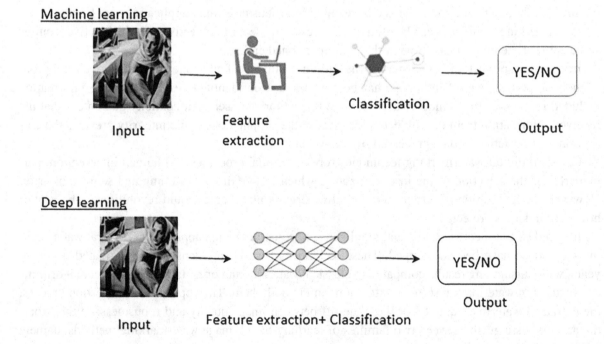

Machine and deep learning are two branches of artificial intelligence, which focus on learning from a data set. They differ in their principles, methodologies and abilities. Machine learning algorithms deal with structured data and with the users themselves who have to manually select and extract features, influencing the prediction as shown in Figure 2. However, deep learning algorithms treat the unstructured data, with the algorithm itself being trained to extract the data influencing the prediction. The data are fed to the network without pre-processing, modification or aggregation. Next, by adjusting a large number of parameters as it trains, the network learns the relationships of all the data on its own. The differences between machine and deep learning are detailed in table 1 below.

Table1. Differences between machine and deep learning

Characteristics	Machine Learning	Deep Learning
Used data	Structured data	Unstructured data
Algorithm	Modifiable algorithm	Neural networks.
Database	Perform well with small to medium	Need large database
Hardware	Can be operated with simple hardware.	Requires powerful computers
External intervention	The process needs to be understood, and the intervention of an engineer is necessary	No need to understand features
Execution time	From minutes to hours	From hours to weeks
Interpretability	Some algorithms are simple, others are difficult to interpret.	Difficult or even impossible to interpret
Application area	Simple tasks	Complex tasks

LITERATURE REVIEW: INTELLIGENT IMAGE WATERMARKING METHODS

In this section, a selection of the existing WI techniques is covered with a detailing and a discussing of the contributions of the studied methods.

Machine Learning-Based Image Watermarking Methods

Rai (Rai, 2017) proposes a robust watermarking method, which assures confidentiality and security for medical images. The SVM classifier with the Radial Basis Function (RBF) kernel is used to subsume the cover greyscale image pixel under two different classes and highlights the Region of the Non Interest (RONI) and the Region of Interest (ROI) of the cover image (Bairagi, 2013).

The ROI region presenting the relevant information of the medical image remains unchanged while the RONI region is the part of the image, which will incorporate the watermark. Two features are extracted and used for the classification: the intensity values and the pixel positions of the input image. For the SVM training, the author uses his own labelled database; the two features are extracted using the appropriate threshold value meanwhile the result is determined by the naked eye. The classification accuracy is 99.80%. Once the classification step is completed, the author applies a Discrete Wavelet Transform (DWT) to the RONI part for the purpose of transforming the cover image to the wavelet field. Later, the Singular Value Decomposition (SVD) is applied to the selected DWT coefficients. The watermark insertion is performed by altering the singular values of the LH and the HL sub-bands.

To ensure additional security for the watermarking method, the watermark greyscale image of the size 128×128 is scrambled before being inserted into the RONI part. A scaling factor is used to assure a highly convenient trade-off between imperceptibility and robustness.

The Rai method leaves promising experimental results, with reasonable imperceptibility estimated by a PSNR of 52.18 dB and an appropriate robustness against various attacks estimated by a SSIM of 0.9872. However, some complexities of calculations are faced.

In the same context, Ramly(Ramly, 2011) begins his medical image watermarking technique with a SVM classification step by means of RBF kernel, very similar to the Rai method .This classification subdivides the greyscale cover image to the ROI and the RONI region. For the SVM training, the author uses his own labelled database; the two features luminosity and the edges value of the images are extracted using the appropriate threshold value. The result is actually determined by the naked eye. The classification accuracy reaches 99.84%.The textual information of the patient is converted into a binary sequence. This sequence is the watermark, which is inserted into the selected DCT coefficient of the RONI zone. The watermark is embedded into the highest frequency coefficient of the 8x8 TCD blocks, which are classified in the RONI using the spread spectrum technique. The spread spectrum procedures guarantee a high level of security to the watermarking approach. In this case, the spreading of the watermark throughout the image spectrum makes it more resistant to attack and even harder to detect, ensuring the confidentiality and the integrity of patient information. The experimental results show a high medical watermarked image quality PSNR of more than 48dB and watermark robustness achieved with similarity ratio (SR) of more than 0.99.

This watermarking method is considered non-blind. Both the cover and the watermarked images are used to extract the watermark. The extracted binary sequence is finally converted to textual information.

The Ramly method underlies a low insertion capacity for the watermark bits are embedded into only one coefficient of each TCD block in the RONI region. The medical image quality is conserved.

Sinhal (Sinhal, 2021) introduces a robust intelligent watermarking method. First, the RVB colour cover image is transformed into YCbCr space. Second, Y standing for the luminance component is divided into 4x4 blocks. The Mersenne Twister random generator(Jagannatam, 2008) is used to randomly choose some blocks for insertion process with a secret key to enhance robustness. The integer wavelet transform(IWT) is applied to the selected blocks, and then to the DCT transform to the LL sub band. Finally, the watermark bits are embedded using an artificial neural network (ANN) with 20 input neurons, a hidden layer of 10 neurons, and an output layer watermarked of 16 neurons. The 16 pixel values of each selected block and four copies of the watermark bit are used to generate 20 input values for the ANN. 16 new pixel values are produced by the ANN to create the DCT block.

The DCT inverse is applied to the modified DCT block in order to obtain the modified LL band. Subsequently, the inverse IWT is performed to obtain the watermarked Y channel blocks. The watermarked image is obtained by converting the updated YCbCr image into an RGB image.The extracting process does not require an original image, which makes this blind IW technique valid and effective for many practical applications. The experimental results reveal remarkable values in terms of imperceptibility with the SSIM and the PSNR. They are up to 40.025 and 0.99 respectively, with robustness to various attacks. BER and NC are used to evaluate the robustness method. Without using the ANN, the average insertion time is 2.23 s while the average extraction time is 1.36 s. The results of the Rishi's method are comparable to those of the four methods shown in the literature section above in terms of robustness and imperceptibility. Rishi develop an ANN using the Matlab toolbox to optimize the integration process and reduce its computational cost to around a quarter.

Zear (Zear, 2018) suggests a multiple hybrid watermarking technique. Its watermarking scheme is classic. Machine learning is used just to optimise the extracted watermark. The author inserts three distinct watermarks in the medical image to assure an identity authentication to two textual watermarks of 190 characters, respectively presenting the doctor's identification code and the patient's diagnosis and an image.

First, the Arnold transformation is applied to the image watermark for more security. Second, the DCT is applied to the scrambled watermark. Then, the SVD is applied to the watermark frequent coefficients to obtain the U, S, and V three matrices. The watermark singular value S_w is inserted into the singular value of the DCT-LH1 sub-band DWT representation of the original image. Using equation (1):

$$S_{wat} = S_c + \alpha * S_w \tag{1}$$

Where α is the scaling factor whereas the Sc the cover singular value

The first symptom text signature is converted to binary coded using lossless arithmetic compression technique and embedded intoLL3 sub-band. The second text is converted to binary sequence. Next, the Hamming error correction code is applied before being embedded into LH2 sub-band.

The insertion reverse process is applied to extract watermarks. The Zear method is non blind; the cover image is required to extract the image watermark. In the same context, in order to obtain the two watermarks of the symptom and the identification texts, the arithmetic and the Hamming decoding are applied respectively to the extracted watermark bits and convert them to text. A BackPropagation Neural Network (BPNN) is used to optimise the extracted watermark quality, to remove noise and to improve their robustness. The proposed Zear method seems of noticeable experimental results in terms of the watermarked image quality with a PSNR 43.88 dB, text watermarks robustness with BER of 0for the first textual watermark, and between 0.2174 and 0.1087 for the second watermark depending on the scaling factor value.

The image watermark robustness is seemingly suitable with a NC of 0.9363 without using the BPNN optimisation and of 0.9888 using the BPNN. The Arnold transformation adds extra security to the Zear method and the Hamming code increases its robustness significantly. However, this method is highly complex while its performance depends on the value of the scaling factor.

Others soft computing techniques are used in new watermarking methods such as the genetic algorithms (GA) and the fuzzy logic.

Kongara introduces (Kongara, 2012) a blind watermarking method based on the GA. The genetic algorithm is an evolutionary one, which turn up by the process of natural selection and living beings to find better solutions to specific problems. In this work, the genetic algorithms are used as an iterative optimization algorithm, which optimizes four parameters; three of them are insertion and one is an extraction process using genetic operators such as selection, reproduction, crossover and mutation. They are inspired by the natural selection, the evolution theory, and the fitness function.

The optimum values of the four parameters used in the watermarking process, which guarantee the best possible robustness and imperceptibility, are determined by the GA. The used fitness function is defined as follow:

$$Fitness_l = PSNR_l + \frac{1}{P}\sum_{k=1}^{P}NC_{k,l}*\alpha_k \qquad (2)$$

Where P is the number of the used attacks, l is the generation number of the GA, and αk is the scaling factor for the NC.

In the light of the Kangora method, first, a third level of the DWT Haar is applied to the cover image. Second, the LH2 and the LH3 coefficients are grouped into blocks. Each block contains one coefficient from the LH3 sub-band and four coefficients from the LH2 sub-band. Then, the first and the second minimum in each block are identified and updated depending on the watermark bit. The three optimised parameters are used as scaling factor for watermark insertion; the fourth parameter is used to control robustness. The obtained experimental results are remarkable; with the NCC values are higher than the traditional methods and a PSNR of 44.95 dB for a 512bit watermark. The used optimization may maximize the values of the NCC and the PSNR, proving the method performances. However, the complexity of the genetic algorithm increases the execution time of this watermarking method.

In the same context, Aslantas (Aslantas, 2008) displays a watermarking method based on the SVD transformation using a genetic algorithm. To ensure robustness without altering the original image, several scaling factors are optimized by means of the GA.

In (Jagadeesh, 2015) Jagadeesh presents a robust and blind watermarking method in the DCT domain by relying on the fuzzy inference System (FIS). The original image is transformed into the DCT domain and meantime decomposed into 8 x8 blocks. The watermark bits are inserted in the central coefficient of each block. Three fuzzy inference rules are used to formulate the calculated Human Visual System (HVS) features to obtain the optimal factor scaling by using an insertion process and fuzzy logic (Hájek, 2013).

The HVS features, notably texture, luminance, frequency and edge sensitivity are calculated for each block of the original image. The obtained results give evidence of the proposed method robustness.

Deep Learning-Based Image Watermarking Methods

After presenting a set of intelligent watermarking methods based on machine learning technique, a range of intelligent watermarking methods using deep learning techniques are depicted. A particular focus is on the insertion and extraction phases. The different deep learning models used in this context are based on CNN (convolutional neural networks) (Krizhevsky,2017) architecture. Its structure is derived from the neurons of the human brain and it is commonly used for classification, pattern recognition and object identification applications. The main advantage of the CNN is its utility to automatically identify the relevant features of the input information without human supervision.

Many intelligent watermarking techniques are utilized with the auto-encoder network structure. An auto-encoder (Pinaya, 2020) is an unsupervised deep learning model composed of two neural networks. An auto-encoder has the same number of neurons on its input and output layers. The hidden layers are smaller than the input ones. This type of architecture is known as a bottleneck. The left side of this bottleneck is called the encoder. It transforms the input into a representation in a lower-dimensional space, also labelled as a latent space. The right-hand side is called the decoder and uses the latent representation of the input. It reconstructs an output as faithful as possible to the input. During the learning process, all the parameters are simultaneously optimized to minimize a loss function on the network output. Watermarking methods, which are based on auto-encoder architecture, contains an encoder, an attack simulator also named noise layer, and a decoder connected to a cascade as shown in Figure 3. The encoder plays the role of embedding the watermark into the cover image and generating the watermarked image. The attack simulator distorts the watermarked image. The decoder is used to extract the signature from the watermarked attacked image.

Figure 3. End-to-end training deep network architecture

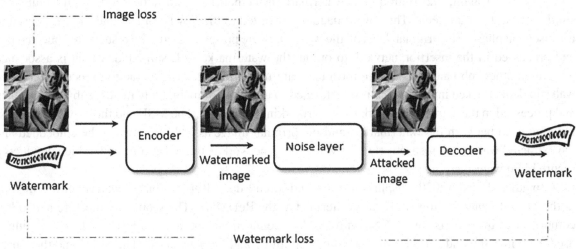

In this context, Jae-Eun Lee (Lee, 2020) proposes an invisible, blind and robust watermarking method, pivoted on four CNN network: two pre-processing network among which one is for the cover image while the other is for the watermark. An encoder named watermark integration network and a decoder termed watermark extractor. The original RGB image is converted to YCbCr (luminance –chrominance space color) and only Y the luminance component is normalized and used for the watermark insertion. The first pre-processing network for the cover image consists of a single convolutional layer of 64 filters with a kernel size of 3x3, consequently preserving the resolution of the original image and produces 64 feature maps to extract the cover image characteristics. The binary watermark is scrambled with a key to ensure more security. To intensify the watermark invisibility, the second pre-processing network is used to increase the watermark resolution, corresponding to that of the cover image. This network consists of four convolutional layers with 512, 256, 128 and 1 filter respectively and a stride of 0.5 for upward sampling of the first three layers. Each convolutional layer is followed by batch normalization, a Rectified Linear Unit (ReLU) activation function, and an average pooling with a kernel sized 2×2. Nevertheless, the last block is made up of only one convolutional layer and an average pooling. A scaling factor is used to control the invisibility and robustness of the watermark. The 64 features map of the pre-processed cover image and one channel of the pre-processed watermark are concatenated and used as input to the watermark integration network. The network consists of four convolutional layers followed by batch normalization and ReLU activation function using 64 filters with a stride of 1 to preserve cover image resolution and one convolutional layer followed by hyperbolic tangent (tanh) activation function. An attack simulator is designed as an incentive for various attacks with the aim of evaluating the robustness of the watermarking method. The watermark extraction network has an inversely symmetric architecture to the watermark pre-processing network which reduces the resolution of the attacked watermarked image and extracts the watermark. It consists of three convolutional layers followed by batch normalization, a ReLU activation function, and one convolutional layer followed by tanh activation function. The number of the used filters is 128, 256, 512, and 1, respectively with a stride of 2 for down-sampling. As the loss functions MSE and MAE are used between the original and the watermarked image as well as between the embedded and the extracted watermark respectively. The Lee's method shows noticeable results, compared with the other IW techniques.

Tavakoli (Tavakoli, 2023) introduces a watermarking method, based on auto-encoder architecture very similar to the Jae-Eun Lee's. The cover image is converted to the DWT domain and the LL is used in the insertion phase. The original data and the watermark are pre-processed. The results are concatenated and processed in the insertion network to output the watermarked LL sub-band, which is associated with three other sub-bands in order to form the watermarked image. The extraction process receives a watermarked attacked image, which is transformed to the DWT domain. Only the LL sub-band is taken and processed in the extractor network for watermarking extraction. The MSE and the MAE are the loss function used between the watermarked and the original image as well as between the embedded and the extracted watermark respectively. The whole deep network is trained end-to-end, which conducts a secure blind watermarking.

Ahmadi (Ahmadi, 2020) displays a blind end-to-end deep learning-based watermarking method in the TCD domain for grey scale images termed as the ReDMark. The global architecture network is comprised of three parts: two CNNs with residual connections and a noise layer. A factor scaling is used to control the trade off between the imperceptibility and the robustness. The SSIM and the binary cross-entropy MAE are the loss function used between the watermarked and the original image as well as between the embedded and the extracted watermark respectively. The obtained result are promising, showing much better performance than a number of the research studies mentioned in the literature section above, particularly the performance of the Hidden (Zhu, 2018) method.

Jiren Zhu (Zhu,2018)comes up with a blind intelligent watermarking method, which labelled the Hidden one. It is also based on auto-encoder network: an encoder for watermark embedding, a decoder for extract the watermark, an attack simulator used to apply divers transformation to the watermarked image and a Generative Adversarial Networks (GAN) (Aggarwal, 2021), which verify the containing message image, either. The GAN architecture has two neural networks termed as the generator and the discriminator network. These networks compete over each other, with their improvement over time. The generator network takes random noise as input and produces realistic data samples, which resembles the real data. During the training process, it ameliorates itself to better produce realistic samples by learning from the feedback provided by the discriminator network, which makes a distinction between the real data from the training set and the fake ones produced by the generator. It takes both the real and the generated data as input. It also learns how to become more accurate in classifying these data into real and fake as soon as the training progresses.

The GAN is used within the Hidden method for the purpose of improving the imperceptibility performance. In this respect, the discriminative network receives a mixture of watermarked and unmodified images. It is expected to differentiate and classify them. During the learning process, the generative network improves its data embedding abilities, ensuring high imperceptibility.

Fierro-Radilla (Fierro-Radilla,2019) proposes a robust semi blind watermarking technique based on the CNN architecture. A CNN network, containing 13 convolutional layers, is applied to the RVB image as a means to extract the most pertinent features. Each convolutional layer is followed by max pooling with a 2x2 kernel size, batch normalization, and a RELU activation function. The network is terminated by two fully connected layers with 100 and 2 neurons respectively and a Softmax activation function to ensure the binary classification of the image target and no image target classes. One hundred real data are extracted from the first fully connected layer, binarized and a xor function is applied between this sequence and the permutated binary watermark. The Fierro-Radilla method is semi blind to extract the watermark. The extraction step requires a master share to be xored with the extracted features. The model is trained using a large dataset containing images, some of which undergoing different attacks. As this method is zero-watermarked (Singh, 2020), it seems that it does not alter the cover image significantly. It retains a convenient visual quality, which is in demand for the medical field. The NCC and the BER are used to evaluate the robustness of this used method.

Chen (Chen, 2021) suggests a deep learning with extraction techniques. It is named the WMNet. A CNN model is used to classify the extracted watermark as "Correct" and "Incorrect". In order to facilitate the creation of the database used to train the CNN model, the author carries out a simulated process, which generates a large number of deformed watermarks. They are collected later to form a training data set. The CNN model includes two successive convolution layers of 3x3 kernel size, which are used to extract features from the input watermark image. Each convolution layer is followed by a max pooling one of 3x3 kernel size, which reduces the size of the obtained features maps. Subsequently, a fully connected layer and a softmax layer are added. The extracted watermark is classified with an accuracy of 97.8%, a specificity of 97.5%, and a sensitivity of 97.8%.Two binary watermarks sized 64x64 and 32x32 are tested in the current work. By using the Chen method, it is worth noting that the insertion process is not specified in detail.

Before moving on to a detailed discussion of the presented techniques, the most prominent specifications of the IW techniques investigated in the last section are delineated in Table 2 and 3:

DISCUSSION

One of the most significant advantages of using the AI in digital watermarking is the ability to automate the process, reducing the need for human intervention. This does not only serve to save time and resources but also to minimize the risk of errors occurring with the classical watermarking. In the light of the current research, it is noticed that the intelligent watermarking techniques outperform the classical ones in relation to robustness and imperceptibility. It proves that the AI plays a significant role in improving the performance of the digital watermarks. Nevertheless, the artificial intelligence techniques and the optimization algorithms used and analyzed in the previous section are apparently complex and costly. They require long computing time and considerable processing power.

Many intelligent watermarking methods combine encryption and watermarking to enhance security, which may even increase more complexity. The Intelligent Watermarking method using transform domain takes the advantages of some different transform processes to assure more robustness and imperceptibility. Nonetheless, it is characterized by low capacity and inversely high complexity. Accordingly, the wavelet transform offers variable spatial resolution enabling precise selection of the cover image regions where the watermark is inserted. This gives greater control over the watermark placement and

Table2. Summary of machine learning-based image watermarking methods

IW Methods	Insertion Domain	Cover Image	Watermark	Architecture	Security Objectives	Detection Schema	Extra security	Scaling factor
(Rai, 2017)	DWT+SVD	Grey scale 256x256	Grey image 128x128	ML / SVM / Insertion process	Confidentiality and security for medical images	Non blind	Yes	Yes
(Ramly, 2011)	DCT	Grey scale 256x256	Textual patient confidential data converted to binary	ML / SVM / Insertion process	Integrity and confidentiality of patients' information	Non blind	No	Yes
(Sinhal, 2021)	IWT+DCT	Colour 512 × 512	Four binary image 32 × 32	ML / ANN / Optimize insertion process / Reduce complexity compute for insertion process	Copyright protection	Blind	Yes	No
(Zear, 2018)	DWT+DCT+SVD	512 × 512	Image 256 x 256 Two texts of 190 characters	ML / BPNN / Optimised the watermark quality	Identity authentication	Non blind	Yes	Yes
(Kongara, 2012)	DWT	Grey scale 256x256	Binary image 32 × 16 32x32 and 64x64 are also tested	Soft computing / GA / Optimise the trade-off between robustness and imperceptibility	Copyright protection	Blind	Yes	Yes
(Aslantas, 2008)	SVD	Gray scale 256x256	Gray scale 32x32	Soft computing / GA / Optimise the trade-off between robustness and imperceptibility	-	Non blind	No	Yes
(Jagadeesh, 2015)	DCT	Gray scale 512 × 512	64x64 Binary image	Soft computing / fuzzy logic	Copyright protection	Blind	No	Yes

Table 3. Summary of deep learning-based image watermarking methods

IW Methods	Insertion Domain	Cover image	Watermark	Architecture	Security Objectives	Detection Schema	Extra security	Scaling factor
(Lee, 2020)	Spatial	Gray scale 128x128	Random binary 8 × 8 image	DL / Auto encodeur(CNN) / Insertion and extraction	Protect intellectual property rights	Blind	Yes	Yes
(Tavakoli, 2023)	DWT	RVB 256, 256	Random 256-bit	DL / Auto encodeur / Insertion and extraction	Protect intellectual property rights	Blind	No	No
(Ahmadi, 2020)	TCD	512x512	32x32	DL / Auto encodeur with residuel connection / Insertion and extraction	-	Blind	-	Yes
(Zhu, 2018)	Spatial	RVB 128x128	30- bit Random	DL / Auto encodeur+ GAN / Insertion and extraction	Data hiding	Blind	No	Yes
(Fierro-Radilla, 2019)	300x300	RVB 300x300	Binary 10×10	DL / CNN / Insertion and extraction	Medical image security	Semi blind	Yes	No
(Chen, 2021)	-	Gray scale 512 × 512	Binary image 64x64 32x32 is also tested	DL / CNN / Extraction	Copyright protection	-	No	No

more improvement to the visual quality (Yong, 2013). Similarly, watermarking in the DCT domain can be performed without a significant alteration of the visual quality. The watermark is spread over the different DCT coefficients. It makes it more and more difficult for attackers to detect the watermark by offering considerable robustness against attacks. However, the transform domain brings about various drawbacks. The DWT is sensitive to the geometric attacks like rotation and image scaling, which can affect the wavelet transform coefficients.The DCT transform may encounter a blocking artefact problem. Transformation requires intense calculations time, which is costly in terms of complexity and processing power. Several intelligent watermarking methods are geared towards using hybrid domains to combine the characteristics of a number of domains, which improve performance and reduce the weaknesses of the watermarking systems. However, this strategy requires a computational complexity. Intelligent watermarking using soft computing like GA, takes the advantage of these algorithms, which need neither initial examples nor a base to learn from. Nevertheless, they do have certain drawbacks, namely the complexity of implementation, long calculation times and uncertain results. There is no guarantee that they will always meet the optimum solution to a problem. The same as the classic watermarking techniques, the intelligent watermarking techniques require a constant need for keeping a trade-off between imperceptibility, insertion capacity and robustness. As these three characteristics are inversely related, this trade-off is often difficult to achieve and remains challenging for most watermarking techniques. Thus, a high insertion capacity reduces the level of imperceptibility and robustness. Similarly, improving robustness against attacks can potentially decrease both insertion capacity and imperceptibility. Some applications, such as the medical field, may require imperceptibility while others may give greater importance to robustness or insertion. The trade-off is rather struck between these three characteristics, depending on the specific requirements of the application. Many WI techniques use scaling factor, giving the user a wide and easy-to-handle compromise between imperceptibility and robustness, depending on the application. Nonetheless, the performance of the watermarking technique becomes dependent on the selected scale factor value. This trade-off can be explicitly managed by the user, due to the adaptable aspect of the watermarking based on deep learning approaches by simply adjusting the training and testing parameters of the network. An additional advantage of watermarking techniques relying on deep learning is their enhancement of the inserted watermark security. The non-linearity of the deep neural models makes it practically impossible for a hacker to retrieve the watermark. Another strength of the deep learning approach is the retaining of the networks to become resistant to new attacks.

Watermarking pivoted on AI techniques improves both the performance of robustness and imperceptibility. It displays much better results than using the classical techniques. Traditional watermarking techniques include an array of limitations, which are practically eliminated by intelligent watermarking. This type of watermarking use artificial intelligence (AI) techniques to smartly adapt the watermark to the specific cover media, its usage, and the intended application IW leverages AI and other dynamic techniques to resist the watermark of various contexts. It enhances content protection and analytics. Accordingly, classical techniques may not be sufficiently capable of concealing watermark information without affecting the quality of the cover media, whereas intelligent watermarking algorithms seek to maximize information dissimulation while maintaining the visual quality of the cover image. Intelligent systems can dynamically adjust the watermark according to content or other external factors; machine learning models can be trained to detect and compensate for distortions in watermarked content. Some classic watermarking methods can be easily detected and eliminated by hackers to appropriate intellectual property. Intelligent watermarking uses advanced detection algorithms, which is sometimes based on AI, to improve the detection reliability. They can even repair themselves after any case of manipulation, offering stronger protection.

Technological advances in automatic watermark removal algorithms can reduce the effectiveness of the traditional watermarks over time. Intelligent watermarking aims to make intellectual property protection more effective by using advanced techniques, which is adapted to the challenges posed by any flow of potential attacks. This adaptability enhances the security and robustness of the watermark.

Intelligent watermarking is particularly relevant in the context of protecting digital media in contemporarily sophisticated digital landscape, where traditional methods can be more susceptible to attack.

However, they are not devoid of some drawbacks. First of all, the IW techniques are characterized by their computational complexity and extended time working. Second, the robustness of the intelligent watermarking techniques is not stable. It depends on the number of the used samples during the training stage as well as on the loss function adopted. Third, the watermarking techniques based on machine and deep learning face the complexity of using databases for training steps. Fourth, the ground truth labelling for an image watermarking task can be ill-defined or time intensive. Fifth, watermarking based on deep learning has a low insertion capacity. Sixth, deep learning remains a black box whose mechanism and principle are enigmatic. Although the network performs well against particular attacks included in the training step, it may encounter suffer low robustness against other new cropping up attacks.

The intelligent watermarking process based on machine learning model used to classify cover image pixels benefits from AI technologies in respect with an adaptation of the embedded watermark to the characteristics of the cover image. This intelligent insertion process is widely used in medical field (Ramly, 2011), (Rai, 2017) to subdivide an image to ROI and RNOI. The watermark will be generally embedded into the NROI region, which improves the conservation of medical information. However, these approaches have several drawbacks. They can be only implemented if an RONI exists and the amount of information to be embedded depends on the RONI area size. As a result, it varies from image to image depending on the type of the medical image.

Concerning the methods based on auto-encoders, although they are blind, they are highly sensitive to hyper-parameters. Several components (the encoder, the decoder and the attack simulator) have to be trained conjointly, which creates a number of drawbacks. First, for every new added attack, all the encoder and the decoder parameters have to be updated simultaneously during the training process, which is computationally expensive. Second, the attack must support back propagation since the encoder and decoder are required to be trained with the attack simulator. However, most attacks, particularly compression, do not meet this requirement and are black boxes.

Before implementing watermarking techniques, it is essential to understand the specific needs of the intended application, to clearly identify the objective requiring an application with the watermark, whether for copyright protection, integrity verification, or other purposes. The characteristics and requirements of the watermark are established in accordance with the intended application, the field of application, and the working context. The integration of strong encryption mechanisms can add further protection to the watermark against fraud and falsification. It would be very interesting to develop dynamic and adaptive watermarking techniques, capable of adjusting to different media characteristics.

Although database preparation is a tedious task for all machine and deep learning methods, whose operation depends entirely on databases, the emergence of new data augmentation algorithms (DA) can limit this challenge and encourage the use of IW techniques (Shorten, 2019).

Several recent watermarking models are used in real-world applications including Imateg (Maho, 2023), which is one of the patented watermarking solutions invested in controlling the use of images on the web and tracking visual content leaks. This security technique has protected brands and agencies from serious reputational and financial damage.

Watermarks have long been one of the most powerful tools available to TV stations and visual artists. They are an efficient way to protect their work, especially in European continent and the USA. They regularly add watermarks to their videos for the sake of drawing the others' attention to the originality of their programs. These traditional watermarks are static. Every copy of a distributed work carries the same watermark, making them both easier to remove. They are of a limited value when it comes to the determination of a copy's origin. Nowadays, Hollywood dynamic watermarks are considered as efficient in preventing plagiarism and privacy. They secure scripts and films (Wu, 2022). It is possible to include the users' details, timestamps, or other identifying features in these dynamic watermarks. The dynamic nature of these watermarks makes them more difficult to remove or manipulate, compared to the static ones. For example, projection dates and video projector identifiers are embedded in videos shown in cinemas. Hollywood can therefore detect in which theater a pirate has recorded a film and put pressure on the theatre owner. In the same context, to guarantee the security of information exchange, Peer-to-

Peer (P2P) networks (Kretthika, 2017) apply watermarking processes. P2P networks are decentralized systems in which participants, known as peers, exchange information or services directly, without having to go through a central server, unlike traditional client-server models. Bit Torrent is an example of a P2P file-sharing protocol designed for the efficient distribution of large quantities of data. Client identifiers can be embedded in files shared on the network for a variety of purposes, including copyright protection, content authentication or tracking the origin of files so that dishonest people who illegally share their versions can be identified, blacklisted or even prosecuted. Thanks to new technologies, dynamic watermarking generates unique watermarks for each copy of a file on these P2P networks, making it more difficult for pirates to remove watermarks by comparing multiple versions of the same content. Additionally, it is possible to cite the case of some companies, which apply digital watermarking as a replacement or a bar code security to anti-counterfeit (Nguyen, 2019), (Soon, 2019).

Future research in this field focuses on developing more advanced techniques, which optimize the trade-off between imperceptibility, robustness and insertion capacity in addition to the satisfaction of the specific requirements of the intelligent watermarking in different applications. To minimize the model training complexity, it is possible to use the transfer learning (Zhuang, 2020), which enables to the user to turn to the pre-trained models. These models are neural networks in relation to the deep learning. They have been previously trained on large datasets like ImageNet and can be reused for watermarking tasks by making small changes. Transfer learning can not only saves time and resources but also improves performance and accuracy of the model.

CONCLUSION

This work is rather an overview of the intelligent watermarking techniques. It begins with covering the background of the watermarking domain. Then, it reviews some IW techniques based on machine and deep learning with some details and discussion. Future research avenues are also raised for an upcoming pursuit. With reference to the analytical and empirical parts in this work, it is no doubt that the intelligent watermarking methods have ensured better results than the classic ones, particularly in term of imperceptibility and robustness. However, the used artificial intelligence techniques and optimization algorithms have not overcome the major problem of the watermarking methods, which is the compromise between robustness, imperceptibility and insertion capacity. This problem still persists, in addition to other added problems, mainly computational complexity, working time and, above all, the difficulty of creating databases to ensure an effective training process. Thus, this study provides an insight into the use of artificial intelligence for watermarking techniques. It is considered as a helpful source of information for researchers to develop optimized intelligent watermarking techniques for different applications.

REFERENCES

Aggarwal, A., Mittal, M., & Battineni, G. (2021). Generative adversarial network: An overview of theory and applications. *International Journal of Information Management Data Insights*, *1*(1), 100004. doi:10.1016/j.jjimei.2020.100004

Ahmadi, M., Norouzi, A., Karimi, N., Samavi, S., & Emami, A. (2020). ReDMark: Framework for residual diffusion watermarking based on deep networks. *Expert Systems with Applications*, *146*, 113157. doi:10.1016/j.eswa.2019.113157

Aslantas, V. (2008). A singular-value decomposition-based image watermarking using genetic algorithm. *AEÜ. International Journal of Electronics and Communications*, *62*(5), 386–394. doi:10.1016/j. aeue.2007.02.010

Bairagi, V. K., & Sapkal, A. M. (2013). ROI-based DICOM image compression for telemedicine. *Sadhana*, *38*(1), 123–131. doi:10.1007/s12046-013-0126-4

Chen, Y. P., Fan, T. Y., & Chao, H. C. (2021). Wmnet: A lossless watermarking technique using deep learning for medical image authentication. *Electronics (Basel)*, *10*(8), 932. doi:10.3390/electronics10080932

Clerc, M. (2010). *Particle swarm optimization* (Vol. 93). John Wiley & Sons.

Cox, I. J., Miller, M. L., Bloom, J. A., & Honsinger, C. (2002). *Digital Watermarking* (Vol. 53). LNCS.

Fierro-Radilla, A., Nakano-Miyatake, M., Cedillo-Hernandez, M., Cleofas-Sanchez, L., & Perez-Meana, H. (2019, May). A robust image zero-watermarking using convolutional neural networks. In *2019 7th International Workshop on Biometrics and Forensics (IWBF)* (pp. 1-5). IEEE. 10.1109/IWBF.2019.8739245

Furon, T., Moreau, N., & Duhamel, P. (2000, June). Audio asymmetric watermarking technique. *Int. Conf. on Audio, Speech and Signal Processing*.

Hájek, P. (2013). *Metamathematics of fuzzy logic* (Vol. 4). Springer Science & Business Media.

Jagadeesh, B., Kumar, P. R., & Reddy, P. C. (2015). Fuzzy inference system based robust digital image watermarking technique using discrete cosine transform. *Procedia Computer Science*, *46*, 1618–1625. doi:10.1016/j.procs.2015.02.095

Jagannatam, A. (2008). *Mersenne Twister–A Pseudo random number generator and its variants*. George Mason University, Department of Electrical and Computer Engineering.

Kallel, I., Lapayre, J. C., & Bouhlel, M. (2008). Medical Image Semi-fragile Watermarking in the Frequential Field. *Journal of Testing and Evaluation*, *36*(6), 540–545.

Kallel, I. F., Bouhlel, M. S., Lapayre, J. C., & Garcia, E. (2009). Control of dermatology image integrity using reversible watermarking. *International Journal of Imaging Systems and Technology*, *19*(1), 5–9. doi:10.1002/ima.20172

Kallel, I. F., Chaari, A., Frikha, M., Kammoun, S., & Trigui, A. (2022, May). DWT based blind and robust watermarking technique using ABCD map for medical image. In *2022 6th International Conference on Advanced Technologies for Signal and Image Processing (ATSIP)* (pp. 1-6). IEEE. 10.1109/ATSIP55956.2022.9805942

Kallel, I. F., Grati, A., & Taktak, A. (2023). 3D Data Security: Robust 3D Mesh Watermarking Approach for Copyright Protection. In Examining Multimedia Forensics and Content Integrity (pp. 1-37). IGI Global.

Kallel, I. F., Kallel, M., Garcia, E., & Bouhlel, M. S. (2006, May). Fragile watermarking for medical image authentication. In *The 2nd International Conference on Distributed Frameworks for Multimedia Applications* (pp. 1-6). IEEE. 10.1109/DFMA.2006.296919

Kamaruddin, N. S., Kamsin, A., Por, L. Y., & Rahman, H. (2018). A review of text watermarking: Theory, methods, and applications. *IEEE Access : Practical Innovations, Open Solutions, 6*, 8011–8028. doi:10.1109/ACCESS.2018.2796585

Katoch, S., Chauhan, S. S., & Kumar, V. (2021). A review on genetic algorithm: Past, present, and future. *Multimedia Tools and Applications, 80*(5), 8091–8126. doi:10.1007/s11042-020-10139-6 PMID:33162782

Kongara, R., & Raja, R. (2012). Wavelet-based oblivious medical image watermarking scheme using genetic algorithm. *IET Medical Image Processing, 6*(4), 364-373.

Kretthika, P., Vinutha Yadav, D., & Ashwini, K. (2017). Survey on copyright protection in peer to peer network. *International Journal of Engineering Research and Applications, 7*(05), 33–40. doi:10.9790/9622-0705013340

Krizhevsky, A., Sutskever, I., & Hinton, G. E. (2017). Imagenet classifcation with deep convolutional neural networks. *Communications of the ACM, 60*(6), 84–90. doi:10.1145/3065386

Kumaraswamy, E., Kumar, G. M., Mahender, K., Bukkapatnam, K., & Prasad, C. R. (2020, December). Digital Watermarking: State of The Art and Research Challenges in Health Care & Multimedia Applications. *IOP Conference Series. Materials Science and Engineering, 981*(3), 032031. doi:10.1088/1757-899X/981/3/032031

Lee, J. E., Seo, Y. H., & Kim, D. W. (2020). Convolutional neural network-based digital image watermarking adaptive to the resolution of image and watermark. *Applied Sciences (Basel, Switzerland), 10*(19), 6854. doi:10.3390/app10196854

Maho, T., Furon, T., & Le Merrer, E. (2023). FBI: Fingerprinting models with Benign Inputs. *IEEE Transactions on Information Forensics and Security, 18*, 5459–5472. doi:10.1109/TIFS.2023.3301268

Mahto, D. K., & Singh, A. K. (2021). A survey of color image watermarking: State-of-the-art and research directions. *Computers & Electrical Engineering, 93*, 107255. doi:10.1016/j.compeleceng.2021.107255

Nguyen, H. P., Retraint, F., Morain-Nicolier, F., & Delahaies, A. (2019). A watermarking technique to secure printed matrix barcode—Application for anti-counterfeit packaging. *IEEE Access : Practical Innovations, Open Solutions, 7*, 131839–131850. doi:10.1109/ACCESS.2019.2937465

Opara, K. R., & Arabas, J. (2019). Differential Evolution: A survey of theoretical analyses. *Swarm and Evolutionary Computation, 44*, 546–558. doi:10.1016/j.swevo.2018.06.010

Pan, J. S., Huang, H. C., & Jain, L. C. (2004). *Intelligent Watermarking Techniques with Source Code* (Vol. 7). Innovative Intelligence. doi:10.1142/5471

Podilchuk, C. I., & Delp, E. J. (2001). Digital watermarking: Algorithms and applications. *IEEE Signal Processing Magazine, 18*(4), 33–46. doi:10.1109/79.939835

Rai, A., & Singh, H. V. (2017). SVM based robust watermarking for enhanced medical image security. *Multimedia Tools and Applications*, 76(18), 18605–18618. doi:10.1007/s11042-016-4215-3

Ramly, S., Aljunid, S. A., & Shaker Hussain, H. (2011). SVM-SS watermarking model for medical images. In *Digital Enterprise and Information Systems: International Conference, DEIS 2011, London, UK, July 20–22, 2011. Proceedings* (pp. 372-386). Springer Berlin Heidelberg.

Sara, U., Akter, M., & Uddin, M. S. (2019). Image quality assessment through FSIM, SSIM, MSE and PSNR—A comparative study. *Journal of Computer and Communications*, 7(3), 8–18. doi:10.4236/jcc.2019.73002

Shorten, C., & Khoshgoftaar, T. M. (2019). A survey on image data augmentation for deep learning. *Journal of Big Data*, 6(1), 1–48. doi:10.1186/s40537-019-0197-0

Singh, A., & Dutta, M. K. (2020). A robust zero-watermarking scheme for tele-ophthalmological applications. *Journal of King Saud University. Computer and Information Sciences*, 32(8), 895–908. doi:10.1016/j.jksuci.2017.12.008

Singh, R., Saraswat, M., Ashok, A., Mittal, H., Tripathi, A., Pandey, A. C., & Pal, R. (2022). From classical to soft computing based watermarking techniques: A comprehensive review. *Future Generation Computer Systems*.

Sinhal, R., Jain, D. K., & Ansari, I. A. (2021). Machine learning based blind color image watermarking scheme for copyright protection. *Pattern Recognition Letters*, 145, 171–177. doi:10.1016/j.patrec.2021.02.011

Soon, J. M., & Manning, L. (2019). Developing anti-counterfeiting measures: The role of smart packaging. *Food Research International*, 123, 135–143. doi:10.1016/j.foodres.2019.04.049 PMID:31284961

Tavakoli, A., Honjani, Z., & Sajedi, H. (2023). Convolutional neural network-based image watermarking using discrete wavelet transform. *International Journal of Information Technology : an Official Journal of Bharati Vidyapeeth's Institute of Computer Applications and Management*, 15(4), 2021–2029. doi:10.1007/s41870-023-01232-8

Wu, S. W. (2014). Research on intelligent image watermarking schemes based on optimization algorithm. *Advanced Materials Research*, 1006, 792–796. doi:10.4028/www.scientific.net/AMR.1006-1007.792

Wu, X., Ma, P., Jin, Z., Wu, Y., Han, W., & Ou, W. (2022). A novel zero-watermarking scheme based on NSCT-SVD and blockchain for video copyright. *EURASIP Journal on Wireless Communications and Networking*, 2022(1), 20. doi:10.1186/s13638-022-02090-x

Yong, B., & Steve, L. (2013). Medical image watermark detection in the wavelet domain using bessel k densities. *IET Medical image Processing*, 7(4), 281–289.

Yu, X., Wang, C., & Zhou, X. (2018). A survey on robust video watermarking algorithms for copyright protection. *Applied Sciences (Basel, Switzerland)*, 8(10), 1891. doi:10.3390/app8101891

Zear, A., Singh, A. K., & Kumar, P. (2018). A proposed secure multiple watermarking technique based on DWT, DCT and SVD for application in medicine. *Multimedia Tools and Applications*, 77(4), 4863–4882. doi:10.1007/s11042-016-3862-8

Zhu, J., Kaplan, R., Johnson, J., & Fei-Fei, L. (2018). Hidden: Hiding data with deep networks. In *Proceedings of the European conference on computer vision (ECCV)* (pp. 657-672). Academic Press.

Zhuang, F., Qi, Z., Duan, K., Xi, D., Zhu, Y., Zhu, H., Xiong, H., & He, Q. (2020). A comprehensive survey on transfer learning. *Proceedings of the IEEE, 109*(1), 43–76. doi:10.1109/JPROC.2020.3004555

KEY TERMS AND DEFINITIONS

Arnold Transformation: It is also known as Arnold's cat map. It is a mathematical transformation, which can be applied to a 2Dimage. It involves an iterative rearranging of the image pixels position in way which preserves the surface but radically alters the appearance. This transformation is often used for encryption purposes.

Batch Normalization (BN): Is a standardization technique used in deep learning network algorithms. It stabilizes the learning process and reduces the number of the learning epochs required to train deep networks.

Rectified Linear Activation Function (RELU): Is the most commonly used activation function in many deep learning networks. It is easy to train and often leads to better performance. If it is positive, it returns the input directly; otherwise it turns back to the zero value.

Chapter 16
Design of a Real–Time–Integrated System Based on Stereovision and YOLOv5 to Detect Objects

Oumayma Rachidi

ENSAM, Moulay Ismail University of Meknes, Morocco

Ed-Dahmani Chafik

ENSAM, Moulay Ismail University of Meknes, Morocco

Badr Bououlid

ENSAM, Moulay Ismail University of Meknes, Morocco

ABSTRACT

Real-time object detection represents a major part in the development of advanced driver assistance systems (ADAS). Pedestrian detection has become one of the most important tasks in the field of object detection due to the increasing number of road accidents. This study concerns the design and implementation of a Raspberry Pi 4-based embedded stereovision system to detect 80 object classes including persons and estimate 3D distance for traffic safety. Stereo camera calibration and deep learning algorithms are discussed. The study shows the system's design and a custom stereo camera designed and built using 3D printer as well as the implementation of YOLOv5s in the Raspberry Pi 4. The object detector is trained on the context object detection task (COCO) 2020 dataset and was tested using one of the two cameras. The Raspberry Pi displays a live video including bounding boxes and the number of frames per second (FPS).

DOI: 10.4018/979-8-3693-0497-6.ch016

I INTRODUCTION

Advanced Driver Assistance System (ADAS) is a vehicle-based intelligent safety system aimed towards improving safety in the automobile industry. ADAS technologies are used in many vehicles today, some of which are integrated as a standard equipment. These systems can improve road safety in terms of collision avoidance, protection and post-crash notification. Intelligent speed adaptation (ISA), electronic stability control (ESC), and autonomous emergency braking systems (AEB), represent a good example of ADAS systems that are offering a significant safety potential (European Commission, 2018). The main purpose of ADAS is to reduce road accidents by providing drivers information about objects in front of the vehicle, to take the necessary actions. Object detection represents a vital tool widely used in computer vision to estimate the location of objects in images or videos for ADAS. There have been many studies in the field of computer vision regarding object detection for real time applications. These studies differ in terms of methodology; however, the objective remains the same: find a detector with high accuracy and high speed.

Deep learning, is a machine learning subset that offers solutions in many complex applications, through deep neural networks. These networks, have improved the performance of smart surveillance, smart city, and self-driving cars-based applications in comparison with machine learning methods. One of the first deep neural networks is the CNN (Convolutional Neural Network), which is used for image classification. This network is aimed to recognize many objects such as vehicles, pedestrians, and traffic signs. The main advantage of CNN, is that it automatically extracts features after training on a dataset, without human intervention (Shin et al., 2016).

Nowadays, deep learning models are used in object detection for real time applications. These models can use different architectures to classify and detect objects, and can be divided into two main categories: Two-stage detectors such as R-CNN and Fast-RCNN (Girshick, 2015), and one stage detectors such as the single Shot MultiBox Detector (SSD) (Liu et al., 2016), and the You Only Look Once (YOLO) (Redmon et al., 2015). In the first category, regions of interest are firstly generated, and then fed to a network to apply classification and bounding boxes regression. These detectors are highly accurate, but take time to process images which makes it harder to deploy them in real time applications. In the second category, the object classification and bounding boxes regression are performed using one network. These models have lower accuracy, but achieve high inference speed.

The main goal of a real time object detection application is to find a good trade-off between the accuracy and the speed of the detector. For YOLO detectors, many improvements have been introduced to reach the best performances. Redmon et al. (2015) have created the first version of YOLO in 2015. In this version, a neural architecture based on GoogleNet model was used. The model was compared to Faster-RCNN on PASCAL VOC 2007 dataset, the results shown that the VGG-16 version of Faster R-CNN was 10 mAP higher, but 6 times slower than YOLO. Few years after the release of the first version, YOLOv2 or YOLO9000 was introduced to detect over 9000 categories with high accuracy and speed compared to YOLO. YOLO suffers from a significant number of localization errors and has a low recall in comparison with region proposed-based methods. Thus YOLOv2, was designed to improve localization errors and recall, while maintaining classification accuracy. In this version, Darknet-19 model was used, and the model was trained on ImageNet for classification and both COCO and VOC for detection. On PASCAL VOC 2007, YOLO gets 63,4 Map and 45 FPS on a GeForce GTX Titan X with a resolution of 448x448, while YOLOv2 gets 77,8 Map and 59 FPS with a resolution of 480x480 (Redmon & Farhadi, 2017). In 2018, YOLOv3 was introduced, with some changes in the architecture to make it better than the previous versions. In this version, Darknet-53 model was used. At 320 x 320 resolution, the model is as accurate as SSD, but three times faster (Redmon & Farhadi, 2018). YOLOv4 was created in 2020 to achieve optimal speed and accuracy. This version uses the architecture of modern detectors with a CSP Darknet 53 as backbone, SPP additional module, PANET path aggregation neck, and YOLOv3 head. It improves YOLOv3 AP and FPS by 10% and 12% respectively (Bochkovskiy & al., 2020).

YOLOv5 is one of the recent versions of YOLO detectors. This model can be used for real time applications, since it provides high accuracy and speed. This version relies on CSP Darknet53 as backbone, SPPF, new CSP-PAN neck, and YOLOv3 head. While YOLOv4 has over 60 million parameters, YOLOv5 provides a YOLOv5s version with only 7 million parameters, making it a lightweight version of all previous YOLO algorithms. A comparison between YOLOv3, YOLOv4 and YOLOv5 was made on three custom dataset, and it was found that the YOLOv5 performs better than other in real time detection.(Murthy et al., 2022). Kim et al. (2022), proposed a YOLOv5 model to detect human on heat map images using a custom dataset. The model has reached high accuracy after training. Jaikishore et al. (2022) developed a model based on YOLOv5 to detect vehicles with a custom dataset, and compared it to YOLOv3. This research has focused on the difference between models with and without pretrained weights. Recently, a monitoring robotic system was designed based on YOLOv5 and Raspberry Pi 4 to recognize and display objects in real time. The system used the pretrained model on the COCO dataset (Al-Tameemi et al., 2023). Zepeda et al. (2022) have proposed an algorithm for lane detection, and an implementation of YOLOv5 for object detection. The algorithms were implemented using Nvidia GPU to get better results.

YOLOv5 has several versions such as YOLOv5L, YOLOV5s and YOLOv5n. These versions have different metrics (mean average precision and speed), and the choice of the version has to be made according to the application. In this work, YOLOv5 was selected since it is a well-known object detector that offers a high computational speed and is easy to train. For the model's version, YOLOv5s was used, as it offers a good trade-off between accuracy and speed, and the model size is 14 megabytes, which facilitates its deployment.

In the proposed work, an embedded system is designed based on stereovision and YOLOv5 to detect pedestrians and estimate distance for traffic safety. The authors have focused on the stereo camera calibration and the implementation of YOLOv5s in the raspberry, to get accurate results regarding distances and object detection.

The rest of chapter is organized as follows: Section II reviews recent pedestrian detectors. In Section III, we present our proposed model for object detection in detail. Section VI provides our results and discussions. The conclusion is presented in Section V with future prospects.

II RELATED WORK

Pedestrian detection represents a critical factor in the development of computer vision systems. Nowadays, different research have been made to improve the efficiency of pedestrian detectors especially for ADAS systems. Thus, many recent neural networks have been designed to address challenges relating to real time pedestrian detection.

Khan et al. (2022) have proposed a Fast Focal Detection Network for pedestrian detection (F2DNet) to improve two stage detector's performance. The proposed network relies on a redesign of two stage detection architecture by replacing region proposal network with a strong focal detection network followed by a fast suppression head to reduce false positives. The detection network is anchor free and based on center and scale map prediction. The model was compared with the state of the art, and has proven its efficiency after evaluation on three of the most used datasets: Caltech, Euro City Persons and City Persons datasets.

One of the most recent pedestrian detectors is the Localized Semantic Feature Mixers for Efficient Pedestrian Detection in Autonomous Driving (LSFM). This model has been designed to improve detection in case of small or heavily occluded pedestrians. It uses a ConvMLP-based backbone, a Super Pixel Pyramid Pooling neck to filter and enrich features extracted in the backbone, and a Dense Focal Detection Network. The model beats all state-of-the-art detectors including the F2DNet for three datasets: Caltech, Euro City Persons and City Persons datasets. However, the model was only evaluated in day scenes and traffic scenarios (Khan et al., 2023).

The above-mentioned models are recent and have not yet proven their performance for real time applications. Besides, state of the art detectors mentioned in these works do not include recent detectors such as the recent versions of YOLO.

Recently, YOLOv5 has gained the attention of many researchers, as it has proven a high accuracy and inference speed for real time applications.

X. Jin et al. (2021) have demonstrated the possibility of usage of YOLOv5 for autonomous vehicles, after training the model with PASCAL VOC2012 dataset. To improve the efficiency of YOLOv5, Reddy and Thale (2021) have modified the structure of the detector, and trained it with the CityPersons dataset. The modification has led to an increase of detection speed with 0.011 sec/image. K. Yang et al. (2022) have created a new model based on YOLOv5s to detect pedestrians in crowds. The main modifications were the substitution of convolutional layers in YOLOv5 with depth separable convolutions, and the activation function with ACON-C. The model was trained on MOT20Det dataset, and was two times faster than the original model while having the same accuracy.

One of the challenges that researchers face while developing deep learning object detectors, is the complexity of deployment in embedded systems .R. Jin et al. (2022), have used the structure of mobilenetv3 in the YOLOv5, and have demonstrated an increase in accuracy and speed of the model, which was trained on a custom infrared dataset with distillation attention to improve accuracy. The use cases of YOLOv5 are numerous and diverse: Zhao et al. (2022) have created a custom dataset based on real pedestrian crossing data and CARLA software. The scenes were used to train the YOLOv5, and tested for detection. Chen et al. (2022) have added an attention module to the YOLOv5 model to increase accuracy, and anchor boxes adjustment with the KITTI dataset, to detect pedestrians and vehicles, and the new model has shown good results after deployment on Nvidia Jetson TX2. For autonomous vehicles, the detector has to be accurate, for this reason Dai (2022) has made a new model based on the fusion of YOLOv5 and CBNet Faster RCNN. The model was tested and compared with other networks, and it was better in terms of accuracy.

Finding a high accurate and fast detector is crucial for Multi-object tracking (MOT) algorithms, hence Cheng et al. (2022) have created a concise model of YOLOv5 based on the reduction of number of channels of the model to increase its speed and deploy it on an end-side device. The new detector was used for a MOT algorithm, and a technique of distillation knowledge was applied to increase the accuracy of the detector. Crowd Human dataset was used to train the detector, and the results showed 28 FPS with a camera used with T40 chip. The training was processed with an NVIDIA Titan RTX.

For ADAS systems, a pedestrian detector has to be accurate even in bad environmental conditions. Recently, many researchers have conducted studies about training object detectors with thermal images.

M. Li et al. (2022) have designed a multimodal detector based on YOLOv5 for RGB and thermal images: The model uses two backbones based on YOLOv5, and a fusion module to get a fusion map based on the data collected from images, the model outperforms the other networks designed for this case in both KAIST and VOT2019 datasets. Ghari et al. (2022) have used YOLOv5s to detect pedestrians at real time. The model was trained on Caltech dataset to ensure a robust pedestrian detection in different environmental conditions. The training process was performed using an NVIDIA GeForce RTX3090, and the final model showed a speed of 69 FPS.T. Li et al. (2022) used K++ clustering method, and added a specific attention module to YOLOv5m in order to increase the accuracy of the model. The training was done using OTCBVS and INO datasets.

Sharma et al. (2022) trained the YOLOv5s with a custom dataset using Roboflow to improve the efficiency of the detector in bad weather conditions. As mentioned above, most of pedestrian detectors rely on large deep neural network models, which makes it harder to deploy them in edge devices, Yan et al. (2022) have reduced the size of YOLOv5s model by eight to make a new lightweight model suitable for deployment. A custom dataset was used to detect six classes including the pedestrian class. The new model was generated using sparsification, pruning and fine tuning, and the training was realized using a GeForce GTX 3090, the precision of the lightweight model has reached 87%. To improve the efficiency of the YOLOv5 detector in complex scenes, C. Yang et al. (2023) have improved the accuracy of the detector by 2%, by changing the structure of the neural network, adding an attention module and modifying the loss function.

Recently, new models have been created to increase the accuracy and reduce the complexity of YOLOv5s model for pedestrian detection. M.-L. Li et al. (2023), have improved the YOLOv5s model by replacing conv and C3 modules with Ghost modules and C3 Ghost modules to get a lightened model while maintaining the original model's accuracy. The new model YOLOv5s-G uses a global attention module GAM to increase accuracy and extract features in complex environments. The αCIoU loss function was applied instead of the GIoU to get better results. The new model was trained on the WiderPerson dataset, and compared with the YOLOv5s. The results have shown an increase of 1% and 1.2% respectively in Map0,5 and mAP0,5:0,95 in comparison with the YOLOv5s.

The majority of research made in the field of pedestrian detection, have focused on the improvement of object detection models and tracking systems. Distance estimation can be considered as an important task in ADAS systems to complete the object detection and implement the necessary actions to avoid collisions, however very few research have studied the combination of this task with YOLO detectors. In this work, we propose a stereovision embedded system based on Raspberry Pi 4 and using YOLOv5s as a detector. Indeed, stereovision method is advantageous because it provides the possibility to estimate depth and distance and the recordings made by the camera can be adapted for different algorithms. In addition, cameras can capture high quality images of traffic scenes and present a more cost-effective solution compared to LIDAR. The deep learning algorithm can be implemented in many embedded devices; however Raspberry Pi 4 was chosen initially as a first open-source test platform, for its availability, low cost, power and high efficiency.

III THE PROPOSED SYSTEM

The proposed system has been designed at ENSAM's laboratory using a 3D printer. The stereoscopic camera was developed using two OV5647 5MP cameras. The system is controlled by a Raspberry Pi 4, and uses computer vision techniques to show real time video with object detection based on YOLOv5s model. The overall design of the system is presented on Figure1.

The research focuses on stereo camera calibration and object detection for Advanced Assistance Driver Systems (ADAS).

Figure 1. Design of the proposed system

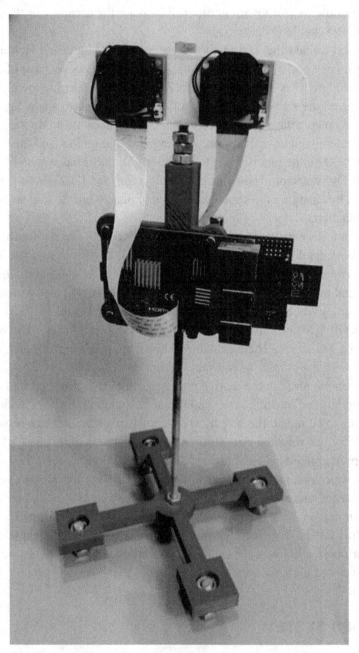

A. Sockets Transmission

The cameras used in the system need to be connected to a CSI port. Thus, each one of them is connected to a Raspberry Pi: The left camera is linked to a Raspberry Pi 4 and the right camera is connected to a Raspberry Pi 2. To ensure a synchronization between the images taken from the left and right cameras, sockets transmission was used.

The TCP/IP protocol was employed to transfer images collected from the right camera into the Raspberry Pi 4. The socket represents the port number and the IP address of the Raspberry Pi.

The client and server of this transmission are the Raspberry Pi 4 and 2 respectively. After identifying the IP address of each Raspberry Pi and the port number, a program is written in Visual Studio code with python language in the two Raspberry.

The Raspberry Pi 4 sends a connection request to the server, which accepts it and starts to send images after converting them into packets of bytes. Once received, the images taken from the right camera are displayed on the Raspberry Pi 4 simultaneously with those taken from the left camera as shown in Figure 2.

Figure 2. Images taken simultaneously from the left and right camera using sockets

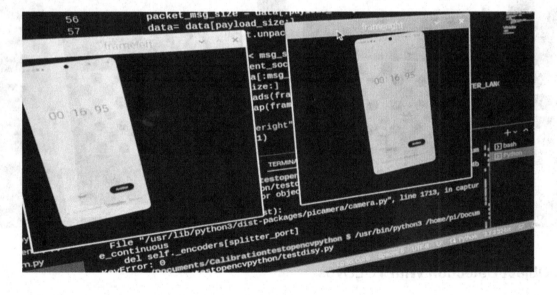

B. Stereo Camera Calibration

Stereo cameras have many advantages in comparison with other sensors used in ADAS systems such as RADAR, LIDAR and monocular cameras. This includes their ability to capture high resolution images with many visual information such as colors and shapes, which are important for object detection. The stereovision is also adapted for occlusion situations and provides a 3D reconstruction of the scene, which allows distance estimation.

Camera calibration is an important task in the field of computer vision: It provides intrinsic and extrinsic camera parameters. The camera coordinates are mapped into the image plane using the intrinsic parameters, and the orientation of the camera regarding the word coordinate frame is represented by the extrinsic parameters. Thus, the 3D word coordinates are transformed into 3D camera coordinates using the external parameters, and the internal parameters are used to transform the 3D camera's coordinates into 2D image coordinates.

In stereovision, these parameters can be used to calculate depth and estimate distance. The two cameras have to be calibrated to ensure a correct distance estimation. While calibrating a camera, an object of known geometry is used. The object coordinates in the word reference and in the image's plane provide the camera's parameters through equations.

In our research, we used OpenCV to calibrate the stereo camera. As shown in Figure 3, chessboard images were generated simultaneously from the left and right camera. The intrinsic and extrinsic parameters were obtained using predefined functions in OpenCV.

The parameters obtained were used in image processing to eliminate distortion and rectify images.

Figure 3. Stereo camera calibration using OpenCV

C. Object Detection With YOLOv5s

Recently, YOLO has been used in many research related to object detection, as it provides a good trade-off between accuracy and speed. In this model, the image is divided into grid cells. Bounding boxes are defined for each grid cell and based on intersection over union (IOU) techniques the object detection is performed. In order to have an efficient object detector, a training process has to be carried out. This process relies basically on a dataset and predefined hyper-parameters such as the number of epochs and images in each batch. During training, a loss function calculates the error between predicted values and ground truth. The main objective of this process is to minimize the loss function to improve the detector's accuracy.

The designed system uses OpenCV to perform image processing and stereo camera calibration, and then the YOLOv5s model to detect object in real time. The YOLOv5 is an ultralytics open-source model implemented on Pytorch. As shown in Figure 4 (Zhou et al., 2021), the structure of the model includes three parts: backbone, neck and output. The input image with 640x640x3 resolution is processed by the focus structure. It then becomes a 320x320x32 feature map after a slicing process and a convolution operation based on 32 convolution kernels. The Conv2D+BatchNormal+LeakyRELU (CBL) represents the basic convolution module. The bottleneck CSP module is used to extract the main features from the image, and reduces gradient information duplication in the optimization process.

By modifying the width and depth of the BottleneckCSP module, four different versions can be obtained: YOLOv5s, YOLOv5m, YOLOv5l, and YOLOv5x.The YOLOv5 uses also a bottom-up feature pyramid structure with the feature pyramid network (FPN), and this makes the model able to detect objects with different scales efficiently. Finally, a prediction of the bounding boxes is performed, and the classification and object detection results are obtained in the output.

The objective of the designed system is to implement YOLOv5s on the Raspberry Pi 4, and show the object detection results in a real time video captured with a raspberry camera. The YOLOv5s pre-trained on the COCO dataset was used. The implementation of this model, requires the installation of deep learning libraries and frameworks in the hardware. The python language was used to import all the necessary packages. YOLOv5s is then loaded from Ultralytics using PyTorch framework. The real time video is obtained by the OpenCV library using a connected camera to the Raspberry Pi. The camera is opened to capture frames, and an algorithm is used to send these frames to the YOLO model for object detection. A loop is used to show the frames at real time with the object detection results until a press exit key "q" from the keyboard. Thus, the object detection results are shown in the raspberry in real time. Figure 5 shows the main steps used for the implementation of the deep learning model in the raspberry.

Figure 4. YoloV5 model architecture

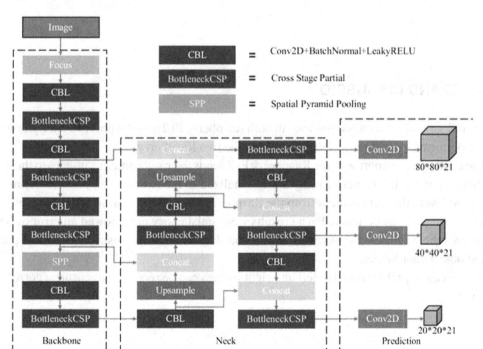

Figure 5. Logigram of the detection model

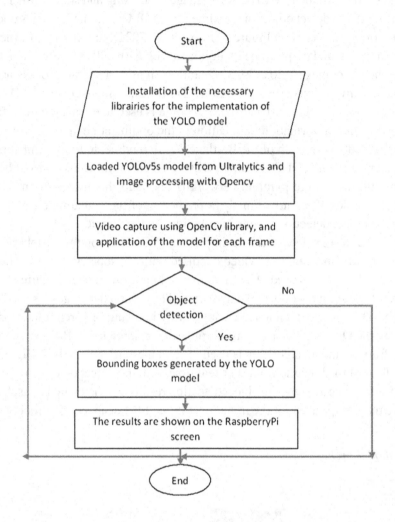

IV RESULTS AND DISCUSSION

After the installation of the required libraries in both Raspberry Pi 2 and Raspberry Pi 4, Python language was used to perform a socket transmission between the two Raspberry.

Once the connection is approved, the Raspberry Pi 2 sends the right camera's images to the Raspberry Pi 4, and both right and left camera's images are visualized in the Raspberry Pi 4 at real time.

Once the access to the right camera from the Raspberry Pi 4 was programmed and executed, the stereo camera calibration was performed: The results were satisfactory and showed an error of 0,6%. This error represents the difference between the object coordinates estimated using the camera parameters, and the real object coordinates.

After stereo camera calibration, the left and right images can be rectified, to ensure a correct distance calculation later.

For the YOLOv5s, a specific algorithm was used in Visual Studio Code to detect objects at real time using the pretrained model on the COCO dataset. At first, the image resolution was set to 300x300 to increase the inference speed while maintaining a good accuracy, and then bounding boxes were generated using the detection algorithm.

Figure 6. Person and chair detection using YOLOv5s

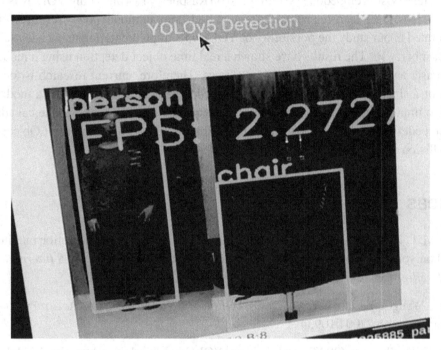

Figure 7. Person detection using YOLOv5s

The results were obtained experimentally using the Raspberry Pi 4, which displays a video including the detections at real time reaching 2.7 FPS as shown in Figure 6 and Figure 7.

V CONCLUSION AND FUTURE PROSPECTS

In this work, a stereo vision embedded system based on Raspberry Pi 4 and using YOLOv5s was designed to detect pedestrians. Deep learning networks require high computational power resources; however, we have demonstrated in our study the possibility of YOLOv5's implementation using a low-cost hardware such as the Raspberry Pi. The results have shown a real time object detection using a model pretrained on COCO dataset and able to detect 80 object classes. Therefore, current research is focusing on the development of a single class detector, namely the pedestrian class. Some model's modifications are also planned to improve its accuracy and speed. Subsequent work will focus on the calculation of distance between pedestrians and vehicles, and the localization of the Most Important Objects for reliable pedestrian collision avoidance.

REFERENCES

Al-Tameemi, M. I., Hasan, A. A., & Oleiwi, B. K. (2023). Design and implementation monitoring robotic system based on you only look once model using deep learning technique. *IAES International Journal of Artificial Intelligence, 12*(1), 106–113. doi:10.11591/ijai.v12.i1.pp106-113

Bochkovskiy A. Wang C.-Y. Liao H.-Y. M. (2020). *YOLOv4: Optimal Speed and Accuracy of Object Detection*. https://arxiv.org/abs/2004.10934v1

Chen, Y., Liu, W., & Zhang, J. (2022). An Enhanced YOLOv5 Model with Attention Module for Vehicle-Pedestrian Detection. *IEEE International Symposium on Industrial Electronics, 2022-June*, 1035-1040. 10.1109/ISIE51582.2022.9831596

Cheng, B., Huang, Y., Xie, X., & Du, J. (2022). A Multi-object Tracking Algorithm Based on YOLOv5-Concise Network. *Proceedings of SPIE - The International Society for Optical Engineering, 12246*. 10.1117/12.2643719

Dai, P. (2022). FYCFNet: Vehicle and Pedestrian Detection Network based on Multi-model Fusion. *2022 3rd International Conference on Computer Vision, Image and Deep Learning and International Conference on Computer Engineering and Applications, CVIDL and ICCEA 2022*, 230-236. 10.1109/CVIDLICCEA56201.2022.9825072

Ghari, B., Tourani, A., & Shahbahrami, A. (2022). A Robust Pedestrian Detection Approach for Autonomous Vehicles. *Proceedings - 2022 8th International Iranian Conference on Signal Processing and Intelligent Systems, ICSPIS 2022*. 10.1109/ICSPIS56952.2022.10043934

Girshick, R. (2015). Fast R-CNN. *Proceedings of the IEEE International Conference on Computer Vision, 2015 International Conference on Computer Vision, ICCV 2015*, 1440-1448. 10.1109/ICCV.2015.169

Jaikishore, C. N., Arunkumar, G. P., Srinath, A. J., Vamsi, H., Srinivasan, K., Ramesh, R. K., Jayaraman, K., & Ramachandran, P. (2022). Implementation of Deep Learning Algorithm on a Custom Dataset for Advanced Driver Assistance Systems Applications. *Applied Sciences (Basel, Switzerland), 12*(18), 8927. Advance online publication. doi:10.3390/app12188927

Jin, R., Xu, Y., Xue, W., Li, B., Yang, Y., & Chen, W. (2022). An Improved Mobilenetv3-Yolov5 Infrared Target Detection Algorithm Based on Attention Distillation. Lecture Notes of the Institute for Computer Sciences, Social-Informatics and Telecommunications Engineering, 416. doi:10.1007/978-3-030-94551-0_22

Jin, X., Li, Z., & Yang, H. (2021). Pedestrian Detection with YOLOv5 in Autonomous Driving Scenario. *2021 5th CAA International Conference on Vehicular Control and Intelligence, CVCI 2021.* 10.1109/CVCI54083.2021.9661188

Khan, A. H., Munir, M., Van Elst, L., & Dengel, A. (2022). F2DNet: Fast Focal Detection Network for Pedestrian Detection. In *Proceedings—International Conference on Pattern Recognition* (pp. 4658-4664). 10.1109/ICPR56361.2022.9956732

Khan, A. H., Nawaz, M. S., & Dengel, A. (2023). Localized Semantic Feature Mixers for Efficient Pedestrian Detection in Autonomous Driving. In *Proceedings of the IEEE Computer Society Conference on Computer Vision and Pattern Recognition* (pp. 5476-5485). 10.1109/CVPR52729.2023.00530

Kim, J., Huh, J., Park, I., Bak, J., Kim, D., & Lee, S. (2022). Small Object Detection in Infrared Images: Learning from Imbalanced Cross-Domain Data via Domain Adaptation. *Applied Sciences (Basel, Switzerland), 12*(21), 11201. Advance online publication. doi:10.3390/app122111201

Li, M., Liu, B., Sun, J., Zhang, G., & Su, W. (2022). Multimodality pedestrian detection based on YOLOv5. *Proceedings of SPIE - The International Society for Optical Engineering, 12456.* 10.1117/12.2659653

Li, M.-L., Sun, G.-B., & Yu, J.-X. (2023). A Pedestrian Detection Network Model Based on Improved YOLOv5. *Entropy (Basel, Switzerland), 25*(2), 381. Advance online publication. doi:10.3390/e25020381 PMID:36832747

Li, T., Song, X., Gao, S., Chen, C., Liu, K., & Liu, J. (2022). Research on Visible Light Pedestrian Detection Algorithm Based on Improved YOLOv5m. *2022 International Conference on Mechanical and Electronics Engineering, ICMEE 2022*, 305-311. 10.1109/ICMEE56406.2022.10093673

Liu, W., Anguelov, D., Erhan, D., Szegedy, C., Reed, S., Fu, C.-Y., & Berg, A. C. (2016). SSD: Single shot multibox detector. Lecture Notes in Computer Science, 9905, 21-37. doi:10.1007/978-3-319-46448-0_2

Murthy, J. S., Siddesh, G. M., Lai, W.-C., Parameshachari, B. D., Patil, S. N., & Hemalatha, K. L. (2022). ObjectDetect: A Real-Time Object Detection Framework for Advanced Driver Assistant Systems Using YOLOv5. *Wireless Communications and Mobile Computing, 2022*, 1–10. Advance online publication. doi:10.1155/2022/9444360

Reddy, E. R. V., & Thale, S. (2021). Pedestrian Detection Using YOLOv5 For Autonomous Driving Applications. *2021 IEEE Transportation Electrification Conference. ITEC-India, 2021*, 1–5. Advance online publication. doi:10.1109/ITEC-India53713.2021.9932534

Redmon, J., Divvala, S., Girshick, R., & Farhadi, A. (2015). You Only Look Once: Unified, Real-Time Object Detection. *Proceedings of the IEEE Computer Society Conference on Computer Vision and Pattern Recognition, 2016-December*, 779-788. 10.1109/CVPR.2016.91

Redmon, J., & Farhadi, A. (2017). YOLO9000: Better, faster, stronger. *Proceedings - 30th IEEE Conference on Computer Vision and Pattern Recognition, CVPR 2017*, 6517-6525. 10.1109/CVPR.2017.690

RedmonJ.FarhadiA. (2018). *YOLOv3: An Incremental Improvement*. https://arxiv.org/abs/1804.02767v1

Sharma, T., Debaque, B., Duclos, N., Chehri, A., Kinder, B., & Fortier, P. (2022). Deep Learning-Based Object Detection and Scene Perception under Bad Weather Conditions. *Electronics (Basel)*, *11*(4), 563. Advance online publication. doi:10.3390/electronics11040563

Shin, H.-C., Roth, H. R., Gao, M., Lu, L., Xu, Z., Nogues, I., Yao, J., Mollura, D., & Summers, R. M. (2016). Deep Convolutional Neural Networks for Computer-Aided Detection: CNN Architectures, Dataset Characteristics and Transfer Learning. In IEEE Transactions on Medical Imaging (Vol. 35, Numéro 5, p. 1285-1298). doi:10.1109/TMI.2016.2528162

Yan, X., He, Z., Huang, Y., Xu, X., Wang, J., Zhou, X., Wang, C., & Lu, Z. (2022). A Lightweight Pedestrian Intrusion Detection and Warning Method for Intelligent Traffic Security. *KSII Transactions on Internet and Information Systems*, *16*(12), 3904–3922. doi:10.3837/tiis.2022.12.007

Yang, C., Fan, H., & Zhu, H. (2023). Research on Target Detection Algorithm for Complex Scenes. *ITNEC 2023 - IEEE 6th Information Technology, Networking, Electronic and Automation Control Conference*, 873-877. 10.1109/ITNEC56291.2023.10082670

Yang, K., Chen, X., Yan, X., & Wu, D. (2022). Yolov5-DP: A New Method for Detecting Pedestrian Aggregation. *Proceedings of International Conference on Artificial Life and Robotics*, 478-483. 10.5954/ICAROB.2022.OS11-5

Zepeda, A. R., Duke, A. M. R., & Castro, R. C. (2022). Applied Computer Vision on Advanced Driving Systems. In *Proceedings of the LACCEI international Multi-conference for Engineering, Education and Technology*. Latin American and Caribbean Consortium of Engineering Institutions. 10.18687/LACCEI2022.1.1.222

Zhao, W., Jia, H., Fang, J., Xue, J., Li, X., & Yu, H. (2022). Virtual PedCross-720 : A Synthetic Benchmark for Pedestrian Crossing Detection in Autonomous Driving Scenarios. In Lecture Notes in Electrical Engineering: Vol. 861 LNEE. doi:10.1007/978-981-16-9492-9_90

Zhou, F., Zhao, H., & Nie, Z. (2021). Safety Helmet Detection Based on YOLOv5. *Proceedings of 2021 IEEE International Conference on Power Electronics, Computer Applications, ICPECA 2021*, 6-11. 10.1109/ICPECA51329.2021.9362711

KEY TERMS AND DEFINITIONS

ADAS: This stands for Advanced Driver Assistance Systems: These systems assist drivers to ensure a safety driving and avoid collisions.

Camera Calibration: This is a technique used to calculate internal and external camera parameters, to calculate metrics form 2D images.

CNN: Convolutional neural network designed to process images and classify objects.

COCO: This stands for Common Object in Context, which is a popular dataset used to train neural networks for object detection. It contains over 330 000 images with 80 object categories.

Computer Vision: This is an artificial intelligence technique, used to teach computers how to process and interpret images.

Deep Learning: Subset of machine learning aiming to process data with algorithms inspired by the human brain.

Neural Network: This is a network used in deep learning and inspired from the human brain architecture: It relies on several layers to teach the machine how to process data for different applications such as object detection.

Object Detection: This is a task aiming to detect object in images by drawing bounding boxes around the objects of interest and classifying them into categories.

Real-Time Object Detection: Process of object's identification and localization in real time video sequences with low inference time

Stereovision: This is a technique used to reconstruct a 3D scene from images taken by different cameras from different angles.

YOLO: This stands for You Only Look Once, which is a recent algorithm used to detect objects in different contexts and for different applications such as autonomous vehicles.

Chapter 17
Prediction of Remaining Useful Life of Batteries Using Machine Learning Models

Jaouad Boudnaya

iD https://orcid.org/0000-0003-3224-2410

Moulay Ismail University, Morocco

Hicham Laacha

iD https://orcid.org/0009-0000-7489-2177

Moulay Ismail University, Morocco

Mohamed Qerras

Moulay Ismail University, Morocco

Abdelhak Mkhida

Moulay Ismail University, Morocco

ABSTRACT

Predictive maintenance is a maintenance strategy based on monitoring the state of components to predict the date of future failure. The objective is to take the appropriate measures to avoid the consequences of this failure. For this reason, the authors determine the remaining useful life (RUL) which is the remaining time before the appearance of the failure on the component. It is an important approach that allows the prediction of aging mechanisms likely to lead components to failure. In this chapter, a new methodology for predicting the remaining useful life of components is proposed using a data-driven prognosis approach with the integration of machine learning. This approach is illustrated in a battery case study to predict the remaining useful life.

DOI: 10.4018/979-8-3693-0497-6.ch017

1 INTRODUCTION

The prediction of the Remaining Useful Life (RUL) of a system is a significant challenge nowadays. It involves understanding, modelling, and forecasting aging mechanisms that may lead to failure.

In the literature, several prognostic approaches exist, and each approach is based on different models. These approaches can be classified according to their application and complexity (Pauline, 2009). Among these methods, it is worth mentioning prognosis based on the use of component failure history data and/or operational usage profile data, which has been employed to monitor the health of a gas turbine alternator (Roemer et al., 2009).

The paper (Tsui et al., 2015) reviews Prognostics and Health Management (PHM) as a crucial framework for enhancing system reliability and competitiveness in the global market. It highlights data-driven approaches and real-world examples to illustrate PHM's applications in practice.

The paper (Sharma et al., 2023) highlights the environmental impact of vehicular emissions and stresses the role of machine learning for accurate estimation of Remaining Usable Life (RUL) in electric vehicles, addressing challenges in lithium-ion battery degradation.

Fault diagnosis has also received considerable attention in the artificial intelligence community (Schwabacher et al., 2007). Frameworks that illustrate the use of artificial intelligence algorithms have been discussed in the literature under the name model-based approach (Schwabacher et al., 2007). Finally, the data-driven approach has been integrated into avionics maintenance architecture (Ghelam et al., 2006). However, some of these models have limitations. They are often restricted to one or two stress factors without incorporating the interactions that may exist among them.

This article presents a novel methodology for predicting the Remaining Useful Life (RUL) of components by using a data-driven prognostic approach with the integration of machine learning. A case study is conducted on batteries to illustrate this approach.

The proposed document is structured as follows: Section 2 introduces maintenance concepts. Section 3 presents the notion of Prognostics and Health Management. Then, Section 4 contains a methodology for predicting the Remaining Useful Life (RUL). Subsequently, Sections 5 and 6 are dedicated to the presentation of machine learning. Part 7 illustrates our case study on battery RUL prediction with results and discussions. Finally, Section 8 concludes the article.

2 CONCEPTS OF MAINTENANCE

Maintenance is an essential step in the lifecycle of any complex system. According to AFNOR's definition, maintenance aims to keep or restore an asset to a specified condition so that it can provide a given service (AFNOR, 2001). There are two main categories of maintenance: corrective maintenance and preventive maintenance.

The first strategy generally incurs additional costs (Lee et al., 2006) and significant system unavailability (Palem, 2013), and it can pose safety issues. Preventive maintenance reduces the risk of unexpected failures and downtime, but it can result in high costs as some components are replaced while still in a slightly degraded operational state (Lee et al., 2006; Le, 2016).

To address these drawbacks, a new form of maintenance has emerged: predictive maintenance (Palem, 2013). It involves regular monitoring of the system's components (Bartelds et al., 2004), which enables the assessment of their proper functioning. Consequently, it becomes possible to predict the occurrence of a system failure before it happens (Lee et al., 2006; Le, 2016; Jardine et al., 2006), to plan the appropriate maintenance tasks at the right time (Mercier & Pham, 2012).

Various types of maintenance are illustrated in Figure 1.

Figure 1. Types of maintenance

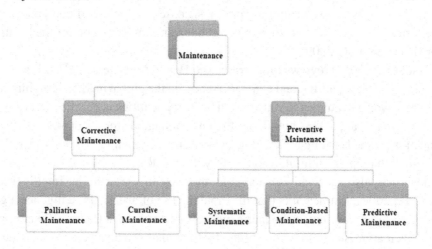

3 PROGNOSTICS AND HEALTH MANAGEMENT

The term "Prognostics and Health Management (PHM)" refers to the set of methods for preventing and predicting failures and their consequences. It is a discipline that focuses on studying the failure mechanisms of real systems to better manage using of information about equipment operating conditions (Gouriveau et al., 2013). PHM addresses the main tasks related to degradation detection, fault diagnosis, and proactive failure prediction and management.

The PHM process consists of seven modules (Hbiche et al., 2022), which are illustrated in Figure 2.

3.1 Data Acquisition

It involves measuring physical quantities such as voltage, current, temperature, etc. using sensors, software, or human observations.

3.2 Data Processing

It analyses and interprets signals to extract information that characterizes the behaviour of the system, either in the time domain and/or frequency domain.

3.3 Current State Evaluation

It will be obtained from these characteristics and assists in detecting various possible anomalies based on the nominal behaviour.

Figure 2. Modules of PHM

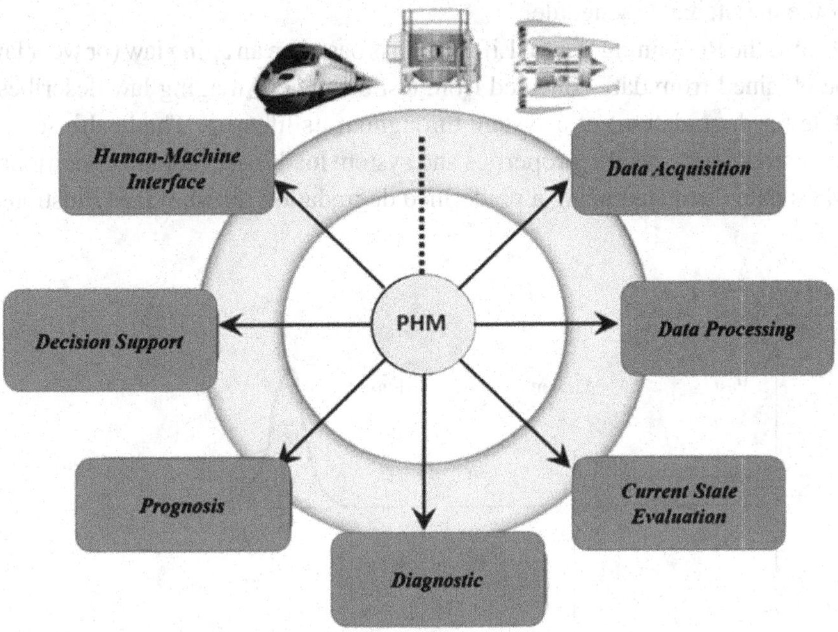

3.4 Diagnostic

It corresponds to the localization and identification of the causes of anomalies or failures.

3.5 Prognosis

It is based on the current state of the system and enables the detection of the diagnosis to predict the remaining useful life (RUL).

3.6 Decision Support

The maintenance strategies to be implemented to keep the system in good condition. This module is based on the collected information (system state, remaining useful life (RUL), basic knowledge, etc.).

3.7 Human-Machine Interface

It is a means of presenting and storing relevant information in various forms.

4 PREDICTION OF REMAINING USEFUL LIFE (RUL)

Prediction plays a vital role in establishing a predictive maintenance strategy. Its objective is to estimate the remaining useful life (RUL) of selected components, which refers to the remaining operating time before these components fail (Boudnaya et al., 2022) (Figure 3). This allows for the adaptation and optimization of the maintenance schedule.

The calculation of the Remaining Useful Life (RUL) is based on an aging law (or wear law, degradation law) that can be obtained from data collected from test benches. An aging law describes the evolution of the health state (or degradation) of a system throughout its lifespan. The health state of a system is defined based on component-specific properties and system loads (operational conditions) (Engel et al., 2000). The RUL is then estimated using a predefined degradation threshold, as illustrated in Figure 4.

Figure 3. Estimation of RUL

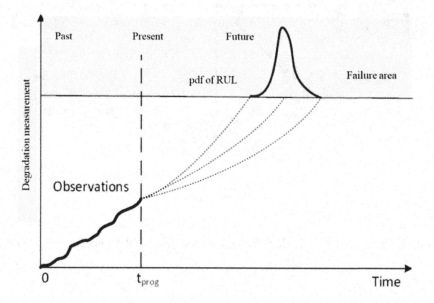

Figure 4. Degradation law for prognostics

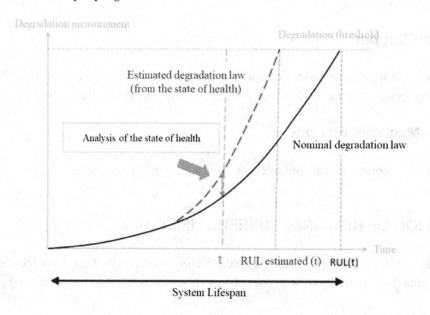

There are three categories of prognostics:

- Prognostics based on physical models: It relies on mathematical and/or physical models of degradation phenomena.
- Prognostics guided by monitoring data: It involves the analysis of datasets to identify indicators of the component's health condition.
- Experience-based prognostics: It is based on leveraging knowledge gained from past failures or degradation of the component.

Figure 5 illustrates the classification of prognostic approaches based on their applicability to different systems, implementation costs, and accuracy (Delmas, 2019; Sikorska et al., 2011).

Figure 5. Classification of prognosis approaches

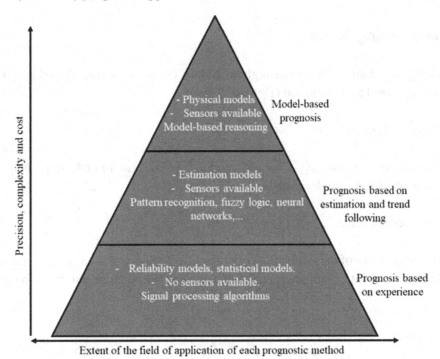

5 MACHINE LEARNING: DEFINITION AND STEPS

5.1 Introduction

Machine learning for predictive maintenance offers significant advantages by utilizing historical data to anticipate equipment failures. Early fault detection, reduced downtime, and cost savings are achieved through proactive identification of potential issues, allowing for timely maintenance interventions. Continuous condition monitoring, optimized maintenance schedules, and increased equipment lifespan are additional benefits. The approach enhances safety by minimizing the risk of sudden failures and enables data-driven decision-making for efficient resource allocation. Ultimately, the scalability of machine learning models makes them valuable for industries with extensive equipment networks, providing a comprehensive and proactive solution to maintenance challenges.

5.2 Machine Learning Definition

"Machine Learning" is a scientific field and a subcategory of artificial intelligence. It involves letting algorithms discover "patterns," which are recurring motifs, in datasets (Chloé-Agathe Azencott, 2022). These datasets can consist of numbers, words, images, statistics, or any digitally stored information that can serve as data for Machine Learning. By detecting patterns in this data, the algorithms learn and improve their performance in executing a specific task.

In summary, Machine Learning algorithms autonomously learn to perform a task or make predictions from data and improve their performance over time. Once trained, the algorithm can identify patterns in new data.

5.3 Machine Learning Steps

Machine Learning applications are increasingly prevalent within organizations today. To use this approach, several steps need to be followed (Delmas, 2019):

- Identify needs and objectives:

Before embarking on constructing a learning model, it is essential to understand why the Machine Learning solution needs to be implemented.

- Collect the necessary data:

The quality and quantity of data directly impact the effectiveness of the resulting model. The more abundant and reliable the data, the more accurate and tailored the outcome will be to the organization's needs.

- Prepare the data:

A successful learning model relies on high-quality data. Therefore, it is necessary to preprocess the collected data to extract its full potential.

- Determine the right model:

Once the data is ready for use, the appropriate algorithm needs to be chosen to address the initial problem (e.g., K-Means, random forest, decision tree).

- Train and evaluate the model:

Among all the steps of Machine Learning, the training and testing phase remains the most characteristic part of automatic learning. By providing the model with data, it is trained over time to progressively improve its ability to react to a given situation, solve complex problems, or perform tasks.

- Test and deploy the model:

This final step of Machine Learning aims to test the model against real-world scenarios. In this phase, test data is used to evaluate the model's performance.

6 MACHINE LEARNING MODELS

In this section, the main machine learning models that are commonly used in practice are presented.
Machine learning models are classified into several categories, such as supervised learning, unsupervised learning, and reinforcement learning (Figure 6).

Figure 6. Classification of machine learning algorithms
Source: Mahesh (2020)

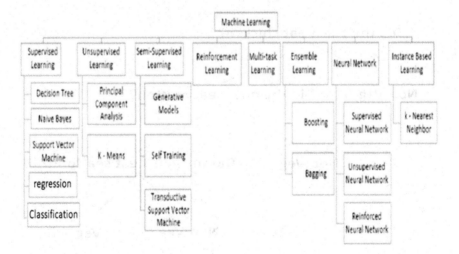

6.1 Supervised Learning Models

Supervised learning (Boudnaya et al., 2023) involves teaching a function to map an input to an output based on known examples (input-output pairs).
For instance, if I had a dataset with two variables, age (input) and height (output), I could implement a supervised learning model to predict a person's height based on their age.

Within the realm of supervised learning, there are several subcategories such as regression and decision trees...

- **Regression:**

In regression models (Sikorska et al., 2011), the output is continuous.

For example, the idea of simple linear regression is to find a line that best fits the data or a plane that provides the best fit in the case of multiple regression. Polynomial regression is another variation, aiming to find a curve that provides the best fit.

Logistic regression is like linear regression, but it is used to model the probability of a finite number of outcomes, typically two.

- **Decision Tree:**

Decision trees (Sikorska et al., 2011) are a popular model used in operations research, strategic planning, and machine learning. Each rectangle below is called a node, and the final nodes in the decision tree where a decision is made are referred to as "leaves". Figure 7 provides an example of a decision tree.

Figure 7. Example of a decision tree
Source: Sikorska et al. (2011)

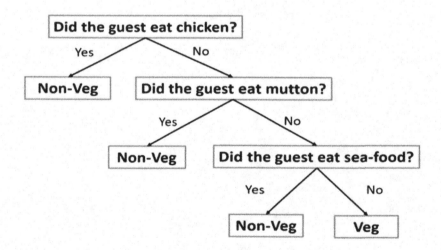

- **Random Forest:**

Random forests (Azencott, 2022), also known as random decision forests, are an ensemble learning technique that relies on decision trees. The random forest model involves creating multiple decision trees using a subset of data sampled from the original dataset and randomly selecting a subset of variables at each decision tree step. The model then selects the mode of all predictions from each decision tree, using a majority voting scheme. The advantage of this method is to reduce the risk of error from an individual tree.

6.2 Unsupervised Learning Models

In contrast to supervised learning, unsupervised learning is used to draw conclusions and discover patterns from unlabelled input data. It returns labelled results and reveals "clusters" or categories. The two main methods used in unsupervised learning include clustering and dimensionality reduction.

- **Clustering:**

    Clustering is an unsupervised technique (Azencott, 2022) that involves grouping, or clustering, data points together (Figure 8). It is commonly used for customer segmentation, fraud detection, and document classification.

    Common clustering techniques include k-means clustering, hierarchical clustering, mean-shift clustering, and density-based clustering. Although each technique has a different method for finding clusters, they all aim for the same objective.

Figure 8. Clustering

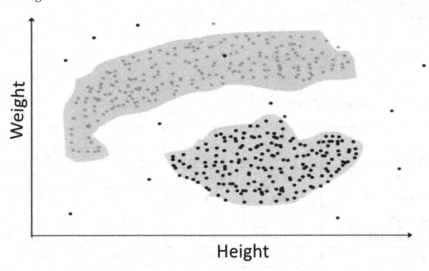

- **Dimensionality Reduction:**

    Dimensionality reduction is the process of reducing the number of considered random variables by obtaining a set of principal variables (Azencott, 2022). Simply put, it is the process of reducing the dimensionality of your feature set (or, in simpler terms, reducing the number of features). Most dimensionality reduction techniques can be categorized into two categories: feature elimination and feature extraction.

    One common method of dimensionality reduction is called Principal Component Analysis (PCA). PCA involves projecting higher-dimensional data (e.g., 3 dimensions) onto a smaller space (e.g., 2 dimensions). This results in lower-dimensional data (2 dimensions instead of 3) while preserving all the original variables in the model.

7 CASE STUDY

7.1 Data Presentation

This section involves the analysis of data sourced from 14 batteries provided by the Hawaii Natural Energy Institute (Dubarry et al., 2017).

The batteries used in the study are NMC-LCO 18650 batteries with a nominal capacity of 2.8 Ah. They have been cycled over 1000 times at 25°C with a charge rate of C/2 and a discharge rate of 1.5C.

The dataset contains the following variables (Table 1).

- Cycle index: number of cycles
- F1: Discharge time (s)
- F2: Time at 4.15 V (s)
- F3: Time at constant current (s)
- F4: Discharge decrement 3.6-3.4 V (s)
- F5: Max discharge voltage (V)
- F6: Min charge voltage (V)
- F7: Charge time (s)
- Total time (s)
- RUL (Remaining Useful Life): target

Table 1. The first five columns of the data

	0	1	2	3	3
Cycle_Index	1,0000	2,0000	3,0000	4,0000	6,0000
Discharge Time (s)	2595,3000	7408,6400	7393,7600	7385,5000	65022,7500
Decrement 3.6-3.4V (s)	1151,4885	1172,5125	1112,9920	1080,3207	29813,4870
Max. Voltage Discharge (V)	3,6700	4,2460	4,2490	4,2500	4,2900
Min. Voltage Charge (V)	3,2110	3,2200	3,2240	3,2250	3,3980
Time at 4.15V (s)	5460,0010	5508,9920	5508,9930	5502,0260	5480,9920
Time constant current (s)	6755,0100	6762,0200	6762,0200	6762,0200	53213,5400
Charging Time (s)	10777,8200	10500,3500	10420,3800	10322,8100	56699,6500
RUL	1112,0000	1111,0000	1110,0000	1109,0000	1107,0000

From this dataset (15064 rows and 9 columns), features representing the voltage and current behaviour in each cycle have been successfully developed. The objective of this study is to predict the remaining useful life (RUL) of the batteries based on these behaviours.

7.2 Methodology

The working methodology comprises a series of steps, succinctly summarized in Figure 9:

Figure 9. Working methodology steps

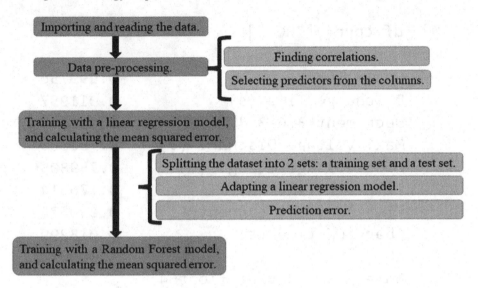

- Importing and reading the data from a CSV file into a Pandas DataFrame using the read_csv method.

```
# Import pandas library
import pandas as pd
# Read Data
df =pd.read csv("/content/drive/MyDrive/Battery RUL/Battery RUL.csv")
#Display column names from  DataFrame df.
print(df.shape)
```

- Data preprocessing:
  - Finding correlations:

The search for correlation between RUL and each of the other columns helps identify the columns that could best predict RUL.

The Pandas DataFrames offers the convenient corr method for easily determining correlations between columns. By applying this method, a correlation matrix is generated, showcasing the correlations between each column and the others. Utilizing indexing, one can extract and focus on the correlations specifically with the RUL column, as illustrated in Figure 10.

The most correlated columns with the rating are observed in the Max. Voltage Discharge (V) and Min. Voltage Charge (V).

- Selecting predictors from the columns:

Prior to initiating predictions, a careful selection of pertinent columns is essential for training the algorithm. Non-numeric columns are excluded to maintain the classifier's objective of predicting the ranking without any prior knowledge. The elimination of columns dependent on target knowledge helps

Figure 10. Correlations

```
[9]  df.corr()["RUL"]

     Cycle_Index                  -0.999756
     Discharge Time (s)            0.011957
     Decrement 3.6-3.4V (s)        0.011998
     Max. Voltage Dischar. (V)     0.782800
     Min. Voltage Charg. (V)      -0.759805
     Time at 4.15V (s)             0.176514
     Time constant current (s)     0.040675
     Charging time (s)             0.018299
     RUL                           1.000000
     Name: RUL, dtype: float64
```

mitigate the risk of overfitting, ensuring that the model performs effectively on both training and future data by promoting better generalization.

```
# Retrieve all columns from the DataFrame.
columns = df.columns.tolist()
# Filter the columns to get the ones you don't want
columns = [c for c ["Max. Voltage Discharge(V)", " Min. Voltage
Charge (V)"]]
# Store the variable we want to predict
target = "RUL"
```

    ◦   Training with a linear regression model, then calculating the mean squared error.
        ▪   Splitting the dataset into 2 sets: a training set and a test set:

To mitigate overfitting, assessing the algorithm on the identical data it was trained on is avoided. The goal is to have the algorithm learn generalized rules instead of memorizing specific predictions. To achieve this, the algorithm is trained on 80% of the data and subsequently tested on the remaining 20%. This separation into training and test sets is accomplished by randomly sampling 80% of the rows for the training set, leaving the remainder for the test set.

```
# Import a function designed to split the sets.
from sklearn.model selection import train test split
# Generate the training set.
# Set random state to replicate results later.
train = df.sample(frac=0.8, random_state=1)
# Select everything that is not in the training set
and put it in the test set.
test = df.loc[~df.index.isin(train.index)]
```

    ◦   Adapting a linear regression model:

Linear regression demonstrates optimal performance when there exists a linear correlation between predictor variables and the target variable. During the model training process, the predictor matrix, encompassing all selected columns from the DataFrame, is passed as a parameter. By passing a list to the Pandas DataFrame during indexing, a new DataFrame is created, incorporating all specified columns. Additionally, the target variable is provided for which predictions are sought. The model learns from the equation that minimizes the error, mapping predictors to the target variable.

```
# Import the model LinearRegression.
from sklearn.linear model import LinearRegression
# Initialize the model class.
model = LinearRegression()
# Fit the model to the training data.
model.fit(train[columns], train[target])
```

    ◦   Prediction error:

After obtaining the predictions, the mean squared error is computed by comparing the predicted values from the test set with the actual values.

```
# Import the error calculation function from scikit -learn
from sklearn.metrics import mean_squared_error
# Generate the predictions for the test set
predictions = model.predict(test[columns])
#Calculate the error between our predictions and the actual values
we know.
mean_squared_error(predictions, test[target])
```

    ◦   Training with a Random Forest model, then calculating the mean squared error.

One of the advantages of Scikit-learn is that it allows us to easily try more powerful algorithms. For example, the random forest algorithm can uncover non-linearities in the data that a linear regression model may not detect.

```
# Import the Random Forest model
from sklearn.ensemble import RandomForestRegressor
# Initialize the model with some parameters
model = RandomForestRegressor(n_estimators=1000, min_samples_leaf=10,
 random_state=1)
# Fit the model to the data
model.fit(train[columns], train[target])
# Make predictions
predictions = model.predict(test[columns])
# Calculation of the error
mean_squared_error(predictions, test[target])
```

Predictions made with random forest typically have fewer errors than those made by linear regression.

7.3 Results and Discussion

Employing two distinct training approaches: training with a linear regression model and training with a Random Forest model, the obtained results are as follows:

- **Linear Regression Model**

Following the completion of model training, predictions were generated for new data formatted consistently with the training dataset. The test set, characterized by the same subset of columns, was carefully selected, and the mean squared error was computed by systematically contrasting the model's predictions with the corresponding actual values. Visual representation through a scatter plot, constructed using MATLAB software (Figure 11), effectively captures the nuanced relationship between the predicted and actual values. Notably, the achieved correlation coefficient of 72.27% serves as a quantitative indicator of the model's efficacy in capturing the underlying patterns within the data, further validating its predictive performance.

- **Random Forest Model**

Following model training, predictions were made utilizing the Random Forest model, known for its capability to capture non-linearities in the data. The resulting scatter plot, visualized through MATLAB software (Figure 12), illustrates a remarkable correlation between actual values and predictions, reflected in an impressive correlation coefficient of 97.86%.

Therefore, the Random Forest model is better at predicting the Remaining Useful Life (RUL) compared to the linear regression model.

Figure 11. Performance for linear regression

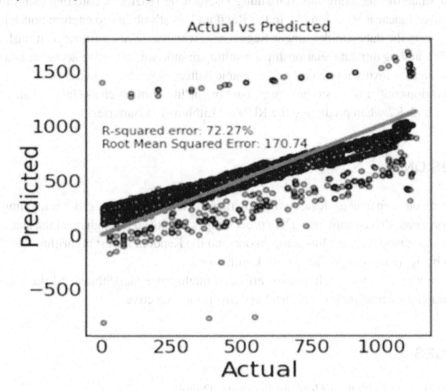

Figure 12. Performance for random forest model

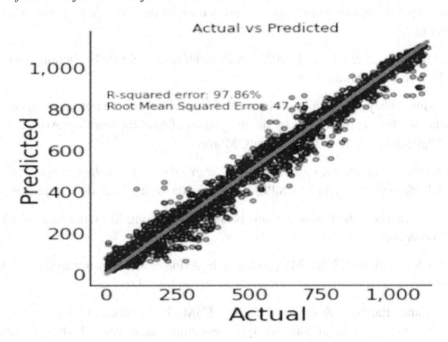

The added value of predicting the Remaining Useful Life (RUL) of batteries using the Random Forest model over Linear Regression lies in the Random Forest's ability to capture non-linearities and complex patterns in the data. Unlike Linear Regression, which assumes a linear relationship, Random Forest excels in handling intricate relationships, resulting in superior predictive accuracy and robustness, especially in scenarios involving diverse and dynamic battery degradation patterns.

This observation confirms the studies carried out on the literature, such as (Jafari et al., 2023) which demonstrates a high R2 when predicting the RUL for Lithium-Ion Batteries.

8 CONCLUSION

The objective of our paper is to develop a predictive model for estimating the remaining useful life (RUL) based on a data-driven approach. Data processing is employed through machine learning models, specifically training models using linear regression and the Random Forest algorithm. Our approach is demonstrated by applying it to predict the RUL of batteries.

In our future work, exploring alternative artificial intelligence algorithms and their application to predictive maintenance in complex industrial systems is our objective.

REFERENCES

Azencott. (2022). *Introduction au Machine Learning*. Dunod.

Bartelds, G., Biemans, C., Boller, C., Breidne, M., Claesson, Å., Delebarre, C., & Worden, K. (2004). *Health Monitoring of Aerospace Structures – Smart Sensor Technologies and Signal Processing*. John Wiley & Sons Ltd.

Boudnaya, J., Marouan, C., & Ilham, G. (2022). A Remaining Useful Life Prediction of a robot with 15 states. *Oran 2 University Journal, 7*(2).

Boudnaya, J., Nina Aslhey, H., & Ouèdan Jhonn, G. (2023). Study of the optimization control of agricultural greenhouse climatic parameters by the integration of machine learning. Artificial Intelligence & Industrial Applications (A2IA 2023), Meknes, Morocco.

Delmas, A. (2019). *Contribution à l'estimation de la durée de vie résiduelle des systèmes en présence d'incertitudes*. Performance et fiabilité (cs.PF). Université de Technologie de Compiègne.

Engel. (2000). Prognostics, the real issues involved with predicting life remaining. *IEEE Aerospace Conference Proceedings*.

Ghelam. (2006). Integration of Health Monitoring in the Avionics Maintenance System. *IFAC Proceedings Volumes*.

Gouriveau, Medjaher, Ramasso, & Zerhouni. (2013). PHM - Prognostics and health management - De la surveillance au pronostic de défaillances de systèmes complexes. Éditions Techniques de l'Ingénieur.

Jafari, S., & Byun, Y.-C. (2023). Optimizing Battery RUL Prediction of Lithium-Ion Batteries Based on Harris Hawk Optimization Approach Using Random Forest and LightGBM. *IEEE Access : Practical Innovations, Open Solutions, 11*, 87034–87046. doi:10.1109/ACCESS.2023.3304699

Jardine, A. K. S., Lin, D., & Banjevic, D. (2006). A review on machinery diagnostics and prognostics implementing condition-based maintenance. *Mechanical Systems and Signal Processing, 20*(7), 1483–1510. doi:10.1016/j.ymssp.2005.09.012

Kwok Tsui, Chen, Zhou, Hai, & Wenbin. (2015). Prognostics and Health Management: A Review on Data Driven Approaches. *Mathematical Problems in Engineering.* doi:10.1155/2015/793161

Le, T. (2016). *Contribution to deterioration modeling and residual life estimation based on condition monitoring data* [PhD thesis]. Université Grenoble Alpes.

Lee, J., Ni, J., Djurdjanovic, D., Qiu, H., & Liao, H. (2006). Intelligent prognostics tools and e-maintenance. *Computers in Industry, 57*(6), 476–489. doi:10.1016/j.compind.2006.02.014

Mahesh, B. (2020). Machine Learning Algorithms - A Review. *International Journal of Scientific Research, 9*(1). Advance online publication. doi:10.21275/ART20203995 381

Matthieu Dubarry, M. (2017, August). State of health battery estimator enabling degradation diagnosis: Model and algorithm description. *Journal of Power Sources, 360*, 59–69. doi:10.1016/j.jpowsour.2017.05.121

Mercier, S., & Pham, H. (2012). A preventive maintenance policy for a continuously monitored system with correlated wear indicators. *European Journal of Operational Research, 222*(2), 263–272. doi:10.1016/j.ejor.2012.05.011

Otman, H., Jaouad, B., Mohamed, S., Abdelhak, M., & Hamza, I. (2022). Datasets analysis in predictive maintenance: prognostics and health management. *The 2nd International Conference on Innovative Research in Applied Science, Engineering and Technology (IRASET'2022), Meknes, Morocco, Proceedings published in IEEE*, 1-7, 10.1109/IRASET52964.2022.9738429

Palem, G. (2013). Condition-based maintenance using sensor arrays and telematics. *International Journal of Mobile Network Communications & Telematics, 3*(3), 19–28. doi:10.5121/ijmnct.2013.3303

Ribot, P. (2009). *Vers l'intégration diagnostic/ pronostic pour la maintenance des systèmes complexes* [PhD thesis]. University of Paul Sabatier-Toulouse III.

Schwabacher. (2007). A Survey of Artificial Intelligence for Prognostics. AAAI fall symposium: artificial intelligence for prognostics, Arlington, VA.

Sharma, P., & Bora, B. J. A. (2023). Review of Modern Machine Learning Techniques in the Prediction of Remaining Useful Life of Lithium-Ion Batteries. *Batteries, 9*(1), 13. doi:10.3390/batteries9010013

Sikorska, J., Hodkiewicz, M., & Ma, L. (2011). Prognostic modelling options for remaining useful life estimation by industry. *Mechanical Systems and Signal Processing, 25*(5), 1803–1836. doi:10.1016/j.ymssp.2010.11.018

KEY TERMS AND DEFINITIONS

Artificial intelligence (AI): It refers to the simulation of human intelligence in machines that are programmed to think, learn, and problem-solve like humans. It involves the development of computer systems capable of performing tasks that typically require human intelligence, such as speech recognition, decision-making, visual perception, and natural language processing. AI encompasses various subfields, including machine learning, robotics, expert systems, and computer vision, and aims to create intelligent machines that can understand, reason, and interact with the world in a human-like manner.

Machine Learning: It is a branch of artificial intelligence that enables computers to learn and make predictions or decisions without explicit programming. It uses algorithms and statistical techniques to analyse data, identify patterns, and improve performance over time. There are three main types: supervised learning (using labelled data), unsupervised learning (finding patterns in unlabelled data), and reinforcement learning (learning through trial and error). Machine learning finds applications in various fields, such as image recognition, natural language processing, and fraud detection, by training models to make accurate predictions and decisions based on data analysis.

Predictive Maintenance: It is a proactive maintenance approach that uses data analysis and predictive modelling techniques to anticipate and prevent equipment or system failures. It involves monitoring and analysing real-time or historical data from sensors, machinery, or other sources to identify patterns, trends, and early indicators of potential issues. By predicting when equipment is likely to fail, maintenance activities can be scheduled in advance, optimizing resources, and minimizing unplanned downtime. Predictive maintenance aims to maximize the operational efficiency and reliability of assets while minimizing maintenance costs and disruptions.

Prognostics: It is a field of study within predictive maintenance that focuses on estimating the remaining useful life (RUL) of a component or system and predicting its future performance and failure behaviour. It involves analysing historical data, monitoring real-time sensor data, and applying statistical and machine learning techniques to determine the health condition and expected future behaviour of the asset. Prognostics aims to provide early warnings of potential failures, enable proactive maintenance strategies, and optimize resource allocation for improved reliability, safety, and cost-efficiency.

Prognostics and Health Management (PHM): It is an interdisciplinary field that combines engineering, data analysis, and predictive modelling to assess and manage the health condition, performance, and reliability of systems and assets. It involves continuously monitoring and analysing data from sensors, diagnostics, and other sources to detect early signs of anomalies, degradation, or potential failures. By using advanced algorithms and statistical techniques, PHM aims to predict the remaining useful life (RUL), diagnose faults, and provide recommendations for maintenance or operational adjustments. PHM enables proactive decision-making, reduces downtime, optimizes maintenance strategies, and enhances the overall performance and availability of complex systems across various industries.

Random Forest Model: It is a machine learning algorithm that combines multiple decision trees to make predictions or classifications. It is an ensemble learning method that operates by constructing a multitude of decision trees during training and outputs the average or majority vote of the individual trees for prediction. Each decision tree in the Random Forest is trained on a different subset of the data, and a random subset of features is considered at each node. This randomness helps to reduce overfitting and improve the model's generalization ability. Random Forest models are widely used for tasks such as classification, regression, and feature selection, and they are known for their robustness, accuracy, and ability to handle large and complex datasets.

Remaining Useful Life (RUL): It is a concept used in predictive maintenance and reliability engineering. It refers to the estimated remaining operational lifespan of a component, system, or asset before it is expected to fail or no longer perform its intended function effectively. RUL is typically determined through data analysis and predictive modelling techniques that consider factors such as historical usage patterns, environmental conditions, and degradation characteristics of the asset. By estimating the RUL, organizations can proactively schedule maintenance or replacement activities, optimize resource allocation, and minimize downtime or unexpected failures.

Chapter 18
Literature Review on the Study of Non–Qualities of a Product Using Neural Networks

Marouane Zaizoune

Laboratory of Industrial Technologies, Faculty of Sciences and Technologies, Sidi Mohamed Ben Abdellah University, Morocco

Brahim Herrou

Higher School of Technology, Sidi Mohamed Ben Abdellah University, Morocco

Hassan Khadiri

ENSAM, Moulay Ismail University, Morocco

Souhail Sekkat

ENSAM, Moulay Ismail University, Morocco

ABSTRACT

The purpose of this study is to use the neural networks method in order to build a neural network system that studies and determines the cause of non-conformities. Companies are regularly confronted with quality problems stemming both from assembly mistakes and also during upstream stages in the process, like design, logistics, technical, and industrial support. These problems would sometimes reach the end customer inducing huge losses for the companies in term of costs and reputation. Therefore, an improvement of non-conformities detection systems as well as the identification of their causes is necessary, which is the purpose of this chapter. First, per the authors, this chapter discusses non-conformities in the industrial field and the management of quality problems. Then, the neural networks method is presented, as well as a review in its recent development and its applications. As a result, the steps to building the neural network system to study non-conformity causes are defined and described.

DOI: 10.4018/979-8-3693-0497-6.ch018

INTRODUCTION

The industrial performances have been a major concern for companies since the beginning of the industrial era. However, its evaluation has evolved from a single productivity indicator to a global and multi-criteria evaluation policy. In recent years, there has been a growing consensus in the operation management field about the benefits of drawing insight from major theories in other fields such as economics, management (Buhman et al., 2005; Handfield, 2006; Sousa & Voss, 2008). Theories in system engineering also recommend thinking in terms of a total system, rather than just a specific discipline (Hasking 2006), especially the risk management field which requires an interdisciplinary approach for better understanding and management of the different industrial risks (Magne & Vasseur, 2006). Industrial risks are defined as risks that have to be considered by organizations that build, run, and control industrial facilities (Magne & Vasseur, 2006). Among these industrial risks, this paper focuses on the risk of non-conformities in product delivery reaching the customer. A product recall represents the worst non-conformity propagation case, in which a defect has reached the final customer. It questions the performance of the protection system of industrial companies set up to protect them against non-conformities.

These protection systems, or quality control systems, are often grounded on the experts' knowledge and risk analyses. There are many risk analysis techniques that exist (Tixier et al., 2002) and can be classified in two main categories: Tree analyses (failures, root causes, butterfly), which start from a feared event in order to find the causes and consequences, and Systematic analyses (FMEA, FMECA, HAZOP).

From these analyses, actions are undertaken, and layers of protection are set up. Layers of protection (Summers, 2003; Gowland, 2006; Duijm, 2009) illustrate the efforts to prevent failures' propagation and to stop them as close as possible from their origin in order to limit their impact at least in terms of costs. In the industrial quality field, these protection layers are, for example, control charts, preventive maintenances, acceptation tests, and inspections. However, the problem remains: how can we study the defects and non-conformities and determine their causes ?

One of the most interesting methods by which we can proceed with this study is Artificial Neural Networks. It's a calculation method that builds several processing units based on interconnected connections. It is a part of a computer system that mimics how the human brain analyzes and processes data. Self-driving vehicles, character recognition, image compression, stock market prediction, risk analysis systems, drone control, welding quality analysis, computer quality analysis, emergency room testing and oil and gas exploration are some of the applications of artificial neural networks.

Neural networks have been applied in many fields and have achieved breakthrough successes, such as those in image and data processing (Tong et al., 2023; Yang, 2023; Chamanbaz & Bouffanais, 2023). Although a deep structure helps a network extract more information than a shallow structure, most deep networks suffer from difficulties in training and theoretical analysis because a deep network involves a great number of parameters and complicated structures (Li et al., 2017). Fortunately, it has been observed that increasing the network width makes training easier (Rudin et al., 2022). It has been suggested in recent papers that if the width significantly exceeds the number of training samples, the training error can be reduced to 0 via gradient descent, and the generalization of the trained network remains good (Lin et al., 2021; Yang et al., 2022).

In this context, this paper focuses on the use of neural networks in the quality field, and more specifically to detect non-conformity causes. First of all, we will talk about non-conformities in the industry and the management of quality problems. Then we will present the neural networks method, as well as a review in its recent development, its applications, and its main architectures. And finally, we will describe the steps to building our neural network system to study non-conformity causes.

LITERATURE REVIEW

Management of Non-Conformities and Quality Problems

Both media and research reports show that product recalls are on a rise (Berman, 1999). The recent case of Toyota and its massive recall illustrates the losses in terms of cost and reputation induced by non-conformities reaching the end customers, but they also question the ability of the company to master its industrial processes . A recall is actually due to non-conformities that have reached the end customers, meaning that they have run through all the defensive mechanisms put in place by the company to prevent such dramatic outcomes, and illustrates the worst propagation case. According to Garvin (1986), quality problems might arise from a number of sources, including poor designs or methods, defective materials, shoddy workmanship, and poorly maintained equipment.

Companies, regulators, investors and customers are gradually recognizing that products recalls are unavoidable parts of conducting a business (Berman, 1999). Even leading companies that put great effort on quality and continuous improvement experienced such hazard. As described by Jacobs (1996), a product recall is a vendor's nightmare from both a financial and an organizational viewpoint. Literature on product recall is mainly directed toward efficient management of recall (reverse logistics, refund policies, insurance, etc.) but gives little insight on how to avoid these dramatic events. Investigating this issue may consist in having a closer look at the propagation mechanism. Bettayeb et al. (2010) propose an inspection allocation model for decreasing uncertainties on products. Their work proposes a quality control plan that insures not to release an amount of non-controlled products above a predefined level. It helps in reducing uncertain products delivered to the market. They contribute to the topic of production recall prevention by actions on quality. However their developments are focused on large-scale productions. These works offer thus a research avenue for low volume productions.

A significant concept relating to the propagation found in the safety field literature is the use of the barrier concept within industrial safety, especially as applied to technical systems in the process and nuclear industries. The best way to ensure a state of safety is either to prevent any occurrence of an unexpected event or to protect against its consequences. The two primary types of responses, prevention and protection, both involve the use of barriers in one way or another. Safety barriers are physical or non-physical means planned to prevent, control, or mitigate undesired events or accidents. The layers of protection illustrate the efforts to prevent failures propagation and to stop them as close as possible from their origin in order to limit their impact. This concept is inspired from the work by Reason (1990) and his "cheese model", as shown in Figure 1. This approach couples an engineering and an organizational model. In this perspective safety relies on successive defense lines or barriers, which protect the organization against dangers. An accident occurs if human or material failures make barriers ineffective. These "active failures" create holes in the different barriers. Other holes may be due to "latent conditions", i.e. errors made prior to the initiating event that triggered the accident, but whose consequences only appear during the accident. Aligned holes let the danger pass through.

Figure 1. Successive layers of defenses, barriers and safeguards
Source: Magne and Vasseur (2006)

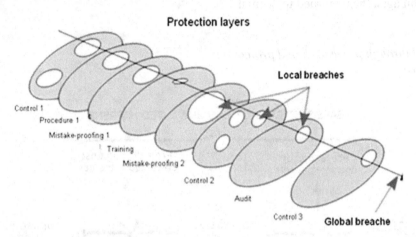

Layers of protection illustrate the efforts to prevent the propagation of failures and to stop them as close as possible from their origin in order to limit their impact, at least in terms of costs (Hollnagel, 2008). In the industrial quality field, these protection layers are, for example, preventive maintenances, control charts, inspections, acceptation tests... The quality performance is measured in terms of scrap, yield or detection quality (sensitivity to detect drifts and the average run length before detection). But how can this performance be managed when statistics are not capable of being generated because of a lack of data?

Prevention in many ways is better than protection. However, it is known that perfect prevention is impossible. This realization has been made famous by the observation that there always is something that can go wrong (Hollnagel, 2008).

According to a common safety model, safety can be brought about either by eliminating hazards, by preventing initiating events, and/or by protecting against outcomes. The best way to ensure a state of safety is either to prevent something unwanted from happening or to protect against its consequences, as illustrated by Figure 2. Since it's practically impossible to completely prevent unwanted events, i.e., to completely eliminate risks, the two approaches are best used together.

In order to ensure safety by preventing something from happening, i.e., through the elimination of risks, it is necessary that the risks are known or can be made known, which is the purpose of risk assessment, and there are a considerable number of well-established methods available for that. The pursuit of safety through the elimination of risks also required that the specific risk source can actually be removed from the system without impeding or changing the system's functioning. In some cases, this condition is obviously violated when the elimination of a risk means the loss of a primary function. For example, the risk of an airplane falling down can only be fully eliminated by not taking to the air, but that is clearly not a viable option, at least in commercial aviation.

The second option is to protect against the consequences of the critical event if or when it happens, all precautions notwithstanding. This can be achieved by reducing or weakening the consequences or by changing their direction either in a real or in a metaphorical sense. Note that, whereas, the first option, prevention, tries to maintain the functioning of the system and to keep it going, the second option, protection, does not need to do that. Indeed, protection may require that the system is shut down when the critical event occurs, as in the case of nuclear power plants, or that the normal functioning is reduced until the situation again has returned to normal.

Figure 2. Safety through prevention and protection
Source: Hollnagel (2008)

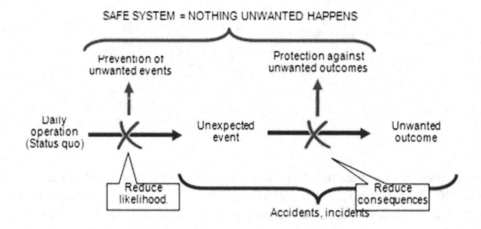

Existing Work and Case Studies on Non-Conformities

The problem of non-conformities detection was covered by many papers in the literature, in many industry related fields, like the detection of the surface defects and non-conformities on steel products, among others. The existing surface defects and non-conformities detection methods in this field are mainly based on classical machine learning algorithms. For example, Ma et al. (2017) proposed an adaptive segmentation algorithm in order to segment defect regions based on the gray features of the mental surface.

Ke et al. (2016) proposed a tetrolet-based method to recognize the surface defects and non-conformities of steel strips. After extracting the sub-band characteristics of surface defects in different scales and directions, a Support Vector Machine (SVM) classifier was used to classify different types of surface defects. Hu et al. (2016) extracted four kinds of defect features and transformed them to a 38-dimensional feature vector, and an optimized SVM classifier was trained to classify 5 types of 101 defect images. Jiangyun et al. (2018) established a dataset of six types of surface defects on cold-rolled steel strip and increased it to reduce over-fitting, by improving the YOLO network and making it all convolutional.

Many studies have been done to detect non-conformities in the automotive industry as well. Doring et al. (2006) and Eichhorn et al. (2005) used the principal of triangulation to detect deformations on unpainted car body panels. A 3D-point cloud is generated, and the data are analyzed for deformations. Borsu et al. (2010) compiled a 3D-point cloud of a car body panel by using stereoscopic images. After detecting the deformations such as dings and dents, the information about the defects and non-conformities is utilized by a robotic system to mark the location of the defect on the panel. Fan et al. (2015) developed a system for the inspection of used car body parts. The goal is to detect surface defects and non-conformities from everyday use, meaning that small defects occurring in the paint shop are not the focus.

Conclusion

In this section, we reviewed the quality management in the industrial field, and the problems that occur from non-conformities and defects, especially product recalls, and non-conformities that reach the end customers. We also reviewed the different concepts and solutions that were proposed in the literature to manage these non-conformity and quality problems, such as the barrier concept and safety through prevention and protection. Furthermore, we reviewed some case studies that exist in the literature on non-conformities in many industrial fields, in order to illustrate the theoretical concepts that are discussed in this paper.

METHODOLOGY

Artificial Neural Networks (ANN)

Inspired by the human brain, the establishment and development of Artificial Neural Networks have seen several directions. The earliest work on computer intelligence goes back to the 18th and 19th centuries, with studies based on Bayes' Theorem creating the fundamentals for Machine Learning. The highlight in this field is brought by Alan Turing, who proposed the idea of 'learning machine' and posed the question – 'Can machines think?'

Importance of ANNs in Quality Management

The quality visual inspection of the products is becoming more and more important in the product quality control (Zhao et al., 2017; Li et al., 2014; Cabral & de Araujo, 2015; Ngan et al., 2011). It aims to ensure the quality of the product by detecting non-conformities, by visual means. However, in order to detect non-conformities, many companies still use methods that rely heavily on the manpower and that consume a lot of financial resources. Since a person's energy is limited, workers with long-time continuous work may reduce production efficiency, due to exhaustion, which will eventually lead to heavy economic losses brought by the human error. Thus, it is necessary to bring automated non-conformities detection into the quality control process.

With the rapid development of computer technology and the expansion of its application fields (Tao et al., 2014; Tao et al., 2014), many methods based on computer vision, including neural networks, have been successfully applied in the quality inspection of various industrial products, including steel slabs, glass products, fabrics, polycrystalline solar wafers, and so on. These methods tend to design different algorithms to extract image features based on actual non-conformities detection conditions.

ANNs Functioning Principal

Artificial Neural Networks is a part of Deep Learning, a subclass of Machine Learning (Hinton et al., 2006). The main idea behind Artificial Neural Networks is to create a network that can mimic the activities of the human brain. A neural network has interconnected nodes, or neurons, that receive signals and deliver output according to requirements, like a neuron. The significant advancements of Artificial Neural Networks from Machine Learning are its capability to handle immense complex relations, learn, and make intelligent decisions on its own through several layers (LeCun et al., 2015). A standard neural network consists of three main layers: an Input Layer, a Hidden Layer, and an Output Layer. The Deep Learning algorithm teaches the system to take the input as an image or text and predict the output through these layers. A simple Artificial Neural Network can be made 'deep' by increasing the number of layers, especially in the hidden layer. The Artificial Neural Network architecture is shown in Figure 3.

Weight, bias, and activation functions are the three major parameters of an Artificial Neural Network (Figure 4). 'Weight' transfers the input of a node onto the hidden layer of the network. The weight is multiplied by the input. The resultant value is observed and passed on to the next node. It is a learnable parameter whose value gets updated during the training period. 'Bias' is another learnable parameter of Artificial Neural Networks, representing how far off the output values are from the intended values. The bias value is added to the multiplication of input and weight before passing on to the next step. Lastly, the 'Activation functions' are differentiable functions added to the Artificial Neural Networks to help the network learn complex patterns from the data. Typically, all hidden layers use the same activation function, and the output layer uses a different one, depending on the type of prediction required.

Figure 3. Artificial neural networks architecture

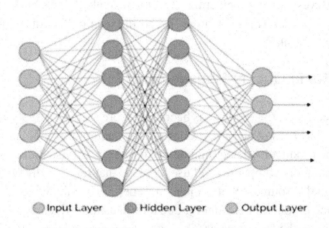

Figure 4. Parameters of artificial neural networks

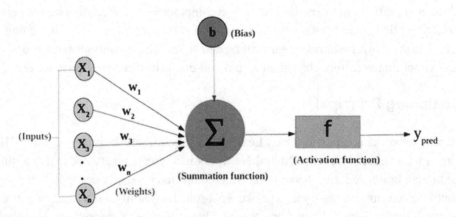

In these networks, if one cell is damaged, the other cells can make up for its absence and contribute to its regeneration. These networks are capable of learning. Basically, the ability to learn is the most important feature of an intelligent system. A learning system is more flexible and easier to program, so it can better respond to new problems and equations. Artificial neural networks, like humans, learn by using the different examples, and a neural network is set up to perform specific tasks, such as identifying patterns and categorizing information, during a learning process. For example, by injecting tactile nerve cells, the cells learn not to go to the hot body, and with this algorithm, the system learns to correct its error.

DEEP LEARNING

Artificial Neural Network systems should be more complex in order to represent more complex features and "read" increasingly complex models for prediction and classification of data based on thousands or even millions of features. Deep learning is a machine learning subfield that focuses on learning successive "layers" of increasingly meaningful representations while learning representations from data (Grekousis, 2019). It is concerned with Artificial Neural Networks (ANNs), which are algorithms based on the structure and function of the brain. Deep Learning allows computational models with multiple processing layers to learn multiple levels of abstraction for data representations. They are neural networks that have more than three layers of neurons (including the input and output layers). These layered representations are learned using models known as "neural networks," which are organized into literal layers that are placed one on top of the other (Schmidhuber, 2015). Simply increasing the number of hidden layers and/or the number of neurons per hidden layer accomplishes this goal. More layers and neurons can represent increasingly complex models, but they also require more time and power to compute. The architecture of Deep Learning technologies is shown in Figure 5 (Santos et al, 2021).

Figure 5. Architecture of deep learning
Source: Santos et al. (2021)

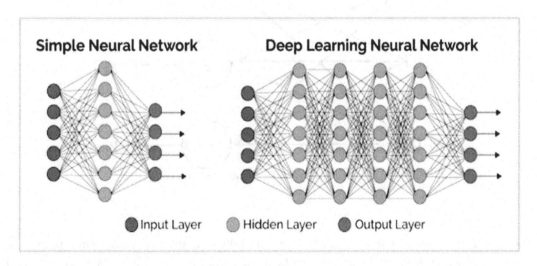

Neural Network Architectures

The architecture of an artificial neural network defines how its several neurons are arranged, or placed, in relation to each other. These arrangements are structured essentially by directing the synaptic connections of the neurons (Da Silva et al., 2016). One of the main challenges of neural network applications is to correctly determine the right neural network architecture to use. There are two main categories of neural network architectures, depending on the type of the connections between the neurons: feed-forward neural networks and recurrent neural networks.

Feed-Forward Neural Networks

If there is no "feedback" from the output neurons towards the inputs throughout the network, the network is referred to as a feed-forward network. In this architecture, the information always flows in a single direction, from the input layer to the output layer. Feed-forward networks fall into two categories, depending on the number of layers: single-layer network and multi-layer network.

A single-layer feed-forward neural network has just one input layer and a single neural layer, which is also the output layer. In this architecture, there is no computation performed in the input layer. Input signals are passed on to the output layer via the weights, and the neurons in the output layer compute the output signals. The architecture of a single-layer feed-forward network is illustrated in Figure 6 (Da Silva et al., 2016). The neural networks belonging to this architecture are usually employed in pattern classification and linear filtering problems.

Figure 6. Single-layer feed-forward architecture
Source: Da Silva et al. (2016)

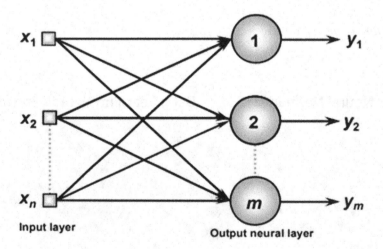

As opposed to a single-layer network, multi-layer networks are composed of one or more hidden layers. The existence of one or more hidden layers enable the network to extract higher order statistics. Figure 7 illustrates a multi-layer feed-forward network composed of one input layer with n inputs, two hidden layers, and one output layer with m outputs (Da Silva et al., 2016). This type of networks is employed to solve diverse problems, like those related to function approximation, pattern classification, system identification, process control, optimization, robotics, and so on.

Among the main feed-forward networks are the multi-layer perceptron (MLP) and the convolutional neural network (CNN). The MLP architecture is the most known and most frequently used type of neural networks. The CNN is a type of feed-forward neural networks used in tasks like image analysis, natural language processing, and other complex image classification problems. It is one of the most significant networks in the deep learning field, and has been making brilliant achievements, becoming one of the most representative neural networks in the field of deep learning. Computer vision based on CNN has enabled people to accomplish what had been considered impossible in the past few centuries, such as face recognitions, autonomous vehicles, self-service supermarkets, and intelligent medical treatments.

Figure 7. Multi-layer feed-forward architecture
Source: Da Silva et al. (2016)

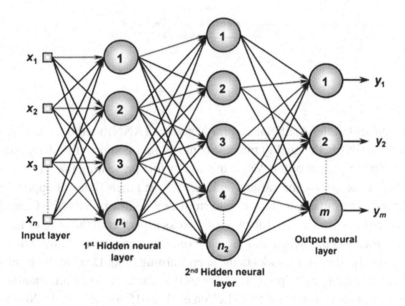

Recurrent Neural Networks

As opposed to the feed-forward networks, if the outputs of the neurons of the neural network are used as feedback inputs for other neurons, the network is called a recurrent network, or a feed-back network. The feed-back feature qualifies these networks for dynamic information processing, meaning that they can be employed on time-variant systems, such as time series prediction, system identification and optimization, process control, and so on. Figure 8 illustrates the architecture of a recurrent neural network, where one of its output signals is fed back to the middle layer. Thus, using the feed-back process, the networks with this architecture produce current outputs also taking into consideration the previous output values (Da Silva et al., 2016).

Figure 8. Recurrent neural network architecture
Source: Da Silva et al. (2016)

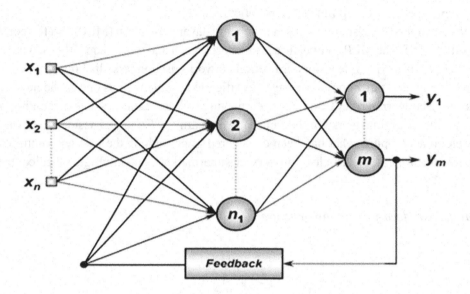

Conclusion

In this section, we presented the Artificial Neural Networks (ANN) method. First of all, we defined the importance of the ANNs in the quality management and non-conformities detection field. Then we reviewed the functioning principal of the ANNs method, before presenting the different neural network architectures. And after comparing the various architectures and their fields of application, we came to the conclusion that the most suitable architecture to study non-conformities is the Convolutional Neural Network (CNN). Indeed, this type of feed-forward networks is perfect in the field of image analysis and complex image classification problems, and its massive advancements in many industrial fields have made it one of the most significant networks in the deep learning field. Deep multi-layer architectures of CNNs are capable of extracting more powerful features that are extracted from training data automatically by using the back-propagation algorithm (LeCun et al., 2015; Bengio et al., 2013). CNNs provide an end-to-end solution from raw defect images to predictions. Furthermore, objects can be detected in a few of milliseconds with accurate location and size information of objects via Convolutional detection networks.

RESULTS

Building the Neural Network System

The purpose of this study is to build a neural network system to determine the causes of non-conformities. The input of the network is then the non-conformity, and the output is its cause. We can now build our neural network following the next steps:

1. Pick a neural network architecture. It implies that we shall be pondering primarily upon the connectivity patterns of the neural network including some of the following aspects:
    - Number of input nodes: The way to identify number of input nodes is to identify the number of features. In our case, the input is the non-conformity. It may be an image of the defective product, or a measure of a parameter (height, weight, temperature…). Therefore, the number of input nodes is the number of all non-conformities, or classes of non-conformities.
    - Number of hidden layers: The default is to use one hidden layer. This is the most common practice.
    - Number of nodes in each of the hidden layers: In case of using multiple hidden layers, the best practice is to use same number of nodes in each hidden layer. In general practice, the number of hidden units is taken as comparable number to that of number of input nodes. That means one could take either the same number of hidden nodes as input nodes or maybe twice or thrice the number of input nodes.
    - Number of output nodes: The way to identify number of output nodes is to identify the number of output classes we want the neural network to process, which means in our case the number of causes classes.
2. Initialize weights randomly. The weights are randomly initialized to a value in between 0 and 1, or rather, very close to zero.
3. Implement the forward propagation algorithm to calculate hypothesis function for a set on input vector for any of the hidden layer.
4. Implement the cost function for optimizing parameter values. One may recall that cost function would help determine how well the neural network fits the training data.
5. Implement the back propagation algorithm to compute the error vector related with each of the nodes.
6. Use the gradient checking method to compare the gradient calculated using partial derivatives of cost function using back propagation and using numerical estimate of cost function gradient. The gradient checking method is used to validate if the implementation of back propagation method is correct.
7. Use the gradient descent or advanced optimization technique with back propagation to try and minimize the cost function as a function of parameters or weights.
8. Test the results and validate the neural network system.

CONCLUSION

Industrial companies set up mechanisms to protect themselves against non-conformities: on one hand, risk analyses are put in place to prevent defects and, on the other hand, detection systems are in place in order to detect them as soon as they occur. These measures can however contain breaches allowing some defects to slip through and propagate. This propagation may lead to huge costs for companies because it creates scraps, a need to rework, stress, accident, delays and potentially product recalls which dramatically impact customer satisfaction. Therefore, detecting non-conformities efficiently is extremely important, and identifying its causes is even more important.

In this context, this paper was interested in studying non-conformity causes, using neural networks. At first we presented some essential notions like the management of quality problems and non-conformities, as well as the neural networks method. Then we tried to build our neural network system to study non-conformity causes.

As a perspective to this work, the neural network model that we built must be more developed, and the parameters must be determined through a case study in order to train the neural network and test the results.

REFERENCES

Bengio, Y., Courville, A., & Vincent, P. (2013). Representation learning: A review and new perspectives. *IEEE Transactions on Pattern Analysis and Machine Intelligence*, *35*(8), 1798–1828. doi:10.1109/TPAMI.2013.50 PMID:23787338

Berman, B. (1999). Planning for the inevitable product recall. *Business Horizons*, *42*(2), 69–78. doi:10.1016/S0007-6813(99)80011-1

Bettayeb, B., Vialletelle, P., Bassetto, S., & Tollenaere, M. (2010). Optimized design of control plans based on risk exposure and resources capabilities. *Semiconductor Manufacturing (ISSM), 2010 International Symposium On*, 1-4.

Borsu, V., Yogeswaran, A., & Payeur, P. (2010). Automated Surface Deformations Detection and Marking on Automotive Body Panels. *IEEE International Conference on Automation Science and Engineering*. 10.1109/COASE.2010.5584643

Buhman, C., Kekre, S., & Singhal, J. (2005). Interdisciplinary and Interorganizational Research: Establishing the Science of Enterprise Networks. *Production and Operations Management*, *14*(4), 493–513. doi:10.1111/j.1937-5956.2005.tb00236.x

Cabral, J. D. D., & de Araujo, S. A. (2015). An intelligent vision system ´ for detecting defects in glass products for packaging and domestic use. *International Journal of Advanced Manufacturing Technology*, *77*(1-4), 485–494. doi:10.1007/s00170-014-6442-y

Chamanbaz, M., & Bouffanais, R. (2023). A sequential deep learning algorithm for sampled mixed integer optimization problems. *Information Sciences*, *634*, 73–84. doi:10.1016/j.ins.2023.03.061

Da Silva, I. N., Hernane Spatti, D., Andrade Flauzino, R., Liboni, L. H. B., & dos Reis Alves, S. F. (2016). Artificial Neural Network Architectures and Training Processes. *Artificial Neural Networks*, 21–28.

Doring, C., Eichhorn, A., Wang, X., & Kruse, R. (2006). Improved Classification of Surface Defects for Quality Control of Car Body Panels. *IEEE International Conference on Fuzzy Systems*. 10.1109/FUZZY.2006.1681903

Duijm, N. J. (2009). Safety-barrier diagrams as a safety management tool. *Reliability Engineering & System Safety*, *94*(2), 332–341. doi:10.1016/j.ress.2008.03.031

Eichhorn, A., Girimonte, D., Klose, A., & Kruse, R. (2005). Soft Computing for Automated Surface Quality Analysis of Exterior Car Body Panels. *Applied Soft Computing, 5*(3), 301–313. doi:10.1016/j.asoc.2004.08.002

Fan, W., Lu, C., & Tsujino, K. (2015). *An Automatic Machine Vision Method for the Flaw Detection on Car's Body*. IEEE 7th International Conference on Awareness Science and Technology (iCAST), Qinhuangdao, China.

Garvin, D. A. (1986). Quality Problems, Policies, and Attitudes in the United States and Japan: An Exploratory Study. *Academy of Management Journal, 29*(4), 653–673. doi:10.2307/255938

Gowland, R. (2006). The accidental risk assessment methodology for industries (ARAMIS)/layer of protection analysis (LOPA) methodology: A step forward towards convergent practices in risk assessment? *Journal of Hazardous Materials, 130*(3), 307–310. doi:10.1016/j.jhazmat.2005.07.007 PMID:16139426

Grekousis, G. (2019). Artificial neural networks and deep learning in urban geography: A systematic review and meta-analysis. *Computers, Environment and Urban Systems, 74*, 244–256. doi:10.1016/j.compenvurbsys.2018.10.008

Handfield. (2006). The state of JOM: An outgoing editor's (retro)spective. *Journal of Operations Management, 24*, 417-420.

Hasking, C. (2006). *Systems engineering handbook*. INCOSE. Version 3.

Hinton, G. E., Osindero, S., & Teh, Y. W. (2006). A fast learning algorithm for deep belief nets. *Neural Computation, 18*(7), 1527–1554. doi:10.1162/neco.2006.18.7.1527 PMID:16764513

Hollnagel, E. (2008). Risk + barriers = safety? *Safety Science, 46*(2), 221–229. doi:10.1016/j.ssci.2007.06.028

Hu, H., Liu, Y., Liu, M., & Nie, L. (2016). Surface defect classification in large-scale strip steel image collection via hybrid chromosome genetic algorithm. *Neurocomputing, 181*, 86–95. doi:10.1016/j.neucom.2015.05.134

Jacobs, R. M. (1996). Product recall—A vendor/vendee nightmare. *Microelectronics and Reliability, 36*(1), 101–103. doi:10.1016/0026-2714(95)00001-I

Ke, X. U., Lei, W., & Wang, J. (2016). Surface defect recognition of hot-rolled steel plates based on tetrolet transform. *Jixie Gongcheng Xuebao*.

LeCun, Y., Bengio, Y., & Hinton, G. (2015). Deep learning. *Nature, 521*(7553), 436–444. doi:10.1038/nature14539 PMID:26017442

Li, D., Liang, L. Q., & Zhang, W. J. (2014). Defect inspection and extraction of the mobile phone cover glass based on the principal components analysis. *International Journal of Advanced Manufacturing Technology, 73*(9-12), 1605–1614. doi:10.1007/s00170-014-5871-y

Li, H., Xu, Z., Taylor, G., Studer, C., & Goldstein, T. (2017). *Visualizing the loss landscape of neural nets*. arXiv preprint, arXiv:1712.09913.

Li, J., Su, Z., Geng, J., & Yin, Y. (2018). Real-time Detection of Steel Strip Surface Defects Based on Improved YOLO Detection Network. *IFAC-PapersOnLine, 51*(21), 76–81. doi:10.1016/j.ifacol.2018.09.412

Lin, S. B., Wang, Y., & Zhou, D. X. (2021). *Generalization performance of empirical risk minimization on over-parameterized deep relu nets.* arXiv preprint, arXiv:2111.14039.

Ma, Y., Li, Q., He, F., Yan, L., & Xi, S. (2017). Adaptive segmentation algorithm for metal surface defects. *Yiqi Yibiao Xuebao.*

Magne, L., & Vasseur, D. (2006). Risques industriels-Complexité, incertitude et décision: une approche interdisciplinaire. *Recherche, 67*(2).

Ngan, H. Y., Pang, G. K., & Yung, N. H. (2011). Automated fabric defect detection—A review. *Image and Vision Computing, 29*(7), 442–458. doi:10.1016/j.imavis.2011.02.002

Pascanu, R., Mikolov, T., & Bengio, Y. (2013). On the difficulty of training recurrent neural networks. *International Conference on Machine Learning, PMLR*, 1310–1318.

Reason, J. T. (1990). *Human error.* Cambridge University Press. doi:10.1017/CBO9781139062367

Rudin, C., Chen, C., Chen, Z., Huang, H., Semenova, L., & Zhong, C. (2022). Interpretable machine learning: Fundamental principles and 10 grand challenges. *Statistics Surveys, 16*(none), 1–85. doi:10.1214/21-SS133

Santos, I., Castro, L., Rodriguez-Fernandez, N., Torrente-Patino, A., & Carballal, A. (2021). "Artificial Neural Networks and Deep Learning in the Visual Arts: A review." Review of. *Neural Computing & Applications, 33*(1), 1–37. doi:10.1007/s00521-020-05565-4

Schmidhuber, J. (2015). Deep learning in neural networks: An overview. *Neural Networks, 61*, 85–117. doi:10.1016/j.neunet.2014.09.003 PMID:25462637

Sousa, R., & Voss, C. A. (2008). Contingency research in operations management practices. *Journal of Operations Management, 26*(6), 697–713. doi:10.1016/j.jom.2008.06.001

Summers, A. E. (2003). Introduction to layers of protection analysis. *Journal of Hazardous Materials, 104*(1-3), 163-168.

Tao, F., Cheng, Y., Da Xu, L., Zhang, L., & Li, B. H. (2014). Cciot-cmfg: Cloud computing and internet of things-based cloud manufacturing service system. *IEEE Transactions on Industrial Informatics, 10*(2), 1435–1442. doi:10.1109/TII.2014.2306383

Tao, F., Zuo, Y., Da Xu, L., & Zhang, L. (2014). Iot-based intelligent perception and access of manufacturing resource toward cloud manufacturing. *IEEE Transactions on Industrial Informatics, 10*(2), 1547–1557. doi:10.1109/TII.2014.2306397

Tixier, J., Dusserre, G., Salvi, O., & Gaston, D. (2002, July). Review of 62 risk analysis methodologies of industrial plants. *Journal of Loss Prevention in the Process Industries, 15*(4), 291–303. doi:10.1016/S0950-4230(02)00008-6

Tong, G., Li, Y., Zhang, H., & Xiong, N. (2023). A fine-grained channel state information-based deep learning system for dynamic gesture recognition. *Information Sciences*, *636*, 118912. doi:10.1016/j.ins.2023.03.137

Yang, A., Li, D., & Li, G. (2022). A fast adaptive online gradient descent algorithm in over parameterized neural networks. *Neural Processing Letters*, 1–19.

Yang, S. (2023). Hierarchical graph multi-agent reinforcement learning for traffic signal control. *Information Sciences*, *634*, 55–72. doi:10.1016/j.ins.2023.03.087

Zhao, Y. J., Yan, Y. H., & Song, K. C. (2017). Vision-based automatic detection of steel surface defects in the cold rolling process: Considering the influence of industrial liquids and surface textures. *International Journal of Advanced Manufacturing Technology*, *90*(5-8), 1665–1678. doi:10.1007/s00170-016-9489-0

Compilation of References

1 Linear codes. (1977). InMacWilliams, F. J., & Sloane, N. J. A. (Eds.), *North-Holland Mathematical Library* (Vol. 16, pp. 1–37). Elsevier. doi:10.1016/S0924-6509(08)70526-9

Abd El Baki, H. M., Fujimaki, H., Tokumoto, I., & Saito, T. (2018). A new scheme to optimize irrigation depth using a numerical model of crop response to irrigation and quantitative weather forecasts. *Computers and Electronics in Agriculture*, *150*, 387–393. doi:10.1016/j.compag.2018.05.016

Abioye, E. A., Abidin, M. S. Z., Mahmud, M. S. A., Buyamin, S., Ishak, M. H. I., Rahman, M. K. I. A., Otuoze, A. O., Onotu, P., & Ramli, M. S. A. (2020). A review on monitoring and advanced control strategies for precision irrigation. *Computers and Electronics in Agriculture*, *173*, 105441. doi:10.1016/j.compag.2020.105441

Abioye, E. A., Hensel, O., Esau, T. J., Elijah, O., Abidin, M. S. Z., Ayobami, A. S., Yerima, O., & Nasirahmadi, A. (2022). Precision Irrigation Management Using Machine Learning and Digital Farming Solutions. *AgriEngineering*, *4*(1), 70–103. doi:10.3390/agriengineering4010006

Acerbis, R., Bongio, A., Brambilla, M., & Butti, S. (2015). Model-Driven Development Based on OMG's IFML with WebRatio Web and Mobile Platform. *Lecture Notes in Computer Science*, 605–608. Advance online publication. doi:10.1007/978-3-319-19890-3_39

Acerbis, R., Bongio, A., Butti, S., Ceri, S., Ciapessoni, F., Conserva, C., Fraternali, P., & Carughi, G. T. (2004). WebRatio is an Innovative Technology for Web Application Development. *Lecture Notes in Computer Science*, 613–614. Advance online publication. doi:10.1007/978-3-540-27834-4_90

Acuña-Zegarra, M. A., Díaz-Infante, S., Baca-Carrasco, D., & Olmos-Liceaga, D. (2021). COVID-19 optimal vaccination policies: A modeling study on efficacy, natural and vaccine-induced immunity responses. *Mathematical Biosciences*, *337*, 108614. doi:10.1016/j.mbs.2021.108614 PMID:33961878

Adewole, M. O., Okekunle, A. P., Adeoye, I. A., & Akpa, O. M. (2022). Investigating the transmission dynamics of SARS-CoV-2 in Nigeria: A SEIR modelling approach. *Scientific African*, *15*, e01116. doi:10.1016/j.sciaf.2022.e01116 PMID:35155878

Adoga, H. U., & Pezaros, D. P. (2022). Network Function Virtualization and Service Function Chaining Frameworks: A Comprehensive Review of Requirements, Objectives, Implementations, and Open Research Challenges. *Future Internet*, *14*(2), 59. doi:10.3390/fi14020059

AFNOR. (n.d.-a). *NF EN 13306 et NF X 60–500, fiabilité maintenabilité disponibilité, recueil des normes françaises*. Author.

AFNOR. (n.d.-b). *Afnor ; fiabilité maintenabilité disponibilité, recueil des normes françaises, afnor-ute*. Author.

Aggarwal, A., Mittal, M., & Battineni, G. (2021). Generative adversarial network: An overview of theory and applications. *International Journal of Information Management Data Insights*, *1*(1), 100004. doi:10.1016/j.jjimei.2020.100004

Ahmadi, M., Norouzi, A., Karimi, N., Samavi, S., & Emami, A. (2020). ReDMark: Framework for residual diffusion watermarking based on deep networks. *Expert Systems with Applications*, *146*, 113157. doi:10.1016/j.eswa.2019.113157

Ahmed, N., De, D., & Hussain, I. (2018). Internet of Things (IoT) for Smart Precision Agriculture and Farming in Rural Areas. *IEEE Internet of Things Journal*, *5*(6), 4890–4899. doi:10.1109/JIOT.2018.2879579

Akhter, R., & Sofi, S. (2022). Precision agriculture using IoT data analytics and machine learning. *Journal of King Saud University. Computer and Information Sciences*, *34*(8), 5602–5618. doi:10.1016/j.jksuci.2021.05.013

Alamdar-Yazdi, A., & Kschischang, F. R. (2011). A Simplified Successive-Cancellation Decoder for Polar Codes. *IEEE Communications Letters*, *15*(12), 1378–1380. doi:10.1109/LCOMM.2011.101811.111480

Alcácer, V., Rodrigues, J., Carvalho, H., & Cruz-Machado, V. (2022). Industry 4.0 Maturity Follow Up Inside an Internal Value Chain: A Case Study. *International Journal of Advanced Manufacturing Technology*, *119*(7-8), 5035–5046. doi:10.1007/s00170-021-08476-3

Ali, N.A., Taha, A.-E.M., & Barka, E. (2020) Integrating Blockchain and IoT/ITS for Safer Roads. *IEEE Network, 34*(1), 32-37.

Aljarhizi, Y. a. (2020). Static Power Converters for a Wind Turbine Emulator Driving a Self-Excited Induction Generator. In *2020 1st International Conference on Innovative Research in Applied Science, Engineering and Technology (IRASET)* (pp. 1--6). 10.1109/IRASET48871.2020.9092319

Aljarhizi, Y. a. (2023). Optimized Wind Turbine Emulator based on an AC to DC Motor Generator Set. *Engineering, Technology & Applied Scientific Research*, 10559–10564.

Alshammari, F. S. (2023). Analysis of SIRVI model with time dependent coefficients and the effect of vaccination on the transmission rate and COVID-19 epidemic waves. *Infectious Disease Modelling*, *8*(1), 172–182. doi:10.1016/j.idm.2023.01.002 PMID:36643866

Alsheikhy, A. A., Shawly, T., Said, Y. F., & Lahza, H. (2022). An Intelligent Smart Parking System Using Convolutional Neural Network. *Journal of Sensors*, *2022*, 1–11. Advance online publication. doi:10.1155/2022/7571716

Al-Tameemi, M. I., Hasan, A. A., & Oleiwi, B. K. (2023). Design and implementation monitoring robotic system based on you only look once model using deep learning technique. *IAES International Journal of Artificial Intelligence*, *12*(1), 106–113. doi:10.11591/ijai.v12.i1.pp106-113

Arikan, E. (2009). Channel Polarization: A Method for Constructing Capacity-Achieving Codes for Symmetric Binary-Input Memoryless Channels. *IEEE Transactions on Information Theory*, *55*(7), 3051–3073. doi:10.1109/TIT.2009.2021379

Arrhioui, K., Mbarki, S., & Erramdani, M. (2018, August 30). Applying CIM-to-PIM Model Transformation for Development of Emotional Intelligence Tests Platform. *International Journal of Online Engineering*, *14*(08), 160. doi:10.3991/ijoe.v14i08.8747

Arsova, S., Genovese, A., & Ketikidis, P. H. (2022). Implementing circular economy in a regional context: A systematic literature review and a research agenda. *Journal of Cleaner Production*, *368*, 133117. doi:10.1016/j.jclepro.2022.133117

Asiain, D., & Antolín, D. (2021). LoRa-Based Traffic Flow Detection for Smart-Road. *Sensors (Basel)*, *21*(2), 338. doi:10.3390/s21020338 PMID:33419026

Aslantas, V. (2008). A singular-value decomposition-based image watermarking using genetic algorithm. *AEÜ. International Journal of Electronics and Communications, 62*(5), 386–394. doi:10.1016/j.aeue.2007.02.010

Assim, M., & Al-Omary, A. (2020). A survey of IoT-based smart parking systems in smart cities. In *3rd Smart Cities Symposium (SCS 2020), Online Conference* (pp. 35–38). 10.1049/icp.2021.0911

Attaran, M., & Celik, B. G. (2023). Digital Twin: Benefits, use cases, challenges, and opportunities. *Decision Analytics Journal, 6*, 100165. doi:10.1016/j.dajour.2023.100165

Azencott. (2022). *Introduction au Machine Learning*. Dunod.

Bairagi, V. K., & Sapkal, A. M. (2013). ROI-based DICOM image compression for telemedicine. *Sadhana, 38*(1), 123–131. doi:10.1007/s12046-013-0126-4

Bartelds, G., Biemans, C., Boller, C., Breidne, M., Claesson, Å., Delebarre, C., & Worden, K. (2004). *Health Monitoring of Aerospace Structures – Smart Sensor Technologies and Signal Processing*. John Wiley & Sons Ltd.

Beauvallet, G., & Houy, T. (2009). L'adoption des pratiques de gestion lean Cas des entreprises industrielles françaises. Revue française de gestion, 7(197), 83-106.

Benaaouinate, L. a. (2019). Emulation of Wind Turbine for Standalone Wind Energy Conversion Systems. *Modeling, Identification and Control Methods in Renewable Energy Systems*, 227-244.

Bengio, Y., Courville, A., & Vincent, P. (2013). Representation learning: A review and new perspectives. *IEEE Transactions on Pattern Analysis and Machine Intelligence, 35*(8), 1798–1828. doi:10.1109/TPAMI.2013.50 PMID:23787338

Berman, B. (1999). Planning for the inevitable product recall. *Business Horizons, 42*(2), 69–78. doi:10.1016/S0007-6813(99)80011-1

Bernaschina, C., Brambilla, M., Mauri, A., & Umuhoza, E. (2017). A Big Data Analysis Framework for Model-Based Web User Behavior Analytics. In J. Cabot, R. De Virgilio, & R. Torlone (Eds.), Lecture Notes in Computer Science: Vol. 10360. *Web Engineering. ICWE 2017*. Springer. doi:10.1007/978-3-319-60131-1_6

Betancourt, M. (2017). *A conceptual introduction to Hamiltonian Monte Carlo*. arXiv preprint arXiv:1701.02434.

Betari, O., Erramdani, M., Roubi, S., Arrhioui, K., & Mbarki, S. (2016, September 23). Model Transformations in the MOF Meta-Modeling Architecture: From UML to CodeIgniter PHP Framework. *Advances in Intelligent Systems and Computing*, 227–234. doi:10.1007/978-3-319-46568-5_23

Bettayeb, B., Vialletelle, P., Bassetto, S., & Tollenaere, M. (2010). Optimized design of control plans based on risk exposure and resources capabilities. *Semiconductor Manufacturing (ISSM), 2010 International Symposium On*, 1-4.

Bidollahkhani, M., Dakkak, O., Mohammad Alajeeli, A. S., & Kim, B.-S. (2023). LoRaline: A Critical Message Passing Line of Communication for Anomaly Mapping in IoV Systems. *IEEE Access : Practical Innovations, Open Solutions, 11*, 18107–18120. doi:10.1109/ACCESS.2023.3246471

BlinowskiG.J.PiotrowskiP. (2020). *CVE based classification of vulnerable IoT systems*. doi:10.1007/978-3-030-48256-5_9

Bluvband, Z., & Grabov, P. (n.d.). *Failure Analysis of FMEA*. Academic Press.

BochkovskiyA.WangC.-Y.LiaoH.-Y. M. (2020). *YOLOv4: Optimal Speed and Accuracy of Object Detection*. https://arxiv.org/abs/2004.10934v1

Bohuslava, J., Martin, J., & Igor, H. (2017). TCP/IP protocol utilisation in process of dynamic control of robotic cell according industry 4.0 concept. *2017 IEEE 15th International Symposium on Applied Machine Intelligence and Informatics (SAMI).* 10.1109/SAMI.2017.7880306

Bootsma, M. C., & Ferguson, N. M. (2007). The effect of public health measures on the 1918 influenza pandemic in US cities. *Proceedings of the National Academy of Sciences of the United States of America, 104*(18), 7588–7593. doi:10.1073/pnas.0611071104 PMID:17416677

Borsu, V., Yogeswaran, A., & Payeur, P. (2010). Automated Surface Deformations Detection and Marking on Automotive Body Panels. *IEEE International Conference on Automation Science and Engineering.* 10.1109/COASE.2010.5584643

Boudnaya, J., Marouan, C., & Ilham, G. (2022). A Remaining Useful Life Prediction of a robot with 15 states. *Oran 2 University Journal, 7*(2).

Boudnaya, J., Nina Aslhey, H., & Ouèdan Jhonn, G. (2023). Study of the optimization control of agricultural greenhouse climatic parameters by the integration of machine learning. Artificial Intelligence & Industrial Applications (A2IA 2023), Meknes, Morocco.

Bounouar, Béarée, Siadat, & Benchekroun. (2020). *Vers un cadre méthodologique de conception des systèmes humains-robots.* 13ème Conférence Internationale de Modélisation, Optimisation et Simulation (MOSIM2020), Agadir, Maroc.

Brahim, H., & Mohamed, E. (2005). L'AMDEC un outil puissant d'optimisation de la maintenance, application à un motocompresseur d'une PME marocaine. CPI'2005, Casablanca, Morocco.

Brambilla, M., Mauri, A., & Umuhoza, E. (2014). Extending the Interaction Flow Modeling Language (IFML) for Model Driven Development of Mobile Applications Front End. *Mobile Web Information Systems*, 176–191. doi:10.1007/978-3-319-10359-4_15

Brambilla, M., Cirami, R., Gasparini, M., Marassi, A., & Pavanetto, S. (2019, Oct). Code Generation based on IFML for the User Interfaces of the Square Kilometre Array (SKA). *Proc. ICALEPCS'19*, 1307-1311. 10.18429/JACoW-ICALEPCS2019-WEPHA093

Brambilla, M., & Fraternali, P. (2014). *Interaction Flow Modeling Language: Model-Driven UI Engineering of Web and Mobile Apps with IFML* (1st ed.). Morgan Kaufmann Publishers Inc.

Brambilla, M., Umuhoza, E., & Acerbis, R. (2017, September 26). Model-driven development of user interfaces for IoT systems via domain-specific components and patterns. *Journal of Internet Services and Applications, 8*(1), 14. Advance online publication. doi:10.1186/s13174-017-0064-1

Bria, D., Assouar, M. B., Oudich, M., Pennec, Y., Vasseur, J., & Djafari-Rouhani, B. (2011). Opening of simultaneous photonic and phononic band gap in two-dimensional square lattice periodic structure. *Journal of Applied Physics, 109*(1), 014507. doi:10.1063/1.3530682

Brisco & Wolfgang. (2018). Design of a Semi-Automatic Artificial Incubator. *European Journal of Applied Engineering and Scientific Research, 6*(3), 4-14.

Brum, A. A., Vasconcelos, G. L., Duarte-Filho, G. C., Ospina, R., Almeida, F. A., & Macêdo, A. M. (2023). ModInterv COVID-19: An online platform to monitor the evolution of epidemic curves. *Applied Soft Computing, 137*, 110159. doi:10.1016/j.asoc.2023.110159 PMID:36874079

Brundtland, G. H., Khalid, M., Agnelli, S., Al-Athel, S. A., Chidzero, B., Fadika, L. M., . . . Botero, M. M. (1987). *Our common future.* World Commission on Environment and Development.

Buhman, C., Kekre, S., & Singhal, J. (2005). Interdisciplinary and Interorganizational Research: Establishing the Science of Enterprise Networks. *Production and Operations Management, 14*(4), 493–513. doi:10.1111/j.1937-5956.2005.tb00236.x

Bwambale, E., Abagale, F. K., & Anornu, G. K. (2023). Data-driven model predictive control for precision irrigation management. *Smart Agricultural Technology, 3*, 100074. doi:10.1016/j.atech.2022.100074

Cabral, J. D. D., & de Araujo, S. A. (2015). An intelligent vision system ´ for detecting defects in glass products for packaging and domestic use. *International Journal of Advanced Manufacturing Technology, 77*(1-4), 485–494. doi:10.1007/s00170-014-6442-y

Cacciapaglia, G., Cot, C., & Sannino, F. (2020). Second wave COVID-19 pandemics in Europe: A temporal playbook. *Scientific Reports, 10*(1), 15514. doi:10.1038/s41598-020-72611-5 PMID:32968181

Car, N. J. (2018). USING decision models to enable better irrigation Decision Support Systems. *Computers and Electronics in Agriculture, 152*, 290–301. doi:10.1016/j.compag.2018.07.024

Chamanbaz, M., & Bouffanais, R. (2023). A sequential deep learning algorithm for sampled mixed integer optimization problems. *Information Sciences, 634*, 73–84. doi:10.1016/j.ins.2023.03.061

Cheng, B., Huang, Y., Xie, X., & Du, J. (2022). A Multi-object Tracking Algorithm Based on YOLOv5-Concise Network. *Proceedings of SPIE - The International Society for Optical Engineering, 12246*. 10.1117/12.2643719

Chen, J., Kudjo, P. K., Mensah, S., Brown, S. A., & Akorfu, G. (2020). An automatic software vulnerability classification framework using term frequency-inverse gravity moment and feature selection. *Journal of Systems and Software, 167*, 110616. doi:10.1016/j.jss.2020.110616

Chen, Y. P., Fan, T. Y., & Chao, H. C. (2021). Wmnet: A lossless watermarking technique using deep learning for medical image authentication. *Electronics (Basel), 10*(8), 932. doi:10.3390/electronics10080932

Chen, Y., Liu, W., & Zhang, J. (2022). An Enhanced YOLOv5 Model with Attention Module for Vehicle-Pedestrian Detection. *IEEE International Symposium on Industrial Electronics, 2022-June*, 1035-1040. 10.1109/ISIE51582.2022.9831596

Choulier & Drăghici. (n.d.). *TRIZ: une approche de résolution des problèmes d'innovation dans la conception de produits*. Academic Press.

Christoforidou, M., Borghuis, G., Seijger, C., van Halsema, G. E., & Hellegers, P. (2023). Food security under water scarcity: A comparative analysis of Egypt and Jordan. *Food Security, 15*(1), 171–185. doi:10.1007/s12571-022-01310-y PMID:36160692

Chu, Y., & Li, S. (2023). Application of IoT and artificial intelligence technology in smart parking management. In *IEEE International Conference on Integrated Circuits and Communication Systems (ICICACS), Raichur, India, 2023* (pp. 1–6). 10.1109/ICICACS57338.2023.10099976

Chu, C., Yin, C., Shi, S., Su, S., & Chen, C. (2022, June). Multidisciplinary Modeling and Optimization Method of Remote Sensing Satellite Parameters Based on SysML-CEA. *Computer Modeling in Engineering & Sciences, 20*.

Clerc, M. (2010). *Particle swarm optimization* (Vol. 93). John Wiley & Sons.

Composition relationships. (2005). *Composition relationships. Introduction to Rational Systems Developer*. IBM Rational Systems Developer Info Center. http://publib.boulder.ibm.com/infocenter/rsdvhelp/v6r0m1/index.jsp?topic=%2Fcom.ibm.xtools.modeler.doc%2Ftopics%2Fccompasn .html

Conde, J., Munoz-Arcentales, A., Alonso, A., Lopez-Pernas, S., & Salvachua, J. (2022). Modeling Digital Twin Data and architecture: A building guide with FIWARE as enabling technology. *IEEE Internet Computing*, *26*(3), 7–14. doi:10.1109/MIC.2021.3056923

Connected Cars Technology Vulnerable to Cyber Attacks. (n.d.). Trend Micro | Newsroom. Retrieved November 4, 2023, from https://newsroom.trendmicro.com/2021-02-16-Connected-Cars-Technology-Vulnerable-to-Cyber-Attacks

Coronavirus, W. H. O. (COVID-19) Dashboard. (n.d.). https://covid19.who.int

Cotrino, A., Sebastián, M. A., & González-Gaya, C. (2020). Industry 4.0 Roadmap: Implementation for Small and Medium-Sized Enterprises. *MDPI. Applied Sciences (Basel, Switzerland)*, *10*(23), 8566. doi:10.3390/app10238566

Cox, I. J., Miller, M. L., Bloom, J. A., & Honsinger, C. (2002). *Digital Watermarking* (Vol. 53). LNCS.

Craig, J. (2005). Trajectory generation. In J. Craig (Ed.), *Introduction to robotics: Mechanics and control* (pp. 201–229). Pearson Education. https://ci.nii.ac.jp/ncid/BA68143739

Cressent, David, Idasiak, & Kratz. (2009). *Apport de SysML à la modélisation des systèmes complexes à fortes contraintes de sûreté de fonctionnement*. ITT 09 (Technological Innovation and Transport Systems 2009), Oct 2009, Toulouse, France.

Critical traffic light system vulnerability could cause 'chaos' on the roads. (2020, June 9). The Daily Swig | Cybersecurity News and Views. https://portswigger.net/daily-swig/critical-traffic-light-system-vulnerability-could-cause-chaos-on-the-roads

Da Silva, I. N., Hernane Spatti, D., Andrade Flauzino, R., Liboni, L. H. B., & dos Reis Alves, S. F. (2016). Artificial Neural Network Architectures and Training Processes. *Artificial Neural Networks*, 21–28.

Dai, P. (2022). FYCFNet: Vehicle and Pedestrian Detection Network based on Multi-model Fusion. *2022 3rd International Conference on Computer Vision, Image and Deep Learning and International Conference on Computer Engineering and Applications, CVIDL and ICCEA 2022*, 230-236. 10.1109/CVIDLICCEA56201.2022.9825072

Dannen, C. (2017). Introducing ethereum and solidity: Foundations of cryptocurrency and blockchain programming for beginners. *Apress Media*. Advance online publication. doi:10.1007/978-1-4842-2535-6/COVER

Dantas, T. E., de-Souza, E. D., Destro, I. R., Hammes, G., Rodriguez, C. M., & Soares, S. R. (2021). How the combination of Circular Economy and Industry 4.0 can contribute towards achieving the Sustainable Development Goals. *Sustainable Production and Consumption*, *26*, 213–227. doi:10.1016/j.spc.2020.10.005

Davenport, T., & Short, J. (1990). The New Industrial Engineering: Information Technology and Business Process Redesign. *Sloan Management Review*, 11–27.

Debongnie, J. F. (2007). Université de Liège, Faculté des sciences Appliquées, Institut Mécanique (Liège.). *Chemin des Chevreuils*, *1*, B-4000.

Deeba, F., Kun, S., Shaikh, M., Dharejo, F. A., Hayat, S., & Suwansrikham, P. (2018, April). Data transformation of UML diagram by using model-driven architecture. *2018 IEEE 3rd International Conference on Cloud Computing and Big Data Analysis (ICCCBDA)*. 10.1109/ICCCBDA.2018.8386531

Dekali, Z. a. (2021). Experimental implementation of the maximum power point tracking algorithm for a connected wind turbine emulator. *Revue Roumaine Des Sciences Techniques—Serie Electrotechnique Et Eneretique*, 111-117.

Delmas, A. (2019). *Contribution à l'estimation de la durée de vie résiduelle des systèmes en présence d'incertitudes*. Performance et fiabilité (cs.PF). Université de Technologie de Compiègne.

DeLuca. (1988). Dynamic control properties of robot arms with joint elasticity. *Proceedings of the 1988 IEEE International Conference on Robotics and Automation*, 1574-1580.

Deneux, D. (2002). Méthodes et modèles pour la conception concourante. Université de Valenciennes, habilitation à diriger des recherches, Valenciennes, France.

Dombrowskia, U., & Mielkea, T. (2013). Lean Leadership fundamental principles and their application. Forty Sixth CIRP Conference on Manufacturing Systems 2013. *Procedia CIRP*, *7*, 569–574.

Doring, C., Eichhorn, A., Wang, X., & Kruse, R. (2006). Improved Classification of Surface Defects for Quality Control of Car Body Panels. *IEEE International Conference on Fuzzy Systems*. 10.1109/FUZZY.2006.1681903

Doron, L. (2017). Flexible and Precise Irrigation Platform to Improve Farm Scale Water Productivity. *Impact*, *2017*(1), 77–79. doi:10.21820/23987073.2017.1.77

Dorri, A. (2017). Towards an optimized blockchain for IoT. *Proceedings - 2017 IEEE/ACM 2nd International Conference on Internet-of-Things Design and Implementation*, *6*, 173–178. 10.1145/3054977.3055003

Dorsch, B. (1974). A decoding algorithm for binary block codes andJ-ary output channels (Corresp.). *IEEE Transactions on Information Theory*, *20*(3), 391–394. doi:10.1109/TIT.1974.1055217

Duijm, N. J. (2009). Safety-barrier diagrams as a safety management tool. *Reliability Engineering & System Safety*, *94*(2), 332–341. doi:10.1016/j.ress.2008.03.031

Eichenfield, M., Chan, J., Camacho, R. M., Vahala, K. J., & Painter, O. (2009a). Optome-chanical crystals. *Nature*, *462*(7269), 78–82. doi:10.1038/nature08524 PMID:19838165

Eichenfield, M., Chan, J., Camacho, R. M., Vahala, K. J., & Painter, O. (2009b). A picogram-and nanometre-scale photonic-crystal optomechanical cavity. *Nature*, *459*(7246), 550–555. doi:10.1038/nature08061 PMID:19489118

Eichenfield, M., Chan, J., Safavi-Naeini, A. H., Vahala, K. J., & Painter, O. (2009). Modeling dispersive coupling and losses of localized optical and mechanical modes in optomechanical crystals. *Optics Express*, *17*(22), 20078. doi:10.1364/OE.17.020078 PMID:19997232

Eichhorn, A., Girimonte, D., Klose, A., & Kruse, R. (2005). Soft Computing for Automated Surface Quality Analysis of Exterior Car Body Panels. *Applied Soft Computing*, *5*(3), 301–313. doi:10.1016/j.asoc.2004.08.002

El-Kady. (2009). Microfabricated phononic crystal devices and applications. *Measurement Science & Technology*.

Eltahlawy, A.M., & Azer, M.A. (2021) Using Blockchain Technology for the Internet of Vehicles. *2021 International Mobile, Intelligent, and Ubiquitous Computing Conference, MIUCC 2021*, 54-61.

Emami, M. R., Goldenberg, A. A., & Türksen, I. B. (1998). A robust model-based fuzzy-logic controller for robot manipulators. *Proceedings of the 1988 IEEE International Conference on Robotics and Automation, 3*, 2500-2505. 10.1109/ROBOT.1998.680717

Engel. (2000). Prognostics, the real issues involved with predicting life remaining. *IEEE Aerospace Conference Proceedings*.

Erol, S., Schumacher, A., & Sihn, W. (2016). Strategic guidance towards Industry 4.0 – a three-stage process model. *International Conference on Competitive Manufacturing 2016 (COMA16)*.

Erraissi, A., Banane, M., Belangour, A., & Azzouazi, M. (2020, October 26). Big Data Storage using Model Driven Engineering: From Big Data Meta-model to Cloudera PSM meta-model. *2020 International Conference on Data Analytics for Business and Industry: Way Towards a Sustainable Economy (ICDABI)*. 10.1109/ICDABI51230.2020.9325674

Error-Correction Coding and Decoding. (n.d.). Retrieved October 19, 2022, from https://link.springer.com/book/10.1007/978-3-319-51103-0

Errousso, H., Malhene, N., Benhadou, S., & Medromi, H. (2020). Predicting car park availability for a better delivery bay management. *Procedia Computer Science, 170,* 203–210. doi:10.1016/j.procs.2020.03.026

Eryarsoy, E., Delen, D., Davazdahemami, B., & Topuz, K. (2021). A novel diffusion-based model for estimating cases, and fatalities in epidemics: The case of COVID-19. *Journal of Business Research, 124,* 163–178. doi:10.1016/j.jbusres.2020.11.054 PMID:33281248

Eureka, W.ERyan, N.E. (1994). *The Customer-Driven Company Managerial Perspective on Quality Function Deployment* (2nd ed.). ASI Press/Irwin.

Fan, W., Lu, C., & Tsujino, K. (2015). *An Automatic Machine Vision Method for the Flaw Detection on Car's Body.* IEEE 7th International Conference on Awareness Science and Technology (iCAST), Qinhuangdao, China.

Farooqi, N., Alshehri, S., Nollily, S., Najmi, L., Alqurashi, G., & Alrashedi, A. (2019). UParking: Developing a smart parking management system using the Internet of things. Sixth HCT information technology trends (ITT), 214–218. doi:10.1109/ITT48889.2019.9075113

Feder, M., Giusti, A., & Vidoni, R. (2022). An approach for automatic generation of the URDF file of modular robots from modules designed using SolidWorks. *Procedia Computer Science, 200,* 858–864. doi:10.1016/j.procs.2022.01.283

Felipe, A. J. B., Alejo, L. A., Balderama, O. F., & Rosete, E. A. (2023). Climate change intensifies the drought vulnerability of river basins: A case of the Magat River Basin. *Journal of Water and Climate Change, 14*(3), 1012–1038. doi:10.2166/wcc.2023.005

Feng, X., Yan, F., & Liu, X. (2019). Study of Wireless Communication Technologies on Internet of Things for Precision Agriculture. *Wireless Personal Communications, 108*(3), 1785–1802. doi:10.1007/s11277-019-06496-7

Fernández-Caramés, T. M., & Fraga-Lamas, P. (2018). A review on the use of blockchain for the Internet of Things. *IEEE Access : Practical Innovations, Open Solutions, 6,* 32979–33001. doi:10.1109/ACCESS.2018.2842685

Fierro-Radilla, A., Nakano-Miyatake, M., Cedillo-Hernandez, M., Cleofas-Sanchez, L., & Perez-Meana, H. (2019, May). A robust image zero-watermarking using convolutional neural networks. In *2019 7th International Workshop on Biometrics and Forensics (IWBF)* (pp. 1-5). IEEE. 10.1109/IWBF.2019.8739245

Fossorier, M. P. C., & Lin, S. (1995). Soft-decision decoding of linear block codes based on ordered statistics. *IEEE Transactions on Information Theory, 41*(5), 1379–1396. doi:10.1109/18.412683

Furon, T., Moreau, N., & Duhamel, P. (2000, June). Audio asymmetric watermarking technique. *Int. Conf. on Audio, Speech and Signal Processing.*

Garcia, J. H., Cherry, T. L., Kallbekken, S., & Torvanger, A. (2016). Willingness to accept local wind energy development: Does the compensation mechanism matter? *Energy Policy, 99,* 165–173. doi:10.1016/j.enpol.2016.09.046

Garg, H. a. (2018). Design and Simulation of Wind Turbine Emulator. In *2018 IEEE 8th Power India International Conference (PIICON)* (pp. 1-6). 10.1109/POWERI.2018.8704424

Garvin, D. A. (1986). Quality Problems, Policies, and Attitudes in the United States and Japan: An Exploratory Study. *Academy of Management Journal, 29*(4), 653–673. doi:10.2307/255938

Gautam, R. (2023). Groundwater Markets structure and its evolution: A study of Karnal District, Haryana, India. *Environment, Development and Sustainability,* 1–36. doi:10.1007/s10668-023-03423-6

Ghari, B., Tourani, A., & Shahbahrami, A. (2022). A Robust Pedestrian Detection Approach for Autonomous Vehicles. *Proceedings - 2022 8th International Iranian Conference on Signal Processing and Intelligent Systems, ICSPIS 2022.* 10.1109/ICSPIS56952.2022.10043934

Ghelam. (2006). Integration of Health Monitoring in the Avionics Maintenance System. *IFAC Proceedings Volumes.*

Girshick, R. (2015). Fast R-CNN. *Proceedings of the IEEE International Conference on Computer Vision, 2015 International Conference on Computer Vision, ICCV 2015*, 1440-1448. 10.1109/ICCV.2015.169

Glaessgen, E., & Stargel, D. (2012). The Digital Twin Paradigm for future NASA and U.S. Air Force Vehicles. *53rd AIAA/ASME/ASCE/AHS/ASC Structures, Structural Dynamics and Materials Conference; 20th AIAA/ASME/AHS Adaptive Structures Conference.* 10.2514/6.2012-1818

Gorishny, Maldovan, Ullal, & Thomas. (2005). Sound ideas. *Physics World, 18*, 24.

Gouriveau, Medjaher, Ramasso, & Zerhouni. (2013). PHM - Prognostics and health management - De la surveillance au pronostic de défaillances de systèmes complexes. Éditions Techniques de l'Ingénieur.

Govers, C. P. (2000). QFD not just a tool but a way of quality management. *J. Production Economics.*

Gowland, R. (2006). The accidental risk assessment methodology for industries (ARAMIS)/layer of protection analysis (LOPA) methodology: A step forward towards convergent practices in risk assessment? *Journal of Hazardous Materials, 130*(3), 307–310. doi:10.1016/j.jhazmat.2005.07.007 PMID:16139426

Grassl, M. (n.d.). *Bounds on the minimum distance of linear codes and quantum codes.* http://www.codetables.de

Grassl, M. (2006). Searching for linear codes with large minimum distance. In W. Bosma & J. Cannon (Eds.), *Discovering Mathematics with Magma: Reducing the Abstract to the Concrete* (pp. 287–313). Springer., doi:10.1007/978-3-540-37634-7_13

Grati, R., Loukil, F., Boukadi, K., & Abed, M. (2023). A blockchain-based framework for circular end-of-life vehicle processing. *Cluster Computing*, 1–14. doi:10.1007/s10586-023-03981-4

Grekousis, G. (2019). Artificial neural networks and deep learning in urban geography: A systematic review and meta-analysis. *Computers, Environment and Urban Systems, 74*, 244–256. doi:10.1016/j.compenvurbsys.2018.10.008

Grieves, M. (2014). *Digital twin: manufacturing excellence through virtual factory replication.* White paper, 1, 2014. pp. 1–7.

GrievesM. (2016). *Origins of the Digital Twin Concept.* Florida Institute of Technology. doi:2016.10.13140/RG.2.2.26367.61609

Grobshtein, Y., & Dori, D. (2008). *Evaluating Aspects of System Modeling Languages by Example: SysML and OPM.* Israel Institute of Technology.

Guardo, E. (2018). A Fog Computing-based IoT Framework for Precision Agriculture. *Journal of Internet Technology, 19*(5), 1401–1411. doi:10.3966/160792642018091905012

Gulati, U., Ishaan, & Dass, R. (2020). Intelligent Car with Voice Assistance and Obstacle Detector to Aid the Disabled. *Procedia Computer Science, 167*, 1732–1738. doi:10.1016/j.procs.2020.03.383

Gupta, A., Singh, G. P., Gupta, B., & Ghosh, S. (2022). LSTM based real-time smart parking system. In *IEEE 7th International conference for Convergence in Technology (I2CT), Mumbai, India, 2022* (pp. 1–7). 10.1109/I2CT54291.2022.9824249

Guven, I., & Parlak, M. (2022). Blockchain, AI and IoT Empowered Swarm Drones for Precision Agriculture Applications. *IEEE 1st Global Emerging Technology Blockchain Forum: Blockchain & Beyond (iGETblockchain)*, 1-6. 10.1109/iGETblockchain56591.2022.10087152

Haag, S., & Anderl, R. (2018). Digital Twin – Proof of Concept. *Manufacturing Letters*, *15*, 64–66. doi:10.1016/j.mfglet.2018.02.006

Hadamard, J. (1893). *Resolution d'une question relative aux determinants - in Bulletin des Sciences Mathematiques, Septembre 1893* (1st ed.). See Description.

Hafian, A., Benbrahim, M., & Kabbaj, M. N. (2021). Design and Implementation of Smart Irrigation System Based on the IoT Architecture. *Lecture Notes in Networks and Systems*, *211*, 345–354. doi:10.1007/978-3-030-73882-2_32

Hafian, A., Benbrahim, M., & Kabbaj, M. N. (2023). IoT-based smart irrigation management system using real-time data. *Iranian Journal of Electrical and Computer Engineering*, *13*(6), 7078–7088. doi:10.11591/ijece.v13i6.pp7078-7088

Hájek, P. (2013). *Metamathematics of fuzzy logic* (Vol. 4). Springer Science & Business Media.

Hallioui, A., Herrou, B., Santos, R. S., Katina, P. F., & Egbue, O. (2022). Systems-based approach to contemporary business management: An enabler of business sustainability in a context of industry 4.0, circular economy, competitiveness and diverse stakeholders. *Journal of Cleaner Production*, *373*, 133819. doi:10.1016/j.jclepro.2022.133819

Hamdani, M., Butt, W. H., Anwar, M. W., Ahsan, I., Azam, F., & Ahmed, M. A. (2019). A Novel Framework to Automatically Generate IFML Models From Plain Text Requirements. *IEEE Access : Practical Innovations, Open Solutions*, *7*, 183489–183513. doi:10.1109/ACCESS.2019.2959813

Hampson, K. (2015). Technical evaluation of the Systems Modeling Language (SysML), Conference on Systems Engineering Research. *Procedia Computer Science, 44*, 403 – 412.

Handfield. (2006). The state of JOM: An outgoing editor's (retro)spective. *Journal of Operations Management, 24*, 417-420.

Haque, K. F., Abdelgawad, A., Yanambaka, V. P., & Yelamarthi, K. (2020). LoRa Architecture for V2X Communication: An Experimental Evaluation with Vehicles on the Move. *Sensors (Basel)*, *20*(23), 6876. doi:10.3390/s20236876 PMID:33271857

Hashemi, S. A., Condo, C., & Gross, W. J. (2016). Simplified Successive-Cancellation List decoding of polar codes. *2016 IEEE International Symposium on Information Theory (ISIT)*, 815–819. 10.1109/ISIT.2016.7541412

Hashemi, S. A., Condo, C., & Gross, W. J. (2017). Fast and Flexible Successive-Cancellation List Decoders for Polar Codes. *IEEE Transactions on Signal Processing*, *65*(21), 5756–5769. doi:10.1109/TSP.2017.2740204

Hashemy Shahdany, S. M., Taghvaeian, S., Maestre, J. M., & Firoozfar, A. R. (2019). Developing a centralized automatic control system to increase flexibility of water delivery within predictable and unpredictable irrigation water demands. *Computers and Electronics in Agriculture*, *163*, 104862. doi:10.1016/j.compag.2019.104862

Hasking, C. (2006). *Systems engineering handbook*. INCOSE. Version 3.

Hazraet, A. (2023). Fog computing for next-generation Internet of Things: Fundamental, state-of-the-art and research challenges. *Computer Science Review*, *48*, 100549. doi:10.1016/j.cosrev.2023.100549

Hern, A. (2017, August 31). Hacking risk leads to recall of 500,000 pacemakers due to patient death fears. *The Guardian*. https://www.theguardian.com/technology/2017/aug/31/hacking-risk-recall-pacemakers-patient-death-fears-fda-firmware-update

Himani, G. a. (2015). Modelling and Development of Wind Turbine Emulator for the Condition Monitoring of Wind Turbine. *International Journal of Renewable Energy Research*, 591-597.

Hinton, G. E., Osindero, S., & Teh, Y. W. (2006). A fast learning algorithm for deep belief nets. *Neural Computation*, *18*(7), 1527–1554. doi:10.1162/neco.2006.18.7.1527 PMID:16764513

Hoffman, M. D., & Gelman, A. (2014). The No-U-Turn sampler: Adaptively setting path lengths in Hamiltonian Monte Carlo. *Journal of Machine Learning Research*, *15*(1), 1593–1623.

Hollnagel, E. (2008). Risk + barriers = safety? *Safety Science*, *46*(2), 221–229. doi:10.1016/j.ssci.2007.06.028

Huang, A., Pan, M., Tian, Z., & Li, X. (2018). *Static extraction of IFML models for Android apps*. doi:10.1145/3270112.3278185

Huang, G., Li, Y., Wang, Q., Ren, J., Cheng, Y., & Zhao, X. (2019). Automatic Classification Method for Software Vulnerability Based on Deep Neural Network. *IEEE Access : Practical Innovations, Open Solutions*, *7*, 28291–28298. doi:10.1109/ACCESS.2019.2900462

Hu, H., Liu, Y., Liu, M., & Nie, L. (2016). Surface defect classification in large-scale strip steel image collection via hybrid chromosome genetic algorithm. *Neurocomputing*, *181*, 86–95. doi:10.1016/j.neucom.2015.05.134

Hui, C. X., Dan, G., Alamri, S., & Toghraie, D. (2023). Greening smart cities: An investigation of the integration of urban natural resources and smart city technologies for promoting environmental sustainability. *Sustainable Cities and Society*, *99*, 104985. doi:10.1016/j.scs.2023.104985

Imad. (2014). *These: Conception et déploiement des Systèmes de Production Reconfigurables et Agiles (SPRA)*. Academic Press.

Immanuel, J., Bersha, B., Boomadevi, M., Soundiraraj, N., Narayanan, K. L., & Krishnan, R. S. (2023). An Efficient IoT based Smart Vehicle Parking Management System. In *7th International Conference on Computing Methodologies and Communication (ICCMC), Erode, India, 2023* (pp. 1224–1228). 10.1109/ICCMC56507.2023.10083977

Iqbal, F., Altaf, A., Waris, Z., Aray, D. G., Miguel, A. L. F., Isabel de la Torre, D., & Ashraf, I. (2023). Blockchain-Modeled Edge-Computing-Based Smart Home Monitoring System with Energy Usage Prediction. *Sensors (Basel)*, *23*(11), 5263. doi:10.3390/s23115263 PMID:37299993

Jacobs, R. M. (1996). Product recall—A vendor/vendee nightmare. *Microelectronics and Reliability*, *36*(1), 101–103. doi:10.1016/0026-2714(95)00001-I

Jafari, S., & Byun, Y.-C. (2023). Optimizing Battery RUL Prediction of Lithium-Ion Batteries Based on Harris Hawk Optimization Approach Using Random Forest and LightGBM. *IEEE Access : Practical Innovations, Open Solutions*, *11*, 87034–87046. doi:10.1109/ACCESS.2023.3304699

Jagadeesh, B., Kumar, P. R., & Reddy, P. C. (2015). Fuzzy inference system based robust digital image watermarking technique using discrete cosine transform. *Procedia Computer Science*, *46*, 1618–1625. doi:10.1016/j.procs.2015.02.095

Jagannatam, A. (2008). *Mersenne Twister–A Pseudo random number generator and its variants*. George Mason University, Department of Electrical and Computer Engineering.

Jaikishore, C. N., Arunkumar, G. P., Srinath, A. J., Vamsi, H., Srinivasan, K., Ramesh, R. K., Jayaraman, K., & Ramachandran, P. (2022). Implementation of Deep Learning Algorithm on a Custom Dataset for Advanced Driver Assistance Systems Applications. *Applied Sciences (Basel, Switzerland)*, *12*(18), 8927. Advance online publication. doi:10.3390/app12188927

Jalajamony, H. M., Nair, M., Jones-Whitehead, M., Abbas, M. I., Harris, N., & Fernandez, R. E. (2023). Aerial to Terrestrial Edge Communication Using LoRa in Drone-Aided Precision Agriculture. *SoutheastCon, 722–723*, 722–723. Advance online publication. doi:10.1109/SoutheastCon51012.2023.10115215

Jamil, F., Ibrahim, M., Ullah, I., Kim, S., Kahng, H. K., & Kim, D.-H. (2022). Optimal smart contract for autonomous greenhouse environment based on IoT blockchain network in agriculture. *Computers and Electronics in Agriculture, 192*, 106573. doi:10.1016/j.compag.2021.106573

Jan, F., Min-Allah, N., & Düştegör, D. (2021). Iot based smart water quality monitoring: Recent techniques, trends and challenges for domestic applications. *Water (Basel), 13*(13), 1729. doi:10.3390/w13131729

Jardine, A. K. S., Lin, D., & Banjevic, D. (2006). A review on machinery diagnostics and prognostics implementing condition-based maintenance. *Mechanical Systems and Signal Processing, 20*(7), 1483–1510. doi:10.1016/j.ymssp.2005.09.012

Javaid, M., Haleem, A., Singh, R. P., Suman, R., & Gonzalez, E. S. (2022). Understanding the adoption of Industry 4.0 technologies in improving environmental sustainability. *Sustainable Operations and Computers, 3*, 203–217. doi:10.1016/j.susoc.2022.01.008

Jdid, T., Benbrahim, M., Kabbaj, M. N., Naji, M., & Benboubker, M. B. (2023, January). A New Compartmental Model for Analyzing COVID-19 Spread Within Homogeneous Populations. In *International Conference on Digital Technologies and Applications* (pp. 976-985). Cham: Springer Nature Switzerland. 10.1007/978-3-031-29857-8_97

Jha, K., Doshi, A., Patel, P., & Shah, M. (2019). A comprehensive review on automation in agriculture using artificial intelligence. *Artificial Intelligence in Agriculture, 2*, 1–12. doi:10.1016/j.aiia.2019.05.004

Jihani, N., Kabbaj, M. N., & Benbrahim, M. (2023). Sensor fault detection and isolation for smart irrigation wireless sensor network based on parity space. *Iranian Journal of Electrical and Computer Engineering, 13*(2), 1463–1471. doi:10.11591/ijece.v13i2.pp1463-1471

Jin, R., Xu, Y., Xue, W., Li, B., Yang, Y., & Chen, W. (2022). An Improved Mobilenetv3-Yolov5 Infrared Target Detection Algorithm Based on Attention Distillation. Lecture Notes of the Institute for Computer Sciences, Social-Informatics and Telecommunications Engineering, 416. doi:10.1007/978-3-030-94551-0_22

Jin, X., Li, Z., & Yang, H. (2021). Pedestrian Detection with YOLOv5 in Autonomous Driving Scenario. *2021 5th CAA International Conference on Vehicular Control and Intelligence, CVCI 2021.* 10.1109/CVCI54083.2021.9661188

Joannopoulos, J. D., Johnson, S. G., Winn, J. N., & Meade, R. D. (2008). *Photonic Crystals: Molding the Flow of Light.* Princeton University Press.

Johnson, S. G., Ibanescu, M., Skorobagatiy, M. A., & Weisberg, O. (2002). Perturbation theory for Maxwell's equations with shifting material boundaries. *Physical Review E: Statistical, Nonlinear, and Soft Matter Physics, 65*(6), 066611. doi:10.1103/PhysRevE.65.066611 PMID:12188855

Jones, D., Snider, C., Nassehi, A., Yon, J., & Hicks, B. (2020). Characterising the Digital Twin: A Systematic Literature Review. *CIRP Journal of Manufacturing Science and Technology, 29*, 36–52. doi:10.1016/j.cirpj.2020.02.002

Juliette, Pierre-Olivier, & Reydellet. (2018). *L'intelligence artificielle au service de maintenance prévisionnelle.* 4ième conférence sur les Applications Pratiques de l'Intelligence Artificielle APIA, Nancy, France.

Jurado Murillo, F., Quintero Yoshioka, J. S., Varela López, A. D., Salazar-Cabrera, R., Pachón de la Cruz, Á., & Madrid Molina, J. M. (2020). Experimental Evaluation of LoRa in Transit Vehicle Tracking Service Based on Intelligent Transportation Systems and IoT. *Electronics (Basel), 9*(11), 1950. doi:10.3390/electronics9111950

Kali, Y., Saad, M., Benjelloun, K., & Benbrahim, M. (2016). Sliding Mode with Time Delay Control for Robot Manipulators. In Studies in systems, decision and control (pp. 135–156). doi:10.1007/978-981-10-2374-38

Kallel, I. F., Chaari, A., Frikha, M., Kammoun, S., & Trigui, A. (2022, May). DWT based blind and robust watermarking technique using ABCD map for medical image. In *2022 6th International Conference on Advanced Technologies for Signal and Image Processing (ATSIP)* (pp. 1-6). IEEE. 10.1109/ATSIP55956.2022.9805942

Kallel, I. F., Grati, A., & Taktak, A. (2023). 3D Data Security: Robust 3D Mesh Watermarking Approach for Copyright Protection. In Examining Multimedia Forensics and Content Integrity (pp. 1-37). IGI Global.

Kallel, I. F., Kallel, M., Garcia, E., & Bouhlel, M. S. (2006, May). Fragile watermarking for medical image authentication. In *The 2nd International Conference on Distributed Frameworks for Multimedia Applications* (pp. 1-6). IEEE. 10.1109/DFMA.2006.296919

Kallel, I. F., Bouhlel, M. S., Lapayre, J. C., & Garcia, E. (2009). Control of dermatology image integrity using reversible watermarking. *International Journal of Imaging Systems and Technology*, 19(1), 5–9. doi:10.1002/ima.20172

Kallel, I., Lapayre, J. C., & Bouhlel, M. (2008). Medical Image Semi-fragile Watermarking in the Frequential Field. *Journal of Testing and Evaluation*, 36(6), 540–545.

Kamaruddin, N. S., Kamsin, A., Por, L. Y., & Rahman, H. (2018). A review of text watermarking: Theory, methods, and applications. *IEEE Access : Practical Innovations, Open Solutions*, 6, 8011–8028. doi:10.1109/ACCESS.2018.2796585

Kamienski. (2018). SWAMP: An IoT-based smart water management platform for precision irrigation in agriculture. *Global IoT Summit (GIoTS)*. doi:10.1109/GIOTS.2018.8534541

Kamienski, C., Soininen, J.-P., Taumberger, M., Dantas, R., Toscano, A., Salmon Cinotti, T., Filev Maia, R., & Torre Neto, A. (2019). Smart Water Management Platform: IoT-Based Precision Irrigation for Agriculture. *Sensors (Basel)*, 19(2), 276. doi:10.3390/s19020276 PMID:30641960

Kapassa, E., Themistocleous, M., Christodoulou, K., & Iosif, E. (2021). Blockchain application in internet of vehicles: Challenges, contributions and current limitations. *Future Internet*, 13(12), 313. doi:10.3390/fi13120313

Katoch, S., Chauhan, S. S., & Kumar, V. (2021). A review on genetic algorithm: Past, present, and future. *Multimedia Tools and Applications*, 80(5), 8091–8126. doi:10.1007/s11042-020-10139-6 PMID:33162782

Ke, X. U., Lei, W., & Wang, J. (2016). Surface defect recognition of hot-rolled steel plates based on tetrolet transform. *Jixie Gongcheng Xuebao*.

Khan, A. H., Munir, M., Van Elst, L., & Dengel, A. (2022). F2DNet: Fast Focal Detection Network for Pedestrian Detection. In *Proceedings—International Conference on Pattern Recognition* (pp. 4658-4664). 10.1109/ICPR56361.2022.9956732

Khan, A. H., Nawaz, M. S., & Dengel, A. (2023). Localized Semantic Feature Mixers for Efficient Pedestrian Detection in Autonomous Driving. In *Proceedings of the IEEE Computer Society Conference on Computer Vision and Pattern Recognition* (pp. 5476-5485). 10.1109/CVPR52729.2023.00530

Khanal, S., Fulton, J., & Shearer, S. (2017). An overview of current and potential applications of thermal remote sensing in precision agriculture. *Computers and Electronics in Agriculture*, 139, 22–32. doi:10.1016/j.compag.2017.05.001

Khan, I., & Kabir, Z. (2020). Waste-to-energy generation technologies and the developing economies: A multi-criteria analysis for sustainability assessment. *Renewable Energy*, 150, 320–333. doi:10.1016/j.renene.2019.12.132

Khanna, A., & Kaur, S. (2019). Evolution of Internet of Things (IoT) and its significant impact in the field of Precision Agriculture. *Computers and Electronics in Agriculture*, 157, 218–231. doi:10.1016/j.compag.2018.12.039

Kharmoum, N., Ziti, S., Rhazali, Y., & Omary, F. (2019, June 1). An Automatic Transformation Method from the E3value Model to IFML Model: An MDA Approach. *Journal of Computational Science, 15*(6), 800–813. doi:10.3844/jcssp.2019.800.813

Khebbou, D., Chana, I., & Ben-azza, H. (n.d.-a). *Decoding of the Extended Golay Code by the Simplified Successive-Cancellation List Decoder adapted to Multi-Kernel Polar Code.* Academic Press.

Khebbou, D., Chana, I., & Ben-azza, H. (n.d.-b). *Single Parity Check Node Adapted to Polar Codes with Dynamic Frozen Bit Equivalent to Binary Linear Block Codes.* Academic Press.

Khebbou, D., Idriss, C., & Ben-azza, H. (2023, May 27). *Adaptation of deep learning-based polar code decoding technique for linear block code decoding.* Academic Press.

Khebbou, D., Benkhouya, R., & Chana, I. (2022). Construction of Some Good Binary Linear Codes Using Hadamard Matrix and BCH Codes. In X.-S. Yang, S. Sherratt, N. Dey, & A. Joshi (Eds.), *Proceedings of Sixth International Congress on Information and Communication Technology* (pp. 523–532). Springer. 10.1007/978-981-16-2377-6_49

Khebbou, D., Benkhouya, R., Chana, I., & Ben-azza, H. (2021). Finding Good Binary Linear Block Codes based on Hadamard Matrix and Existing Popular Codes. *International Journal of Advanced Computer Science and Applications, 12*(11). Advance online publication. doi:10.14569/IJACSA.2021.0121150

Khebbou, D., Chana, I., & Ben-azza, H. (2021). Simplified successive-cancellation list polar decoding for binary linear block codes. *Journal of Southwest Jiaotong University, 56*(6), 6. Advance online publication. doi:10.35741/issn.0258-2724.56.6.54

KhebbouD.IdrissC.Ben-azzaH. (2022). *Décodage des codes en blocs linéaires par les techniques des codes polaires.* doi:10.13140/RG.2.2.15406.08002

Khlif, W., Elleuch Ben Ayed, N., & Ben-Abdallah, H. (2018). From a BPMN Model to an Aligned UML Analysis Model. *Proceedings of the 13th International Conference on Software Technologies.* 10.5220/0006866606570665

Kim, J., Huh, J., Park, I., Bak, J., Kim, D., & Lee, S. (2022). Small Object Detection in Infrared Images: Learning from Imbalanced Cross-Domain Data via Domain Adaptation. *Applied Sciences (Basel, Switzerland), 12*(21), 11201. Advance online publication. doi:10.3390/app122111201

Kirikkaleli, D. a. (2021). Do public-private partnerships in energy and renewable energy consumption matter for consumption-based carbon dioxide emissions in India? *Environmental Science and Pollution Research, 28*, 30139-30152.

Kitchenham, B., & Charters, S. (2007). *Guidelines for Performing Systematic Literature Reviews in Software Engineering.* Technical Report EBSE 2007-001 Keele University and Durham University Joint Report. Récupéré sur https://www.elsevier.com/__data/promis_misc/525444systematicreviewsguide.pdf

Kochovski, P., Gec, S., Stankovski, V., Bajec, M., & Drobintsev, P. D. (2019). Trust management in a blockchain based fog computing platform with trustless smart oracles. *Future Generation Computer Systems, 101*, 747–759. doi:10.1016/j.future.2019.07.030

Komurcugil, H., Biricik, S., Bayhan, S., & Zhang, Z. (2021). Sliding mode control: Overview of its applications in power converters. *IEEE Industrial Electronics Magazine, 15*(1), 40–49. doi:10.1109/MIE.2020.2986165

Kongara, R., & Raja, R. (2012). Wavelet-based oblivious medical image watermarking scheme using genetic algorithm. *IET Medical Image Processing, 6*(4), 364-373.

Koren, I., & Klamma, R. (2018). The Exploitation of OpenAPI Documentation for the Generation of Web Frontends. *Companion of the Web Conference 2018 on the Web Conference 2018 - WWW '18.* doi:10.1145/3184558.3188740

Kowsari, K., Meimandi, K. J., Heidarysafa, M., Mendu, S., Barnes, L. E., & Brown, D. E. (2019). Text Classification Algorithms: A Survey. *Information (Basel)*, *10*(4), 150. doi:10.3390/info10040150

Kraus, S., Breier, M., & Dasí-Rodrígue, S. (2020). The art of crafting a systematic literature review in entrepreneurship research. *The International Entrepreneurship and Management Journal*, *16*(3), 1023–1042. doi:10.1007/s11365-020-00635-4

Kretthika, P., Vinutha Yadav, D., & Ashwini, K. (2017). Survey on copyright protection in peer to peer network. *International Journal of Engineering Research and Applications*, *7*(05), 33–40. doi:10.9790/9622-0705013340

Krishnan, R. S., Narayanan, K. L., Bharathi, S. T., Deepa, N., Murali, S. M., Kumar, M. A., & Prakash, C. R. T. S. (2022). Machine learning based efficient and secured car parking system. In *Recent advances in internet of things and machine learning* (pp. 129–145). Springer. doi:10.1007/978-3-030-90119-6_11

Krizhevsky, A., Sutskever, I., & Hinton, G. E. (2017). Imagenet classifcation with deep convolutional neural networks. *Communications of the ACM*, *60*(6), 84–90. doi:10.1145/3065386

Kumaraswamy, E., Kumar, G. M., Mahender, K., Bukkapatnam, K., & Prasad, C. R. (2020, December). Digital Watermarking: State of The Art and Research Challenges in Health Care & Multimedia Applications. *IOP Conference Series. Materials Science and Engineering*, *981*(3), 032031. doi:10.1088/1757-899X/981/3/032031

Kuran, M. S., Carneiro Viana, A., Iannone, L., Kofman, D., Mermoud, G., & Vasseur, J. P. (2015). A Smart Parking lot management system for scheduling the recharging of electric vehicles. *IEEE Transactions on Smart Grid*, *6*(6), 2942–2953. doi:10.1109/TSG.2015.2403287

Kushwaha, M. S., Halevi, P., Dobrzynski, L., & Djafari-Rouhani, B. (1993). Acoustic band structure of periodic elastic composites. *Physical Review Letters*, *71*(13), 2022–2025. doi:10.1103/PhysRevLett.71.2022 PMID:10054563

Kwok Tsui, Chen, Zhou, Hai, & Wenbin. (2015). Prognostics and Health Management: A Review on Data Driven Approaches. *Mathematical Problems in Engineering*. doi:10.1155/2015/793161

Laaz, N., Wakil, K., Mbarki, S., & Jawawi, D. N. (2018, September 1). Comparative Analysis of Interaction Flow Modeling Language Tools. *Journal of Computational Science*, *14*(9), 1267–1278. doi:10.3844/jcssp.2018.1267.1278

Lachgar, M., & Abdali, A. (2014, October). Generating Android graphical user interfaces using an MDA approach. *2014 Third IEEE International Colloquium in Information Science and Technology (CIST)*. 10.1109/CIST.2014.7016598

LaClair, A. (2016). *A Survey on Hadamard Matrices*. Chancellor's Honors Program Projects. https://trace.tennessee.edu/utk_chanhonoproj/1971

Lameche. (2018). *Proposition d'une méthodologie pour la conception des systèmes de production reconfigurables et d'un outil associé d'aide à la décision par simulation de flux* [Thesis]. Université de Nantes, Soutenue.

Lasnier, G. (2011). *Sûreté de fonctionnement des équipements et calculs de fiabilité*. Lavoisier.

Le, T. (2016). *Contribution to deterioration modeling and residual life estimation based on condition monitoring data* [PhD thesis]. Université Grenoble Alpes.

LeCun, Y., Bengio, Y., & Hinton, G. (2015). Deep learning. *Nature*, *521*(7553), 436–444. doi:10.1038/nature14539 PMID:26017442

Lee, J. E., Seo, Y. H., & Kim, D. W. (2020). Convolutional neural network-based digital image watermarking adaptive to the resolution of image and watermark. *Applied Sciences (Basel, Switzerland)*, *10*(19), 6854. doi:10.3390/app10196854

Lee, J., Ni, J., Djurdjanovic, D., Qiu, H., & Liao, H. (2006). Intelligent prognostics tools and e-maintenance. *Computers in Industry*, *57*(6), 476–489. doi:10.1016/j.compind.2006.02.014

Leo Brousmiche, K., Durand, A., Heno, T., Poulain, C., Dalmieres, A., & Ben Hamida, E. (2018). Hybrid Cryptographic Protocol for Secure Vehicle Data Sharing over a Consortium Blockchain. *Proceedings - IEEE 2018 International Congress on Cybermatics: 2018 IEEE Conferences on Internet of Things, Green Computing and Communications, Cyber, Physical and Social Computing, Smart Data, Blockchain, Computer and Information Technology, iThings/GreenCom/CPSCom/SmartData/Blockchain/CIT 2018*, 1281-1286. 10.1109/Cybermatics_2018.2018.00223

Leone, G. R., Moroni, D., Pieri, G., Petracca, M., Salvetti, O., Azzarà, A., & Marino, F. (2017). An intelligent cooperative visual sensor network for urban mobility. *Sensors (Basel)*, *17*(11), 2588. doi:10.3390/s17112588 PMID:29125535

Li, H., Xu, Z., Taylor, G., Studer, C., & Goldstein, T. (2017). *Visualizing the loss landscape of neural nets.* arXiv preprint, arXiv:1712.09913.

Li, M., Liu, B., Sun, J., Zhang, G., & Su, W. (2022). Multimodality pedestrian detection based on YOLOv5. *Proceedings of SPIE - The International Society for Optical Engineering*, *12456*. 10.1117/12.2659653

Li, D., Liang, L. Q., & Zhang, W. J. (2014). Defect inspection and extraction of the mobile phone cover glass based on the principal components analysis. *International Journal of Advanced Manufacturing Technology*, *73*(9-12), 1605–1614. doi:10.1007/s00170-014-5871-y

Li, J., Su, Z., Geng, J., & Yin, Y. (2018). Real-time Detection of Steel Strip Surface Defects Based on Improved YOLO Detection Network. *IFAC-PapersOnLine*, *51*(21), 76–81. doi:10.1016/j.ifacol.2018.09.412

Li, M.-L., Sun, G.-B., & Yu, J.-X. (2023). A Pedestrian Detection Network Model Based on Improved YOLOv5. *Entropy (Basel, Switzerland)*, *25*(2), 381. Advance online publication. doi:10.3390/e25020381 PMID:36832747

Lin, S. B., Wang, Y., & Zhou, D. X. (2021). *Generalization performance of empirical risk minimization on over-parameterized deep relu nets.* arXiv preprint, arXiv:2111.14039.

Lin, C.-Y., Huang, Y.-C., Shieh, S.-L., & Chen, P.-N. (2020). Transformation of Binary Linear Block Codes to Polar Codes With Dynamic Frozen. *IEEE Open Journal of the Communications Society*, *1*, 333–341. doi:10.1109/OJ-COMS.2020.2979529

Lin, J., Chen, S. Y., Chang, C. Y., & Chen, G. (2019). SPA: Smart parking algorithm based on driver behavior and parking traffic predictions. *IEEE Access: Practical Innovations, Open Solutions*, *7*, 34275–34288. doi:10.1109/ACCESS.2019.2904972

Lin, N., Wang, X., Zhang, Y., Hu, X., & Ruan, J. (2020). Fertigation management for sustainable precision agriculture based on Internet of Things. *Journal of Cleaner Production*, *277*, 124119. doi:10.1016/j.jclepro.2020.124119

Lin, T., Rivano, H., & Le Mouël, F. (2017). A survey of smart parking solutions. *IEEE Transactions on Intelligent Transportation Systems*, *18*(12), 3229–3253. doi:10.1109/TITS.2017.2685143

Lin, W., Huang, X., Fang, H., Wang, V., Hua, Y., Wang, J., Yin, H., Yi, D., & Yau, L. (2020). Blockchain Technology in Current Agricultural Systems: From Techniques to Applications. *IEEE Access : Practical Innovations, Open Solutions*, *8*, 143920–143937. doi:10.1109/ACCESS.2020.3014522

Lin, Y.-P., Petway, J., Anthony, J., Mukhtar, H., Liao, S.-W., Chou, C.-F., & Ho, Y.-F. (2017). Blockchain: The evolutionary next step for ICT e-agriculture. *Environments (Basel, Switzerland)*, *4*(3), 2076–3298. doi:10.3390/environments4030050

Li, Q., Guan, X., Wu, P., Wang, X., Zhou, L., Tong, Y., Ren, R., Leung, K. S. M., Lau, E. H. Y., Wong, J. Y., Xing, X., Xiang, N., Wu, Y., Li, C., Chen, Q., Li, D., Liu, T., Zhao, J., Liu, M., ... Feng, Z. (2020). Early transmission dynamics in Wuhan, China, of novel coronavirus–infected pneumonia. *The New England Journal of Medicine, 382*(13), 1199–1207. doi:10.1056/NEJMoa2001316 PMID:31995857

Li, T., Song, X., Gao, S., Chen, C., Liu, K., & Liu, J. (2022). Research on Visible Light Pedestrian Detection Algorithm Based on Improved YOLOv5m. *2022 International Conference on Mechanical and Electronics Engineering, ICMEE 2022*, 305-311. 10.1109/ICMEE56406.2022.10093673

Liu, W., Anguelov, D., Erhan, D., Szegedy, C., Reed, S., Fu, C.-Y., & Berg, A. C. (2016). SSD: Single shot multibox detector. Lecture Notes in Computer Science, 9905, 21-37. doi:10.1007/978-3-319-46448-0_2

Lucas, A., Geneiatakis, D., Soupionis, Y., Nai-Fovino, I., & Kotsakis, E. (2021). Blockchain technology applied to energy demand response service tracking and data sharing. *Energies, 14*(7), 1881. doi:10.3390/en14071881

Luis, T. (2010). *Modèles et méthodes pour une conception hautement productive orientée vers la fabrication: application à l'ingénierie routinière de pièces plastiques* [Thesis]. Université de Technologie de Belfort-Montbéliard-UTBM.

Lu, M. H., Feng, L., & Chen, Y.-F. (2009, December). Phononic crystals and acoustic metamaterials. *Materials Today, 12*(12), 34–42. doi:10.1016/S1369-7021(09)70315-3

Lu, Y. (2017). Industry 4.0: A survey on technologies, applications and open research issues. *Journal of Industrial Information Integration, 6,* 1–10. doi:10.1016/j.jii.2017.04.005

Lyonnet, B. (2010). *Amélioration de la performance industrielle: vers un système de production Lean adapté aux entreprises du pôle de compétitivité* [Thesis]. Arve Industries Haute-Savoie Mont-Blanc.

Ma, Z., Richard Yu, F., Jiang, X., & Boukerche, A. (2020) Trustworthy Traffic Information Sharing Secured via Blockchain in VANET. *DIVANet 2020 – Proceedings of the 10th ACM Symposium on Design and Analysis of Intelligent Vehicular Networks and Applications,* 33-40.

Mackey, A., Spachos, P., & Plataniotis, K. N. (2020). Smart parking system based on Bluetooth low energy beacons with particle filtering. *IEEE Systems Journal, 14*(3), 3371–3382. doi:10.1109/JSYST.2020.2968883

Magne, L., & Vasseur, D. (2006). Risques industriels-Complexité, incertitude et décision: une approche interdisciplinaire. *Recherche, 67*(2).

Mahesh, B. (2020). Machine Learning Algorithms - A Review. *International Journal of Scientific Research, 9*(1). Advance online publication. doi:10.21275/ART20203995 381

Maho, T., Furon, T., & Le Merrer, E. (2023). FBI: Fingerprinting models with Benign Inputs. *IEEE Transactions on Information Forensics and Security, 18,* 5459–5472. doi:10.1109/TIFS.2023.3301268

Mahto, D. K., & Singh, A. K. (2021). A survey of color image watermarking: State-of-the-art and research directions. *Computers & Electrical Engineering, 93,* 107255. doi:10.1016/j.compeleceng.2021.107255

Maldovan & Thomas. (2006a). Simultaneous complete elastic and electromagnetic band gaps in periodic structures. *Appl. Phys. B, 83,* 595-600.

Maldovan, M., & Thomas, E. L. (2006b). Simultaneous localization of photons and phonons in twodimensional periodic structures. *Applied Physics Letters, 88,* 251907. doi:10.1063/1.2216885

Manju Bala, Usharani, Ananth Kumar, Rajmohan, & Pavithra. (2022). Blockchain-Based IoT Architecture for Software-Defined Networking. *Blockchain, Artificial Intelligence, and the Internet of Things: Possibilities and Opportunities,* 91-115.

Manoj, T., Krishnamoorthi, M., & Narendra, V. (2023). A trusted IoT data sharing and secure oracle based access for agricultural production risk management. *Computers and Electronics in Agriculture, 204*, 107544. doi:10.1016/j.compag.2022.107544

Manyonge, A. W. (2012). *Mathematical modelling of wind turbine in a wind energy conversion system: Power coefficient analysis*. Academic Press.

Martínez-Márquez, C. I.-B.-M.-G.-S.-C., Twizere-Bakunda, J. D., Lundback-Mompó, D., Orts-Grau, S., Gimeno-Sales, F. J., & Seguí-Chilet, S. (2019). Small Wind Turbine Emulator Based on Lambda-Cp Curves Obtained under Real Operating Conditions. *Energies, 12*(13), 2456. doi:10.3390/en12132456

Martín-Gómez, A. M., Aguayo-González, F., & Bárcena, M. M. (2018). Smart Eco-Industrial Parks: A Circular Economy Implementation Based on Industrial Metabolism. *Resources, Conservation and Recycling, 135*, 58–69. doi:10.1016/j.resconrec.2017.08.007

Mason, M. T. (1981). Compliance and force control for computer-controlled manipulators. *IEEE Transactions on Systems, Man, and Cybernetics, 11*(6), 418–432. doi:10.1109/TSMC.1981.4308708

Mathieu, E., Ritchie, H., Rodés-Guirao, L., Appel, C., Giattino, C., Hasell, J., Macdonald, B., Dattani, S., Beltekian, D., Ortiz-Ospina, E., & Roser, M. (2020). *Coronavirus Pandemic (COVID-19)*. Retrieved from: https://ourworldindata.org/coronavirus

Matthieu Dubarry, M. (2017, August). State of health battery estimator enabling degradation diagnosis: Model and algorithm description. *Journal of Power Sources, 360*, 59–69. doi:10.1016/j.jpowsour.2017.05.121

Matulis, M., & Harvey, C. (2021). A robot arm digital twin utilising reinforcement learning. *Computers & Graphics, 95*, 106–114. doi:10.1016/j.cag.2021.01.011

Ma, Y., Li, Q., He, F., Yan, L., & Xi, S. (2017). Adaptive segmentation algorithm for metal surface defects. *Yiqi Yibiao Xuebao.*

McDonough Braungart Design Chemistry, M. B. D. C. (2021). *Built Environment Herman Miller*. (MBDC) Récupéré sur https://mbdc.com/case-studies/herman-miller/

Mendiboure, L., Chalouf, M. A., & Krief, F. (2020). Survey on blockchain-based applications in internet of vehicles. *Computers & Electrical Engineering, 84*, 106646. doi:10.1016/j.compeleceng.2020.106646

Mercier, S., & Pham, H. (2012). A preventive maintenance policy for a continuously monitored system with correlated wear indicators. *European Journal of Operational Research, 222*(2), 263–272. doi:10.1016/j.ejor.2012.05.011

Mhamdi Taoufik, B. A. (2018). Stand-alone self-excited induction generator driven by a wind turbine. *Alexandria Engineering Journal, 57*(2), 781–786. doi:10.1016/j.aej.2017.01.009

Mizumoto, K., Kagaya, K., Zarebski, A., & Chowell, G. (2020). Estimating the asymptomatic proportion of coronavirus disease 2019 (COVID-19) cases on board the Diamond Princess cruise ship, Yokohama, Japan, 2020. *Eurosurveillance, 25*(10), 2000180. doi:10.2807/1560-7917.ES.2020.25.10.2000180 PMID:32183930

Model Driven Architecture (MDA). (2014). Object Management Group. https://www.omg.org/mda/

Mogili, U., & Deepak, V. (2018). Review on Application of Drone Systems in Precision Agriculture. *Procedia Computer Science, 133*, 502–509. doi:10.1016/j.procs.2018.07.063

Mohammed, H. a. (2017). Simulation and experimental verification of PID controlled DC/DC buck converter in wind energy conversion system. In *2017 4th IEEE International Conference on Engineering Technologies and Applied Sciences (ICETAS)* (pp. 1-6). IEEE.

Mousarezaee, E. a. (2020). Wind turbine emulator based on small-scale PMSG by fuzzy FOC. In *2020 21st international symposium on electrical apparatus & technologies (SIELA)* (pp. 1-4). 10.1109/SIELA49118.2020.9167128

Moussa, I., Bouallegue, A., & Khedher, A. (2019). New wind turbine emulator based on DC machine: Hardware implementation using FPGA board for an open-loop operation. *IET Circuits, Devices & Systems, 13*(6), 896–902. doi:10.1049/iet-cds.2018.5530

Murthy, J. S., Siddesh, G. M., Lai, W.-C., Parameshachari, B. D., Patil, S. N., & Hemalatha, K. L. (2022). ObjectDetect: A Real-Time Object Detection Framework for Advanced Driver Assistant Systems Using YOLOv5. *Wireless Communications and Mobile Computing, 2022*, 1–10. Advance online publication. doi:10.1155/2022/9444360

Nabdi, S., & Herrou, B. (2018). Contribution to Integrating Maintainability into Preliminary Design. *Triz, Engineering Journal, 22*(5).

Naveiroa & de Oliveira. (2018). *QFD and TRIZ integration in product development: A Model for Systematic Optimization of Engineering Requirements*. Academic Press.

Nazzal, B., Zaid, A. A., Alalfi, M. H., & Valani, A. (2022). Vulnerability classification of consumer-based IoT software. *Proceedings of the 4th International Workshop on Software Engineering Research and Practice for the IoT*, 17–24.

Negri, E., Berardi, S., Fumagalli, L., & Macchi, M. (2020). MES-integrated digital twin frameworks. *Journal of Manufacturing Systems, 56*, 58–71. doi:10.1016/j.jmsy.2020.05.007

Nelder, J. A., & Mead, R. (1965). A simplex method for function minimization. *The Computer Journal, 7*(4), 308–313. doi:10.1093/comjnl/7.4.308

Neshenko, N., Bou-Harb, E., Crichigno, J., Kaddoum, G., & Ghani, N. (2019). Demystifying IoT Security: An Exhaustive Survey on IoT Vulnerabilities and a First Empirical Look on Internet-Scale IoT Exploitations. *IEEE Communications Surveys and Tutorials, 21*(3), 2702–2733. doi:10.1109/COMST.2019.2910750

Ngan, H. Y., Pang, G. K., & Yung, N. H. (2011). Automated fabric defect detection—A review. *Image and Vision Computing, 29*(7), 442–458. doi:10.1016/j.imavis.2011.02.002

Nguyen, H. P., Retraint, F., Morain-Nicolier, F., & Delahaies, A. (2019). A watermarking technique to secure printed matrix barcode—Application for anti-counterfeit packaging. *IEEE Access : Practical Innovations, Open Solutions, 7*, 131839–131850. doi:10.1109/ACCESS.2019.2937465

Niu, K., & Chen, K. (2012). CRC-Aided Decoding of Polar Codes. *IEEE Communications Letters, 16*(10), 1668–1671. doi:10.1109/LCOMM.2012.090312.121501

Nova, S. H., Quader, S. M., Talukdar, S. D., Sadab, M. R., Sayeed, M. S., Al Islam, A. B. M. A., & Noor, J. (2022). IoT based parking system: Prospects, challenges, and beyond. In *International Conference on Innovation and Intelligence for Informatics, Computing, and Technologies (3ICT), Sakheer, Bahrain, 2022* (pp. 393–400). 10.1109/3ICT56508.2022.9990838

Nova, K. (2023). AI-enabled water management systems: An analysis of system components and interdependencies for water conservation. *Eigenpub Review of Science and Technology, 7*(1), 105–124.

Núñez-Gómez, C., Caminero, B., & Carrion, C. (2021). HIDRA: A Distributed Blockchain-Based Architecture for Fog/Edge Computing Environments. *IEEE Access : Practical Innovations, Open Solutions, 9*, 75231–75251. doi:10.1109/ACCESS.2021.3082197

Núñez-Gómez, C., Carrión, C., Caminero, B., & Delicado, F. M. (2023). S-HIDRA: A blockchain and SDN domain-based architecture to orchestrate fog computing environments. *Computer Networks*, *221*, 109512. doi:10.1016/j.comnet.2022.109512

Nuspire, T. (2023, March 30). The Ongoing Rise in IoT Attacks: What We're Seeing in 2023. *Security Boulevard*. https://securityboulevard.com/2023/03/the-ongoing-rise-in-iot-attacks-what-were-seeing-in-2023/

NVD - Data Feeds. (n.d.). Retrieved May 18, 2023, from https://nvd.nist.gov/vuln/data-feeds

NVD - Home. (n.d.). Retrieved May 18, 2023, from https://nvd.nist.gov/

Ofualagba, G. a. (2008). Wind energy conversion system-wind turbine modeling. In 2008 IEEE power and energy society general meeting-conversion and delivery of electrical energy in the 21st century (pp. 1-8). doi:10.1109/PES.2008.4596699

Ohno, T., & Setsuo, M. (1988). *Just-In-Time: For Today and Tomorrow*. Diamond, Inc.

Omali, K. O., Kabbaj, M. N., & Benbrahim, M. (2021). Fault detection and isolation using sliding mode observers with sensor fault in robot manipulator. *International Journal of Digital Signals and Smart Systems*, *5*(2), 182. doi:10.1504/IJDSSS.2021.114560

Omali, K. O., Kabbaj, M. N., & Benbrahim, M. (2022). Fault-tolerant control with high-order sliding mode for Manipulator Robot. *International Journal of Power Electronics and Drive Systems*, *13*(3), 1854. doi:10.11591/ijpeds.v13.i3.pp1854-1869

OMG-BPMN. (2011). *Business Process Model and Notation (BPMN)-Version 2.0*. OMG. Available at: https://www.omg.org/spec/BPMN/2.0/PDF

OMG-IFML. (2015). *Interaction Flow Modeling Language (IFML)- OMG*. Available at: https://www.omg.org/spec/IFML/1.0/Beta1/PDF

OMG-XML. (2015). *XML Metadata Interchange (XMI) Specification*. Available at: https://www.omg.org/spec/XMI/2.5.1/PDF

Ömür Bucak, İ. (2021). An in-depth analysis of sliding mode control and its application to robotics. IntechOpen eBooks. doi:10.5772/intechopen.93027

Opara, K. R., & Arabas, J. (2019). Differential Evolution: A survey of theoretical analyses. *Swarm and Evolutionary Computation*, *44*, 546–558. doi:10.1016/j.swevo.2018.06.010

Otman, H., Jaouad, B., Mohamed, S., Abdelhak, M., & Hamza, I. (2022). Datasets analysis in predictive maintenance: prognostics and health management. *The 2nd International Conference on Innovative Research in Applied Science, Engineering and Technology (IRASET'2022), Meknes, Morocco, Proceedings published in IEEE*, 1-7, 10.1109/IRASET52964.2022.9738429

Otunuga, O. M. (2021). Estimation of epidemiological parameters for COVID-19 cases using a stochastic SEIRS epidemic model with vital dynamics. *Results in Physics*, *28*, 104664. doi:10.1016/j.rinp.2021.104664 PMID:34395184

Palem, G. (2013). Condition-based maintenance using sensor arrays and telematics. *International Journal of Mobile Network Communications & Telematics*, *3*(3), 19–28. doi:10.5121/ijmnct.2013.3303

Pan, J. S., Huang, H. C., & Jain, L. C. (2004). *Intelligent Watermarking Techniques with Source Code* (Vol. 7). Innovative Intelligence. doi:10.1142/5471

Papageorgiou, V. E., & Tsaklidis, G. (2023). An improved epidemiological-unscented Kalman filter (hybrid SEIHCRDV-UKF) model for the prediction of COVID-19. Application on real-time data. *Chaos, Solitons, and Fractals, 166*, 112914. doi:10.1016/j.chaos.2022.112914 PMID:36440087

Papp, D., Ma, Z., & Buttyan, L. (2015). Embedded systems security: Threats, vulnerabilities, and attack taxonomy. *2015 13th Annual Conference on Privacy, Security and Trust (PST)*, 145–152.

Parmentola, A., & Tutore, I. (2023). Unveiling the Positive and Negative Effects of Blockchain Technologies on Environmental Sustainability in Practice. In *Industry 4.0 Technologies for Environmental Sustainability: Intended and Unintended Consequences* (pp. 59–78). Springer International Publishing. doi:10.1007/978-3-031-40010-0_4

Pascanu, R., Mikolov, T., & Bengio, Y. (2013). On the difficulty of training recurrent neural networks. *International Conference on Machine Learning, PMLR*, 1310–1318.

Patil, A., Dwivedi, A., Abdul Moktadir, M., & Lakshay. (2023). Big data-Industry 4.0 readiness factors for sustainable supply chain management: Towards circularity. *Computers & Industrial Engineering, 178*, 109109. doi:10.1016/j.cie.2023.109109

Pennec, Djafari Rouhani, El Boudouti, Li, El Hassouani, Vasseur, Papanikolaou, Benchabane, Laude, & Martinez. (2010). Simultaneous existence of phononic and photonic band gaps in periodic crystal slabs. *Opt. Express, 18*(13), 14301-14310.

Pennec, Y., Djafari Rouhani, B., El Boudouti, E. H., Li, C., El Hassouani, Y., Vasseur, J. O., Papanikolaou, N., Benchabane, S., Laude, V., & Martnez, A. (2011, February). Band gaps and waveguiding in phoxonic silicon crystal slabs. *Zhongguo Wuli Xuekan, 49*, 100.

Pennec, Y., Vasseur, J., Djafari-Rouhani, B., Dobrzynski, L., & Deymier, P. A. (2010). Two-dimensional phononic crystals: Examples and applications. *Surface Science Reports, 65*(8), 229–291. doi:10.1016/j.surfrep.2010.08.002

Pérez-Lombard, L., Ortiz, J., & Pout, C. (2008). A review on buildings energy consumption information. *Energy and Building, 40*(3), 394–398. doi:10.1016/j.enbuild.2007.03.007

Petajajarvi, J., Mikhaylov, K., Roivainen, A., Hanninen, T., & Pettissalo, M. (2015). On the coverage of LPWANs: Range evaluation and channel attenuation model for LoRa technology. *Proc. 14th Int. Conf. ITS Telecommun. (ITST)*, 55-59. 10.1109/ITST.2015.7377400

Peyal, M. M. K., Barman, A., Tahiat, T., Ul Haque, Q. M. A., Bal, A., & Ahmed, S. (2021). IoT based cost effective car parking management for urban area. In *4th International Symposium on Agents, Multi-Agent Systems and Robotics (ISAMSR), Batu Pahat, Malaysia, 2021* (pp. 70–75). 10.1109/ISAMSR53229.2021.9567826

Pietre-Cambacedes. (2010). *Des relations entre sûreté et sécurité* [Thesis].

Pincheira, M., Vecchio, M., Giaffreda, R., & Kanhere, S. S. (2021). Cost-effective IoT devices as trustworthy data sources for a blockchain-based water management system in precision agriculture. *Computers and Electronics in Agriculture, 180*, 105889. doi:10.1016/j.compag.2020.105889

Piscitelli, G., Ferazzoli, A., Petrillo, A., Cioffi, R., Parmentola, A., & Travaglioni, M. (2020). Circular Economy models in the Industry 4.0 era: A review of the last decade. *Procedia Manufacturing, 42*, 227–234. doi:10.1016/j.promfg.2020.02.074

Planas, E., Daniel, G., Brambilla, M., & Cabot, J. (2021, August). Towards a model-driven approach for multiexperience AI-based user interfaces. *Software & Systems Modeling, 20*(4), 997–1009. doi:10.1007/s10270-021-00904-y

Podilchuk, C. I., & Delp, E. J. (2001). Digital watermarking: Algorithms and applications. *IEEE Signal Processing Magazine, 18*(4), 33–46. doi:10.1109/79.939835

Population by Country. (2023). *Worldometer.* https://www. worldometers.info/world-population/population-by-country/

Pranto, T. H., Noman, A. A., Mahmud, A., & Haque, A. K. M. B. (2021). Blockchain and smart contract for IoT enabled smart agriculture. *PeerJ. Computer Science*, 7, 1–29. doi:10.7717/peerj-cs.407 PMID:33834098

Prasad, D., Rahul Reddy, P., Sreelatha, B., Jeevan Reddy, K., Jayabalan, S., & Kumar Panigrahy, A. (2021). Recent developments in code compression techniques for embedded systems. *Materials Today: Proceedings*, *46*, 4128–4132. doi:10.1016/j.matpr.2021.02.643

Puri, V., Nayyar, A., & Raja, L. (2017). Agriculture drones: A modern breakthrough in precision agriculture. *Journal of Statistics and Management Systems*, *20*(4), 507–518. doi:10.1080/09720510.2017.1395171

Qian, C., Liu, X., Ripley, C., Qian, M., Liang, F., & Yu, W. (2022). Digital Twin—cyber replica of Physical Things: Architecture, applications and future research directions. *Future Internet*, *14*(2), 64. doi:10.3390/fi14020064

Qin, H., Xu, N., Zhang, Y., Pang, Q., & Lu, Z. (2023). Research on Parking Recommendation Methods Considering Travelers' Decision Behaviors and Psychological Characteristics. *Sustainability (Basel)*, *15*(8), 6808. doi:10.3390/su15086808

Queiroz, A., Oliveira, E., Barbosa, M., & Dias, K. (2020) A Survey on Blockchain and Edge Computing applied to the Internet of Vehicles. *International Symposium on Advanced Networks and Telecommunication Systems, ANTS.*

Quy, V. K., Hau, N. V., Anh, D. V., Quy, N. M., Ban, N. T., Lanza, S., Randazzo, G., & Muzirafuti, A. (2022). IoT-Enabled Smart Agriculture: Architecture, Applications, and Challenges. *Applied Sciences (Basel, Switzerland)*, *7*(7), 3396. doi:10.3390/app12073396

Ragheb, M. a. (2011). Wind turbines theory-the betz equation and optimal rotor tip speed ratio. *Fundamental and advanced topics in wind power*, 19-38.

Rai, A., & Singh, H. V. (2017). SVM based robust watermarking for enhanced medical image security. *Multimedia Tools and Applications*, *76*(18), 18605–18618. doi:10.1007/s11042-016-4215-3

Rajbhandari, S., Thareja, B., Deep, V., & Mehrotra, D. (2018). IoT based smart parking system. In *International Conference on Innovation and Intelligence for Informatics, Computing, and Technologies (3ICT), Sakhier, Bahrain, 2018* (pp. 1–5). 10.1109/3ICT.2018.8855787

Raj, P., & Deka, G. C. (2018). *Blockchain technology: platforms, tools and use cases.* Academic Press.

Raj, V., & Sadam, R. (2021). Performance and complexity comparison of service oriented architecture and microservices architecture. *International Journal of Communication Networks and Distributed Systems*, *27*(1), 100–117. doi:10.1504/IJCNDS.2021.116463

Ramasamy, M., Solanki, S. G., Natarajan, E., & Keat, T. M. (2018). IoT based smart parking system for large parking lot. In *IEEE 4th International Symposium in Robotics and Manufacturing Automation (ROMA), Perambalur, India, 2018* (pp. 1–4). 10.1109/ROMA46407.2018.8986731

Ramly, S., Aljunid, S. A., & Shaker Hussain, H. (2011). SVM-SS watermarking model for medical images. In *Digital Enterprise and Information Systems: International Conference, DEIS 2011, London, UK, July 20–22, 2011. Proceedings* (pp. 372-386). Springer Berlin Heidelberg.

Rasheed, A., San, O., & Kvamsdal, T. (2020). Digital Twin: Values, challenges and enablers from a modeling perspective. *IEEE Access : Practical Innovations, Open Solutions*, *8*, 21980–22012. doi:10.1109/ACCESS.2020.2970143

Ray, R. L., & ... . (2022). The Role of Remote Sensing Data and Methods in a Modern Approach to Fertilization in Precision Agriculture. *Remote Sensing (Basel)*, *14*(3), 778. doi:10.3390/rs14030778

Reason, J. T. (1990). *Human error.* Cambridge University Press. doi:10.1017/CBO9781139062367

Reddy, E. R. V., & Thale, S. (2021). Pedestrian Detection Using YOLOv5 For Autonomous Driving Applications. *2021 IEEE Transportation Electrification Conference. ITEC-India, 2021,* 1–5. Advance online publication. doi:10.1109/ITEC-India53713.2021.9932534

Redmon, J., & Farhadi, A. (2017). YOLO9000: Better, faster, stronger. *Proceedings - 30th IEEE Conference on Computer Vision and Pattern Recognition, CVPR 2017,* 6517-6525. 10.1109/CVPR.2017.690

Redmon, J., Divvala, S., Girshick, R., & Farhadi, A. (2015). You Only Look Once: Unified, Real-Time Object Detection. *Proceedings of the IEEE Computer Society Conference on Computer Vision and Pattern Recognition, 2016-December,* 779-788. 10.1109/CVPR.2016.91

RedmonJ.FarhadiA. (2018). *YOLOv3: An Incremental Improvement.* https://arxiv.org/abs/1804.02767v1

Renier, R., & Chenouard, R. (2011). *De SysML à MODELICA aide à la formalisation de modèles de simulation en conception préliminaire.* 12ème Colloque National AIP PRIMECA, France.

Renosi, P., & Sapriel, J. (1994, May 23). Near-resonance acousto-optical interactions in GaAs and InP. *Applied Physics Letters, 64*(21), 2794–1994. doi:10.1063/1.111427

Reyna, A., Martín, C., Chen, J., Soler, E., & Díaz, M. (2018). On blockchain and its integration with IoT. Challenges and opportunities. *Future Generation Computer Systems, 88,* 173–190. doi:10.1016/j.future.2018.05.046

Rhazali, Y., Hadi, Y., Chana, I., Lahmer, M., & Rhattoy, Ab. (2018). A model transformation in model-driven architecture from business model to web model. *IAENG International Journal of Computer Science, 45,* 104–117.

Rhazali, Y., Hadi, Y., & Mouloudi, A. (2015, December 31). A Methodology of Model Transformation in MDA: From CIM to PIM. *International Review on Computers and Software, 10*(12), 1186. doi:10.15866/irecos.v10i12.8088

Ribeiro, F. M. (2021). Data resilience system for fog computing. *Computer Networks, 195,* 108218. doi:10.1016/j.comnet.2021.108218

Ribot, P. (2009). *Vers l'intégration diagnostic/ pronostic pour la maintenance des systèmes complexes* [PhD thesis]. University of Paul Sabatier-Toulouse III.

Rodriguez-Echeverria, R., Preciado, J. C., Sierra, J., Conejero, J. M., & Sanchez-Figueroa, F. (2018, December). AutoCRUD: Automatic generation of CRUD specifications in interaction flow modeling language. *Science of Computer Programming, 168,* 165–168. doi:10.1016/j.scico.2018.09.004

Rolland, Q., Oudich, M., El-Jallal, S., Dupont, S., Pennec, Y., Gazalet, J., Kastelik, J. C., Leveque, G., & Djafari-Rouhani, B. (2012). Acousto-optic couplings in two-dimensional phoxonic crystal cavities. *Applied Physics Letters, 101*(6), 061109. doi:10.1063/1.4744539

Romaric, Hamid, & Nabil. (2012). *Base De Connaissances Sysml Pour La Conception De Systemes Complexes Surs De Fonctionnement.* Academic Press.

Rong, C., & Liu, X. (2020). IFML-Based Web Application Modeling. *Procedia Computer Science, 166,* 129–133. doi:10.1016/j.procs.2020.02.034

Rosa, P., Sassanelli, C., Urbinati, A., Chiaroni, D., & Terzi, S. (2020). Assessing relations between Circular Economy and Industry 4.0: A systematic literature review. *International Journal of Production Research, 58*(6), 1662–1687. doi:10.1080/00207543.2019.1680896

Roubi, S., Erramdani, M., & Mbarki, S. (2016, April 19). A Model-Driven Approach for generating Graphical User Interface for MVC Rich Internet Application. *Computer and Information Science*, *9*(2), 91. doi:10.5539/cis.v9n2p91

Rudin, C., Chen, C., Chen, Z., Huang, H., Semenova, L., & Zhong, C. (2022). Interpretable machine learning: Fundamental principles and 10 grand challenges. *Statistics Surveys*, *16*(none), 1–85. doi:10.1214/21-SS133

Sadat-Saleh, S., Benchabane, S., & Baida, F. I. (2009). *Simultaneous photonic and phononic band gaps in a two-dimensional lithium niobate crystal*. IEEE International.

Sadat-Saleh, S., Benchabane, S., Baida, F. I., Bernal, M.-P., & Laude, V. (2009). Tailoring simultaneous photonic and phononic band gaps. *Journal of Applied Physics*, *106*(7), 074912. doi:10.1063/1.3243276

Sadorsky, P. (2009). Renewable energy consumption and income in emerging economies. *Energy Policy*, *37*(10), 4021–4028. doi:10.1016/j.enpol.2009.05.003

Sah Tyagi, S. K., Mukherjee, A., Pokhrel, S. R., & Hiran, K. K. (2021). An Intelligent and Optimal Resource Allocation Approach in Sensor Networks for Smart Agri-IoT. *IEEE Sensors Journal*, *21*(16), 17439–17446. doi:10.1109/JSEN.2020.3020889

Said, A. M., Kamal, A. E., & Afifi, H. (2021). An intelligent parking sharing system for green and smart cities based IoT. *Computer Communications*, *172*, 10–18. doi:10.1016/j.comcom.2021.02.017

Sajji, A., Rhazali, Y., & Hadi, Y. (2022, October 1). A methodology for transforming BPMN to IFML into MDA. *Bulletin of Electrical Engineering and Informatics*, *11*(5), 2773–2782. doi:10.11591/eei.v11i5.3973

Sakthi. (2023). Blockchain-Enabled Precision Agricultural System Using IoT and Edge Computing. *Smart Trends in Computing and Communications*, 397–405. doi:10.1007/978-981-99-0769-4_35

Samigulina, G. (2020). Development of Industrial Equipment Diagnostics System Based on Modified Algorithms of Artificial Immune Systems and AMDEC Approach Using Schneider Electric Equipment. *2020 International Conference on Industrial Engineering, Applications and Manufacturing*.

San Emeterio de la Parte, M., Martínez-Ortega, J.-F., Hernández Díaz, V., & Martínez, N. L. (2023). Big Data and precision agriculture: A novel spatio-temporal semantic IoT data management framework for improved interoperability. *Journal of Big Data*, *10*(1), 1–32. doi:10.1186/s40537-023-00729-0 PMID:36618886

Santos, I., Castro, L., Rodriguez-Fernandez, N., Torrente-Patino, A., & Carballal, A. (2021). "Artificial Neural Networks and Deep Learning in the Visual Arts: A review." Review of. *Neural Computing & Applications*, *33*(1), 1–37. doi:10.1007/s00521-020-05565-4

Saracco, R. (2019). Digital Twins: Bridging physical space and cyberspace. *Computer*, *52*(12), 58–64. doi:10.1109/MC.2019.2942803

Sara, U., Akter, M., & Uddin, M. S. (2019). Image quality assessment through FSIM, SSIM, MSE and PSNR—A comparative study. *Journal of Computer and Communications*, *7*(3), 8–18. doi:10.4236/jcc.2019.73002

Schmidhuber, J. (2015). Deep learning in neural networks: An overview. *Neural Networks*, *61*, 85–117. doi:10.1016/j.neunet.2014.09.003 PMID:25462637

Schumacher, Pokornib, Himmelstoßa, & Bauernhansla. (2020). *Conceptualization of a Framework for the Design of Production Systems and Industrial Workplaces*. Academic Press.

Schumacher, A., Nemeth, T., & Sihn, W. (2019). Roadmapping towards industrial digitalization based on an Industry 4.0 maturity model for manufacturing enterprises. *Procedia CIRP*, *79*, 409–414. doi:10.1016/j.procir.2019.02.110

Schumpeter, J. (1935). Théorie de l'évolution économique. Traduction française Dalloz, Paris.

Schwabacher. (2007). A Survey of Artificial Intelligence for Prognostics. AAAI fall symposium: artificial intelligence for prognostics, Arlington, VA.

Šebestová, J., & Sroka, W. (2020). Sustainable development goals and sme decisions: The czech republic vs. Poland. *Journal of Eastern European and Central Asian Research, 7*, 39–50.

Seifert, M., Kuehnel, S., & Sackmann, S. (2023). Hybrid Clouds Arising from Software as a Service Adoption: Challenges, Solutions, and Future Research Directions. *ACM Computing Surveys, 55*(11), 1–35. doi:10.1145/3570156

Sekkat, S., & El-hassani, I. (2021). What approach using to digitize quality management? *International Conference on Artificial Intelligence and Emerging Technologies (AIET) 24-25 November 2021.*

Sekkat, S., El-hassani, I., & Cherrafi, A. (2023). *Maturity Models as a support for Industry 4.0 implementation: Literature review. Artificial Intelligence & Industrial Applications A2IA'2023 February 17th and 18th, 2023.*

Sénéchal, O. (2003). *Le cycle de vie du système de production. Evaluation des performances des systèmes de production.* Lavoisier.

Sharma, A., Awasthi, Y., & Kumar, S. (2020). The Role of Blockchain, AI and IoT for Smart Road Traffic Management System. *Proceedings - 2020 IEEE India Council International Subsections Conference, INDISCON 2020,* 289-296.

Sharma, K. D., & Srivastava, S. (2018). *Failure Mode and Effect Analysis (FMEA) Implementation: A Literature Review.* Academic Press.

Sharma, P., & Bora, B. J. A. (2023). Review of Modern Machine Learning Techniques in the Prediction of Remaining Useful Life of Lithium-Ion Batteries. *Batteries, 9*(1), 13. doi:10.3390/batteries9010013

Sharma, R., Sibal, R., & Sabharwal, S. (2021). Software vulnerability prioritization using vulnerability description. *International Journal of System Assurance Engineering and Management, 12*(1), 58–64. doi:10.1007/s13198-020-01021-7

Sharma, T., Debaque, B., Duclos, N., Chehri, A., Kinder, B., & Fortier, P. (2022). Deep Learning-Based Object Detection and Scene Perception under Bad Weather Conditions. *Electronics (Basel), 11*(4), 563. Advance online publication. doi:10.3390/electronics11040563

Shen, M., Zu, J., Fairley, C. K., Pagán, J. A., An, L., Du, Z., Guo, Y., Rong, L., Xiao, Y., Zhuang, G., Li, Y., & Zhang, L. (2021). Projected COVID-19 epidemic in the United States in the context of the effectiveness of a potential vaccine and implications for social distancing and face mask use. *Vaccine, 39*(16), 2295–2302. doi:10.1016/j.vaccine.2021.02.056 PMID:33771391

Shieh, H., & Hsu, C. (2008). An adaptive Approximator-Based backstepping control approach for Piezoactuator-Driven stages. *IEEE Transactions on Industrial Electronics, 55*(4), 1729–1738. doi:10.1109/TIE.2008.917115

Shin, H.-C., Roth, H. R., Gao, M., Lu, L., Xu, Z., Nogues, I., Yao, J., Mollura, D., & Summers, R. M. (2016). Deep Convolutional Neural Networks for Computer-Aided Detection: CNN Architectures, Dataset Characteristics and Transfer Learning. In IEEE Transactions on Medical Imaging (Vol. 35, Numéro 5, p. 1285-1298). doi:10.1109/TMI.2016.2528162

Shingo, S. (1989). *A Study of the Toyota Production System from an Industrial Engineering Viewpoint.* Productivity Press.

Shorten, C., & Khoshgoftaar, T. M. (2019). A survey on image data augmentation for deep learning. *Journal of Big Data, 6*(1), 1–48. doi:10.1186/s40537-019-0197-0

Shrestha, S., Aihara, Y., Bhattarai, A. P., Bista, N., Kondo, N., Futaba, K., Nishida, K., & Shindo, J. (2018). Development of an objective water security index and assessment of its association with quality of life in urban areas of developing countries. *SSM - Population Health*, *6*, 276–285. doi:10.1016/j.ssmph.2018.10.007 PMID:30480077

Shyamala Devi, M., Suguna, R., Joshi, A. S., & Bagate, R. A. (2019). Design of IoT Blockchain Based Smart Agriculture for Enlightening Safety and Security. *Communications in Computer and Information Science*, *985*, 7–19. doi:10.1007/978-981-13-8300-7_2

Sikorska, J., Hodkiewicz, M., & Ma, L. (2011). Prognostic modelling options for remaining useful life estimation by industry. *Mechanical Systems and Signal Processing*, *25*(5), 1803–1836. doi:10.1016/j.ymssp.2010.11.018

Singh, M., & Kim, S. (2018). Trust Bit: Reward-based intelligent vehicle commination using blockchain. *IEEE World Forum on Internet of Things, WF-IoT 2018 - Proceedings.*

Singh, A., & Dutta, M. K. (2020). A robust zero-watermarking scheme for tele-ophthalmological applications. *Journal of King Saud University. Computer and Information Sciences*, *32*(8), 895–908. doi:10.1016/j.jksuci.2017.12.008

Singh, P., & Sharma, A. (2022). An intelligent WSN-UAV-based IoT framework for precision agriculture application. *Computers & Electrical Engineering*, *100*, 107912. doi:10.1016/j.compeleceng.2022.107912

Singh, R., Saraswat, M., Ashok, A., Mittal, H., Tripathi, A., Pandey, A. C., & Pal, R. (2022). From classical to soft computing based watermarking techniques: A comprehensive review. *Future Generation Computer Systems.*

Sinhal, R., Jain, D. K., & Ansari, I. A. (2021). Machine learning based blind color image watermarking scheme for copyright protection. *Pattern Recognition Letters*, *145*, 171–177. doi:10.1016/j.patrec.2021.02.011

Slim, Houssin, & Coulibaly. (2019). Une approche d'intégration de la méthode SMED dans la conception des systèmes de production. *16e Colloque National S-mart, Les Karellis*, (73).

Sloane, N., Reddy, S., & Chen, C.-L. (1972). New binary codes. *IEEE Transactions on Information Theory*, *18*(4), 503–510. doi:10.1109/TIT.1972.1054833

Slotine, J. E., & Li, W. (1991). Sliding Control. In *Applied Nonlinear Control* (pp. 276–307). Prentice-Hall International. http://ci.nii.ac.jp/ncid/BA11352433

Smith, R. C. (2013). *Uncertainty quantification: theory, implementation, and applications* (Vol. 12). Siam. doi:10.1137/1.9781611973228

Soon, J. M., & Manning, L. (2019). Developing anti-counterfeiting measures: The role of smart packaging. *Food Research International*, *123*, 135–143. doi:10.1016/j.foodres.2019.04.049 PMID:31284961

Soto, F. (2018). *Operational Excellence: The fundamentals for succeeding where others have failed*. Endeavor Management.

Souad, N., & Brahim, H. (2017). *Integration de la maintenabilité en phase préliminaire de conception en se basant sur la théorie TRIZ. 3ième Congrès International du Génie Industriel et du Management des Systèmes (CIGIMS'2017), May 2017*. Meknès.

Sousa, R., & Voss, C. A. (2008). Contingency research in operations management practices. *Journal of Operations Management*, *26*(6), 697–713. doi:10.1016/j.jom.2008.06.001

Srai, A., Guerouate, F., Berbiche, N., & HilalDrissi, H. (2017, November 2). Generated PSM Web Model for E-learning Platform Respecting n-tiers Architecture. *International Journal of Emerging Technologies in Learning*, *12*(10), 212. doi:10.3991/ijet.v12i10.7179

Stan Development Team. (2017). Stan Modeling Language User's Guide and Reference Manual, Version 2.32.0. Author.

Sultan, M. (2023). UAV-Based Wireless Data Collection from Underground Sensor Nodes for Precision Agriculture. *AgriEngineering, 5*(1), 338–354. doi:10.3390/agriengineering5010022

Summers, A. E. (2003). Introduction to layers of protection analysis. *Journal of Hazardous Materials, 104*(1-3), 163-168.

Sundaresan, S., Suresh Kumar, K., Ananth Kumar, T., Ashok, V., & Golden Julie, E. (2021). Blockchain architecture for intelligent water management system in smart cities. In *Blockchain for Smart Cities* (pp. 57–80). Elsevier. doi:10.1016/B978-0-12-824446-3.00006-5

Sun, Q., Miyoshi, T., & Richard, S. (2023). Analysis of COVID-19 in Japan with extended SEIR model and ensemble Kalman filter. *Journal of Computational and Applied Mathematics, 419*, 114772. doi:10.1016/j.cam.2022.114772 PMID:36061090

Su, Q., & Karthikeyan, R. (2023). Regional Water Stress Forecasting: Effects of Climate Change, Socioeconomic Development, and Irrigated Agriculture—A Texas Case Study. *Sustainability (Basel), 15*(12), 9290. doi:10.3390/su15129290

Tang, B., Wang, X., Li, Q., Bragazzi, N. L., Tang, S., Xiao, Y., & Wu, J. (2020). Estimation of the transmission risk of the 2019-nCoV and its implication for public health interventions. *Journal of Clinical Medicine, 9*(2), 462. doi:10.3390/jcm9020462 PMID:32046137

Tanwar, R., Chhabra, Y., Rattan, P., & Rani, S. (2023). Blockchain in IoT Networks for Precision Agriculture. *Lecture Notes in Networks and Systems, 471*, 137–147. doi:10.1007/978-981-19-2535-1_10

Tao, F., Cheng, Y., Da Xu, L., Zhang, L., & Li, B. H. (2014). Cciot-cmfg: Cloud computing and internet of things-based cloud manufacturing service system. *IEEE Transactions on Industrial Informatics, 10*(2), 1435–1442. doi:10.1109/TII.2014.2306383

Tao, F., Zhang, H., Liu, A., & Nee, A. Y. (2019). Digital Twin in industry: State-of-the-art. *IEEE Transactions on Industrial Informatics, 15*(4), 2405–2415. doi:10.1109/TII.2018.2873186

Tao, F., Zuo, Y., Da Xu, L., & Zhang, L. (2014). Iot-based intelligent perception and access of manufacturing resource toward cloud manufacturing. *IEEE Transactions on Industrial Informatics, 10*(2), 1547–1557. doi:10.1109/TII.2014.2306397

Tavakoli, A., Honjani, Z., & Sajedi, H. (2023). Convolutional neural network-based image watermarking using discrete wavelet transform. *International Journal of Information Technology: an Official Journal of Bharati Vidyapeeth's Institute of Computer Applications and Management, 15*(4), 2021–2029. doi:10.1007/s41870-023-01232-8

Taveiros, F. E. (2013). Wind turbine torque-speed feature emulator using a DC motor. In *2013 Brazilian Power Electronics Conference* (pp. 480--486). 10.1109/COBEP.2013.6785159

Tavera-Romero, C. A., Castro, D. F., Ortiz, J. H., Khalaf, O. I., & Vargas, M. A. (2021). Synergy between Circular Economy and Industry 4.0: A Literature Review. *MDPI. Sustainability (Basel), 13*(8), 4331. doi:10.3390/su13084331

Tezel, A., Papadonikolaki, E., Yitmen, I., & Hilletofth, P. (2020). Preparing construction supply chains for blockchain technology: An investigation of its potential and future directions. *Frontiers of Engineering Management, 7*(4), 547–563. doi:10.1007/s42524-020-0110-8

Tixier, J., Dusserre, G., Salvi, O., & Gaston, D. (2002, July). Review of 62 risk analysis methodologies of industrial plants. *Journal of Loss Prevention in the Process Industries, 15*(4), 291–303. doi:10.1016/S0950-4230(02)00008-6

Tong, G., Li, Y., Zhang, H., & Xiong, N. (2023). A fine-grained channel state information-based deep learning system for dynamic gesture recognition. *Information Sciences, 636*, 118912. doi:10.1016/j.ins.2023.03.137

Torky, M., & Hassanein, A. (2020). Integrating blockchain and the internet of things in precision agriculture: Analysis, opportunities, and challenges. *Computers and Electronics in Agriculture*, *178*, 105476. doi:10.1016/j.compag.2020.105476

Trifonov, P., & Miloslavskaya, V. (2013). Polar codes with dynamic frozen symbols and their decoding by directed search. *2013 IEEE Information Theory Workshop (ITW)*, 1–5. 10.1109/ITW.2013.6691213

Trifonov, P., & Miloslavskaya, V. (2016). Polar Subcodes. *IEEE Journal on Selected Areas in Communications*, *34*(2), 254–266. doi:10.1109/JSAC.2015.2504269

Tripathi, G., Ahad, M. A., & Sathiyanarayanan, M. (2019). The Role of Blockchain in Internet of Vehicles (IoV): Issues, Challenges and Opportunities. *Proceedings of the 4th International Conference on Contemporary Computing and Informatics, IC3I 2019*, 26-31.

Uddin, A. E., Stranieri, A., Gondal, I., & Balasubramanian, V. (2021). A survey on the adoption of blockchain in IoT: Challenges and solutions. *Blockchain: Research and Applications*, *2*(2), 100006. doi:10.1016/j.bcra.2021.100006

Ulrich, K. T., & Eppinger, S. D. (2008). *Product Design and Development* (5th ed.). McGraw-Hill.

Vacchi, M., Siligardi, C., Cedillo-González, E. I., Ferrari, A. M., & Settembre-Blundo, D. (2021). Industry 4.0 and Smart Data as Enablers of the Circular Economy in Manufacturing: Product Re-Engineering with Circular Eco-Design. *MDPI. Sustainability (Basel)*, *13*(18), 10366. doi:10.3390/su131810366

Välja, M., Korman, M., & Lagerström, R. (2017). A study on software vulnerabilities and weaknesses of embedded systems in power networks. *Scopus*, 47–52. Advance online publication. doi:10.1145/3055386.3055397

Vasconcelos, G. L., Brum, A. A., Almeida, F. A., Macêdo, A. M., Duarte-Filho, G. C., & Ospina, R. (2021). Standard and anomalous waves of COVID-19: A multiple-wave growth model for epidemics. *Brazilian Journal of Physics*, *51*(6), 1867–1883. doi:10.1007/s13538-021-00996-3

Vidhyalakshmi, R., & Kumar, V. (2014). Design comparison of traditional application and SaaS. *International Conference on Computing for Sustainable Global Development*, 541–544. 10.1109/IndiaCom.2014.6828017

Wagner, C. (2009). *Specification risk analysis: Avoiding product performance deviations through an fmea-based method* [Thesis]. L'université téchniques, München, Allemagne.

Waheed, F., & Azam, F. (2020). Model Driven Approach for Automatic Script Generation in Stress Testing of Web Applications. doi:10.1145/3397125.3397137

Wakchaure, M., Patle, B. K., & Mahindrakar, A. K. (2023). Application of AI techniques and robotics in agriculture: A review. *Artificial Intelligence in the Life Sciences*, *3*, 100057. doi:10.1016/j.ailsci.2023.100057

Wang, X. V., & Wang, L. (2019). Digital Twin-Based WEEE Recycling, Recovery and Remanufacturing in the Background of Industry 4.0. *International Journal of Production Research, 57*(12), 3892–3902.

Wang, X., Zeng, P., Patterson, N., Jiang, F., & Doss, R. (2019). An improved authentication scheme for internet of vehicles based on blockchain technology. *IEEE Access, 7*, 45061-45072.

Wang, Q., Gao, Y., Ren, J., & Zhang, B. (2023). An automatic classification algorithm for software vulnerability based on weighted word vector and fusion neural network. *Computers & Security*, *126*, 103070. doi:10.1016/j.cose.2022.103070

Wang, Q., Li, Y., Wang, Y., & Ren, J. (2022). An automatic algorithm for software vulnerability classification based on CNN and GRU. *Multimedia Tools and Applications*, *81*(5), 7103–7124. doi:10.1007/s11042-022-12049-1

WebRatio Learn Center. (2023, February 16). WebRatio. https://my.webratio.com/learn/content?nav=65&link=oln208a. redirect&so=pcu1a

Wellsandt, S., Foosherian, M., & Thoben, K.-D. (2020). Interacting with a Digital Twin using Amazon Alexa. *Procedia Manufacturing*, *52*, 4–8. doi:10.1016/j.promfg.2020.11.002

Wen, Q. a. (2021). A comprehensive review of miniatured wind energy harvesters. *Nano Materials Science*, 170-185.

Wen, T., Zhang, Y., Wu, Q., & Yang, G. (2015). ASVC: An Automatic Security Vulnerability Categorization Framework Based on Novel Features of Vulnerability Data. *Journal of Communication*, *10*(2), 107–116. doi:10.12720/jcm.10.2.107-116

Wiktionnaire. (2023). https://fr.wiktionary.org/wiki/s%C3%BBret%C3%A9_industrielle

Wu, S. W. (2014). Research on intelligent image watermarking schemes based on optimization algorithm. *Advanced Materials Research*, *1006*, 792–796. doi:10.4028/www.scientific.net/AMR.1006-1007.792

Wu, X., Ma, P., Jin, Z., Wu, Y., Han, W., & Ou, W. (2022). A novel zero-watermarking scheme based on NSCT-SVD and blockchain for video copyright. *EURASIP Journal on Wireless Communications and Networking*, *2022*(1), 20. doi:10.1186/s13638-022-02090-x

Xiang, Z., & Pan, J. (2022). Design of intelligent parking management system based on ARM and wireless sensor network. *Mobile Information Systems*, *2022*, 2965638. Advance online publication. doi:10.1155/2022/2965638

Yablonovitch, E. (1993). Photonic band-gap structures. *Journal of the Optical Society of America. B, Optical Physics*, *10*(2), 283. doi:10.1364/JOSAB.10.000283

Yadav, G., Luthra, S., Jakhar, S. K., Mangla, S. K., & Rai, D. P. (2020). A framework to overcome sustainable supply chain challenges through solution measures of industry 4.0 and circular economy: An automotive case. *Journal of Cleaner Production*, *254*, 120112. doi:10.1016/j.jclepro.2020.120112

Yang, A., Li, D., & Li, G. (2022). A fast adaptive online gradient descent algorithm in over parameterized neural networks. *Neural Processing Letters*, 1–19.

Yang, C., Fan, H., & Zhu, H. (2023). Research on Target Detection Algorithm for Complex Scenes. *ITNEC 2023 - IEEE 6th Information Technology, Networking, Electronic and Automation Control Conference*, 873-877. 10.1109/ITNEC56291.2023.10082670

Yang, K., Chen, X., Yan, X., & Wu, D. (2022). Yolov5-DP: A New Method for Detecting Pedestrian Aggregation. *Proceedings of International Conference on Artificial Life and Robotics*, 478-483. 10.5954/ICAROB.2022.OS11-5

Yang, S. (2023). Hierarchical graph multi-agent reinforcement learning for traffic signal control. *Information Sciences*, *634*, 55–72. doi:10.1016/j.ins.2023.03.087

Yan, X., He, Z., Huang, Y., Xu, X., Wang, J., Zhou, X., Wang, C., & Lu, Z. (2022). A Lightweight Pedestrian Intrusion Detection and Warning Method for Intelligent Traffic Security. *KSII Transactions on Internet and Information Systems*, *16*(12), 3904–3922. doi:10.3837/tiis.2022.12.007

Yariv & Yeh. (1984). *Optical Waves in Crystals*. Academic Press.

Yong, B., & Steve, L. (2013). Medical image watermark detection in the wavelet domain using bessel k densities. *IET Medical image Processing*, *7*(4), 281–289.

Yu, X., Wang, C., & Zhou, X. (2018). A survey on robust video watermarking algorithms for copyright protection. *Applied Sciences (Basel, Switzerland)*, *8*(10), 1891. doi:10.3390/app8101891

Zbicinski, I., Stavenuite, J., Kozlowska, B., & van de Coevering, H. P. (2006). *Product Design and Life Cycle Assessment*. The Baltic University Press.

Zear, A., Singh, A. K., & Kumar, P. (2018). A proposed secure multiple watermarking technique based on DWT, DCT and SVD for application in medicine. *Multimedia Tools and Applications*, *77*(4), 4863–4882. doi:10.1007/s11042-016-3862-8

Zelenkov, Y., & Reshettsov, I. (2023). Analysis of the COVID-19 pandemic using a compartmental model with time-varying parameters fitted by a genetic algorithm. *Expert Systems with Applications*, *224*, 120034. doi:10.1016/j.eswa.2023.120034 PMID:37033691

Zeng, H., Dhiman, G., Sharma, A., Sharma, A., & Tselykh, A. (2023). An IoT and Blockchain-based approach for the smart water management system in agriculture. *Expert Systems: International Journal of Knowledge Engineering and Neural Networks*, *40*(4), e12892. doi:10.1111/exsy.12892

Zepeda, A. R., Duke, A. M. R., & Castro, R. C. (2022). Applied Computer Vision on Advanced Driving Systems. In *Proceedings of the LACCEI international Multi-conference for Engineering, Education and Technology*. Latin American and Caribbean Consortium of Engineering Institutions. 10.18687/LACCEI2022.1.1.222

Zhai, Z., Martínez, J. F., Beltran, V., & Martínez, N. L. (2020). Decision support systems for agriculture 4.0: Survey and challenges. *Computers and Electronics in Agriculture*, *170*, 105256. doi:10.1016/j.compag.2020.105256

Zhang, L., Pingaud, H., Lamine, E., Fontanili, F., Bortolaso, C., & Derras, M. (2022). A Model-Driven Approach to Transform Business Vision-Oriented Decision-Making Requirement into Solution-Oriented Optimization Model. *Advances and Trends in Artificial Intelligence. Theory and Practices in Artificial Intelligence*, 211–225. . doi:10.1007/978-3-031-08530-7_18

Zhao, W., Jia, H., Fang, J., Xue, J., Li, X., & Yu, H. (2022). Virtual PedCross-720 : A Synthetic Benchmark for Pedestrian Crossing Detection in Autonomous Driving Scenarios. In Lecture Notes in Electrical Engineering: Vol. 861 LNEE. doi:10.1007/978-981-16-9492-9_90

Zhao, Y. J., Yan, Y. H., & Song, K. C. (2017). Vision-based automatic detection of steel surface defects in the cold rolling process: Considering the influence of industrial liquids and surface textures. *International Journal of Advanced Manufacturing Technology*, *90*(5-8), 1665–1678. doi:10.1007/s00170-016-9489-0

Zhao, Y., Wang, Y., Wang, P., & Yu, H. (2022). PBTM: A Privacy-Preserving Announcement Protocol With Blockchain-Based Trust Management for IoV (2022). *IEEE Systems Journal*, *16*(2), 3422–3432. doi:10.1109/JSYST.2021.3078797

Zheng, Q., Lin, N., Fu, D., Liu, T., Zhu, Y., Feng, X., & Ruan, J. (2023). Smart contract-based agricultural service platform for drone plant protection operation optimization. *IEEE Internet of Things Journal*, 1. Advance online publication. doi:10.1109/JIOT.2023.3288870

Zhou, F., Zhao, H., & Nie, Z. (2021). Safety Helmet Detection Based on YOLOv5. *Proceedings of 2021 IEEE International Conference on Power Electronics, Computer Applications, ICPECA 2021*, 6-11. 10.1109/ICPECA51329.2021.9362711

Zhu, J., Kaplan, R., Johnson, J., & Fei-Fei, L. (2018). Hidden: Hiding data with deep networks. In *Proceedings of the European conference on computer vision (ECCV)* (pp. 657-672). Academic Press.

Zhuang, F., Qi, Z., Duan, K., Xi, D., Zhu, Y., Zhu, H., Xiong, H., & He, Q. (2020). A comprehensive survey on transfer learning. *Proceedings of the IEEE*, *109*(1), 43–76. doi:10.1109/JPROC.2020.3004555

About the Contributors

Idriss Chana received the Ph.D. degree from ENSIAS, Mohamed V University of Rabat, Morocco in 2013. He is currently an Associate Professor at Moulay Ismail University of Meknès, Morocco. His research interests include information and communication technologies, IoT, channel coding and Artificial Intelligence. A large part of his research projects are related to Error correcting codes and Turbo codes. Idriss Chana has published more than 40 papers in major journals and conferences in Information Theory and Artificial Intelligence.

***

Mariselvam A. K. completed his B.E Degree in Electronics and Communication Engineering (ECE) from Anna University in 2008 and M.E Communication systems from Anna University in 2011 and Ph.D., Degree from Anna University in 2022. He gained his Post-Doctoral fellowship from IIT Kanpur in 2023. He has published 13 research articles in National and International Journals. He has a 6-year teaching and 6 years in research. He is working as an Assistant Professor in Department of ECE, SRM Valliammai Engineering College, Tamil Nadu.

Okacha Amraouy obtained his B.Sc. degree in Mechatronics and Embedded Systems from Sidi Mohamed Ben Abdellah University, Fez, Morocco, in 2019, and his M.Sc. degree in Smart Industry from the same university in 2021. He is currently a Ph.D. Student at Laboratory of Engineering, Modeling and Analysis of Systems at the Faculty of Sciences, Sidi Mohamed Ben Abdellah University. His research interests include Intelligent Irrigation as a Service, IoT, Wireless Network Technologies, Blockchain, Fog and Cloud computing, IA, expert systems, intelligent and complex distributed systems, automatic control, data mining and knowledge discovery, supervised and unsupervised learning, predictive analytics, optimal intelligent irrigation scheduling and planning, optimal automatic management of precision irrigation, and optimization in precision agriculture.

T. Ananth Kumar received his Ph.D. degree in VLSI Design from Manonmaniam Sundaranar University, Tirunelveli. He received his Master's degree in VLSI Design from Anna University, Chennai and Bachelor's degree in Electronics and communication engineering from Anna University, Chennai. He is working as Associate Professor in IFET college of Engineering afflicted to Anna University, Chennai. He has presented papers in various National and International Conferences and Journals. His fields of interest are Networks on Chips, Computer Architecture and ASIC design. He is the recipient of the Best Paper Award at INCODS 2017. He is the life member of ISTE, and few membership bodies.

Aissa Ben Yahya is a Ph.D. Student in Department of Information Science at Moulay Ismail University, Morocco. He received his Master degree in Networks and Embedded Systems from Moulay Ismail University, Morocco, in 2020. His research interests include Embedded Systems, Internet of Things, and Resource constrained systems security.

Mohammed Benbrahim received the B.Eng. degree in electromechanical engineering from the Higher National School of Mines, in 1997 and the M.Sc. and Ph.D. degrees in automatic and industrial informatics from the Mohammadia School of Engineers, in 2000 and 2007, respectively. Currently, he is a Full Professor at the Department of Physics and the program coordinator for the Master Smart Industry at the Faculty of Sciences, Sidi Mohamed Ben Abdellah University. His research interests include robotics, automatic control, intelligent systems, predictive maintenance, modeling, and optimization.

Aziz Bouazi is a professor of Electrical Engineering in High School of Technology, UMI, Meknès.

Jaouad Boudnaya was born in Taounate, Morocco. He earned his engineering degree in Electromechanical Engineering in 2012 from ENSAM, Moulay Ismail University, Meknes, and completed his Ph.D. in Automatics and Dependability in 2017 from the same university in collaboration with the University of Technology of Compiègne in France. Currently, he works as a Safety and Diagnostics Engineer at Stellantis Group, holds a part-time teaching position at ENSAM Meknes, and is an associated member of the research team: Multidisciplinary Engineering and Mechatronic Systems (IMSM), within the Research Laboratory: Mechatronics Mechanics and Control – L2MC. His research interests encompass safety, reliability, and risk analysis, particularly in industrial systems, with a focus on the railway and automotive industries.

Yassine Boukhali received his B.Sc. degree in Computer Systems and Software Engineering from cadi ayyad University, Essaouira, Morocco, in 2019, and his M.Sc. degree in Smart Industry from Sidi Mohamed Ben Abdellah university in 2021. He is currently a Ph.D. Student at Laboratory of Engineering, Modeling and Analysis of Systems at the Faculty of Sciences, Sidi Mohamed Ben Abdellah University. His Main research interests are Industry 5.0 and Software Engineering.

Badr Bououlid Idrissi was born in Marrakech, Morocco. He received the Ph.D. degree from Faculté Polytechnique de Mons, Mons, Belgium, in 1997 and the engineer's degree from Ecole Nationale de l'Industrie Minérale, Rabat, Morocco, in 1992. Since 1999, he has been working at Ecole Nationale Supérieure d'Arts et Métiers (ENSAM-Meknès), Moulay Ismaïl University, Meknès, Morocco, where he is a Professor in the Department of Electromechanical Engineering, in the areas of power electronics and electrical machines. His research interests are mainly electric drives, industrial control systems, DSP/FPGA based ADAS systems and Electrical Vehicles.

Chaymaâ Boutahiri is a Ph.D. Student at Moulay Ismail University, Laboratory of Computer Science, Applied Math and Electrical Engineering (IMAGE), IEVIA team, EST, Meknes,Morocco.

Imane Cheikh received the B. Eng in electrical engineering from the Hassania School of Public Works in 2020. Since 2021, she is a PhD Student at the faculty of Sciences, Sidi Mohamed Ben Abdellah University. Her research includes the control of manipulator robots and fault detection.

Anass Cherrafi is an Associate Professor at Cadi Ayyad University, Morocco. Holding a Ph.D. in Industrial Engineering, he has nine years of industry and teaching experience. He has published a number of articles in leading international journals and conference proceedings, and has been a Guest Editor for special issues of various international journals. His research interests include Industry 4.0, green manufacturing, Lean Six Sigma, integrated management systems and supply chain management.

Chafik Ed-dahmani received the Engineering degree in Mechatronics engineering from the National School of Applied Sciences, University of Abdelmalek Essaadi, Tétouan, Morocco, in 2014, and the Ph.D. degree in electrical engineering from the Mohammadia School of Engineers, Mohamed V University, Rabat, Morocco, in 2020. He is currently working as a Professor with National Graduate School of Arts and Crafts, Moulay Ismail University, Meknès, Morocco. His research interests include electric power systems, protection and control of Microgrids, and Advanced Driver Assistance Systems.

Hicham El Akhal received his master degree in Networks and Embedded Systems from Moulay Ismail University, Morocco, in 2020. He is currently working toward a Ph.D. degree in the Department of Information Science, Faculty of Sciences, at Moulay Ismail University, Meknes, Morocco. His research interests include artificial intelligence and agriculture.

Abdelbaki El Belrhiti El Alaoui received the PhD degree in optoelectronics from Metz University, France, in 2002, the accreditation to supervise research degree from Moulay Ismail University, Morocco, in 2009. He is currently a professor in the department of Computer Science, Faculty of Sciences Meknes, Moulay Ismail University. His current research interests include fault tolerance, mobility and security in wireless sensor networks, wireless multimedia sensor networks and embedded systems.

Ibtissam El Hassani, serving as a Professor in Industrial & Manufacturing Engineering at ENSAM, Moulay Ismail University, and Associate Professor at UQAR Canada, specializes in artificial intelligence applications in industrial engineering. She earned her engineering degree in 2006 and her Ph.D. in 2014 at ENSAM Meknès, teaching subjects like Lean Manufacturing, Six Sigma and artificial intelligence industrial applications.

Youssef Hadi received his Ph.D. degree from Mohammed V University, Faculty of Sciences Rabat, Morocco in 2008. Currently, he is an Assistant Director for Educational Affairs at the Higher School of Technology (EST) Kenitra, Morocco, and responsible for many Masters Formations sections at the same university. He's a leader of research teams on Software engineering and Multimedia Database indexing. He has valuable contributions and publications in those topics of research.

Abdallah Marhraoui Hsaini is a professor at Moulay Ismail University, Laboratory of Computer Science, Applied Math and Electrical Engineering (IMAGE), IEVIA team, EST, Meknes, Morocco

Komala James is a highly esteemed educator and researcher with a distinguished career in the field of Electronics and Communication Engineering (ECE). Currently serving as the Professor & Head of the Department of ECE at SRM Valliammai Engineering College, a prestigious institution under the SRM Group, has made significant contributions to academia and the wireless communications domain. She completed her Bachelor's degree in Electronics and Communication Engineering, followed by a

Master's degree in Applied Electronics. Building on this strong foundation, she pursued a Ph.D. focusing on the Mobility in Fourth Generation Wireless Networks, showcasing a passion for cutting-edge research and technological advancements. With an impressive teaching experience of 27 years and 3 years of industrial experience, she has consistently demonstrated a commitment to academic excellence and student success. She published more than 25 research articles in esteemed International Journals and Conferences. She received "100 Most Dedicated Professors" award by the World Education Congress in 2018 and were named the "Best Professor in Communication Engineering" at the 11th Innovative Education Leadership Awards in 2019. She is a Fellow member of IETE (Institution of Electronics and Telecommunication Engineers) and Life Members of ISTE (Indian Society for Technical Education) & CSI (Computer Society of India). Additionally, an Annual Member of the Indian Science Congress Association and a Member of IAENG (International Association of Engineers). In recognition of their contributions to academia and the engineering community, she received a grant of Rs. 1.5 Lakhs from AICTE (All India Council for Technical Education) for organizing the National Conference on "Recent trends in Wireless Communications and Networking" in 2014. Her area of interests is Wireless Communication, Networking and Internet of Things.

Touria Jdid received an M.S. in Smart Industry from the Faculty of Sciences, Sidi Mohamed Ben Abdellah University, in 2020. Currently, she is a Ph.D. candidate at the same university. Her research interests include intelligent systems, infectious disease modeling, statistical modeling, Bayesian inference, data analytics, AI, data science, IoT, and Cloud Computing.

Mohammed Nabil Kabbaj is a Full Professor at the Faculty of Sciences, University of Fez, where he is the Program Coordinator of Mechatronics and Embedded Systems Bachelor. His research interests include control engineering, fault detection, and diagnosis of complex systems. Before joining the University of Fez, he received a Ph.D. degree from the University of Perpignan in 2004 and has been a postdoctoral researcher at LAAS-CNRS in Toulouse.

Imen Kallel is a research member at ESSE (Advanced Electronic Systems and Sustainable Energy), ENET'COM –Tunisia. Research interests include image processing, digital watermarking and data hiding, multimedia authentication, human machine interaction (HMI), computer vision and environmental health and agriculture.

Mohamed Kallel is a research member at ESSE (Advanced Electronic Systems and Sustainable Energy), ENET'COM –Tunisia. Research interests include image processing, digital watermarking and data hiding, multimedia authentication, human machine interaction (HMI), computer vision and environmental health and agriculture.

Abdelhak Mkhida works as a Professor at ENSAM-Meknès, the specialty is related to Safety-Critical Systems and electronics.

Jothy N. is an accomplished academician with a passion for Electronics and Communication Engineering. She completed her B.E degree from Anna University in 2005, followed by an M.Tech degree from Pondicherry Engineering College in 2010, and a Ph.D. from the same institution in 2022. Her commitment to excellence in education has been recognized, and she was honored with the prestigious Best Teacher

Award from Sri Manakula Vinayagar Engineering College, Puducherry. With a teaching experience of over 15 years, she is currently serving as an Assistant Professor in the Department of Electronics and Communication Engineering at SRM Valliammai Engineering College, Tamil Nadu. As a life member of IEI (Institution of Engineers India) and ISTE (Indian Society for Technical Education), she actively engages in professional networks, staying abreast of the latest developments and advancements in her field. Her expertise spans various domains, including Ad-hoc Networks, Internet of Things, Machine Learning, and Deep Learning.

Subhashini N. received her B.E. Degree in Electronics & Communication Engineering from the University of Madras in 1998 and received her M.Tech. in Communication Systems from SRM University in 2007 and Ph.D. degree from Anna University, Chennai in the year 2020. She is a life member of ISTE, IETE, CSI and IAENG. She has Co-Authored a book titled Microwave Engineering. She has published 16 research articles in International and National Journals. She has a total teaching experience of over 22 years and presently serving as Assistant Professor in the Department of Electronics and Communication Engineering, SRM Valliammai Engineering College, Kattankulathur, Tamil Nadu. Conducted national level seminars, FDPs and co-convened International Conference and AICTE sponsored National level Conference. Received Grant of Fifteen Lakhs from DST-SERB for her project. She received Best Teacher Award from SRM Valliammai Engineering College. She serves as reviewer for many International Journals. She was recognized by DST and Texas Instruments for fostering an ecosystem bridging Government, Industry and Academia and for preparing the Texas Instruments: DrishTi online contest Questionnaire .Her research interest includes Wireless Sensor Networks, Machine Learning, Electromagnetic Fields, RF and Microwave Engineering.

Ayoub Nouaiti is a professor at Moulay Ismail University, Laboratory of Computer Science, Applied Math and Electrical Engineering (IMAGE), IEVIA team, EST, Meknes,Morocco

Khaoula Oulidi Omali received the M.S degree in Engineering of Industrial Automated Systems, and Ph.D. in electrical engineering from the University of Sidi Mohamed Ben Abdellah, Fez, Morocco, in 2016 and 2021, respectively. She is currently a Professor at National School of Computer Science and Systems Analysis in Rabat, University Mohammed V. Her main research interests are in engineering sciences, robotics, and automatic control.

Kanimozhi P. received her B.E degree from Vellore Engineering College in 2000 and M.Tech degree in the field of Computer Science and Engineering from Sri Manakula Vinayagar Engineering College in 2008, India. She completed her research in the area of Cloud Compuitng at Anna University, Chennai, India. Her area of interest includes Cloud computing, Data Mining and Internet of Things. She has also published 3 papers in International journal, 6 in International Conference. She is currently working as a Professor and Head in IFET College of Engineering for the department of Computer Science and Engineering.

Mohamed Qerras is a promising young talent in the field of engineering. Currently in the final phase of his studies at ENSAM Meknes, he is preparing to become an engineer specializing in electromechanical engineering, with a focus on control and industrial management. With an insatiable curiosity and a passion for new technologies, Qerras stands out for his dedication and constant desire to learn and excel.

Currently involved in the Final Industrial Project at OCP, he is actively working on the development of a fuel monitoring system based on IIoT (Industrial Internet of Things) and AI (Artificial Intelligence). His work aims to improve the efficiency, safety, and sustainability of industrial processes. Throughout his academic journey, Qerras has acquired a solid foundation of theoretical and practical knowledge in the fields of electromechanical engineering, control management, and industrial management. He also possesses in-depth skills in analyzing technical problems, problem-solving, and project management.

Oumayma Rachidi was born in Rabat, Morocco. She is a second year Ph.D. student and received an engineer's degree from National Graduate School of Arts and Crafts, Meknes, Morocco, in 2021. She is actually working as an electromechanical engineer in the industry field. Her ongoing dissertation studies the pedestrian detection in ADAS systems, and explores deep learning techniques for object detection. She is particularly interested in industrial control systems, FPGA based ADAS systems and Electrical Vehicles.

Yassine Rhazali is a Moroccan professor, he obtained his Ph.D. in computer science at Ibn Tofail University, Kenitra, Morocco, more specifically in software engineering, his specialty is the Model Driven Engineering, he proposed several approaches in model engineering, and his approaches are validated in various scientific papers published at international scientific conferences and international scientific journals. He is now a professor, researcher, reviewer, editorial board member, and scientific committee member in several international scientific journals and at various international scientific conferences He has taught computer science in varied universities and institutes.

Abir Sajji received her Master's Degree in Software Quality from the Ibn Tofail University, Faculty of Sciences Kenitra, Morocco, in 2010. She later worked at the presidency of the same university as an administrator, currently, she prepares her Ph.D. degree in the Ibn Tofail University, Faculty of Sciences Kenitra, Morocco, in 2021. Her research interest focuses on conceptual modeling, and software processes.

Souhail Sekkat is a professor at ENSAM Engineering school in Meknes (Morocco). His research focuses is in the field on operations management. He holds a PhD in Engineering Sciences and a DEA (Diplôme des Etudes Approfondies) in Management Sciences.

Index

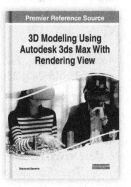

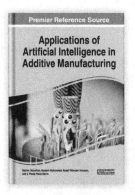
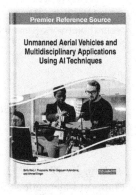

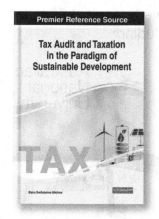

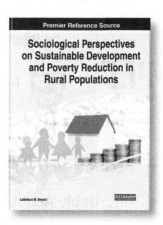

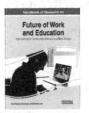